For Georgia, Joseph, James, Joanna, Stuart and Sarah-Jane

thanks to :

Hughes for photographs,
l for maps,
ne Hoare for archaeological pointers,
Smith at LMA for illustrations,
ouglas for the proof reading,
brey for Mac.

shed 2013

ry Press
Brimscombe Port
oucestershire, GL5 2QG
istorypress.co.uk

x, 2013

rary Cataloguing in Publication Data.
ie record for this book is available from the British Library.

7509 5291 0

g and origination by The History Press
India

OLD EAST E[ND]

A History of the Tow[er]

Speci[al]
Yvon[ne]
Jane S[...]
Katha[rine]
Jerem[y]
Patsy
Nell [...]

JANE COX

First [published]

The [...]
The [...]
Strou[d...]
www[...]

© Ja[ne...]

The [...]
of th[e...]
Copy[right...]

Brit[ish...]
A ca[talogue...]

ISBN[...]

Typ[...]
Prin[ted...]

CONTENTS

PREFACE

East London was the oldest and greatest of the suburbs of London, the country home of her merchant princes, the open spaces, hunting grounds and playing fields of her citizens, the muster-grounds of her trained bands, the practising ground of her archers, as well as the refuge of craftsmen seeking to escape the regulation of her guilds, the receptacle of the overflow of her industrial population, and one of the principal sources of supply of her necessaries of life.

Sir Hubert Llewellyn-Smith, 1930

The East End is a vast city, as famous in its way as any city men have built. But who knows the East End? It is down through Cornhill and out beyond Leadenhall Street and Aldgate Pump, one will say; a shocking place where he once went with a curate. An evil growth of slums which hide human creeping things; where foul men and women live on penn'orths of gin, where collars and clean shirts are not yet invented, where every citizen wears a black eye, and no man combs his hair. Our street is not a place like this.

Arthur Morrison, 'A Street', *Macmillan's Magazine*, 1891

Introduction

LONDON'S BACKYARD

'The East End' is generally taken to mean poverty, deprivation and the vibrant subculture that grew up in the slum which, for about a hundred years, seethed like a boil on the side of the richest city in the world. Historians of London are strangely neglectful of the earlier times, while recollections of this 'Jewish East End' abound. It is as if there was no life in the East End before that era of modern folklore. Tales are endlessly told of the sufferings and of tough East Enders struggling through, of the good old, bad old days of eel and pie shops, of cheery costermongers, of the sharing and caring that went on in the dark hovels. Just over a hundred years ago Walter Besant wrote his famous and despairing description of the East End, broadcasting the 'unparalleled magnitude of its meanness and monotony … line upon line, row upon row, never ending lines' of dingy houses up squalid courts. No carriages were to be seen in any of its 500 miles of streets; no one of any account went there except, briefly, for good works. This 'Unlovely City', as populous as Berlin or Philadelphia, was the ugly underbelly of the booming metropolis, where orphans slept on rooftops, the dead bodies of children were left to rot in the streets, women worked at their needle for eighteen hours a day, match girls died of phossijaw, drunks reeled and prostitutes plied their trade.

It was not always so, but neither did the Tower Hamlets turn overnight from a scattering of pretty little cottages among market gardens and windmills. There was a time when carriages rattled merrily east of Aldgate pump, passing along the busy, thriving highways to elegant houses among the lush watermeadows. As we shall see, the East End has a history that is quite as much worthy of attention as the City which spawned it and the West End which despised it.

This book is the story of that old East End, before the Docks, before Jack the Ripper, when the suburbs, villages and hamlets east of the Tower were independent places, with their own identities, before they became subsumed into London.

The area defined

I have, like my eminent predecessor Sir Hubert Llewellyn-Smith, taken only the area covered by the borough of Tower Hamlets as my subject. The term 'East End', which I have used anachronistically, throughout, only came into general usage in the late nineteenth century. It is a very vague term, embracing what are now the London boroughs of Newham, Hackney, parts of Islington, as well as Tower Hamlets. The true East End, however, is the area to the immediate east of the City of London. I regret the omission of Shoreditch, which has rich history, not least for being the cradle of London's theatre, but it belongs to the history of Hackney.

The borough of Tower Hamlets comprises most of the ancient parish of Stepney, including its hamlets (see below); the ancient parish of St Leonard Bromley; some areas bordering on the City, including the Tower, Tower Hill, the precinct of St Katherine, the Liberties of East Smithfield and Norton Folgate, the parishes of St Botolph Aldgate (part, including the Old Artillery Ground) and Holy Trinity, Minories, St Botolph Bishopsgate (part). The Portsoken was the ancient name of the strip of land running from Bishopsgate down to the river, including the precinct of St Katherine's, East Smithfield, the parishes of St Botolph, Aldgate and Holy Trinity Minories, incorporating part of what is now Spitalfields, Whitechapel and Wapping. Its eastern boundary was Nightingale Lane, now Thomas More Street.

The London Borough of Tower Hamlets was created in 1965, merging the old (1899) boroughs of Stepney, Bethnal Green and Poplar. The 1899 Local Government Act had created three metropolitan boroughs: Bethnal Green, coterminous with its parish; Poplar, which included Stratford Bow and Bromley; and Stepney, which was all the rest, including Whitechapel, East Smithfield, the Liberty of the Tower, Holy Trinity Minories, the Old Artillery Ground and Norton Folgate. The name Tower Hamlets seems to have been first used in the sixteenth century, when the Constable of the Tower was Lord Lieutenant of Tower Hamlets and commanded the bands of the Tower Hamlets Militia.

Stepney parish jurisdiction evolved from the Bishop of London's vill, which included Hackney and Bromley. In 1086 the bishop tried to take over Bromley parish, unsuccessfully; it is not known when they separated. It covered the area bounded by the Lea, the eastern boundary of Middlesex, the Thames and the City until Whitechapel parish was created in 1338 (*c.* 211 acres). The boundaries were delineated in 1703: the Thames to the south, Bromley to the east and West Ham (across the Lea), Hackney to the north, Shoreditch to the north-west, Bishopsgate Without and Portsoken wards, and the parishes of St Botolph's Bishopsgate and Aldgate to the west; East Smithfield and St Katharine's lay in the Portsoken and Aldgate parish.

The ancient parish of Stepney was 4,150 acres at its greatest. It comprised Mile End Old Town, Mile End New Town, Ratcliff, Whitechapel, Wapping Whitechapel (the little riverside strip), Wapping Stepney (St George's in the East), Stratford Bow, Shadwell, Spitalfields, Bethnal Green Limehouse, Poplar and the Isle of Dogs with Blackwall, Millwall and Cubitt Town. During the latter part of the seventeenth century and the eighteenth new parishes were created as the population grew; these were St Paul Shadwell (68 acres) in 1670; Christ Church Spitalfields (73 acres) and St George's in the East (244 acres) in 1729; St Mary Bow (565 acres) and St Anne Limehouse (244 acres) in 1730; St Matthew Bethnal Green (755 acres) in 1743; and All Saints' Poplar (1,158 acres) in 1817. Stepney now comprised three hamlets: Mile End Old Town (677 acres), Mile End New Town (42 acres) and Ratcliff (111 acres).

Part I

LONDON'S OLDEST SUBURB

from earliest times to c. 1500

Chapter 1

OLDER THAN LONDON ITSELF

Prehistory, Romans and Saxons

The very first Londoner of whom we have mortal remains happens to be an 'East Ender', a Neolithic lass whose skeleton was recently found in Blackwall, lying on her left, curled round in a foetal position, with a pot and a flint knife. She was buried there about 6,000 years ago, but there are signs of human life around London stretching back many millions of generations before that.

Humans, or something like humans, first appeared in the London area in about 400,000 BC, when the weather was Mediterranean and a land bridge joined Britain to the Continent. In those days lions roared in Limehouse, bears roamed in Bethnal Green, rhinoceroses in Ratcliff, elephants in East Smithfield and Neanderthals, smaller than us, seriously carnivorous, with beetling brows and receding chins, hunted by chasing herds of animals to their death over cliffs or into marshes. Traces of these near-human creatures have been found in Rainham and Woodford.

Over thousands of years it got colder and colder, and the land was covered with ice. The Neanderthals probably retreated to southern Europe, returning about 60,000 years ago to hunt the woolly mammoths, reindeer and horses that now lived in the British arctic tundra, where winter temperatures might be as low as -25°C. By c. 30,000 BC they had died out and were replaced by modern humans who, it is thought, originated in Africa. By c. 13,000 BC Britain had warmed into fruitful life, and the vast freezing plains were covered first in pine forests and then with oak and birch. People lived in the Thames and Lea valleys more or less continually from this distant era, only forced to retreat to higher ground when, about 8,500 years ago, the sea rose, submerging the area and turning Britain temporarily into a group of islands.

Archaeologists have found evidence of the earliest British *homo sapiens* living in the early Neolithic period (8,000–3,000 BC) around London, in Essex at Rainham, Ilford, Upminster and Dagenham. Semi-nomadic hunter-gatherers, they built wooden huts to live in, mainly on the river terraces, and hunted the roe, wild cattle, red deer and boar which ran in the forests. Between 3,500 and 350 BC farming started, the growing of cereals and the herding of cattle; clearings were made in the forests and something like villages started to dot the land. Traces of enclosures have been found to the west of London, with entrances aligned with the setting or rising sun. In the east a late Neolithic (3,500–2,500 BC) track-way has been found in Silvertown, and a handful of burnt grains of wheat in Canning Town hint at early arable farming. There are signs of the beginnings of the human preoccupation with an afterlife, as people, like the Blackwall lass, started to be buried with equipment for their journey into the great unknown. The river Thames, which provided so many of the necessities of life, became an object of veneration, and votive gifts were thrown into the waters to gratify or appease the powerful spirits.

By the late Bronze Age, (1,000–750 BC), when women wove woollen cloth and men fashioned fine metal utensils and ornaments, the countryside was beginning to have an appearance that we might recognise, with field systems and hedges planted to divide farm from farm. At some point river levels appear to have risen again, and wooden tracks were built across the new marshy meadows: on the Isle of Dogs a timber platform was recently discovered at Atlas Wharf. At Old Ford, where the river Lea was readily crossable and where there are hints of a much older settlement, there grew up a village, presumably a collection of round huts, with perhaps a forge, where Lefevre Walk now is. Signs of Bronze Age life have been found in Stepney village and in Bromley.

So, before the Romans came to Rye, and before there was any London, or any London of significance, there had been habitation in the 'East End' going back deep into the Celtic twilight and beyond. The gravel soils of Stepney, Bow and Bethnal Green, lying on top of London clay, lightly wooded with oak and beech, interspersed with glades and open grasslands, were among the most fertile in the south of England. The woods were easily cleared to make cornfields and the oak trees provided food for pigs and timber for building. In the alluvial parts, Wapping and the Isle of Dogs, where river mud was deposited, there was excellent pasture when water levels were low.

Lying as it did between two navigable tidal rivers, the Thames and the Lea, our area was a good place to live; it was easy to travel around by boat, to trade with neighbours and continental Europe; and there was a plentiful supply of water not just from the rivers but from abundant springs and wells, as at Shadwell. This and others were on the edge of the flood plain, where the water that has sunk through the gravel around, unable to permeate the clay below, trickles along until it can find a way out. The whole triangle of land was criss-crossed with streams. The brook (hence Brook Street in Poplar) that was to be christened the Black Ditch in the eighteenth century rose near Spitalfields, crossed the Mile End Road at Cambridge Heath Road, then ran along north of Stepney church, turning south to join the Thames at Limehouse Dock. Another short stream rose in Wellclose Square, ran along Nightingale Lane (now Sir Thomas More Street) and into the Thames at Crassh Mills in Wapping. One rose in the gravel near Shadwell Well (where St Paul's Shadwell now stands); another started in Bromley and crossed Poplar High Street; another rose in Goodman's Fields (Whitechapel) and ran south into the Thames where now Tower Bridge stands.

By the time of the first Roman invasions (55 and 54 BC) this rich and watery place was well settled, and, as all over the country, the people of what we call the Iron Age were organised into tribes or embryonic kingdoms. According to Roman sources these were warlike bands of rough folk, recent immigrants from northern Gaul, whose so-called towns were timber fortresses in thickets defended with ditches and banks. Their villages were collections of large round dwellings, with barns for storage of grain and stockades for beasts; their gods were the wee folk of good and evil, spirits lurking in trees and springs, hobgoblins, animal-headed men and squinting hunchbacks. From their headquarters far away in Anglesey the powerful priests and judges, the Druids, held some considerable sway over all the tribes in the Midlands and south-east, supervising wide-scale human sacrifice. In this fierce world of faery and wickermen, into which the great Caesar marched his legions, the site of Greater London seems to have been peripheral to the politics of the time, a sort of no-man's land lying where four kingdoms met. These were the territories of three major Belgic tribes: the Trinovantes of Essex, with a capital near Colchester, the Catuvellauni ('good in battle'), of Hertfordshire, the Atrebates, to the west, with their fortress at Silchester, and in Kent the Cantiaci. Overlooking the fields and marshes to the east of London's site, in what is now Ilford, rose an enormous fortress, at 60 acres one of the largest in Britain, with ramparts 20ft high, towering over Barking Creek and watching over the valley. Built in the second century BC, Uphall Camp marks the boundary of Trinovantes territory, guarding Essex from the Catuvellauni, who ruled from their headquarters at Wheathampstead.

It was the ambition of the Catuvellauni that brought Julius Caesar to these shores, or was at least his excuse for intervention. Invited by the Trinovantes to protect them from their neighbours, he trounced the aggressors, with their 4,000 war chariots and, having received their submission, retired, leaving the Celtic warlords to their own devices. By the time of the Claudian colonisation of Britain, some hundred years later, Cunobelin (Shakespeare's Cymbeline), King of the Catuvellauni, had forged a new kingdom, adding to his possessions in Hertfordshire, South Cambridgeshire, Buckinghamshire and Oxfordshire the Essex territory of the Trinovantes and that of the Cantiaci in Kent. His sons, Caractacus and Togodomus, ruled this wide domain from Camulodunum (Colchester), the old Trivonantes' fortress. So when Aulus Plautius, commander of the emperor's forces, led the invasion of Britain in AD 43, the British capital at

Colchester was the focus of the attack – and Tower Hamlets was on his route. Our entry into the historical East End starts with the glittering and terrifying martial rhythm of the legions, marching from the Thames to the Lea, led by the Emperor Claudius, the youthful Vespasian at his side, with elephants, horses and soldiers crashing through the shallows at Old Ford.

Although Roman sources are not specific enough about topography to allow us to trace the invaders' route exactly, it is almost certain that the Romans used the Old Ford to cross the Lea. Aulus Plautius and his troops landed in Kent, fought their way to the Thames, which they crossed, possibly at Greenwich or perhaps 1 mile to the west of the City, where the roads to Verulamium and Canterbury align, and where the river might be crossed through about 5ft of water at low tide. There, having got into difficulties, they camped and awaited the arrival of Claudius from Italy, at least six weeks later. There followed a victorious march to Colchester and the annexation of Britain to the Empire.

Much rests on the account of Roman historian Dio Cassius, not least regarding the founding of London itself, so it is worth quoting the relevant passage in full:

> The Britons withdrew to the Thames at a point where it flows into the sea and at high tide forms a lake. This they crossed with ease since they knew precisely where the ground was firm and the way passable. The Romans, however, in pursuing them, got into difficulties here. Once again the Celts swam across, while others crossed by a bridge a little way upstream and they engaged the enemy from several sides at once, cutting many of them down. However, in pursuing the garrisons without due precautions, they got into marshes from which it was difficult to find a way out and lost a number of men.

According to R.G. Collingwood the swamps they got lost in were those of the numerous branches of the lower Lea. This may or may not have been the case; Dio Cassius was writing at least 150 years after the event. No firm conclusions can be drawn as to where they crossed the Thames, although their camp was presumably on the twin hills that grew speedily into Londinium, and within two decades was, according to Tacitus, a flourishing city. The probability of the army using the ancient ford over the Lea, however, is very high; it was the obvious route to take. The emperor's forces needed to cross the river to get to Colchester, and there was an ancient turf chariot trackway that led there, passing through the river at Old Ford. Westwards it probably followed the line of Bethnal Green Road, Old Street and so into Oxford Street, thence running towards the major settlement at Brentford and on to the capital of the Atrebates at Silchester.

Within ten years or so of the invasion this road, more ancient than any of the City's streets, was made into a three-lane highway, Roman style. It appears to have stayed in use until Bow Bridge was built at Stratford in the twelfth century. In 1845 traces of the old road were discovered, running closely parallel to today's Roman Road, where a colourful market has sold the necessities and fripperies of life to East Enders since 1888. Masses of Roman herringbone masonry found in the bed of the Lea nearby indicates that there was a paved ford here, and very recent excavations at nearby Le Fevre Walk and Parnell Road have placed the ribbon development along this road and around the river crossing among the major inhabited sites in the London area both in Roman and pre-Roman times.

So the village of Old Ford is older than London itself – perhaps. There is, to date, no archaeological evidence of any pre-Roman settlement where the great port grew, which was to fashion and finally absorb the hamlets between the Thames and the Lea. On the face of it this seems unlikely, as the 'square mile' offered a prime site, a natural fort on twin hills that rose above the largest river in the country, set in a wide, fertile valley and naturally embanked with steep gravel banks. It was an excellent spot for landing ships and men and for lively trade with the Continent, which was much in evidence in the decades before Roman colonisation. According to Stow it was chosen as the 'royal city' because it 'reaches furthest into the belly of the land' and 'openeth indifferently upon France and Flanders'. The entomology of its name is debatable; traditionally it was thought to derive from Llyndin, meaning a lake fort; these days it is said to derive from Plowonida, which means a river that is too wide to ford. Either way it is an ancient British name, which might argue that there was a settlement there, although the Romans are said to have adopted indigenous names for new towns in conquered territories. The most significant evidence for a pre-Roman settle-ment at London is the fact that, according to Tacitus, there was a flourishing city there within eighteen years of Plautius's arrival. From a mere camp arose, in an astonishingly short time, a new town, an *oppidum* 'celebrated for the gathering of dealers and commodities'.

When considering the origins of London or, indeed, the prehistory of its east side, it is worth remembering that archaeology has only evolved recently into a serious and systematic pursuit. Although our forebears were fascinated by acci-dental finds, as John Stow was by the discovery of a Roman vessel still containing liquid in Spitalfields in 1576, it is really only since the 1920s that it has become a scientific study, bolstered by new dating methods. In the 1860s Colonel Lane Fox (Pitt Rivers) thought he had discovered the remains of the London 'lake fortress' of Cassivellaunus, Caesar's protagonist, in pile structures on the banks of the Wallbrook. In 1928 Sir Mortimer Wheeler's investigations revealed that it was no such thing, being Roman works of a much later date. The western market area of Lundenwic, now thought to be the main site of Saxon London, was only discovered in 1985 at the Aldwych (old market). As we have seen, ongoing exca-vations at Old Ford are revealing a continuity of occupation since the Bronze

Age, and this, with discoveries made at Shadwell since 1975, have quite changed the traditional view of the Roman East End. The story of London may shift at any moment. Sir Christopher Wren noted some Roman work below the foundations of the medieval cathedral when he was building St Paul's; who knows what lies beneath that?

As legends have a comforting way of turning out to be true, or partially true, it should be remembered, that, in medieval and early modern times London was believed to have been a great city 1,000 years before the Romans came, founded in 1,074 BC by one Brutus, great-grandson of Virgil's Aeneas. Like Rome itself, London was the creation of a fugitive from Troy. A Welsh bishop, Geoffrey of Monmouth, composed a *History of the Kings of Britain* in the twelfth century, based on 'lost' sources and oral traditions. According to this book, Brutus's city, New Troy or Nova Troia, was the city of Trinovant to which Caesar refers. The name London was coined when it was rebuilt by one King Lud, remembered in Ludgate. This story, presumably written to elevate London by giving it both a classical and Celtic pedigree, was eagerly accepted and held sway for some 400 years. It only began to be questioned in the sixteenth century, when it was observed that the chronicler had used a misunderstanding of Caesar's word *civitas*, thinking that he had referred to a city rather than the territory of the Trinovantes. Nevertheless the story still hung around: in 1805 Thomas Pennant, in his serious *Some Account of London*, refers to the Celtic lake city. Even today, even though scholars have long dismissed the tale of King Lud's topless towers, you may find some version of it repeated in websites whose authors seek, as did that journalist monk, to find a fine and fancy ancestry for the City that in due course superseded Rome as the greatest city in the world.

The Romans said they founded London, and as far as we can tell at present they seem to have done so, with archaeological evidence dating it to *c.* AD 50. Ten or eleven years later the Old Ford witnessed a scene probably even more awesome to the locals than the advance of the legions, when the terrible, tall, tawny-haired Queen of the East Anglian Iceni, Boudicca, led her army of 100,000 men, women and children crashing through the Lea. You can see her, magnificent in a war chariot, just by Westminster Bridge.

Boudicca's husband had left a will leaving the client kingdom of the Iceni divided between his two daughters and Emperor Nero, hoping thereby to secure inheritance for his dynasty. At his death the reverse happened; the Romans plundered his kingdom, had his widow publicly flogged and his daughters brutally raped. The queen, in revenge, raised an army and led in person the only sustained resistance against the invaders in all their time in Britain. The revolt focussed first on Camulodunum, now settled with Roman army veterans, where thousands were slaughtered and buildings were burnt to the ground. She and her troops then turned towards London; they would have taken the established route through the Lea at Old Ford. Tacitus writes in his *Annals*:

> Suetonius [the Roman governor, who was in Anglesey suppressing the Druids] … marched amidst a hostile population to Londinium, which, though undistinguished by the name of a colony, was much frequented by a number of merchants and trading vessels. Uncertain whether he should choose it as a seat of war, as he looked round on his scanty force of soldiers, and … he resolved to save the province at the cost of a single town. Nor did the tears and weeping of the people, as they implored his aid, deter him from giving the signal of departure and receiving into his army all who would go with him. Those who were chained to the spot by the weakness of their sex, or the infirmity of age, or the attractions of the place, were cut off by the enemy.

Londoners, Romans and 'friends of Rome' were massacred, hanged, burned and crucified, and the new town went up in flames. Traces of charred earth in the eastern side of the City have confirmed the Roman accounts of the destruction of London, but the City rose again, and grew and flourished.

The town, although never classified as a *municipium* or a *colonia*, as were the tribal capitals at St Albans and Colchester, rapidly became the leading city of the province, a trading centre with roads radiating out from it all over the country. In the fourth century Londinium was to be awarded the honorary title of Augusta as a mark of imperial favour. It was a polyglot society in this great mercantile city, with people drawn from all over the Empire, as many as 45,000 of them at the City's height in the second century. Gauls, Nubians, Spaniards, Greeks, Turks, Germans, along with native Romanised Britons and the Italians themselves, lived and worked among the colonnades and giant statues that proclaimed the might of Imperial Rome. For the wealthy there were fine houses with painted plaster walls and mosaic floors, elegant furniture, gardens laid out with fountains sprinkling into pools, while ordinary folk had narrow thatched 'town houses'. The streets were lined with shops, inns and workhouses, and, down by the riverside were quays and warehouses stacked full of precious oil, wine and cloth imported from the Continent. At the 'town centre' (Cornhill) was a great square, dominated by a vast building housing administrative offices, the biggest basilica outside Italy. Nearby stood a palace (by Cannon Street), which may have been the governor's residence. For recreation there were public baths and an amphitheatre where the Guildhall now stands.

The face of the 'Home Counties', the new boom town's *pagus* or hinterland, must have been transformed; it has been argued that the area was more extensively Romanised than other parts of the country, although farming probably went on much as before. So what lay to the east? The City was enclosed by

20ft walls of Kentish ragstone, built in about AD 200; Aldgate, which guarded the Colchester Road and was to divide the City from the East End for 1,000 years, was one of the original four gates. Looking east from the gate you might have seen smoke rising from the funeral pyres of the City's main cemetery, 50 acres in extent, in what is now Whitechapel. This vast citadel of the dead, where over 100,000 corpses are thought to have been buried, covered the area later known as Goodman's Fields, now crossed by the Minories, Mansell Street, Leman Street and Prescot Street, and extended north of the Colchester (Mile End) Road. Other smaller burial grounds were located near today's Liverpool Street, at Smithfield and in Southwark. All were outside the City walls, as Roman law prescribed. The eastern cemetery was divided into a series of enclosures, with a minor road running through, from west to east, a road that must have witnessed many a torch-lit procession accompanied with wailing and music as biers were trundled out from the City.

Beyond the cemetery, along the routes of the modern Mile End and Commercial Roads, lay cornfields and market gardens stretching towards the Lea. By the late Roman era most of the London area was intensively cultivated, and it is unlikely that this swathe of fertile land, adjacent to a populous city, would not have been exploited, as it was later by the nuns of the Minories, successive Bishops of London and canons of St Paul's. The lower-lying alluvial soils near the two rivers provided meadow and grazing, and the flourishing village or town at Old Ford on the old Colchester Road may, it seems from the number of bones found there, have had a cattle market. Old Ford, which flourished until the fifth century, was one of a number of large settlements ringing London; others were at Brentford, Staines, Brockley Hill, Crayford and Ewell. Other known Roman villages farther east were at Little London, Chigwell, possibly Stratford, Romford, Upminster, Rainham, North Ockenden, Fairlop and Beckton.

Three major roads went out from the City across the Tower Hamlets triangle. The most northerly was the Staines to Colchester road, which crossed the Lea at Old Ford, probably following westwards the line of the Bethnal Green and Hackney roads, as described above. Following the line of the modern Mile End Road out of Aldgate was the slightly later straight road, which crossed the Lea at the ford. The third was a Thames-side route, running along the gravel ridge in the marshes from just east of the City Tower to Shadwell and Ratcliff; most of the modern road follows the age-old route and is known as the Highway.

The Highway started just east of the Tower of London site, where there were certainly some buildings, perhaps even a fortress; our forebears were convinced that the White Tower was built by Julius Caesar. The road led directly to Ratcliff, which was Stepney's port in the Middle Ages, focusing on the point where today the road goes into the Limehouse Link tunnel. Below Tower Hill the riverbank was low and swampy on the north side, and at high tide the unbanked river probably flowed over large tracts of land, hence Wapping in the Wose (Wose being derived from Wash or Ouze). A bit further east the riverside was protected by a line of low bluffs, the cliffs of Ratcliff, making access to the river easier than at any other place between the City and Blackwall. In the absence of any archaeological evidence of Roman occupation of this area, historians of the East End have always assumed that the Romans must have used the Ratcliff landing place, as the road does not lead anywhere else. Recent excavations have proved their assumptions well founded, and seem to herald a seismic shift in the view of the Roman East End.

Eight years ago archaeologists discovered the remains of a huge public bath-house on the south side of the Highway at Shadwell, just near St George's in the East. It was established that the baths had two phases of occupation, one in the second century and one in the fourth, and that they were demolished soon after 400 BC. Adjoining the baths site are the remnants of a series of clay and timber structures, possibly including an inn. To the immediate east, discovered in 1975, are the foundations of a stone tower. Originally this was thought to have been a signal tower, but the unearthing of a cremation cemetery close by suggests that it may have been a mausoleum. Nearby, on the west side of Wapping Lane, are the remains of what may have been granaries. Decorated plates from Gaul were found at these sites, with oyster shells scattered like crisp packets, stacks of beef and mutton bones, jewellery and even a leather bikini.

So 1½ miles east of the City on the riverside, about halfway along the major road which led from the City to a natural landing place, there were public buildings, a cemetery, farms and people living well. It seems there was a port complex, extending along from Shadwell to Ratcliff, dated from the first to the fourth centuries, namely practically the whole time of the Roman occupation, at its busiest in the third century. When there was a dramatic drop in the water level of the Thames between the first and third centuries the port operation may have concentrated on the eastern port, which, it seems from the dating of the bath-house, was already established. The Pool was no longer suitable for seagoing ships and the building of quays and revetments in the City stopped between AD 250 and 270. A defensive wall was built along the Thames, cutting the City off from its river.

A quarter of a mile inland from the Ratcliff landing place, lying to the north on higher ground and safe from flooding, was a pleasant wooded glade, which was to become in later years the heart of the East End, the village of Stepney. St Dunstan's church, which stands there as it has for 1,000 years or more, has a tradition of very great antiquity, and although there is no hard evidence to prove its great age the claim is worth consideration.

No Roman finds have been made in Stepney village; indeed, nothing much has surfaced between the Bronze Age and the late Middle Ages, and the earliest documentary reference to Stepney, as Stybbanhythe, was not made until AD 1000.

Common sense suggests, however, that the strong tradition of a very ancient settlement here may not be without foundation. It was an ideal spot: good for cereal cultivation, a stone's throw from the eastern port, on higher ground, safe from the inundations of the river, lying between two Roman roads. The lack of archaeological finds may be happenstance, perhaps occasioned by extensive medieval gravel quarrying, the digging of clay for bricks or by regular flooding in the lower-lying parts.

When St Dunstan's church was under major reconstruction in 1885 some Roman tiles were found near the south porch and arches of Roman brick in the north wall. This does not, of course, necessarily mean that a Roman temple or even a church stood on the site; all the fragments of the City's Saxon churches that have been found show evidence of the reuse of Roman building materials, and there are Roman traces in thirty-five Essex churches. For many years after the collapse of imperial rule in these islands there must have been huge quantities of bricks and tiles lying around, the remains of long-ruined villas and abandoned public buildings, ready for medieval masons to use when they set about building churches.

Nevertheless there is much to be said for the continuity of religious sites, and it is quite possible that Stepney church is, as has been claimed, one of the oldest Christian places of worship in Britain. Followers of the expanding 'Jesus cult' started arriving on these shores in the late third century, some no doubt landing at Londinium or even Ratcliff. Like the Druids they were regarded by the imperial authorities as a threat and were persecuted, until the Emperor Constantine, perhaps with an eye to the main chance, took the first steps towards establishing Christianity as the religion of the Empire in 313. The British Church was organised enough to send three bishops to the Christian Council held at Arles in the year following the initial edict of toleration.

Hardly any archaeological evidence has been found concerning Romano-British churches, but there must have been places of worship for what was now the official cult. Sir Montagu Sharpe, who made a study of Roman Middlesex a hundred years ago, produced an intriguing theory that seeks to prove the Roman origins of a number of churches in Middlesex and Essex. Using the alignment of traces of ancient roads he argues that London's canton was divided up by imperial surveyors into a number of equal size squares, making up rectangular subdivisions called *centurias*. This vast chequerboard of settlement plots was then, presumably, allocated to individuals. Where estates converged, or at village crossroads, were, he surmises, public 'chapels' or *compita* where ploughmen and millers, herdsmen and their families went to appease their gods with sacrifices and to celebrate the coming of spring and the joyous harvest. These deities would have been the strange Romano-British conflation of the Olympian cast, which the Italians had brought with them, and home-grown spirits, like Sulis of wells and streams

(Minerva) and Taranis the wheel god (Jupiter). Stepney church was, Sharpe claims, the site of one such *compita*, later adopted, as many were, by the Christians.

There yet remains to be found concrete evidence about any shrine, temple or Romano-British church in Stepney village. Sharpe's 'chequerboard' is rather far-fetched, but as we have seen the archaeological story of the East End is unfolding dramatically. Within a few decades perhaps finds will be made to confirm the opinion of the parish clerk who headed the 1748 vestry minute book 'The most ancient parish of Stepney'.

At all events Roman Tower Hamlets was a busy place, a patchwork of fields, gardens and meadows, crossed by main roads, and well watered by two large rivers and numerous springs and pools. Probably the air hummed with the clack of watermills, which were such a vital feature of this watery place in medieval times; they are said to have been introduced into the province by an early Roman governor. There were granaries stocked with corn in Wapping, ships riding on the river, warehouses and quays along the riverside, a thriving social and commercial centre at Ratcliff, cattle driven along the lanes to the market at Old Ford. Even the swampy peninsula later known as Stepney Marsh and then the Isle of Dogs (Dykes) may have been drained, providing the lush pastures for which it would become famous. Roman tiles were used when the chapel of St Mary in the Marsh was built there in the early Middle Ages, brought from the ruins of some nearby villa, perhaps.

In the early decades of the fourth century, after 350 years, the Roman administration collapsed, apparently quite suddenly, and England became England, the 'land of the Angles', barbarians from Denmark. German and Danish warrior bands had started raiding these islands in the early third century, and by the fourth the situation was severe enough to warrant the appointment of a general to guard the 'Saxon Shore'. London's defences were overhauled, bastions put on the east side and a riverside wall built. In 406–7 the Germans invaded Gaul and Britain was cut off from the empire. There followed a rapid economic collapse, and Roman government was withdrawn from Britain between 406 and 410. According to Gildas, a sixth-century Romanised Welsh monk, 'They [the inhabitants] took to looting from each other, since there was only a very small stock of food to give nourishment to the desperate people; and the calamities from abroad were made worse by internal conflict, and consequently, the whole area became almost devoid of food, except for what hunters could find.'

The last literary appearance of London as a Roman city is dated 457, when, according to the Anglo-Saxon Chronicle, Britons took refuge behind its walls, fleeing from their crushing defeat at Crayford at the hands of the probably legendary Hengist, the Jutish 'stallion'. What happened to London and its environs thenceforth is hotly debated, as is the nature of the Saxon invasion and settlement in general. The only near contemporary account is the apocalyptic *Ruin of Britain*, written by Gildas a hundred years later and based, on his own admission, on hearsay. His was a Christian polemic, deploring the pagan invaders and presenting the cataclysm as punishment for the sins of the land-grabbing and debauched Romano-British:

> Lamentable to behold, in the midst of the streets lay the tops of lofty towers, tumbled to the ground, stones of high walls, holy altars, fragments of human bodies, covered with livid clots of coagulated blood, looking as if they had been squeezed together in a press; and with no chance of being buried, save in the ruins of the houses, or in the ravening bellies of wild beasts and birds.

All that is certain is that Roman buildings fell into decay and that 'lowland' Britain was taken over by pagan Saxon rulers during the course of the following 200 years, with some survival of British culture and Christianity in the Celtic fringes. Petty kings established themselves, Old English replaced the existing language and Romano-Celtic place-names, apart from that of London itself and that of some rivers, were wiped from the face of England. Augusta the magnificent was either abandoned, or became what Sir Mortimer Wheeler described as a 'sub-Roman slum'. The Saxons were not city dwellers and, apparently from superstitious fear of the haunted Roman ruins, they created their new villages, or adopted old ones, outside the City, alongside riverbanks. Early settlements and cemeteries have been found to the west and south of London, with nothing nearer to the City than 4 miles, at Hanwell, Hammersmith, Ham, Greenwich, Brentford and Mitcham, and at Rainham and Enfield in Essex.

Saxons: Blida, Stibba, Waeppa and the Knights' Guild

By the early seventh century a new Saxon London had emerged, an important trading centre, until *c.* 604 under the sway of the East Saxon monarchs, then ruled by the Kentish kings and taken over by the Mercian dynasty in the 730s. Archaeological evidence indicates that this Lundewic was centred outside the old Roman walls, round the area later known as the old market, the Aldwych, with its port located along the riverside parallel to where the Strand is now. But there is reason to think that the seat of government was within the walls, and that the old Roman fort, still standing secure among the ruins on the western hill, was a royal headquarters.

As to what happened to the east of the City, in the absence of any serious scholarly attention or archaeological evidence, commonsense and guesswork must prevail. We know that the eastern cemetery was abandoned in the fifth century, the baths at Shadwell were demolished – and there does not seem to have been much sign of life at Old Ford. When the Saxons came sailing up the Thames and the Lea they would have found an undefended outpost of the City in the Tower Hamlets triangle. Sir Hubert Llewellyn-Smith, east London's first modern historian, surmised that the East Saxons arrived in our area in the last half of the sixth century, making their first permanent settlement at Stepney (Stybbanhythe) on the high ground just above Ratcliff, where there was a good haven (or hythe) at which Stybba's band could land. Perhaps they sailed up the Black Ditch, the brook that flowed from Spitalfields and emptied into the Thames at Limehouse Dock.

The place-names around are Saxon in origin and bespeak the settling of the area with small autonomous groups; whether they came as raiding parties or as peaceful wanderers we shall probably never know. Thus Blida came with his clan and gave his name to Bethnal Green, Hacca to Hackney, Deorlof to Dalston. It used to be thought that Wapping (Waeppingas) was the place where Waeppa's extended family made their village; the ingas element is a possessive, as in the Gillingas of Ealing, the Berecingas of Barking and the Gumeningas of Harrow. Today a more likely derivation is thought to be from Walpol, meaning a marsh. The bank of brambles rising from the Lea they called Bramlege (Bromley), and the name of the old Roman port was lost, replaced by 'red cliff' (Ratcliff), because of the colour of the sandy gravel that was exposed there. They named the fields and wells and streams: Shadwell, the shallow well, Shacklewell, Snecockswell, Copatswell and Schadfliet.

Sir Mortimer Wheeler's thesis that Grim's Dyke and other earthworks around London marked a Romano-British enclave in the south-east might make the date of the Saxon settlements in Tower Hamlets of a later date than Llewellyn-Smith suggested. But we are sailing through uncharted waters in the fifth and sixth centuries, with only Gildas for company, and it is not until the opening years of the following century that there is some slight clearing of the mists. Bede's *Ecclesiastical History*, written in the early eighth century, gives us the first substantial clue about the origins of Stepney as an episcopal manor.

Using reliable Vatican and Kentish sources, Bede says that in 604, following the successful Christian mission of Augustine to the King of Kent, a cathedral, St Paul's, was built; it is thought to have been approximately on its present site. Ethelbert, the king, assigned lands for the sustenance of the diocese around London and in Essex. The foundation endowment may have included Stepney:

In the year of our Lord 604, Augustine, archbishop of Britain, ordained two bishops, viz. Mellitus and Justus; Mellitus to preach to the province of the East-Saxons, who are divided from Kent by the river Thames, and border on the Eastern sea. Their metropolis is the City of London, which is situated on the banks of the aforesaid river, and is the mart of many nations resorting to it by sea and land. At that time, Sabert, nephew to Ethelbert by his sister Ricula, reigned over the nation, though he was under subjection to Ethelbert, who, as has been said above, had command over all the nations of the English as far as the river Humber. But when this province also received the word of truth, by the preaching of Mellitus, King Ethelbert built the church of St. Paul, in the City of London, where he and his successors should have their episcopal see ... he also bestowed many gifts on the bishops [of London and Rochester] ... and added both lands and possessions for the maintenance of those who were with the bishops.

Although the Stepney estate is not mentioned by name until 400 years later, in a list of cathedral properties, the medieval canons believed that Stepney, the Bishop of London's own manor, was part of the grant made by Ethelbert to the Church. The cathedral was endowed with a wide belt of land, encircling the City on the north and east, 24 hides in Moorfields, St Pancras and modern Camden and 55 in Stepney with Hackney and Clerkenwell. This area of about 7,600 acres (including Tillingham in Essex) was to be used to supply food for the teams of clergy and an income for the running of the diocese, which was, according to Bede, coterminous with the kingdom of the East Saxons. Thus, if the canons were right, began the long rule of the Church in east London, which only ended when Stepney manor was handed over to Sir Thomas Wentworth in 1550, with all its appurtenances: Shoreditch, Holywell Street, Cleve Street, Brook Street, Whitechapel, Poplar, North Street, Stratford atte Bow, Ratcliff, Limehouse, Mile End, Bethnal Green, Old Ford, and all Hackney.

It was not a continuous thread, however. Only twelve years after the creation of the bishopric Ethelbert and Sebert both died, and the common folk who had adopted Christianity at their behest lapsed into paganism. In spite of Mellitus's best efforts Woden, the mighty sky god, Freya, the mother goddess, Tiw, the protector of warriors, and the rest came back into play, and it was not until Bishop Erkenwald (675–93) appeared on the scene that London's Church was set to rights again. What happened to the Stepney estates and the rest of the diocesan endowments is anybody's guess.

By the mid- to late seventh century the Christian Church was firmly established; its Continental missionaries brought back to rough and roaring England literacy and learning, culture and sophistication, the art of building with stone, the true legacy of the imperial Roman civilisation. St Aldhelm, Abbot of Malmesbury, wrote in the 680s, 'Where once the crude pillars of the ... foul snake and the stag were worshipped with coarse stupidity in profane shrines, in their place dwellings for students, not to mention holy houses of prayer, are constructed skilfully by the talent of the architect.' Minsters peppered the land. These were largely royal and aristocratic foundations, churches-cum-monasteries, with accommodation for resident priests, some secular, some monks and nuns, with chapels for prayer, baptistries, cemeteries for the burial of the holy dead and farms for the sustenance of the workforce. Many later became mother or parish churches. Tradition puts the foundation of Stepney church in this period; what would become the mother church of a huge parish on the east of the City may well have started life as an outpost of St Paul's, lying as it did halfway between the cathedral and Barking Abbey, founded by Erkenwald in 666.

We can picture this early Stepney, a cluster of thatched huts (like those at the recreated Anglo-Saxon village at West Stow) with a little wattle church in their midst, dedicated, as many Saxon churches were, to All Saints, standing perhaps where St Dunstan's still stands, with cattle in enclosures and pigs rooting for acorns and beechmast. A little to the north ran the old Roman road to Colchester, overgrown, no doubt, but probably still in use. North of the road was Blida's village (Bethnal Green) on the borders of the dense woodland, a hunting ground for deer and wild boar. A short walk to the south took the villagers down a track, later given the name of Cleve (Cliff) Street, to the river, rich in salmon and eels. To the south-east snipe and curlew wheeled over reeds and irises in the great marshy peninsula that would become the Isle of Dogs.

Little is known about the organisation of government in these times, when London was an important port but not yet a capital city, and kingdoms came and went. The rich paraphernalia found recently near Southend, in the tomb of a Christian warrior king known to archaeology as the Prince of Prittlewell, is a reminder that this was no mud hut society. London came under the sway of different ruling houses and its hinterland was known as Middlesex, a no-man's land that lay between the territories of the East and West Saxons. The earliest reference to 'the province called Middelseaxan' is in a 704 grant to the Bishop of London of lands at Twickenham. This was made by Swaefred, sub-king of the East Saxons, under Mercian rule. Church councils are known to have met at Chelsea, Brentford and in London itself. Little hard evidence has surfaced of any activity, ecclesiastical or otherwise, in eastern Middlesex; although, as we have noted, Bishop Erkenwald founded a house of nuns for his sister on the other side of the Lea, at Barking in Essex. Only a handful of seventh-century charters survive, mainly recording grants of lands to monasteries and churches by Mercian kings, but none relate to our area.

Possibly the Bishops of London from the seventh to tenth centuries were lords of the estate known as Stibbanhythe; they may even have lived at Bethnal Green as their successors did. These lordly priests, Erkenwald's successors, the 'bishops of the East Saxons', are little more to us than names: Waldhere (693) Ingwald, Ecwulf, Wigheah, Eadbert, Eadgar, Coenwalh, Eadbald, Heathobert, Osmund, Aethelnoth, Ceolberht, Deorwulf, Swithwulf, Heahstan, Wulfsige, Aethelweard, Leofstan, Theodred and Brihthelm (d. 957). They appear in the scanty records witnessing charters, attending councils, receiving the odd grant of land. Only for the saintly Theodred is there a little more, notably a will, but no specific mention is made of Stepney; although fifty years after his death the estate certainly belonged to St Paul's. As landlords of the Anglo-Saxon East Enders, the bishops would have taken rents and services from the farmers and millers who presumably supplied grain for the people of London, as their descendants would for generation upon generation. It is not until the appointment of the great Dunstan as bishop in 957, however, that the mists hanging over the eastern fields and marshes begin to clear a little more.

But before that came the terrible Viking raids that ravaged the country from the late eighth century and culminated in about half the country being assigned as Danelaw. These fierce Norsemen, it was said, never wept for their sins or the death of their friends, and cooked victory feasts in cauldrons placed on top of the corpses of their enemies. There is an old tale that links Stepney with the Viking attacks. It is unlikely to be based in fact – but as it is so unlikely you never know! White Horse Street, which runs from the Mile End Road to Stepney church, and originally went right down to the river, along the line of what is now Butcher Row, has been known by that name for about 400 years. They say that the body of a Kentish warrior, slaughtered by the Danes, was brought along the river to be buried in the hallowed ground by the little Saxon church of All Saints. In commemoration there was erected nearby the emblem of a white horse, the well-known badge of Kent.

The inhabitants of Lundenwic, and doubtless those living in the eastern villages named after the old Saxon bandits, together with the farmers from the marsh islands of Thorney, Chelsea, Bermondsey and Battersea, moved into the ancient ruins of the Roman metropolis, abandoned so long ago, and took shelter behind its high stone walls. London was repeatedly attacked, and was occupied from 871/2 until 886, when it was recovered by Alfred the Great. The eastern approaches were extremely vulnerable over this period; Stepney was only a few miles from the easily fordable river Lea, which was the boundary with the Danelaw set by treaty in 878. Raiding still went on after 878, and in 895 a flotilla of Danish ships poured up the Thames and the Lea. The following summer, in the fields near the City says the chronicler, Alfred's army had to guard the harvesters as they reaped the corn. Like many other churches and monasteries, Barking Abbey had been destroyed (in 870); the lands stretching east from the City walls towards the Danish boundary at the Lea were a war zone, and we can surmise that the Tower Hamlets triangle was laid waste, with the little All Saints' church and the dwellings it serviced being burnt to the ground.

In 886, according to the Anglo-Saxon Chronicle, 'gesette Alfred Lundenburh and gave the burh to Aethered the ealdorman to hold'. Archaeological evidence indicates that London was indeed rebuilt at this time, but some historians, notably

Sir Hubert Llewellyn-Smith and W.R. Lethaby, have interpreted the words of the Chronicle as meaning that Alfred established a military colony to garrison the citadel of London, to occupy what later became Tower Hill and to protect the eastern approaches to the City. Herein Lethaby sees the origins of the strange Knights Gild or Cnihtengild, of which more anon.

Under Alfred's grandson Aethelstan, England came under one rule, and the reign of his great grandson, Edgar the Peaceable (957–75), is often referred to as a 'golden age'. It was during this time of religious reform and a respite from Viking onslaughts that Stepney church was apparently rebuilt. According to an oft-repeated story, it was in the year 952, in the reign of Edgar's predecessor, Eadred, that St Dunstan refounded the ancient All Saints' church, which after his canonisation in 1029 adopted a new dedication. Although the origins of this tradition are lost, it makes sense.

The tenth century was the great era of church-building, with large minsters replaced by the one church, one priest, one village system. Unlike continental Europe, where churches of this era were mainly episcopal foundations, English churches were mainly built by thegns and attached to their estates as an insurance policy for a place in heaven or to acquire local kudos. Dunstan, however, is known to have founded a number when he was Archbishop of Canterbury (959–88), notably at Mayfield in Sussex, 'as also in the other places of his hospices'.

In the year 952 Dunstan, a scion of the royal house of Wessex, a saintly, charismatic man and Abbot of Glastonbury, was chief adviser to King Eadred. In 955 he was sent into exile for questioning the marriage of the new sixteen-year-old king, Eadred, but was recalled two years later by his successor, and became the leading royal counsellor. He was made Bishop of London and of Worcester, and was then raised to be Archbishop of Canterbury. For nearly thirty years he was probably the greatest man in the country, more influential and longer in power than Becket or Wolsey. As elder statesman to a number of very young monarchs he dominated the political scene, reviving the almost extinct monastic life, securing the election of Edward the Confessor and devising a coronation service, part of which is still used today. It is quite reasonable to suppose that as Bishop of London Dunstan refounded a church in what became his vill, the old church having, perhaps, fallen prey to the Vikings. It has been suggested that he might also have been responsible for the foundation of Bromley Abbey, although this is disputed.

It is in Dunstan's day, during the relatively peaceful reign of King Edgar (959–75), that the legend of the Knights' Guild, with its fairytale jousting competition, is set. It concerns the Portsoken, and according to John Stow, who probably had it from the cartulary of Holy Trinity Priory (which took over its jurisdiction in 1125), the folk living here in the tenth century had left it 'because of too much servitude'. No one seems to know exactly what this means, but at all events the beleaguered area of wasteland adjoining the City, perhaps the haunt of thugs, was put under the special charge of a band of young men, known as the Knighten Guild or the Anglissh Knightgelda, as it appears in the City records. Such guilds seem to have existed in Canterbury and Winchester, but they remain something of a mystery. The term 'cniht' was not used in the Anglo-Saxon period, as the equivalent of a knight in the age of chivalry; it meant either a lad or an attendant or servant. It has been surmised that the Knights' Guild may have been either an association of thegns' sons who had not yet come into their estates, or of the personal attendants of various lords. W.R. Lethaby saw it as a military garrison dating from Alfred's day, when London was under attack from Vikings, although there does not seem to be any real evidence for its existence pre-Edgar.

Whatever the origins or function of this guild, whether it was a 'police force' or just a way of rewarding men for military service with a grant of land that no one else would touch, it remained the effective ruling body for the western strip of the Tower Hamlets for something in the region of 150 years, with its charter renewed in turn by Edward the Confessor, William Rufus and Henry I.

The Danish wars broke out again after the death of St Dunstan in 988, and the laws of Aethelred the Unready advised: 'It is a wise precaution to have warships ready every year soon after Easter.' Appropriately for a parish that was to become the heart of the seafaring end of town, its church was known as 'the church of the high seas', the earliest known mention of Stepney by name (as Stybbanhythe) being in a list of 'scipmen' required for manning a ship, dated AD 1000. Warships of this date needed sixty sailors, and this document lists the king's requirements from the places that belonged to St Paul's Cathedral and the bishop, there being no distinction made yet between episcopal lands and those belonging to the canons. A note is made of the number of men each estate is to supply for the navy: the total is fifty-eight, with Stepney and Islington (Gislandune) assigned to produce two.

It is nearly 1,000 years since the Romano-British East Enders loaded their ships at Shadwell and herded their cattle to market at Old Ford. At last the records give us a name for somewhere in the East End, Stibba's Haven, the village that will become over the next 1,000 years Stibbenhede, Stebenee, Stepney; the place at the heart of it all. The Saxon East End is a shadowy place, with only hints and legends allowing a very partial picture of the great episcopal estate that lay east of Lundenburgh. From these Dark Ages, however, there survives *in situ* one very concrete reminder of the ancient past. Set into the east wall of Stepney church is a stone rood, a panel measuring 3ft 2in high by 2ft 3in across, with the crucifixion in relief and the 'human' figures of the sun and moon veiling their eyes in grief. It is much weathered, having hung for many centuries outside the south porch. Expert opinion agrees that it is certainly pre-thirteenth century, and the likelihood is that it dates from the eleventh.

Chapter 2

THE TOWER AND ITS HAMLETS

1066–1200

The Norman Conquest and Domesday

The Norman invasion brought the Tower to the Tower Hamlets; in due course the post of Constable of the Tower would become combined with that of Lord Lieutenant for the hamlets. With the Conqueror's Domesday survey of 1086 comes the first contemporary account of the East End. The precious statistics illuminate the dim and distant ploughlands and meadows, naming the great land-owners and counting the peasant labourers; describing the land manor by manor, both as it was at the time of the Conquest and twenty years later. 'Not one ox nor one cow nor one pig which was there was left out,' wrote the chronicler, with some exaggeration.

When the brutal Normans, themselves of Viking descent, took the prize of England, sixty-six years had passed since the first mention of Stepney in the records, the list of sailors required to fight off the Danes. Since then there had been a Danish king, the powerful and wise Canute, ruling for nearly twenty years, and now the throne was back with the West Saxon line. London had been the headquarters for the defence of the realm against attack and the largest conurbation by far. Although the idea of a capital city was not yet established in western Europe and the centre of government moved around with the court, London, with its large population and its extensive trading connections, was the lead-ing town and crucial for William's conquest. It stood almost entirely within the Roman walls, with the vill of Westminster and its church of St Peter a little to the west. To the immediate east was the strip of land guarded by the City's Knights' Guild; it included what is now Houndsditch and the Minories and the open ground at East Smithfield (on the east side of Tower Hill) where a great watermill whirred and clattered, the biggest in the country, grinding corn for the City's bread. The villages and hamlets between the walls and the Lea, Wapping, Stepney, Bethnal Green, Shadwell, Bromley, with Hackney and Dalston to the north, lay undefended, and we can only guess how they fared in that terrible autumn and winter of 1066 when William the Bastard and his army, having defeated the Saxons at Hastings, wrought devastation in Middlesex and Surrey. Both the surviving accounts of his campaign and Domesday evidence suggest that the eastern villages suffered appreciably less than the rest of London's hinterland.

Accounts vary slightly, but it seems clear that after Hastings William, having gained the submission of the other chief city, Winchester, 'directed his march to where populous London gleamed'. His army burned its southern suburbs and turned west, crossing the river at Wallingford and making for Berkhamsted, where, according to one version of events, William took the surrender of Archbishop Ealdred, Edgar the Ætheling, the Earls Edwin and Morcar, and 'all the best men from London' and was offered the Crown. The Normans finally came down into London through Hackney and Clerkenwell, slaughtering and burning as they came. Siege engines may even have been brought up to the City walls. At all events, the terrified Londoners offered their surrender at some point.

The Tower Hamlets triangle, then, seems to have escaped the worst ravages of the invader. Domesday records that in Stepney manor, a great block of land of some 7,000 acres flanking the City on the east and encompassing lands to the north as far as today's Muswell Hill, the overall loss in value between 1066 and 1086 was 23 per cent. Although it is not possible to identify all the individual estates within the manor, it does seem to have been the case that the greatest depreciation was in the Fafiton lands at Kingsland and the Brian lands in Clerkenwell, both of which were probably on William's route to London from Berkhamsted.

After being crowned at Westminster William went to Barking Abbey, presumably marching along the Colchester (Mile End) road through the East End, while fortifications were undertaken in London to contain what the chronicler describes as 'the restlessness of its vast and savage population'. According to the king's biographer, William of Poitiers, the Conqueror sent an advance guard to London to construct a fortress in preparation for a triumphal entry into the City; the first reference to the Tower of London. Whatever the details of the chronology, archaeological evidence confirms that these early defences used the Roman wall in the south-east corner of the City, and that East London's great royal castle, the White Tower, was under construction on this site by the 1070s and completed by 1100. It was built of limestone brought from Caen, protected by the old walls on two sides with wide ditches to the north and west, a massive structure dominating the skyline, a reminder to the 'restless' Londoner, the Wapping miller, the Stepney ploughman, the shopkeeper up at Aldgate Street, of the military force of the Frenchmen who were now their masters.

Not, one imagines, that they would have needed reminding. Thousands had been slaughtered, and in the upper echelons of society the process of

Normanisation was complete. The court spoke French, children were given Norman names, men were brought over from the Continent to take the top jobs in the Church and, perhaps most immediate of all, there was a revolution in landholding. The 5,000 men who came over with William were well rewarded; of the 180 or so tenants-in-chief with large estates in Domesday only two were Englishmen; of the 1,400 lesser tenants-in-chief about 100 were English; among the 6,000 sub-tenants there were more English. As to the villagers and cottagers, the smallholders, craftsmen, labourers and their like, although they are not named, they were probably to a man of old English stock.

In Stepney manor, although a virtual clean sweep was made of the tenants, the man at the top remained the same. He was the Bishop of London, one William, a Norman and a favourite of King Edward the Confessor's; he had been bishop since 1051, and continued in post and in charge of Stepney until his death in 1075.

In black gall ink, on sheep's skin, written with a sharpened goose quill 923 years ago, is the undoubted evidence that Stepney was held by the Bishop of London. The entry in Great Domesday sets the estate in the Hundred of Ossultone. Under the Saxon kings the shires (formed in the late tenth century) had been divided up into hundreds, notionally containing about a hundred families, or ten tithings; there were six in Middlesex. Ossultone's name was derived from Oswulf's stone, which marked the meeting place of the hundred court, somewhere near Park Lane. The bishop's manor of Stepney encompassed the later parish of Stepney (including Whitechapel, Wapping, Shadwell, Ratcliffe, Bethnal Green, Bromley, Old Ford, Poplar, Limehouse, Stratford, Mile End and the Isle of Dogs), Hackney, part of Shoreditch, Clerkenwell, Islington and Barnsbury, covering some 7,000 acres. In 1066 the only lay tenants were Alwin Stichbare ('King Edward's man'), two mill-owners and Earl Godwin, the father of King Harold, killed at Hastings.

Before we attempt to interpret what Domesday tells us about Stepney (there is no Domesday for London; Stow says there was but it was lost), we will look at the wider picture. Nearly 200 years of raids and unremitting war had drawn the country into close-knit units, a strong monarchy at the head, with a handful of tremendously powerful families, underpinned by a thegnly class. Tenant farmers, villeins, the yeomen of England, some of them with farms as big as 100 acres, and below them peasants and slaves, bought and sold like cattle, were defended by the military might of these landlords, to whom they were tied by obligations and taxes. No man could be without a lord, said King Athelstan's law code of 930. For many thousands of Englishmen their 'lord' was an abbey, a cathedral or a bishop. About half the land in the tiny county of Middlesex (only 278 square miles, as opposed to 1,524 in Essex) belonged to the Church, to the Archbishop of Canterbury, the Bishop of London, the canons of St Paul's, and the Abbot of Westminster.

Although the Conquest saw much looting of Church treasures and destruction of ecclesiastical buildings, the ancient Church estates by and large remained intact. Thus in the great confiscation, although Bishop William lost about 1,200 acres of his Stepney demesne lands (lands devoted to the lord's profit) to three Norman tenants, he was compensated with an important castle at Bishops Stortford. The canons lost their Barnsbury land, but were compensated with gains in Essex.

The land was measured in hides (a sort of rateable value, the equivalent of about 120 acres in Middlesex), arable land in numbers of ploughteams, and woodland in terms of the number of pigs that could be fed from acorns and beechmast. In post-Conquest Middlesex the largest estate described in Domesday is that given under the heading *Terra Episcopi Lundon et Canonicorum*, the lands of the Bishop of London and the canons of the cathedral chapter at St Paul's, with a total assessment of 162 hides, 1 virgate. Of this 40 hides was the Fulham estate and 32 was Stepney.

Although place-name evidence suggests that there were villages, hamlets or farmsteads at Wapping, Bromley and Bethnal Green, and there were enough people living in the Marsh (the Isle of Dogs) to warrant a chapel there within fifty or so years of the survey, Stepney is the only east London place named in Domesday. It is the only east London place-name to appear in any government records until the twelfth century. The bishop's manor was a large and valuable holding, worth £48, only a drop of £2 since 1066.

Two lay Norman tenants-in-chief held land in Stepney directly from the king, although the bishop laid claim to both of these manors. The two takeovers are thought to have been respectively at Bromley, where Robert son of Roscelin held 3½ hides, which had in the Confessor's day belonged to one Alwin Stichehare, 'King Edward's man', and in Kingsland, where Robert Fafiton was in possession of 4 hides that had belonged to a Saxon canon of St Paul's called Sired, the father of Ailward, prebendary of Stoke Newington. Fafiton, who was a minor landholder, with small estates in four counties, also had 53 acres that had been seized by Hugh de Berners (one of the bishop's tenants) from the canons of St Paul's.

The bishop had ten sub-tenants in 1086, and of them only two had been there at the Conquest. The only tenant who was a significant figure was Ranulf Flambard. He held 3½ hides that had belonged to Earl Godwin, father of King Harold, now under the bishop's overlordship. Flambard was to become one of the leading men of the realm, Bishop of Durham and then chief minister to William Rufus. He had been attached to the household of Maurice, Archdeacon of le Mans, then the royal chancellor and, in 1086, created Bishop of London. The Stepney lands may have been a gift from Maurice.

One Hugh de Berners, who also had small manors in Essex and Cambridgeshire, had an estate of 5 hides, 1 virgate and a mill. The 5 hides had formerly belonged to the canons of St Paul's and were partly located, as their names suggest, in Canonbury and Barnsbury. Half of the canons' land had been the personal property of Canon Sired, who had held some of the Fafiton lands.

From our point of view Berners' industrial acquisition in Stepney is most interesting. The most valuable watermill in the country, and perhaps the largest, was his, with 30 acres of land attached to it. There is a fair chance that this was on the site of the famous twin watermills on the Thames, later known as Crassh Mills (see plan), near the Wapping Swans Nest Hermitage and St Katharine's. The lane leading to it was once called Toddyneslane (before it became Nightingale or Cnihtengild Lane and then Thomas More Street). The lane ran by a pond called Dodding's, according to John Stow, and according to Domesday the pre-Conquest mill-owner, paying rent to the bishop, was one Doding. In 1362 a Burners descendant of Hugh held two mills on the St Katharine's site and in 1375, according to the will of Sir Nicholas Loveyn, there were two mills hereabouts, 'les Molynes appellez Eastmills' and Crassh Mills.

A Norman lady, referred to in the Domesday text only as 'the wife of Brian', had 5 hides, taken from the bishops' demesne, part of which lay in Clerkenwell, and later granted to the priory of St Mary, Clerkenwell and the Knights Hospitallers. It is possible that she was the wife of Count Brian, son of Eude, Count of Brittany; Brian had led the suppression of the invasion of Harold's sons from Ireland in 1069.

Another portion of the bishop's demesne was assigned to William de Vere of the great de Vere clan, from which were descended the Earls of Oxford. This was 1 hide, which may have been in Hackney or possibly the Isle of Dogs. Two other portions of the bishop's demesne were given to members of the royal household. King William's personal physician and chaplain, Gilbert Maminot, Bishop of Lisieux, 'very learned but not very spiritual', had 1½ hides; he was well rewarded with small fiefs of the king in six counties and under-tenancies in others. William the Chamberlain, who also had various other manors in different parts of the country, held 1 hide, 3 virgates in Stepney, possibly the manor of Topsfield in Hornsey. In addition Alvric Chacepul had 1 hide, formerly the bishop's demesne, but no plough, and Canon Edmund fitz Algot had a large, newly constructed mill on the Lea at Old Ford.

The two survivors of the great confiscation were Alwin, the son of Brihtmar, who kept on the 20s mill that he had in 1066, and Canon Englebric, a major land-holder and chancellor of the Diocese of London, whose small estate, probably at Shadwell, may have been a prebend (canon's personal estate), as Domesday says that he was not allowed to sell it.

The bishop's own demesne was in 1086 only 14 hides (1,680 acres); it had been 24 hides in 1066. There were only three plough teams, compared with twenty-two belonging to the husbandmen; this may indicate that not much demesne farming went on (by the mid-fourteenth century it had stopped altogether), or it may merely be a reflection of the fact that much of the demesne was wooded, as it continued to be for hundreds of years, with Victoria Park as a modern reminder. The bishop's own arable land lay between Bethnal Green and Shoreditch, extending down to the Whitechapel Road.

The people of eleventh-century Stepney were disposed among the scattered villages, farms, cottages and inns that may have gathered outside the City's eastern gates. The population of London, although there is no Domesday entry to guide us, is thought to have been about 10,000 at this time, and the total number of people living in England possibly something in the region of 2 million. In rural Middlesex there were perhaps 2,000, of which between 800 and 900 were in Stepney manor. Presumably the bishop spent some time at his manor house (it was certainly there by 1169), as bishops would for several hundred years, and Roger, the sheriff of Middlesex, may have lived on the 60-acre estate in Clerkenwell that he rented from the wife of Brian. There is no way of knowing how many of the new Norman masters lived in the area, whether the men who ran the estates as stewards or bailiffs were countrymen of theirs, or whether there was any significant immigrant presence. There are no 'Frenchmen' listed in the Domesday Book for Stepney, as there are in some manors.

Most families were those of villeins or villagers, the highest class of dependent peasantry; on the bishop's estate there were sixty-one men of this category of which most (forty-four) had 30 acres of farmland. Seven of them had much larger holdings of 65 acres and nine had smaller ones of 15 acres. They would have owed labour services to the lord, although it is possible that cash rents were already being paid in lieu; the process of commutation in Stepney was well in advance of other places, being complete on the episcopal manor by the mid-fourteenth century. On the wife of Brian's estate two of the villeins paid cash rent for their houses; at 8s and 4s a year respectively they must have been substantial properties.

An extract from a management text in a volume of Anglo-Saxon law gives some indication of what was expected of villeins in terms of work and dues:

> The gebur's [villein's] duties vary; in some places they are heavy, in other moderate. On some estates it is such that he must perform such work as he is told for two weekdays each week throughout the year, and three weekdays at harvest time, and three from Candlemas to Easter; if he performs cartage he need not work while his horse is out. At Michaelmas he must pay 10d tax, and at Martinmas twenty-three sesters of barley and two hens: at Easter one young sheep or twopence. And from the time when they first plough until Martinmas he must plough one acre [of his lord's land] each week and prepare the seed in the lord's barn himself … When death befalls him, his lord is to take charge of what he leaves.

Forty-six cottars or cottagers (the next rank down) shared 120 acres between them, paying 30s to the bishop. From the size of the rent and the proximity to London it has been deduced that these men were possibly craftsmen, artisans, shopkeepers or market gardeners from the urbanised areas of ribbon development outside the City in Alegate Street (Whitechapel) of Haliwell Street (Shoreditch), both of which lay partly in the manor. The wife of Brian's fifteen bordars (similar to cottars) paid 9s for their 10 acres and may have also been of this order.

William of Poitiers described England as the 'granary of Ceres', and the rich lands to the east of London were, like most of south-east England, predominantly arable, with good meadows, rich pastures over towards the Lea and woodland, which provided timber to spare and food for 750 pigs, with deer and wild bulls for the chase. Wheat, oats and barley were the main crops, grown in vast fields, much larger than any today. The heavy ploughs, drawn by a team of eight oxen, were cumbersome and difficult to turn, so the land was divided into long strips, about 22yds wide, each of which was reckoned as a separate unit.

'On the north [of London],' wrote William FitzStephen, some hundred years after Domesday, 'are pasture lands and a pleasant space of flat meadow, intersected by running waters, which turn revolving mill-wheels with a merry din.' Windmills were not introduced until the twelfth century and the countryside murmured with the sound of waterwheels; 3,500 mills are mentioned in Domesday and there were probably many more. The Stepney mills, or some of them, presumably ground grain for London's bread, as the mills at Stratford and Old Ford would for years to come. There were seven mills in all: four small ones on the bishop's demesne, worth only £4 16s 4d a piece; the great Doding/ Berners mill at East Smithfield/Wapping, worth 66s 8d; a newly constructed mill at Old Ford, held by a canon of St Paul's, Edmund FitzAlgot, (later a fullers' mill called Allgodsmill), worth 33s 6d; and another, worth 20s and with no land attached, still in the hands of its old English tenant, Alwin son of Brihtmare. Both Crassh Mills and Algot's mill would pass in the fourteenth century to St Mary Graces, the abbey on Tower Hill.

The millers at Dodings and Old Ford grew dusty at their toil, as all England groaned under the Norman Yoke. Rebellions in the west, east and north were quashed with increasing ferocity and castles rose everywhere. There were three in London alone, on the eastern side: the White Tower, Montfichet, to the southwest of St Paul's, and Baynards, south of Ludgate. Our villagers went on as usual through seedtime and harvest, aware, perhaps, of the goings-on in the hundred court, where some of them may have testified that the Norman lord Hugh de Berners had seized land from the canons of the cathedral. Orderic Vitalis, the Anglo-Norman historian, observed in the 1120s: 'The English are concerned only in the tilling of their fields: feasts and convivialities are more to their taste than battles.'

In the time of Thomas a Becket

Sixty-eight years after the Conqueror's survey, in 1154, comes the first reference to Stepney church in the records. Its omission from Domesday is without significance; many, many churches that are known to have been in existence at the time were not recorded. The probability is that a very old church stood where St Dunstan's is now, serving the 500 or so people in the hamlets around; in the City there were about 300 people to each church, and the pattern in the countryside of village churches was well established.

St Dunstan's parish, which was delineated by this time, comprised about 4,500 acres, the whole of the triangle of land bounded by the City, the Thames and the Lea, with only Bromley assuming independent parochial status. Stepney parish included the suburb of Whitechapel (Algate Street), the villages at Bow and Old Ford, a number of scattered hamlets and isolated farmsteads (Mile End, Shadwell, Wapping, Poplar, Bethnal Green, Limehouse) and Stepney Marsh. East Smithfield and the Portsoken in due course become part of the parish of St Botolph Aldgate.

The church at the centre of the Tower Hamlets was firmly established now, with a collection of farms and cottages around it, no doubt – although gravel quarrying and flooding have left no archaeological indicators of domestic habitation at that time. The landlord bishop was in his palace at Bethnal Green, from time to time, while the bailiffs of the Norman aristocracy took rents in kind and cash, and English peasants were at the plough. We have enough in the way of evidence, deeds and charters mainly, to create a reasonable picture of the twelfth-century East End and to see what changes took place during the reigns of William Rufus and Henry I, and the civil war that followed.

The first year of the reign of Thomas Becket's stormy king, Henry II, was 1154. His accession rescued the realm from seventeen years of civil war and the devastation that racked the kingdom while Matilda, granddaughter of William the Conqueror, and her cousin Stephen fought for the throne, with London taking Stephen's part. According to the chronicler, in these chaotic and lawless times poor men starved, taxes were high and corn, meat, cheese and butter were in short supply. Swine and cattle plagues had savaged the land; in 1131 a tenth of all ploughs were laid up for want of beasts to pull them. For the eastern villagers, especially the farmers in Stepney Marsh, the great floods of November 1099 and August 1115 must have wrought havoc.

Looking west from Stepney church, across the wide, flat cornfields, traversed by quiet ways and dotted with farms, you could see the towers, turrets and walls of the City of London, guarded by its three castles; a metropolis of some 50,000 souls, the largest city north of the Alps. The eleventh and twelfth centuries saw the phenomenal growth of London; it was said to have been, with Cologne, one of the two 'urban phenomena' of northern Europe. William FitzStephen's famous description, written in about 1180, is of a demi-paradise, marred only by 'the immoderate drinking of fools' and the frequency of fires. Twice between Domesday and the accession of Henry II it had been burnt to the ground; the cathedral was rebuilt, the new one being the largest church in England, with the tallest spire. The streets, alleys and wharves buzzed with life and trade; there was gold from Arabia, spice and incense from Scythia, palm oil from Baghdad, gems from Egypt, silk from China, wine from France, and furs from Norway and Russia. The king's palace 'exalts its head and stretches wide', situated at the end of a road lined with mansions to the west of the City.

Stepney village was slightly farther to the east of the City than Westminster was to the west. From 1052 Westminster had been the king's London headquarters, and as such was to attract courtiers, bishops and the nobility, and the high-class tradesmen who serviced them; thus the ancient origins of the West and East Ends. City merchants, made rich by trade and commerce, tended to look east for their suburban retreats and investments in land.

Midway between the Colchester Road and the Roman riverside highway, Stepney village lay among fields and meadows that were criss-crossed with streams, half a mile from the riverbank and high enough above it to be safe from flooding. To its north was a dense and immense forest. On the fringe of this was the hamlet of Bethnal Green, a few cottages and city merchants' houses clustered around St Winifred's well and the clearing known as the Green. Among the trees was the bishop's palace, with its farms and outbuildings. The earliest reference to the hamlet by name is a thirteenth-century grant by Mathilda le Vayre of Stepney to Henry Dariere, wheelwright of Aldgate Street, and his wife Agatha, of a parcel of land next to her house in Blithehale. You can walk the route from Stepney village to the bishop's manor house today by setting off from north of the church up Whitehorse Lane, crossing the Mile End Road into Globe Road and then taking Approach Road up to Victoria Park. The mansion lay just to the right of the gate into the park.

To get to Stepney from the City you could leave via the eastern gate (Aldgate), newly rebuilt, facing onto the Colchester Road, then turn right towards the river after 1 mile (at Mile End). Along here was some ribbon development, spilling out from the City. It would become Whitechapel, but was known for some years to come as Algatestreet. Alternatively you could take the southern route. Down by the river, north-east of the Tower, was a postern, St Peter's gate, which opened onto East Smithfield; thence there were two routes to Stepney and the old port of Ratcliff (La Rede Clive in 1294). The northerly one, which would become Cable Street and Brook Street (at the Ratcliff end), was Hachestreet, meaning Gate Street (by 1250). By 1542 the west end was called Hog Lane, by 1607 Rosemary Lane, later Royal Mint Street. Running parallel to Hache Street, nearer the river, was the old Roman road to Ratcliff. By 1272, and probably before, it was called

Shadwell Street ('vicum de Shadwell') and would later become The Highway. A turning off this road, down across the marshy land that bordered the river, led to Wapping Mill, along what is now Wapping Lane. The Roman highway known as Ermine Street led north from Bishopsgate through Spitalfields; another Roman road probably ran along the line of Bethnal Green Road; and the Cambridge Road ran north from Mile End to Hackney.

Eight hundred years ago, then, eight of the East End's main thoroughfares were already marked out; and there would be little change until the nineteenth century. The greatest change in the topography of the area since Domesday was probably along the Colchester Road at the ford over the Lea. According to tradition, Henry I's Scottish queen, Matilda, on her way to visit the nunnery at Barking and riding through the swollen river, lost some of her attendants in the floodwaters. She had two bridges built, between 1110 and 1118, one over the Lea itself and one over its tributary, the Channelsea. The main one had three round arches supported by massive piers, and is thought to have been the first arched stone bridge in the country, predating London Bridge by some years. The good queen, says Lysons, 'caused the road to be turned'; the Colchester Road, which had crossed the Lea at Old Ford, is thought to have been diverted from its old course, a new one being thrown across the marshes by Bromley, probably along the line of existing footpaths. These days the roaring Bow Flyover marks the spot where a pretty little medieval bridge stood for over 700 years.

The three bowed arches were obviously something of a local talking point, and when cottages, mills (three were built after the construction of the new causeway) and bakehouses gathered near the bridge, the village on the Middlesex side came to be known as Stratford atte Bow, meaning the street by the ford at the bowed bridge. Leland wrote: 'The town of Stratford [was] nowe called Bowe, because the bridge was arched like unto a bowe, a rare piece of work'. On the Essex side, where apparently thorn bushes grew in abundance, the hamlet (of West Ham parish) was known as Stratford Langthorne. Although the earliest reference to Stratford in the records is dated 1177, there was evidently already some settlement round the ford, otherwise the villages might, perhaps, have been called something like Bridgeside or Thornbridge.

Barking Abbey was originally made responsible for the upkeep of the bridge, but quite soon the maintenance of the bridges and causeway between Stratford Bow and Ham was assigned to the new abbey of Stratford Langthorne. This was built in 1135 in the marshes on the Channelsey river, about half a mile south of the road, on the Essex side. Founded by the Essex magnate William de Montfichet, it became a rich and important centre, visited by royalty.

On the Middlesex side of the Lea, in Bromley, was the more modest house of St Leonard's, Bromley. The nunnery was to become famous in years to come by its association with Chaucer's character sketch of the Canterbury pilgrim, the

Prioress Madame Eglantine, who spoke the French 'in the manner of Stratford atte Bow'.

St Leonard's was an older foundation than the abbey over the river at Stratford; the Victorian historian of Bromley supposing that it had been there since Dunstan's day, but much more likely it was founded between 1086 and 1122 by Maurice, Bishop of London or his successor. It was endowed with 2 hides of episcopal lands and the 3½ hides of Domesday Roscelin lands, William Roscelin being the probable co-founder with the bishop. As well as the manor of Bromley, the priory had tenements in Southwark, and lands in Kent, Essex and Cambridgeshire. Apart from their home manor of Upper Bromley, with its farm-lands and two watermills, the main source of income for the nuns came from four churches, one of which was Islington. The ownership of the latter was in dispute between 1163 and 1183 with the canons of St Paul's; Bishop Gilbert Foliot finally adjudicated, and it was agreed that the priory was to hold the church from the canons for the annual payment of 1 mark, and were to appoint and pay a priest to serve it. The priory's chapel, dedicated to St Mary, came to be used as the parish church of Bromley, and the parish and manor of Upper Bromley belonged to the nuns, who took the tithes from the parishioners and the manorial dues from their tenants. Meanwhile the great city house of Austin Canons, Holy Trinity, had started acquiring land in Bromley between 1144 and 1165, and by the late thirteenth century were lords of the manor of Lower Bromley. The small parish of Bromley was the only part of the Tower Hamlets triangle that lay outside the jurisdiction of Stepney church, until Whitechapel was accorded parish status in the fourteenth century.

Today there is nothing left of St Leonard's Priory or the church except street names: Priory Street and St Leonard's Street. About a quarter of a mile to the east of the priory site, however, on the opposite side of the roaring dual carriage-way of the Northern Approach Road to the Blackwall Tunnel, just near a giant Tesco's, is a spot that helps the imagination to recreate the distant past. This is the heritage site of Three Mills Island, on land once belonging to Stratford Abbey but very close to the site of St Leonard's Priory. In an unexpected peaceful oasis the channels of the Lea curve and bubble through grassy banks, presided over by graceful eighteenth-century mill buildings. This mill, the largest extant tide-mill in the world, was operational until 1941. Here is the place to conjure up those days when the gigantic wheels ground corn for the black-clad daughters, sisters and widows of city merchants. They were sent to live in Bow, in rural isolation on the banks of the river, to rise at dawn for prayers, to speak to no man, without bed linen or fun, to fast and mortify their fleshly desires, to be punished for gossiping or swearing by eating alone. That was the rule, not necessarily the practice, and the priory had by the thirteenth century acquired a reputation for 'goings-on'. In 1282 Archbishop Pecham, whose attempts to get a deformed girl into the nunnery had been blocked by the prioress who objected to her handicap, said that he wished that not only the Stratford nuns, about whom there were so many scandals, but all other worldly nuns were deformed, so that they might lead no one into sin.

Domesday records eight mills on the Lea and its tributaries, and Bow, Bromley and Stratford were already baking communities, supplying bread for the City, although the first reference to this is not until the mid-thirteenth century. Mills and bakehouses lined the riverbanks and early morning carts, piled high with loaves, rumbled into the City through Aldgate. There would be ongoing squabbles with the City bakers, who were in competition for an expanding market as the population of the City grew.

At least as important as the corn mills were the fullers' mills. In the twelfth century a technical revolution brought mills to the most arduous task of fulling cloth. Woven cloth, taken from the loom, has a loose, open texture, and in order to tighten and thicken the material it was soaked in water and fullers' earth, then pounded with clubs or stamped on. The watermill was adapted to mechanise this process: heavy hammers were attached to the great beam, and as it turned the hammers pounded the cloth. The earliest reference to a fulling mill on the Lea is to the mill at Old Ford, which belonged to St Helen's Priory and is dated 1293, but local mills had probably already been adapted for fulling before that. There was one at Stratford in 1297, and both the City Bridge House and the priory of St Thomas of Acon owned fulling mills there in 1303. In 1318 there was one on the Bishop's Stepney manor.

Leaving the villages around Bow Bridge, with their mills and bakeries and the two new abbeys, either side of the Lea, we will turn back to London and take the Thames-side route out of the City towards Stepney village and Ratcliff, starting at the postern gate north of the Tower. The gate opened onto the open ground of East Smithfield, where long ago the Saxon knights of the Cnichtengild held their tournaments, on what are now the approaches to Tower Bridge.

By mid-century the City knights' guild was no longer in charge of this patch. In 1125 the guild gave up, or was forced to relinquish its jurisdiction over the Portsoken, the strip of land that stretched from the Thames up to Bishopsgate. It was probably one of the most significant moments for the history of the East End when the City guild of English Knights gave up its considerable powers over the eastern suburbs of the City; perhaps it can be viewed as the final postscript to the Norman Conquest. The knights had hung on through the turmoil of the invasion, having their rights reaffirmed by William I and renewed by Henry I. Now the guild members, described by Stow as the 'progeny of those noble English knights ... Ralph Fitalgod [an alderman, prebend of Rugemere and a descendant of Edmund FitzAlgot who had the Domesday mill at Old Ford], Wilmarde le Deucreshe, Orgar le Prude, Edward Hupcornehill,

Blackstanus, Alwine, his kinsman and Robert his brother, the sons of Leafstanus the goldsmith, Wiso his son, Hugh Fitzvulgar and Algare Sescusme', attended the chapter house of Holy Trinity, alias Christchurch Priory, and surrendered their powers to the canons there.

The new, flourishing priory, a house of Augustinian canons, stood on the site of the ancient church of Holy Cross and St Mary Magdalene, just inside the City walls at Aldgate. The church of St Katharine Cree marks the site of its cemetery, and the priory buildings covered the area of St James's Place, Duke Street and Mitre Street. It had been founded in 1107–08 by Henry I's queen, Matilda, and endowed with the income from various city churches, the gate of Aldgate itself, a basket of fabulous jewels from Constantinople and a precious piece of the True Cross. Under the tutelage of its first prior, a go-ahead protégé of Archbishop Anselm, it became an enormously successful institution, popular with Londoners; by 1291 it had properties in seventy-two city parishes and, as we have seen, owned the manor of Lower Bromley. In 1125 the prior took over from the Knights' Guild as lord of the manor for the 'inner East End', responsible for law and order, land transactions and the regulation of trade, and the taking of tithes.

The transfer of the Portsoken to the priory was not smooth; various constables of the Tower claimed the southern part as theirs, and the row rumbled on for some thirty years. In 1136 a panel of twenty-one men (all evidently of English rather than Norman stock, and some certainly members of the Knights' Guild) swore that this part of the soke had belonged to the guild since Edward the Confessor's time.

In 1157 there was a major row between the priory and Ailward, the priest at St Peter's Chapel in the Tower, as to who had the right to bury people living in the southern part of the Portsoken (and hence the fees). The priest at St Botolph's Aldgate, the priory's church, one Witthulfus, had administered the last rites to Godlune, the wife of Eilricus, an East Smithfield '*rusticus*', evidently a sheep farmer. The chaplain at the Tower appropriated the body for burial, claiming that the deceased was his parishioner. The archdeacon found in favour of St Botolph's and the widower duly handed over to Witthulfus six sheep, a roebuck and a cloak, by way of compensation or as his 'mortuary gift'. Although from now on 'All the street and all the ponds of Dudyngspond were adjudged to be in the parish of St Botolph as it had been in the time when Robert had been priest of St Botolph and Derman(n)us priest of St. Peter', the Tower continued to make its claim. The matter seems to have been settled in favour of St Botolph's in 1166.

East of the Tower, along towards Doddings Pond, was a vineyard. The climate was slightly milder than it is today and the sun was hot enough in those long-ago summers to ripen the grapes that flourished on many an aristocratic and monastic field. Another Queen Matilda, King Stephen's feisty French wife, grieving for the death of her two small children Baldwin and Maud, bought this vineyard and the adjoining watermill (where Irongate Stairs are now, on the river frontage of the Tower Hotel) from the new priory. She had a hospital built there in 1147–48 where a master, brothers and sisters were to say daily prayers for the souls of her children and to take care of thirteen paupers. The priory was to run the hospital with the queen reserving to herself and her successors the appointment of the master. At that time crusaders were returning from the east with tales of the martyrdom of Katharine of Alexandria, whose body had been torn apart on a wheel. She was to become England's favourite saint, and the queen's house for the poor was one of the first institutions to bear her name. In 1273, when the hospital was refounded by Eleanor of Provence, there were twenty-four inmates, mainly old or fallen women. In years to come St Katharine by the Tower was well known as a scandalous house, little better than a brothel.

The foundation of St Katharine's might be seen as the beginning of the special relationship of the queens of England with the East End; the hospital, as it was under royal protection, was the only monastic establishment to survive the Dissolution, supposedly thanks to Anne Boleyn's intervention. It still exists today, relocated to Limehouse as a religious retreat and conference centre. The nineteenth-century dock and the twentieth-century marina on its original site kept the name of St Katharine's and prayers are still said for Matilda, Stephen and the royal babies at the coronarium among the fancy yachts and tourist boutiques.

In medieval times the black-clad canons from Queen Matilda's Priory at Aldgate and the brothers, sisters and reformed prostitutes from the other Queen Matilda's hospital down by the river were a common sight about the streets and lanes. They were familiar enough to find their way into the jingle about executions at the Tower, which turned into Oranges and Lemons:

> Old father Baldpate
> Say the bells of Aldgate
> Maids in white aprons
> Say the bells of St Katharine's

Passing St Katherine's and taking Shadwell Street, the lower, riverside route in the direction of Stepney and Ratcliff, you would pass Toddyneslane, curving down to the right, leading by Dodding's pond to Crassh Mills. The rector of Stepney, William de Sancte Marie Ecclesie, and his vicar, Roger, were involved in a dispute with Holy Trinity Priory at Aldgate over the valuable tithes from the mills in 1233. There were at least five mills on the Thames hereabouts, including Crassh Mills, St Katharine's Mill, Wapping Mill, at the end of what is now Wapping Lane, and Shadwell Mill a little farther east.

The damp marshes of Wapping lay to the south of Shadwell Street, a soggy place with clumps of rushes, covered with pools and meres and often flooded at high tide. Part of modern Wapping, probably the eastern part, known as Walmarsh, was drained in the twelfth century or even earlier, and the hamlet was a cluster of cottages around the area of Wapping Mill, where corn was ground for St Paul's, who owned it. In 1218 Terricus of Aldgate leased it for 5 marks a year. According to an inquest of 1324, in 'ancient times' 100 acres had been recovered in Walmarsh, and the plots in this area, between St Katharine's Marsh and the vill of Shadwell, had been granted by an unknown lord of the manor to his freemen and bondmen, in return for the service of keeping the river wall and the dykes in good repair. Two 'wall reeves' were in charge; they reported to the manor court.

Shadwell, the place of the shallow well, was the next place along the riverside road, with a mill and a manor house, and maybe not much else. By the late twelfth century it was in the hands of one Brice of Shadwell, who probably lived there; the mill is first referred to in 1198. Brice's lands included two plots in Walmarsh, which he acquired from Thomas Becket's nephew, Theobald of Helles. In 1228 the Shadwell manor was granted by the bishop to the Dean of St Paul's for the maintenance of the Dean and Chapter, and became known henceforth as Dean's Linches. Linche was the name given to the balks dividing the strips into which sloping fields were divided.

Shadwell Street and Hache Street, with a stream called Cropet's Ditch lying between them, led to Ratcliff, the old Roman port. The earliest references to it by name are in 1294, 'la Rede clive', and in 1307, 'la Redeclyve juxta Stubenheth'. The derivation of the name is not clear, although Kevin McDonnell supposed that the low cliff formed by the sharp descent from a gravel terrace 'revealed the red sandy gravel and stood in striking contrast to the green of the surrounding countryside'. Although there is no archaeological evidence of any medieval habitation here before the fifteenth century, it became the hub of the riverside settlement part of the East End, with a busy market at Ratcliff Cross and a dock in use certainly in the fourteenth century and probably before. What scant documentary evidence there is shows that by 1300 there were houses in Cleve (Cliff Street) and in Forby Street (now Limehouse).

Cleve Street (now Butcher Row and Whitehorse Road) led up from the landing place at the cliffs past the church, following for 2 miles the line of a Saxon trackway that went to the bishop's palace at Bethnal Green. The heart of Stepney was Cleve Street and the area around the church, where in all probability Domesday villagers had their cottages.

St Dunstan's is a wealthy church. In the list of churches paying Pope Nicholas's tax in 1292 it appears as one of the richest in the diocese. It was evidently well established by the time of its first appearance in the records in 1154, servicing a wide area. Today's church has nothing of its Saxon or Norman predecessor, except the stone plaque of the crucifixion and the font; it was rebuilt in the thirteenth century and again in the fifteenth. It reigned supreme over the eastern marches, except for Bromley, which belonged to the nuns. There was only one chapel of ease or daughter church, down in the Marsh, of which more anon. The church's ties were firmly with St Paul's and, as one would expect, the bishop; the rectors were almost all canons of the cathedral. The first rector known to us by name was the bishop's steward, and some of his medieval successors were relatives of Bishops of London.

The hamlet of Poplar, the place of the poplar trees, lay to the south-east of Stepney village. Although its name does not appear in the records until 1327 (as Popeler), there was a largish settlement here by the twelfth century, perhaps because of its proximity to the landing place at Blackwall. A row of thirty houses were strung across the neck of the peninsula, along the line of today's High Street and going up into North Street. There were nine at 'Westwall' and eleven at 'Newbiggin'. The manor house of Bernard of Stepney, a tenant in chief of the king, probably stood just north of the High Street, with its ten fields and a vineyard. A shallow stream, the Schadfliet, flowed under a bridge in Poplar, and gave its name to an estate which was held by Bernard's daughter.

To the south lay the wild and windswept Stepney Marsh, later called the Isle of Dogs, patterned with dykes and marsh walls, a place of sandpipers and curlews. At the tip of the peninsula was the ferry to Greenwich. The marsh had been drained long ago, and even though there was still an ever-present threat of flooding it was far from uninhabited. The chief landholder was William de Pontefract, William of the broken bridge, perhaps. He was the bishop's steward for his manor at Stortford in the 1180s and '90s and had a manor house and farms in the centre of the south of the peninsula, 750 acres of land in all; he also owned the ferry. William (or one of his predecessors) had built a chapel for his tenants, dedicated to the Virgin. The Marsh folk evidently used it as their parish church, which got the Pontefract family in trouble with the mother church. Some time between 1163 and 1179 the pope wrote a letter about the dispute to the Bishop of London; the chapel had been built while the rector was away on study leave, it was claimed, and the locals had started paying tithes to the chapel rather than to the mother church. William de Pontefract's reply was that the chapel had been there for a long time. St Mary in the Marsh continued to serve as a chapel of ease for the locals until it was swept away in the Great Flood of 1448.

North of Stepney village was the 'pleasant meadow' at Mile End, stretching along the Colchester Road, a place for recreation and assembly for Londoners. This became, during the Middle Ages, the prize residential location in the east for city merchants. On its south side was the manor of Hulls or Helles. In later years this was acquired by Sir John Philpot, Stepney's most prominent fourteenth-century resident. The manor house was well set back from the road, slightly to the west of its junction with the Cambridge Road to Bethnal Green; the site is remembered today in the name of Philpot Street. The manor had its origins with the twelfth-century Helles family, Thomas Becket's sister Agnes had married Thomas Fitz Theobald e Helles, the founder of the Cheapside monastery of St Thomas of Acon. Looking at the street today, a scruffy side-turning off Commercial Road just behind the Royal London Hospital, it is well nigh impossible to imagine that this might possibly have been the home of the sister of Thomas the magnificent, chancellor and archbishop, and the English Church's most venerated saint.

Walking towards the City from the Helles territory one would pass along what later became Whitechapel High Street, at that time Alegatestreet; this was the name used for an area larger than the later Whitechapel parish, extending into the City, to Lime Street and Fenchurch Street. There is little evidence for housing in Whitechapel in Becket's day, but it is likely that there was some city overspill, with cottages, shops and workshops, perhaps, lining the highway. There were enough people around for a chapel of ease to be built by 1282, just outside the Bars (posts linked by a chain). It stood where Whitechapel church was until it was bombed in the Second World War; it is marked now by a patch of green that used to be known to the locals as Itchy Park. By 1320 it had its own parish, which meant there were enough folk around to make the tithes worth having. This little white-washed chapel gave its name to the area, but originally it was known as St Mary Matfelon or Matfallon, it is assumed after the family who founded it.

About three-quarters of a mile along the road to the west was the City gate and, standing outside it, the church of the Knights' Guild, dedicated to St Botolph, patron saint of travellers. Just inside the gate was a well or fountain, ancestor of the famous Aldgate Pump. Both church and gate were rebuilt in the twelfth century, the gate between 1108 and 1147. John Stow thought that Aldgate meant old gate, but the 'd' did not appear until 1486–87; before that it was called Ealsegate (1070) or usually, from 1108, Alegate: this may have brewing connotations or, more likely, once belonged to or was built by someone called Ealh. The church, Saxon in origin and taken over by Holy Trinity Priory in 1125, had a parish that lay partly in the City and partly outside, the Middlesex portion extending from Petticoat Lane down to the river and East Smithfield. It still stands today, though many times rebuilt.

Our tour of the Tower Hamlets finishes as we leave the muddy highway (the Mile End Road), the lanes across cornfields, with willows and dyke walls, meres and streams, watermills, isolated farmsteads, clusters of cottages, manor houses and monasteries. We go through the massive gateway into the narrow, bustling streets that were Becket's London. Before we take a look at the few East Enders that have left some account of themselves from those days, we will go up to the Bishops Gate and out into Spitalfields.

Ermine Street was the Saxon name for the road to York built by the Romans. It left London at Bishopsgate, and the London end of the highway became a fashionable place for suburban mansions. So far it was probably open ground, with perhaps some city overspill and inns – as one might expect on a main road at the entrance to a great city. In Norton Folgate, a soke or liberty that belonged to St Paul's, perhaps the 9 acres that in Domesday was *ad portam Episcopi* (by the bishop's gate) was the priory of St Mary. Later known as St Mary Spital, it gave Spitalfields its name. This house of Austin canons stood on the east side of Bishopsgate Street. It was founded by a citizen of London called Walter Brown and his wife Rosea in 1197. Twelve canons, five lay brothers and seven lay sisters (in 1303) worshipped God and tended the needy, lighting lamps between the beds in the infirmary 'for their comfort'. It was primarily a lying-in hospital, charged also with entertaining pilgrims, caring for the sick and for the children born there whose mothers had died; the little charges were kept by the sisters until they were seven years old. The hospital served London well for nearly 350 years. When it was dissolved, much against the wishes of the citizens, it had 180 beds.

By the close of the twelfth century, when King John took the throne, London was three times richer than any other city in England and its population was about five times as great as it had been at the Conquest. How many people lived outside the walls on the east is impossible to say, but it is certain that there were a good many more than the 900 or so estimated from Domesday. There is every reason to think that London expanded eastwards as much as it did to the west, perhaps more so. At least one deed (1216) refers to the 'town' of Stepney. The public buildings we know about, the East End's large contribution to the explosion of religious building in and around London, were the two hospitals in Wapping and Bishopsgate, Bow nunnery (all three newly built), a rich church, an episcopal palace and one (possibly new) chapel of ease. Two new stone bridges spanned the Lea. As to the dwelling places of the ordinary folk, the cottages, shops and workhouses, breweries and bakehouses, evidence is piecemeal, as there was no record of tenure at this date. Manor houses cannot be positively placed, so far, and their very existence is largely surmise.

The people themselves are shadowy figures. Most Londoners are said to have been of Saxon descent, and presumably the same applies in our area. In any case, a hundred years after the Conquest the great-great-grandchildren of the original Norman invaders would hardly have considered themselves foreigners. Although Frenchmen continued to come and settle (Becket's father, a port reeve of London, being a case in point) and to take senior posts in the church, there is generally thought to have been a good deal of integration. Christopher Brooke maintained that after the first generation of immigrants names lose their significance, as it became the fashion for the English to give their children French names.

The bishops, as lords of Stepney Manor and sometimes resident at Bethnal Green, are the chief local celebrities, and the best-known East Enders from these days. They were all Norman, or of Norman descent: Hugh D'Orival, Maurice,

Richard de Belmeis, Gilbert the Universal, Robert de Sigillo, Richard de Belmeis II, Gilbert Foliot, Richard FitzNeal, William of Sainte-Mère Eglise. As magnates, royal advisers, diplomats and administrators, and rulers of the church in the largest city in the Anglo-Norman Empire, they were very important men indeed. Some attracted the attention of the chroniclers more than others.

Maurice (bishop 1086–1107), reputedly 'worldly and lascivious', was said to have had sex on prescription from his doctors, and was owner of a particularly extravagant chasuble, ornamented with gold and precious stones. He was chaplain and chancellor to the Conqueror. As we saw at Domesday, Ranulf Flambard, chief minister to William Rufus, had been a member of Maurice's household and had about 420 acres in Stepney, perhaps given to him by Maurice. The Flambard clan was to dominate the chapter at St Paul's for many years.

Richard de Belmeis (bishop 1108–27), probably from Beaumais-sur-Dive in the Calvados, came to England as a tenant of the first Norman Earl of Shrewsbury, and had extensive lands in Shropshire. He served the king as his seneschal in Shrewsbury and was only ordained as a priest just before his consecration as bishop in 1108. As much a layman as Becket, he was a true family man who saw to it that his sons and nephews got all the best posts in the cathedral chapter. In the first half of the century clerical marriage was common, and a quarter of the canons of St Paul's were married men. His nephew, of the same name, followed him as bishop some twenty years after his death.

Gilbert Foliot, a relative of the Belmeises, is much better known than any of his fellow bishops of London. He was bishop for twenty-five years (1163–87), and as the arch-enemy of Thomas Becket has had a great deal of attention from chroniclers and hagiographers; a large volume of his correspondence has also survived. Ascetic and high born, a former monk at Cluny, he took against the king's favourite on account of his worldliness and relatively humble birth, and was jealous of his promotion to archbishop. The king, he said famously, had wrought a miracle by turning a secular man and a soldier into an archbishop. He is known to have been at his Stepney residence on Ascension Day in 1169, when he received with fury the news that Becket's letter, excommunicating him for 'disobedience and contempt', had been delivered on the high altar at St Paul's. We even have the words he wrote in his rage: '[Becket] puts his scythe to another's corn, since he has power neither over my person nor my church – my person since I never made profession nor promised obedience to him, nor to the church of Canterbury in the name of this church, that is the church of London, my church, since the church of London claims back what was taken from it long since.'

Richard Fitzneal (bishop 1189–98), originally a lawyer, is best known for being the author of the Dialogue of the Exchequer. He was much involved in disputes between Richard I's brother John and William de Longchamp, when the king was away on crusade, and in 1193 he was made one of the guardians of the king's ransom.

Becket's family had some connections in Stepney, as we have noted; his sister Agnes, their father's heir, had lands in Shadwell that passed to her son. A pretty story is told about Becket's mother, Mathilda of Mondeville, near Caen. The first Prior of Holy Trinity (lord of the Portsoken) spent so much money on books and vestments that there was no money left for food. Mathilda and other locals, paying their Sunday visit to the priory, saw the poor canons starving, and vowed to give them a loaf every Sunday thenceforth.

We know something of the rectors of Stepney. They were not rectors as we understand them today but the landlords of the church, taking most of its income from tithes, fees and oblations, and paying a vicar or a parish chaplain for the cure of souls, to celebrate mass, take confession, baptise, marry and bury and look after the flock. The king and the pope needed this money to keep Christendom on the road, using the rectorial incomes as salaries for civil servants and to finance ecclesiastical scholars. Stepney's rectory was held by a number of extremely influential men, senior royal servants, ambassadors and powerful churchmen.

In 1154 the post was held by one Roger le Brun (Roger Brown), a swarthy man perhaps. He was the bishop's steward, his agent in charge of all his manors, and a prebend of St Paul's, holding the ecclesiastical manor of Brondesbury. Le Brun may have lived in a parsonage house to the east of the church, as later rectors did (we have no way of knowing), but it is reasonable to assume he had a Stepney establishment because he was on hand to run the bishop's estates. His successor, another canon, was Henry of London (known to have been rector sometime between 1163 and 1179). He was Master of the Schools at St Paul's, secretary to the Dean and Chapter, librarian and supervisor of teaching in the City. Canon Henry probably had few hands-on dealings with Stepney; he would have spent his time among the chained books and manuscripts in the cathedral's bell tower, abroad on study leave or about the business of education.

The effective administrator of the church was the vicar. Deputies for the incumbent of the church, vicars were now a commonplace, with about a quarter of all parish churches in the land being owned (appropriated) by monasteries, who appointed vicars with a perpetual benefice to run the churches on their behalf. In a church of Stepney's size and status there would also have been a parish chaplain, a stipendiary priest whose levels of learning and living standards were probably not much different from the farmers, fishermen and artisans in the congregation. We know nothing of any parish chaplains or assistant priests at Stepney from this date, but they must have existed and perhaps, like many of their fellow priests, they kept *focariae* (literally 'hearthmates'); the chronicler Gerald of Wales noted that 'the houses and hovels of the parish clergy are full of bossy mistresses, creaking cradles, new-born babies and squawking brats'.

As to the lay landholders, they are little more than names. Ralph the Clerk had a meadow called Sunneswinchesham and house in Shadwell; Bernard of Stepney had a house and vineyard in Poplar in about 1178; Salomon of Stepney (our first East End Jew, perhaps) had land in Walmarsh from 1140 to 1203; the Trentmars family had rents in the Portsoken (later the Manor of Berners/Barnes) held of the Knights' Guild, the Cole family in Old Ford and William de Pontefract's estate in the Marsh.

The pattern for the next few hundred years in the Stepney triangle is set during the reigns of the Norman kings and their fierce Angevin successors, Henry II and Richard (reigning 1154–99). London had grown greatly in size and wealth since Domesday, now sporting a splendid stone bridge over the Thames, the wonder of the western world, a new cathedral, religious houses and over a hundred churches within its walls. Over at Westminster William Rufus built a banqueting hall of gigantic proportions for his palace. As the City grew so did its suburbs and the villages around.

By 1200 the castle, roads and villages of the Tower Hamlets were in place, and the nuns of Bromley had their house on the banks of the Lea, providing a church for the locals. The hospital of St Katharine's will survive for over 850 years, and the Bishopsgate hospital stood, ready to give its name to Spitalfields. Down by the Thames mills clattered away in Wapping, and over at Bow, near the fine new bridge, a baking community was gathering; soon, like the village outside Aldgate, to have its own church. The bishop ruled most of the area from Bethnal Green, while the Prior of Holy Trinity Aldgate oversaw the 'inner East End' and the Pontefracts ran the ferry to Greenwich. Stepney church and the canons of St Paul's were responsible for the East End soul, while Marsh families attended the little chapel of St Mary. There was no hint that the east was the 'working end of town'.

Chapter 3

THE BLIND BEGGAR OF BETHNAL GREEN AND CHAUCER'S EAST END

1200–1400

The first seventy years of the thirteenth century were troubled times of civil strife, with the kings, John and Henry III, at war with their barons and asserting control over the unruly, wealthy City of London. Both in the rebellion of 1215 and the barons' wars of 1258–65 citizens took up arms against their monarch. Henry III frequently interfered with the election of city officers; in 1239 there was a dispute over the choice of mercer Ralph Eswy (of Asshews Manor in Mile End) and Reginald de Bungay as sheriffs, and the king refused to accept the duly elected mayor. One John de Stepney, head of the fishmongers, a landowner with his own ship, was prominent in the City revolt of 1263. He joined with others from the rising middle class of craftsmen and merchants who took power under the aegis of rebel baron Simon de Montfort in 1263. Over to the east the Tower brooded with royal menace, a constant reminder to the citizens of the might of their sovereign. When Edward I, the strongest of the Plantagenets, took the throne he tightened his grip on London by enlarging and strengthening his castle in the east, between 1275 and 1285.

The City and its hinterland were swelling: the population of London peaked in 1300, with perhaps as many as 100,000 inhabitants. According to Stow it was the western wards of London that grew more than those to the east of the Walbrook; by 1394 the ward of Farringdon was so populous that it was divided into two, within and without the walls (the Holborn and Fleet Street area). Surviving tax lists from the late thirteenth century show the areas between the Tower and Blackfriars and those around Cheap as the wealthiest parts, while the Portsoken ward (London's oldest suburb) appears to have been poorer; in 1292 there were twenty-three taxpayers here, as opposed to sixty in the Vintry. The part of Bishopsgate outside the walls had eighteen taxpayers. This is not necessarily an indication of the actual numbers of residents, however, and it may well be that the eastern suburbs were as much inhabited as those in the west – but there were fewer rich households.

For the area outside the City's jurisdiction to the east we have no figures, but the chapel of ease at Whitechapel was evidently serving a good number of people, as it was made a parish church in the early part of the thirteenth century. Likewise, the thriving town of Bow acquired its own chapel of ease in about 1311, when the community of craftsmen, bakers, fullers, farmers and millers was numerous, confident and organised enough to get together and to petition for their own place of worship. Stepney church was too far away, they argued, and in winter the roads were impassable. The request was granted and the little chapel of St Mary was built, about 100yds from the bridge, right in the middle of the highway – where its successor still stands. It would, however, be 400 years before the mother church finally let busy, baking Bow break free to have its own parish.

It has been estimated that there may have been about 1,500 people living in Stepney and its hamlets. There may have been considerably more; twelve men who are known as 'de Stepney' appear in the register of City recognisances, known as *Letter Book B* (1275–1312). This is more than any other group of individuals with place cognomens; others are five 'de Stratford', nine 'de Hackney', three 'de Shoreditch', six 'de Enfield', five 'de Fulham', eight 'de Greenwich', ten 'de Oxford' and 'de St Albans', eleven 'de Gloucester' and 'de Northampton', nine 'de Cambridge', seven 'de Canterbury', eight 'de Winchester'. Thus, if Stratford and Hackney are included, there are twenty-nine individuals with an East End surname, nearly three times as many as hailed from any other particular place. This must indicate that there were a lot of people living to the east of London, and had been for some generations. It also emphasises what is obvious, that the links between our area and the City were very strong, that the sons and grandsons of the semi-servile sons of the soil of Domesday were already leaving the plough and the hoe and getting themselves apprenticed to City craftsmen and traders. Mile End Green was the parade ground for the citizens of London 'mustering in arms' there in 1232, and in 1299 city carpenters held something like a modern strike meeting there to oppose city ordinances about their trade. Meanwhile successful merchants were acquiring lands and manors to the east.

At least two thirteenth-century mayors had Stepney connections. Ralph Aswy (Eswy), whose election to sheriff was disputed by Henry III, was mayor three times from 1241 to 1244. He had Stepney lands that included the manor later known as Ashweys, neighbour to the Hulls estate, on its city side.

Just to the north-west of Stepney church was the very grand country house of mayor Henry de Waleys, a Gascon vintner who made his fortune by importing wine and selling it to the royal household. Excavations have confirmed that this was the site of Waleys' house, as fragments of fine pottery have been found which date from 1270 to 1350 and come from the part of France where de Waleys' family had property. He was mayor six times between 1273 and 1299 (and mayor of Bordeaux in 1275), one of the most enterprising and impressive of medieval mayors. He built a covered market for the sale of meat and fish, and cleaned up Cheapside. He fell foul of Edward I, who suspected he had been a supporter of Simon de Montfort, the leader of the baronial revolt against his father.

De Montfort was the swashbuckling hero of Londoners, hailed as the founder of Parliament and even as the champion of the common man, and no account of the East End is complete without the story of the Blind Beggar, which links, albeit fancifully, the Montfort family with Bethnal Green. The legend of the Beggar is a robust and enduring one; there is a block of flats in Bethnal Green today called Montfort House and a street named after Besse. Everyone knows of the Blind Beggar pub in the Whitechapel Road, where Ronnie Kray murdered one of his many enemies in 1966. The story, which appears in various forms, tells of an old blinded soldier called Montfort, who begged around the Green, and his beautiful daughter Besse. Unable to find a local suitor, she sets off in search of a husband to Stratford Bow and then to Romford, where eventually a young knight takes her on. They return to Bethnal Green. At her father's house the beggar invites the knight's family to 'drop angels', that is to throw down coins, by turns, until one side has no more money. The floor is soon covered with gold and the beggar reveals himself to be a man of enormous wealth. The earliest version of the ballad is the manuscript in the collection of the eighteenth-century collector Thomas Percy, and is dated about 1649; the earliest reference to a ballad of this name was registered at Stationer's Hall in 1624. Twenty-four years before this, in 1600, a play by John Day on the theme of the beggar story had been performed by the Admiral's Men, but the extant published version of this (1659) presents a rather different story, with Momford, the beggar, as the governor of Calais in the days of Henry VI. The ballad enjoyed wide popularity and was adopted by the local tradesmen in Bethnal Green; Samuel Pepys was a visitor to the 'very house built by the blind beggar of Bednal Green, so much talked of and sang in ballads'. He thought, perhaps, that the outhouses were the remnants of the old place. In the late eighteenth century Lysons tells us that every inn in the village sported a sign depicting the beggar, or besse. In 1690 the beadle's staff was ornamented with a beggar badge, which was incorporated into a coat of arms when the London borough was set up in 1900.

It was Thomas Percy, who published a version of the ballad in the 1750s, who seems to have made the Montfort or Momford of the old tale into Simon de Montfort's son, forced to disguise himself after the defeat of the barons' army and the death of his father at the Battle of Evesham in 1265:

Sir Simon de Montfort my subject shall bee
Once chief of all the great barons was he

Simon de Montfort had three well-documented sons, Simon, Guy and Amaury, all of whom fled into exile abroad. Two Bishops of London (and lords of Stepney Manor) are known to have had connections with Amaury in the 1270s, but apart from this there is no evidence of any Bethnal Green link. A John de Montfort of Bromley is noted in the City's *Calendar of Letter Book B* (1309). It remains for some devoted scholar to delve further into the affair and perhaps establish some historical basis for this good old tale.

To return to more solid matters, the mother church of Stepney was rebuilt during the thirteenth century, and there are still some remnants of the work today. On the south side of the chancel are three sedilia, priests' seats, of Early English style and dating from this time. Celebrants at mass sat here: the priest, the deacon and a sub-deacon. A wealthy church like Stepney's, serving an enormous parish with perhaps ten times as many parishioners as the average, would have had a good flock of assistant chaplains for the celebration of a daily mass, supplemented by lesser services, or 'offices'. The church was probably rather smaller than it is today and may have had an apsidal sanctuary, which was then the fashion; an example can be seen in the nearby church of East Ham, built in the 1130s. On the outside of the church, probably on the west wall, there was a tablet of the annunciation, depicting the moment when the Angel Gabriel tells the Virgin Mary that she is with child by the Holy Ghost.

As we have seen, the chapel that was to give Whitechapel its name was built at this time. For many years it was known as St Mary Matfelon, having almost certainly been built by a family of that name. A Richard Matefelun, a wine merchant, is referred to in the area in 1230, but a picturesque story grew up about its origins, recounted by Stow. A devout widow loved and kept for a long time a Frenchman or Breton, who most 'unkindly and cruelly' murdered her and afterwards fled, taking her jewels and anything else he could carry. He was found out and pursued, and took sanctuary in the church of St George, Southwark. The constables brought him into London, but as they went through Whitechapel the wives there pelted him with 'missiles and filth' and killed him. Thus, it was said, the parish acquired the name of Matfellon. Stow sets this tale in 1428, when something like this may well have happened, but the church was known as Beatae Marie Matfellon a hundred years or more earlier!

Henry III's long reign of fifty-six years, though troubled with battling barons, has been seen as an 'Age of Faith'. With a pious, though ineffectual, man at the helm, churches were built or rebuilt all over the country. Over to London's west the king rebuilt, at vast expense, his sumptuous Abbey of Westminster (consecrated in 1269). In the east, as well as the building of a church in Alegate Street, there appeared two hospitals and a nunnery.

The hospital of St Mary of Bethlehem or Bedlam, as it soon became known, the famous madhouse, was founded as a priory in 1246–47. It stood on the west side of

Bishopsgate Street, closer to the City than its neighbour, the Spital, on the site of today's Liverpool Street station. In those crusading days, when young men still sallied forth to fight the infidel for the Holy Land, a sheriff named Simon FitzMary gave land to the Bishop of Bethlehem (who resided in Burgundy) to found a priory of canons, brothers and sisters of the order of St Mary of Bethlehem, to receive members of the order when they came to London. There were to be perpetual prayers for the soul of FitzMary and various other Londoners, including Ralph Ashew of Ashews in Mile End, the mayor noted above. How soon it became primarily a lunatic asylum is not known; certainly there were lunatics in residence by 1403. Stow says that the inmates of the Stonehouse asylum at Charing Cross were transferred there, because the then monarch (probably Richard II) had objected to having a madhouse so near his palace at Westminster. The hospital was maintained by the fees paid by relatives of the inmates and voluntary aid, with collecting boxes being rattled around the City by the brothers and sisters, wearing cloaks embroidered with the star of Bethlehem. The second hospital to come to the East End at this time was the leper or lazar house of St Mary Magdalene, first mentioned in 1274. Leprosy became widespread in the eleventh century, and this was one of ten isolation hospitals that ringed London; it stood where the Mile End Road crosses the Regent's Canal today, well away from any habitation. Pesthouse Lane is marked on Gascoyne's map of 1703; it is now Canal Road. The fearful, disfiguring disease was thought, wrongly, to be very contagious and sexually transmitted, and the unfortunate sufferers were banned from churches, markets and fairs, and had to cover themselves from head to foot and carry a rattle to warn of their approach. They even had the burial service read over them.

At the very end of the century a convent came to the Portsoken, which was to give its name to one of London's best-known streets, the Minories, running down to the river from Aldgate. Here in 1293 Edmund, Earl of Lancaster, known as Crouchback, brother of Edward I, founded the house of the Grace of the Blessed Mary, for enclosed nuns of the Order of St Clare, also called Minoresses. The first members of the convent were brought probably from France by the earl's wife Blanche, Queen of Navarre. This was a privileged and up-market nunnery, exempt from the powers of the archbishop and bishop, and endowed with London and country properties. Henry de Waleys, the vintner mentioned above, gave the nunnery property, and by his will set up a chantry there, with five priests praying for his soul in perpetuity.

Of the eight thirteenth-century Bishops of London, lords of Stepney manor, two were Chancellors of England and most were men of some note. Two of them are known to have died at their Stepney palace, and although their working base was in Westminster, Stepney was evidently as important a residence as Fulham. Two of them, Henry of Sandwich and Richard Gravesend, had close links with Amaury de Montfort, Simon's youngest son.

Little is known of the first of these bishops, William de Sancte-Mere-Eglise (1198–1221), from Manche in France. The rector of Stepney (fl. 1233) had the same name and must have been a relative. Eustace of Fauconberg, bishop for eight years from 1221, son of the Lord of Rise in Holderness, was a lawyer and treasurer of the Exchequer (1217). A 'discreet, merciful and jocund' man, says a chronicler, he collected *objets d'art* and was the owner of a fine jewelled crozier that encased a piece of the true cross. In his will he left Stepney lands and a mill to the Dean and Chapter of St Paul's, and 5 marks a year for a chantry priest. This was the manor of Shadwell, which would stay in the hands of St Paul's for many years to come.

His successor, Roger Niger, was revered as a saint after his death at Stepney in 1241. A learned, honourable and handsome man, if Matthew Paris is to be believed, on good terms with Henry III, he combined piety with good living; his statutes for the regulation of the Archdeaconry of London stipulated that fines for non-attendance at meetings should be paid in wine. Fulk Basset, bishop from 1244 to 1259, was an aristocrat, the son of Henry III's justiciar and ally against the barons, Philip. He engaged in a prolonged feud with his archbishop, Boniface, and refused to support the baronial attempt to curtail the king's powers, known as the Provisions of Oxford.

Henry of Wingham (bishop 1260–62), was a life-long royal official, serving in the important posts of escheator for south of the Trent and then chancellor. He was one of the committee of six who investigated charges against Simon de Montfort. He died at Stepney. Henry of Sandwich, who followed him and was bishop for ten years, was essentially a scholar; he spent most of his life at Oxford. He took on the barons' cause and was their leading spokesman in negotiations with Henry III; he was the only bishop to serve on de Montfort's baronial council, appointing de Montfort's son Amaury as one of his prebends at St Paul's. After the Battle of Evesham he was exiled to Rome, but was reinstated in 1272. John Chishull/Chishall (1274–80) was a royal clerk serving in the Chancery and was chancellor twice, receiving the bishopric of London in his old age as a reward.

Richard Gravesend (1280–1303) tried to enclose part of the Bishops Woods in Bethnal Green as a private hunting ground. Although the king (Edward I) was agreeable, the City authorities were violently opposed to the scheme, claiming that the citizens of London had from 'time immemorial used to hunt within the aforesaid forests and without, hares, foxes, conies and other beasts, where and when they would'. He interceded on behalf of de Montfort's son Amaury when, en route for Wales in 1275, he was captured and imprisoned by Edward.

William de Sancte Marie Ecclesie was rector of Stepney in 1233, Prebend of Harleston and Archdeacon of London, and may well have been the son of the eponymous Bishop of London; as mentioned earlier, clerical marriage was common at this time. He may have been the same William de Sancte Marie Ecclesie who was Dean of St Paul's from 1241 to 1243. We know the names of three other thirteenth-century rectors: Adam de Boxgrave, William of London and John de Silverstone (Shelverstone/Selverstone/Selston). Virtually nothing is known about the first two. Silverstone was another canon of St Paul's, and a Prebend of Ealdland. He was appointed to the benefice in 1294 by Edward I, and along with a number of other clergy was awarded special protection by the king in that year, for granting the king part of the income from Stepney to pay for his campaign in Scotland. Perhaps his appointment, which was made by the king, was conditional on the gift to the Crown. It is, as we have seen, unlikely that any of the canons were directly concerned with the practice of religion in Stepney in those days, or even spent any time there. John de Silverstone had a house adjoining the cathedral, but may have had an establishment in the village, as there is mention of John, his chaplain, suing for debt in the Stepney Manor Court records for 1318. This John, however, may actually have been the parish chaplain. Rector Silverstone also left the income from some property to fund a chantry in the church. Although this came to nothing, because no mortmain licence was obtained, it does bespeak a genuine attachment to the church.

The vicar ran the church, and his glebe included part (or all) of the vast field called Erthbury 'abutting towards Hachestrate' (Cable Street), a long strip of land that stretched westwards from Ratcliff, lying along what is now the Commercial Road, and nearly as far as the walls of the nunnery in the Minories. We know nothing about the individual vicars at this time, except that there was one called Roger in 1233.

As for the laity, there is scant reference to any ordinary folk of Stepney parish among the records. There are no manor court accounts or rent rolls yet, and surviving records relate by and large to freehold transactions and the estates, which were Asshews and Hulls in Mile End, Shadwell Manor, Pomfret in the Isle of Dogs, Poplar Manor and the widespread Trentemars holdings in Aldgate and East Smithfield, Whitechapel and other parts of Stepney vill.

For the inner suburbs there is more. City records tell us something about the individuals who were living outside the eastern walls, although under the jurisdiction of the commune. Medieval London was as much a manufacturing community as it was a port and trading centre, and in the City's out-parishes of St Botolph without Aldgate (in the city ward of Portsoken) with East Smithfield and Bishopsgate were the workshops of tanners, ironmongers and blacksmiths, potters, breweries, bakeries, butchers, girdlers and all manner of other 'shops'. The bellfounding craft was established in Aldgate by the mid-thirteenth century and continues today at the Whitechapel Bell Foundry. We hear of William le Moyne who had an Aldgate brewery and William de Houndesditch who has a tannery and brewery outside Bishopsgate (1280s). Thomas de la More, a tanner of East Smithfield, who was said to have lost his reason in his last years, evidently did very well for himself; at his death he had three houses, two in East Smithfield and one in Houndsditch (1281/2). The important baking family of Poyntell, whose mills and bakeries dominated the riverside at Ratcliff in the days of Henry VIII, were probably descended from William Poyntell, who leased a mill at Stratford (1305), lived outside Bishopsgate and contracted to gather the reeds in the marshlands around Bedlam.

The cartulary of Holy Trinity Priory, which had taken over rule in the Portsoken from the English Knights in 1125, gives the names of property owners and tenants in Houndsditch, Aldgate and the Minories: the Trentmar family had properties along Aldgate and down towards the Tower; the houses of William the Shoemaker, Solomon le Teuler (tiler) and John Goldcorn stood where the new nunnery would be built; we hear of Lambert the Glover, Fulcher the Limeburner, Roger the Tiler, Wurthing the Carpenter, Geoffrey Waterladere, Stephen and Ralph the Tanner and John le Poter.

The 1292 tax list gives us the names of the wealthy men of the Portsoken: John le Lung, carter, Jordan le Macegref, butcher, Robert Jordan, butcher, Philip le Tanner, Gervase le Tanner, Laurence le Hodere, butcher, John de Billirica, brewer, Walter le Seytnure, girdler, Geoffrey Danyel, possibly a carter, Alan le Potere de Suffolk, Salaman le Tuelere, tiler, Walter Cope junior, tiler, Edmund Trentmars, Peter Berneval, vintner, Walter Cope senior, tiler. In the ward of Bishopsgate without eighteen taxpayers are listed: William Lindraper, Robert Canun and John de Sancto Salvatore, Thomas Broning, Hugh de Ponte, John le Gardiner, Johm de Hackneye, tanner, Geoffrey Dreye, William Pointel, currier, John Miles, John Gode, Walter Sklefol, John Lingedraper, Geoffrey de Houndsditch, tanner, Richard le Seinture, girdler, William le Pinour, combmaker, Hugh Mulgas, possibly a woolmonger.

The inner East End was already something of an immigrant community, with foreign merchants, notably Flemings and Italians (encouraged by Henry III and Edward I), Jews and the inevitable presence of folk from the shires, especially Essex and East Anglia, who came to London to make their fortune. The gatekeeper at Aldgate, Nicolas de Gypeswick (Ipswich), had a house in East Smithfield (1274/5); Alan de Suthfolck had a potters' 'werkus' in Aldgate; Roger de Nasing (Nazeing) had a house in Matfelon in 1282–83; and there were Lombards in Bishopsgate. We hear of Jorninus, son of Abraham the Jew (1272), and Walter, son of Robert le Fleming (1291/2), both having houses in East Smithfield. A Walter le Flemyng is named in the cartulary of Holy Trinity as the gatekeeper at Aldgate (no date). Immigrants from the Low Countries, especially Flanders, were a significant element in the life of the East End, as we shall see in later chapters. The Jews, whose commercial skills and banking know-how made such an important contribution to early medieval cities, were subjected to bouts of vicious persecution, with tales of child crucifixion and all manner of horrors spreading like wildfire. There were two areas of Jewish settlement in London, one near the Guildhall (now

Old Jewry) and one in the Liberty of the Tower and, probably around Aldgate. According to Stow, the gate was repaired with stones from Jewish houses smashed up in the 1215 anti-Semitic riot, fuelled by the barons. In 1229 the synagogue at Old Jewry was destroyed, by command of the king, and replaced by a church. It is reasonable to suppose that Jewish families drifted east, and that the main concentration was near the Tower in the Portsoken. In 1290 they were expelled from the country. It would be nearly four centuries before a Jewish community made London its home again, putting down roots in Duke Street and Goodman's Fields, either side of the City gate that had once been shored up with stones from the ruined homes of their ancestors.

Out east in the countryside, although there were commercial bakers in Bow and craftsmen and artisans, no doubt, both there and in Stepney village, most people worked on the land and the river, employed by the bishop and the great landlords. Some were free and some were serfs: ploughmen, haywards, farmhands, fishermen, swineherds, shepherds, millers and woodcutters.

Occasionally names and occupations occur in surviving legal records, and a story or two surface to remind us that these old East Enders were flesh and blood. One Henry of Stepney was in a lawsuit over a smallholding with Adam the Ironmonger; and a locksmith was one of the jurors presenting the bishop's hayward for breaking into the Stepney house of Alice Wyldegar and murdering a stranger there. The *London Eyre* of 1244 has an account of Edward Bray, a tiler, who assaulted the daughter of Richard Wilton in the fields near Stepney, breaking her arm in two places. She died of the wounds and her sister continued the prosecution, but died before it could be resolved. On a roll of felonies for 1277/8 there is the lively story of William Cole, perhaps of the landowning Old Ford family mentioned above, although he is described as a citizen of London. One day, when he was reaping his corn in the fields near Stratford (Bow), John, parish clerk of the village (this must have been the clerk of Bromley parish), stole some of his sheaves. He seized them back and a fracas ensued, with John getting assistance from Richard, chaplain to the Prioress of St Leonard's, and one John Scheld, a Fleming, perhaps. Cole was beaten black and blue from the soles of his feet to the top of his head and died from his wounds. The felons fled to the parish church, and then disappeared.

King Edward I himself spent quite a lot of time in Stepney between 1274 and 1303, for days and weeks at a time. In 1291 he was at the Shadwell manor house of the Dean and Chapter of St Paul's, but exactly where he stayed for most of his sojourns 'apud Stybenhithe' (at Stepney) is something of a mystery. It would have to have been a large mansion with sufficient stabling and out-houses for his entourage, and a hall large enough to accommodate the lords and clergy who attended the parliament that convened at Stepney in May 1299. The Stepney parliament may have been held after a fire in the lesser hall of the king's palace at Westminster, which broke out on 29 March. According to Stow, the venue was the house of mayor Henry de Waleys, the aforementioned wealthy Gascon vintner. Although official records confirm that a parliament met in Stepney in May 1299, Stow is the only source for it being in de Waleys' house. On the face of it this seems unlikely; by 1299 de Waleys was severely out of favour with the king, who had taken the government of London into his own hands between 1285 and 1298, suspecting that the lord mayor had been a supporter of Simon de Montfort. However, the parliament certainly met in Stepney and the king confirmed the provisions of Magna Carta there to appease the barons, and to ensure their cooperation in fighting the Scots. Did he perhaps take over the Waleys' mansion as he had taken over the government of the City?

A mysterious entry on the Patent Rolls, dated 10 July 1297, tells us that the Bishop of Bath and Wells paid 'rent' to the king for the advowson of Rokeleye in the time of Henry III by carrying a goshawk from the gates of Shrewsbury to Stepney.

We will leave thirteenth-century Stepney, as the great lords of parliament, with their packhorses and servants, their armed retainers, clatter off away from 'King John's Palace', past the scattered farms and the windmills between Hache Street (Cable Street) and Shadwell Street (the Highway). Eight years later the mighty 'Hammer of the Scots' will be dead and the throne will have passed to his ignominious son. A clearer picture of our area emerges. Manorial records for Stepney start in 1318 and bishops' registers in 1304, tax records from mid-century. From the later part of the century wills survive for at least a few of the people, providing us with names and hints about lifestyle and preoccupations.

Chaucer's East End, 1300–1400

The troubled reign of the weak Edward II (1307–27) culminated in a rebellion led by his queen, Isabella, the She-Wolf of France, and the monarch's deposition and grisly death. Mid-century we find the forceful, martial Edward III (1327–77) asserting his claims over the Church against the French pope at Avignon, and conquering much of France, his mother's inheritance. For the arrowmakers and armourers of Aldgate and East Smithfield the glorious, victorious battles of Sluys, Crécy and Poitiers meant hard work and money in their coffers. Jingoism and anti-French rage were the order of the day. The Black Death, a plague worse than anything since, plundered the population; rival popes claimed St Peter's throne and Christendom was cut in half. Oxford scholar John Wycliff made an attack on Church abuses, striking at the very heart of its doctrine and castigating clergy and monks with their 'red and fat cheeks and great bellies'. Wat Tyler led a rebellion of peasant labourers, and the century ended with a *coup d'état* and the murder of the unstable fop king, Richard II.

Our East Enders must have often lain uneasily in their beds. As troubles brewed between the king and his subjects in the summer of 1325, by night guards from St Paul's could be seen patrolling the Dean and Chapter's fields in Shadwell. In 1377 threats of a French invasion saw the Alegate fortified with a portcullis and chained 'barbykanes'. Most terrifying were the events of 1381, when thousands of angry peasants swarmed onto the wide expanse of common known as Mile End Green, brandishing scythes and pitchforks.

A new London, and sundry folk

Against this backdrop of tumult a new London emerged, and with it a new East End. We have been, so far, in a land of legends and surmise, of crusades and mysterious palaces, with the soft chanting of nuns and the cries of lepers. Now, as the City and its hinterland grew, a more lively and bustling world arrived, brought to life by the poet Chaucer, who lived over the gate at Aldgate for twelve years. Men blossomed into tight, figure-hugging garments of brilliant hues, very short, sexy doublets, slashed shoes and jewelled girdles. Laws had to be passed to stop people dressing above their station. Sir John Poultney, draper, mayor four times in the 1330s and Lord of Poplar Manor, had sixteen fur-lined robes; his sumptuous bed-hangings were patterned with fleur-de-lis, eagles, lions, popinjays, griffins and apple blossom in gold, blue, red, violet and pink, with white roses decorating the story of Tristan and Isolde, set against a green background. Merchants' houses were a riot of colour, their whitewashed walls ablaze with hangings all the colours of the rainbow.

London had more churches than any city in Christendom, and was now effectively the capital city. Westminster, where the king's chief treasury had been housed since the twelfth century, was the home of government, with the courts of Chancery, Exchequer and Common Pleas fixed there from 1338; while the Great Wardrobe, the storehouse of royal and military supplies, settled in the City in 1361 (remembered in the church of St Andrew by the Wardrobe).

The City flourished as an industrial centre, and most of all as a port. The export of wool and later woollen cloth was the foundation of the country's wealth. By 1362, 45 per cent of all English wool was exported through London, and 70 per cent of this wool was handled by native merchants. Money was to be made and fortunes were amassed, and a new breed of seriously rich merchants emerged, a force for the Crown to reckon with. All this was celebrated with colourful civic extravaganzas: when the future Edward III was born in 1312 the City exploded with delight. There was singing and street parties, and the fishmongers organised a stunning pageant, carrying a vast model ship in full sail through the streets, emblazoned with the arms of England and France.

A hundred years earlier the City had been firmly in the hands of a small oligarchy of patrician landholders, some of whom might have been engaged in trade as a sideline. Now the trade and craft guilds had consolidated themselves, and the major ones, especially the victualling companies, were taking over civic government. Old feudal mansions were bought up by some of these newly chartered guilds, and some built splendid new halls for their headquarters. While bishops and the nobility built themselves mansions out west along the Strand, with fine gardens overlooking the river and handy for Westminster, City 'millionaires' tended to have 'inns' within the walls and country houses in the pleasant fields beyond Aldgate. Although riverside mansions were not an option in the marshy land east of the Tower, by the mid-fourteenth century inland Stepney, famous for the beauty of its landscape, was a suburban retreat for rich Londoners; here the 'swaggering persons' of the merchant classes could build themselves houses with room for orchards and gardens, dovecots and stables, only half an hour, or less, by horse or river from the City.

Some courtiers and lawyers, as well as City merchants, found Stepney a pleasant place to live or have a country house, although most were to be found in the 'west end'. Thomas Morice, a lawyer of great wealth, as many were, 'a pleader' in the king's court, bought himself what was later known as Cobhams Manor, just near Whitechapel church. He was buried in St Dunstan's in 1368, leaving to his son armour and a silver piece enamelled with roses, a sapphire ring to the bishop of London, a blue girdle for the shrine of St Erkenwald in St Paul's and legacies for the 'poor and impotent' of Stepney, Bromley, Stratford and Hackney.

There was even a royal presence mid-century. Over among the poplar trees, near the flourishing village that had grown up on the neck of the peninsula, was a mansion often occupied by the dashing Black Prince, heir to the throne and hero of Crécy and Poitiers, Prince of Aquitaine and Gascony.

The Black Prince's Register shows that he was in residence in Poplar on various occasions between 1354 and 1365, when he was not campaigning in France. It has been assumed that he was staying in Poplar Manor House, the country residence of the Poultney family, but it is perhaps more likely that he was staying with the family who became his in-laws. In 1361 he married the stunningly beautiful Joan, the 'Fair Maid of Kent' who was the heiress of the Wake family; she inherited their Poplar mansion in 1381. The Stepney field survey of *c.* 1400 makes reference to Lady Wake's house (between Limehouse and Poplar) and the rental of *c.* 1390 calls the area 'Wakeslond'.

The main lay landholders in Stepney, however, apart from the bishop and the religious houses, were City merchants, 'Dick Whittingtons' who had made fortunes in trade. At the end of the century they were: Henry Vanner/Fanner, a vintner with a considerable export trade, sheriff from 1391 to 1392, and living in the Vintry, Adam le Changeour (alias Adam of St Ives), fast talker, pepperer and mayor, and John Hadley, lord of the two great manors of Asshews and Cobhams (from Sir John Cobham, who had inherited it from his grandfather Morice, the 'pleader').

The link between the East End and the new capitalists that was forged at this time endured for many hundreds of years, but there was no real East-West divide yet. It is too easy to see the East End from a view of what it would become. The area was not by any means just the City's backyard, and although it is often said that the prevailing wind, blowing the smells and smoke from workshops towards the east, was the occasion of 'dirty' trades being practised on the City's east side, there is no real evidence of this. Tanneries and tallow chandlers, two of the worst offenders, were to be found within the walls and in the northern and southern suburbs; there was a concentration of tanners in the Fleet Ditch area.

The other oft-mentioned factor in the growth of the working end of town is the lack of trade and craft restrictions outside the City, which encouraged industry here; later the guilds embraced the 'suburbs' in their jurisdiction. Life outside the great stone gates was rather more relaxed in many ways. Inside the City limits there were numerous rules, such as no walking about after curfew time, no selling of sweet wine in the same tavern as dry wine, and no Christmas fun (in 1393 an ordinance forbade anyone to go about the City 'with visors or false face during this solemn Feast of Christmas'). There was a positive obsession with health and safety as far as food was concerned.

The rulers of the City were fierce and forceful. The mayor himself might supervise the weighing of loaves; when John Hadley did this in 1387 he caught Robert Porter, servant to Bow baker John Gibbe, who, knowing his master's bread to be underweight, put a 4oz piece of iron into a loaf. Punishments were horrible and public. Bakers might be dragged on hurdles or flung into Newgate for selling light loaves in the City markets, whereas the bishop's court only imposed a modest fine if you did the same thing in Stepney village. Shoes sold in the City had to be made of a certain quality leather; selling small (overpriced) quantities of hay was forbidden; there were numerous restrictions on prices charged for commodities. The City fathers were particularly vigilant about bad fish and stinking meat. The favoured punishment was to put the offending butcher, fishmonger or salesman in the pillory with the bad food burning in a fire underneath. In 1320 Thomas the Smythe of Stepney was prosecuted for buying bad meat from Alice la Coureors to bring into the City. He was, however, found innocent; the court decided that one Nicholas Schyngal had been the real culprit. One John Gylessone found a pig thrown into a ditch outside Aldgate in 1348. He flayed it and cooked it and sold it to Agnes la Ismonger (ironmonger) for 4*d* and she sold it in the City. Gylessone was put in the pillory on Cornhill over a fire of bad pork.

Wages were strictly regulated, especially after the Black Death, when the chronic shortage of labour gave the opportunity for workmen to put their prices up. Masons, plasterers, carpenters, tillers and labourers were instructed to charge no more than 6*d* a day in 1350. Likewise the price of foodstuffs was regulated – 7*d* for a capon pie, 2*d* for a shoulder of mutton, for instance, in 1363.

Most historians of London, concentrating on the growth of the western suburbs and Westminster, assert that these areas were more developed than the east. A.R. Myers, for instance, speaks of the thinly populated east side. Extant tax records, however, make it clear that this was not the case. Although they are difficult to interpret, it seems undeniable that the east (outside the walls) was more heavily populated than the west. The records for 1334, for instance, show Stepney paying three times as much as Westminster; it was either considerably more populous or much richer. As we have seen, Algatestreet (Whitechapel) had grown sufficiently by 1311 for it to become a parish of its own, taking about 200 acres from Stepney.

Records of the 1377 Poll Tax list the number of people taxed, namely all adults except beggars. As in 1334, the East End is shown to have more inhabitants than the west. In Bromley and East Smithfield 156 heads are counted, paying £2 12*s*; in Stepney, Bow, Halliwell (Shoreditch) and Whitechapel there are 855, paying £14 5*s*. In the western suburbs St Giles, Grays Inn and Bloomsbury had 180 tax-payers, St Mary le Strand 160, St Clement Danes 228, Ebury and St Martin in the Fields 48, Westminster 280. Thus the East End total, excluding the City's out-parishes of Aldgate and Bishopsgate, which were probably the most populous, is 1,011, while the West End's total is 896. Allowing for evasion (which was consider-able) and children, this gives a population of perhaps 1,700 for the East End. If the out-parishes of the two St Botolph's are taken into account, the figure for the area is probably well over 2,000. The East End without these parishes, namely Stepney, Whitechapel, Shoreditch, Bow, Bromley and East Smithfield, had about the same number of people as the wool town of Wells in Somerset (901 taxpayers). If notional numbers are added for Aldgate and Bishopsgate, the headcount for the area was probably, and astonishingly, somewhere between the great towns of Ipswich (1,507 taxpayers) and England's second city, Norwich (3,952 taxpayers). Bearing in mind that perhaps 40 per cent of the population was wiped out by the Black Death, figures suggest that in the early part of the century the area had a population of over 4,000, while Westminster is estimated to have had 3,000.

Enough survives in the way of tax, manorial and probate records to give us the names of a good many of these East Enders, even of the more humble folk, the peasants working their 1-acre strips, carting loads of dung, threshing corn and dig-ging ditches. Surnames for the lower orders of society were still in the process of becoming fixed: they may tell us what a man did, where he lived or came from, or perhaps what his father or grandfather did or where he came from. Marsh families (from Poplar and the Isle of Dogs) tend to have distinctive names that reflect the watery nature of the place. The first known Limehouse limeman was called Dyk (dyke); this name was probably given to individuals who held their property in return for the responsibility of maintaining a section of river wall. The atte Ferry family presumably lived down at the tip of the peninsula, where a ferry crossed to Greenwich. There were families called Langdych (longditch), Othordych (possibly of the ditch), Attewall (living by the river wall), Etgoos (at the marsh), Conewall (rabbit wall), Attewater, Atte Marsh, Bythestronde (by the beach). Some of the family names that recur over the generations in Stepney's manorial records are atte Hache (at the Gate), Potter(giving their name to Pottersfield), Elond/ Eldelond (a Marsh family for over a hundred years), Batte, Reyson, Spylman (giving their name to Spylman Street, which ran south of Stepney church towards Cleve Street), Browning, Saykin, Gaywode, Sweeting. Not all the bishop's tenants belonged to old Stepney families by any means: when Solomon Waleys collected his rents in 1361, among the tenants were families who, according to their names, hailed from Croydon, Staines, Shoreditch, Holywell, Tottenham and Waltham.

Two Stepney manorial documents provide an almost complete census of the bishop's tenants, great and small, at the end of the century; these are a survey dated 1400 and a rental from *c.* 1390. The rental lists every parcel of land, field by field, in Wapping, Limehouse, Ratcliff, Poplar, the Isle of Dogs and part of Mile End. It starts in Churchstrete (now Stepney High Street), by the church, and Spillmanstrete (White Horse Road), and goes south along Cleve Street and Redecleve (Cable Street and Butcher Row). It then goes north to Stepney Green and Whitechapel and thence south-east to Shadwell, Ratcliff and Wapping Marsh, finishing at Aldgate. Old Ford is omitted from the survey. All the tenants are named; in some cases they were the occupiers of the house or cottage listed. Some of the tenements were held by ancient forms of tenure called 'smoke pennies' or 'hel pennies', and these probably indicate the oldest areas of settlement: in Stepney's Church Street (by St Dunstan's), in Cleve Street, going down towards the river at Ratcliff, along Poplar High Street and in the Marsh. Houses for which money rents were paid lined the road from Aldgate to Whitechapel church, thence eastwards towards Mile End is an area of open ground (manorial waste). There were twenty-one houses in Cleve Street and thirty-four in Poplar High Street. In Cleve Street and 'Redcleve' (now White Horse Lane and Butcher Row) there were between seventy and a hundred people living. Names here include John and Nicholas Joye, Adam Swetynge, Thomas Harrell, John Fordryngheye, Alice Hesew (?Hughes), William Owens, John Whelp, John Pynnock, Amerce de Chemestre, John Pynnocks and Alice Pynnocks, John Bordeland, Richard Elond, Roger Gate, William Comere, Roger Whelp, Roger Coteler, Ralph Godelok, Roger ate Stoke, Richard Sthirbourne, Adam Eldelonde, Lettitia Gaywode and Simon Gaywode, Richard Wyllesden and John Hore. John Maryne and Walter Saykin held one cottage 'newly built' (perhaps they were builders) on the 'cliff' at Ratcliff. There seems to have been something of a Welsh presence, as the names Hughes and Owen testify, as does the existence of the big new house le Welshdyk, in Stanycoft (a field lying south of the church), occupied by Lady Wake.

Occupational names speak for themselves, and we find more of them in the urbanised inner East End than in the countryside. In workshops and cottages outside the walls at Bishopsgate and Aldgate, in Whitechapel and around the Tower in East Smithfield we find tanners, ironmongers, blacksmiths and potters, leatherworkers, fullers, girdlers (working in leather and metal) butchers, brewers and a whole variety of other craftsmen and tradesmen, some of whom are still known by their occupation. A subsidy roll for 1319 lists the following taxpayers in Bishopsgate Ward (I have only listed those who are of the parish of St Botolph, namely those living outside the walls): John le Mareschal, a farrier, the gate-keeper of Bishopsgate, William Preston, warden of the Dyers and Fullers' Company, John le Hornere, Thomas le Brewere, Hugh de Ponte, William de Pountefreyt, a skinner, Walter de Bedefunte, a kisser, John Brid, a poulterer, Geoffrey le Wyttawere, Mathilda la Braceresece (Breweress), Walter le Fanner (possibly a haymonger), William ate Gatte, Warden of the Cutlers Company.

The forty-two taxpayers in the Portsoken Ward in 1319 (see map) include John Hoder, butcher in East Cheap, Gervase of Houndsditch, Walter Ruso, John Fabro, smith, William le Clerk, potter, from Suffolk, Estmar de Lung and John Cob, both butchers, Agnes Centuraria, girdler, Henry Gamene, possibly a saddler, William de Redyngs, possibly a tiler, John Bigge, potter, John Eliot, carter, Stephen Talp, brewer, John le Brewere of Estsmethefeud (East Smithfield), Simon Pottario, William Ladyl, Estmar Parno, butcher, Adam de Ridegraver, brewer, John le Hottere, possibly a basketmaker, Henry le Sunor, possibly a shoemaker, William Godefray, William Molendario, miller, John Chapman, John ate Walle, John Pardieu, Nicholas Semer, Jacobus le Bruer, Robert Sutore, Walter Vynour, butcher, William Centurario, girdler, Robert Carpenter, Hugh de Hecham, limeburner (he had a house in East Smithfield in about 1324), Alexander ate Grene, William Lymbrenner, John de la Warde, possibly a watchman, James Centurario, girdler, Thomas Ceseario, cheesemonger, Nicholas Dereman, butcher, Robert de Raughtone, potter of metal pots, and John de Billerica.

Prominent among the craftsmen in our part are the celebrated bellfounders or beliters (remembered in Billiter Street). They were originally attached to the Potters' Company, and may appear as potters in the records. Founders listed in 1311 include Henry in the Lane (the Lanes were a Stepney family), John atte Marsh (presumably Stepney Marsh) and William de Alegate. William Burford of Aldgate is the first named bellfounder, with a workshop at the sign of the Three Nuns next to Aldgate church. In the will of Joan Burford, his widow, he is described as a brazier (1397). Braziers, smiths and founders seem to have been interchangeable terms, and it is evident from the will archive that metalworking was the predominant craft in Aldgate and Whitechapel. Armour, cannon and arrow boxes were made in workshops in the vicinity of the Tower, where the royal armoury was housed; in 1339 there was an arms depot called La Bretaske near the Tower and one 'beyond the gate' at Aldgate, stocked with crossbows and arrows. Alan Birchore was making bowstrings in a workshop near Tower Hill in 1386.

With the increasing demand for church bells and the need for armaments for the French wars, metalwork was a very profitable business. At his death in 1391 Burford left numerous sums of money to local religious institutions, including a remarkably lavish £100 to the two chaplains at St Botolph's to say masses for his soul; evidently he had made a fortune. Joan Burford, a brewer in her own right, was directed by her husband to keep a beam light burning in the church as long as she lived. She followed her husband to the grave after six years. By 1414 the foundry incorporated a brewery. Metalworking and brewing seem to have made good bedfellows. William Marowe, who had the Vine brewery in Bishopsgate, was also a smith.

In later years the area was famous for its breweries, especially that owned by the City monastery of St Thomas of Acon in Wapping, probably near where the Prospect of Whitby now is (sold for an astronomical sum of money by Henry VIII at the Reformation) and the brewery at the Hermitage near St Katharine's. The number of prosecutions for breaking the assize of ale at the Stepney Manor Court (giving short measure) in 1384 indicates that numbers of people, especially women, were making and selling beer. Thomas Haywode had a brewery called the Ram on Tower Hill in 1361; it was one of many, no doubt. There was a concentration of brewers in Bishopsgate, men like Adam Mitchel (d.1417) who kept the Dragon, Richard Sonday (d.1415), whose wealth is indicated by the large mortuary gift he left in his will, William Marowe, mentioned above, who had lands and tenements locally, and whose son would become mayor of London in 1455, John de Wodestock, William Mokeron, with lands in Essex and shops in Bishopsgate, and buried by the rood in St Botolph's (a prime place).

An ordinance of 1371 forbade the slaughter of oxen, sheep and pigs in the City; the beasts were to be taken to Stratford Bow and Knightsbridge. There were butchers all over London, but there seems to have been a concentration of them out east, men like Richard atte Hoke of Whitechapel who had amassed enough money to pay 8 marks for a year of chantry masses, and generous sums to his relatives, 2s each to all the London and suburban hospitals and a legacy for the repair of the road that ran from his house to Whitechapel church. In 1319 more than six butchers are mentioned in the list of taxpayers in the Portsoken Ward, more than any other occupational group, including Estmar de Lung, warden of the Butchers' Company.

Down by the riverside there was work for the locals on the king's ships. The Tower was the base for the few royal ships and the keeper of the king's ships had his office there. Although most vessels were imported from the Low Countries, there was a small community of shipwrights in Thames Street, Queenhithe and the parish of All Hallows Barking, there is evidence for some shipbuilding activity along Stepney's riverside. Little Alan le Palmere, scion of a shipbuilding dynasty of Thames Street, was left a wharf in Ratcliff for his maintenance when his parents died in the Black Death. This wharf may, of course, just have been a landing place for timber; the earliest actual mention of the industry in Ratcliff is in 1354, when John de Alkeshull is instructed to get eighty-three trees from Guildford Park to 'La Redeclyve' for building the king's ships. Two years later Guy de Saintcler and John Straunge were authorised to conscript ships' carpenters in East Anglia for the construction of the king's ships at Ratcliff. Robert Crull, Stepney rector from 1368 to 1404, was 'clerk of the king's ships'. The 1390s rental for the bishop's estates has a field in the Limehouse area called 'Schypmade' (shipmead). In 1401 Henry IV had a special dock constructed there, where his small ship, *Gracedieu de la Tour*, was built, by forty-six men. It was painted in bright colours with a golden eagle on the bowsprit and a golden crown on the stern.

As to the loading and unloading of merchant vessels and the docks with which the area would be identified in later centuries, there is not much known. The chief operation of the port of London was along the City's riverside, between the Tower and Blackfriars, which was lined with quays and wharfs. Small ships and barges were unloaded there, while larger vessels lay out in the river and discharged their cargoes into lighters. The easterly reaches were certainly in use, perhaps for the coastal trade. At the time of the French invasion threat in 1377 royal ships were moored along the riverside from the bridge, extending as far east as Ratcliff, for the safe-keeping of the shipping on the Thames. In 1380 Sir John Philpot (of whom more anon) proposed the building of a barricade across the river from Ratcliff to Greenwich, with two stout 6oft-high stone towers and a chain between them. Any tendency for the port operation to move east, where the river was deeper, was halted in the sixteenth century by the Act that restricted unloading to certain 'legal quays'. Nevertheless wharves and warehouses are beginning to make their appearance; the first wharf for which we have a precise date of construction is that built in 1395 by William Danyell on the Wapping estate of the priory of St Thomas of Acon.

Fish for the markets and tables of London was supplied from the river, a rich source for trout, salmon and eels, but there does not seem to have been much fishing along Stepney's Thames waterfront, except on the eastern side of the Isle of Dogs. Most London fishermen, or those who have left any account of themselves, operated from Barking, Poplar, Deptford and Greenwich. Presumably this was to do with the river traffic; in 1488 all net fishing was banned from Wapping

Mill to London Bridge. There were, however, fisheries on the Lea and in and around the many watermills; manor court records show fisheries in and around Bullivant's Mill at Bow.

The mills needed manpower: strong men were required to operate the heavy machinery and hump the sacks of grain; labourers or 'scavellmen' were needed for scouring out the ditches. Crassh Mills, Wapping Mill, Algot's and Bullivant's at Stratford and seven others are known of, and there may have been more. Shadwell's mill was derelict and its watercourse dried up by 1334. There were windmills too; at least one whirred away on Stepney Marsh, belonging to Pontefract Manor. The bishop's mill, or one of them, stood just south of the west end of what is now Cable Street; it seems to have been destroyed by fire, giving its name to Brendmill [Burntmill] Hill. It would be nice to think that Chaucer's roughest pilgrim, with the coarsest of tales to tell, might have been modelled on one of the great strapping Stepney millers the author encountered when he lived in these parts.

Wool was the country's most important commodity and the East End played its part. There were sheep around, though probably not many; in 1335 some wool from the bishop's estate was sold to a wool dealer in Hackney, and there are some references to sheep grazing on Stepney Marsh. Cloth woven in the shires was brought to London for finishing and much of it was sent for fulling to mills at Bow and Stratford. In 1376 the radical draper John of Northampton stood up for the hurers (capmakers), who complained that their livelihood was threatened by the fulling watermills. Bullivant's was adapted for fulling and Algot's or Fullers' Mill was restored by Sir John Poultney and was working in 1383/4. Roger ate Pond, a wool merchant, had seven shops in East Smithfield in 1328–29. John Hardy was a wealthy fuller of Bishopsgate. After his death his widow, Alice, seems to have run the workshop for over twenty years, with the help of her trusty servant John Sowson. She evidently did well for herself, and at her death in 1400 had an abundance of costly clothes, gold, silver and sapphire jewellery and an amber necklace with a silver crucifix to leave to her friends.

It was during the fourteenth century that Limehouse became Limehouse. The lands lying between Ratcliff and Poplar are called 'Le Lymhostes' in 1367, which suggests that lime may have been made there for some time. Lime, produced by burning chalk and made into mortar, was an essential material for the building trade, and as London grew there was an increasing demand. The chalk was brought up from Kent by river to the Stepney kilns, which stood near what would become Limehouse Dock. In 1335 lime used on the manor for building repairs came from the 300 sacks received by the bishop each year as rent for the lime-kilns. In 1362/3 one John Dik gave twenty-five sacks of lime as rent to the bishop. In 1398–99 there were five kilns; the manor received fifty sacks of lime from the kiln of one tenant, and twenty-five each from the kilns of another four. The two Dyk/Dyke kilns had passed, with other property in the area, to the atte Haches, along with the portion of river wall that Philip Dyke (hence the family name) was responsible for. In 1380 John Hadele, leading City merchant and Stepney landlord, granted a cottage and gardens by 'les lymhostes' to Peter atte Hache, the bishop's beadle and a major landholder in Poplar and the Marsh; one of his properties is described as in 'Lymstret'. Other kilns were rented by members of the Golding and Kent families and William Edwin and Thomas Warris, who made wills in 1404 and 1443 respectively. The two atte Hacche kilns passed to John atte Hacche, presumably Peter's son, and William Hacche, perhaps his brother, was a benefactor to Stepney church when he died in 1400. During the years that followed the lime 'millionaires' were to become most important men in the running of Stepney parish.

Bread for the City's markets was made in the Bow bakeries, as we have seen; early in the morning carts trundled through Aldgate bound for 'The Cartes' in Cheapside, for Bishopsgate, Queenhithe, Fleet Bridge and the Carfax at Leadenhall. There was serious rivalry between the bakers from Stratford Bow and those of the City, and it was stipulated that the 'Bremble' (Bromley) or Stepney loaf should be heavier than the London loaf. While the men toiled at the hot ovens their wives and daughters did the marketing. Women and servants were sent into the City to sell bread there, as 'aliens' were, strictly speaking, not allowed to: wives and daughters, apprentices and journeymen were not accounted personally liable, as the bakers would have been. In 1310 sheriff Roger le Palmer arrested a whole bunch of 'bakeresses' for selling underweight loaves: Sarra Foting, Christina Terrice, Matilda de Bolingtone, Christina Prichet, Isabella Sperling, Alice Pegges, Johanna de Cauntebrigge and Isabella Pouveste. They were found to be innocent; the incident was probably just part of the ongoing rivalry between the City bakers and those on the banks of the Lea. But the Stratford bakeries continued to be the main supplier; Langland, in *The Vision of Piers Plowman*, wrote of the alarm caused in a spring drought:

> When no cart came to towne
> With breed fro Stratforde

The blacksmiths, founders, brewers, bakers, brick- and tilemakers, fullers and limemen, fishermen, wharfingers, millers and scavellmen comprised a significant, but a small percentage of the East Enders. Most men were agricultural workers of one sort and another, working on the large estates known as manors. The Bishop of London's manor was still by far the largest, although a number of other freehold estates had been built up by the accumulation of small plots, eating into his extensive Domesday property. A rental of 1381 shows some 160 customary (later copyhold) tenants, some of whom were city men, holding plots of varying sizes. Gradually the acre strips were brought together through purchase or exchange, with land changing hands regularly. The manorial partible inheritance system, known as gavelkind, meant that on a tenant's death his property, allowing for his widow's 'free bench', would pass first to sons (equally), then to daughters, then to next of kin in equal degrees. When Roger Goderde's widow died in Stepney in 1384 the heirs are named in the court records as two sons and the widow's stepdaughter.

As the years passed the enormous patchwork quilt fields were parcelled up; some were called after the families to whom they belonged, like Galeysfield, Pottersfield, Gromettsland. Most of the arable land belonging to free and customary tenants lay south of the Whitechapel Road. Corn was grown on the rich lands reclaimed from the river in Walmarsh and East Marsh. A marsh called the Wylde in Limehouse was meadow and pasture. The field pattern created in the late Middle Ages was largely that which still pertained when the parish was first properly surveyed in the eighteenth century, and can be seen in Gascoyne's 1703 map.

The ancient feudal arrangement whereby tenants held their land in return for labour services had long ceased to operate in Stepney; the liabilities of wodelode and timberlode, nedreps and falcones (reaping and mowing) and the rest had been sold off, and the term molmen (which means tenants who paid cash rent for their property) disappears from the records, as everyone now paid rent. Previously tenants, or, more likely their labourers, had helped out with hoeing, threshing, making drainage channels, purifying rye seed, bundling straw for thatching, taking produce to market and bringing in the harvest, for which last they received a generous allowance of bread and cheese. In 1362, 2s an acre was paid in lieu of labour services for lands held by the forms of tenure known as cotland and shirland, 4d for molland and 14d for hideland.

In 1336 the bishop employed three carters, three herdsmen, three ploughmen, a dairymaid, a shepherd, a swineherd and a stockman. There was a small breeding herd of pigs (about sixty of them), some cattle and sheep, but grain and hay production were paramount; in 1336 the bishop had 82½ acres put to hay. A huge amount of hay was needed for horses in London that had no pasture, and it was bulky to transport and store – hence the artificially high price of meadow in Stepney, vastly more expensive than arable land. Geese, cranes, cygnets and peacocks were reared for bishops' lavish banquets. Farming on the bishop's demesne stopped somewhere between 1339 and 1362, and only the home farm was worked by the episcopal employees, to supply the immediate needs of the household at Bethnal Green.

Little survives to show us how the bishop's tenants and the freeholders farmed their land, but mixed farming seems to have been general, with wheat and barley as the main crops. On Pomfret Manor, down in the Marsh, 80 acres that had been arable in 1323 had been given over to sheep grazing by 1362, but this may have

been because the manor house was unoccupied. Wheat and other crops continued to be grown on the peninsula until the Great Flood of 1448. William Potter
of the Marsh, who died in 1380, makes reference in his will to 2 acres of wheat,
two oxen and two plough teams. Walter Page (whose will is dated 1364) had
nearly 50 acres, mainly sown with wheat and barley, with just 2 acres of meadow.
In 1393 Adam Chaunger of St Ives, one of the biggest landholders in Poplar and
Limehouse, had 50 acres of wheat, 23 acres of barley, 16 acres of beans, peas, and
vetches, 16 acres of pasture and 5 acres of meadow.

Tales of the Tower Hamlets, the Poet and the Church

Of the momentous events that affected the lives of the fourteenth-century East
Enders, the first was the collapse of Bow bridge, which may well have happened
even before the century opened. According to John Leland, one Godfrey Pratt,
appointed by the Abbot of Stratford Langthorne to keep the bridge and paid
with a daily allowance of loaves, started imposing a toll, and the abbot stopped his
bread allowance. Pratt gave the job up and the bridge fell into disrepair. According
to the official report, an inquest of 1303, one Hugh Pratt introduced a voluntary
toll and his son and heir, William, got permission to levy a compulsory toll, which
paid for an iron railing called Lock Bridge, presumably a tollgate. One day Philip
Basset (royal justiciar, who died in 1271) and the Abbot of Waltham drove over
the bridge with wagons and broke it down. After that William abandoned repairs
and it remained broken, presumably for many years, until Edward I's wife Eleanor
had it repaired. The nursery rhyme 'London Bridge is broken down, dance over
my Lady Lea' may well refer to this incident, although there are many far-fetched
theories about its origins.

Six years after the inquiry into the bridge over the Lea something much more
fascinating to the locals occurred. In the early spring of 1309 a great whale was
washed up by the tide and stranded on the bank of the Thames. Both the bishop,
as Lord of Stepney Manor, and the Dean and Chapter of St Paul's, whose fields lay
by the river at Shadwell, claimed possession of the creature.

A series of major floods affected the lives of the ordinary folk more than the
politicking at Court or goings-on at the Guildhall. In 1323 a 'mighty floud, proceeding from the tempestuosness of the Sea' made a breach in Wapping's river
wall. The jurors who looked into the matter decided that it was not the fault of the
bishop or his servants, and that all landholders should share in the repairs, maintaining the banks, dykes and sewers 'according to the Custome of those parts'. At
the time of the flood the area of 32 acres belonged to prominent City families, to
John Gisors (twice mayor), John Pertun and Maud de Cauntebrig, Walter Crepyn
had half an acre and 10 acres belonged to the monastery of St Thomas of Acon.

In 1369 much of Stepney's manor lands was again flooded. Nicholas Carter and the bishop's beadle, Solomon Waleys/Salviano Watley (a probable descendant of Henry de Waleys, see above), were instructed to employ carpenters, ditchers and other labourers to repair the river wall.

A terrible storm in the early spring of 1390 was written up by the St Albans chronicler Thomas Walsingham: great old trees were blown down, roofs torn off, houses upturned and cattle drowned. John Wadham, William Skrene and William Cressewyk were commissioned to inspect and repair damage to river walls and ditches between Stepney and Bromley, while the poet Chaucer, with others, was sent to deal with the ditches between Woolwich and Greenwich.

Far worse than the intermittent flooding was the 'pestilence'. The most dire and dreadful time for East Enders, and for everyone else, came mid-century, with the terrifying swellings, or buboes, which killed man, woman or child within a couple of days of their appearance. The plague, which became known as the Black Death, arrived in London at the beginning of November 1348, brought by a Genoese ship. Within a few weeks it had reached Stepney. This most devastating of the many late medieval plagues killed perhaps 3 million people in England, left villages deserted, houses empty, crops rotting in the fields for want of labourers and churches empty for want of priests. Long-term it wrought a radical change in the social order and in religious practices. In Stepney a possible third of the inhabitants were lost. Manor court records for 1348–49, with their lists of dead, give some idea of the scale of the calamity. By December 1348 four members of one family had died, mother, daughter and two sons. In the following spring the clerk noted that the suit pending between William of Huntingdon and Edmund Cobbe had been dropped: '*mortuus est*' is written over their names. By Easter the aletasters at Stratford, Aldgate Street and Halliwell Street were all dead. It was during that summer and autumn that most people died, with 105 holdings vacated by tenants and, in many cases, no heirs to take them over. Agnes ate Wall's 2 acres went to non-relatives, as did Margaret Godyng's cottage; for William le Pulter no heirs could be found in the county, and the bishop took Christine ate Nok's cottage as her daughter, Margery, failed to appear. No heirs could be found for Hugh Baronn's cottage and 3 acres. A total of 121 dead tenants are listed in the legible parts of the documents. There were many more.

The defeudalisation of the country at large was hastened by the Black Death. With the loss of a great part of the workforce, landlords were unable to work their estates and land was sold off cheaply. Wages rocketed; in Stepney in 1362 tilers got 8*d* a day, double what they had earned before the plague. Peasants acquired their own farms, and some drifted towards well-paid work in the local and City breweries, bakeries, tanneries, smithies and carpenters' shops.

Over at East Smithfield a cemetery was made for London plague victims, on the City side of Doddings Pond and Crassh Mills, just south of Hog Lane, where later the Royal Mint would be built, now Royal Mint Flats. Here some 2,400 corpses were laid in orderly graves, dressed in their ordinary clothes, not shrouds, as was usually the case. This was known as the New Churchyard of Holy Trinity, to which the land had belonged; one John Corey, a senior official in the service of the Black Prince, had acquired a toft of land from the priory to be used as a graveyard.

In 1350 Edward III founded a Cistercian monastery on the site of the plague cemetery. It is now thought that John Corey had been acquiring land on behalf of the king or the prince for this purpose before the plague called a temporary halt to the plans. The house of white monks was dedicated to the Virgin, whom the king believed had rescued him from a storm at sea; it was called the Abbey of St Mary Graces, nicknamed Eastminster. This was Edward III's favourite monastery. The rents bequeathed by the rector of Stepney, John Silverstone, for a chantry priest to sing for his soul in St Dunstan's were confiscated by the king, because a mortmain licence had not been procured, and given to the abbey. A well-endowed and prestigious establishment, enjoying royal patronage and papal favours, in 1396 it was the chosen venue for a great meeting of the Chapter General of the order. At the time of the Dissolution it was the third largest Cistercian abbey in the country, a red-roofed building with a dove house, cattle yard and a grove of conifers lying to its east, known as the Pineapple Garden. The Abbot of Tower Hill, as he became known, was Lord of Eastminster Manor, ruling over the rowdy brothels and gaming houses of East Smithfield; he also acquired Poplar Manor from the Loveyn family in 1375. A very old monk, giving evidence in a tithe suit in the Exchequer in 1577, remembered in the days of his youth collecting rents for the abbot; he recalled the manor house with its fishponds and orchards, and the hay and corn grown in Birdingbushe field and Ashfield.

The king buried his mother, the She-Wolf, in 1358, the French princess whose inheritance was now his. For thirty-one years Edward III had kept her confined at Castle Rising, where she went mad. A procession accompanied the corpse of the tragic Isabella along the Colchester Road, resting at Mile End before the last stage of the journey to London; board and lodging for the stay cost the king £10. The sad and solemn retinue then passed along Alegate Street and through the gate, with its massive twin towers, and finally came to the Greyfriars at Newgate, where the queen was buried with her lover, Roger Mortimer.

In the summer of 1374 the eastern gate of the City was honoured by the arrival of the first great poet of the English language, Geoffrey Chaucer. A protégé (and later brother-in-law) of the king's brother, the magnificent John of Gaunt, he was appointed Comptroller of Wool Customs and, courtesy of his patron, moved into accommodation over the gate at Aldgate. He lived there for eleven years, during which time he is thought to have started writing his most famous work, *The Canterbury Tales*. The gate stood astride the Colchester Road, a famously muddy highway. Sir John Hadley and others left money for its improvement in their wills; Nicholas Dereman, a butcher, left 100s and 'his olden white horse on which he was wont to ride … to mend the way where most needful from the Church of St. Mary de Matfolone toward Myle End'. The gate lay from just east of Jewry Street to somewhere between Houndsditch and Duke Street, having a frontage of about 75ft; the road running between its towers was just 20ft wide. It was locked from sunset to sunrise, and the great gates swung open when the first bell of the day rang out from St Thomas of Acon in Cheapside. Underneath Chaucer's probably quite palatial apartment was the weighhouse, where corn was weighed at the Great Beam before going to be milled. The gate was busy with traffic; in 1376 a toll system was in operation, whereby 2d was charged for every iron-bound cart bringing victuals into the City by Aldgate, and every cart bringing in blood and entrails of slaughtered beasts, 1d for ordinary carts and ½d for every grain cart.

Looking east from his windows, Chaucer must have felt lord of all he surveyed. His father, John, a wealthy vintner, had land in Stepney and Whitechapel, twenty-four shops, and two gardens in St Mary Matfelon, his wife's inheritance from her uncle, Hamo de Copton, a moneyer at the royal mint in the Tower. The properties included a large brewery, which the Abbey of St Mary Graces had taken over in 1341. In 1349 one Nigel of Hackney brought a plea of intrusion into a house in St Botolph's parish against the poet's parents; in 1361 they were involved in litigation with John de Goseborn and his wife Idonea in the Stepney Manor Court. Agnes Chaucer, *née* Copton, is thought to have grown up in Aldgate, and Geoffrey was probably familiar with the sights and sounds, the streets and the residents, the fishmongers, butchers, potters, bakers, chandlers, goldbeaters, fell-mongers, vintners, saddlers, cobblers, brewers, hatters, spurriers, cooks, janitors, bellfounders, bucketmakers, pail and metal potmakers. He would have mixed with the religious and the great merchants and, more than likely used them as models for the characters in his famous work.

The Prioress in *The Canterbury Tales*, the simpering 'Lady Sweet Briar', Madame Eglantine, with her little lapdog and her pretty ways, spoke French 'after the school of Stratford atte Bow', and it is a reasonable assumption that Chaucer based her on someone he had met from Bromley Priory:

Ther was also a nonne, a prioresse,
That of hir smylyng was ful symple and coy;
Hire gretteste ooth was but by seinte loy;
And she was cleped madame eglentyne.
Ful weel she soong the service dyvyne,
Entuned in hir nose ful semely,
And frenssh she spak ful faire and fetisly,
After the scole of stratford atte bowe,
For frenssh of parys was to hire unknowe

Chaucer moved in elevated circles. The priory had become fashionable and was now quite the place for royalty to patronise, visit and even take retreat. Queen Philippa's sister, Elizabeth of Hainault, seems to have been a resident; she was buried in the chapel of St Mary and left a psalter to one of the Bow nuns (of which there were about thirty) named Argentyn, Madame Eglantine perhaps! The manor of Cobhams was left to one Giles Argentem by John Hadley in his will of 1405.

Another of the Canterbury pilgrims was a merchant, a solemn single-minded man with a forked beard and a Flemish beaver hat, whose conversation ran on money-making and the worries of pirates in the North Sea. Although the identification is not so clear-cut as that of the Bow nun, he can be matched with the man who was, without doubt, the foremost 'celebrity' of the fourteenth-century East End, Sir John Philpot, whom we met as Lord of Hulls Manor. His widow, although she remarried twice after his death, persisted in calling herself Lady Philpot to her dying day. At his death in 1381 he left her a life interest in Stepney Manor, which suggests that this was their home. Hulls Manor House, with its great 50-acre field, lay south of the Whitechapel Road, standing well back from the highway, near the junction with the road to Bethnal Green. Philpot had over 100 acres in Stepney, land in Mile End, Galeysfield and Limehouse. A fishmonger by trade, according to Higden's *Polychron*, but a freeman of the Grocers' Company, he became fabulously wealthy, owned Hoxton and was rich enough to launch his own fleet to clear the Channel of pirates, earning the undying hatred of Chaucer's patron, John of Gaunt, whose own expedition to France had failed.

Philpot and his neighbour John Hadley, pepperer, grocer and lord of two Stepney manors, near the white chapel, were both leaders in the great city war that raged from the 1370s to 1384, and both served as mayor. Hadley (mayor in 1379–80 and 1391–92), and previously mayor of Calais, was said to be 'outwardly the finest talker but inwardly the falsest' of all the four previous mayors. A merchant prince, like Philpot, he lent large sums of money to the king. When the victualling companies mounted a campaign against foreigners trading in the City, their chief opponent was John of Northampton, a draper, a radical and reformist alderman, who gained the support of the all-powerful Gaunt. In 1378 they had Philpot and William Walworth removed from their offices as war treasurers to parliament, and managed to get a statute passed that allowed free trade in all foodstuffs except wine. The victualling lobby finally won and Nicholas Brembre, grocer, became mayor in 1384.

Philpot was much acclaimed for his philanthropy, and left the residue of his fortune to provide a water supply and latrines for the City; but posterity remembers Philpot not for City lavatories nor for ridding the seas of pirates but as hero of the Peasants' Revolt. The summer of 1381 brought a peasant army, 50,000 strong, to London, led by Wat Tyler from Maidstone. Essex rebels joined him from the east and Aldgate was opened up, letting the furious mob swarm into the City's narrow streets. Inflamed by the crippling Poll Tax, and possibly encouraged by Wycliffe's teaching that anyone in a state of grace was his own master, the rioters sacked the palace of the hated John of Gaunt at the Savoy and decapitated the archbishop, Simon of Sudbury, on Tower Hill, along with a friar, a farmer of the public revenue and 'one Richard Somenour of Stepney parish'. This Richard may well have been a summoner, one of the hated Church officials satirised by Chaucer. The rebels made a camp not far from the Philpot mansion, on Mile End Green. With remarkable bravery the fourteen-year-old Richard II rode out to meet them, and promises were made. There was a further confrontation at Smithfield; Wat Tyler lost his temper, and in the ensuing fracas Walworth, the lord mayor, stabbed him. The 'Commons', as the chronicler calls them, bent their bows, intent on revenge. The mayor, with John Philpot at his side, flew to the City to raise help, while the dying peasant leader was dragged from St Bartholomew's hospital, where he had been put in the master's room. His head was cut off, stuck on a pole and paraded before his followers. 'They felt like men discomforted', writes the chronicler, and went 'crying to the king for mercy'. John Philpot and his friend Walworth were both knighted in recognition of their bravery and quick thinking.

According to Chaucer, the fourteenth-century Church employed a number of nasty people: randy monks, crooks, conmen and hypocrites. But then piety is not much of a subject for a satirical poet and, moreover, Chaucer was probably sympathetic to Wycliffe and the Lollards who were attacking corruption in the Church. How many of these characters may have had their origins in individuals encountered by Chaucer when he lived in Aldgate is anybody's guess; apart from Madame Eglantine, there is no mention of any local connection. We will probably never know whether the monster of a summoner, with 'knobbes sitting on his cheeks', was based on the Stepney parish summoner lynched by the pro-Lollard mob during the Peasants' Revolt.

The presence of the Church in the Tower Hamlets was overpowering, with religious institutions ringing the eastern city walls from the Spital in the north to St Katharine's down by the river, and eight churches and chapels. The streets and lanes were full of monks, canons, nuns, priests and other religious personnel. London was a busy market for 'choppe churches', traffickers in benefices, who might sell a rich benefice for ready cash, buy a poor one and pocket the difference. St Botolph's Bishopsgate changed hands six times in twenty-one years. It is difficult to overestimate the power of the Church, especially after the calamity of the Black Death. The loss of a third of one's family and friends drew folk closer to eternity, made the prospect of heaven and hell real and imminent. As we shall see in the next chapter, religious observance was dramatically changed, and people were more and more inclined to use what money they had to pay priests for a guaranteed place in the afterlife. Langland, in *The Vision of Piers Plowman*, written at this time, describes the life of a poor priest, like many, come to London to cash in on the new demand:

> The looms that I labour will be my livelihood to earn
> Is the pater noster and my primer: Placebo and Dirige
> And my psalter sometime: and my seven psalms
> That I say for the souls: of such as me help

The survival of some testaments (wills of cash, chattels and leases) from the fourteenth century, mainly from the 'middling sort', tell us something about the economic status and possessions of East Enders, but more about their relationship with their parish church and the nearby hospitals and monasteries. These testaments are in the main short, formularised documents, death bed wishes dictated to the parish chaplain, probably very much under his direction, and tidied up by the clerk in the registry at St Paul's, where they went for probate. Belongings are not usually itemised, but some prized or expensive items may feature. In the standard will the testator simply leaves the residue of his personal estate to his wife or children, appointing the widow, sons or trusted friends as executors. These documents were authorised by the Church and, as such, are not concerned with the disposal of freehold and copyhold land, over which it had no say. The former descended by law to the 'heir-at-law' and copyhold was dealt with by the manorial lord, while the City's 'Custom of London' made sure that widows and orphans were cared for. City wills were enrolled in the Court of Hustings.

The proliferation of testaments of personal estate at this time, especially in the East End, was occasioned by the growing wealth of ordinary folk, who now had rich clothes and valuable plate, pots and pans to leave to their loved ones, and by the increasing tendency of landlords to grant leases (which might be bequeathed in testaments). In the year after the Black Death much land in Stepney was let on lease. Perhaps even more instrumental in the number of testaments (which increased substantially in the fifteenth century) was the tighter grip that the Church was able to take over the money of its flock, for whom the fields of purgatory were as real as Mile End Green. A 'mortuary gift' to the parish church was *de rigueur*, and the amount left (nominally a gift for 'tithes forgotten') seems to have been related to the wealth of the testator. Most people left 1*s* (two days' wages) but some left as little as 2*d*, with wealthy and/or pious men giving more. Legacies to Bedlam, the hospitals at Bishopsgate (the Spital), St Thomas's and St Bartholomew's feature in the wills of the wealthy City men, and the parish chaplain, clerk, sometimes the vicar, and very often the friars were usually left a reasonable sum. Money was left for masses to be said for the soul of the testator, and often for the souls of everyone they knew or all Christians. Bellfounder

Burford, as we have seen, left a huge sum for this purpose. Margaret in the Lane, widow and executrix of a wealthy Stepney cooper, Adam, married John Robart after Adam's death in 1392. Her extravagantly pious will, made in 1399, is a foretaste of the preoccupation with the purchase of relief from purgatory and the wholesale endowment of chantries, such a feature in the next century. The whole of the extensive landed estates left to her by her first husband, apart from a small parcel left to her son, Marun, were directed to be sold for the benefit of the souls of herself and Adam. Land was also given to the monastery of Holy Trinity at Aldgate, where she and her husband were buried.

Some of these wills, though not many, allow us a glimpse of something a bit more lively than hours, days, months or even years of murmuring priests. Alice Collier of Stepney died before her husband, leaving him, among other things, her luxurious gowns of silver and scarlet, silver buttons and a scarlet cap. Brass pots and vats (for dye?) are mentioned in her will, and she left a generous £2 to the fabric of the church, with 2s for the vicar, Thomas de Hengham ad Castra. It would be nice to think of her all in scarlet at mass on Sunday, like the Wife of Bath, 'quite put out of charity' if any other dame 'dared stir to the altar steps in front of her'.

The ground landlord over all, or nearly all, was of course the Bishop of London. Throughout the century bishops continued to spend time in Bethnal Green. The episcopal palace, with its fine bath-house, was refurbished in 1371. Richard of Newport died suddenly in August 1318 at the vicar's house in Ilford, and was taken by night to Stepney and thence for burial at St Paul's. He thoughtfully left money for two boys in the choir of St Paul's 'when they shall change their voice'. Ralph Baldock died there in July 1313 and Ralph de Stratford in April 1354. Robert Braybrook, bishop from 1382 until his death in 1404, was the last bishop to spend any time in the Stepney Manor House. He offended the Wycliffite Londoners by refusing to proclaim the nullity of statutes directed against the preachers of heresy. In 1392 he tried to stop London cobblers working on Sundays by threat of excommunication.

Holy Trinity Priory kept surveillance over the inner East End, with the prior as *ex officio* alderman of the Portsoken Ward and lord of one of the Bromley manors. St Mary of Clerkenwell, St John of Jerusalem and St Bartholomew's were major landholders in Stepney, St Thomas of Acon had estates in Wapping and the Dean and Chapter of St Paul's had Shadwell Manor; their lands along by the river were called Dean's Lynches.

The area was now directly served by fourteen religious institutions. There were four independent parish churches, the two St Botolph's (Aldgate, probably a Saxon foundation, and Bishopsgate, certainly there by 1212), St Mary Matfelon at Whitechapel, the mother church of Stepney, St Dunstan; and four hospitals, St Katharine's by the Tower, St Mary Spital, St Mary of Bethlehem and the Mary Magdalene Mile End Leper Hospital. Two religious houses had churches attached: Madame Eglantine's Bromley nunnery and the convent of the Poor Clares in the Minories. There were two chapels of ease to Stepney church, St Mary in the Marsh (which William Pottere called the chapel of 'Fisshbrigge') and St Mary, Bow. The new Abbey of St Mary Graces (Eastminster) ruled on Tower Hill, and by the end of the century in Poplar too, The Tower had its own church, appropriately dedicated to St Peter in Chains, and there was a hermitage in Wapping; one John Ingram lived in seclusion among the swans' nests near Crassh Mills. Of the religious houses, the grand royal foundation of Eastminster and the convent in the Minories were the most prestigious. The latter attracted a whole raft of royal and noble benefactors, including Queen Isabella herself and John of Gaunt. It had especially close associations with the family of Thomas Woodstock, Duke of Gloucester (1355–97), youngest son of Edward III and prime leader in the attack on Richard II. The Gloucesters' London mansion was next door to the convent's church; the duchess died there and their daughter, Isabella, was put into the care of the nuns there when she was just a little girl, rising in adulthood to become abbess. At St Katharine's work began on a new church, with carved wooden stalls in the chancel. In 1351 Edward's queen, Philippa, drew up new regulations for her hospital: the brothers and sisters were to wear a dark cloak emblazoned with a Katharine wheel, there was to be no private conversation between the sexes, and the chapter was to meet once a week.

As for the others, Bedlam, now that the Holy Land was lost to Christendom, was taken over by the City, and operated as a sick and lunatic asylum, while the Spital struggled for money, especially after the Black Death reduced the value of its property. At St Katharine's matters had to be taken in hand, as we have seen, and we know nothing of the leper hospital at this period. As to Stepney's chapels of ease, at Bow and in the Isle of Dogs, presumably they went on asserting their independence from the mother church; by 1497 the clergy at St Mary Bow were burying their own dead, rather than carting the corpses over to Stepney village.

Before we look at the mother church itself, about which we know a good deal, we must make the acquaintance of the ubiquitous friars. Members of the four orders of begging monks intruded themselves into parishes, holding public confessions and stealing members of the congregation. They specialised in thunderous sermons and offered a special power of absolution. Very popular with the nobility, gentry and, indeed, royalty, they were the bane of the lives of the regular parish clergy, and regarded by many as little better than market traders in God's mercies, greedy conmen who flattered the rich to get legacies, cadged the best food from susceptible householders and seduced girls. Friary churches, particularly the Greyfriars' church at Newgate, attracted people away from their home parish, and though tithes and mortuary gifts still went to the mother church, legacies and payments for masses might be made to the friars, and often were. Sir John Philpot, the Stepney 'millionaire', was buried at the Greyfriars. Bellfounder William Burford left 10s to the friars to pray for his soul. When Roger Atte Nook of Stepney died in 1392 he left only 1s to St Dunstan's fabric (where he was buried), and 2s 6d each to the Carmelite Friars and to the Austin Friars to say masses for his soul.

There is no sign today of any of the churches, chapels and monasteries here mentioned, they are all lost or rebuilt beyond recognition, except the mother church itself. St Dunstan's was rebuilt in the fifteenth century, but some remnants of its forebear can be seen in the jamb shafts and caps of the east window, and the second window from the east in the north aisle, with its simple flowing tracery in the decorated style. There is no documentary evidence that the church was rebuilt in the fourteenth century, but the architectural signs suggest that a north aisle was added, and the chancel was either remodelled or a new east window was added in the fashionable style.

The church, perhaps rather squat in appearance, something like the church of East Ham, stood in a wide, flat churchyard, surrounded by drainage ditches, like a moat. To the south was a tall Pauline cross, where the parish chaplain sometimes preached, and a lych-gate leading towards Cleve Street, where most people lived. Over to the east a gate led into the grounds of the parsonage house, which lay in Churchfield. The storage of the corn tithes of corn from such a large arable parish would have necessitated a large barn. A porch probably protected the main doorway at the west end of the south wall; here the first part of baptism and marriage ceremonies took place. The floor was strewn with rushes and branches of box and yew were used for decoration, except on some festival days. Candles flickered on the walls, which were painted with brightly coloured 'strip cartoons' to warn, encourage and instruct the faithful. The popular virgin saint Katharine of Alexandria stood among other painted wooden statues of saints, on altars and in niches; there would have been a statue of St Dunstan in the chancel. Benches lined the walls for the sick and elderly (hence the expression 'the weakest go the wall'), and the font, the Norman bowl of which survives today, stood at the west end, just inside the door, perhaps accompanied by a statue of John the Baptist.

The 1381 clerical Poll Tax records show that the church was wealthy and, as we have seen, the rectory was held by a succession of powerful churchmen and senior civil servants, many of them were involved in politics or diplomacy. Stephen of Gravesend, a nephew of Richard Gravesend, Bishop of London, was the first of three consecutive rectors related to Bishops of London. He farmed the rectory out and went to study in Paris for three years from 1306. His successor Stephen Segrave was related to Gilbert Segrave (Bishop of London 1313–16), and to Nicholas Segrave, a baron high in the king's favour and Warden of Scotland. Stephen was also Archdeacon of Essex and Chancellor of Cambridge University. In 1323 he resigned Stepney on being made Archbishop of Armagh by the pope.

Edward II then granted the rectory to Richard de Baldock, of the family of the Bishop of London, Ralph de Baldock, and of Robert de Baldock, a favourite of the king's and Chancellor of England. In 1326 this Robert was lynched by the London mob when they turned on the king, in support of the rebels led by Queen Isabella. Edward of Carnavon was cruelly dispatched and his young son was put on the throne. Rector Baldock was evidently involved in these events, as in June 1327 the queen's lover, Mortimer, issued a pardon to 'Master Richard Baldock' for 'adhering to Master Robert Baldock, a rebel'.

While all this was going on the reforming French pope John XXII appointed a French cardinal, John Gaucelin, Bishop of Alba, to Stepney. Baldock, however, continued to be named as rector of Stepney in the records for ten more years; it seems that the papal provision did not hold. In February 1344 Edward III put another 'king's clerk' into Stepney, William de Shrovesbury, a pluralist with six prebends and the Archdeaconry of Salop. His patent was revoked the following year and Gaucelin's confirmed. When a new rector was granted the living in 1348 Gaucelin was named as his predecessor. Whether or not the Frenchman ever took the corn in the great tithe barn or the fees paid by Stepney's folk for their rites of passage is a moot point. It is unlikely that he ever came near the place; he certainly neglected to pay his English taxes.

Conflict between the king and the pope over benefices was now rife. Edward III, in need of money for his expensive military campaigns, took a firm hold over the Church, seizing benefices to pay his officials. Moreover, from 1308 the papacy had been kidnapped by France and the curia was now in Avignon. Soon the English king was to launch his bid for his mother's hereditary lands across the channel; France was to be the enemy for a hundred years, and her priests unwelcome in English parishes. In 1351 and 1353 two statutes, Provisors and Praemunire, made papal appointments and appeals to Rome illegal, and patriotric parliaments clamoured against foreign priests. Ironically a Frenchman was claiming an income from the people of Stepney while the king's warships were being prepared to fight the French, just a stone's throw from the church at Ratcliff.

In the month that the Black Death struck London Richard de Saham, Professor of Civil Law, recently returned from a diplomatic venture in Portugal, acquired Stepney rectory. In 1345 he had been sent to negotiate a marriage between the Black Prince and the daughter of the King of Portugal, and although it was unsuccessful Stepney may have been a reward for his efforts. For reasons that are not apparent this rector, with a gang of retainers or armed bandits, raided the priory of St Mary Spital. At his death in 1368 Saham left ornaments, books and other items to St Dunstan's, which suggests that he may have had a rather closer association with his parish than any of his immediate predecessors.

When Saham died the Bishop of London, Simon of Sudbury, a former papal chaplain, presented his brother, Thomas Thebaud, to Stepney. The king had other plans, and Sudbury was ordered to inspect his registers and other papers for evidence for the bishop's right to appoint to Stepney rectory over the previous sixty years. Unable to find any foundation for his claim, Sudbury was forced to rescind the appointment, and the king's candidate, Robert Crull, became rector.

Crull's rule at Stepney lasted thirty-six years from 1368 to 1404; he was a 'king's clerk' and was well supported by the income from many church posts. He held an Exeter prebend (1370), was Keeper of the Woods in the Isle of Axholme and had land in Redenesse in Yorkshire. In 1374 he was licensed by the pope to have the canonry and prebend of Skipwith in Howden in Yorkshire in addition to Stepney rectory, and in 1377 he was granted the prebend of Swords in Dublin. His civil service posts were his main job: he was appointed Clerk of the Works to survey all royal castles and manors with a view to repair, and he was Treasurer of the Irish Exchequer. Although much of his time was spent in Ireland, it seems he had an establishment in Stepney village; in March 1384 his servants, Hugh Resan and John Fyssher, who may have been his steward and his bailiff, were fined at the Manor Court for contravening a by-law. He was made Clerk of the Kings' Ships, and in the autumn of 1380 might have been seen down at Ratcliff docks inspecting the king's old warships, 'le *Gracedieu*, la *Migel*, La *Nawe Seinte Marie* and a galley' with a view to selling them off to pay royal creditors, with all their 'tackle, old iron, seacoal and utensils'. In July 1384 he was assigned to find labourers to save the flooded Barking Marsh. For the next sixteen years he was back and forth from Ireland, but finally settled in Stepney; in January 1400 the king gave him permission to stay in England while still enjoying the fruits of his Irish benefices.

So much for the tubby, worldly canons – in 1382 parliament complained that the king's clerks were 'too fat in body and in purse'. For the folk of the hamlets, trudging through the lanes to mass on Sunday, bringing their babies for baptism, their dead for burial, taking their marriage vows in the church porch or joining in the processions at Easter and Corpus Christi, the rector was almost as remote a figure as the king himself. His deputy, the vicar, was the effective administrator of the church, though even he was probably not much concerned with pastoral care or regular celebration of the mass.

Vicars might live in the parish and served for about ten years, on average. We know some names of Stepney vicars, but not much else about them. Richard de Norton served from 1326 and went on to become rector of Greenford Magna; nothing more is known about him, but he is worth mentioning as the first vicar known to us by name – except the shadowy Roger who made a single appearance in 1233. In the vicarage when Saham first took Stepney was John at Lee, appointed by royal patent in 1346, having exchanged with the previous vicar, James Pondrick. With the loss of parishioners during the Black Death clerical wages doubled, such was the lack of priests. According to the chronicler, Knighton: 'So great was the scarcity of priests that many churches were desolate,

being without divine office ... Hardly a chaplain could be got under £10 or
10 marks to minister to any church.' No one would accept a vicarage for less than
£20 or 20 marks; Stepney's vicarage was worth the good sum of £33 6s 8d a year.

At Lee had only been in Stepney a few years when the pope attempted to put
a Frenchman in his place, John de Hiere. This does not appear to have worked;
two years later a Welshman, John de Swanseye, came for eleven years. In 1366
he left for Stoke in the Diocese of Winchester, exchanging with one John de
Middleton. In Stepney over this period there were four vicars and a series of
parish chaplains and clerks, to keep the show on the road while Crull was about
his master's business.

The honest parson is the only one of Chaucer's clerics to get a good character:

> Wide was his parish, with houses far asunder
> Yet he neglected not in rain or thunder,
> In sickness or in grief to pay a call
> On the remotest, great or small.

Wide was Stepney parish, and if anybody visited the scattered farmhouses and
cottages along the highways at Poplar, Mile End and Ratcliff, it was the humble
stipendiary clergy, known as parish chaplains, earning about £4 a year and performing all the duties that we now associate with parish clergy. Chaucer's 'poor
parson', as a ploughman's brother, was probably based on one such. St Botolph's at
Aldgate had eight chaplains in 1361.

How many priests served Stepney church altogether is not known; with a flock
of several thousand, all of whom over five years old had to be confessed in the
six weeks of Lent, there are likely to have been a good number. When Richard
Bethishal was presented as vicar in 1374, the mandate for his induction went to
the parish chaplain, Henry. In 1383 two parish chaplains are named: William de
Shoreham and John Ramesby. It was usually a chaplain who was at the bedside of
dying parishioners; they are often mentioned in wills, getting a standard bequest
of 4d, 6d or 1s.

In a big parish the work of the parish clerk was considerable; there were two
at St Botolph's Bishopsgate at this time. The clerk carried holy water at the head
of processions, he cut up the holy loaf for distribution at mass, read the Epistle
in the service and sang the responses. It was up to him to make sure that banns
were read, and he might help hold the cloth over the couple during the marriage
service. He took the money for burials and arranged for the great bell to toll, and
made sure the church windows were cleaned and the statues dusted or scrubbed
up twice a year. In Stepney one of his most important tasks was clearing out the
churchyard ditches. Doubling as attorney, scrivener or even barber for the parish,
he was a most useful chap. It would be nice to think that Chaucer's parish clerk,

who features in 'The Miller's Tale', might have been based on a clerk at a local church, perhaps St Botolph's Aldgate. This Absalom, with his long golden hair, flounced blue jacket and shoes cut like the tracery in old St Paul's, enjoyed flirting with the wives of his parish and entertaining in the taverns with his hurdy-gurdy. When it was Easter and time for the play, he took the opportunity of showing off by taking the part of Herod.

By the late fourteenth century Stepney had two clerks, respectively responsible for the northern and southern parts of the parish, what would later become the Spitalfields and Ratcliff divisions. In a will of 1383 they are named as John Large (perhaps he was) and John Pope. The Popes were a Barking family. In 1395 Pope was still in post, and had been joined by John Herlowe. Another John Clarke makes an appearance in the 1383 manorial records, providing us with a few facts about his life. He was a haymonger with a cottage, rented from Isolda Coleworth and standing in 2 acres of pasture. He ran an alehouse with his wife and gave short measure from time to time. His daughter Idonia rented her own cottage from a (bounder?) called John Lovechild, and got behind with her rent. On at least one occasion Clarke neglected to clear out the ditches.

It is time to leave the fourteenth century, and with it Chaucer's flash parish clerk, his honest parson, his beetle-browed summoner, his humourless merchant, his prioress with her pretty ways and pet dogs. Before we move into the years of Agincourt and then the Wars of the Roses, we will take a final look at the Tower hamlets.

The king's gilded ships bobbed about down by the shore at Ratcliff, lime-kilns smoked alongside, furnaces roared at Whitechapel, haycarts rumbled up from the Marsh and Bow breadcarts rattled into Cheapside. Fine merchants were to be seen in gorgeous silks of scarlet and Lincoln green, azure and silver, trimmed with fur, and peacocks strutted around the gardens of the bishop's palace in Bethnal Green. The air rang with the whirr of mill wheels, the ching of hammers, the click of hooves, and the constant tintinnabulation of bells, calling across the marshes and fields: Milleacre, Sevenacre, Hailmary Field, Fullersfield, Galey Field, Ashewsy Great Field, Le Wyld, Northhyde, Charteyfield, Summerleas, Walmarsh, Stoneyfield, Brewersfield and the rest.

Cottages and workshops spilt out along the roads leading out of the walled city to the east at Bishopsgate, and at Aldgate, with habitation petering out beyond Whitechapel church along the muddy road that led to the leper hospital and a few scattered farms at Mile End. In Bethnal Green a hamlet had grown up around the bishop's palace; the bishop had eleven tenants there in 1392–93. Down towards the Tower in East Smithfield there were shops, houses and gardens, stretching out west and south of the new abbey towards St Katharine's land, Doddings Pond, the Swans Nest and Crassh Mills; there was a pottery in Toddyneslane in 1362 (now Sir Thomas More Street). A river wall, built long ago to keep Wapping dry, was kept under repair and the occupants of the houses by the wall were, as they had been since time immemorial, responsible for the maintenance of the dykes, sewers and banks. Stratford Bow, at the bridgehead on the Lea, was a populous working village, almost a town by fourteenth-century standards; houses lined the steep road that ran down to the river from Stepney church and the 'high street' among the poplar trees, across the top of the peninsula known as Stepney Marsh. It was a mixture of town and country, as it was for hundreds of years more.

The great houses were not, it has to be said, as numerous as in the City itself and along towards Westminster, but as we have seen they were there. The religious ones dominated: the bishop's sumptuous palace at Bethnal Green, the inns and mills of the Dean and Chapter of St Paul's at Shadwell, the imposing abbey on Tower Hill, the fashionable nunneries in the Minories and at Bromley by Bow (with a cluster of houses around) the humbler Spital and St Katharine's. As to the establishments of the lay lords, there were large manor houses: Cobhams on the south side of the Mile End Road, Mewes on the north-east side of Cambridge Heath Road, Ashhews Manor House with its neighbour Hulls/Helles in the vicinity of the Royal London Hospital, to the east of Whitechapel church, Poplar Manor House on the north side of Poplar High Street (south of East India Dock Road), the Wake family mansion in Limehouse and Pomfret Manor at the southern end of the Marsh.

We must not forget the East End's castle. Although mainly used to house prisoners of rank, it was still a royal residence from time to time. As the century ended Richard II was there. His great lords took up arms to rescue the realm from an increasingly despotic and crazy sovereign and his coterie of loathed favourites. 'Thou hast always been rewlid be fals flaterers, folowyng thair counsel and thaym avaunsyng befor alle other trew men', wrote Archbishop Thomas of Arundel to his sovereign; 'thou hast also livid incontinently and lecherously, and with thi foule and cursed ensample thou hast enfectid thi court and thi reme.' Thirty-three accusations were levelled against him by a parliament packed with hostile Londoners. And so Richard took shelter in the Tower, from where he had long ago ridden to his coronation, all in white, 'looking as beautiful as an angel'. He gathered up his jewels and relics, including the vial of oil supposedly given by Our Lady herself to St Thomas of Canterbury. Soon he would be dead and the precious oil used to anoint his cousin as king. On 3 September 1399 Henry of Bolingbroke, son of John of Gaunt, led his army into the City: 'Long Live Henry of Lancaster, King of England'.

Chapter 4

FOREIGNERS, FLOODS AND FIGHTING

the Fifteenth Century

'Dyvers Dowchemen and their bere houses'

The streets of London were paved with gold in the sunshine days of prosperity and faith that came with the Lancastrians. The usurper Bolingbroke died after twelve years and was succeeded by his popular and glamorous warrior son, Henry V, whose return from victory over the French at Agincourt was greeted by ecstatic Londoners with flag-waving delight and a magnificent procession, led by giant figures of Gog and Magog. Even during the long and disastrous reign of Henry VI, when, said the chronicler, the realm of England was 'out of good governaunce', things were not so bad for ordinary folk. The civil wars of 1455–85, known to posterity as the Wars of the Roses, caused little disruption to day-to-day life for the generality; it was an aristocratic wrangle with a bare thirteen weeks of fighting in thirty years; life for Londoners and East Enders for the most part probably went on much as usual.

These good times, years of opportunity for the peasant and artisan population, followed in the wake of the Black Death. With the population decimated, labour was in short supply and wages rose dramatically. The income of ordinary folk was probably relatively higher than at any time before the nineteenth century. This was particularly so in London and its hinterland, where wages were 25 per cent higher than in other parts of the country. It became easier for servile farmhands to free themselves from their feudal ties, especially those near the great market and port. East Enders did well for themselves, becoming smallholders or running industrial enterprises, some amassed lands and houses, ran fishing fleets, built and fitted out ships, bought wharves or engaged in trade.

Trade flourished and the City's guilds proliferated, while labourers and merchants alike were increasingly drawn towards London; the story of Dick Whittington, a country lad who became lord mayor, was recounted to children and hopeful apprentices.

As London grew, its increased demand for building materials, for mortar and bricks for the newly fashionable Flemish-style brick houses, saw the industry taking a firmer hold on its eastern flank. As we have seen, Brick Lane had acquired its modern name by the mid-fifteenth century, and it is clear from the wealth accumulated by the limemen that their business was flourishing. Whitechapel's bellfoundries were busier than ever. A frantic religious devotion took hold in the years following the great pestilence; death was brought into life in an unprecedented way, and millions of pounds was spent on the purchase of relief from the torments of purgatory, on priests and masses, on church buildings, on steeples, and on bells.

The waterfront was being developed; There are references to wharves in wills, like that owned by the Dryrer family (see below); the Cely family had a ship repaired at Blackwall. Sailing up river to the pool of London, you would have passed a jumble of wharves and warehouses on the north bank, stretching from Limehouse and Wapping Dock (with its mill and brewhouse belonging to St Thomas of Acon) to the spire and outbuildings of St Katharine's and the great white tower of the royal castle. Smoke belched from the riverside lime-kilns, from the chimneys of forges, foundries and brickworks up at Whitechapel, from the Wapping breweries and the bakeries over to the east at Stratford Bow.

But the area was still predominantly a country place, with more dovecotes and orchards than workshops, more hayfields and cornfields than brickyards, more pasture than garden plots. Houses, shops and work sheds were gathering together in the cityside parts, in East Smithfield, Aldgate, Whitechapel and Bishopsgate, around the kilns in Limehouse, in the town of Stratford Bow at Ratcliff and St Katharine's, but Stepney village and its hamlets of Bethnal Green, Mile End, Poplar, Blackwall and the Marsh were farming and fishing places. The area was still renowned for its pastoral peace, and Londoners of substance, especially city merchants, continued to have country houses here for many years to come. Bells from fourteen belfries rang out over marshes and fields standing high with wheat for London's bread, hay for London's horses and barley for the local breweries. Mid-century Stepney village offered a pretty scene, with carpenters, stonemasons and glaziers busy about the work of rebuilding their church in a nursery rhyme place, with fine houses and snug cottages, ducks on the pond, a ducking stool and a cosy inn, the Harts Horn, kept by a landlord called Geoffrey. The roads and lanes were as muddy as ever, as might be expected in such a well-watered terrain; the main highway, the Whitechapel/Mile End Road, was notoriously so; brickmaker John Brampston made provision for a load of gravel to be 'laid in the highway … where most mede is'. The riverside lanes and those in the Marsh were in constant need of attention. Watermen with their wherries down at Ratcliff were ready to take passengers to St Paul's Wharf or Westminster and there was a ferry station at the tip of the marshy peninsula which went to

Greenwich, where Duke Humphrey of Gloucester had built a splendid palace in 1427. At Mile End there was a wide common where apprentices strolled with their girls, and further north, at Bethnal Green, there were the bishop's woods for hunting, and where on May Days the aldermen and sheriffs of the City could be seen, parading to their annual feast.

This collection of villages was servicing the growing city and in parts was beginning to take on the characteristics of the working end of town. It was also attracting the foreign immigrants who in years to come lent the East End the cosmopolitan air for which it is celebrated.

Foreign trade was booming. There was a marked increase in the export of woollen cloth, which brought Continental merchants to London and took Londoners to the Continent. Venetian galleys brought in spices, soap, carpets, silk and glassware, and took away cloth, pewter and tin. The Italians were especially unpopular, their 'nifles and trifles' thought to be unnecessary luxury items that the good burghers of London could well do without. They spoke of 'Lombards and Galeymen' in the Abbot of Tower Hill's court in East Smithfield. The Spanish and French brought wine and the Portuguese oranges, sugar and cork. Mistress Say, a widow, was said to keep a house of Spaniards, Lombards, Presbyters' women and suspicious persons in Aldgate. London merchants had dealings with Italian banks: Sir John Crosby of Crosby Hall in Bishopsgate was on terms with the Friscobaldi of Florence. The German Hanseatic League maintained the gate at Bishopsgate from the thirteenth to the sixteenth century. This gate opened onto the main route to the east and north-east coast, from where their goods were brought into their fortress in the City, the Steelyard. Inevitably this drew Germans to the suburbs outside the north-eastern walls.

By far the largest and most influential foreign group in this century was the 'Doche' or 'Flemings'; they were most numerous in the East End. Spaniards, Italians, Germans and Portuguese may be found here, as in the City and Southwark, but the 'Doche' were here in significant numbers, not just merchants who came and stayed but refugees seeking a fresh life. The community flourished and continued to attract newcomers from their homelands for the next 200 years. 'Doche' and 'Flemings' were terms applied to people from the Low Countries, from modern Belgium and Holland and parts of northern France. They came from the county of Flanders, with its weaving towns of Ypres, Ghent and Bruges, from Holland, Zeeland and Guelders, from the Duchy of Brabant, with the great trading city of Antwerp at its heart, from the county of Hainault, from Picardy and Artois, where Calais lay. Trade with these parts had been lively in the previous century but now, with the rise of Antwerp under Burgundian rule and the increased demand for English wool for the looms of Ypres, Ghent and Bruges, the Thames teemed with Flemish ships. London merchants, mainly under the auspices of the Merchant Adventurers' Company, flocked to the cloth fairs at Antwerp and set up 'English Houses'. Meanwhile, at home Flemish-style houses (built of brick instead of stone or wattle and daub), tapestries and painted panels were all the rage. One such, the amazing Ashwellthorpe triptych (now in Norwich Museum), was commissioned by Christopher Knyvet, brother-in-law of Stepney's leading 'merchant prince', Sir Henry Colet (of whom more anon). It was not just luxury items that came from the Low Countries; there was regular import of fish, beer and even fruit and vegetables into London from Holland and Zealand.

Flemish traders had been a familiar sight about London for years, as had families who came to make their home in a new land. A lack of natural resources had pushed the densely populated Low Countries in the direction of manufacture and trade, and late medieval 'Dochemen' were considerably more technically and economically advanced than the English, with expertise in weaving, brewing and brickmaking, and a sophisticated banking system centred at Bruges. Since the 1330s, when Edward III encouraged Flemish weavers to bring their skills to his realm, they had been coming to England, especially to London. Now they were coming in much greater numbers, driven from their home towns by high taxes, poverty and mob violence. They settled in the south and east of the country, most of them in London and its suburbs.

The main concentration of foreigners in London was not, as is often claimed, in St Clement Danes and Southwark. As the alien tax lists show, there were as many if not more 'Doche' living to the east of the City, most of them in the precinct of St Katharine's, in Whitechapel and down near the Tower, in East Smithfield. Poor Flemish girls plied their trade as prostitutes and rich madams ran brothels and gaming houses. They worked in a whole range of trades, notably as brick- and tilemakers and printers, also as hatters, goldsmiths, haberdashers, hosiers, tailors and butchers, and were well known for their breweries, cooperages and alehouses. In Stratford Bow they worked in the bakeries. The 1439–40 tax list includes sixteen 'alien' families in Bow. John De Opiris, rector of Stepney, was involved in the brewing industry, as many rectors were, and employed Dutch or Flemish brewers; he may even have owned the great Ratcliff beerhouse. In a tax list of foreign residents dated 1439–40, he has a servant listed as Mokaele Cooper; two years later he had four 'Dochemen' in his employ: Gerard Barehouse (Beerhouse), Adrian, George and John. At the Hermitage in Wapping, where there was a big brewery, seven foreigners were named in 1456–57. In the early 1480s the Ratcliff beerhouse was owned by a 'Docheman' called William Harman, employing five fellow countrymen, a stoker, a cooper, a drayman and two others. John Elond of Limehouse had a foreign servant called Matthew, and Thomas Atkins of Mile End had four Dutchmen working for him; presumably this was another brewery.

Their skills were recognised and their presence welcomed in some quarters, as a 1469 letter written at Havering ate Bower in Essex bears witness. A local man is looking for someone to build a brick chimney and wants 'a mason that ys a Ducheman or a Flemyng that canne make a dowbell chemeney of brykks for they canne best fare therewith. I wolde have seche as cowed maket to voyde smoke.' But there was also a good deal of resentment. The newcomers invited the same sort of abuse and attacks that were reserved in later years for Huguenots and then for the Jews. In 1440 two bargemen were hanged for murdering three Flemings and a child on board a Flemish ship riding in the river. Their bodies were propped up and left for the tide to flow over them as an example to sailors coming up river. The rebels of 1471, who sacked and looted in St Katharine's and Ratcliff, 'Robbed and dispoyled dyvers Dowchemen and their bere houses'. The clever, hard-working foreigners were both an example and an irritant, successful in their business ventures and strange and unfamiliar in their habits, and speaking a language that was near enough to English to be laughed at: they said 'brode and kese' instead of bread and cheese.

A few decades later the religious reformers in the Low Countries and Germany were turning Christendom upside down, and more immigrants came and joined their families in the East End. It is little wonder that in Stepney, Whitechapel and Aldgate folk allied themselves so firmly with the reformed faith in the great religious divide of the next century.

The roughest spots on London's east side were Tower Hill and St Katharine's, both known for their immigrant communities, the courts and alleys just outside Aldgate and the notoriously lawless liberty of Norton Folgate, up near Shoreditch. Some records survive that allow us to visit these dirty and unruly places, recognisably East End in character. The Correction Book of the Bishop's Commissary Court records a string of moral prosecutions for Whitechapel, where the goodwives regularly brawled, shouting insults such as 'horemoth', 'strongharlot' and 'cocold'. Near the Spital, in the extra-parochial precinct of Norton Folgate, gambling, brothels and affrays caused problems for the canons residentiary of St Paul's, whose court sat in solemn judgement on the rowdy locals. In June 1466 John Palmer was accused of serving a false measure of beer 'vocat [called] a pynt'.

Tower Hill was a grim and terrible place, echoing to the screams of burning 'Lollers', as the Lollard proto-Protestant heretics were known. In 1443 a woman was burned here for murdering her husband. In 1440 gallows were put up just by St Katharine's and two traitors were hanged. It became a place of political executions, of which there were many in those tumultuous years. For whores, swindlers and others there was a great pillory, just near the Abbey of St Mary Graces.

The abbot, as Lord of East Smithfield Manor, was responsible for law and order here; prostitution and gambling were rife among the Flemings, Italians and French, the seafarers, riverworkers and artisans. In 1438 a sawyer called Gerard, for instance, was fined for keeping a prostitute called Katerina; they were both 'common dice players'. In 1453 Henry Buskyn was prosecuted for keeping a gambling wheel. John and Joan Lovell kept a brothel for at least eighteen years, turning up regularly at the abbey court to pay their fines. Cloysh alleys were a major problem, both here and in Norton Folgate. Cloysh was a gambling game, rather like croquet, introduced by the 'Doche', in which a wooden bowl was hit with a chisel-shaped implement through a hoop and bets were cast. It evidently caused a great deal of excitement and tumult and was forbidden by a whole series of fifteenth- and sixteenth-century statutes.

In marked contrast to the red light district outside its walls was the abbey itself, an influential institution enjoying the favour of Lancastrian and Yorkist monarchs alike. It stood among beautifully laid out gardens and groves of trees, a house of piety, power and elegant living, ruling over the manors of East Smithfield and Poplar. The only hints of its old splendour that survive today are some German drinking cups and a collection of bright blue and yellow glazed stove tiles in the Museum of London. Not that it was without its internal troubles. In the opening years of the century a monk from a Lincolnshire abbey, one Ralph Bikere, took refuge there having been sentenced to a term in prison for attacking his abbot. He confessed his crime and was allowed to stay, but was soon up to his old tricks, laying violent hands on the Abbot of Tower Hill and stealing what he could. In 1427 the abbey was said to have been much impoverished because of the mismanagement of Abbot Pascal; the matter (among others) was investigated by no less a person than Humphrey, Duke of Gloucester, one of the rulers of the country during the minority of his nephew, Henry VI. In 1491 Peter James, the warden of St Anthony's foundation in the abbey, ran off with jewels and ornaments belonging to the fraternity.

Just a stone's throw from the abbey was St Katharine's Hospital, a very different institution though likewise patronised by the great and the good; the Duke of Exeter was buried here in 1446. Here the brothers and sisters (accorded equal status) cared for the elderly, the infirm and for orphans; for many years it had also specialised in 'fallen women'. These inmates lived in the almshouses that adjoined the sisters' houses, and some at least carried on with their trade, offering their services to the locals in the increasingly rough precinct. One such was Margaret Morgan alias Smith, dispatched by her local alderman to St Katharine's for prostitution in Fenchurch Street, and later sent off to St Bartholomew's, perhaps for treatment for venereal disease. The evidence produced in the bishop's court by a gang of unsavoury characters in a matrimonial suit over a dodgy marriage in an Aldgate alehouse suggests that St Katharine's was little better than a whorehouse.

Whores had good pickings in St Katharine's precinct. Following the grant of a royal charter in 1442 the immediate vicinity of the hospital had become an attractive place for artisans, craftsmen and small-time traders to work free of restrictions, and for criminals and lowlife to lurk. The hospital and its precinct were exempted from all jurisdiction save that of the Lord Chancellor, and the master was accorded exclusive rights over the liberty, holding courts, punishing crime, regulating weights and measures and generally running the show. As we have seen, it was especially attractive to the 'Dochemen' and other foreign immigrants, who probably landed at St Katharine's Quay. It became known for its Dutch and Flemish breweries and alehouses, a lawless liberty with brewers, sailors, carpenters, blacksmiths and tallow chandlers living and working in its 14 acres of cottages and workshops, crossed by narrow, muddy lanes, Pottlepot Alley and Maidenhead Alley among them.

For three weeks in high summer Tower Hill was a riotous place. Jugglers and players, stallholders and merchants, goodwives and good-time girls, apprentice boys and farmhands all gathered for St Katharine's Fair, authorised by the same royal charter that gave the precinct its independence. I dare say the cloysh alleys and brothels did a roaring trade. All manner of things were sold, including toys, souvenirs, sweets and gingerbread in the shape of Catherine wheels. East London's fair was a major rival to the three-day marathon at West Smithfield, Bartholomew Fair, held just a few weeks later, and the City authorities made several attempts to have it stopped. Eventually, in the sixteenth century, the City bought St Katharine's Fair, but until then it provided a good boost to the hospital's income from the tolls paid by stallholders.

As to the other religious houses in the area, there is little to report. The small house of nuns at Stratford Bow had had its heyday: by the time of the Dissolution there were only eight residents. The nuns in the Minories continued to flourish and acquired more endowments; a 'plummer' (worker in lead) called Colston left them the reversion of his Tower Hill premises, 'le Bole on the Hoop', in 1441. Many of the nuns were fine ladies, such as Anne de la Pole, daughter of the second Duke of Suffolk, and Dame Syble Christemas, a cousin of the 'millionaire' merchant Sir John Crosby. St Mary without Bishopsgate (the Spital) was well supported by Londoners' wills (as were the hospitals of St Bartholomew and St Thomas); nothing much surfaces from the bishop's ordinances of 1431, except that the sisters who attended the sick were given to raiding the pantry.

Bedlam, on the other hand, was in a dire state in the opening years of the century, with no brothers or sisters at all, a poorly equipped chapel, only six lunatics cared for and three sick persons. Under the management of porter Peter Taverner, the place had been all but wrecked. He set up an alehouse with his wife in his house in the close, stole the alms, sold the beds and spent his time playing dice and draughts.

The Great Flood and the 'Cousins' War

So much for 'nifles and trifles', for nibbling of gingerbread at the fair, nuns raiding the larder and the Taverners selling off beds at Bedlam. So much for men about their work in foundries, brickyards and bakeries, Flemings making beer, merchants making a mint, so much for gambling and fun. Just a hundred years after the last great disaster, the Black Death, God struck again, this time with water.

On Lady Day 1448 a freak spring tide brought an angry Thames bursting through the river walls that banked Stepney Marsh, drowning cattle, sweeping away farms and cottages, destroying the chapel of St Mary. We do not know how many human lives were lost. For sixteen years at least, probably much longer, there was a vast lake, said to be 1,000 acres, bounded by St Katharine's Mill, Whitechapel, St Dunstan's, St Leonards Bromley, the Thames and the Lea. If this was really so, as the instructions for the public enquiry claimed, then Wapping, Shadwell, Ratcliff and even parts of Limehouse were affected, as well as Poplar and the Marsh. Archaeological evidence indicates that there was flooding in what is now Butcher Row, the road that runs south from Commercial Road, the bottom half of the old Cleve Street. It seems unlikely that the floodwaters reached as far as Stepney church, but it is perhaps more than a coincidence that it was two years after the Great Flood that work re-started on the rebuilding of the church.

The Abbot of St Mary Graces, who, as Lord of Poplar Manor, had lands in the Marsh, was directed to look into the matter. An inquiry was held, and forty-one Marsh tenants turned up at the abbey on 8 December to give their evidence. As lists of inhabitants are something of a rarity at this time, the names are worth a mention: Simon Cok, Roger Resyn, Richard Calowe, John Norfolk, Robert Bryche, William Halewood, John Staunton, John Fremet, Thomas Motte (Limehouse), William Cureys, William Brytte, John Parker, John Buntyng, Thomas Helder, John Eland, John Potter, Simon Kelk, John Rotny, Laurence Hay, William Canon (fisherman), Reginald Hoggekyn, William Wryght, John Baker, Thomas Potter, William Bocher, Simon Wilkyn, William Potter, Roger Whitbarigh, Ralph Penyngton, Richard Ford, Robert Pod, Richard Smyth, Nicholas Smyth, John Deyer, Thomas Shefeld, William Helder, Thomas Atkin, John Bore, John Fuller and John Pekker. The final decision was that John Harper, landlord of the old Pomfret Manor, was to blame. He had apparently been neglecting his river embankments down in the south-west corner of the peninsula.

The flood caused devastation. William Chedworth, the bailiff of Stepney Manor, reported to the manor court sixteen years later that the manor's 400 acres in the Marsh had been 'utterly submerged' and that the income from rents was reduced to a mere £23 6s 8d from the £373 6s 8d it brought in before the flood. The bishop's tenants who lost houses were John Porter, Richard atte Wall, Richard Blitheworth, Richard Assher, John Perours, John Brygge, William

Childe, Richard Batte, Thomas Port, John Elsy, William Bocher and John Eland. The Elands/Elonds had been Marsh farmers for at least a hundred years When John died in 1472, twenty-four years after the disaster, he left his drowned copyhold lands to his son-in-law William Graunger, to 'do hys best therwyth'. Some people did well out of the disaster. The workmen who were employed to repair the East Wall and 'le Blackwall' on the East Marsh got paid over the odds at 5*d* a day, and Thomas Shipman and Richard Danyell bought fishing rights over the whole area for just £2 a year. With the Marsh chapel of ease gone, legacies and mortuary gifts that once had benefited St Mary's now went to the parish church of St Dunstan's. Bishop Thomas Kempe drained his 400 acres, but by 1524 it had been inundated again. The 'wet marsh' was let to William Morowe/Marowe, who drained it again and used it as fisheries. Most of the Marsh families seem to have moved into Limehouse. For the next few hundred years the Marsh was a desolate place, its farming families gone, given over to fishermen and later becoming pasture. It would soon become known as the Isle of Dykes, later corrupted into Dogs.

Whether or not Harper was at fault is debatable. The wall was breached again at the same spot in March 1660 (according to Pepys); it was known as Old Breach until the eighteenth century. It was later called Poplar Gut, and finally became absorbed into the West India Docks.

In these years when Stepney's Marsh was a lake, there was trouble brewing all over the land, and in the spring and summer of 1450 came East London's first direct involvement with the civil strife that would culminate in war. Bands of brigands, old soldiers back from defeats in France for the most part, roamed the streets of England. With the great lords gathering private armies and fighting for mastery over the weak king Henry VI, with laws disregarded, lands seized, taxes at a new high and the wool trade badly affected by the loss of Normandy, the 'commons' of Kent and Essex rose. Their leader, one Jack Cade, may have been related to the Yorkist clan that was making claims to the throne. The state of affairs was, as is usually the case, blamed on false counsel: 'We sey owr sovereyn lord may understond that his fals cowncell hath lost his law, his marchandyse is lost, his comon people is dystroyed, the see is lost, Fraunce is lost, the kynge hym selffe is so set that he may not pay for his mete nor drynke.' The rebels stormed London (where they were initially welcomed), making an attempt on the Tower itself and terrifying the life out of the Abbot of St Mary Graces:

> The Abot of the Towre Hyll, with his fate face
> Tremelyth and quakythe for Domine ne in furore

This dirge was ascribed to the rebels. Leading 'traytors' were lynched. William Crowmer, Sheriff of Kent, was taken by this 'multytude of ryffe raffe' and beheaded at Mile End, in a spot said to be just near the mansion house of Robert Clopton, a major local landholder, who had been lord mayor in 1441. At Whitechapel they beheaded one John Bayle. Cade was taken and the rebellion quashed, but five years later battle commenced between York and Lancaster with a major conflict at St Albans. Richard of York defeated the king's forces and Henry VI was taken. For thirty years all was change and change about in the higher echelons of society, and although the strife of the 'Cousins' War' must have filtered down to the humble folk and involved them in some measure, this was not a civil war in any modern sense. Ploughmen and limemen, butchers, bakers and candlestick makers kept their heads down and carried on regardless. There were no major battles that impinged directly on the East End, although the Tower was central to the conflict and was besieged by the Yorkists in 1461. Each takeover of power was marked by pageantry and punishment. Kings and queens spent the eve of their coronations at the castle in the east before processing to Westminster, with as much impressive show as could be mustered. When Edward, Earl of March, the Yorkist warlord, was victorious in the spring of 1461 and took the throne as Edward IV, he had the Earl of Oxford and his other leading opponents brought one by one to a scaffold on Tower Hill. Henry VI himself was incarcerated behind its thick walls for five years, and finally was slaughtered while at prayer in the Wakefield Tower. The culmination of the horrors of these bloodthirsty times was the fate that met the thirteen-year-old Edward V, awaiting his coronation in the Tower in 1483 along with his little brother. A contemporary wrote: 'He and his brother were withdrawn to the inner apartments of the Tower and day by day began to be seen more rarely behind the bars and windows, till at length they ceased to appear altogether.' 'And the two sonnyes of kynge Edward were put to cilence,' wrote the chronicler.

For East Enders, then, the machinations of the powerful were experienced at first hand: the parades and pomp, bloody heads rolling, doomed royal children let out for a play on Tower Green. But as far as we know the Wars of the Roses brought only one direct hit on the suburbs and hamlets, in May 1471. This was soon after the Yorkist victory at Tewkesbury, when Thomas Neville, known to history as Shakespeare's Bastard Fauconberg, made a last bid for the Lancastrians, bringing a vast fleet up the river. The ships were moored near the Tower and an army, 5,000 strong and armed with clubs, staves and pitchforks, unable to get into the City, smashed up the suburbs, setting fire to sixty houses and looting and burning the breweries at St Katharine's and Ratcliff. On 11 May they assaulted Aldgate and got in, but the portcullis was brought down and they were trapped. The alderman and recorder of Aldgate ward let them out, fought them back as far as St Botolph's church and then chased them to Mile End and Poplar.

Londoners tended to be for the 'white rose', its merchants having suffered much at the hands of Henry VI. When the Earl of March took the City and the throne in 1461 (aptly in the month of March), according to one chronicler there was a spirit of optimism in the air: 'Lette us walke in a newe wyne yerde, and lette us make us a gay gardon in the monythe of Marche with thys fayre whyte ros and herbe, the Erle of Marche.' Of the possible 8,000 people living in the Tower Hamlets, those who had political opinions were probably of a mind with the City dwellers. We know of something of the allegiance of important local families. The de la Pole family had local connections; William de la Pole, first Duke of Suffolk and a great magnate, did homage for a Poplar estate, and his sister, Katharine, was Abbess of Barking. The family was aligned with the Yorkist cause and John, the second duke, married Edward IV's sister, Elizabeth. After her husband's death the dowager duchess evidently lived in their Stepney mansion; as noted in 1502 in the account book of her niece, Queen Elizabeth of York. Her daughter, Anne (d.1495), was a nun in the Minories.

One of Stepney's foremost families was the Chedworths. William Chedworth, probably the chief landowner in the second half of the century, was the father-in-law of one of London's richest merchant princes, the grocer, wool dealer and alderman John Crosby. Crosby supported the Yorkist cause with fervour and it is reasonable to suppose that the Chedworth clan did likewise. He was knighted for his part in rescuing the City from the Fauconberg raid, and after his death in 1475 his widow, Ann Chedworth, gave over the Bishopsgate mansion, Crosby Hall, to the future Richard III, the last Yorkist king. Here Richard Crookback held his court and, according to Sir Thomas More, 'little by little all folks drew unto him'. He may even have plotted the murder of the little princes, his nephews, from here, and it was in the council chamber at Crosby Hall that the mayor and a deputation of citizens offered him the Crown in 1483. The house, referred to three times by Shakespeare in *Richard III*, still stands; it was moved to Chelsea in the 1930s and now overlooks the river.

A new church

Apart from the Tower itself, there is precious little left in the East End to remind us of these days when the blood of overmighty subjects was spilt on Tower Hill, when the Isle of Dogs was a great lake, when the fat-faced Abbot of St Mary Graces fined brothelkeepers, and the women of St Katharine's got such a name for themselves. The only structure left in the East End from the fifteenth century is Stepney church. Though much restored, St Dunstan's today is essentially the church that was rebuilt before and during the Wars of the Roses, possibly with the help of Chedworth money.

As we have seen, devotion among the laity reached a new peak following the cataclysm of the Black Death. Merchants and yeomen spent money on their parish churches, old ones were extravagantly refashioned with fine tracery in the Perpendicular style and coloured glass was put into the windows. Brand new churches were built and filled with rich ornaments and painted statues. Saints were all the rage and, with literacy on the increase, people were able to read stories about them for themselves. In 1383 Caxton published the thirteenth-century *Golden Legend* in English, an immensely popular book of saints. The Virgin Mary took pride of place: her six principal feasts were celebrated with much fervour, lady chapels were created, and songs were sung about her: in Stepney; they even had a field named after her: Hailemaryfeld. Every day at noon the ploughman stopped in the field and the women in the market to listen to the angelus bell, reminding them of the Annunciation.

In Stepney the church was rebuilt in grey ragstone, brought up the river from northern Kent to Ratcliff. This was an immensely hard and intractable limestone, the principal building stone of London until the seventeenth century. Meanwhile at Bow a 'great work of renovation' began on the chapel of St Mary. At the parish church there were two phases of rebuilding, the first between about 1409 and 1431 and the second between 1450 and 1474. Perhaps the Great Flood called a halt to the work, or perhaps it damaged the building and they had to start again, although it is difficult to imagine that the floodwaters reached that far. Perhaps the second phase was the scheme of John Chedworth, rector from 1450 to 1471. Evidence of what went on has to be pieced together from the wills of its benefactors, local brewers, farmers and widows. It is noticeable how many of them had no family to provide for. In 1408 Roger Edwyn, a childless bachelor or widower, left the large sum of £5 for work on the church. The following year Robert Brownyng left 20s *ad sustenacionem corporis ecclesie* (for the body of the church). In 1411 there was a site manager in charge; Warryn Bocher of Forbelane, Limehouse, left his best gown to be sold for the church works, entrusting the money to the keeper of the works. In 1419 Vincent Syward, a Limehouse brewer, left debts owing to him from a baker and one other towards a new belltower. John Batte of the Marsh left 5s for the belfry fund in the same year, stipulating that it should not be paid until the work was near completion. A cleric from Somerset, Nigel Honyngton, left a bequest for the belfry in 1422. In 1431 the rood loft was repaired; apparently childless William Bryche left 6s 8d for this purpose. The rood, an enormous tableau with giant statues of Christ on the cross, the Virgin and St John, stood above the screen that divided the chancel from the nave, dominating the church. For about a hundred years London churches had been building lofts or galleries, so that the tableaux could be lit with candles, like footlights. Staircases were constructed, so that the parish clerk or verger could climb up and light the candles. He also needed to get up there to see to the Lenten veil: during Lent the rood was covered up with a shroud and, in a dramatic presentation at Easter, this covering was slowly winched up. The little tower on the south side of

St Dunstan's, shown in its original form in the print of 1792, is almost certainly a relic of the outside staircase built at this time, and inside there are still the remains of the rood staircase.

A property adjoining the church was acquired by the vicar, Nicholas Norton, and others in 1438; this may have been a church house, perhaps for the chaplains to live in, or a church hall for church ales (fundraising events) and other celebrations.

There seems to have been a hiatus at this point, and then in 1450–51 there are indications that work started anew, perhaps with the advent of the new rector, in the aftermath of the flood. John Symond, a wealthy brewer from the Vintry, whose wife was a relative of Aubrey, the chaplain, in his will of 1451 instructs that his Stepney copyhold land should be sold (if his daughter leaves no heirs) and the profits divided into three, with a third going to the rector and churchwardens for the nave. Constance Swynford, a childless widow from Limehouse whose husband had died eleven years before, left 6s 4d for the vestry work and 13s 4d for the fabric in general in 1450. John Hunden, an organmaker from St Stephen Walbrook, left 3s 4d for the nave in 1455. It is tempting to think that he provided the organ or even played it. John Buntyng, a Poplar farmer, formerly of the Marsh, where he had grown grass on the wall at East Marsh, left 6s 8d for the repair of the church in 1456. The mid-century renovations seem to have included plans for a south aisle, the usual place for a lady chapel. In November 1449 a Bethnal Green widow, Margaret Brace, left 20d for 'St Mary of Stepney'. She may, of course, have had the chapel in the Marsh in mind, even though it had apparently been destroyed beyond repair in the flood. Mistress Brace was a wealthy lady, with tenements that she left to two women, who were appointed, unusually, her executrixes. The properties were to be sold and the money distributed for the benefit of her soul. She had two black heifers, a black cow and a brindle one, a fur-lined cloak, a fine tablecloth and other prized possessions, which she carefully itemised in her will and distributed among her friends.

What happened to the south aisle and the lady chapel remains a mystery. Some years later, in 1464, Thomas Mott of Limehouse, formerly of the Marsh, and a friend of the rich widow Swynford, who endowed the vestry, wrote a will directing that a generous 100s should be paid to the church if, at any time in the future they should build another south aisle. It was eventually built. Thomas Browne left 13s 4d to the lady chapel in 1472, and Richard Colton and John Elond were buried there.

More work was undertaken in 1474; a new rood loft was built in the new nave, another rood of Our Lady was put up, presumably in the lady chapel, and the belfry was repaired. William Sellers of the Marsh family left 13s 4d 'to the making of the rode lofte', 6s 8d 'to the rode of Our Lady' and 3s 4d for the repair of the belfry.

It is more than likely that the expensive business of rebuilding the church was partially financed by the Chedworth family. The rector from 1450 to 1471 was the son of William Chedworth, 'lord of the place of Stebenhythe', who may have been the tenant of the bishop's manor house, now that the bishops were no longer there. He was the manor bailiff from 1464 to 1465. A man of wealth and connections, a relative, perhaps the brother, of John Chedworth, Bishop of Lincoln (1451–71), he acquired extensive properties in Stepney, Whitechapel, Hackney and Barking, including the Clopton Stepney estates, the manor of Cobhams and some of the drowned lands in the Marsh. In 1461 he and his wife, Joan, bought a house adjoining Stepney churchyard, which he seems to have set up as a shelter for poor local girls. Thomas Browne, who died eleven years later, left 2*s* for each of the five girls in Master Chedworth's house. His daughter Ann was Lady Crosby of Crosby Hall, his daughter Joan was wife of William Marowe, grocer, landowner and lord mayor in 1455. His son Nicholas had estates in Hackney and his son, the rector of Stepney, was also Archdeacon of Lincoln and prebendary of St Paul's.

A fourth aisle seems to have been added to the church by 1524, when John Gardyner of White Hart Street asked to be buried there. It may have accommodated the new Trinity chapel, where it was now fashionable for the quality to sit during the service. John atte Fen, a wealthy merchant, asked to be buried in the Trinity chapel, beside his pew 'as I was wont to sit', as did Elys Gymer of the leper hospital, who used to sit there too, her husband's body being in the churchyard with his first wife.

St Dunstan's must have been a splendid sight, probably larger than it is today, spreading out cathedral-like in bright new stone, with four aisles and numerous chapels, decked with all the glittering ornaments that local devotion could provide. An array of saints was there to intercede for the faithful: St Katharine, for maidens, wheelwrights, attorneys and scholars, St George, St Ann, St Nicholas, for sailors, St Dunstan, as patron standing in the sanctuary, and St John the Baptist near the font. In the chancel (where Sir Henry Colet's tomb now is) was the brand new sepulchre, which had its part to play in the dramatic presentation of the passion at Easter. Churches everywhere were amassing wealth as the cult of purgatory peaked. The place where souls went for cleansing was seen as a wide open space, full of wheels of fire, where the dead called out to the living to save them from torment. Would you not, asked Sir Thomas More, reach out to snatch your mother from the fire?

Huge sums were spent on chantry priests, over the years many millions of pounds. In St Dunstan's, the two St Botolph's, St Mary at Bow, St Mary at Whitechapel, St Leonard at Bromley, in Bedlam, the Spital, St Katharine's, St Mary Graces and at the Minories there was an almost continual murmuring of prayers as priests said masses for the local families who had commissioned them to rescue their dead, and ensure their own place in paradise. The going rate was 4*d* a mass (a day's wages), 10*s* for a trental, the popular marathon of thirty masses. Indulgences (tickets to get you or your loved ones out of purgatory)

might be bought for cash or obtained through various exercises. The frontis-
piece of a mass primer found in the convent of Syon near Isleworth promised
32,755 years' worth of indulgence to those who recited a modest number of
prayers while looking at the woodcut of the suffering Christ there displayed.
Many thousands of pounds were spent on the great tapers and candles that burnt
continually on altars, at shrines and round corpses.

In 1438 the old Burford house in Aldgate, along with 'le Ship', 'le Wollesakke'
and the Crown Brewery, were all given over to the Prior of Holy Trinity as *ex
officio* rector of St Botolph's, by vintner Alexander Sprot. The income from these
premises was to finance the saying of masses before the statue of St Nicholas for
ever, for the souls of Sprot, Robert Burford the bellfounder and John Romney,
potter (probably also a bellfounder). Sir John Crosby of Crosby Hall left 400
marks for masses to be said for his soul for forty years. Amy Stepkyn left her
house in Blackwall for a priest 'syngung and redying' for the soul of her husband
William. Sir Henry Colet, one of Stepney's richest and most influential merchant
gentlemen, left £220, the equivalent of perhaps £500,000 today, for fifteen years'
worth of masses. Thomas Dalton, a glover of Aldgate, even left expenses for a local
priest to ride up to Penrith to the graveyard where Dalton's family were interred,
to supervise the saying of masses there for them.

Richard Calowe, a husbandman from the Marsh, promised Stepney's vicar
Nicholas Norton 2s a year for life if he would regularly commend the souls of
him and his wife from the pulpit. If he refused the money was to go to the poor.
This instance of a parishioner taking a firm line with the clergy is not unusual
and is a foretaste of things to come, a hint of the challenge to the clergy that
was part and parcel of the Reformation, which would turn the world upside
down in the next century. The laity were increasing their foothold in the running
of the Church. Wardens might be responsible for administering the considerable property portfolios acquired by some churches. Parishioners at Stepney and
Aldgate churches in particular had a core of rich, strong, self-made men among
their number, merchants and manufacturers, brewers, smiths, founders, tanners,
vintners, tailors and the like, a powerful 'middle class', prepared, as will become
apparent, to take the lead.

The proliferation of religious guilds is one manifestation of the growing
power of laymen. These fraternities were like burial clubs or benefit societies,
poor men's cooperative chantries, offering a mutual support system, a feeling
of belonging and a relatively inexpensive way of buying time out of purgatory.
As well as guilds attached to churches, there were trade guilds, like the Trinity
Guild for sailors, and guilds attached to monasteries, like the Anthony's Guild at
St Mary Graces and the Guild of Our Lady at St Katharine's. Like any exclusive
club, they had their own rules and practices. Members of the guild of Holy
Trinity at St Botolph's Aldersgate were expected to greet one another in an

especially friendly way, like a Masonic handshake perhaps? The Fraternity of St Anne at St Laurence Jewry were strict about their membership and threw out lie-a-beds and tavern haunters. Some were devoted to raising money for church fabric and ornaments; some appointed their own chaplain. Henry Hanslip of Stepney may have been one such: he left the St Dunstan's Guild of Our Lady and St Anne 3s 4d in his will.

Stepney's Guild of Our Lady and St Anne starts appearing in wills soon after the loss of St Mary in the Marsh and the construction of the lady chapel; Thomas Sheffeld left 3s for the 'brithrid' (brotherhood) of Our Lady and churchwarden and limeman Dryver left a mark for the maintenance of the brothers of the guild. Members would have been responsible for keeping the candles lit in the lady chapel and for processions on the Virgin's feast days with special masses when the names of dead members were read out. A Trinity guild was flourishing by the early years of the sixteenth century. The Brotherhood of Jesus at St Botolph's Aldgate, among other things, funded funerals for those who could not afford the expense; glover Dalton left the eight torches that burned on the altar at his own burial to the brotherhood 'for to bery the pore people withal and they to paye nothing'. At St Mary Whitechapel there were guilds of Corpus Christi, St Katharine and St Margaret.

The Protestant/Evangelical movement which was soon to smash the medieval Church took a firm hold in the East End. Although there is no evidence, England's 'homegrown' heresy of Lollardy, which anticipated Luther in so many ways, may have enjoyed more support in London and its suburbs and villages than is generally supposed. In 1414 there was a Lollard rising led by Sir John Oldcastle, an old soldier who had fought with Henry IV in France (Shakespeare's Falstaff was based on him). The leaders were arrested at the sign of the Axe outside Bishopsgate. Oldcastle escaped and was tried three years later at Westminster, then paraded through the streets to Tower Hill, from where he was dragged on hurdles to the 'Lollers gallows' at St Giles. After this Lollardy went underground. We have no way of knowing how many heretics were gathering in 'safe houses' to read the forbidden English Bible and to work each other up in a frenzy of rage against Holy Mother Church and the greed of her fat officials. In the summer of 1440 there was a strange event that seems to point at popular sympathy for those who attacked the Church, combined with a deep commitment to its 'magic'. The vicar of Harmondsworth, Richard Wyche, was burnt on Tower Hill for heresy, to his last breath cursing the Four Orders of Friars. Tourists flocked in; 'meny menne and wommen', says the chronicler, 'went be nyghte to the place where he was brent'. They brought offerings of money and wax images, kneeling down and kissing the ground, carrying away scraps of his ashes as relics, and causing enough of a stir for the City's watch to be alerted. The vicar of the nearby church of All Hallows Barking, obviously delighted with the publicity his church was getting, mixed sweet spices with the ashes so that they gave off a perfume, as the remains of saints were said to do. 'The symple peple was deceyved', and the vicar was arrested.

Heretics were burnt from time to time, but Lollardy was to surface in a major *cause célèbre* sixty-two years later in Whitechapel, when, as we shall see in the next chapter, Richard Hunne, of Lollard sympathies, took on the Church.

Some 'great places' and the nouveau riche

The bishop himself, after Braybrooke's death in 1404, no longer kept house in his Bethnal Green palace; Bishop's Hall was let, with its groves of trees, its sparrow-hawk garden, dovecots and stables, to wealthy men of the City, probably William Chedworth among them. Of the fine and famous the young Edmund, Earl of March, Richard II's rightful heir, was keeping a mistress in Poplar in 1415; in 1452 Jasper, Earl of Pembroke, half-brother to Henry VI (son of Queen Katharine and Owen Tudor) took a house in Poplar's Brook Street called Garlick. The de la Poles had a Stepney establishment, as we have seen.

As to other great houses, there was Lord Mayor Clopton's 'place' in Mile End (where the rebels beheaded the Sheriff of Kent in 1450), and Lord Mayor William Marowe's 'place' in Poplar. Bernes or Barnes Manor House in what was later Goodman's Fields, with imposing gates opening out onto the Minories, now belonged to the Cornwaleys family. In 1472 it was described as a 'great messuage in St Botolph, with Homefield of 50 a. in Stepney (recte Whitechapel) and tenements north and south of the great gate by the highway'. Poplar Manor House belonged to the Abbot of Tower Hill; there were two houses, two cottages, a dovecote, barns, gardens and orchards. Philpot's descendants were still at Hulls/Helle. In Old Ford there was a great house, according to Lysons, who knew of its ruins; it had once belonged to Humphrey, Duke of Gloucester, and was called King John's Palace.

In the heart of Stepney village, flanking the church, were three mansions standing in extensive grounds; to the east the parsonage house with its enormous tithe barn, and to the west and north the two 'great places'. One, opposite the church on its north-western side, where in days past le Waley's mansion stood, belonged to one John atte Fen (d. 1474), of the Fishmongers' Company, a merchant of the Staple. Nothing much is known about the appearance of this property, but it was evidently a very grand house indeed, with an imposing gatehouse. For hundreds of years this sturdy and medieval-looking structure stood just north-west of St Dunstan's church; these days a ruined archway in Ben Jonson Road, the remains of the entrance to a nineteenth-century training college for Baptist ministers, stands as a reminder of the old 'palace'. John atte Fen referred to the house as his 'gret ples'; it might have been built in the early years of the sixteenth century on the site of the Waleys' mansion, or it may have been part of the later structure built by the Marquis of Worcester. It was obviously a building of con-siderable local interest, and prints survive from the eighteenth century, but no topographer or antiquarian has come up with any explanation of its nickname. Was it called King John's Palace because of some folk memory of a long-ago royal association, or was the King John simply the *nouveau riche* John atte Fen, mocked for the grandiose style of his 'gret ples' – as, in similar vein, an Elizabethan house in Bishopsgate was, according to Stow, 'mockingly called Fisher's Folly ... being so large and sumptuously built by a man of no great calling'. At all events the property was in 1512 deemed suitable accommodation for one of the greatest magnates in the land, Lord Thomas Darcy. Atte Fen's son John, having built him-self another house in the village (enclosed with a brick wall), let the mansion to Darcy for 35s a quarter.

The better known 'Great Place', just to the south, was a vast, rambling, half-timbered structure, surrounded by a moat and approached through groves of elms and poplars. This too was a very splendid house, with its own chapel, turkey carpets and luxurious wall hangings. It would survive for at least 300 years, to become a place of leisure called the Spring Garden in the eighteenth century, a rather downmarket Vauxhall, where 'jack tars' took their girls to drink under the lamps that twinkled in the trees. For now it was the country seat, or suburban retreat, of a family whose presence in Stepney was momentous. Henry Colet, a mercer of great wealth, bought the house possibly from one John Crosse in 1482, along with over 100 acres of copyhold land (later converted to freehold), including Cleve Street/White Hart Street, part of London Field and 5 acres in Limehouse Field. Colet was the third son of Robert Colet of Wendover; he was twice lord mayor (in 1486 and 1495) and was knighted in 1487. The family's town house was in Budge Row in the Vintry, but it is clear from the account of the dis-pute over Bow chapel, recounted below, that Sir Henry took the lead in Stepney's parish affairs and that Great Place was their home base. In 1505 he died at Stepney and was buried in the Easter sepulchre in the chancel of the church. His fine table tomb was erected later by the Mercers Company; it is still there, the only surviv-ing monument to a man from this period in Tower Hamlets.

Dame Christian, Colet's wife, was the daughter of Sir John Knevet of Ashwellthorpe in Norfolk. A remarkable woman, learned and feisty, she bore her husband eleven boys and eleven girls, of whom only the first boy survived, John. How much effect a childhood thus surrounded by deaths had on the surviving child may be guessed at; he must have been much treasured and perhaps indulged by this rich and pious couple. As his little brothers and sisters left their cradles empty, one after another, and only he was left playing on his rocking horse and with his 'painted dolls', John perhaps felt he was someone special, which he was.

John Colet, albeit unwittingly, would lead the dance that took Stepney and the country at large towards the abolition of the medieval Church. We shall see in due course how monks and nuns were turned out of doors, saints were banished, candles were snuffed and purgatory was 'pissed owte', as one man put it.

The Colets, Stepney's leading family, were of merchant stock. The mobility of society in England is often commented on, perhaps more in connection with the rise of trading and manufacturing families in Shakespeare's day; but it is clear from the extraordinarily rich will archive that documents life in the eastern suburbs and villages that by the time of the Wars of the Roses the working man was already on the up. Great lords had houses here but the new 'middle class' was a force to be reckoned with. Let us start with Grocer William Marowe, the lord mayor who had a place in Poplar and bought up part of the Isle of Dogs after the Great Flood. His father, William Marowe senior, had made his money as a brewer and smith in Bishopsgate. At his death in 1498 the son had, as well as his Stepney estates, a house and a number of quays (one called Marowe Quay) in the Vintry and extensive lands in Essex and Middlesex.

The Dryver and Etgoos families ran the Limehouse kilns for several generations and intermarried. William Dryver, who died in 1487, had a wharf and was rich enough to be buried in the sepulchre in St Dunstan's, the prize spot. His son, limeman Richard (d. 1520), was wealthier than his father; his household in Limehouse boasted a fleet of servants, fur-lined gowns, feather beds, silver cutlery, a 7ft dining table and a quantity of fine bedlinen. Richard held the important post of churchwarden and had his own brass holy water stoop. His was a happy marriage: he lent £20 to his eldest son, Richard, 'on condition that he be good to his mother and comfort her at all times'. I hope he did – in due course he would marry Elizabeth Etgoos, the lime-kiln heiress.

Elizabeth Etgoos was the granddaughter of limeman and property developer Richard Edgose (Etgoos), by 1497 one of the foremost men of the parish. He first appears in the records as a fisherman (more likely the owner of a fishing fleet), fined 4d for poaching the bishop's fish in the flooded Marsh in 1481. By his death in 1503 he had a ninety-nine-year lease from the bishop of lands in Limehouse; he ran local lime-kilns and also kilns in Greenwich; chalk for burning was brought up from Kent to his wharf in a boat which he called the *Kateryn*. He had 2 acres in London Field (formerly Galey's field, west of the church), where gravel was dug for ships' ballast, and 28 acres in the Marsh. He built himself a new house, with a brewery and four other new houses adjoining it. On the wharf that he had bought from Joan Dryver, the churchwarden's widow, he erected eight tenements. He also had 50 acres in the Marsh, a farmhouse, a barn and an orchard in Limehouse. His wife Alice was well furnished with jewellery.

When Etgoos was 'pinched by the messengers of death' he directed that he should be buried before the Pauline cross in the churchyard in the tomb of John and Margaret Laskes. He left a generous corpse present of 20s, and a chantry priest was directed to 'sing for his soul' for two years and get paid 9 marks. If his neighbours were prepared to club together for a communal chantry, the period was to be extended to ten years. The £2 that he left towards the construction of the new Easter sepulchre was given on condition that it be 'began and forthward in makyng' within two years of his death. The limeburner was a businessman who sounds as if he was used to giving orders.

Richard Dryver (d.1549) the younger, who united the lime dynasties by marrying Elizabeth Etgoos, widow of another limeman, Richard Marche (d.1540), was rich indeed, with houses and land, four-posters hung with tapestries and green and red silk, a fine array of silver gilt plate, a brickworks, two wharves, farms, carts, cattle, horses, timber, coals, sacks of lime and 2,000 reeds. He left £100 for the completion of his new house (with garden and orchards), which was under construction adjoining the kilns. This must have been some mansion, when one considers that King Henry VIII himself paid £177 9s 1d for a property he bought in Bethnal Green.

The supply of lime and bricks for an expanding city brought money into the pockets of East Enders and made their sons into gentlemen. John Bramston/ Brampston, brickmaker of Whitechapel, had a sizeable operation and made a mint, leaving 10,000 bricks to the Charterhouse 'that they may have my sould the more in rememberance', 10,000 bricks to his son Hugh and 4,000 to St Bartholomew's, and a load of gravel to be laid as soon as possible after his death in the Whitechapel Road. His son Hugh was quite the gentleman, with a diamond ring, a black velvet doublet and all manner of fine and fancy clothes. His grandson entertained Queen Mary, no less, when she entered London as sovereign for the first time, fifty years after our brickman's death.

Richard Hill took over the bellfoundry at Aldgate from the Burfords in the early part of the century; twenty-three of his bells ring even today in the belfries of England, as far afield as Gloucestershire and Devon. For a short while after his death his widow Johanna ran the show, and seven of her bells (made in one year) are still extant. Theirs was a sizeable operation with a substantial workforce, and must have been very lucrative.

Founders, braziers and 'potters', making brass pots, swords, pewterware, leadware, lattenware, candlesticks and all manner of household items, were numerous in London and congregated in Whitechapel, Aldgate and outside Bishopsgate. John Shrouesbury, blacksmith of Norton Folgate (d.1461), had acquired a number of tenements by his death in 1461. There was an arrowsmith called William Sheffeld living in Stepney in the 1430s, a friend of Walter Colte, a Mile End brazier and brassworker. Perhaps William, or his father or his grandfather, had come down from Sheffield to make arrows for the French wars. A relative, maybe his son, Thomas Sheffeld, a Marsh man, was rich enough to pay for a good number of masses for his soul and had property in Stepney and East Ham. Walter Colte had a black russet gown, outlived two wives and was nursed at the end by Margery Hyde, to whom he left her a quarter of a mark for her pains. His melting bellows and other equipment were left to a family member.

The service industries are well represented in the will archive. Whitechapel barber Thomas Hudson, who died in 1486 (and was buried before the St Thomas window in Whitechapel church), had lands and tenements, silver spoons, mazers (bowls) and fur-trimmed gowns. In spite of his wealth he was obviously a working barber, leaving his late apprentice 'all my rasors' and 'all myn instruments for tooth drawing and blode letynge'. A kindly man, this 'dentist' willed 'that continually 3 poor folk have their dwelling free within the haussyng of the said tenements [his Whitechapel estate] whoever owns it'.

Bow

Perhaps most striking among the records of East Enders who did well for themselves are the numbers of men from Stratford Bow. The manorial roll for 1404 lists Stepney's hamlets: Stratford, Old Ford, Poplar, Forbelane (in Limehouse), Clyvestrete (Ratcliff), Mylehynd and Blethenhale, Marsh (Isle of Dogs) and Lymehostes. Of these, the hamlet of Stratford Bow (first on the list), 2 miles east of the City, was the most populous and independent, with its flourishing bakeries, fullers' mills and dyehouses. The mills on the Lea at Stratford Bow, Old Ford, Bromley (an independent parish) and Stratford Langthorne (in Essex) had been in operation since Domesday. The locals, as fullers of the all-important woollen cloth and the main suppliers of London's bread, were making a mint, much to the chagrin of the City bakers. When Henry Colet was mayor the Bow bakers complained to him that the City's inspectors of loaves often dropped and damaged them, as if by accident, so they were unsaleable.

One of the many successful bakers was Edward Waryn, baker and tallow chandler. He died in 1497 leaving his extensive freehold and copyhold lands in Bow, Stepney, Hornchurch, Havering and Waltham Cross in trust for the benefit of St Leonard's chapel (in the nunnery in Bromley); 13s 4d a year was set aside for an annual mass for his soul and everyone else's, and a party, with supplies of drink and bread and cheese, ringing of the bells and the giving of alms to the poor. His family got his two bakeries, one in the town of Bow, called the Rose in the Hope, and one in north Bow, and four barns, which were presumably used for storing grain. Waryn evidently lived in Bromley, where the inhabitants worshipped and were buried in the nunnery church. The people of Stratford Bow hamlet had of course had their own chapel for nearly 200 years; they buried their dead in its churchyard and, as the list of chantry property (1548) and wills bear witness, were enthusiastic in their support of their local place of worship, resenting their subjugation to the mother church at Stepney and failing to pay their dues.

In the year of Waryn's death there was a major falling out between the people of Bow and the people of Stepney over the status of St Mary's chapel; it had been brewing for ten years at least. The leading men of both places attended two meetings. Stepney's contingent was led by Sir Henry Colet, with limemen Richard Dryver, Richard Edgoose and Thomas Brett (Byrte). There were forty-eight delegates for the mother church, from the hamlets of Stepney, Poplar, 'Lymose', 'Redclyffe', Mile End and 'Bednalgrene' (in that order); the great matter of Bow was clearly something that was taken very seriously, and the 'public meetings' are a measure of the laity's concern with the Church at this time, giving a foretaste of the years to come.

Bow's 'ancients' met in the chapel of St Leonard's Priory at the same time as the Stepneyites were meeting in St Dunstan's. They were led by a gentleman, John Raymond, and are named as John Porter, John Newbaud, Thomas Awsten, John Cannon, John Mondewe, Christopher Smyth, William Bote, Thomas Sawyer, John Awood, Thomas Pole, John Sturmyn. William Parker, Clemens Maltby, William Johnson, William Mason, George Dyson, John James, Robert Armetsted, William Price, Nicholas Trynley, John Parcenson, John Dyconson, James Pewle, Robert Trynley and John Lane. The doctors of civil law decided that the people of Stratford/Bow were to accept St Dunstan's as their mother church in perpetuity. As a sign of their subjection, twice a year they were to go in solemn procession to Stepney, to hear mass and make their oblations. One of these processions was to take place on St Dunstan's Day. They were also ordered to go in company with the parishioners of Stepney church on the annual pilgrimage to St Paul's. For repair of the church and ornaments they were to pay the churchwardens 24s a year, half at Michaelmas and half at Easter. They were not, however, required to contribute towards the Sunday bread, the parish clerk's stipend or to the office of churchwarden. If they failed to pay up, their chaplain would be removed and there would be a ban on burials in their chapel. It was not until the eighteenth century that Bow finally managed to break free.

Postscript

With Bow put in its place, the civil wars at an end and a new dynasty established on the throne, we must leave the medieval East End behind and move into the Tudor era, when Stepney will take the limelight, but before we do, just in case you might think that these long-lost medieval East Enders were a different breed from us, listen to a conversation overheard in Houndsditch.

One day, just before Christmas 1491, a woman named Isabella attacked a man called Newport, who claimed she had promised to marry him. She threw him in the ditch, as she told a witness at the bishop's court: 'Y met Newport And had the hooreson by the face And put him in the ditch,' uttering the words, 'A hooreson, yf I might have had my will y should have kylld the[e] that wold to Godds passion I had so done – hooreson that thowe art.' Someone else heard her say, 'Y had liever [rather] the bald hooreson Cokkoold wer hangyd than he should be my husband. And I tryst that y shall fynde sum goode fellowe that for my sake other evyn or morowe shalt make hym to pysse above his gydylsted'. This must surely mean a kick in the balls.

Part II

UNDER THE TUDORS AND STUARTS

Chapter 5

THE TUDORS

1500–1600

Against a bloodstained tapestry of religious revolution and then the long golden years of exploration and endeavour under Elizabeth I, the countryside east of the Tower would be transformed. Countryfolk trooped into London, its suburbs and nearby villages, drawn by the gold-paved streets and driven by the enclosure of common land and changes in farming methods, inflation and bad harvests, to seek their fortune or just make a decent living. There grew up a large shanty town population of newcomers – country East Enders, living in tiny, cheap cottages thrown up in haste, or in 'bedsits' in old houses divided up by rapacious landlords. From the end of the century the City guilds were continually pressing for power over crafts in the eastern suburbs. The riverside hamlets became the haunt of sailors and ships' chandlers.

Concurrent with the invasion of the East End was the end of the medieval Church. Bells were hushed, saints banished and candles snuffed out, the murmuring of anniversary masses replaced by stern sermonising. Monasteries were closed and churches stripped of all their gorgeous paraphernalia, and the clergy were excluded from commercial enterprises. No more would clergy run breweries, as the rector of Stepney had done. No more would taxes be paid to the pope; there would be no appeal to his court and no regard for his works. For the East Enders, most of them well to the left in matters of religion, the old 'Popish' mass would become 'of no more effect that the bleating of a cow to her calf and the calf's answering call'.

London was swelling at an accelerated pace. Between 1530 and 1600 the population of the capital rose, at a conservative estimate, from *c*. 50,000 to *c*. 200,000, with the eastern suburbs taking a heavy load. By the 1550s the East End had considerably more licensed alehouses than the western and northern suburbs: Stepney (with Bow) had forty-four, two more than Westminster, thirty-one more than Islington and thirty-four more than Clerkenwell. St Botolph's Aldgate (like Southwark) doubled its numbers between 1548 and 1620, while Shoreditch expanded sixfold. Likewise Stepney and its hamlets grew; by the 1540s there were probably something in the region of 13,000 inhabitants. In 1580, 'because of many houses builded in the parish', a gallery was put up in Stepney church. If we accept Sir William Petty's method of calculating the number of residents by multiplying the numbers of burials in a parish by thirty, then the East End, including the liberties and out-parishes of Bishopsgate and Aldgate, may have accommodated some 30,000 souls by the opening of the seventeenth century. According to Sir Hubert Llewellyn-Smith, the East End had about 48,000 inhabitants by 1630, excluding the Portsoken. Stepney's hamlets of Limehouse, Poplar, Bethnal Green, Ratcliff and Mile End were small towns by the standards of the day, and each had their own chapel within the parish church by 1532. Bow, with 'much people there inhabiting', had its own church, as we have seen.

When Henry VII took the throne the outer East End was a rural place; its woods and parklands provided a retreat from the City and its evils, the plague and the pox. Early in the sixteenth century the boys from St Paul's School were sent to Stepney for safety during plague times. A hundred years later, as we shall see, the plague hit hardest here, an indication of overcrowded, poor living.

The out-parishes of St Botolph's Bishopsgate and Aldgate spread out along the highways and joined with their neighbouring villages, Shoreditch in the north and Whitechapel to the east. Every spare plot was covered; even the ditch that ran round the City walls was filled in and divided into strips where residents could grow beans and cabbages. Norton Folgate and East Smithfield got rougher, while along the riverbank Wapping, Ratcliff, Limehouse, Poplar and Blackwall turned from fishing villages into 'sailortown'. Young men arrived Dick Whittington-style, perhaps on a carrier's cart, perhaps on foot. There was work available in the marine and cloth trades, in Ratcliff's new sugarhouse, in the lime-kilns in Limehouse, the brick-kilns in Spitalfields, the breweries, cooperages, and the Bow bakehouses. Their sisters went into service, joined the burgeoning silk trade, and worked as barmaids, prostitutes, midwives and wetnurses.

What changed the East End most in these years was the growth of the riverside and the seafaring connection. The Armada Map of 1588 shows a built-up area stretching along the river from Wapping to Blackwall, in what looks to be an area half the size of the whole conurbation of London and Westminster. The riverside was developing both east and west of Ratcliff. There were docks at Limehouse, Ratcliff and Wapping. Blackwall, where there was a reef in the Thames providing a natural harbour, was to become a passenger port, where travellers often disembarked and made their way into London by road, instead of waiting for the ship to go round the Isle of Dogs.

The young Henry VIII built up his navy to restart the Hundred Years War. When the king arrived at Calais in 1513 his fleet astonished one observer: it was, he said, 'a sight such as Neptune had never seen before'. Royal dockyards were opened at Woolwich (1512) and Chatham (1513), although the north bank of the river played its part. From 1512 several royal ships, including the *Mary Rose*, were fitted out in Blackwall and Wapping; in 1525 royal galleons were lying at Ratcliff for repair. There was some actual shipbuilding and the great Pett family, which took over the industry in years to come, was already in residence. But it was for ships' chandlery and marine crafts that the north bank became renowned, for anchorsmiths, ropemakers, carpenters, mastmakers, sailmakers and allied trades. Ships were fitted here and got ready for sail; food and men were taken on board. Hence the growth of the local seafaring community and all the associated traders; the slopsellers, physicians, apothecaries, midwives, barmaids and victuallers, pimps and prostitutes. Local butchers, bakers and brewers were now victualling the navy and merchant vessels.

There were lodging houses and alehouses for the accommodation and entertainment of sailors and fishermen. Galleons swayed down river from Blackwall and Wapping, taking locals, perhaps trained in their father's fishing vessels, and young men from all over the country, setting out for the New World in hopes of filling their pockets with foreign gold.

All this change, and much more about the early modern East End, is well documented. Parish registers provide systematic recording of the people from mid-century: Bow from 1538, Whitechapel, St Botolph's Bishopsgate and Aldgate from 1558, Holy Trinity Minories from 1563, Stepney from 1568, with vestry minutes, St Katharine's from 1584. There are some maps: the Armada Map gives an overview of riverside development; Frans Hogenberg's map of 1559 shows the north-western part, Spitalfields and Bethnal Green, the Copperplate Map of 1559 shows Spitalfields. There is biographical information supplied by witnesses in the Church courts, which tell us where the country East Enders came from and when. Even more wills went to probate than before, as locals enriched themselves with Spanish gold; and all manner of sources bring the people to life – with plays and even a diary surviving, as we shall see. As Stepney takes the limelight in events of national importance, there are multifarious government records. Perhaps the most telling of all, however, is the first-hand account of London written at the end of the century by John Stow, who lived in Leadenhall Street, near Aldgate, and had a special interest in this part of town.

With an old man's nostalgia Stow yearned for the days of his youth, when teasels grew by Bishopsgate Street, hedgerows lined the lane down to Aldgate Bars, and 'fair elm trees' shaded the highway to Ratcliff. He describes Wapping High Street as a 'filthy straight passage'; from the Bars to Shoreditch, as a 'continual building of small base tenements'; the 'common field' east of Whitechapel church, in spite of government attempts to prevent building outside the City walls, being encroached upon by filthy cottages, rubbish dumps and dung heaps. This urban mess spilt over into the road, so that there was not room enough for droves of cattle or carriages to pass; it was 'an unsavoury and unseemly an entrance' to 'so famous a city'.

A delightful garden: before the Reformation

But all that is yet to come. Before we watch the Reformation played out in Stepney and Aldgate and move on into the world of the country East Enders, we will take a look at the suburbs and villages as they were before the sea-change. In these days Bluff King Hal was young and glamorous, went to mass three times a day, wrote pretty songs, rode to battle and wore out horses with hunting, some-times in Bethnal Green. In 1512 he gave £1 as a New Year gift to St George's chapel on the waste there, and in 1517 he bought a property in the hamlet, paying £177 9s for it; it was probably a lodge for hunting or hawking in Bishopswood.

Bow, its houses and workshops gathered around a 'great thoroughfare with much people there inhabiting', baked bread for the king's sailors. Whitechapel and Aldgate made guns for the king's arsenal while, on Thursday afternoons up near the Spital you could hear the blasts of cannon as the gunners from the Tower practised their skills in the fields nearby. Artillery Lane marks the spot today. The *Mary Rose* rode at Blackwall, and along the riverside the sound was the clink of hammer on anvil as the king's galleons were fitted out for war.

In Stepney village, secluded among chestnuts and elms, behind high walls and dykes, were luxurious residences, the Colet's Great Place and Fen's Great Place, rented by Privy Councillor and Yorkshire warhorse Sir Thomas Darcy (from 1512 to 1536) and hung with tapestries depicting Achilles, King David and Abigail. Down Cleve Street, now known as White Hart Street, was the house belonging to the High Master of St Paul's School, approached along a tree-lined avenue. Along the road across the fields to Whitechapel, now known as Whitehorse Lane, were the butts for archery practice. The Whitehorse tavern and the 7-acre field to the east of the parsonage, churchfield, belonged to Richard Dryver, the limeman.

Thomas More famously compared Stepney to a garden abutting an inn (the City), and wrote to his friend, John Colet, trying to persuade him to return home from the country:

> Wherever you turn your eyes, you are charmed by the smiling aspects of the fields, and refreshed by the pleasant coolness of the air, and delighted by the very sight of the sky. You see nothing but the bounteous gifts of nature and traces of holy innocence ... granting that you dislike the discomforts of the City, yet the country of Stepney ... will afford you no less delights than where you are now residing. And from there you can now and then turn aside into the City ... as into an inn.

In this delightful garden, there was, on the surface at least, precious little hint of the revolution to come, with the mighty Cardinal Wolsey in charge of affairs of state and the king, 'Defender of the Faith'. The Abbot of St Mary Graces divided his time between his grand abbey on Tower Hill and his Poplar Manor House, with its well-stocked fishponds, rabbit warrens and doves. The convent in the Minories was burnt down but rebuilt hastily with a generous personal subvention from the king, whose mother had been so attached to the nunnery. Up at Bishopsgate the Spital made major acquisitions of property, in 1509 and 1514, while at Mile End the ancient house for lepers, Lazercottes, operated as a rather superior private hospital, or so it seems from the wills of the couple who owned and ran it, John and Elys Gymer. It had six beds hung with fine tapestry hangings (for poor people and lepers), plentiful linen and silver plate, its own chapel with silver gilt chalice and patten, rich vestments, a bell at the door and a little handbell. Elys had one son, an Augustinian friar. She left him a cloth painted with St John the Baptist and 10s for his friary to 'make them a breakfast all together', at which they were to remember her soul; she was a jolly woman by the sound of it. In 1522 John left instructions that the hospital should be kept as it was and entrusted it to the care of the parish. It would be handed over to St Bartholomew's in 1549.

The newly built parish church at Stepney was filled with painted saints; a Mile End smith's widow gave 1s towards a statue of St George. A high cross was put up on Mile End Green to remind passers-by of their maker. Purses were emptied and houses were sold to enrich the Church and secure everlasting bliss for the donors and their families.

But trouble was stirring. Sir Henry Colet's son John, friend of rising star Thomas More, was vicar of Stepney when the century opened. We met him in his nursery in the previous chapter. There is no record of Colet's presentation to the vicarage, but it is assumed to have been made in 1499; and he resigned on becoming Dean of St Paul's on 21 September 1505. As he was arguably the most celebrated East Ender of his day, the so-called Father of the Reformation, we should make his acquaintance. Always dressed in black, this stern, fastidious figure looked to a Church 'purified of the dross of observance and ritual which had accrued to it'. He had no time for the credulous, with their relic-kissing and image worship, and was horrified on a trip to Canterbury by the tourist attraction of Becket's shrine, with its fabulous collection of jewels and the supposed 'holy arm' of the martyr, with flesh clinging to it. His dream of a return to the primitive Church was shared with other London humanist reformers and his great friend Erasmus. The Dutchman was often at Great Place and was a favourite of the dean's mother, Dame Christian, a cheerful and erudite old lady who evidently shared her son's views. At her death she left no money to help herself or anyone else out of purgatory; there is nothing for anniversary masses or even a month's mind.

The reformers urged a rigid application of the actual word of the scriptures, in their purest, original, form, and sought an expansion of the Christian faith drawn from the philosophical culture of the classics. Whenever Erasmus heard Colet speak, he said, it was like listening to Plato himself. Like Wycliffe and the 'Lollers' before him, although he never attacked the basic dogma of the Church, the radical dean frequently launched into the clergy. In a much-publicised sermon of 1511 he declaimed: 'They [the higher clergy] give themselves to feasts and banqueting; they spend themselves in vain babbling; they give themselves to sports and plays; they apply themselves to hunting and hawking; they drown themselves in the delights of this world.' His outspoken preaching got him into trouble on many occasions, notably his Good Friday sermon before the court at Greenwich in 1513 when he urged his audience, which included the king, to follow Christ, not Caesar, proclaiming that an unjust peace was preferable to a just war. On the opposite side of the river, at Ratcliff, ships were being got ready for the king's 'just war' against France, in defence of the papacy. Colet was summoned to the royal presence and, apparently, withdrew his remarks. In later years clerics lost their lives for less.

Colet's Great Place was known as a 'safe house' for reformers, and the dean had good 'press coverage', with shops in St Paul's churchyard and pedlars selling books and pamphlets to an eager public. How much effect the publicised fulminations of the son of the 'big house' had on the locals can only be guessed, but in the conflict to come Stepney became a strongly evangelical parish. Seeds sown by Colet flowered as Lutheran and radical Anabaptist ideas started to filter into the East End, brought by the sailors on German ships and by Flemish and Dutch refugees.

For the time being, however, the most immediate impact that Dean Colet had on the locality was his refoundation of St Paul's School, with its endowment of Stepney property. All his inherited Stepney estate, comprising some 100 acres, was given over to the endowment of this new school. The management of the school and its estates was not, as one might expect, given to some ecclesiastical body, but to the livery company of which the dean's father was a member, the Mercers. Thus began a 400-year association between Stepney and the Mercers; in 1843 half the original 100 acres still belonged to the Mercers.

It was a sign of the times that a dean of St Paul's should attach to his cathedral a school controlled by a lay body, at a time when education was largely a clerical matter. Colet's distrust of the Church authorities ran very deep. According to Erasmus he took this step because 'There was no absolute certainty in human affairs but, for his part, he found less corruption in such a body of citizens than in any order or degree of mankind.' By 1512 the school was up and running, with humanist William Lily as the first high master. During plague time the boys were brought to Stepney and taught in a barn between Midsummer and Allhallowtide (November). In 1528 seventeen boys came, including the young Thomas Gresham. The boys learned their Latin from Erasmus's books and not the corrupted and adulterated Latin 'which ignoraunt and blyende fooles brought into this woarld', according to the dean. Literature had been so abused it should, he wrote, be called 'blotterature'.

After Dame Colet's death Great Place was divided and let out to a series of wealthy court and city men, many of them Mercers, and the houses in Whitehorse Street were often let to Company men. In the seventeenth century a Mercer's widow endowed almshouses just near the church; they were rebuilt in 1842 and can still be seen, now private villas. The manufacture of silk, which was soon to occupy most people in Bethnal Green and Spitalfields, must surely be associated to the Company's strong local presence.

The most celebrated Company tenant of Great Place was Thomas Cromwell, the organising genius of the Dissolution of the Monasteries and, we will see in due course, organiser of the part played by the Mercers in the attacks on the mal-practices of the Church which fired the Reformation Parliament of 1529. This richest of the livery companies, with its jurisdiction over the manufacture and sale of fine cloth, had a strong evangelical bent and carried on the Puritan tradi-tion in the following century. Its close involvement in the religious revolution parallels what happened in Germany, where the wealthy trade guilds were the leading agents in the adoption of the reformed faith.

Richard Pace, also Dean of St Paul's and another humanist scholar, was vicar of Stepney from 1519 to 1527. His story is hardly part of the East End's history (he was probably the vicar who saw least of his parish), but he deserves a mention. He was taken up by the increasingly powerful King's Almoner, Thomas Wolsey, in 1514 and spent most of his career abroad, sent by his master on a series of unrewarding and gruelling rounds of diplomatic negotiations in Europe, not least a futile attempt to get his master elected pope. Following a spell in the Tower for arranging a meeting with the Spanish ambassador on Catherine of Aragon's behalf, he went mad, died and was buried in the chancel of St Dunstan's. His monument was still there in 1631.

Members of the 'Colet set' in Stepney were the Gibsons, Nicholas, a grocer and sea-captain's son, and Avice, his wife. After Nicholas's death Avice married Sir Anthony Knevytt, a relative of Dame Christian's. Like Dean Colet they set up a school that was given over to a livery company and still functions to this day. The old Ratcliff Free School became the Coopers' Company School and in 1971 combined with the Bow Coborn School for Girls. The school is now in Upminster.

Ratcliff was the most populous of Stepney's hamlets, with about 4,000 inhabit-ants by the end of the sixteenth century. The riverside here wore an industrial aspect, with yards for ship repair, warehouses and the chimneys of the Dryver lime-kilns and the Poyntells' bakery smoking over the rooftops. It was mostly a place of ships and sailors, and a survey of immorality and crime made by Wolsey in 1519 listed at least ten victualling houses in Stepney's port. Nicholas Gibson grew up in Ratcliff, a sea captain's son and a member of the Grocers' Company. Unable to have children, the wealthy Gibsons decided to 'relieve the poor' by 'mutual consent'. By June 1536 the building of Ratcliff school and almshouses was underway, situated on the north side of what is now the Highway, with a 115ft frontage, bounded by Schoolhouse Lane on the west. On the eastern side were the almshouses, where fourteen old folk were housed in single rooms. Next door was the school and the master and usher's house. A walled garden enclosed the whole, with 2,800 rose bushes, pear trees and crab apples; strawberries and all manner of herbs were cultivated for the residents; and there was a bowling alley for their entertainment. A chapel was added later. This fine establishment had provision for sixty children; it never actually took more than thirty poor (non-paying) pupils at a time. The master and usher were paid generous salaries, £10 and £6 13s 4d a year respectively, and were permitted to take boarders and paying pupils to augment their incomes. Even the gardener was well paid, at a rate of 9d a day. Nicholas died on 25 September 1540 and Avice and her new husband looked after the school. After Knyevtt's death Avice made the school and alms-house over to the Coopers' Company, on 20 February 1552. The inscription on the Gibson monument in Stepney church begins:

> Here was I borne, and here I make myne end
> Though I was Citizen and Grocer of London
> And to the office of Schrevalty did ascend
> But things Transitorie pass and vanische sore
> To God be geven thanks of that I have right
> That to his honowre and to the bringing up of youth
> And to the succowre of the Age; for siwerly this is soth.

The monasteries dissolved

Fifteen years after Dean Colet's death, the very house where he had discussed the iniquities of the clergy with the Dutch 'prince of Renaissance scholarship' was occupied by Thomas Cromwell. Together with his staff of Stepney clerics, he was busy about the Dissolution of the Monasteries and much more besides. The 'Defender of the Faith' would become head of the English Church; the pope would become 'anti-Christ' and his adherents 'papists', bogeymen for most of the yeomen of England. Instead of legacies to buy masses and fund priests, money went into the poor box. Abuses that Chaucer and others had vilified long-ago were dealt with by an avenging laity led by a power-hungry monarch. Stepney was so much bound up in the Henrician Reformation that the full story should be told.

The East Enders joined with vigour the attack on the old Church. There is nothing particular to link the area with Lollardy, the indigenous brand of proto-Protestantism that had been rumbling around for about 150 years, but as we saw in the previous chapter the movement had gone underground and there may well have been lingering pockets. However, the first serious outburst of popular attacks on the Church involved a man of known Lollard sympathies, and it happened in Whitechapel. City people commonly put their babies to wetnurse in the suburbs, and one such was Richard Hunne, a tailor of St Margaret's Bridge Street, said to be a Lollard. Hunne's baby son died and was buried by the parson of Whitechapel, who claimed the child's winding sheet as a mortuary gift. This was a sort of church death duty, which everybody usually paid. The angry father was of another mind and took proceedings to the king's court on a writ of *prae-munire*, the basis of which was that the Church had no rights over his property. One evening, just after Christmas 1512, the parish priest of Whitechapel, Henry Marshall, threw Hunne out of his church, declaiming, 'Hunne thou art accursed, and thou standest accursed.' Marshall was taken to court by Hunne in a defamation suit, and the Church authorities countered by accusing Hunne of heresy; they had him imprisoned in the Lollards' Tower at St Paul's. There he was found strangled, and the Bishop of London's chancellor, a court summoner and a bell-ringer stood accused of the murder. Meanwhile Hunne's body was exhumed and burnt at Smithfield. Although the chancellor and his fellows were found not guilty, the scandal of the much-publicised case sent shockwaves through the Church, heralding the cataclysm to come. 'Poor men and idiots,' asserted Hunne, 'have the truth of Holy scriptures, more than a thousand prelates.' Any London jury, commented the Bishop of London, would condemn a clergyman, though he were as innocent as Adam.

This anticlericalism was boosted by resentment of the extraordinary extravagance, display and greed of Cardinal Wolsey, the subject of many popular ballads and rhymes. It would be unleashed only fifteen years after the Hunne scandal by the king himself; the door was opened to reformist ideas coming in from Europe only six years after the king had written his attack on Luther. Henry's obsessive need for a male heir, combined with a growing megalomania and a passion for the beautiful, ambitious and evangelical Anne Boleyn, had changed everything. By August 1527 Henry and Anne were probably informally betrothed. A Cambridge academic, Thomas Cranmer, suggested he procure an annulment of his marriage to Catherine of Aragon, pleading that it was uncanonical by virtue of her previous contract with his brother. Wolsey's attempts to procure an annulment from the pope failed, and sealed his own downfall. 'I wonder,' pondered Erasmus, 'whither this savagery of the king will lead.'

The organising genius of Henry's Church coup and his vicar general was Thomas Cromwell, a protégé of Wolsey's. Cromwell had various houses in

London and the suburbs, in Austin Friars, Mortlake and Chelsea, but he seems to have made Stepney his headquarters for the main thrust of his attack on the Church. Before he took the lease on Great Place he had Stepney connections; his wife died there in 1527, and he 'moved office', out into the comparative safety of the sympathetic Mercers' stronghold outside the capital, just as things were coming to a head (in 1534), spending a considerable amount of time there during the next six years. Whether or not the religious temper of the locals had anything to do with it can only be guessed. Certainly the rector's inclinations and person-ality did. Richard Layton, a brutal and arrogant fanatic, who had held Stepney rectory since 1522, was employed by Cromwell as his chief visitor, leading the hunt for evidence of corruption in the religious houses.

The son of a Putney blacksmith, Cromwell was a self-made man who at some stage had worked as a cloth dresser, hence his association with the Mercers' Company. He came from a business and legal background, and had spent some time in Antwerp and Italy. Although probably motivated primarily by personal ambition, there seems little doubt that he was in genuine sympathy with the Continental reformers; when he went to Rome in 1517–18 he took Erasmus's New Testament with him and learned it off by heart. He entered parliament in 1523, and as Wolsey's secretary handled all his legal affairs. In 1525 he was on a commission set up to look into the affairs of the smaller monasteries and was known as Wolsey's 'chefe doer … in the suppression of abbeis'.

In November 1529 Henry threw in his lot with anticlericalism and called par-liament. The first session, meeting at the Blackfriars monastery, with the king's blessing fell on the clergy, led by the Mercers' Company with Cromwell pushing from behind. The first four of the Mercers' Five Articles concerned the redress of City grievances; the fifth urged parliament to:

> Have in remembrans howe the kynges poore subjectes principally of London, bean polled and robbed without reason or conscience by th'ordenarys [Church authorities] in probatying of testaments and taking of mortuarys and also vexed and trobled by citacions with cursing oon day and absoulyng the next day, et hec omnia pro pecuniis [all for money].

Pluralism, worldiness and non-residence were attacked, as well as the fees for probate and death duties. Priests, they said, let orphans go begging rather than allowing them to keep the cow that was their mortuary fee. Draft bills for reform, based on these debates, were drawn up. In the legislation that resulted, clergy were ordered to be resident; only in special circumstances might they be absent from their living or hold in plurality, in theory at least. The abolition of clerical leases and the restrictions imposed on economic activity, meant that the days of the priest as developer and businessman were at an end. Appeals to Rome were forbidden and anti-papist material was circulated under royal auspices. Bishop Fisher called the legislation a 'violent heap of mischief'; meanwhile, encouraged by their betters, the criminal classes started stealing from churches. In August 1530 an ex-gaoler from Newgate, Roger Horton, with three London accomplices, George Hopye, Humphrey West and James Mychell, broke into St Dunstan's and stole a cross, chalices and other plate. The previous February Horton, this time with a clerical accomplice, had burgled the Abbot of Abingdon's house, stealing £100.

Anne Boleyn was now openly living with the king, and while negotiations with the pope about the 'great matter' of the royal marriage rumbled on, Henry's team was gathering scholarly support for an annulment from universities at home and in Europe. In May 1532 a battered rump of Convocation surrendered to the king the Church's powers of legislation; this Submission of the Clergy was the final straw for the chancellor, Sir Thomas More, who resigned. By the early months of 1533 Anne was pregnant, and still nothing had been resolved as regards the divorce. Archbishop Warham had died the August before, and in March Thomas Cranmer was consecrated as his successor. On 23 May, in a court con-vened at Dunstable, Cranmer declared the king's first marriage invalid. In June Anne was crowned, the elaborate festivities surrounding the coronation being masterminded by Cromwell.

Meanwhile in Stepney, Alice Atkyson would have been pleased if no one else was; a few days before the coronation she got a pardon for stealing money and clothes from Nicholas Wilcockes.

In 1534 the succession was settled on Anne's children. A series of statutes eliminated papal authority and made the King Supreme Head of the Church of England. Cromwell was riding high; by early 1533 he had become the king's chief adviser and the following year he was made principal secretary. John Stow, who was a teenager, remembered him as a new Wolsey, keeping great state, fol-lowed always by a retinue of retainers, wearing an embroidered grey livery lined with velvet. Twice a day food and drink was distributed to 200 poor people from his gate.

In the summer of 1534 Cromwell took a fifty-year lease on the Mercers' Great Place with 12 acres, lately Sir John Aleyne's and 6 acres, lately Robert Studley's, and the house and garden that were formerly William Gresham's. All these tenants were members of the Company. The rent was 46s 8d a year, rising to £6 13s 4d after ten years. Cromwell quickly got rid of Stepney's vicar, Miles Wyllen, who was also a canon of Windsor, depriving him for delaying payment of his first year's income into the Exchequer and for covering up seditious words spoken by Christopher Plommer, a fellow canon. Along with Plommer and a number of other priests and monks accused of resistance to the Supremacy, Wyllen was sent to the Tower. From there he sent a petition to Cromwell, explaining that he had entered into a bond for the payment due and declared himself to be a 'true man unto my prince'. He dreaded the coming of winter in that terrible dungeon: 'yf I tarry her this winter I have nother [neither] fewell nor mony to help me withal'. In place of Wyllen, Cromwell appointed Dr Simon Haynes in March 1535, a scholar and a keen reformer, who especially hated the veneration of holy statues: 'the common people ... esteem more virtue in images and adorning of them, kissing their feet or offering candles unto them ... the curates knowing the same and fearing the loss of their offerings, do rather encourage the people to continue after this sort'. Haynes was sent to Europe to try and lure the reformer Melancthon to England, in company with Robert Barnes, a noted evangelical preacher, of whom we shall hear more anon.

In 1535 the king reinforced his position by executing Chancellor Sir Thomas More and John Fisher, Bishop of Rochester, for denying the royal supremacy; both were beheaded on Tower Hill. From the pulpit of churches countrywide proclamations were read out, explaining the implications of the break with Rome; the pope's name was to be erased from all mass books and other devotional books. The great survey of Church incomes, known as the *Valor Ecclesiasticus*, was underway, and Cromwell's visitors were crawling all over the country's religious houses, led by the rector of Stepney, who concocted the articles of interrogation. Rector Layton was said to have had thirty-two brothers and sisters; he had a law degree from Cambridge and was generally feared and loathed. The spitting venom of his reports on the monasteries are the stuff of propagandist revolutionary invective. The 'blake sort of dyvelisshe monks (Benedictines) ... be passed amendment', he wrote. The people of Norfolk were 'more superstitious than virtuous, long accustomed to frantic fantasies and ceremonies ... right far alienate from true religion'. In August 1535 he was gathering up the holy bric-a-brac from Bath Abbey and dispatching it to Stepney: 'I send vincula S Petri [St Peter's chains] which women put about them at the time of their delivery ... I send you also a great comb called St Mary Magdalen's comb and St Dorothy and St Margaret's comb.' In February of the following year he got a 'lewd canon' to surrender his house in York and, with his colleague Legh, swept through the midlands and the north, exposing sexual activity and superstitious practices. At Garadon monastery, near Loughborough, in the Diocese of Lincoln, he reported, there were five named sodomites, one with ten boys; they had the shirt of St Francis for pregnant women and St Guthlac's bell for toothache. At Shelford Priory, near Nottingham, there were three sodomites, three incontinents and three monks anxious to get out of holy orders; they venerated the milk and girdle of Our Lady. The Abbot of Dale, near Derby, had two mistresses, and one of his monks had five women. In Thurgarton Priory, near Mansfield, there were ten sodomites and Prior Dethyck had several women. In Carlisle the monks worshipped the sword with which Thomas Becket was murdered; the prior of Holland in Lincolnshire had seven women and the arm of St Margaret. The rich monastery at Bury St Edmunds was the scene of regular feasting and sexual junketing, and they had Becket's boots! Down in Sussex Layton found corruption of both kinds at Lewes Priory, 'avowsters' (fornicators) and sodomites.

In 1536 the lesser monasteries were closed; the bill was passed in March. Their abbots and priors petitioned Queen Anne in a body, but were dismissed with the rebuke that their dissolute life had brought God's judgement on them. On 19 May, St Dunstan's Day, Anne was beheaded on Tower Green. Among these small houses was the Bow nunnery, St Leonards, only valued at £108 1s 11½d. There had been some trouble of late in the nunnery and the Bishop of London may have attempted some reform. The prioress, Eleanor Starkey, resigned in 1528, but continued to live in the nunnery, and the bishop put in her place Sybil Kirke, Prioress of Kilburn. According to petitions for her removal, presented to the king and to Cromwell, the new prioress was a bully who kept the nuns, especially her elderly predecessor, short of food and drink. Bishop Stokesley had no truck with the complaints, and his chancellor urged Dame Sybil to be firm. Presumably she was, and she continued to draw her 'state pension' for many years after the Dissolution. The nuns' manor of Upper Bromley was sold off to Sir Ralph Sadler, and the Romanesque chapel was used as Bromley parish church.

While in one Stepney Great Place the Church revolution was being brought into effect by Cromwell, the tenant of Stepney's other Great Place, Lord Tom Darcy, now an elderly and sick man, was of a very different mind. Although he had joined in the initial attack on the clerics in the Reformation parliament, and had been in on the initiation of the abolition of the monasteries, he became a vocal opponent of the divorce and a defender of the Old Faith. Henry banned him from attending parliament and he was 'grounded' in Stepney. Darcy may have contemplated joining forces with the emperor to overthrow the government and put a stop to the religious changes; Charles V's ambassador in London reported in 1534 that the old man had been sounding him out about using Princess Mary, Catherine of Aragon's daughter, as a focus for English discontent.

In the autumn of 1536 a widespread revolt against the closure of the monasteries, known to history as the Pilgrimage of Grace, posed a real threat to the monarchy. Robert Aske raised a force of between 30,000 and 40,000 men in the north; like Darcy's archers in his campaign against the Spanish Moors, years before, they marched under the banner of the Five Wounds of Jesus. The Archbishop of York and local gentry were forced to take refuge in Pontefract Castle, and Darcy opened the gates of the castle to the rebel force. He pleaded necessity and was pardoned in consideration of his suppression of Sir Francis Bigod's rebellion in Beverley, only to be rearrested on treason charges and beheaded the following June, together with Sir John Neville, a Stepney neighbour.

With Simon Haynes gone off to sweep Exeter Cathedral clean of images (where he was 'marvelous hated and maligned at'), in 1537 William Jerome became vicar of Stepney. A former monk from the Cathedral Priory in Canterbury, he was a firm Lutheran and a well-known preacher.

In the summer of 1538 John Harrydance, a Whitechapel bricklayer and hot gospeller, gained some notoriety by preaching twenty-two sermons, each of two hours' duration, among other things ordering the absentee rector, William Longford, to reside in the parish. He was cursed from the pulpit by the curate. In September Cromwell issued his second set of royal injunctions for Church reform. A copy of the Great Bible (in English) was to be kept in every church for the instruction of the people and the checking of superstition. Sermons were henceforth to urge works of charity and faith rather than 'works devised by men's phantasies … as in wandering to pilgrimages, offering of money, candles or tapers to images or relics, or kissing or licking the same, saying over a number of beads'. Statues were to be removed and the number of candles restricted. The populace at large were perhaps most alarmed at the order issued for the keeping of registers of baptisms, marriages and burials, fearing that it heralded the imposition of a tax on these rites.

During 1538 and 1539 the great monasteries were closed down. St Mary Graces, one of the wealthiest monasteries in the country, worth £547 0s 6½d (half the value of the whole bishopric of London), was surrendered by Abbot Henry More in September 1538 and the ten monks pensioned off. Abbot More had recently been involved in the reform of various Essex monasteries and had been granted the abbey at Coggeshall *in commendam*, in 1536, after the incumbent abbot had accused Cromwell of being 'the maintainer of all heretics'. More got a good pension when the two houses were closed down: 100 marks a year for both Tower Hill and Coggeshall. In March 1545 he was also given the vicarage of Stepney where, in spite of his acclaimed zeal in deposing 'the old unthrifty abbot' of Tiltey, he would, as we shall see, stick to his papist guns and fight his parishioners for the maintenance of the Old Faith. The abbey buildings on Tower Hill were converted into a victualling house for the navy; ironically Sir Arthur Darcy, old Tom's youngest son, fitted it out with ovens to bake ships' biscuits.

Sir Thomas Gresham, realising the value of the work done by the Tower Hill monks among the 'impotent poor', had petitioned in vain for this abbey and the hospital of St Mary outside Bishopsgate to be handed over to the City. The hospital was worth £504 12s 11½d and had 180 beds for poor Londoners who could not afford a 'nurse keeper' at home. The king allowed the patients to stay put (presumably until they died or were discharged), but the priory was dissolved and its buildings converted into what Stow described as a 'fair house for the receipt and lodging of worshipful persons'. Its lands were disposed of, including some in Stepney Marsh.

Ironically, St Katharine's, which enjoyed the patronage of the Queen of England (whoever she might be in these dangerous times), survived. Some say it was because of intervention by Anne Boleyn, but more likely it was Jane Seymour who saved the hospital; the king not only spared this house but in 1537 remitted the annual tenth, and the first fruits due from Gilbert Latham, who had been appointed master by Queen Jane. The income of the house in 1535 was said to be £315 8s 4d; there were three brothers and three sisters, three priests, six clerks, ten bedeswomen, six children, with a master in charge of them, a steward, butler, cook and undercook. After Henry VIII's death Katharine Parr's second husband was appointed master and their work carried on.

Bedlam survived too, with its 'religious arm' removed. The priory itself was abolished and the hospital operation, with all its income, given over to the City as a lunatic asylum. The Minories nunnery, so favoured by the king's mother, was rather surprisingly not saved, although Elizabeth Salvage, the abbess, got a good deal (a pension of £40 a year) as did her nuns. The house, worth £318 8s 5d, was surrendered in March 1539 and its twenty-four nuns and six lay sisters turned out.

The grabbing of monastic land went on a pace here as everywhere in the country. Thomas Stepkyn, a brewer, bought part of Shadwell manor. The Dethick family acquired the abbey's manor of Poplar with its dairyhouse, gatehouse, barns and grain store, dovehouse, gardens and fisheries. The Mercers' Company bought the Wapping brewery and 6 acres of marsh by the Compass Ditch (where the Prospect of Whitby now stands), which had belonged to the monastery of St Thomas Acon, for the huge sum of £1,100. Stepney church bought four bells from the priory of Holy Trinity at Aldgate, according to Stow. Meanwhile, up at Shoreditch, two theatres sprang up on the site of Holywell Priory, but that is another story.

Returning to the events of 1539, with monks and nuns turned out of doors and the whole Church under threat, the papist powers of France and the empire were threatening to take action against 'the most cruel and abominable tyrant'. A show of military splendour and might was put on. On a fine May morning in 1539 a body of 15,000 militia men assembled on Mile End Green, a good number of Cromwell's men among them. With harnesses, coats of cloth of gold and white silk and gold chains gleaming in the sunlight, they marched along Whitechapel, through Aldgate, along Holborn to Westminster and back again.

There followed, that June, a sudden about-turn in government policy, a halt to the advance of Lutheranism, which was probably a panic attempt to draw the teeth of the Catholic threat from abroad. Parliament, pushed by the king, passed the Act of Six Articles, which reaffirmed the doctrine of purgatory, vetoed clerical marriage and made mandatory the burning of heretics who denied the doctrine of transubstantiation. 'Our king,' commented the reformer Dr Robert Barnes, 'holds religion and the Gospel in no regard.'

Next came a greater disaster for the reformers: the new queen. In January 1540 the king, single since the death of Jane Seymour in October 1537, married the

Princess of Cleves, Cromwell's Lutheran candidate for the royal bed. Henry's disappointment with this unattractive girl was almost certainly the occasion of the vicar general's sudden fall from grace. Cromwell's enemies were everywhere, headed by the powerful Duke of Norfolk and the conservative bishops, led by Stephen Gardiner of Winchester. Unable even to make love to his 'Flanders Mare', Henry was only too eager to believe the calumnies whispered about the man who had procured her. Arguably, if Ann had been a pretty filly, Cromwell might have continued in power and Jerome, the vicar of Stepney, would not have been consigned to a Smithfield bonfire.

At three o'clock on Saturday 10 June 1540 the vicar general was arrested at the council table, taken to the Tower and attainted for various offences; for denying the real presence, and openly declaring support for the Lutheran dogma and for the teaching of Dr Barnes. He went to the scaffold on 28 July, speaking, at the last, of his lowly origins and protesting his innocence of heresy. Meeting Lord Hungerford on the way down Tower Hill, also destined for the block, he told him to be of good cheer: 'Though the breakfast which we are going to be sharp, yet, trusting to the mercy of the Lord, we shall have a joyful dinner.'

With Cromwell went William Jerome, his vicar at Stepney, Robert Barnes, who had helped negotiate the Cleves marriage, and preacher Thomas Garret, a protégé of the radical Bishop Latimer. All three had been in trouble with Bishop Gardiner for their open attacks on the Act of Six Articles; Jerome had preached a thunderous Lent sermon from St Paul's Cross, the cathedral's outside pulpit, calling the burgesses of parliament 'butterflies, fools and knaves'. The text of his sermon survives, with angry notes scribbled on it by Gardiner. All three had preached inflammatory Easter sermons from the open air pulpit at Spital Cross, on the dissolved hospital site, and were immediately sent to the Tower where they languished for nearly four months.

Two days after Cromwell's death, and the king's fifth wedding day, the vicar of Stepney, with his two fellow Lutherans, were taken out from prison and dragged on hurdles to Smithfield, attainted for being Anabaptists (extreme evangelicals). The three martyrs took each others' hands, kissed one another and 'quietly and humbly offered themselves to the hands of the tormentors'. So moved were the crowd watching that one observer said that if someone had taken the lead there would have been a riot.

On the same day three other priests, who had been in custody for over a decade, were hanged, drawn and quartered for denying the Supremacy and opposing the king's divorce. 'Which spectacle,' commented the martyrologist, Richard Foxe, 'brought the people into a marvellous admiration and doubt of their religion, which part to follow and take; as might so well happen amongst ignorant and simple people, seeing two contrary parts so suffer, the one for popery, the other against popery, both at one time.' A London pamphleteer reckoned that the three martyrs had gone to their death because of their social teaching: 'Well, the poor well feeleth the burning of Dr Barnes and his fellows ... they barked upon you to look upon the poor.' They had looked to a new Commonwealth with the wealth of the monasteries divided among the poor, teaching that smacked of Anabaptist ideas of communism. Their deaths were part of a purge on heresy; according to Hall's *Chronicle* 500 Londoners were arrested in a fortnight that fateful July.

The slow erosion of the old order went on, halted from time to time by conservative measures. Meanwhile there were still Cromwells in Stepney. Thomas Cromwell's nephew, Sir Richard Cromwell, a wordly courtier, probably of a reformist inclination lived there in some style; he had the farm of the rectory and Stepney property in right of his wife, Frances Murphyn, as well as extensive estates in other parts of the country. Richard was the son of Morgan Williams and Thomas Cromwell's sister, and had changed his name when he entered his uncle's service in October 1530. At his death in 1545 there was a very grand sale of his Stepney effects. Sir Edward North, one of Richard's executors, Chancellor of the Court of Augmentations, bought a quantity of stuff, doublets of red and white satin and of quilted satin, white velvet breeches, a crimson velvet jacket, a girdle encrusted with seventy-two pearls, three masks, a crossbow, hangings embroidered with water lilies, a patchwork quilt with a fountain on it, a purple velvet chair embroidered with the Cromwell coat of arms, three studded velvet collars worn by the Cromwell greyhounds, a great carved four-poster, carpets and kitchen equipment, linen and three pewter chamberpots. Lord and Lady Dennys bought clothes and jewellery to the value of £124 3s 4d: emerald and pearl brooches, a gold girdle encrusted with pearls, cameos galore, and any number of pearl buttons. William Burrell, of the great shipbuilding family, who we shall meet anon, bought table cloths, napkins, some pewterware, curtains and coverlets, one of 'olde imagery' (out-of-date design). He also bought forty 'morris pikes', which had been in the parsonage house. One of the Darcys bought a jewel with a great emerald, a ruby and a pearl hanging from it, worth £6. In the barns and outhouses were three wagons, twelve carthorses and thirteen other horses. The hay in the barn was bought by Lady Margaret Douglas, the king's niece no less, daughter of Margaret, Queen of Scots. She and her husband Matthew, Earl of Lennox, must have been near neighbours in Stepney. Lennox, second in line to the Scottish throne and leader of the English party, had just come to court to plan an invasion of the Highlands with Henry VIII and to marry Lady Douglas. Their first-born child, Henry Stuart, Lord Darnley, died in Stepney aged nine months in 1545, and was buried in the church.

Gabriel Donne, rector of Stepney, bought some furniture, curtains, bedding and pots and pans in the house sale. An Oxford-educated man, he had been a monk at the Cistercian house at Stratford Langthorne, and organised the arrest of

William Tyndale at Antwerp in 1535. He seems to have been taken up by Thomas Cromwell who made him Abbot of Buckfastleigh in Devon, where he alienated much of the monastic property. He did very well out of the Dissolution, getting a generous pension of £120 a year and acquiring a lucrative prebend at St Paul's as well as Stepney rectory, worth £50 a year. He was a close friend of Richard Cromwell's and was put in charge of the education of his younger son, Francis, who was the heir of the Stepney estates. In spite of his role in the arrest of Tyndale, he must have thrown his lot in with the reformers, as Cranmer put him in temporary charge of the London diocese when Bishop Edmund Bonner was imprisoned for opposing Protestant measures in 1549.

All was turbulence and confusion in these years, with one local lord executed for being a Protestant and one for his allegiance to the Old Faith, a Protestant vicar consigned to the flames, a popish vicar (Abbot More from Tower Hill) put in by a Protestant patron, a reformist archbishop in Cranmer and a traditionalist bishop and lord of the manor in Edmund Bonner. How did it stand with Our Lady and the rest of the cast of saints? Exactly which candles could be lit in church?

As the old monster king, racked with pain and savage to the last, drew near to death, most of the East End was on course for a Protestant alignment. Here the Flemish and Dutch reformist influence was probably stronger here than anywhere else in the country. Traditional preacher Roger Edgworth said that in the port of Bristol 'the Germans and Saxons bring in their opinions'. In Stepney, likewise, there were German sailors and 'Dochemen' in abundance, and a strong reformist core of the manufacturing and merchant classes, families like the Ivies, Marches and Poyntells, underpinned by a increasing number of poor landless folk. This large population of newcomers, getting work onboard ship, with anchorsmiths or ropemakers, or in the myriad trades and industries that served the City, were more receptive to the revolutionary ideas than conservative peasants.

Whatever the religious temper of Stepney's vicar, the curates led their flock along a middle path, steering between the old faith and the new, assisted by the popular constable and churchwarden, baker Thomas Poyntell, and the parish clerk, Thomas Nosterfilde. Curate John Crosse was particularly assiduous in his attendance at death beds, advising on the disposition of parishioners' money and belongings, and even writing out some of the wills in his own hand. The wills drawn by him are all much of a pattern: wives are executrixes, the 'whole distribution' being assigned to them at the beginning of each document. The dedication of the soul is to God and the Virgin and there is usually no mortuary or mass prescribed for the soul of the departed. The king's final word on things doctrinal, the 'King's Book' of 1543, forbade the use of the word purgatory. As someone had remarked, 'purgatorie was piss'd oute'.

'The old faith taken clene awaie': a Limehouse Gospeller and a stout popish prelate

When Henry expired in January 1547 all was set fair for a Church revolution proper; there would be no more trimming or hedging. The Protestant faction at court took over, led by Edward Seymour, Duke of Somerset, the uncle of the child king, Edward VI. Stepney's vicar More, and traditionalists countrywide, must have been shaking in their shoes.

Churchwardens' accounts and Exchequer records chart events at Aldgate, and Limehouse gospeller Edward Underhill has left us an account of what happened in Stepney. Both parishes, like many in London and the south-east, were a battleground between clergy and reformist leaders. Revisionist historians of the Reformation have of late made much of popular opposition to the reforms in the countryside, but in the East End, with the exception of Bow, it was with undoubted glee that the parishioners fell upon the treasures horded in their churches and attacked what a local gospeller called their 'old mumsymnissis', ignorant old conservative priests. They were not alone: at St Matthew Friday Street, St Benet Gracechurch Street, St Laurence Poultney, St Mary Magdalene Milk Street, St Martin Ludgate and St Martin Outwich they started pulling down altars 'long afore' the orders came so to do.

During the six and half years of Edward VI's reign the world was turned upside down. No longer did tonsured priests, bearded and celibate, dressed in embroidered robes, perform the mystic magic of the mass, cut off from the congregation by a screen, murmuring to themselves and their fellow officiants in a strange, obsolete, foreign tongue 'which the people understood not'. Dressed in a plain surplice, they served their parishioners from an ordinary table standing lengthways in the body of the church, and the ancient ritual wherein bread and wine was changed into the very flesh and blood of God became a commemorative act. They paid 10s for their holy table at St Botolph's. Priests could marry, and many did with alacrity; by the time Mary came to the throne there were about 200 married clergy in the Diocese of London alone.

A royal visitation of the Church began in August. Its injunctions stipulated no more processions at the beginning of the mass, no bells in the service (just one before the sermon), no elevation, no sharing of the holy loaf. The holy loaf rota was replaced by a levy to pay for the bread and wine at communion; in Stepney, and elsewhere this was known as Pascal Pence, a penny paid at Easter. There was to be no more recitation of the rosary and the only candles permitted were those on the high altar. All churches were to have a locked poor box, and priests were to enjoin their parishioners to leave money for that on their death-bed instead of ornaments.

Towards Christmas 1547 a proclamation ordered that communion in both kinds was to be administered to the people; henceforth the congregation, as well as the priests, were to be given wine as well as bread. Edmund Bonner, Bishop of London, was put into the Fleet prison for opposing the royal visitation. Orders for the king's visitors to destroy images that attracted idolatrous worship was an excuse for the smashing of stained glass windows and roods, the giant tableaux of the crucifixion that were the focus of worship. On 16 November the attack was launched on St Paul's, a stronghold of the old faith; statues and pictures were taken 'clene awaie'. As the workmen took down the towering cross from the rood loft it toppled and fell on top of some onlookers, injuring several and killing one. The 'papish priests' opined that it was the will of God. At St Botolph's they got 1s for the 'reffuse wood of the Roode loft'. Edward Underhill took it upon himself to remove the pyx (the box for the host) from the altar in Bow chapel, from under the curate's very nose, thereby arousing the fury of the conservative locals. Mistress Tawe, the wife of a local papist justice, led the women of Bow in a conspiracy to have Underhill murdered, but he was saved by a 'Godly' woman who warned him of the plot.

Next came the blow that must have hit the churches hardest: the abolition of the chantries. Churches and cathedrals were stripped of the considerable incomes that had been granted to them over the years for prayers for the dead, and the whole business was proclaimed to be a nonsense: 'superstition and errors … vain opinions of purgatory'. For the generality, perhaps, it was welcome; Londoners, the more wealthy ones at least, had recently ceased to endow chantries. Around the chilly lanes in December 1547 the parish beadles went, announcing the sale of Church property and the abolition of religious gilds and chantries. In March 1548 the king's commissioners were sent out to survey all colleges, free chapels and chantries. Only one chantry and one chantry priest is referred to in Stepney's chantry certificate, the report made to the Exchequer. It is of a tenement in Forby Street, Limehouse, enfeoffed by Thomas Brett for prayers for the souls of Dennys Rewlyn and her husband, benefactors. In 1547 the house was let to a fisherman called John Phellipes, a friend of the Dryvers; he paid St Dunstan's 33s 4d a year for it, to pay a priest to say masses. Some sort of 'right to buy' seems to have been in operation, and Phellipes bought the house from the Crown for £25, fifteen years' purchase.

St Dunstan's was remarkable in having only one chantry endowment, and there was little for the king to seize in Whitechapel, although there were far fewer chantries in London than in other parts of the country. While the Church only lost an income of 33s 4d a year from Stepney's single chantry, Bow chapel had twelve items on its list: tenements, pieces of land and quit rents, in the parishes of Stepney and West Ham, which brought it in £13 6s 8d a year, used for the main- tenance of the curate (£8) and the repair of roads. The locals appealed against the confiscation of their income and 'Payd for a learned counsell, at suche tyme as the Kyng's commissioners demaunded our lands, whyche we thought had been without the compas of the statute … All the olde Latin boks were caryed to the chancellor of the Bishop of Westminster, according to the statute.' In Aldgate Alexander Sprot's Crown brewery, left to St Botolph's in 1438, fetched £114.

Cranmer's 1548 visitation articles included instructions for sacred images to be rooted out of private houses, for all stained glass images, statues and pictures in their church destroyed, and that rosaries were not used. Curates left in charge of benefices were not to be 'rude and unlearned' and all clergy without a degree were to be provided with a copy of Erasmus's *Paraphrase of the New Testament.* St Botolph's paid 10s for theirs.

At Aldgate a vigorous vestry, strong in their evangelical convictions, took matters into their own hands, conducting a major battle with their farmer and 'dedde soule priest', William Grene, who, they claimed, could neither preach nor teach. Their leaders were merchants and manufacturers, brewers, smiths, founders, tanners, vintners, tailors and the like, led by the Owens, of the great gunfounding family with a works in Houndsditch and another gunsmith Richard Martyn. Four old Latin service books, which the people 'understood not', were sold for 18s in November 1548; by December the new poor box was installed and gravestones, statues and the small bells sold. The chapels were whitewashed and a petition sent to the government to get rid of Grene. In July 1548 they bought psalm books in English, but curate Rofford refused to conduct the service in English, and he and Grene had churchwarden, Robert Owen, the gunfounder, arrested. The vestry bailed him out and appealed to the lord mayor, who removed the offending curate and replaced him with a man of their choice, William Dobbes. In May 1550 they sold the organ.

The reforms were welcomed, too, by the 'Godly men' of Stepney, led by the evangelical coterie at its heart, the churchwardens and chief men of the parish. The most prominent among them were Thomas Ivy of Limehouse, shipowner and anchorsmith, 'ernest in the Gospel' according to Underhill, later high constable and a churchwarden, Richard Dryver, the limeman, Thomas Poyntell, the baker (both churchwardens) and John Marche, Dryver's stepson, who was in the family lime business. Other gospellers who served as wardens were John Dove, Thomas Esterfeld and Richard Thompson.

Evangelical preachers and lecturers were brought by the lay leaders to preach in the church, much to the fury of vicar More. The old monk rang the bell during these sermons and hectored the unfortunate man in the pulpit from the body of the church. No one dared stop him, until Edward Underhill, a close friend of Ivy's and his next door neighbour, took things in hand. Underhill was a gentleman, a soldier and courtier. He moved in elevated circles, had served under Richard Cromwell, had gone to Boulogne with Henry VIII, was a gentleman pensioner; Lady Jane Gray was godmother to one of his children. According to his own account, Stepney's 'Godly' 'durst nott medelle with hym [the vicar] untylle it was my happe to cume dwelle amongst them; and that I was the kyng's servauntt'. Underhill even abducted the elderly abbot and took him off to the archbishop at his Croydon Palace and demanded that Cranmer 'unvicker' him. When the archbishop simply administered a mild rebuke, the gospeller was outraged: 'My Lord, methinks you are too gentle unto so stout a Papist.'

All over London there was a wholesale purge of images, and popish paraphernalia was sold off. St Botolph's had a vast collection of fabulously costly ecclesiastical garb accumulated over the years, much of it given by the rich local bellfounders and brewers. Between 1548 and 1551, together with all other 'Popish trappings', these garments were sold off in the church jumble sale to end all jumble sales. They were good times for the local rag trade. The profits were used for repair of the building and any surplus for the building of houses for the maintenance of the church. The royal commission that investigated what was left led to the final seizure of church goods in 1552–53. The list sent into the Exchequer records sales made between 1547 and 1551 and contains pages and pages, itemising priceless ecclesiastical bric-a-brac, of silver and silver gilt, and vestments galore. A local tailor paid 41s for three copes with lions and flowers, given to the church by a bellfounder about a hundred years before. A 'broiderer' of St Lawrence Jewry bought some embroidered items, including a red altar cloth with bells and flowers on it. Giles Harrysone, brewer, bought a blue velvet cope for 23s 4d; there was a blue velvet vestment embroidered with St James's cockleshells, nine white damask vestments with 'Jesus of Nazareth' on them, copes of crimson and purple velvet with golden flowers, copes of red silk and red and black velvet. Thomas Cordye, a bowyer, paid 6s 8d for a green damask vestment given by bellfounder Richard Hill. A Portuguese bought various items, including a white damask vestment given by a curate at the beginning of the century. Anthony Anthony paid £25 5s 9½d for a silver gilt cross and censer and £4 5s 6d for a blue velvet vestment and other items. Two massive silver candlesticks fetched £35 5s. John Owen the elder, gunsmith, bought a blue altar cloth and one with gold birds on it. The mass books, the chalices and a silver cross brought the church £15 17s 9d, enough to buy a house or two. The pyx and the pax (the tablet with the crucifixion on, which was kissed) went; the organ made 2s, and even some of the tombstones were sold, along with bowls, chalices, basins, censers and candlesticks of gold, silver gilt and silver. All non-essential linen was given to Christ's Hospital, the new charity school that now occupied the old Greyfriars Monastery.

No such detailed account survives for the other churches. At Stepney the Dryver family probably bought the silver gilt chalice weighing 2½lb, left to the church by vicar Walter Stone. When Elizabeth Dryver, widow of Richard the limeman, died in 1578, she left her 'standing cup commonly called the Comunyon cupp' to her son, Justinian.

In October 1549 Bonner was deprived of his bishopric and put in the Marshalsea prison where he stayed until 1553, leaving Gabriel Donne as caretaker of the diocese until it was given to Nicholas Ridley. With Ridley's appointment came a major transfer of East End property. On the day of his enthronement, the twelfth day of Christmas 1550, Ridley handed over to the king the vast episcopal manors of Stepney, Hackney and Stepney Marsh; he was well compensated with estates in other parts of the country. The old bishop's palace at Bethnal Green, meanwhile, had been leased, three years previously, to Sir Ralph Warren, protégé of Thomas Cromwell's, a Master of the Mercers' Company and former lord mayor. He paid 4d a year for it.

Within a few months Edward VI gave to his lord chamberlain, Sir Thomas Wentworth, for services rendered, the Manor of Stepney with all its appurtenances: Shoreditch, Holywell Street, Cleve Street, Brook Street, Whitechapel, Poplar, North Street, Stratford atte Bow, Ratcliff, Limehouse, Mile End, Bethnal Green, Old Ford, and all of Hackney besides. The bishop's 900-year rule in Stepney was at an end and that of the Wentworths had begun; it would last for 170 years, remembered today only in Wentworth Street. Henceforth the locals would pay their dues to a lay lord who would also appoint the rectors of their parish church. Stepney's first Sir Thomas was a significant member of Edward's government and, whether from conviction or convenience, a supporter of Church reform. Miles Coverdale preached at his funeral in March 1551.

While Dr Ridley started his examination of every parson and curate in his diocese there was a blitz on prostitutes and scolds; in Bishopsgate a Jewish physician from Portugal was banished for whoring. By the autumn of 1551 there was talk of the 'great abuses' of the Duke of Somerset, the lord protector of the realm. Early in the morning the following January he was taken to Tower Hill to be beheaded, escorted by the royal guard and a great body of militia men from 'the Towre, [Ratcliffe,] Lymhowsse, Whyt-chapell, Sant Kateryn, and Strettford [Bow], as Hogston [Hoxton] and Sordyche'. Just before the axe-man struck his blow, reported one chronicler, there was a strange rumbling noise like gunfire or 'grett horsys commyng'. The crowd panicked: some tumbled down into the Tower moat; others rushed away in terror, falling over one another as they went. It was probably only part of the scaffold collapsing, and the execution proceeded. The great duke 'tooke his death very patiently'. The Duke of Northumberland was now protector of the realm.

These were tense and anxious times, and chroniclers noted signs, portents and strange events. At Blackwall six dolphins were sighted; the smallest was the size of a small horse. In April a gunpowder factory blew up in Hog Lane; at Whitsun it rained blood.

Bloody Bonner rides

When the young king died in July 1553 all was in turmoil and London was on the alert. The gates were watched and aldermen were on the prowl. The Protestant claimant to the throne, little Jane Grey, Northumberland's candidate and daughter-in-law, was proclaimed queen on 10 July. Bishop Ridley preached from St Paul's Cross, whipping up the mob in her support, and declaring the dead king's sisters, Mary and Elizabeth, both bastards. He was met with stony silence. Then all was change and change about, and news came of a rising in Norfolk in support of the Catholic Mary. Before you could say 'God save the Queen' there was the lord mayor riding into a packed Cheapside with heralds to announce the accession of another queen. The trumpets blared and everyone threw up their caps: 'God save Queen Mary'. Alarm and confusion reigned. Little Jane and her husband were dispatched, but in the eastern suburbs the headlines were stolen from these momentous events by tales of the enormous size of the bladderstones of old Ralph Warren. The Mercer and former lord mayor had died in his Bethnal Green mansion (formerly the bishop's palace) at this most critical moment in English history.

At the beginning of August Mary left the manor of Wanstead and, with a procession 1,000 strong, started the journey west to take charge of her capital. Along the Mile End Road came heralds and horsemen, trumpeters, knights and ladies, clattering to a halt just outside the City at Whitechapel, where the queen went into the house of Mr Bramstone, the 'millionaire' brick manufacturer, to change her clothes. She emerged, to be welcomed by the lord mayor, with all a true Tudor's flair. Her gown was cut in the French fashion and was of purple velvet with a purple satin over skirt 'thick set with goldsmith's work' and 'great pearl'. The sleeves glittered with precious stones and she wore a heavily jewelled collar. The crowds at Aldgate Bars pressed close to hear her speak: 'My Lord Mayor, I hartely thanke you and all your brethren the aldermen, of your gentleness shewed unto me, which shall not be forgotten.'

When they came to St Botolph's, the children of Christ's Hospital were there to welcome the queen. The charity school, founded by Edward VI on the site of the Greyfriars' monastery, was one of the showpieces of the Protestant revolution. To Catholic Mary they were a sore reminder of the crimes committed against her faith. A boy addressed her in Latin, but she turned away because, wrote the treasurer of the school, 'she did not like of the blew boys'. The procession narrowed down to file through the gateway as the cannon from the Tower roared its welcome to the new monarch. The houses along the way had silks and tapestries hanging from the windows, and there were stages with musicians playing on them. Down Mark Lane they went, three abreast. The crowd sobbed with tears of joy: 'God save her Grace'.

And so began the five-year struggle to restore the Old Faith in England. On the night of 4 August at 10 p.m. in Limehouse, Thomas Ivy, now High Constable, knocked anxiously on the door of his friend and next-door neighbour Edward Underhill, to tell him that the sheriff and a company of pikemen were on their way with a warrant for his arrest for publishing an anti-popish ballad. Ivy begged the sheriff to stay outside for fear of upsetting Mistress Underhill, who had just given birth. Underhill was arrested and taken to the Tower, and thence to Newgate, from where he wrote home to his wife asking for his lute, nightgown and Bible. He was let out after a month, so weak that he had to be carried on a horse litter home to Limehouse, but was forced out of the parish by vicar More and his supporters, led by papist John Banbury, a 'shifter, a dycer, a hore-hunter'. A Whitechapel bricklayer bricked up Underhill's books for him, and he fled to the anonymity of the crowded City.

Edmund Bonner was restored to his see of London, and he and the other traditionalist bishops were 'set lose to worry the poor flock'. The winter of 1553–54 was a hard one; soon after Christmas London apprentice boys pelted with snowballs the grand Spanish retinue, harbingers of Philip II, soon to come to England to marry the queen.

With the coming of spring the purge of clergy began in earnest: 200 clerics were thrown out in the diocese of London alone, mostly for being married. Of these, the majority separated from their wives, did the required penance and were put into another living. John Thomas, the new vicar of Stepney (More had died) was a Protestant and may have been married at this time; if he was he kept quiet about it, and stayed in post. In Whitechapel the zealous reforming rector George Mason resigned and was replaced by a priest from Kent called Yaxley.

On Wednesday 25 July 1554 the queen married Philip of Spain, the royal nuptials being celebrated at Winchester Cathedral. Edward Underhill, rather surprisingly, attended the feast, in his role of gentleman at arms, and made off with an outsized venison pie. He had managed to stay at court, in spite of various attempts to oust him from his position, declaring that court was a good place to 'shift the Easter time', i.e. avoid receiving communion. Bells rang out from London's steeples on 18 August as the newly-weds processed over London Bridge and entered the City, welcomed by the giant figures of Corineus and Gog Magog.

Now the wholesale execution of Protestants started, and terrible human bonfires sent up their smoke from Smithfield and from Stratford Bow. Between February 1555 and November 1558 300 heretics were executed and many others died in prison; 85 per cent of the victims were from the south-east; most of them were Londoners, many East Enders among them. Heresy was rife in Essex, hence the siting of a major place of execution at Stratford Bow. Nearly all of the martyrs were artisans (the gentry took flight); the very first was a Shoreditch weaver, Thomas Tomkins. 'Bloody Bonner', the Bishop of London, the man responsible for the death of numbers of heretics in his diocese, earned the enduring hatred of East Enders and many others besides. In later years a tale grew up that his ghost rode in a coach around Bethnal Green, drawn by a team of black horses, a harbinger of imminent death to anyone who saw it. According to guides who take you round Victoria Park and its environs, the ghost rides still.

One of the first martyrs was the saintly Rowland Taylor, vicar of Hadleigh in Suffolk. On a January day in 1555 he was brought out of the City by the sheriff of London to overnight at the Woolpack outside Aldgate, on his way to be burnt at Aldham Common. His wife Margaret, William Tyndale's niece, kept watch all night in St Botolph's with her children. In the early hours of the morning, while it was still dark, the company set off. 'O my dear father!', called out little Elizabeth, his adopted daughter, 'Mother, mother, here is my father led away.' The martyr took his own little Mary in his arms and they all knelt down and prayed together. When he arrived at the place of execution he introduced his young son to the mob gathered there: 'Good people, this is mine own son, begotten in lawful matrimony; and God be blessed for lawful matrimony.'

Cranmer was executed and Cardinal Pole was made archbishop; he was also the queen's chief adviser. In the sodden autumn of that year, when weeks of torrential rain saw Stepney's hamlets flooded out, the Bishop of London, Nicholas Ridley, was burnt alive. The following June, 1556, the East End was the scene of one of the most horrific events of the Maryan persecutions, when eleven men and two women, all ordinary, humble folk, all but three from Essex, were brought from Newgate in three carts to 'the end of the towne of Stratford the Bowe' to be tied together in a circle and burnt. Twenty thousand people watched the spectacle. By the following summer Bonner was so nervous of tumults that he suggested clandestine burnings in the early hours of the morning.

Meanwhile all the trappings of the Old Faith were being brought back into church buildings. St Botolph's Aldgate had fallen into 'great ruin and decay' and major repairs were put in hand. The Protestant gunsmith Robert Owen contributed £20! Pews, stairs and vestry were repaired and new pews were put into the choir, where Sir Arthur Darcy and his wife sat. They laid out £60 for a new rood loft, and 2d to have it brought over from Cripplegate, 20s for three new altar stones, 1d for incense. Four loads of lime were bought from John Marche, the limeman of Limehouse, loads of sand and gravel were supplied by John Collyns of Whitechapel and 500 bricks by Mr Bramstone, who had accommodated the queen at her entry into the City. A new sepulchre was built in front of the high altar, curtains put round it and four stave torches placed around it. Anthony Anthony gave back the blue velvet vestments that he had bought for £4 5s 6d in the 'jumble sale'. Thomas Deven gave back the rood cloth. Brand new statues of the Virgin, St John and St Botolph were procured at a cost of £8 2s. Inexpensive pewter and latten vessels were bought to replace the silver and silver gilt plate that had been sold off. A new high altar and a new curtained sepulchre were installed and the side altars and the tabernacle put back. They traded in their old chalice for a heavier one at a Cheapside goldsmith.

No doubt there were some who welcomed back the gaiety of the Old Faith: streamers on Holy Thursday, processions with candles around the parish on St Nicholas's night, holly and ivy at Christmas. But, as we have seen, the lay leaders at Stepney and Aldgate were predominantly reformist. With the smell of charred flesh in the air, they and their fellows lay low, and many clergy went through Catholic motions, even if they found them abhorrent. The vicar of Stepney, John Thomas, seems to have been one such. As Mary's reign progresses the wills he drew for his parishioners became increasingly Catholic in tone, stipulating burial 'according to the catholyk order nowe used' or 'as the holy Catholyck Churche hathe appointed for the health of my soul'. Robert Collop, who died in January 1558, asks for mass and dirige (a special service for the dead) for his soul.

A covert reformist group met at various venues in Stepney, Aldgate and on the east side of the City, led by a series of ministers: Master Scamler, Thomas Foule, Master Rough, the Augustinian Berher and finally Thomas Bentham, later Bishop of Coventry and Lichfield. At Mistress Warner's tavern in Ratcliff, the King's Head, about twenty men, French, Dutch and young English merchants, who called each other 'brother', gathered in the back room at seven or nine o'clock in the morning on Sundays and holy days and stayed until early afternoon. There were two services, taken from the second Edwardian Prayer Book, with a meal eaten in front of the fire in between, consisting of bread, roasted pig and faggots, washed down with several pints of beer. There were readings and sermons, and the Nunc Dimittis and Magnificat were read in English. Two deacons collected money, most people contributing about 2*d*, which was given to the poor. The landlady, when examined by Bonner, claimed to know nothing of what was going on in her back room. Sometimes the secret church met in the house of a man appropriately called Church, by the riverside at Wapping, sometimes in the Swan at Limehouse and occasionally on board a ship, the *Jesus*, riding on the river between Ratcliff and Rotherhithe. There were occasional meetings in Billingsgate, at Aldgate, Blackfriars and Horsleydown.

As Mary's reign of terror drew to its close her unhappy people were restive, angry and fearful. Some were brave enough to make a public stand: in 1557 a satirical play attacking the establishment, *A Sackful of News*, was performed in an Aldgate tavern.

At the end of the following year the bitter, childless queen went to meet her maker.

The Elizabethan East End: a brave new world

Mary's Protestant sister, the Lady Elizabeth, was proclaimed queen and defender of the faith on 17 November 1558; the 'Great Landlady', as playwright Thomas Dekker called her, was to guide the church along a 'middle way', steer her realm into glory and her East End sailors towards gold. In many hearts the Virgin Queen took the place of the Virgin Mary.

A new Act of Uniformity was passed. Clergy who refused to take the oath of supremacy were deprived and royal injunctions ordered churches to 'take away and utterly destroy all shrines, covering of all shrines, all tables, all candlesticks, trindals, and rolls of war, pictures, paintings, and all other monuments of feigned miracles, pilgrimages, idolatry and superstition, so that there remain no memory of the same in walls and glass windows'. At St Botolph's, Aldgate, all the popish ornamentations bought in Mary's reign was disposed of: the sepulchre, the altar stones, the painted cloths; all the latten, pewter and brass sold for a mere 27s 1d. An odd job man was paid 16d to take down the rood and get rid of the statues. John Owen the gunsmith paid 16d for 'old gere'. The altar was replaced by a communion table, which cost 10s. The provision of plain surplices (and repair of the old ones) cost only 20d – how different from the enormous sums spent on pre-Reformation copes and chasubles. With much ceremonial linen disposed of, the years' washing bill was reduced from 10s to 6s 8d.

At Stepney church the elderly vicar, John Thomas, took a new young and rich wife, the daughter of a Hoxton 'moneyer', and lived openly as a married man; the children, which he continued to bear into his old age, were seen running around in the orchard. The organs at Whitechapel, Stepney and St Botolph's were disposed of, following instructions that there should be no more 'curious singing and playing of the organs'.

There were many who could not come to terms with the Church settlement, and regarded the new prayer book as something 'pick'd out of a Popish dunghill'. These extreme Protestants came to be known as Puritans, and by the mid-1580s had taken a strong hold in London. The movement was fed by the extraordinary flamboyance and luxury of the court and the upstart nouveau riches, made wealthy by trade, manufacture and Spanish gold. Stephen Gosson, the 'reformed' playwright, curate at Stepney from 1585 to 1586 and later rector of Bishopsgate (and vicar of Sandridge) was a 'Puritan' in the strict sense of the word, celebrated for his preaching against the immorality and materialism of Londoners. A focus of his invective was the 'newfangled gentlewomen' with their elaborate wigs, ruffs, spangles, chains and laces, fans, flaps and feathers, farthingales, naked paps, 'the baudie busk that keeps down flat the bed wherein the babe should breed'.

In the East End, with its evangelical traditions, dissent from a Church that still smacked of popery was exacerbated when war started against Catholic Spain

in 1585. Anti-popery became the government's propaganda tool and pulpits rang
with ranting tirades against the monster pope and his band of demons. 'Satan is
from us banished in his old Popish pride,' declaimed Anthony Anderson, vicar of
Stepney; the realm is delivered from the 'innumerable Hostes of Popish Locustes'.
For the seafaring men of Stepney, many of whom had direct contact with the
Catholic enemy from Spain and Portugal, the fight was against a flesh and blood
devil. Likewise, the old soldiers who went with the expedition to the Low
Countries in 1585 had fought with the cruel Spaniards. The religious temper of
the locals was also much influenced by the Calvinist and Anabaptist refugees who
invaded the East End in the second half of the century. French, Dutch, Walloons
and Flemings came fleeing prosecution from the Catholic powers of Spain and
France. In 1550 Edward VI had granted a charter for a Dutch church in Austin
Friars, and a great number of Dutch and Flemings arrived in 1567 when the
Spanish invaded the Netherlands. Some 100,000 people were said to have taken
flight within the space of a few days. A survey of strangers of 1568 shows 3,500
in London. There followed another influx, this time of Frenchmen following the
massacre on St Bartholomew's Day in 1572 and more 'Doche' came after the sack
of Antwerp in 1585.

There was, of course, resentment directed against the immigrants, who
arrived *en masse*, worked hard and made money that might have gone into
English pockets. 'Their children,' said Sir Henry Finch, sergeant at law, 'are
no sooner able to go, but they are taught to serve God and to flee idleness.'
Apprentices rioted in protest against them in 1586, and a bill was brought
before the Commons to restrict foreign retailers in 1593; it was unsuccessful.
Nevertheless, talk of horrors perpetrated on the Continent must have spread
like wildfire and fuelled fears of popery.

As one might expect, the refugees were drawn to the parts of London where
their compatriots might be found. The main concentration of newcomers was in
St Katharine's, East Smithfield, Aldgate and Shoreditch, with a few families settling in Poplar, Mile End, Bethnal Green, Bromley and Norton Folgate. So many
Frenchmen set up house in Bishopsgate that the patch next to the church became
known as Petty France. St Katharine's became virtually a 'Doche' ghetto; the
'way to the Flemish church' there is shown on a map of 1597, and Ben Jonson's
character Iniquity went to 'drink with the Dutch there'. The Dutch were apparently well integrated, and of 1,972 aliens in St Katharine's, Whitechapel and East
Smithfield in 1571, 61 per cent went to an English church, 21 per cent to a Dutch,
21 per cent to a French and 6 per cent to none.

Life for the country East Enders

In Shakespeare's *Henry VIII*, the porter describing the crowd at the christening of the Princess Elizabeth refers to 'youths that thunder at a playhouse and fight for bitten apple that no audience but the Tribulation of Tower Hill or the Limbs of Limehouse their dear brothers are able to endure'. Thus Shakespeare (or Fletcher) referred to the rough element from east of the Tower: the Tribulation and the Limbs may have been organised gangs. For Stow the area had 'gone down' and 'ignorant swains' (as Thomas Middleton called them) had invaded his boyhood home, with their bowling alleys, alehouses, workshops, noise and muck. Developers hastily painted over old houses 'scarce worth the daubing' and raised the rent, preferring to let their properties to drunken Flemings, rather than Englishmen, said Dekker.

The high walls that still enclosed the City's square mile made a physical barrier between the wealthy old town, with its five- or six-storey houses, and the lower buildings of its rowdy out-parishes, 'dark dennes for adulterers, thieves, murderers, and every mischief worker', as playwright Henry Chettle described them.

To picture the eastern suburbs, conjure up market day in the centre of some small Suffolk or Essex town, where plastered and weatherboard cottages still stand around in companionable disorder, with their own garden plots. Hang signboards up and add some tall half-timbered Christmas card coaching inns. String their galleries with washing lines and fill the narrow streets, courts and alleys with sailors, knots of gossiping sailors' wives, silk weavers, errand boys, hawkers, peddlers, washerwomen, scolds and prostitutes. Add workshops and patches of vegetable garden, heaps of woods, piles of tiles and bags of lime. Fill the air with the stench of burning tallow, saltpetre, smoke from brewery chimneys and smiths' forges, festering humanity, 'necessary houses' and horse dung. Listen to the noise of carts and coaches rolling along the wide Whitechapel Road (paved in 1572) up from Bishopsgate through Shoreditch and along the highway to Ratcliff, making 'such thundering as if the world ran upon wheels'. You may also hear the clip of smarter hooves; no gallant in Sir Philip Sidney's day, said the gossip John Aubrey, would have been seen dead riding in a coach. Down by the river the sound was the clink of hammers. When a new house was built next to the school in Ratcliff in the 1570s the Coopers' Company stipulated that it should not be let to 'a smith or pewterer or to any hammer man'. Every house in four was an alehouse; many were just two-up two-down cottages with one room as tap room. Larger more impressive affairs for travellers stood just outside the gates, like the Dolphin at Bishopsgate and the Three Nuns at Aldgate. All sorts of business was conducted in taverns and alehouses: mariners were recruited and paid off, deals made between masters and owners of vessels and victualling contracts drawn. 'Corner shops' were everywhere, selling a variety of commodities, from candles to cheap food and drink.

Life was more communal than it is today. Few ordinary homes had ovens, and even the 'rag tag' folk ate out at 'short order cafés'. A group of Wapping ditchers who had occasion to report their daily lives to the bishop's court in a suit over a will, in 1594, regularly took breakfast out, sometimes at the Rose Tavern on Tower Hill, where rolled lamb or bacon might be on the menu. Tom Davies, the 'scavellman' whose will was in dispute, though only a humble labourer, had a woman to clean his cottage and dress his meat, when he wasn't eating out.

Women were, in general, in rather short supply, with a continual influx of countryfolk, more boys and men than girls. Widows were quickly snapped up. European visitors often commented on the freedom of English women, and it is clear from Church court records that East End women, of the labouring classes, frequented drinking houses quite as much as their menfolk. Their favoured tipple seems, as now, to have been white wine. Alehouses run by sailors' wives were a commonplace along the riverside, many of them left to shift for themselves while their husbands were at sea. Many East End wives worked to support themselves while their husbands were away at sea. They dressed wigs, ran market stalls, nursed the sick, delivered babies, cleaned other people's houses and washed other people's linen. The heavy, expensive clothing now fashionable needed a good deal of beating and brushing. Prostitution paid well, and there were plenty of sailors wandering about with jingling pockets.

'Many vicious person get liberty to live as they please', it was said of the suburbs, and it was not unusual for husbands and wives to simply run off and set up home with someone else. Adulterous couples did run the risk of being presented by the churchwardens, and they might then have to go over to the west side of the City, to Christchurch, Newgate, and put in an appearance at the archdeacon's court. There would follow a shaming penance; they would have to put on white shifts and be publicly admonished during divine service in their parish church. In times of moral purge there might be a worse punishment, like being paraded round the streets in a cart. Those who provided shelter and aid for pregnant girls might also find themselves in trouble. During morning prayer at St Botolph's Aldgate on 10 April 1598 Ellen Wright came, white wand in hand, and 'in the middest of the whole congregation fell upon her knees' and in a loud voice confessed that she had harboured an unmarried mother and even taken the bastard over to the Savoy to be baptised.

Families were small because marriage was late, as it was all over northern Europe at this time, and children had a struggle to survive in the harsh living conditions. In the parish of St Botolph Aldgate between 1583 and 1599, 70 per cent of children died before they reached fifteen, and most died before they were six. Life expectancy was short; most of the burials in Aldgate churchyard in the 1590s were of people between twenty and thirty-nine. Walking around the streets and alleys in these times, as in Canary Wharf today, you would have seen few children and fewer old people. It was a world of the young, regularly fed with hopefuls from the agricultural districts. There was more chance of babies dying here than at home and women, delivered by 'mercenary midwives', were more likely to die in childbirth than their country cousins. Anxiety took its toll. These men and women had been uprooted, and there was unlikely to be a family support group to help out in times of trouble, although the newcomers tended to cling together in regional groups, like Tom Davies's scavellmen, a colony of Shropshire men in Wapping. Coming to town, risking a dose of the pox and the plague shortened lives. 'Till death us do part' rarely committed the couple to a thirty- or forty-year partnership in the insanitary suburbs, where every year, with sickening predictability, the spectre of plague stalked the hot summer alleys. Major epidemics swept through London in 1563 and 1593. In 1592–93 the eastern suburbs and hamlets were worst hit, with the pestilence striking first in Spitalfields. These were terrible days with 'The daily jangling and ringing of the bells, the coming of the minister to every house ... the digging up of graves, the sparring in of windows, and the blazing forth of the blue cross'. At Aldgate the sextons buried 1,463 bodies.

It was a turbulent, bad-tempered society, with a good deal of shouting and brawling. When they squabbled they called each other 'copper nose', 'whore', 'harlot', 'rogue' and all manner of sexual insults; even sermons were passionate and violent and larded with sexual innuendo. Witchcraft reared its head as neighbours fell out. In 1598 Richard Nelson, a sorcerer of St Katharine's, was indicted for bewitching an eleven-year-old girl and Alice, the wife of Anthony Cutler of Whitechapel, bewitched the baker's wife so that she wasted away and died. If you could afford it, a slander action in the bishops' court was a good way of getting at someone who had upset you. And many did. Elizabeth, the daughter of Anthony Anderson, Puritan vicar of Stepney, sued the couple who had thrown her and her family out of the vicarage after her father's death in 1593. Quite a slanging match, or 'brabbling', had gone on in the vicarage garden, with Elizabeth's little brother Thomas shouting out that the 'bailiff' had twelve pricks and that his wife was a poxy-arsed whore. 'Twelve pricks' responded by calling the deceased vicar a whoremaster and his daughter a bastard, begotten of a milkmaid.

Bitches snarl and dogs fight, and it was mainly women who attacked with the 'lavish of their tongues'. Their mates, many of them sailors and soldiers, tended to resort to violence, and fights were frequent. The swathe of open ground stretching westward from Stepney church to the windmills was a popular venue for duels. These were not duels as we might imagine them; gentlemen in lace with fine steel swords and seconds. Brawls and serious fallings out might be settled by an organised fight, and any old weapon might be used. Five Stepney fights that ended in death came before the Sessions between 1549 and 1603; undoubtedly there were many more. In the summer of 1580 a couple of sailors had a spat in Ratcliff Wall and ended up going to fight it out with 'Danske javelins' at 'Hemynges Close near the windmill'.

To us, as to the do-gooders going into the horrors of the Victorian and Edwardian East End slum, the appearance of what Stow called the 'meaner sort' would seem rather appalling, stunted from poor living, with bad complexions. Syphilis often reached epidemic proportions, and many of the fresh-faced young men and women soon succumbed to the pox. Thomas Warde, schoolmaster at the Ratcliff School, was sacked by the Coopers' Company for having a dose of 'that grete and notorious distress called the P'. It made your hair fall out, your breath stink, your voice hoarse and, at worst, your penis fall off. Thick make-up was used to cover up blemishes; patches were common from the 1590s, and masks were the fashion. Layers of padded clothes were worn to cover every part of the body to protect it from the noxious air. Even the poor were fastidious about wearing underwear to absorb dirt and vermin and protect the costly outerwear.

You would have heard a jangle of different accents in the alehouses and around the streets; Sir Walter Raleigh spoke Devonshire until his dying day, according to Aubrey, and there is every reason to suppose that the Scots and the Welsh, the West Countrymen and the East Anglians, the Northerners and the Midlanders who made up the country East Enders likewise kept their accents. Most records present a tidied up version of speech; only occasionally can you get a clue as to how they spoke. A Limehouse sailor called William Borgine wrote out his own will, spelling the words as he spoke them: 'parffet memrey' for perfect memory, 'atorati' for authority, 'viage' for voyage, 'acsetter' for executor, 'shallanges' for shillings, 'delleth' for dwelleth.

The government was concerned to prevent parishes in the capital and its immediate hinterland (within 3 miles) being 'Overcharged and burdened with sundry sorts of beggars and evell disposed persons'. In October 1595 Henry Miller was bound over on his own recognisances and those of two friends not to build any more houses in East Smithfield. A Star Chamber order of October 1598 directed that two men, Rice Griffin and John Crippes, should be put in the Fleet and fined for dividing tenements up and letting them to 'base persons', contrary to the royal proclamation of July 1580. The properties, in Hog Lane (Petticoat Lane) and Shoreditch, were to be 'razed to the ground' and the developers fined and put in the Fleet prison. The proclamation of 1580 prohibited new building in the City and within 3 miles of any of the gates, and in any house already inhabited in future only one family was allowed to live. 'Indwellers' were given a few months to find alternative dwelling. Poor occupants were to be kept by the parish (with a subsidy from the landlords), for life. Early in the next century the survivors petitioned James I about their right to live rent free in Hog Lane. Eighteen families are named; they include three men with no legs, four men with only one leg, three lame and diseased people and two lame widows. The men may have been old soldiers or sailors who had lost their limbs in battle, perhaps in the Low Countries, or perhaps in the nearby gunpowder factory. A statute of 1589 reinforced the proclamation of 1580 against building, but it is generally agreed that it was of little effect.

Vagrancy was a matter of increasing urgency for the late Elizabethan government, with bands of 'sturdy beggars' roaming the country and in Stepney parish, as in Aldgate, with folk pouring in from the shires, the problem was particularly acute. Beggars took shelter in barns and bodies were found floating in the river, in the fields, especially up by the brick kilns in Spitalfields and in reed stacks. Dekker wrote of bodies lying 'stinking and unburied' outside the City walls: 'Looke ... over thy walls into thy Fields, and thou shalt heare poore and forsaken wenches lye groaning in ditches, and travailing to seek out Death upon thy common hye wayes.'

Church and parish were increasingly burdened with unemployed vagrants and unsupported bastard children, born to servant girls, prostitutes and beggar girls, sired, many of them, by sailors and soldiers. They were spawned in the dingy alleys, dumped in barns, found on the slimy stairs that led down to the river. Often they were dumped or even born in the church porch, like the baby who was found in St Dunstan's porch in August 1582 'with a not written in the breast of it, that it was a Christian sole named Jane ... we call her Jane'. She was cared for by the parish but only survived a few weeks.

Although a poor tax had been introduced in 1572, there was no proper system of relief yet, and in Stepney the vestry and vicar made an attempt to deal with the problem in their vast parish by setting up a shelter in the enormous parish tithe barn, which lay just east of the church. Unmarried mothers, beggars, old soldiers and the destitute gathered in the warmth of the barn, which had once been stacked high with sheaves. The first mention of the shelter is in January 1585 when a poor woman was buried 'out of the parsonage barn'. For some fourteen years there are regular reference to burials and baptisms 'out of the parsonage barn': baby Ellen, daughter of a soldier fighting in Flanders (according to the mother) in spring 1586, baby William, son of a 'poor wanderer from the Isle of Wight' in August 1591, and numerous others. Foundlings, or some of them, were cared for by one Mother Bartholomew, who occupied the church house and presumably was paid for her pains. One such, a 'poor child found in the fields', she named John Fortune.

Bastards were a problem for any parish and in Stepney, where the declared illegitimacy rate was about 10 per cent, therefore probably much higher, since the Act of 1575 that imposed a prison sentence for both parents. It was important for the parish clerk to establish the paternity of children brought for baptism, so that the authorities could at least attempt the payment of maintenance. Bridget, servant of Goodman Stanes of Limehouse, named a city alderman as her baby's father and the midwife attested to it. Many girls obviously invented fathers' names, or perhaps their procurer did it for them. Some, like a servant girl from John Lock's house in Hog Lane, named soldiers who had, they said, been killed in Flanders, on the expedition to save the Low Countries from Spain in 1585. Only the most bold and inveterate of whores refused to supply a father's name. Elizabeth Duckett of Poplar was obdurate when her baby was christened in May 1589; the clerk noted that she was 'an ancient harlott'.

Conditions were especially bad in the 'starvation years' at the end of the century, when real wages dropped dramatically. It is little wonder the pastoral was so popular a form of literature, with its nostalgic tales of shepherds and shepherd-esses set in the rustic idyll of a childhood enchanted by distance. One of the most famous was *The Shepherd's Calendar*, written by Edmund Spenser, who grew up in East Smithfield (although he denied it), a humble clothworker's son. His publisher, John Wolfe, of Dutch extraction, also lived in East Smithfield.

Around the parishes and hamlets

But this was no nineteenth-century slum, with row upon row of squalid housing and no space between; there was still much open ground, stretches of pasture and parkland with room for market gardens, orchards and playing fields. Thirty thousand people in 7 square miles is not overcrowding by modern standards. Even in the working parts of the Tower Hamlets there was a country feel, with strips of garden plots, where cottagers grew 'all manner of herbs': bay, rosemary, sage, hyssop, thyme and parsley. Chickens pecked in the yards, pigs wandered around, cows grazed and cartloads of grain trundled along the lanes to barns at Lammastide (August). Not far away, secluded among chestnuts and elms, stood grand country houses.

The East End was a collection of suburbs, little towns and villages still, each with its own character with the parish organisation at the centre of things. Local government activity was at parish level and the vestries ran affairs. Most important was the enormous parish of Stepney, including its hamlets of Ratcliff, Mile End, Poplar with Blackwall and the Marsh (the Isle of Dogs), Bethnal Green, Limehouse and Stratford Bow with Old Ford. By 1532 Poplar, Limehouse, Ratcliff, Mile End and Bethnal Green had their own special chapels in the parish church. By the end of the century, if not before, the hamlets had acquired a good deal of independence from Stepney parish.

The only surviving record of 'hamlet government' from this period is the 'book of accounts wherein all actions are registered for the hamlet of Poplar' for the period 1593–1675. Poplar's chief inhabitants met every two years to elect constables, head boroughs, churchwardens and ale tasters. They chose scavengers,

supplied arms for the constables, men and weapons for the militia and maintained the butts for archery practice. Money was collected for poor and plague
relief and kept in the town chest. Almshouses were maintained for poor widows
and orphans provided for. Even then there was a winter fuel allowance; just
before Christmas 1595 Mistress Vassal contributed £5 for the purchase of coal
to be distributed to the needy. Presumably this was Judith Vassal, the third wife
of John, one of the founders of the Virginia Company and a wealthy colonial
adventurer.

Aldgate, East Smithfield, St Katharine's, Whitechapel and Bishopsgate: the suburbs

When contemporaries spoke of 'the suburbs' they were not referring to Stepney's
outlying hamlets, Mile End, Bethnal Green and Bow, or even to the riverside, but
to the areas just outside the walls, to Aldgate, East Smithfield and St Katharine's,
Bishopsgate, Norton Folgate and the new rough spot, Spitalfields.

The church of St Botolph's Aldgate was in charge of an area of about 40
acres immediately outside the City gate, including East Smithfield to the south,
Houndsditch and part of Spitalfields to the north. Holy Trinity in the Minories,
a tiny parish of only 4 acres, had taken a bite out of Aldgate's patch when it
was created from the Abbey of Poor Clares after the Dissolution. Whitechapel
parish had about 200 acres to the east of Aldgate, including the riverside part of
Wapping; the rest of Wapping belonged to Stepney. The church at Bromley served
the tiny village and about 600 acres, mainly farmland. St Botolph at Bishopsgate
had about 44 acres outside the gate and St Katharine's ran its own show, ruling
over a rowdy precinct of some 14 acres. The Tower precinct had its own parish
church of St Peter ad Vincula.

The parish of St Botolph's Aldgate was a true suburb, busy with industry, apart
from the High Street, a crowded and insalubrious place that suffered terribly in
the plagues of 1563 and 1593. In 1587 the curate, Christopher Therkill, died from
'inward grief of mind', a clergyman's natural melancholy perhaps exacerbated by
conditions in the parish. Thomas Harrydance (of the family of John the bricklayer who had preached marathon sermons in 1538), appointed parish clerk in
1594, bought ' a newe booke of parchament' for the grim job of recording the
births, marriages and deaths in a parish that probably had the highest mortality
rate of anywhere in the country. There was a real poverty problem: in December
1583 a distribution was made to eighty needy souls of 'all the collection gathered
at the communions and put into the poor box'. At the Easter communion of
17 April 1595 they collected 3s 7d from twenty-nine people, gave 1s to old Father
Bates in Ship Alley and put the rest in the poor box.

Aldgate had a population of about 6,000 people, perhaps 1,500 more than its sister parish at Bishopsgate, having 'mightily increased', multiplying about four-fold between the Armada and Shakespeare's death. The church that Chaucer knew had been rebuilt by Holy Trinity Priory and by Stow's day was 'pestered' with lofts and extra seating for the newcomers. Next to the churchyard, on the north side of the High Street, were 'fair and comely buildings' along towards the Bars, and on the south side there were crowded alleys.

Houndsditch, the road up to Bishopsgate, its eastern side largely taken over by the Owen gunfoundries in the early part of the century, was these days full of downmarket secondhand clothes shops, market traders and 'houses of pleasure', according to Stow. He remembered the good old days when Holy Trinity Priory had almshouses for the infirm there, and pious Londoners took a Friday walk, distributing money to the poor souls who hung a sheet out of their windows to show that they were bedridden. Along the High Street were inns for travellers: the Three Nuns, the Woolpack, the Blue Boar, the Crown, where a gentleman from Maldon died in 1594: 'for want of a trusse', wrote the parish clerk, 'the Bowells of the said Richard Pellett ded issue owt of his Bodye'. The King's Head, run by vintner George Clarke in the 1590s, was the venue for parish functions. A visitation dinner held there in 1595 was attended by thirty people, including the curate and his wife and the wardens and their wives. They consumed a double rib of beef, a sirloin, three legs of mutton, a loin and breast of veal, two capons, oranges and lemons, fruit and cheese, all washed down with claret and sack. Clarke supplied the wine for the monthly communion at St Botolph's and made a good profit out of it. On Easter Sunday 1595 he supplied 9 gallons and a pot of claret for 663 people; that was probably enough for a small glass each!

There were rows of shops of all sorts, with swinging signs, like the chandlers' shop at the sign of the Black Bull in the High Street. The Mot family now ran the famous bellfoundry; in June 1596 Robert Mot delivered a new treble bell to the church. The age-old local industries of founding, armament manufacture and brewing were still in operation, but the new demand for fine clothes saw Aldgate and its neighbour, Whitechapel, gradually taken over by the trade for which the area would become famous. There were silk weavers, winders and twisters, makers of velvet, linen, fustian, taffeta and felt, dyers, wool winders and loom-makers. When the cloth was made it was handed over to the local tailors, seamstresses, embroiderers, collarmakers, stockmakers, pointmakers, glovers and girdlers. Hot-pressers finished the garments off, and they were ready for fashion-conscious Londoners to buy. All the accoutrements were made here too: buttons, pins and needles, starch (for ruffs), perfume and looking-glasses. There were hatters and hat-trimmers, hat band-makers, cobblers and shoe-cleaners. James Burbage employed two silk weavers as stewards in the theatre in nearby Shoreditch.

Flemish and Dutch names appear increasingly in the records of the parish; in Armada year there was even a Dutch dustman; the 'scavenger' for Houndsditch was one Peeter de Measter. Mostly they seem to have congregated, however, in the south part of the parish, in East Smithfield, and, as we have seen, in St Katharine's, its near neighbour.

Coming from the City, if you turned right just by the church you were in the Minories, the road down to the Tower. On the right, the City side, was the town ditch, banked up and confined to a narrow channel. New houses were interspersed with garden plots, carpenters' workshops and bowling alleys. On the east side of the road were the small church of Holy Trinity and the armouries, where the nunnery had stood. 'In place of this house,' wrote Stow, 'is now built divers fair and large storehouses for armour and habiliments of war, with divers workhouses serving to the same purpose.' One workshop belonged to an aptly named smith, Vulcan Skinner. In 1594 he was cuckolded by John Wolfe, a Dutch butcher of Mores Alley. The resulting baby (another Vulcan) only lived to three years and succumbed to the smallpox.

South-east of the nunnery site was (and still is) Goodman's Fields and Goodman's Yard. Stow remembered fetching milk fresh from old Goodman's dairy farm there when he was a boy in Henry VIII's reign. At the bottom of the Minories were East Smithfield and Little Tower Hill, open ground with a pump, a 'great tree', tenters for the clothworkers to peg out their cloth and for washerwomen to lay out clothes to dry. A new brick-built complex housed the almshouses for the Merchant Taylors' Company (erected in 1593). Where once the great Abbey of St Mary Graces had stood was the victualling house for the navy, where animals were slaughtered and biscuits and bread were baked to feed the men of Wapping and Limehouse when they took to the high seas.

East Smithfield was the roughest part of Aldgate parish. Just before the Dissolution the rolls of the abbot's court at St Mary Graces record the prosecution of ruffians, dodgy lodging house keepers, brawlers, prostitutes and gamblers and 'fly tippers', many of them foreigners, Italians, French and the ubiquitous 'Doche'. Fifty years later it was full of bowling alleys, lodging houses, breweries, brothels, tailors and clothworkers' shops. In St Botolph's parish registers of 1587–95 we read of the Hartshorne brewhouse, the Ship brewery run by Jeanes de Meatris, a brewery in Kercombe's Alley by the Tower, run by Henrick up den Acker, a cooperage at the sign of the Haddock, a tallow chandler's shop, a cutler called Abraham van Wingen, a Flemish weaver, a mariner from Flushing, a Dutch sailor from Delft. In January 1587 the curate went down to a victualling house called the Oliphant to christen the landlord's weak baby son.

Hog Lane, which ran east along the north side of the abbey site, was renamed Rosemary Lane in the early seventeenth century, or 'Rag Fair' after its notorious market for stolen goods. This is Royal Mint Street and Cable Street in modern times. In 1594 the parish had so many bodies to dispose of that a new burial ground was opened in Hog Lane. To the south-east, near the river, was Nightingale Lane (now Sir Thomas More Street), which wound its way down to Crassh Mills, the twin flour mills, dividing St Katharine's from a sort of industrial park. On the site of the old hermitage here was the Swan's Nest brewery; there is a picture of this in a contemporary plan of the area; a great half-timbered structure.

Iniquity flew to St Katharine's, as we have seen, to drink with the Dutch. The 14-acre precinct was notorious: a liberty free from city restrictions, it attracted foreigners, the disreputable and 'dirty trades' like tallow-chandling. Stiff with little Dutch breweries, sailors' cottages and the workshops of blacksmiths and carpenters, it was criss-crossed by narrow muddy lanes, Pottlepot Alley and Maidenhead Alley among them. There was a Flemish church, and the only monastery in London to survive the Dissolution was a hospital for 'the better sort of mad-folks', according to Ben Jonson, and a reformatory for fallen women.

Beyond Aldgate Bars was Whitechapel, with its own church and parish, taking in the riverside strip of Wapping. According to Stow's account the parish seems to have been most affected by the arrival of the country East Enders, and both sides of the main road were 'pestered with cottages and alleys'. In the 1560s there were about 2,000 inhabitants, growing to 5,000 by 1600. In its 200 acres there was much more open ground than in Aldgate parish, but its 'common field ... sometime the beauty of this city ... is so encroached upon by filthy cottages, and with other purpressors, inclosures, and laystalls', spilling over into the road, which was now hardly passable. Whitechapel had become 'no small blemish to so famous a city'.

A little to the east of Aldgate, on the north side of the highway, was another Hog Lane. Stow remembered it as a country lane lined with elms, wandering up through the fields to the Spital, where citizens strolled to 'refresh their spirits with the wholesome air'. Now it was built up on either side with cottages, tentergrounds for the clothworkers and bowling alleys. By 1607 the lane, which had taken its name from the pigs that were driven down it from Hoxton, has been rechristened in accord with its new function: Petticoat Lane. Around this Hog Lane there grew up a new hamlet of Stepney, called Spitalfields, populous enough to have its own warden in the church by 1635. Clay pits had been dug in the field that had belonged to the Spital and a brickworks sprang up. From the number of fatal accidents noted in Stepney's burial register it is clear that the brick factory was a dangerous place to work. 'Base persons' lived around here, like the desperate bunch of cripples we met in Crippe's 'bed sits' in 1598; in 1600 Anthony Warren was prosecuted for building three 'base cottages' in Hog Lane. There were bowling alleys, gambling dens and lodging houses, like those kept by a man called William Dickes/Dix and the Widow Dales in the 1580s.

Petticoat Lane led into Bishopsgate Street, the highway that led up to Shoreditch and beyond. Less populous than Aldgate parish, though roughly the same in area, it was similarly accounted one of the City's poor parishes, and had enough of an immigrant population to acquire the name Petty France.

Three large coaching inns stood outside the gate, the best known being the grand Dolphin on the east side. Next to it, where Devonshire Square is now, was the extravagantly grand house known as Fishers' Folly, with pleasure gardens and bowling-greens. This was built and laid out by Jasper Fisher, one of the six clerks in Chancery, a Justice of the Peace, and a freeman of the Goldsmiths' Company. The house, being considered far too splendid for a mere Chancery clerk, much in debt, was nicknamed Fisher's Folly.

Adjoining the Folly on the other side was an estate of small houses built for the newcomers. Up towards Shoreditch on this side of the highway were more small new properties. Russel's Row, or Rotten Row, comprised some twenty-five cottages that had previously been Spital almshouse, bought by a developer called Russel, a wealthy draper, who did them up using cheap labour and charged vast sums in 'key money'. Adjoining to the south was the old monastery precinct, approached through an imposing gatehouse. The priory buildings had been converted into exclusive residential accommodation much favoured by wealthy Roman Catholics: one such was the celebrated Father Garnet, executed for supposed complicity in the Gunpowder Plot. An old mansion north of Russel's Row, once priory property, was converted into what would today be called luxury flats and let out to Italian, Dutch, Spanish and French merchants. On the other side of the main road, near the church, was Bedlam, with its stone gatehouse. For a small sum you could go and gawp at the lunatics there. Outside the bars was Norton Folgate, known for its 'soldiers and wenches'.

Bishopsgate probably had more of a mixture of folk than the rest of the East End: wealthy Catholics, rich foreign merchants and poor foreign refugees, tinkers, soldiers, weavers, prostitutes and players.

Merrie England: plays and players

Before we go down to the riverbank and look at the 'Limbs of Limehouse', the theatrical fraternity must have its say. Now there were no more church theatricals, no more 'Jesuses with moving parts' and the Robin Hood costumes had been confiscated, Londoners were hungry for fun and stimulation. It was supplied in spades by bearbaiters, dancers, swordfighters and tumblers. Shakespeare and his fellow players drew crowds to inn yards and purpose-built playhouses at the Theatre and Curtain in Shoreditch, at the famous Globe and the other playhouses on the south bank, in the Boar's Head Inn Yard theatre and the Red Lion in Whitechapel. The impact of these great public attractions was enormous, with the rowdy gatherings, of as many as 3,000 people frightening the life out of the authorities and horrifying the Church, with gangs of thugs from Limehouse and Tower Hill and apprentices fighting over apples in the pit. Plague spread like wildfire in the playhouses and clergy were appalled at the bawdiness of some performances, especially the rude 'jigs' that were often performed like a B movie at the end of the show. Stephen Gosson, curate of Stepney and rector of St Botolph's Bishopsgate (whom we met berating 'newfangeld gentlewomen') wrote *The Schoole of Abuse*, 'a pleasant invective against Poets, Pipers, Plaiers, Jesters and such like Catterpillars of a Commonwealth'.

Shoreditch and Bankside are, of course, the celebrated theatrical places, but Whitechapel, a similar sort of area, near to the City but free of its restrictions and with enough open ground to allow for the building of large structures, had its day. In fact the earliest purpose-built playhouse in London was in what has been described as a sort of 'theatre-land' east of Aldgate Bars. This was the Red Lion, said to have been on the site of the old Asshews/Ashwyes Manor House (now the Royal London Hospital site). It was a short-lived affair, opening in 1567 and closing the following year, but it was the first, predating James Burbage's Shoreditch Theatre by nine years. The only surviving records of the Red Lion are of two lawsuits involving the owner, John Brayne, city grocer and brother-in-law of James Burbage. Brayne sued the two carpenters who built the cheap, makeshift playhouse, which cost only about £20 (Shoreditch Theatre cost £700), accusing them of shoddy, incomplete work. Built in the garden of the former Starke House Farm, it seems to have been a single gallery multi-sided theatre, with a fixed stage standing above the audience; attached was a 30ft turret, perhaps for aerial stunts and for a flagpole. As far as we know the only play performed there was called *The Story of Sampson*. This was the first of Brayne's theatrical enterprises, the next being his partnership with Burbage at the Theatre (1576). This ended, for Brayne at least, in disaster and he then (1599–1600) invested in yet another Whitechapel playhouse, the George, just to the east of the Red Lion. He quarrelled with his partner, Robert Miles, went bankrupt and died in 1586; he was buried in Whitechapel church.

A playhouse that never came to fruition was in Nightingale Lane, not far from the Swan's Nest brewery and the tidemills. This was the speculative venture of John Wolfe, launched in 1599–1600 after he had made a fortune as the most successful publisher in the country. This one fell victim to the government's concerns about the dangers of plague and sedition, and was ordered to be dismantled before it was even finished.

Actors and entertainers of one sort and another took lodgings or even bought houses in this area, although the main colony was in Shoreditch. They were a rough crew, classified by the government as vagrants and much given to violent squabbling. Shakespeare himself lived for a short time in Bishopsgate, in the parish of St Helen's, within the walls so not part of our patch, but he must have walked many times up past Bedlam and the Spital on his way to the theatre where his company regularly played before the Globe opened in 1599. Brayne and his wife Margaret moved to Whitechapel after their financial collapse forced them to sell their house in Bucklesbury.

Edward Alleyn, celebrated player and theatre manager, was the son of a Bishopsgate innkeeper, baptised at St Botolph's in 1566. He endowed three sets of almshouses locally, including one in Lamb Alley off Bishopsgate Street. Christopher Marlowe was living in Norton Folgate in 1589 when he was involved in a brawl in Petticoat Lane. On 21 May 1588 the baby son of Robert Wilson, the famous comic actor, was buried in Stepney churchyard, from the Poplar house of John Mead, a wealthy Puritan. Wilson had been a member of the Earl of Leicester's Company and was one of the twelve selected by the lord chamberlain to be of the Queen's Company in 1583. What the Wilsons were doing at Mead's house is anybody's guess; perhaps they were lodging there during a performance at the Theatre. In September 1590 Elizabeth, the wife of Thomas Kidd, was buried in Stepney churchyard. It is possible that this was the wife of Thomas Kyd the playwright, who wrote *The Spanish Tragedy*, a precursor of *Hamlet*. In April 1595 the sexton at Aldgate buried the one-year-old son of Thomas Goodaell at St Botolph's Aldgate, 'a player of Enterludes' living at Mr Gaskins' Rents at the Flowr de Luce in Houndsditch. The baby had been 'long sick'.

The riverside: Ratcliff, Limehouse, Wapping, Poplar and Blackwall

The leading characters in the real life dramas and comedies of the Elizabethan East End, were, however, not the actors and tumblers, the actor managers and impresarios, they were the mariners. The riverside from St Katharine's to Blackwall lay at the heart of the age of exploration and the emergence of England as a seaborne superpower. From here explorers set off on voyages of discovery and plunder. Between 1589 and 1591, about 200 English vessels went on privateering voyages, to the coasts of Spain and Portugal and the West Indies. Of these the overwhelming majority were London vessels, with crews recruited from the pool of men in Ratcliff, Limehouse, Wapping, St Katharine's and Rotherhithe. By the end of the century ships were regularly setting off from Blackwall, taking miscreants and adventurers to the New World.

Swaggering sea captains and wealthy shipwrights built themselves 'stout houses' and took over the running of Stepney vestry. The great Sir Walter Raleigh himself was around, a frequent visitor to his brother-in-law's house in Mile End, as we shall see. In 1596 he set sail from Limehouse on his third voyage to Guiana, in a pinnace named after his son, Watte.

All was bustle and excitement down by the riverbank, where the broad seas of adventure lapped up against the landing stages, wharves and warehouses. At Ratcliff Cross and in the alehouses that pepper the riverside, old hands told tales of frozen lands and bizarre beasts, of countries where natives cooked with solid gold pots and pans. Here the great galleons were fitted and victualled and their crews and passengers taken aboard. In small workshops anchors, ropes, masts, sails and all manner of fittings for ships were made, but there were some big yards where ships were built. Best known were those of the Pett family. William Pett laid down and launched the *Greyhound* in Limehouse in 1586. Phineas Pett set up home in Limehouse and in 1597 was in the employ of his brother Joseph. He records: 'I was employed by my brother ... in his yard at Limehouse, upon the repairing of a great Flemish ship, of whom the master was Mr John King of Limehouse.' Young hopefuls from all over the country joined with local lads, perhaps trained up by their fishermen or waterman fathers, to take their chance riding the seven seas. The fishermen of Stepney had been doing well for themselves, like Richard Leverocke of Poplar who died in 1544, possessed of a fishing boat and two houses. Aping the gentry, he created an entail, leaving one of his houses to his daughter Elizabeth with the injunction that she should not sell it 'out of their kindred'. Some 2,000 wherries plied for hire along London's riverbanks, and the watermen who manned them provided a pool of labour with some sailing know-how for the ocean-going galleons. Like modern taxi drivers, watermen, according to Sir Thomas Overbury, had the reputation of 'telling strange news'.

The first major exploratory expedition from Stepney was that led by Sir Hugh Willoughby at the end of Edward VI's reign (1553), setting off from Ratcliff in search of a sea route to China. Only one of the three ships returned and many Stepney lads were lost in the frozen seas. The *Edward Bonaventure*, with Richard Chanceler as captain, got to Moscow and opened up trade with Russia. Three years later Stephen Borough of Limehouse, brother of William, the great navigator and author, set off as master of the *Serchthrift* and explored Lapland and Finland, seeing 'white foxes and white bears'. The first two of Martin Frobisher's three great voyages in search of a north-west passage to China set off from Ratcliff and Blackwall respectively, in 1576 and 1577. The crew were fascinated by the Eskimos, who ate raw meat with their hands and used black wolf-like dogs to draw their sledges. They found what they thought was 'Eskimo gold' and a 'sea-unicorn', which they brought back and presented to the queen. In 1588 two City merchants funded an expedition to Benin in the *Richard of Arundel*, which brought back to Blackwall a cargo of wool, linen, iron, copper bracelets and glass beads. In 1590 the *Richard* went again to Africa, returning to Limehouse with 589 sacks of pepper, 150 elephants' teeth and 32 barrels of palm oil.

The war against Spain changed the activities of the East End seafarers, who took to privateering; you could make £10–15 on an average raid while pay in the navy was 10s a month. With government sanction in the form of letters of reprisal, raiding parties set off to plunder Spanish ships. Following Sir Francis Drake's example, mariners and old soldiers, according to John Hooker, 'travelled every place at the seas where any proffite might be had'. Usually there was a gentleman captain with a professional master and crew. Captains who showed an aptitude for trading or managing often bought shares in vessels, as did many East Enders from all walks of life. Katherine Brooke, a Poplar widow, sent her servant off in the *Quaker* to bring her riches from abroad. Rich spoils were to be had: pearls, silver and gold, precious stones, indigo, balsam, sugar and hides. When Michael Geare, captain and part-owner of the *Michael and John*, docked in 1595, local goldsmiths swarmed onto the ship to get their hands on the bullion and gems. There were weird and wonderful cargoes: William King, captain of the *Salomon*, brought home to Ratcliff two ships laden with 'great tortoises' from the Caiman Islands and forty live hogs from Cuba.

Fortunes were made by ordinary men from humble origins. One of the best known is Limehouse vestryman Christopher Newport, originally from Harwich, who led nine expeditions to the West Indies. His raid with the *Margaret* in 1591 brought back booty worth an extraordinary £32,000. In 1606 he was put in charge of the Virginia Company's expedition to America. At his death, in Java in 1617, he left a substantial dowry for one of his daughters, and only £5 to the other because of her disobedience to him. Sailor William Rafe leased the Ship on Ratcliff Wall and made enough to buy himself three houses. William Borgine's pickings were more modest; he had gold earrings, two barbary ducats and a purse of Spanish gold. George Frood of Wapping who had come from Newcastle on a collier boat, entrusted his shipmate with a bag of 'chickens' (sequins; Turkish coins) for his wife. Limehouse merchant Henry Smith of the *Salamander* left 1,060lb of currants, four looking-glasses and chinaware.

It was tough and rough aboard these ships; the governor of Havana described the English corsairs as low drunkards. 'Shite on thy commissions, coppernose!' roared William Ivey/Ivy of Limehouse, master of the *Tiger*, at his captain when he was told that his commission did not allow him to break bulk (touch the cargo). William Ivy was the son of Thomas who had opposed the 'stout Popish prelate' in the 1550s. He was active on Stepney vestry, and in 1613–14 was Master of Trinity House. Thomas Ivy's father William, grandfather of this William, was an anchorsmith and shipowner of some wealth, as indicated by his will: he had silver and silver gilt plate. He owned ships, a stock of anchors, coals and a herd of cattle. His witnesses and overseers were his friends, the limeman Dryver and the Limehouse baker Thomas Poyntell. In the will of John Hall he is described as a smith.

During Elizabeth's forty-five years the trade and shipping of London assumed worldwide importance. With the discovery of America and sea routes to the east, the focus of European trade was now on the Atlantic, on the ports of Cadiz, Lisbon, Antwerp, Bristol and London. England's capital was literally at the centre of the world, and its merchants and sailors seized their share of the new trade with America and the Indies, which the pope had appropriated for the Catholic empires of Spain and Portugal.

Since early medieval times the quays between Baynard's castle and the Tower had been the main port area, where vessels were discharged. As ships grew larger it would have been natural for the port operation to move east, where the river was deeper. This was prevented by an Act of 1558 that restricted the landing of foreign cargoes to the 'legal quays' west of the Tower. It would be another 250 years before the loading and unloading of cargoes became the main business of the East End when the enclosed docks were built.

Exceptions to the 1558 Act were made for cargoes of coal, beer and corn, and the coastal trade came increasingly into the East End, notably coal from Newcastle. There were numerous privately owned wharves, like those of Gardiner's sugarhouses in Butcher Row. Sir Arthur Throckmorton of Mile End had wood (165,130 billets) costing £3 brought down from Manningtree, presumably by Lea barge, paying 2d per thousand wharfage to John Gardiner and 22s to the carter who brought the wood up from the river. Thomas Poyntell, Puritan churchwarden, had a wharf adjoining his riverside bakeries at Limehouse, where wheat was delivered. As the City grew more and more overcrowded, merchandise of all sorts was stored in East End warehouses.

Before we leave the commotion of the riverside and make for the inland villages, we will take a last look at the hamlets of sailortown as they were at the end of the century.

A rare pictorial map of Poplar survives from 1600. It shows rows of small red-roofed houses lining the High Street, a brewery and a lock-up, with some larger residences in North Street with long gardens. These houses belonged, as did 'Master Garter's Pale', to the Dethick family. A road ran down across the Marsh to the ferry from the centre of the village, and the whole area was criss-crossed with water channels, dykes and locks. The peninsula, now known as the Isle of Dogs, had few inhabitants (there were only four baptisms between 1586 and 1593). After the Great Flood and subsequent inundations it was used for cattle grazing, and city butchers took leases on this most lush of pasture.

Not many people lived in the village of Blackwall on the east side of the peninsula, although it was rapidly developing as a passenger port for ocean-going vessels. Here mooring were protected by the 300ft long and 150ft wide reef known as Blackwall Rock.

The old lime-burning village of Limehouse, west of Poplar, was now becoming a place of seaman and shipwrights, with a population of about 3,000. A Jacobean map shows a cluster of some thirty houses around the Dock and what are now Three Colt Street, Narrow Street and Limehouse Causeway. Substantial houses were built, three-storeyed gabled affairs, with garrets under the eaves; a modern imitation of these can be seen alongside the Limehouse Link. One such was occupied by a Scandinavian merchant called John Dagge and, courtesy of his probate inventory, we can look inside what was an average house for the 'middling sort'. There were three bedrooms, one of which was described as the 'new chamber', perhaps an extension built on to accommodate a growing family. All had feather beds. The master's clothes were in the new chamber: three doublets, two pairs of breeches and six shirts. Downstairs in the hall was a fine new dining table, stools and a very costly walnut cupboard, a court cupboard, a glass case, three chairs and a settle. There was a green carpet, six cushions and eighteen china dishes, which cost Dagge nearly 1s a piece. In the fireplace there were brass fire irons. The kitchen was equipped with five spits, five brass kettles, five little skillets, pewter dishes and candlesticks and three dripping pans. His plate comprised a silver salt cellar, a beaker, a broad bowl and six spoons.

Sir Humphrey Gilbert, Raleigh's half-brother, lived in Limehouse for part of the time between 1573 and 1578, and was visited by the poet George Gascoigne, who was taken up into the great man's study and shown 'sundry exercises which he had perfected painfully with his own pen' in his attempts to discover a northeast passage to China.

West of Limehouse was the ancient port of Ratcliff, 'that same hath now taken hold of Lime hurst', records Stow. Ratcliff, 2½ miles in circumference, was the heart of the seafaring East End, long settled, with its famous cross, a place for the exchange of gossip, its school and almshouses, sugarhouse, breweries, workshops, wharves and warehouses. Stow remembered it as a village with high hedgerows and elm trees, but these had now been cut down and 'strong houses' built by marine men and cottages for sailors. There were coopers and chandlers, carpenters and shipwrights, brewers and bakers, ballasters, anchormen and sailmakers, ropemen and watermen, merchants and mechanicals. One of Ratcliff's best-known residents was John Vassal, who lived on Ratcliff Wall. He was a man of very great wealth who fitted out two ships at his own expense to fight the Armada, and was one of the founders of the colony of Virginia.

Shadwell, was the next place west, where a mill and a manor house had stood since Domesday. The riverside meadows still belonged to St Paul's and continued to do so until a developer bought the area in the next century. By the time Stow was writing his description of the area, 'in place of elm trees' there were 'many small tenements raised towards Ratcliff'.

Shadwell's much larger neighbour, Wapping, was expanding fast, and its riverside strip, which belonged to Whitechapel parish, was populous enough to have its own church by 1617. 'Wapping in the Wose' (renamed Wapping in the

West), 130 acres of marsh lying between the Hermitage and Old Gravel Lane, had been drained in 1536–41 by Cornelius Vanderdelft, from Brabant. A mercer called Richard Hill took part of these newly drained lands from the Dutchman, who owed him 'greate somes of money'. They were left to his son Jasper in 1553, tied up with an entail to keep them in the family. A new wharf and wall 'commonly called Wapping Wall' was built by John Stepkine on the frame of his father's old wharf, by Wapping Mill. Between 1560 and 1570 Wapping Wall was again destroyed by the tide. In 1580 the Commissioner of Sewers recommended that houses should be built along the wall and the owners induced to maintain it. William Page leased 110ft of wall, strengthened it and laid foundations – only to be stopped by the queen's proclamation against building. A new road was built in about 1570, along the riverside from the Tower to New Crane Wharf. This 'filthy straight passage', as Stow called it, is now Wapping High Street.

Although, imports from abroad could not be landed at Wapping, much smuggling went on, and theft from ships riding in the river was rife. Wapping in the Wose was the usual place for the execution of pirates; thirteen pirates were executed here between 1577 and 1587, and buried in Aldgate churchyard. Later the gibbet was moved east to the site of Execution Dock.

Stepney village and Mile End, Bethnal Green and Bow; fine houses and famous people

Only a short walk from the buzz of the port, up White Hart Street, lined with twenty Mercers' Company houses, past the White Hart tavern and the big house built for the High Master of St Paul's School, was Stepney church, with its wide leafy churchyard, great pond and tithe barn. Here, and in the fashionable village of Mile End beyond, were the country residences of lawyers, courtiers and merchants, and the homes of some of the wealthier seafarers.

Mile End Green was a stretch of parkland, about half a mile in length. All that is left now is the small wedge-shaped Stepney Green. On the old common, where 'penny royal grew in abundance', locals took the air and from time to time the militia were put through their paces. Shakepeare's Justice Shallow remembered, as a 'little quiver fellow', playing Sir Dagonet the fool there in a springtime pageant called *Arthur's Show*, which the lawyers of Clements Inn had laid on for entertainment of the soldiers. In the fearful summer of 1588, when Philip II's Armada was ready to invade, there was a mock battle on the Green, watched by a great crowd who were 'not a little encouraged against the enemy'. Mistress Merrythought in Beaumont and Fletcher's *Knight of the Burning Pestle* may have been recalling this: 'Mile End is a goodly matter; there has been a pitch-field … between the naughty Spaniels and the Englishmen; and the Spaniels ran away …

and the Englishmen followed: my neighbour Coxstone was there … and killed them all with a birding piece.'

The Green was fringed with the houses of the well-to-do, among them Lord Morley, father of Lord Monteagle to whom the Gunpowder Plot was revealed. A neighbour was Michael Geare, Master of Trinity House, a surveyor of the navy, on the vestry from 1585 to 1595 and knighted in 1625. William Ryder's house was in Mile End; he was collector general of the Customs, knighted in 1601 for loyalty during Essex's rebellion, when he was lord mayor. It was Geare who first introduced stockings of knitted woollen yarn into this country.

A wedding of note took place in St Dunstan's in 1589, when William Borough, one of the foremost navigators of the age, married Jane Wentworth, widow of the Lord of Stepney Manor. She was probably living in the manor house on the north-east side of the churchyard. Borough, a Devonian, had sailed before the mast in Richard Chancellor's 1553 expedition to Russia and, rising through the ranks, became chief pilot to the Muscovy Company and comptroller of the navy. He surveyed the Baltic and was second in command to Drake in the Cadiz expedition of 1587. He commanded the *Bonavoglio* when the English fleet defeated the Armada. He owned Mews Manor, the White Horse in Mile End and, in spite of his demanding career, was very active as Limehouse vestryman between 1581 and 1594.

Five years after Borough had taken to himself a 'good wife' in Lady Wentworth, there was a wedding of even greater splendour in Stepney church. The old Colet mansion, Great Place, was let by the Mercers to a number of wealthy or high-ranking tenants, including the queen's godson, her 'saucy poet', Sir John Harrington. His daughter, Lucy, to become patroness of John Donne and Ben Jonson, was married in Stepney church to Edward Russell, Earl of Bedford on 12 December 1594. Sir Arthur Throckmorton, Sir Walter Raleigh's brother-in-law, was one of the guests; the excitement brought on one of his funny turns! Of all the fine and famous local residents, this Sir Arthur must top the list, not just because he was related to the great Sir Walter but because he left a very personal account of his life in Elizabethan Mile End among the court circle. He kept a diary, a Pepysian sort of journal, lapsing into French or Italian when he wanted to record something intimate. The three volumes were discovered in 1956 and, if you can make out the handwriting, you can read it in the archives of Canterbury Cathedral. Among other things it brings home the huge divide between rich and poor.

On Joel Gascoyne's map of 1703 a house called Frogmortons is marked, where the Mile End mosque now stands. Just before Christmas 1587 Sir Arthur Throckmorton and his wife Ann (*née* Lucas) moved into a house facing Mile End Green, a little to the east of Whitechapel church. Peter Porter of Houndsditch charged £9 10s to put up railings. (The boundary of Mile End hamlet was just to the east of Whitechapel church.)

The Throckmortons were a very important family. Sir Nicholas, Arthur's father, had been close to the queen, a powerful politician and diplomat, part of the Protestant coterie led by Sir Francis Walsingham. The family's townhouse was in the parish of St Katharine Cree, near Aldgate, and there were Stepney connections. A Simon Throckmorton was tenant of Great Place in 1577 and Thomas Throckmorton, Arthur's brother, had a room at the Limpet in Mile End in 1588. It was Arthur's sister Elizabeth, known to the family and to posterity as Bess, who would bring Mile End into the limelight.

Arthur's diary reveals an anxious man, a hypochondriac, always pill popping and purging, consulting physicians and apothecaries (at great expense), reading his stars, concerned about his wife's periods and post-natal depression (*douleur du laice*). Apart from the odd mention of a christening, wedding or funeral there is no mention of church or religion in the diary, except a note that he paid £3 for a copy of Luther's works. He spent three times as much in a day on doctors than he gave to Stepney church as his annual tithe of 3s 4d. He played the lute, drank Canary wine and Muscatel, smoked a pipe, gambled, worried about his wife's temper and whether or not she would sleep with him.

The household at Mile End had fourteen servants, including a coachman, footmen, a blackamoor from Guinea, maids and a cook. The maids were paid £2 a year 'all found'; the cook and Lady Throckmorton's personal maid got £4 and the coachman £3. Arthur paid his barber 1s for 'trimming', his farrier 1s 6d to shoe a horse and 10s to vicar Anderson to 'church' his wife at St Dunstan's (the going rate was 9d). The household consumed eight loaves of bread a day; herrings cost 2s a barrel and sugar loaves were a luxury item at 14d a pound. Arthur's tobacco was an expensive treat, costing 11s 6d for a mere 3oz. A Turkey carpet cost £8 and a grey horse from a hacker in Ratcliff £6 13s 8d; Arthur was very proud when he stabled it in the royal stables. For families of such status gorgeous attire was a necessity, and it came at a very great price. One of Anne's velvet gowns cost £15, russet satin was 12s 6d a yard, shoes 7s a pair, a pair of black silk stockings 35s, a good ruff 10s, gloves 4s a pair, five dozen gold and pearl buttons £10. In July 1591 Arthur got himself a new outfit of purple velvet with a white plush girdle with silver lace.

To 'Frogmortons' in the autumn of 1591 came Bess Throckmorton, Arthur's feisty and ambitious sister, lady of the bedchamber to the queen. She was pregnant and had married in secret the father, the fabulous Sir Walter Raleigh, tall, dark and glittering with jewels, one of the queen's favourites. If Gloriana found out about the marriage everyone would be in dire trouble. One wonders how many pills Arthur had to take when he was told the news. Bess stayed at Mile End for her confinement and went into labour on the morning of 29 March 1592; a boy was born between 2 p.m. and 3 p.m. Dick the footman was given 10s to run to Chatham to tell Raleigh. Walter, apparently deserted by most of his friends, sent his half-brother Adrian Gilbert to Mile End to give Bess some money, £50, for which he was never reimbursed. On 10 April, the diary records, the child was baptised Damerei, reinforcing Raleigh's claimed descent from the Plantagenets and the daughter of de Amerie of Clare. No mention is made of the clergyman who officiated. The Earl of Essex himself was godparent, along with Arthur and Ann Throckmorton. On 27 April Bess returned to court, and the baby was sent to an Enfield wetnurse. Raleigh set sail but was called back by Elizabeth. On 19 May he signed an *ex-post facto* marriage settlement and Bess went back to Mile End with the baby. Within a few days she was arrested and sent with the baby to the Tower. Raleigh was put under house arrest. In December both were released, but the baby had died. When things calmed down Bess went to live in Raleigh's mansion in Dorset. Walter was often at Mile End with his in-laws, in 1595 and in May and August 1596, when one of his servants died and was buried in Stepney churchyard.

Up from Mile End Green, a little eastwards of the Throckmortons' house, a lane with very few houses either side led through Lord Wentworth's fields to the sleepy and superior village of Bethnal or Bednal Green. By 1649 the lane was called Dog Row; later it became the Cambridge Heath Road.

Bishop's Hall, the old episcopal palace, about half a mile east of the village, had long ceased to have any church connections and was occupied by a series of rich men, like 'Judge' Fuller, who died in 1592 and endowed the famous Fuller almshouses in Stepney and Shoreditch. The Wentworth lords of the manor had a house in Stepney village.

In Bethnal Green village St George's chapel stood on the Green, in what is now Victoria Park Square, and there were a few large houses, of which one was of great notoriety and awarded the nickname Kirby's (or Kirkby's) Castle. Like King John's Palace and Fisher's Folly this was a Beckingham Palace of a house, one of many sumptuous dwellings built by men of 'no greater calling possession or wealth'. Stow says that rude rhymes were made up about them. Kirby's Castle had been occupied (from *c.* 1550) by a most suitable copyholder, Sir John Gresham, courtier, merchant founder of the Muscovy Company, lord mayor, four times master of the Mercers' Company and one of the jurors who found Catherine Howard guilty. It was rebuilt by the upstart Kirby in about 1570. By Pepys's day the story had grown up that Kirby's Castle, now Sir William Ryder's residence, was the original Blind Beggar's house (see chapter 3). Strype joked that it was thus named because Kirby had beggared himself building it. In 1726 it was a lunatic asylum, and to this day that part of the Green (on the east by Roman Road) is known as Barmy Park.

Finally, we may go out along the Whitechapel Road in the direction of Bow in the company of William Kemp, Shakespeare's comic actor, as he did his marathon morris dance to Norwich. Either for a wager or for publicity, in 1599 Kemp performed this 'nine days' wonder', which certainly caught the public imagination. He wrote it up the following year, telling his audience that 'Mile-end is no walke without a recreation at Stratford Bow with Creame and Cakes'.

Stratford Bow, with its pretty bridge spanning the Lea, full of water irises in the summer, was quite the beauty spot in those days, better known for its cream teas than for the bakeries that had steamed away supplying bread for the City in medieval times. The mills still ground and there were still some bakeries, but by the time Stow wrote his account of London in 1598 the supply of bread to the City from the Stratfords had ceased. This was probably quite a recent development: during the bread shortage of 1527 people had flocked to Mile End and besieged the bread carts that were coming in from the villages on the Lea. Barges still brought wheat for grinding and malt for the breweries down from Enfield and Ware. In 1580 the river was cleaned out and made more navigable.

Bow had the feel of a little country town, surrounded by farmland, with its sub-hamlet of Old Ford where folk went to bathe in the river. King John's Palace was in the occupation of a Mr Woodall by 1598. There were some millers and mealmen and bakers, a good number of hackneymen, brewers, vintners and distillers, together with basketmakers, silk-weavers, painters, carpenters, butchers and chandlers. Goodwife Waldon kept a lodging house called The Ship; a tinkers' family were staying there in 1595. William Poyntell had a pub called The Bear and the Saracen's Head was kept by Henry Thomson (1599). Virtually independent from the mother parish of Stepney, the church of St Mary, in the middle of the High Street, looked after its own. There the locals took their babies for baptism and their corpses for burial, and there they were married. An unusually high proportion of gentry make their appearance in the marriage registers. Some are City couples; as in later years Bow, it seems, was a fashionable place for Londoners to marry, far enough away to be private, easy of access and an attractive venue.

As William Kemp hops and jigs away out of the town of Bow and towards the Essex marshes, his bells jingling and ribbons fluttering, we will leave Merrie England for what the Royalist vicar of Stepney described as the 'tottering times' of the seventeenth century.

1 East London, 1935.

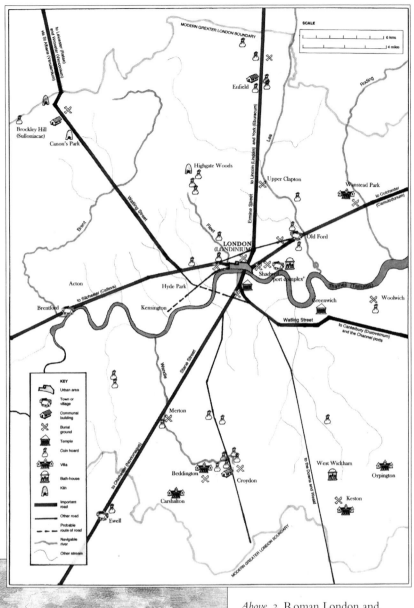

Above 2 Roman London and its environs. Map by Jane Seal.

KEY

Urban area
Town or village
Communal building
Burial ground
Temple
Coin hoard
Villa
Bath-house
Kiln
Important road
Other road
Probable route of road
Navigable river
Other stream

SCALE

6 kms
4 miles

MODERN GREATER LONDON BOUNDARY

to Leicester (Ratae) and Wroxeter (Viroconium) via St Albans (Verulamium)

Brockley Hill (Sulloniacae)

Canon's Park

Watling Street

Brent

Acton

Brentford

Kensington

Hyde Park

to Silchester (Calleva)

Wandle

Stane Street

Merton

Beddington

Carshalton

Ewell

to Chichester (Noviomagus)

Enfield

Highgate Woods

Upper Clapton

Lea

Ermine Street

to Lincoln (Lindum) and York (Eburacum)

Fleet

LONDON (LONDINIUM)

Old Ford

Shadwell 'port complex'

Thames (Tamesis)

Watling Street

Greenwich

Woolwich

Wanstead Park

to Colchester (Camulodunum)

Roding

to Canterbury (Durovernum) and the Channel ports

West Wickham

Croydon

Orpington

Keston

to the Downs and Weald

MODERN GREATER LONDON BOUNDARY

Left 3 Stepney parish church, an eighteenth-century print.

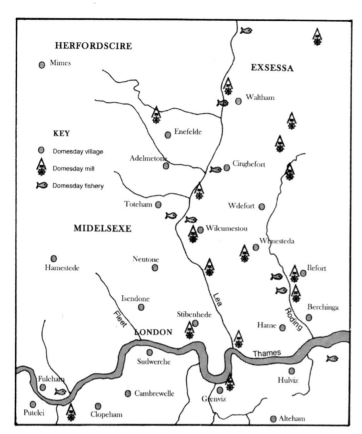

Left 4 East London at the time of Domesday. Map by Jane Seal.

Below 5 The manor house of Upper Bromley and the remains of Madame Eglantine's nunnery, 1758.

MANOR HOUSE, ST. LEONARD, BROMLEY

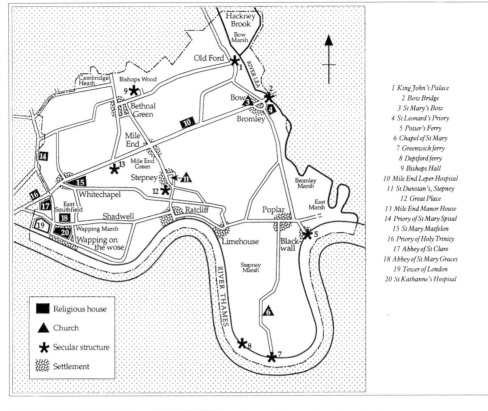

Above 6 The medieval East End.

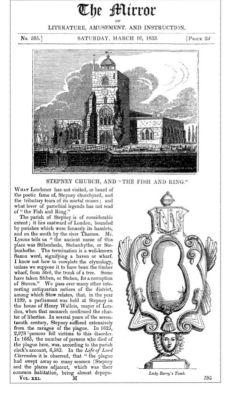

Left 7 Stepney church, 1830s.

8 King John's Palace, Old Ford.

A Curious GATE at Stepney.

This House by Tradition is call'd King Johns Gate from what Authority is not known, but will serve as a specimen of Variegated Brick work, It is reputed to be the oldest House in Stepney. In this Village Edward the 1 held a Parliament Anno 1291 and in Doomsday Book it occurs as a Place of great Antiquity.

Pub: Jan 1: 1791 by N. Smith G? Mays Buildings.

9 The Tudor gatehouse of King John's Palace.

Right 10 A Tudor house on Tower Hill: the engraving dates from 1792.

AN OLD HOUSE which is now standing on LITTLE TOWER HILL

This House was erected about the time of Henry VIII when it was much the fashion to ornament the fronts of buildings with figures in Plaister or Stucco of the heads of the Roman Emperors, the cardinal Virtues or other emblematic figures. It was not unusual whenever coins were found upon a particular spot whereon a house was to be erected, to cause such coins to be represented in plaister upon the house. Stow mentions a Roman Coin being found in digging the foundation of Aldgate, which Mr Martin Bond one of the Surveyors of that work, caused to be carved in Stone, and fixed on either side of the Gate.

London Pub.d May 10.1792 by N.Smith. Gt Mays Buildings S.t Martins Lane

Below 11 The ruins of Holy Trinity Minories Priory, Aldgate, 1800.

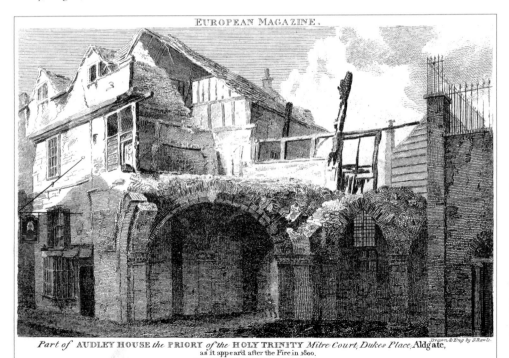

EUROPEAN MAGAZINE.

Drawn & Eng.d by S.Rawle.

Part of AUDLEY HOUSE *the* PRIORY *of the* HOLY TRINITY *Mitre Court, Dukes Place,* Aldgate, as it appear'd after the Fire in 1800.

Published by J.Sewell Cornhill. Sept.1.1800.

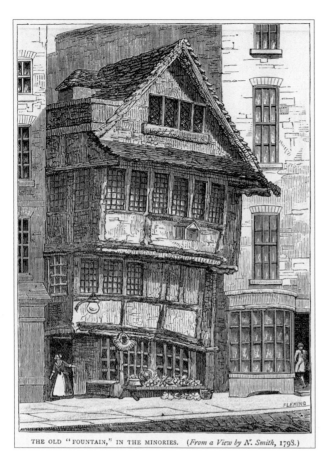

THE OLD "FOUNTAIN," IN THE MINORIES. (*From a View by N. Smith,* 1798.)

Left 12 The old Fountain in the Minories, from a view by N. Smith, 1798.

Below 13 Although this engraving is of Southwark, Whitechapel would have been very similar.

JEREMIAH BURROUGHES Late
Gospell = Preacher To two of the Greatest
Congregation in England viz: Stepney
and Cripplegate London.

Above 14 The East London Mosque – on the site of Sir Walter Raleigh's brother-in-law's house. Photograph by Yvonne Hughes.

Left 15 Jeremiah Burroughs, famous Stepney preacher.

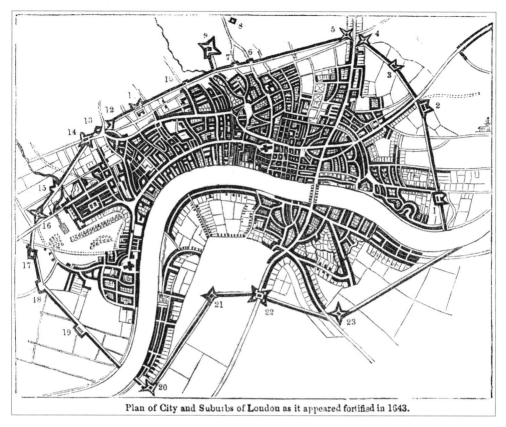

Plan of City and Suburbs of London as it appeared fortified in 1643.

Above 16 The fortifications around the city and suburbs of London, 1643.

Right 17 Matthew Mead, the celebrated Puritan divine.

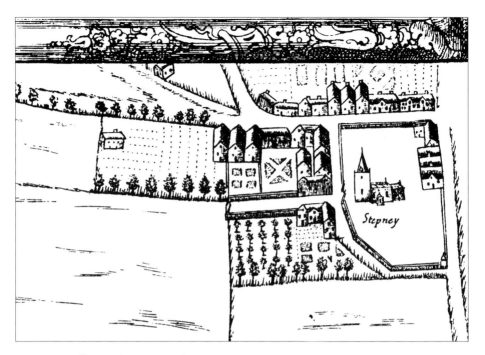

18 Stepney village in the seventeenth century.

Of Carthage wall I was a Stone,
Oh Mortals, read with pity,
Time consumes all it spareth none,
Man, Mountains, Town, nor City.
Therefore Oh Mortals, now bethink
You, whereunto you must,
Since now such lately buildings,
Lie buried in the dust.

Thomas Hughes, 1663.

Pub.ª March 1ˢᵗ 1804

Drawn & Engraved by S. Jones & I. Greig

19 The Carthage Stone, Stepney churchyard.

20 Mansell Street, Goodman's Fields. Photograph by Yvonne Hughes.

21 The Royal London Hospital. Photograph by Yvonne Hughes.

22 Prescot Street, Goodman's Fields. Photograph by Yvonne Hughes.

23 Ireland Row: eighteenth-century houses along the Mile End Road. Photograph by Yvonne Hughes.

24 No. 37 Stepney Green. Photograph by Yvonne Hughes.

25 Old houses by the Bow flyover. Photograph by Yvonne Hughes.

26 Bromley Hall, stranded on the Blackwall Tunnel approach road. Photograph by Yvonne Hughes.

Above, left 27 Meridien House, Poplar, built for the chaplain to the East India Company almshouses. Photograph by Yvonne Hughes.

Above, right 28 The Town of Ramsgate at Wapping Old Stairs, Wapping Whitechapel. Photograph by Yvonne Hughes.

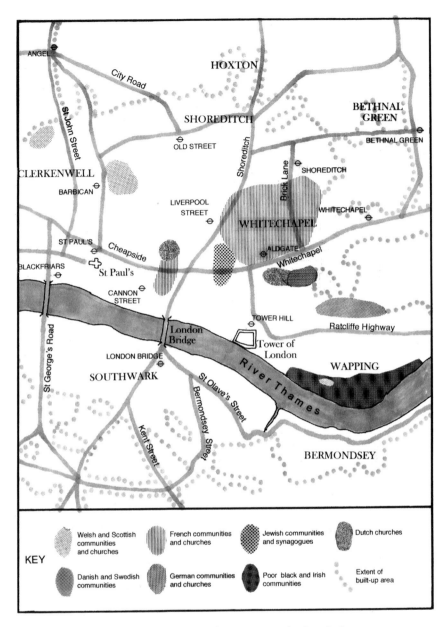

KEY

Welsh and Scottish communities and churches	French communities and churches	Jewish communities and synagogues	Dutch churches
Danish and Swedish communities	German communities and churches	Poor black and Irish communities	Extent of built-up area

29 Immigrants to London in the eighteenth century. Map by Jane Seal.

30 The German Lutheran church, Alie Street, built in 1762. Photograph by Yvonne Hughes.

View of TRINITY ALMS~HOUSES, *Mile End Road*

31 The Trinity House almshouses.

Chapter 6

THE STUARTS

1603–1689

In the great seventeenth-century conflict the East End was staunchly Parliamentarian. While the City was the Presbyterian stronghold, that great, rackety seafaring conurbation on its eastern flank became a hotbed of extreme Puritan sects, with Stepney and, to a lesser extent, Whitechapel taking the limelight as the flagships of Independence, the creed adopted by Oliver Cromwell and most of the new Model Army. Nonconformist ideas from the Continent combined with a home-grown Puritanism to swell the ranks of separatism, especially in London and notably in Stepney, where, as we have seen, there was a good deal of Dutch influence, much more since the new waves of religious exiles. One contemporary described Puritans as 'fluttered from the cage of Amsterdam'. The first General Baptist church in England was in Spitalfields, established in 1612 by Thomas Helwys on his return from Holland.

From the early years of the century, moreover, there was a growing alienation from the king's mercantile policies. Peter Paul Rubens thought that the mercantile connections of the Puritans, and their close relations with the Dutch, represented a real threat of rebellion to which the king was strangely indifferent.

Stepney vestry was a strong and forceful body, dominated by 'Godly mariners' who would increasingly find themselves out of sympathy with 'bishop and king', along with much of the country, seeing popery at every turn. All East India Company ships carried a copy of *Foxe's Book of Martyrs*, with its graphic tales of the sufferings of Protestants under Bloody Mary. Trinity House, moreover, had no love for James I, who had removed their ballasting monopoly and other privileges. As time passed this unrest was exacerbated by the distress of the lower orders of society, desperate unemployed clothworkers and angry sailors who had rioted after the ill-equipped and underpaid expedition to Cadiz in 1625. It would become a classic revolutionary situation, with a powerful dissatisfied middle class leading an angry mob. The war, said Puritan divine Richard Baxter, started in the streets. As C.V. Wedgwood put it, 'The rumbling discontent of London, the great angry Protestant seaport suddenly burst into a roar of rage.'

James I: plague, Puritans and poverty

Things started badly for the Stuarts. With the 'Great Landlady's' departure it must have seemed as if a curse had fallen upon her country, and especially upon her fine capital: the City of London lost about 30,000 people to a devastating plague, its worst attack since the Black Death.

They rang a celebratory peal at Stepney church when the Scottish king was crowned as James I in that pestilential summer of 1603, and the churchwardens allowed themselves a lavish banquet. Not that there was much to celebrate for anyone except the 'merry sextons', 'hungry coffin makers' and the herb wives, able to command an extortionate 6s a bunch for rosemary. London and her suburbs presented a 'vast silent charnel house, hung with dimly lit lamps'; bells tolled mournfully over the rush-strewn streets; stinking corpses were tumbled into pits or left to stand bolt upright in their winding sheets. The watermen of Wapping and Southwark were busy, carrying families who could afford it to the cleaner air of the countryside. The plague 'pitched his tents in the sinfully polluted suburbs' of the overcrowded tenements and cottages of Spitalfields, Ratcliff, Limehouse and Wapping. The sextons at Aldgate buried 1,948 bodies, while at Whitechapel, at the height of the plague, some thirty bodies were buried every day. Not that the more salubrious areas of Mile End, Bethnal Green and Stepney village escaped. Those deaths noted as plague deaths in Stepney's burial registers are spread evenly over the parish, with nearly as many from Mile End as from the waterside slum areas. Knockfergus (now Cable Street), however, was especially hard hit.

The visitation came early to the East End, brought, no doubt, as it was to the ports of East Anglia, by ships from continental Europe (there were a significant number of burials of people from East Friesland in the parish). Already, in the warm days of May 1602, burials were alarmingly up on other years, and parish clerk Cottesford and his six-year-old son were among them. By and large women and boys succumbed before men and girls. Corpses littered the fields. They found them on Cambridge Heath, in Blackwall Fields, Poplar Fields, Wellclose Fields, Ratcliff Fields and Spital Fields. In September, when deaths were at their peak, they buried a child kept by the hamlet of Mile End; she had been found in a haystack, and she had been given the name Mary Haycocke. They buried a tinkers' child from Bow, a 'poor man out of the straws in Brickhills', a corpse found in the Limehouse 'dusthill'. Whole families were wiped out: a Dutch anchorsmith from Limehouse, Justus Mallet, and his five children died within three days. In November, among others, they buried a Norfolk vagrant found in a barn in Mile

End and a beggar child who had died in the church porch. In September they buried Agnes, a 'niger of Mr Paules of Stonehouse'. Vicar Edward Muns, aged thirty-five, in his fifth year at Stepney, brother of a leading East India Company merchant and married to a liveryman's daughter, fell victim. He was buried on the day of his infant son's baptism, 10 May, three days after the king's arrival in London. In September John Thomson, the curate who had been holding the fort, died. Bennet Johnson, probably a lady of ill repute, thought she was dying and had someone pen a pathetic letter to her mother in Kent, leaving her the house she had in Blackwall: 'My most deare and lovinge mother my moste humble commendacions unto you.' She asks to be remembered to her father, brother and friends: 'I bed you all farweel for at this tyme I am vearye syck. So I reste, disireinge my dear mother to have patience for me.' She recovered, and lived for another four years.

'Let us see what doings the sexton of Stepney hath,' wrote Thomas Dekker in his account of the plague year. Such was the severity with which the pestilence struck in the east that it was Stepney the writer chose as the location for his hideous comic tale of the drunk who fell into a grave. One midnight, 'when sprites walke and not a mowse dare stirre, because cattes goe catter-walling', out of one of the many alehouses in Stepney reels a drunk. So drunk is he that 'houses seemed to turne on the trees and athings went round'. He keeps bumping into trees and challenging them to a duel. Eventually he collapses into an open grave, full of plaguey corpses, and, mistaking it for his bed, falls asleep. Along comes the Stepney sexton, greedily 'casting up how much money he will make from today's burials'. So absorbed is he that he falls into the open grave, scattering bones and skulls about. One of the bones strikes the sleeping drunk on the head and he cries out: 'Zoundes, what do you mean to crack my Mazer!' The terrified sexton, thinking a corpse is talking, rushes off pursued by the drunk. So traumatised is he that he goes mad and dies. The Stepney sexton at the time was Edmund Purser, a Poplar vestryman. There is no mention of him in the vestry minutes after his appointment in 1601, so this might have been a true story.

There were more positive events. In 1606 the newly chartered Virginia Company sent an expedition to North America, under the command of Christopher Newport. Three ships set off from Blackwall, and just over a hundred colonists arrived to found Jamestown. From this time on there was a steady stream of emigrants, numbers of them East Enders, and the term 'Virginia widows' was commonplace in Wapping and Ratcliff.

Of even greater importance for the area were the activities of the East India Company. In the early years of the new century that most successful and prestigious of trading companies bought a yard in Stepney. Likewise, the Corporation of Trinity House made a Stepney house its headquarters. Both had moved their operations north of the river. The East India Company was founded in 1600 and was soon trading in ivory, pearls, diamonds, calicoes and many tons of spices, from the East Indies and India, even venturing as far as Japan. Some idea of the immense value of the luxury items can be had from the auction of velvets in July 1614, where one coverlet would sell for as much as £20, seven times the annual value of a small Stepney house. Sailors pressed for government service were the left-overs, the men not good enough for the company's ships. This was the largest commercial operation in London; its great ships 'mobile maritime fortresses' dominated the river. In 1614 William Burrell of Ratcliff, the foremost builder of the company's vessels and the greatest shipbuilder of his day, suggested that ground should be bought in Blackwall, and the company's dock moved there from Deptford. The land was held in copyhold, one Thomas Jones, a Ratcliff gentleman and vestryman, being lord of the manor. The purchase was achieved and Jones was ordered to hold a 'great dinner' for his copyhold tenants to attend and surrender their rights in the land; the menu was to be appropriate to the 'credit and reputation of the company'. It must have been some banquet that initiated the East India Company's long rule in Stepney.

The company's presence in the parish became overwhelming. It gave direct or indirect and lucrative employment to great numbers of men, and its leading officers, merchants and shipbuilders, particularly the latter, had houses built for themselves in Limehouse, Blackwall and Poplar. The company built houses for seamen in Blackwall in 1614 and provided generously for the relief of local women whose husbands had been wounded or killed in their employ.

Trinity House was originally established in 1514, perhaps having its origins in a medieval Trinity Guild. It was a body of great influence that extended its activities to all matters of navigation in coastal waters and provided shelter and pensions for seamen and their families. In the early years of the century, certainly by 1610, the Corporation had acquired a house in Stepney, probably where the sugarhouse had been, where they held meetings. Richard Nottingham, who was Ratcliff churchwarden from 1615 to 1616, was clerk to the Corporation from 1610 to 1613 and from 1613 to 1614 William Ivy was master – the roistering privateer we met in the last chapter. Although they still had their Deptford house, by 1621 Stepney was evidently regarded as the Corporation's headquarters and the elders erected a monument to a former master, Thomas Spert, in St Dunstan's, in that year, eighty years after his death. The monument is still in the church and claims Spert as the founder of Trinity House. There is no evidence for this, but he was master of the *Mary Rose*, the *Henri Grace a Dieu* and the *Great Harry*.

The riverside hamlets were now overwhelmingly concerned with ships and seafaring, and the Shipwrights' Company moved their hall to Ratcliff. The shipbuilding clan of Petts was already established there. Phineas rented a house in Limehouse from William Borough in 1597 (for £11 a year) before moving to Chatham, and his brother Joseph lived in Limehouse and had a yard there. When he died in November 1605 he was buried in the chancel of Stepney church and his funeral was attended by the 'principal officers of the Navy', Sir Robert Mansell, Sir Henry Palmer and Sir John Trevor.

The East India Company and Trinity House had a virtual monopoly of places on Stepney vestry. Ratcliff vestrymen included Thomas Best, East India Company captain, the founder of English power in India and a master of Trinity House (1633), William Burrell, the Company's shipbuilder, pulleymaker John Crane, Sir John Lee, keeper of ordnance stores at the Tower, Thomas Manning, a ship's carpenter of the Highway, Richard Nottingham, clerk of Trinity House, Robert Rooke, a tailor and coal-merchant, and Augustine Badicott, a Wapping butcher who supplied the Company's meat. The men who represented Limehouse were nearly all shipbuilders: Nicholas Diggins of the East India Company (1594–1621), Mr John Bennet, described as waterman and shipwright, Sir Michael Geare, surveyor of the navy and master of Trinity House (1603–25), Joseph Pett (1604), Edward Stevens, the Petts's main rival, and Thomas Andrewes (1603–11), a shipbuilder in partnership with William Jones and Robert Rickman.

The Church of England was in an uneasy, wretched condition in those days. With the loss of endowments and gifts to the church that came with the Reformation, it was in dire financial straits and the clergy were forced into pluralism. There were complaints about their lack of education and many church buildings lay neglected for lack of funds to keep them in good order. Meanwhile there was an increasing divide between a predominantly 'High Church' hierarchy and a strong underswell of Puritanism. Puritan leaders had high hopes of the new king, but they were in for a gross disappointment. In 1604 a conference assembled at Hampton Court to settle differences between the Puritan wing of the Church and the bishops. But James had been made wary of nonconformists because of his experiences with Presbyterians in Scotland, and no concessions were made. That autumn eighty ministers (out of a total of about 8,000) were expelled for not subscribing to the surplice, the cross, confirmation and other High Church practices. As a sop, however, it was agreed that a new translation of the Bible should be made to replace the Bishops' Bible of 1568. The director of this enterprise was Lancelot Andrewes, brother of Thomas Andrews, the Limehouse shipbuilder. Their father was a sea captain and Lancelot had been educated at the Ratcliff School, before going on to Merchant Taylors. He was now Dean of Westminster, Master of Pembroke College, Cambridge, soon to become a bishop, an ardent ceremonialist and as keen as his master to 'harry them (the nonconformists) out of the land'. The new Bible was published in 1611, the finest flower of seventeenth-century prose, the King James Bible.

The planned terrorist attack on king and parliament in November 1605, masterminded by the Roman Catholic lunatic fringe and whose reverberations have swung down the centuries even to this day, gave a huge boost to anti-popery. It was close to home for the East Enders; Lord Monteagle, to whom the famous anonymous letter of warning was sent, lived on Mile End Green. Gunpowder Plot sermons were preached on the anniversary, their published versions bestsellers for many years.

Undoubtedly the corruption and ostentatious luxury of the court, what Dekker called a cluster of 'spangle babies', combined with the hints of Popish ceremonial creeping back into parish churches, fostered the growth of Puritanism and separatism. In Jacobean Stepney, home of the sailors and merchants who, as we have seen, encountered enemy papists on their foreign voyages, there was added cause for anxiety. Captain Thomas Best, for instance, assiduous vestryman for nearly forty years, 'a man of substance and repute, well known in Ratcliff and Limehouse', became well acquainted with the Portuguese devils and their Jesuit anti-Christs, as did his crews, when fighting in India. On 13 December 1613 Robert Johnson moved a motion at the East India Company's Court of Assistants to consider the relief of their employees' souls. It was decided that 'some sufficient preacher to be sent with the latest fleet to remain at Surat, who might be of learninge and courage to oppose the Jesuits'. For this service of anti-popery the company was prepared to pay 100 marks a year.

After the initial purge of clergy following the Hampton Court Conference, however, there was something of a lull in this Church divide. Alehouse keepers across the country might dread the arrival of a 'Godly' parson or curate in their parish who would clamp down on the jollifications that went on in their establishments after churchings and christenings. A series of good harvests kept everyone relatively content. If contemporary literature is to be believed, the Godly were regarded by the generality as harmless if irritating fools, who 'spoke through their nose', while it was the Catholics who were the 'reds under the bed'.

In Stepney parish George Gouldman, a 'quiet man', vicar for nearly all of James I's reign and most of Charles I's, was engaged in a number of tithe prosecutions, usually a sign of a Puritan presence. There was not much sign of open religious conflict in the church yet, although there was a High Church curate in Edward Edgworth and a High Church sexton in William Culham. The signs suggest that the powerful Puritan vestry was in charge; certainly the organ was not replaced and there was a lecturer (another sign of Puritanism) in attendance at the 1607 visitation. Whitechapel and Aldgate remained strongly Puritan.

Isolated groups of the 'elect' fled the country for the freedom of Holland or the New World. In the summer of 1620 the East End's riverside was the scene of one of the most celebrated events in world history. Had you been down in Wapping or Blackwall, on a morning in mid-July, you would have seen sixty-five passengers embarking onto a ship of 200 tons named the *Mayflower*. She was a London vessel, and one of her part-owners was a Blackwall man, Robert Sheffield. Of this company some were off to seek their fortune; some were in search of freedom to practise a simpler form of Christianity than was imposed in England. Many came from Whitechapel and Aldgate, which the *Mayflower* historian Charles Banks named, along with Shoreditch, as the 'pilgrim heart' of London. The ship sailed down to Southampton and eventually, at Plymouth, picked up the religious refugees, mainly from the north of England, who had fled to Holland in 1608. Tired of the struggle with poverty in Leyden and the unhealthy influence of the Dutch youth on their children, they too were off to make a new life. The Pilgrim Fathers arrived at Cape Cod on 11 November, and the rest is history. The following year the *Fortune* sailed to the embryonic colony in New England, taking more 'pilgrims'. On board this vessel were at least two Stepney men. One was Thomas Prence/Prince, a carriagemaker's son, who was to become Governor of Massachusetts. His family had come to London from Gloucestershire and the boy grew up in Ratcliff. The other was William Bassett, a gunsmith from Bethnal Green.

The main preoccupations of the leaders of Stepney parish during the Jacobean years were the growing size of the flock, and the poor, 'which do daily increase'. The East End's population explosion went on apace in the new century, reaching well over 50,000 by 1630. As in Southwark and the northern suburbs, people were still pouring in from the countryside in search of work. The riverside was crowded and Spitalfields was growing. 'Cruel and covetous landlords' did up hovels and raised rents to £3 a year. 'Filthy wide mouth'd bardogs they are,' wrote Dekker, 'that for a quarter's rent will pull out their ministers throte, if he were a tenant.' The authorities were slow to react to the problem of parish growth; the folk of Wapping Whitechapel got their own chapel of ease in 1617, but Wapping Stepney would have to wait over a hundred years – as would Limehouse and Spitalfields.

As for the areas closer to the City, Aldgate, Whitechapel, St Katharine's and East Smithfield, an alarmist report written in the early years of James I's reign describes the desperate situation: 'Many lewd and badd people harbour themselves near the Citie'; artisans and tradesmen who had never served as apprentices, men with no trade at all, porters, ostlers, labourers and broom-men haunted the alehouses, gambling dens and brothels, along with 'cheaters, shyfters and cuttpurses'. The influx of these unsavoury characters caused rack-renting and the building of poor-quality housing: 'the desire of profitte greatly increaseth buyldinges' and 'everie man secketh out places, high wayes, lanes and coverte corners to build upon'. Old mansions were rented out to the 'rag tag' people or papists, while some were converted into gaming houses or brothels and some used as factories for the processing of 'indigo, cochineal, saffron, nutmeg, quicksilver and wax steele'. In many parishes, the author claims, there were as many as 2,000 people on poor relief. The immigrants, he says, have mercenary midwives, bawds and panders in their pay, and babies are often delivered in secret. Many of the tradeless acquired alehouse licences for 10s and two sureties; every fourth house in the liberties and out-parishes was a drinking establishment of some kind. There was a brisk trade in stolen goods among these people, who 'shroud themselves in corners and covert places near unto the Citie, only thirsting after the spoyle thereof'.

Rosemary Lane's celebrated Rag Fair in East Smithfield became one of the most notorious spots for the trade in stolen goods. Crime and disorder, according to the records of the Middlesex Sessions, was at its worst in Whitechapel, East Smithfield and Wapping, with the East End accounting for about half the crime in London's suburbs.

Charles I: 'loud clamour'

Within a few months of the accession of Charles I in 1625 the plague returned with terrible ferocity. Deaths in London were about 5,000 up on the 1603 total and Stepney lost 2,978 souls. Sexton William Culham was to become rich on the proceeds of his grim task, and took the lease of the Rose tavern.

Diarist John Ward wrote of:

> empty streets deoderized with oak and juniper smoke, musket fumes, rosemary garlands and frankincense, and peals of bells ... dormant houses, the staring eyes of their inhabitants glimpsed through windows thrown open to let in the fragranced air and the clarions ... stray dogs who had lost their masters, ditches left undredged for fear of stirring up pestilential airs, lone pedestrians chewing angelica or gentian or wearing arsenic amulets to ward off infection, some coming to a sudden halt and holding out their arms in curious positions, as though carrying invisible pails of water-signs of the first twinges of the characteristic plague sores or 'buboes' that appear under the arms.

Nehemiah Wellington of Whitechapel reported that 300 children died in one alley. All the men, women and children in Red Lion Court were taken, while in Shoreditch sixty pregnant and nursing women died in one week. At the usual April vestry meeting in Stepney the 'contagion of sicknes' was discussed. There had already been a number of deaths, and goodwives were appointed as searchers for dead bodies and infected households in the most densely populated parts of the parish. Mary Oswell and Elizabeth Scott earned 4d a household for their task in Ratcliff, while Joan Hassam and Rose Write did the same in Limehouse. There had been a number of plague burials near the church; the vestry now ordered that new graves were to be kept at least 17ft away from it. During the summer the vestry met twice in emergency sessions under the chairmanship of curate Edgeworth. On 24 July 1625 the orders about burial were changed as the graveyard was now so full, and the diggers were told that graves should be just 7ft from the church.

From the hamlets came the carts of bodies, the bearers carrying red wands, cloakless, so they could be easily spotted and people might keep away. At the height of the pestilence, in August, they were able to command large sums for carting corpses, and the vestry set a table of rates: for collecting bodies from Ratcliff, Limehouse, Mile End or Bethnal Green they were to charge 6*d*, 4*d* if the church had to pay, 8*d* if they used the church cloth. The clergy were taking funerals all day, every day; the curate at Bow, John Forster, was taken in July. Stepney's parish clerk, John Robinson, was so busy that a deputy was appointed to take charge of the entering of names in the registers.

The stench was terrible; the churchyard was 'noisome … by reason of so many bodies … entered there', and it was decided to gravel over part of it and use the burial fees that had accrued to buy an extra burial ground. Evidently this was not enough, and the wardens were ordered to hand over any monies they had collected as 'church duties' for the purpose. Shipbuilder and East India Company magnate Robert Bell, Ratcliff warden, refused to do so, and the vestry took him to court. The outcome is not known, but he left the parish for Rotherhithe and did very well for himself, becoming a gentleman of the privy chamber and receiving a knighthood.

A much-needed new churchyard was purchased and walled, paid for by a levy from all the hamlets, with a contribution of £15 from the Mercers' Company. Thomas Green of Mile End filled in the 'great pond' that lay to the south-east of the church to make room for it, and built the walls.

The wills make sad reading. Joan Lane of Stepney, whose husband was sailing to the East Indies, made hers when she was 'stricken with the sicknesse'. She left her husband her wedding ring 'for a remembrance of my love', trusting that her sister, the wife of a Wapping mariner, who had been nursing her, would take 'loveing and kind care' of her three children. Widow Mary Drinkall of Limehouse spoke her dying wish on 3 September, asking one John Donne to look after her little boy Luke. By the time the will went to probate, twenty-five days later, Luke too was dead. John Smith Ratcliff, carpenter, 'not very well', signed his will with a trembling hand, leaving his damson cloak to his brother, his ruff to 'Silvester's wife' and the residue to his mother and sister. John Billman, Ratcliff shipwright, left £5 to the 'poor infected of the hamlet of Ratcliffe' and 30*s* to the woman who had nursed him. Robert Westover, lighterman of Stepney, dictated his will to his 'onlie mother', leaving her his house on Wapping Wall. Nicholas Hitchman, victualler of Ratcliff, left his brother his feather hat.

William Ferrers, a young gentleman of Bromley and the son of a rich merchant, died in August, as did his wife and baby. A pathetic inscription was put on the child's memorial tablet in St Leonard's church:

As Nurses strive their Babes in Bed to hie,
When they too liberally the Wantons play;
So, to prevent his future grievous Crimes,
Nature, his Nurse, got him to Bed betimes.'

The plague bled the parishes and hamlets dry, and the poverty problem was acute. The accommodation over Stepney's new vestry house, currently occupied by the sexton, curate and clerk, was ordered to be given over to the poor as the rooms became vacant. When the churchwardens' accounts were rendered in August 1627 all four wardens had overspent.

There were serious riots in Wapping and Ratcliff in 1628 when the unpaid sailors from the Duke of Buckingham's poorly equipped expedition to the Ile de Ré were quartered there.

In July of that year William Laud, a disciple of Lancelot Andrewes, was made Bishop of London; five years later he was to become Archbishop of Canterbury, with his protégé William Juxon taking over in London. With Laud's elevation there began in earnest the religious revolution so close to the king's heart. A tireless regime of visitations and prosecutions in the Church courts with the vicious and powerful court of High Commission at the head, brought back candles and images, stained glass and vestments, music and bowing to the altar, and all the trappings of popery, or so it appeared to the Godly. To Laud and his followers this was 'the beauty of holiness'. Having the communion table in the body of the church, with tavern pots instead of silver chalices, made churches into alehouses, said Laud – who held that although the Roman Catholic Church had fallen into error, the Calvinist and other Protestant sects were heretics. Such was the antagonism to all this among those who had a say that in 1629 parliament refused to grant the king the income from tunnage and poundage (taxes on imports) unless he reformed his High Church policy. The stubborn monarch dissolved his parliament and ruled without it for eleven years.

On a summer day in 1629 Charles I, out hunting in Wanstead, chased a stag all the way into Wapping, and finally killed it in Nightingale Lane. A crowd gathered to watch, and trampled down a vegetable garden. The fact that so unimportant a tale was repeated and handed down is, perhaps, some indication of what the locals thought about their monarch. If we look at what happened in the East End during these years of King Charles's 'personal rule', it becomes a matter of little wonder that they joined with such fervour in the cry 'Hunt Laud, the fox', and that their support was overwhelmingly for the Roundhead cause in the conflict to come.

Laud set about cleaning up the East End. Hundreds of men and women were summoned to St Paul's over these years, to appear before the doctors of civil law and answer the charges of 'tippling', Sunday and holy day trading, bearing bastards, running brothels, adultery and keeping alehouses open during divine service. The churchwardens and court officials were on the look-out for Virginia widows who entertained themselves with other men while their husbands were abroad, for card parties and dancing on Sundays, for costers selling their wares when they should have been in church. A rash of presentments followed each holy day.

All this is very ironic if one considers the traditional view of the period, with solemn Puritanical spoilsports ranged against maypole-dancing Cavaliers. The world was turned upside down in Stepney, with Puritan churchwardens, like the brewer Francis Zachary, Ratcliff warden, implementing High Church policies and getting stick for being tainted with popery. There is no doubt that the alehouse keepers, barmaids, labourers, sailors and their women associated the harassment with the popish innovations; this is especially true of the Dutch victuallers, of whom there were quite a number. When the house kept by George and Anna Hooth was raided in November 1638 Mistress Hooth let out a stream of abuse, accusing the officer, among other things, of being an 'incense promoter'.

Concurrent with the efforts of the agents of the Church to spoil everybody's fun and ruin local trade, Stepney vestry imposed a swingeing church rate to raise money to shore up the crumbling church building. Not surprisingly there was widespread resistance. Ratcliff warden Robert Salmon presented twelve individuals for refusing to pay, and warden William Pyot named seven from his hamlet of Mile End.

The first rash of prosecutions for drinking, immorality and Sabbath-breaking came just when the parishioners were smarting from the imposition of the new church tax. In August 1632 twelve parishioners were presented to the Commissary Court for 'tippling', many, many more than any other parish, and the following May, along with the church rate refusers, Matthew Venn at the Cross and another publican were summoned for Sunday opening; there were four cases of 'incontinence'; and Solomon Stryder, the miller of Knockfergus, was hauled up for grinding on a Sunday. From Limehouse there were two cases of 'incontinence' and one of harbouring a single mother. Victuallers Gilbert Pickering from the Hen and Chickens and Master Pollard from the Mitre in Ratcliff were presented. In June the court met twice with similar prosecutions; on the 19th thirty-four people from St Botolph's Bishopsgate were indicted for moral offences and not taking communion. In July the court's time was taken up with Stepney alehouse keepers: there were eight prosecutions for opening during service time in Mile End, twenty-three in Ratcliff, Henry Doggett on Wapping Wall, the landlord of the King's Head in Upper Shadwell, Master Goddin at the White Hart in White Horse Street, the keeper of the Close Style, William Saunders at the Three Hatts. Solomon Strider the miller had to pay 3s 4d to the poor as a penalty for Sunday grinding. Mary Title was accused of selling figs and other fruit from her stall during divine service. On 25 October the prosecutions came in from the north of the parish, Spitalfields and Petticoat Lane, with summonses for the landlords of three houses in Wentworth Street, the Golden Cross, The Ship and the Sugar Loaf. William Norman was presented for having dancing on Sunday and, from Stepney village itself, the landlord of the Three Mariners in Whitehorse Street and Master Kirby at the Rose in the village were presented. In January 1635 there were prosecutions of victuallers from all over London, including thirteen from Stepney. In February miller Solomon Stryder was fined again for Sunday milling. In the opening months of 1636 numbers of landlords had to pay the penalty for opening their houses on New Year's Day. Robert Hill and his brother's wife, of King Street, Wapping, were brought before the court because they, 'induced by temptacons of the Devil, did commit the filthy sin of incest' while Hill's brother was away at sea. Proceedings against Josia Draper (for living in sin with Agnes Clark) were so traumatic that he died. Agnes, the wife of George Peters, a King Street shipwright, was fined 7s for having a sailor's baby.

It was, however, Sunday drinking that, as usual, took up most of the court's time. In February presentments were made against the landlords of The Bell, The Christopher, the Sugar House in Poplar, the Cross Keys and the Princes Arms in Mile End, the houses on the Green, the Bull Head and The Gunne, The Exchange, in King Street, the Carpenter's Arms, The Wheatsheaf in Fox Lane, the pub at Ratcliff Cross, The Swan in Ratcliff, the Sun and Gun in Limehouse, The Bull in Stepney village, the Black Bull on Bethnal Green, The Estridge in Limehouse. William Stevenson of Poplar was summoned for having a card party during service time on 14 January. The widow Tilman from The Bell in Wapping escaped her fine by claiming that she 'hath not victualled this half yeare'. Thomas West from the Grave Morris in Ratcliff refused to answer the court 'clamouring and railing', shouting out that 'he would see his accuser'. Andrew Adamson at the White Horse in Wapping's Hermitage had refused to open his doors when the churchwarden came spying, but the warden was able to see the company drinking through the windows. He was fined 6s.

That summer the vestry reported that the large sum of £300 was needed to repair the north side of the church, and the hamlets were to be taxed accordingly, with Ratcliff paying the lion's share. The plague struck again, raging until spring 1639; yet another levy would be made on the over-burdened hamlets for plague relief. Plans were also afoot to pull down the old gallery in the north aisle and replace it to match the new one in the south aisle.

Meanwhile the government was becoming dangerously unpopular, with its persecution of Puritans, favours shown to Catholics and repeated attempts to raise money without parliament.

Failure to observe the holy days of SS Simon and Jude and All Saints brought forth a further rash of prosecutions in November; twenty-two 'tipplers' were presented from Stepney, with a further twenty-nine prosecutions in December: landlords, weavers, bakers and labourers. Robert Frauncis was before the court for keeping a bawdy house, having been shopped by his own prostitutes.

In July 1637 Stepney vestry stopped payments for wounded soldiers and hospitals, and regulated the payments for ransoms for captive seamen; henceforth applicants for a parish ransom were to provide security and the money raised was to go to the poor. The parish had been under severe financial strain in paying out pensions to soldiers wounded in the king's expedition to the Ile de Ré. By October Ratcliff was behind with its payments, but still the vestry pressed on with plans to re-lead the steeple, and gave the go-ahead for the new north gallery.

The attack on alehouses and brothels continued in 1638, while Bow, still technically a chapel of ease to St Dunstan's, made another bid for freedom. The Stepney churchwardens' tasks were insurmountable and dangerous. Francis Zachary had the worst job as Ratcliff warden. At the Commissary Court in December 1638 Margaret, the wife of James Jackson, appeared accused of 'scandalously abusing and reviling' him on the previous 8 October, saying, 'You are a base churchwarden and the devil himself chose you churchwarden.' She then rushed into the George tavern and said things which were 'ten times worse'. In December Henry North was fined for having his pub open at illegal times, as he had been many times before, and also for not following the court order to pay Walter Cooke, the Mile End churchwarden, 3s 9d for the poor. December's prosecutions included Mistress Cooke of the Green Dragon and Master Whitbread, a strongwaterman (a member of the brewing family, no doubt). Jane Dryver was summonsed for having a bastard in her house and 'conveying her away'. In January 1639 Master Harvey of Poplar was fined for beating tobacco and delivering it round the parish in time of divine service. John Downeing from the Blue Boar and Matthew Owen from the Blew Anchor were summonsed in February. One Mistress Chiswell lost her temper with the apparitor who came after her, and shrieked out at him that he was a 'sherking rascal, one of the clerks of Paul's who live by the swett of our brows', making it quite clear what the East Enders thought of church officials. No wonder they made their own arrangements for worship, away from their oppressors. In the same month Limehouse warden Daniel Darling, the brewer, presented Mark Whitlock of Ropemakers' Fields, Limehouse, for having a conventicle. In May Master Wright was summonsed for selling calves on holy days. Costers and chandlers, mealmen and butchers were called to court for trading at illegal times. Prostitutes were picked up by the watchmen and brought to book, and William Tindall, landlord of the Three Mariners in Whitehorse Street, was prosecuted for bedding his maidservants. A Gloucester man was fined a crippling £500 for adultery, and had to do penance in St Dunstan's church porch.

While the East Enders stung from the Church's purge, parish officers were struggling with acute financial problems. Organisation in all of London's large suburban parishes was in a state of near collapse; population growth and high turnover, combined with the effects of the plague, saw administration disintegrating. Stepney was the most extreme case, because of its unwieldy size and the nature of its population. The plagues of 1625 and 1637–39 had bankrupted the parish. As well as the funding for searching and the carting of bodies for those who could not afford it, the parish had to pay burial expenses for the poor and a new burial ground had to be provided and paid for. Levies were high, and the collectors of plague rate had a tough time. John Jenney, collector for Wentworth Street, Spitalfields and Artillery Lane, had to appeal to the privy council for protection. In December 1640 the wardens complained to the Sessions that a Shadwell shipwright and an East Smithfield cooper had 'created tenements for the poor in several Shadwell houses' and were refusing to pay plague expenses. East India Company director Robert Salmon spoke of the 'common beggars up and down the streets of Limehouse'. In December 1637 it was reported to the Mercers' Company Court of Assistants (at St Paul's School) that all the tenants in their White Hart Street properties were poor and four were on the parish. Churchwardens were having to pay out of their own pocket for plague and poor relief. John Dalby, Ratcliff warden and later a captain in Cromwell's navy, paid out £879 14s 4d, and in January 1639 the Sessions ordered the vestry to raise £50 to reimburse warden Zachary. Five years into the Civil War the wardens made desperate plea to the local magistracy: 'The poor of the parish are so numerous and their necessities so great' that they were likely to 'perish for want of relief'.

It is no wonder that the continual demands made for money to shore up Stepney church met with little success. The presence of the great old building in their midst must have been a constant reminder to parishioners of the hated authorities, which not only added an extra burden of taxation to that extorted by the king but also stopped drinking and dancing, closed down Sunday markets and cleared gaming houses. In October 1638 Zachary reported that he was having trouble collecting the church rate, and £54 2s 9d was owing. Anger and desperation stalked the streets, with Solomon Stryder, the miller, stopped from grinding on holy days, many alehouse keepers fined, costers and good-time girls having their livelihoods threatened, and Master Harvey interrupted in his 'tobacco round'. All over the country the battle of the rival creeds was surfacing, with vicars, wardens and patrons at each others' throats, and Puritan lecturers, employed for the most part by the laity, exhorting congregations to abominate altars and incense, candles and coloured glass, and all the luxury and loose living with which they were said to be associated.

In Stepney the dry tinder was to be ignited by two firebrands known as the 'Morning and Evening Stars', Jeremiah Burroughs and William Greenhill, lecturers of the persuasion known as Independents, both ordained clergymen who had been thrown out of their East Anglian parishes by the notorious

High Church Bishop Wren. Burroughs came in 1640 and Greenhill a year later; Burroughs preached at seven o'clock in the morning and Greenhill at three in the afternoon. They were accounted 'the sailors' favourites', the 'Morning and Evening Stars'. Independents, mocked by their detractors for having long hair and wearing unfashionable clothes, demanded from candidates for admission to communion not only a profession of faith but also an 'account of Christian experience', what we would call 'witness' today. They stressed toleration and were against any sort of hierarchy or structured government of the Church. The split in the Parliamentarian cause, which would crystallise within the next few years, was between the Independent Divines with the Army, and the Presbyterian faction supported by the City authorities. This was mirrored in Stepney, with a Presbyterian minister notionally at the helm but actually quite overborne by two of the nation's most important Independent divines. Burroughs, the morning lecturer, had fled to the exiled church run by William Bridges in Rotterdam, where he had been a teacher. On returning to England he took up lectureships in Stepney, St Giles Cripplegate, St Mildred Bread Street and St Michael Cornhill. Though accounted a moderate and scholarly man (with a forceful wife), Burroughs was a spellbinding preacher with a flair for gruesome dramatic crescendo. If you listen to the dark and violent sexual world he preaches of you can imagine the sailors of Wapping turning up in the early morning and flocking into the church. Here is an extract from a work published some years later and based on some of his sermons. He is speaking of the Roman persecution of early Christians, perhaps with the nearby Limehouse kilns in mind:

All the policy, wit, strength of invention, of men and evils were exercised and stretched [*sic*] out to the utmost, for devising the most miserable torments and exquisite tortures; as plates of iron burning hot laid upon their naked flesh, pinsers red hot pulling off the flesh from the bones; bodkins pricking and thrusting all over their bodies; casting into lime kilns, and into caldrons of scalding lead; whipping until almost all the flesh was torn off their bodies and their bones and bowels appeared.'

Taking an example of a woman or two, he describes, with undeniable relish, the execrable things done to Blandina and Eulalila: 'How lamentable is the hearing of these things unto nice and curious women who now must not have the wind to blow on them, who are ready to dye, if they but crossed a little of their wills.' 'Earth', ends the Morning Star of Stepney, 'is not the place for pleasure: this is the place of sorrw [*sic*], of trouble, of mourning, of affliction.

The year 1640 was turbulent. The king was forced, after eleven years of arbitrary government, to call parliament to try and raise money to quell the Scottish rebels who had taken arms against the Laudian measures. In April the 'Short Parliament' met, with a crowd of clamouring MPs led by the Somerset man John Pym. They refused to grant the king money for the Bishops' War in Scotland, and were dismissed on 5 May. Meanwhile London was in turmoil. Sailors, dockhands and watermen, mainly from Stepney and Southwark, joined with the apprentices who were enjoying their rollicking May Day holiday, and rioted through the streets. This was triggered by the king's demands for further money from the City, but the roots of the anger of the seafaring community lay deeper. Their merchant ships were held up, and the once proud navy was held in scorn; their preachers were imprisoned and papists abounded at Court. With beating drums they marched on Laud's palace at Lambeth and Thomas Bensted, a nineteen-year-old sailor, struck the archbishop's door with a crowbar. He was hanged, drawn and quartered. It is not difficult to imagine how the news of this was received at Ratcliff Cross, in the Green Dragon and the other East End hostelries. Direct action against the Laudian innovations began all over London. In November zealots at All Hallows Barking sawed the angels off the altar rails. In the same month the king was forced to recall parliament, and the revolution began in earnest. The 'Long Parliament' set about its business of punishing those responsible, and making sure that tyranny was at an end. The Earl of Strafford, the king's chief adviser, and Archbishop Laud were sent to the Tower. The courts of high commission and star chamber were abolished, and plans were afoot to get rid of the Church hierarchy root and branch. On May Day the apprentices rioted in East Smithfield; some 500 of them gathered to rescue those apprentices who had been pressed to go to fight in Flanders 'under the Archduke'.

In August a new vicar took charge in Stepney, or attempted to. This was William Stampe, a staunch Laudian, an Oxford man appointed by the lord of the manor. He was a noted preacher, quite as charismatic and compelling as his Puritan rivals. He was to have a rough ride, with Burroughs (the other lecturer was soon to be appointed) stirring up an already disaffected flock. Although his curate, the elderly Edgworth, was sympathetic to his views, as were the parish clerk and the sexton, and he had the support of Lord Wentworth and his own brother, Timothy, a local JP and steward at the manor house, his vestry was largely of another mind. At least the Mile End churchwarden, Hilary Mempris, was a Royalist. A list of the prominent vestrymen who confronted Stampe indicates just how overpowering the maritime and Puritan interest was in the parish. They were Anthony Tutchen, an Independent, a master of Trinity House and former master assistant of the navy, Walter Cooke, master of Trinity House, a Mile End warden, wealthy Ratcliff mariner Jonas James (warden 1639–41), William Goldston of Wapping Wall, timber merchant to the East India Company, Edward Stevens, leading Limehouse shipwright, Captain Henry West of Limehouse, once the master of a privateer, Mr John Heaman, mariner, Limehouse churchwarden, Mr John Ducy of Poplar, timber measurer and surveyor of timber to the navy, John Southerne,

Poplar shipwright, brewer Francis Zachary, Independent, Ratcliff warden, soon to be a colonel in Cromwell's army, Robert Clements, churchwarden for the new 'Wapping Side', mastmaker master and naval shipwright.

Within three weeks of vicar Stampe's arrival the revolutionary 'Long Parliament' sanctioned the first official lectureship, and it was to his parish. On 6 September 1641 parliament granted the parishioners of Stepney permission to set up a 'lecture at their own charge every Sunday'; this was the very first act of its kind, and two days later, on a motion by Oliver Cromwell himself, this precedent was set forth as a general principle. Stepney was leading the way. William Greenhill was appointed; he had been deprived of his parish of Oakley in Suffolk by Bishop Wren. A most learned and deeply pious man, like Burroughs, of mild temperament, he was to become one of the most influential divines of the day, and would later be appointed by parliament as chaplain to the king's children. As with Burroughs, there was a good deal of sexual content in his sermons, talk of harlots, whores, nakedness and adultery, with all the deadly sins not far behind.

With the authority of the Church collapsing, strange new sects started to proliferate. A list of 'Divelish and Damnable sects' published early in 1641 itemises, among others, Brownists, who went in for *ex tempore* prayer, Pan worshippers, practitioners of free love (the Family of Love), Adamites (nudists), Chaldeans, who worshipped the Devil, sun worshippers, Bacchanalians, who achieved heaven through drink, Thessalonians, who rejected the Old Testament, Electricians, who broke up families, Junoneans, who worshipped Juno, Queen of Heaven. In September John Spilsbury's Particular Baptist group, the first of its kind, was discovered in Ratcliff. There were twenty-nine of them, of whom thirteen were women.

All over the country there were attacks on clergy, organs were smashed and prayer books thrown around. Churchwardens and clergy were accused of stealing from the collections made for the poor and sextons and clerks attacked for making money out of private plague burials for wealthy families. The people of Chigwell in Essex petitioned parliament for the removal of their High Church vicar, Emmanuel/Samuel Utye, because of his popish ways, kissing the altar and, according to his wife, wearing a crucifix. Utye was to become vicar of Stepney in 1661.

As the leaves from the fruit trees in the orchards fell and the days shortened, the East Enders must have become increasingly terrified and bewildered. There was daily news of bloodshed in Ireland (rebellion broke out in October) and Scotland, wild rumours of papist plots, tumultuous assemblies of 'Brownists and Separatists', soldiers back from Scotland looting in the streets. The dreaded pestilence recurred; someone sent Pym, the Commons leader, a plaster infected with the plague. All was chaos. In November the *Bonaventure*, a merchant ship docked at Blackwall, was set on fire by someone to whom the master had refused a butt of wine. News came from Westminster that the Commons were baying for reform. The parliament's 'Grand Remonstrance', listing their grievances, was published ten days before Christmas. It deplored monopolies, enclosures, forced loans, illegal taxes, mutilation and banishments by Star Chamber, and, what must have struck home in the East End, the activities of the bishops' courts', which, 'lighting upon the meaner sort of Tradesmen and Artificers, did impoverish many thousands'.

During 1641 parliament had organised a sort of referendum, a national protest against 'an arbitrary and tyrannical government', wherein all males over eighteen were required to take an oath of loyalty to the Protestant religion and Crown and in support of the rights and privileges of parliament. The 'protestation returns', which came in the following year, provide a partial census of the country just before civil war broke out and, although the population figures available from them are far from reliable (the returns show that Stepney's population was in the region of 15,500; it was certainly much more), the documents give a firm indication of the relative size of the hamlets. The riverside hamlets of Limehouse and Ratcliff had by far the greatest number of inhabitants, Poplar with half as many. The growing immigrant area of Spitalfields was next, having nearly as many people as Poplar; about a third of the names were French or Dutch – the names ascribed to some of the newcomers being clearly plucked out of the air and giving an idea of how the locals felt about them: Charles Lepoxon and Jacques Monsieur, for instance. Mile End and Bethnal Green were still select. The ancient breadmaking village of Bow flourished and the tiny village of Old Ford made an appearance, with just thirty-six names listed. Vicar Stampe, Richard Popjoy, minister of St Leonards Bromley, James Cowper, curate of Stratford-Bow and William Greenhill, lecturer, signed the list along with curate Edgworth, now an old man with arthritis from the look of his signature.

In January 1642 matters came to a head. Thousands of mariners, hit by the trade slump, petitioned the committee at Grocers' Hall and a mob of poor artificers marched to Westminster, waving their petitions against bishops and lords. On the 4th the king went to Parliament House to arrest the five leaders of the Commons, only to find his 'birds had flown' into the safety of the City, where he pursued them. London was in uproar; barricades were erected and chains put across the streets, cannon were rolled out; and the City and the Inns of Court declared themselves for parliament.

From Stepney, Wapping and St Katharine's came the seafaring community in force, about 2,000 of them, to guard 'that Great Vessel the Parliament House'. Sea captains, masters of ships and ordinary mariners, 'hearing the whole City to be in compleat arms', sailed their barges and long boats, armed to the teeth, up to Westminster. A flotilla of longboats, lighters and barges, with flags, and streamers, drums and trumpets, 'joined the thunder of powder with the City muskets at the entrance to the House'. A vice-admiral, writing a justification for the mariners' 'ebbing and flowing to and from the Parliament House', wrote: 'We who are always abroad can best tell no government upon Earth is comparable to [parliament].' Their aim in defending the narrow seas was, he said, 'the firme establishing of our Protestant religion'. He prays to that 'great Pilot of Heaven and Earth, who steers the world with his finger'. 'Our appearance above the bridge', he said, was 'a passage the Histories of England cannot exemplifie.' Eleven years later William Stampe, the Royalist vicar of Stepney, addressing himself to the Corporation of Trinity House and his former parishioners from his exile in the Hague, wrote: 'It is no slight contribution that you have given to the miseries we complain of, when you went to Whitehall in your long boats with the mouth of your cannon toward your Sovereign, instructing the whole kingdom to follow you in that loud clamour.'

At home in the houses and cottages along the river, around the Green at Mile End, across the fields at Spitalfields, folk were alarmed and arming themselves. A Royalist constable, Richard Cray, was terrorising the neighbourhood with a small gang of soldiers from the Tower, seizing arms from the locals and preventing them from going to hear Greenhill and Burroughs preach. Thumping the table with his fist, Cray shouted that all Puritans should be tortured and torn apart, and he would do it. Another constable defiantly organised the setting up of a maypole in East Smithfield. The parishes of Stepney, Shoreditch, Whitechapel, Wapping, St Katharine's and St Peter Ad Vincula combined to petition parliament, asking for permission to raise their own 'citizens' army'. Most of the male population were seamen and soldiers, often away from home, and the defence of houses was left to the 'handy crafts men' who were untrained in military affairs.

John Walter of Limehouse was shopped to parliament for accusing a band of honest folk of being 'damned Puritan whores and rogues'. Thomas Burgie was heard to say that he would join the papists if they rose, and Matthew Owen claimed that Pym had 'two faces under his hood', publicly expressing his opinion that papists would be all right if they were left alone. No more angry congregations have ever assembled in Stepney church, with the High Church Royalist vicar and curate facing a predominantly 'Godly' multitude. Poor old Edgworth was called a 'damned dogg' by one woman parishioner; she said she would 'rather go to hear a cartwheel creake and a dogg bark, than to hear him preach'. A scrivener called him a 'mass priest'. In July the vicar went too far. On Sunday the 24th three journeymen from outside the parish, led by an apothecary's apprentice, came as a recruiting party for the Earl of Essex, newly appointed as lord general of the Parliamentary forces. Standing outside the church, waiting to catch young men as they left the morning service, they were having some success when Stampe strode out, calling them 'Roundhead rascals'. Constable Cray arrested them, and the vicar's brother, magistrate Timothy Stampe, had them put in prison. The next day the vicar and constables were sent for by the Commons, ordered to release the recruiters and to invite all those who wished to volunteer to enlist at New Artillery Yard in Moorfields.

The following Wednesday was a public fast day, and the Commons had recommended that Burroughs and Greenhill should preach. When curate Edgeworth rose to his feet to start the proceedings there was a riot; the curate was attacked and clumps of hair were pulled from his head. A gang of sailors and Justice Stampe came to the curate's aid; the latter was astonished 'that he had so many friends there'. It was generally supposed that the Stampe brothers had deliberately provoked the violence 'with an intent to mischief those that had complained of them before parliament'.

A contingent of the Tower Hamlets Militia was stationed in Stepney and the Commons continued to investigate the parish. The maypole, put up by constable Arnold, was pulled down. Justice Stampe and his brother were put in prison, and the vicar was ejected from his 'very good living of Stepney' for 'being a proved prelatical innovator of Romish ceremonies and a desperate malignant'. Curate Edgworth disappeared. After eight months in prison William Stampe fled to join the Royalists at Oxford, where he enjoyed the king's 'high favour'. With the king's fall he took a cure at Charenton near Paris and then at the Hague, where he died in 1653 aged forty-three.

Overall some 2–3,000 clergy were ejected from their livings. Thomas Swadlin, Laudian vicar of St Botolph's Aldgate, was dispatched, as was John Squire from Shoreditch. There was a terrible rift in Squire's parish; he was a devoted parson and had been indefatigable in his visiting during the plague of 1625. When he was finally released from prison twenty celebratory bonfires were lit around the parish by his loyal supporters.

'Oh Stepny, Oh Stepny, thou hast had thy time of peace'

On 22 August 1642 the king set up his standard at Nottingham and in October Cavalier and Roundhead were engaged in the first major pitched battle of the war, at Edgehill. Meanwhile a 'paper war' was raging; thousands of propaganda pamphlets came off the press and were circulated among the literate (about 70 per cent of men) and read aloud in alehouses and taverns.

A satire on the Roundhead women of Ratcliff and Wapping takes us into the company of some local women and shows what the Royalist 'tabloid press' thought about the vulgarity and stupidity of these daughters of the revolution, determined to make the most of the freedom of their new 'levelling' religion. John Lillburne, the Leveller leader, whose wife Elizabeth was the member of a local sectarian congregation, insisted that women were 'by nature all equall and alike in power, dignity, authority and majesty [to men]'. Mistress Warden, a pretentious drunk, midwife, teacher, and the wife of a liveryman, is the rather Dickensian character who stars in the pamphlet, Stepney's very own Madame Defarge, with a touch of Sarah Gamp. The scene is Mistress Warden's house, where a group of six women are gathered, Mistress Spritsale and Gamaer Toad-Fish among them, eating eggs, washed down with jug upon jug of muscatel. The hostess addresses the company on the subject of her 'most ever Roundheaded husband', who has recently, with his shoes highly polished for the occasion, delivered a speech and petition. Leaning back in her chair, like a bear about to perform tricks, she speaks: 'Most pure and Chosen of the Times, my Daughters and Companions in Predestination ... Our owne invention [is the] onely and infallible rule of our Faith, Hope and Charity.' There follows a fairly incomprehensible ramble, oiled with four quarts of wine, after which she calls for a chamber pot and uses it. Another woman takes the floor, dropping a 'Wapping curtsey' and delivering a drunken tirade against the king and the prayer book, going black in the face on the subject of prerogative. Gamaer Toad-Fish expresses her outrage that the speech and petition presented by Mistress Warden's husband have been mocked. Proceedings draw to a close with Mistress Warden addressing Goodwife Toad-Fish: 'I perceive, by the fervent twinkling of your eyes, and the ardent licking of your lips, you would be at your devotions.'

By autumn 1642 the building of London's fortifications was in full swing. Volunteers were called for from pulpits, and it was said that about 20,000 people turned out, including women and children, with any implements they had to hand, supervised by sailors and trained bands. They dug a great ditch all around the capital and threw up 9ft-high ramparts, with a ring of twenty-four forts blocking all the main roads; there was one in Whitechapel, where the Royal London Hospital is now, one at the north end of Gravel Lane in Wapping and one in Bethnal Green. About half of the East End lay outside the new 'city walls'. The forts were completed by May 1643, and an observer described the Whitechapel structure: 'I saw a nine-angled fort, only pallosaded and single ditched, and planted with seven pieces of brazen ordonance, and a court du guard, composed of timber, and thatched with tyle-stone, as all the rest are.'

A new vicar of Stepney, appointed by parliament to replace the Royalist Stampe, arrived in June 1643. Josuah Hoyle, also minister at Blackfriars, was a scholar, an eminent Presbyterian theologian, Professor of Divinity at Trinity College Dublin, who had assisted in sifting the evidence against Archbishop Laud. This academic Presbyterian was not to the parishioners' taste, and he certainly did not have the charisma and fortitude to stand up to the two lecturers, Greenhill and Burroughs. When, the celebrated hellraiser Hugh Peters, once minister at Salem in Massachusetts, came to Stepney to stir them up, he made no bones about Hoyle's position: 'O Stepney, Stepny [*sic*], thou hast had thy time of peace, and the day of visitation by two famous and worthy lights; you have had your morning Star [Burroughs] and your evening Star [Greenhill] … never taking notice of a third, Dr Hoyle, the Minister of the place.' Hoyle was one of the 'Godly divines' called by parliament to settle the government of the Church at the Westminster Assembly in the same month as he came to Stepney. At this assembly came the first sign of the complete rift between Presbyterians and Independents. Five 'Dissenting Brethren' emerged, all of whom had been in exile in Holland in the 1630s, and among them was Stepney's Jeremiah Burroughs. They published their apology, an attack on Presbyterianism, denying that anyone had authority in Church affairs apart from God. 'As for the new conformity,' said the Morning Star, 'God kept me from it.'

But as yet, Hoyle was holding Stepney to the 'new conformity' as best he might. The day after Christmas the 'ancients' of the parish met in emergency session in the freezing vestry house; with Newcastle blockaded there was no coal to warm London's houses. The new vicar and magistrate William Mellish, together with the wardens, addressed the problem of the parish clerk, Laurence Spence, and the sexton, William Culham. There had been complaints about both, presumably concerning their religious and political affiliation, and they were given 'until Sunday next' to reform their ways and take the Covenant. They evidently complied.

Meanwhile the militia committee for Tower Hamlets asked the East India Company to pay for trained bands at Blackwall. It being 'a place altogether consisting of seamen' they could only find seven men capable of bearing arms! The following November (1644), with the Parliamentarians now holding thirty-seven of the fifty-seven counties and most of the important towns, the draft of a Presbyterian form of government for the Church was presented. Eight men dissented, including Greenhill and Burroughs.

It was sometime during this year that Greenhill, together with the famous Henry Burton, who had his ears cut off by Archbishop Laud, set up their breakaway congregation, which came to be known as Stepney Meeting, the oldest Independent (Congregationalist) chapel in the world. The tradition is that its first meeting place was a house in what is now Ocean Street, or in the Walnut Tree tavern, but it may have met in St Dunstan's itself: when in August 1645 Katharine Chidley, leader of the Leveller women, visited Stepney and Greenhill's 'gathered church', she attacked him bitterly for 'using a parish church where idolatrous services had been once performed'.

On 14 June 1645 the Parliamentary army won a resounding victory at Naseby, and in August the government tried its Presbyterian experiment. The Book of Common Prayer was made illegal and replaced by the Directory of Public Worship. Henceforth the Church was to be ruled by a series of councils, with parish elders chosen by the parish and minister. The whole Church would be divided into 'classes': for London there would be ten, and above them were provincial and national assemblies. Stepney was joined with All Hallows

Barking, All Hallows Stayning, St Dunstan in the East, St Gabriel Fenchurch Street, St Katharine Coleman, St Katharine by the Tower, St Margaret Pattens, St Olave Hart Street, St Peter ad Vincula, Holy Trinity Minories, Wapping and Whitechapel, forming a super parish stretching along the river from Limehouse into the City. The plan was ill received in Stepney.

The petition for settling the government of the Church was given to Dr Hoyle by one Mr Alley sometime in September. Hoyle ordered that it should be read in St Dunstan's after Burroughs had finished his morning lecture, and signatures were to be collected. Burroughs preached against it, as did Greenhill in the afternoon. And Alley, although he was only the messenger, was 'baited and rated' by sectaries. The next fast day Greenhill attacked the petition violently, 'for a moderate man'; both he and Burroughs maintained that to adopt the Presbyterian scheme was ungrateful to the army 'who had done so much for us'. Burroughs preached against it again that morning, and later at Cripplegate. On 25 September some Presbyterians went to Burroughs's house, presumably to discuss the matter. Apparently Burroughs was unforthcoming, but his wife was not! There is no indication from the vestry minutes that any part of the government's reforms were adopted by the parish. It was, in fact, a general flop.

In the following year Burroughs, the Morning Star, went to meet his maker, and in the wettest of winters, with 'floods to a wonderment the like not known', his friend and mentor William Bridge, the Independent divine who had run an exiled church in Rotterdam, came to Stepney to replace him.

In the summer of 1647 the king was seized by the army and on 2 August Cromwell and his New Model Army were let into London; the country was now under military rule. The all powerful army council wanted to extend the franchise and there were plans for a great demonstration of solidarity, using local weavers. Men from Spitalfields and Whitechapel were to march in their thousands to a designated rendezvous where the army were to meet to 'settle things'. The great meeting set for 15 November never happened as planned; things were disrupted by the king's escape from his captivity at Hampton Court. He fled to the Isle of Wight.

Meanwhile Stepney's Royalist sexton, Culham, was in trouble for 'scoffing' at the Godly and being abusive to parishioners. He had, moreover, openly defied the vestry in their intention to close down his (presumably rowdy) pub, The Rose, by putting his son in as landlord and stocking it up with beer. He craved forgiveness and was given it, on condition that the pub was closed down.

It was about this time that Cromwell's close friend Maurice Thomson appeared on the Stepney scene, taking up residence in Worcester House, the great mansion north-west of the church. He was to become the most powerful man in the parish during the ensuing decade. Starting his career as a 'poor fellow in Virginia', he made a fortune out of tobacco and was to become an influential member of Cromwell's government, the author of the anti-Dutch First Navigation Act, which gave the countries of the British Isles a monopoly in the carrying trade. He was one of three founders of the East India Company's chapel in Poplar, which opened in 1654. A story was told that he showed his humility at the opening service at the chapel by going into the clerk's desk and leading the first psalm.

For the next eighteen months the tumultuous events of state rolled on, with army and parliament engaged in weary negotiations with the king; parliament and the City's common council were purged of opponents of military rule. Government lay effectively in the hands of the senior officers of the New Model Army and Parliamentarians of like mind, ruling without law, radical in politics and Independent in religious affiliation. Fairfax ended the City's control over the Tower Hamlets trained bands and made himself Constable of the Tower. Josuah Hoyle struggled to keep the Presbyterian show on the road at St Dunstan's, always in competition with his lecturers and their newly formed Independent congregation, the Stepney Meeting, supported by many of his vestrymen and a stronghold of the navy.

It was in June 1648 that the East End had its only slice of Civil War action – in Stratford Bow. There was a widespread Royalist reaction and the Earl of Norwich marched from Kent to Blackheath, pursued by Parliamentary forces under Colonel Whalley. In response to a rumour that thousands had risen for the king in Essex, he left his men and made for Bow where he was expecting to meet 2,000 Royalist supporters in arms. Finding nothing of the sort, he crossed Bow Bridge and went into Essex, and was again disappointed. Most of his men had in the meantime dispersed, but a body of some 500 managed to cross the Thames in boats, with their horses swimming, and found themselves in Stepney facing a regiment of the Tower Hamlets Militia. Their commander, Sir William Compton, allowed them to pass, extracting a promise from them that they would disband. The Royalists forced the turnpike at Bow Bridge to let them over into Stratford where they met Norwich, returning from Chelmsford. They stayed at the bridge awaiting Royalist moves from within the City, but only a few loyalists crept out to join him. Whalley led his force of cavalry to Mile End; and the Royalists were ambushed and forced to retreat to Bow, pursued by the Tower Hamlets trained bands. The latter were, however, forced to take refuge in the church, which was surrounded by the Royalists, and were released on condition they all went home. Norwich placed guards on the fords over the Lea and set out for Colchester, where an eleven-week siege ended in the capitulation of the town to the Roundheads.

What reverberations there were in the East End when the king was executed in January 1649 is anybody's guess. The register for St Mary, Whitechapel records that on 2 June 1649, four months after the execution, Richard Brandon, 'a man out of Rosemary Lane', was buried. Against this entry the clerk added the following memorandum: 'This R. Brandon is supposed to have cut off the head of Charles I.' He was the son of Gregory Brandon, and claimed the headman's axe by inheritance. There is some debate as to whether he actually performed the deed; according to some he refused. One account says that he was paid £30 in half crowns for his work and was offered 20s by a bystander for the pomander and handkerchief that he had taken from the king's pocket. He refused the sum, and later sold the orange for 10s in Rosemary Lane.

That spring, 1649, the navy was purged of all but good Independents, and in May Francis Zachary the brewer and Hilary Mempris, a former Royalist, were put in charge of the Tower Hamlets Militia with Philip Skippon and others. In October, at a meeting of justices of the 'Publique peace of the Commonwealth' (the word 'kingdom' was crossed out in the vestry minute book) with Stepney parishioners the 'needfull repare of their Parish church' was discussed, and it was decided that a rate should be imposed to raise the necessary £160. Whether or not the money was collected or any repairs were done is unclear; the poverty of the parish was becoming a matter of extreme urgency. When the case of Mary Jennings, a 'poor impotent creature' from Spitalfields, came before the Sessions, it was decreed that she should be sent to her rich brother in Kent; Stepney parish was 'poor enough'.

The problems of administering such a huge and diverse parish were considerable. When the Ratcliff warden had applied to the magistracy for financial help from some of the adjoining parishes, he was told firmly to apply to the wealthier hamlets of Stepney, Mile End, Poplar and Limehouse. The church building itself was also much too small; it was reported to the Mercers' that 'The parish church is not of capacity to contain the 10th part of the parishioners'. The Parliamentary committee sitting to consider the state of ecclesiastical benefices proposed to divide Stepney into four. This was never achieved, but two chapels were built to relieve the situation, one at Poplar, funded by the East India Company and completed in 1654, and one built between 1656 and 1658 in the newly developed hamlet of Shadwell, funded by property developer Thomas Neale, helped by a grant from the Mercers' Company.

Hoyle seems to have retired to the peace of Oxford sometime in 1650 or 1651, leaving the field to William Greenhill, who would be officially appointed in his place a few years later. Meanwhile the wardens were preoccupied with the poor. On Christmas Eve 1651 they decided to let the old pesthouse and its grounds to Michael Barks of Rogueswell House for 45s a year 'for the present and future good of the poore of the Parish'.

The eclipse of the sun in March 1652 had all the astrologers foretelling doom. Nicholas Culpepper of Spitalfields forecast the onset of democracy and the second coming of Christ in his *Catastrophe Magnetum*. Most of Stepney's mariners, the while, were away fighting the Dutch, their natural religious allies but fierce commercial rivals. The war was fought entirely at sea and lasted from July 1652 to 1654.

In 1653 Cromwell finally dispatched the Rump Parliament and replaced it with a hand-picked assembly of Godly men, the so-called Barebones Parliament. Although only of short duration, this body accomplished a good deal, setting up a probate system to replace the chaotic mess left by the abolition of the Church courts and also regularising civil marriage. Henceforth East Enders, along with everyone else, had to take or send all wills to be proved in one central court, and weddings in church were conducted by a magistrate. In Stepney, more often than not, it was Maurice Thomson who officiated.

On 2 June 1654 William Greenhill was appointed vicar of Stepney by the Keepers of the Liberties of England, taking with him the congregation from Stepney Meeting. In January 1658 Matthew Mead, an eminent Independent divine, was put in as the first minister at Shadwell and another, Thomas Walton, was minister at the new chapel in Poplar. All the local pulpits were occupied by Independents.

Meanwhile, at a 'general meeting of parishioners' in Stepney's vestry house, the affairs of the parish were taken firmly in hand. There were to be no more 'tumolteous appearances', and there were to be regular meetings of a select vestry that the vicar was to attend. Maurice Thomson headed the Mile End team, with Thomas Mempris, former employee of the Wentworths, James Dantier of Spitalfields and eight others. There were twenty vestrymen for Ratcliff (which included Wapping and Shadwell), led by JP William Mellish. Naval captain John Limbrey led the Limehouse band of ten, and for Poplar and Blackwall there were ten, mainly 'old hands'. Their first minuted action was a further examination of the seditious and troublesome sexton, Culham. Seven weeks before he had been let off with a reprimand; now, with Thomson in charge, he was sacked and Francis Tivell was appointed in his place for a year, conditional on his good behaviour. Anyone who swore at or abused fellow vestrymen was to be thrown out, and the whole business of 'disorders' at burials and the registration of the births of children (no longer baptisms) was to be addressed. A good sum of money ($£232$ $12s$ $11d$) was collected for distressed fellow Protestants in Savoy.

In July, led by Thomson, this reforming vestry set about implementing the repressive regime introduced by Cromwell's newly appointed team of major generals, the 'flying squad for righteousness'. This was the nadir of the Puritan revolution, with the military, through constables and JPs, clamping down on Sabbath-breaking, feasting, dancing, wrestling, shooting, parties and masques. Adultery was to be punished by death, fornication by three months in prison and there was even a Swearing and Cursing Act. Ironically, Stepney had never had it so bad since Archbishop Laud had done almost the same twenty years ago.

Captain John Crowther, once in command of the Irish Seas and now Mile End warden, and Edward Keeling, Ratcliff warden, were given the task of getting copies of all the new government orders about Sabbath-breaking and having them pinned up in the church and around the parish, 'to the end that all idle and disorderly persons whoe walk uppe and downe on the Lord's daye or lyers on the ground in the churchyard may bee timely forewarned'.

All the wardens were told that they must confer with Greenhill about the disposition of the £400 that the government had given to the parish from the coal tax, that is to say, they were to keep an eye on what he did with it. The vestry house was to be repaired and, most important of all, a lock-up and stocks were to be erected near the church for the punishment of offenders. By spring 1656 the church had been thoroughly repaired at a cost of £326, aisles relaid and the whole church repaved, pews repaired and a new churchyard wall built. In 1659 it was decided that every individual in receipt of poor relief was to wear a pewter badge.

On 16 August 1657 the parish clerk, William Bissacre/Bissaker, triumphantly noted, in an especially large and flowery hand, that Mr Andrew Collace, 'the curate of Stepney church', had conducted a marriage. True it was witnessed by magistrate George March, but surely it is an indication that some folk in Stepney, like others countrywide, were ready for the restoration of Church and Monarchy.

'The King is now coming to hang you all up': the Restoration of the monarchy

On 29 May 1660 the king returned to his own again under the auspices of General George Monck and the army. Diarist Samuel Pepys was astonished at the 'greatness and suddenness' of events. At the west end of Stepney church, set into the wall, is the rough stone tablet that commemorates 'honist Abraham Zouch', a Wapping ropemaker who died during the Civil War. His widow remarried and then died, according to the same tablet, on 29 May 1660, the very day that Charles II entered London. Too much dancing and free wine flowing from the public conduits, perhaps.

London was aglow with joyful bonfires, and the whole country seemed ecstatic as the tall, dark man returned warily from exile to take his father's throne. The King's Declaration of Breda promised that no one should be 'disquieted or called in question for their religious opinions'. Most people were sick of the turbulence of the last two decades and the harsh oppression of the major generals. 'Old Noll' was dead now and, perhaps, with the Black Boy on the throne there might be a return to the good old days of Queen Bess. The stocks in the churchyard might be taken away and the maypoles put back up at East Smithfield and Mile End Green. East Enders had witnessed trade being killed off by the Spanish and Dutch wars; bread was expensive in 1659 and everyone was bled dry to pay for the hated army. In the months leading up to the glorious 29 May boys in the

City threw turnips at passing soldiers and thousands of watermen, many of them from Stepney, marched to Westminster to demand the dismissal of the 'Rump' of parliament. In Wapping a vintner shouted at a group of Baptists at their devotions, 'Do you see what you have done by your fasting and praying ... for the king is coming now to hang you all up.'

It was certainly not the king's personal intention to 'hang them all up' and, to begin with at least, all seemed to be forgiveness and light. Bishops and their courts and all the trappings of the old Church of England were reinstated, but the king had promised indulgence to the nonconformists and 'Indemnity and Oblivion' to his former enemies. Those individuals who had been actively involved in his father's murder were disposed of, but for the first months it seemed that all might be well for the Presbyterians and Independents, and even the 'fanatics'.

In November Pepys noted that in his parish of St Olave's Hart Street the people began to 'nibble at the Common Prayer ... But the people have beene so little used to it that they could not tell what to answer.' The playhouses were opened again, and Ben Jonson's *Bartholomew Fair* was staged for the first time in forty years. In Stepney the lords of the manor, the Wentworths, were back. When the king came into London Thomas Wentworth, Earl of Cleveland, that valiant old Cavalier, had led the band of 300 noblemen and gentlemen in triumphal procession wearing his 'plain grey suit'. Soon he would be restored to his heavily mortgaged Stepney estate, would reappoint Timothy Stampe, the Royalist vicar's brother as steward and reassume the patronage of the church.

Most people, especially those who had something to lose, trimmed their sails to the prevailing wind and got on with life. But for some of the ordinary men and women who had led the cry of 'Hunt Laud the fox', the mariners who had sailed up the Thames to protect the parliament house from their tyrannical king, the restoration of the old order was not welcomed with such joy. At the Middlesex Sessions House, Hicks Hall in Clerkenwell, the magistrates were busy dealing with those who spoke seditious words against the king. There were men and women from the western suburbs, but most were East Enders. Edward Medbourne, a Wapping glazier, said he would like to hang the king and General Monck (who had brought him back), and would spend 5s for joy when he had done it. Richard Cheltham of Nightingale Lane said he hoped to meet the king at the gallows. John Harper of Wapping wanted the Roundhead General Lambert as king. William Sparkes, also of Wapping, said that Charles was 'a poor and beggarly king'. Wentworth Day spoke seditious words at a private meeting in Wapping. Anne Allin, wife of a Whitechapel barber surgeon, declared 'The Queen [the king's mother, Henrietta Maria] is the Great Whore of Babilon.'

Restoration London was a world of plots and plotting, real and imagined. Not surprisingly, the government was jittery and suspicious of anything that smelled of republicanism and the possibility of a recurrence of the 'late troubles'. Following the attempted insurrection of the Fifth Monarchy Men in the City in January 1661, it clamped down; all worship was forbidden except in parish churches. In February Captain Thomas Hodgekins arrested Henry Johnson, a Whitechapel tobacco pipemaker, and seven others 'unlawfully and riotteously assembled together on the Lords Day at a private meeting or conventicle in the dwelling-house of Thomas Hinton of Whitechappell tobacco-pipe maker'. In the same month there was an unlawful assembly at Spittle Yard and at the end of March another 'seditious meeting' in Spitalfields, attended by a silk throwster, a shoemaker, a turner and a tobacco pipemaker. In June thirteen men were arrested at a Stepney meeting; they came from Bishopsgate, Petticoat Lane, Shadwell, Rosemary Lane, Ratcliff Highway, Whitechapel and Wapping, weavers, ropemakers, smiths, sawyers, lightermen and mariners. John James, Minister of a Seventh-Day Baptist congregation in Bullstake Alley Whitechapel was arrested and hanged. William Hammond of Sprusom's Island in Wapping was arrested for saying he had lent Cromwell £1,000, and that the king was 'a very knave as Oliver was'.

In the spring of 1662 Stepney parish was a focus of public attention. Three regicides, John Barkstead, Miles Corbet and John Okey, were dragged to Tyburn and hanged, their hearts and intestines ripped out, and what was left of them boiled and put into baskets. The ghastly stewed remains of Barkstead and Corbet were put on the City gates, while Baptist John Okey's 'quarters' were, on the king's special orders because of his contrition, to be conveyed in a cart to Stepney, where his wife was to have him buried. Such was the throng of sightseers hustling around the grisly procession that the remains were taken into the Tower of London and interred there.

However much the king himself favoured religious toleration, the young, vengeful men of the Cavalier Parliament were of a different mind, and bad times were ahead for the Presbyterians, Independents and sectaries, especially the Quakers, who had burst upon the London scene in the 1650s, preaching the 'Kingdom of God' in bold, loud voices. Quaker Anne Douner had shouted at Greenhill, from the body of the church when he was preaching, declaring herself publicly 'against the minister in Stepney Steeple House'.

With the passing of the 1662 Act of Uniformity and the introduction of a new revised prayer book, nearly 1,000 nonconformist incumbents had to leave their livings or wrestle with their consciences. There began a period, albeit intermittent, of vicious persecution of Dissenters and 'conventicling' as it was known. The East End was under fire, a dark and troubled place in these years, with 'saints' huddled in secret rooms and grinding poverty in the riverside hamlets.

The stringent Conventicles Act came into force on 1 July 1664 to last for three years, forbidding religious meetings of more than five persons. Within three weeks the Middlesex constables had arrested men and women from eleven conventicles, of which six were in the East End. The largest gathering was at the house of one William Beanes at Stepney, where there were 134 people at the meeting of 17 July. Over a period of eight months 347 convictions were made. Eight meetings were raided at the 'building or a room' in the possession of an unknown man in Stepney, one at the house of 'one Brock' in Mile End (Captain James Brook, the Quaker), one in Limehouse at the house of widow Sybil Heaman, one in the dwelling-house of Peter Burdett in Westbury Street in Stepney and one at Joseph Robinson's in the Liberty of Norton Folgate. Offenders were dragged to prison where they were kept until they paid their fines: for the first offence this was only about 6*d*, but for the third offence the Godly were required to pay £100 or they were sent to the colonies. The Constable of the Tower, Sir John Robinson, enforced the Act with great severity, especially with regard to that most troublesome of sects, the Quakers, who openly defied the law, refused to take oaths, to pay church taxes or serve in the militia, running a 'state within a state'. Between July and October 1664, 296 members of Captain Brook's congregation were arrested. John Otter, cobbler of Mile End, brought before the magistrates in December 1664, was asked for his address: 'I have a dwelling where neither thief, murderer, not persecutor can come.' 'Where is it?' asked the JP. 'In God,' replied the brave, but infuriating, cobbler. He was deported. The Wheeler Street meeting in Spitalfields (now remembered as Quaker Street) was raided eight times. The Mile End Meeting moved to the corner of School Lane, Ratcliff in 1666–67 and the building continued to be used as a Friends' Meeting House until 1935.

Quaker distiller John Selwood was to spend three years (1662–65) faithfully attending Stepney parish church, trying to accommodate himself to the faith of his forefathers. Unable to stomach what he regarded as the chilly neglect of the vicar, Dr Clarke, and the ignorance of the rest of the congregation 'in those things which they … call a Worshipping of God', he slipped an anonymous note through the vicarage door and took himself off to the Friends. He admonished the vicar not only for his absenteeism and his sermons, but for his personal wealth and failure to visit the poor: 'Let thine own filthy Lucre and Laziness be laid aside … Do not think it below thee to go into the poor, dark cottages of those under they charge, their souls are as precious as those of princes.'

The Five Mile Act of 1665 forbade ejected ministers to go within 5 miles of their old parish. The wife of the curate of Wapping told her brother, historian John Strype, that she and her husband had been forced out of their home by the Five Mile Act and were having to pay an exorbitant 1*s* a week to rent lodgings.

William Greenhill had left his living of Stepney by July 1660 and devoted himself to his Independent chapel, Stepney Meeting. In June 1661 he and Matthew Mead, curate at Shadwell, were bound over in £300 each for suspected involvement in a plot. Mead fled to Holland; he would return in 1669 to help Greenhill at Stepney Meeting, and take over when he died in September 1671. From 1660 to 1668 the chapel went underground, and the faithful met in the Walnut Tree. Greenhill only took a handful of his flock with him, but the congregation grew and grew and was, within twenty-five years, said to be attracting the biggest crowds in London.

In Whitechapel there had been a series of Puritan rectors for years, including John Johnson, who turned Laudian and was ejected in 1641. He was restored at the Restoration but was deserted by most of his parishioners, who took themselves off to a meeting house in Brick Lane with the ejected minister, Whalley.

In Stepney an elderly Laudian, Emmanuel/Samuel Utye, was appointed as vicar by the lord of the manor, now the Earl of Cleveland. Utye had been ejected from Chigwell before the war for his popish ways and no doubt anticipated a rough ride with his new, famously Dissenting congregation. In tune with the temper of the times in the early honeymoon days of the Restoration, he was prepared to be accommodating. At his very first vestry, when confronted by the fierce Cromwellian worthies who had been in charge for so long, he let them have their way. Two lecturers were to be chosen by the parish and 'Hee [the vicar] shall freely consent to the Exercise of a Lecturers paines in this place … and shall give no interruption to him.' Each was to be paid a handsome £50 a year, as Burroughs and Greenhill had been.

That old bounder, the Royalist High Church sexton William Culham, seized the opportunity of the restoration of a sympathetic regime to try and get his job back, without success. He lived to see the Great Plague of 1665, dying the following year, and must have suffered much chagrin to have missed out on the profits made from so many thousands of burials.

In March 1662, two months before the passing of the Act of Uniformity, Dr William Clarke came to Stepney as vicar, to take in hand the 'most factious hamlet of the Tower Division'. Clarke, a wealthy cleric, from humble origins, was sixty-seven when he began his seventeen years at Stepney. Not that he was there much, according to Quaker Selwood, who claimed that one Sunday sermon was all he offered the parish, and then it was a 'cold and lazy performance'. In 1665 Clarke was made Dean of Winchester but remained in Stepney; in 1671 he turned down a bishopric because he didn't need the money.

High on Dr Clarke's agenda when he arrived must have been the question of the vestry, dominated by Cromwellians, mainly naval men. The navy was a big problem for the king; every ship was in the hands of his former enemies when he took the throne. He said of his former Commonwealth commanders that they had 'all had the plague but they were quite sound now and less accessible to the disease [republicanism] than others'. The Pett clan remained in control at the royal dockyards, accepting Charles II as readily as they had abandoned his father. Pepys called Navy Commissioner Peter Pett 'a fawning rogue'. Only the more obvious malcontents were removed from the Fleet; the Master of the Happy Entrance, a member of Stepney Meeting, was turned out for refusing to take the oath of supremacy and allegiance.

The Corporation Act required conformity from all vestrymen on pain of expulsion. In September 1662 a document was issued by the Bishop of London's office, apparently in response to a petition from Clarke and the parish. The vicar had argued that a general meeting of parishioners was unsuitable for so large a parish and similarly that there were too many parishioners to make a free vote an option. The document named a handpicked list of forty-four men who were to form the new select vestry. Most of the old guard are gone from the list; all eight of the Shadwell vestrymen were new men. The Limehouse team was headed by a JP, George Marsh of the Tower, who was to become well known for his hounding of conventiclers. Samuel Pepys's friend Baltic merchant Sir William Ryder led the Mile End contingent. Also representing Mile End was Timothy Stampe, the Royalist vicar's brother, now steward at the manor house. Just in case there was any trouble from what had been a notoriously powerful vestry, a stern injunction came from Sheldon, Bishop of London. They were not to meddle with the ministers in strictly ecclesiastical matters, or with the churchwardens, their presentments, or anything that appertained to the jurisdiction of the church courts.

In the hot summer of 1665 the plague struck again, starting in St Giles and the western suburbs. The highway in Whitechapel was thronged with wagons, carts, coaches and servants leading horses, all piled up with baggage, as the nobility and gentry took flight. The East Enders, according to Daniel Defoe, had a 'mighty fancy that they should not be visited ... some people fancied that the smell of pitch and tar, and such other things as oil and rosin and brimstone, which is so much used by all trades relating to shipping, would preserve them'. It did not. When it came to the east it struck hard and long. 'They dug the great pit in the churchyard of our parish of Aldgate,' wrote Defoe:

> A terrible pit it was ... it was about forty feet in length, and about fifteen or sixteen feet broad, and at the time I first looked at it, about nine feet deep; but it was said they dug it nearly twenty feet deep afterwards in one part of it, till they could go no deeper for the water ... For though the plague was long a-coming to our parish yet, when it did come, there was no parish in or about London where it raged with such violence as in the two parishes of Aldgate and Whitechapel.

The first plague burial at Stepney church was a Spitalfields weaver's son who died at the end of June. In July the master of the Ratcliff school and his assistant went to the Coopers' Company and asked for it to be closed, but the court ordered them to carry on as usual. But soon the numbers of plague deaths mounted as the pestilence moved south and east, spreading more quickly among the dark hovels and overcrowded alehouses that huddled in the stifling alleys and courts of the riverside hamlets. A committee of the East India Company scheduled to meet at Sir William Ryder's house in Bethnal Green decided against meeting there.

Thomas Marriott, elected lecturer the previous November, decided that Stepney was too dangerous a place to work, and the vestry had difficulty replacing him because of the 'spread of the Infection'. By late August the Stepney sextons were burying over seventy corpses a day; in September it was ninety-five. At night cartloads of corpses, announced by the ringing of bells, trundled up and down White Horse Street and along to the great stinking burial pits at Mile End and Bethnal Green. Bonfires flickered everywhere in the streets, lit to burn away the infected air; shops were closed; and the great river lay hushed, between Ratcliff and Rotherhithe full of ghostly vessels. 'Does anyone go by water these days?', asked the observer in Defoe's *Journal of the Plague Year*. A Blackwall waterman explained: 'Do you see there ... ships lie at anchor ... All those ships have families on board, of their merchants and owners ... who have locked themselves up and live on board ... for fear of infection; and I tend on them to fetch things for them.' The 'lower rank' got into hoys, smacks, lighters and fishing boats; many of them watermen, going from ship to ship to provision the floating 'richer sort', caught the plague and died alone in their wherries, their corpses left to rot.

People literally died of terror, some distracted souls flinging themselves into the great plague pits. Infected houses were locked up, the families shut in and a red cross painted on the door. The watchmen put to guard them ran errands, fetching food and medicine, and the dead cart when the time came. Defoe has several tales to tell of families who took advantage of the watchman's absence to escape from the house of death into which they had been sealed. Doctors, nurses and sextons did well out of the situation, if they survived. The executors of a Bow sugar merchant's wife paid out various sums to nurses, 6gns to washerwomen, and £7 to the Dutch doctor who had taken over the care of the family after their own doctor had died attending them. Thomas Somerlie and Henry Maggott, sextons at Shadwell chapel, were burying corpses at a great rate and charging, without informing the local doctor, who was responsible for supplying information for the bills of mortality. In all 6,583 plague deaths were noted in Stepney's burial register, but there were almost certainly many more which were not accounted for. The very last plague death was noted in December 1666; widow Cooper of Shadwell died a month after the public thanksgiving for the end of the epidemic. One in five of the parishioners had perished, as opposed to the one in eight who had died in 1625. The Earl of Clarendon, speaking of the difficulties of recruiting men for the navy, commented that 'Stepney and the places adjacent, which were their common habitations, were almost depopulated.'

The story was that 116 sextons, gravediggers, bearers, bellmen and carters were employed by Stepney parish within the year. How the parish organisation fared under this appalling burden is not apparent from the records. The vestry met three times in the plague months and no discussion of the arrangements is noted by the clerk. The problems that arose in trying to cope with a crisis such as this in such an enormous and disparate parish almost certainly contributed to its subsequent break-up. Dr Clarke seems to have stayed in the vicarage and did not, like so many of those who could afford it, take refuge in the country. While the vicar of St Olave's Hart Street was, according to Pepys, the first to go and the last to return, Dr Clarke and his curate Edward Turner were certainly around for the bishop's visitation at Whitechapel church in October 1665.

Churches stood empty during these terrible months; the Spitalfields churchwarden reported in May 1666 that the parish church was in good repair, but to little avail: 'Concerning parishioners, the one half of them that are left alive to the best of my knowledge are not willing to come to their parish church either to hear Divine Service or to receive the blessed sacrament.' No wonder the women of the parish drank and swore at each other. One day in June, the month when the pestilence first struck, Sarah Overy was sitting in the sun, knitting with some friends, on her neighbour's doorstep in Wapping's Ropemakers' Fields. Elizabeth Sherman was nearby, knitting in her own porch. Fuelled no doubt by drink a row blew up, and Overy shouted out for all to hear: 'I care not for that whore Sherman, the curse of God light upon that Sherman's whore. Shee was so drunke at the Christening of my child that the minister and her husband were forc'd to carry [her] upstairs into a chamber ... I care not a fart for that whore Sherman.' Sarah Overy then turned on another neighbour, Elizabeth Browne, accusing her of being 'Churchwood's whore' and a thief: 'You went over a brick wall and stole a peck loaf out of Goodwife Powell's cupboard. And you came up to London and left your bastard in the country.' The assembled knitting party started 'fleering and laughing' at Elizabeth Browne and 'hitting her in the teeth therewith'. Ever afterwards, whenever Sarah Overy encountered any of Elizabeth Browne's children she called after them: 'Sequestered whores!'

The strong east wind that was blowing on 2 September 1666 saved the eastern suburbs from the next disaster that hit the capital, the Great Fire. Stepney, on the fringes of this calamity, provided safe storage and refuge for beleaguered citizens. Pepys, still in his nightgown, going with his precious belongings (including his diary) to Sir William Ryder's at Bethnal Green, passed carts and people in their hundreds on similar missions. Dr Clarke, the vicar, took in fine cloth, treasures, ledgers and papers belonging to the East India Company; two carmen were paid at the emergency rate of 36s to convey nine bales of cloth to the vicarage. Captain Disher was paid the large sum of £25 for taking other Company stuff to Stepney, to the houses of Captain Crowther and Captain John Proud.

The Michells, parents of one of Pepys's wenches, shopkeepers in Westminster Hall, lost their house in the Fire and moved to the riverside 'new town' of Shadwell. Many others moved into the eastern suburbs and hamlets, and St Dunstan's, from being the empty place it was in the plague months, was overflowing with Londoners on Sunday mornings. Widow Adams, who had been the pew-opener, was pensioned off, and a number of 'bouncers' replaced her. The vestry appointed 'sober men of the poorer sort' to organise the seating and exclude from the pews anyone who presumed to 'sit above their quality and condition'. The new pew-warders were warned that they must welcome the Fire refugees and treat them kindly.

While the goodwives at home coped with sickness and death, many of their husbands were away at sea for periods of time, fighting the Dutch. Since March 1665 war for command of the seas had been waged, employing numbers of locals. Sometimes the Ryders could hear the roar of cannon from their house in Bethnal Green. As clerk of the acts for the navy, Pepys saw much of the 'seafaring end of town' and was deeply involved in the preparation of the Fleet for war. We will spend a little time in his company before moving on to the next disaster that struck Restoration London.

Pepys had a house in the navy office's gated community of dwellings, offices and gardens in Seething Lane, just north-west of the Tower. As a senior civil servant he spent a good deal of time at Whitehall mingling with the mighty, but he regularly went along the north bank of the river, as well as to Chatham and Rotherhithe, to inspect the fitting of ships and to arrange contracts with suppliers of shipbuilding materials and victuals. It was but a short step from his home to the Victualling Office across Tower Hill, where once the Abbey of St Mary Graces had stood. Sometimes he walked or went by boat; more often he took a hackney carriage to the yards of Wapping and Blackwall. Sir William Warren, supplier of masts for the navy, had yards in Wapping and Rotherhithe; Pepys was fascinated when Warren showed him round his yard, explaining what the different timbers were. The main contracts for hemp and canvas, for rope and sails, went to Sir William Ryder, who lived in the mansion at Bethnal Green that used to be known as Kirby's Castle, where Pepys took his diary and other belongings during the Fire. There were social gatherings at Ryder's house: at one very jolly summer dinner party old sea dogs' tales were told and Pepys took a turn round the beautiful garden with the ladies, and was astonished at 'the greatest quantity of strawberrys I ever saw'. The Bethnal Green 'tourist trade' had by now adopted the tale of the Blind Beggar, and claimed that Ryder's house had been built by the beggar. 'But they say', commented Pepys 'it was only some of the outhouses of it.'

He went down to Blackwall and saw the East India Company's warehouses and new wet dock, with a 'brave new merchantman to be launched there shortly, the *Royal Oak*'. On another occasion he was taken into the hold of an East Indiaman and wondered to see the 'the greatest wealth lie in confusion ... pepper scattered through every chink, you trod upon it; and in cloves and nutmeg', all among bales of silk and boxes of copper. In June 1663 Pepys was at Blackwall, watching 200 drunken soldiers embarking to join the Four Days battle that was raging at the mouth of the Thames: 'But Lord, to see how the poor fellows kissed their wives and sweethearts in that simple manner at their going off, and shouted and let off their guns.' He went to inspect repairs that were being made to naval vessels at Blackwall twice in March 1667. On the second visit the party was entertained by East India Company shipbuilder Henry Johnson, and became 'mighty extraordinary merry'. 'Too too merry for me whose mother died so lately,' writes Pepys, 'but they know it not, so cannot reproach me therein.'

Although the headquarters of Trinity House were now in Deptford, the Corporation still had their Stepney house in Butcher Row, which they used for dinners and such like. One Trinity Monday the members were celebrating the election of a new master with a dinner, or so Pepys thought. He took a boat over from Deptford to Ratcliff and hung about, hoping to meet some of them. To pass the time he wandered into Stepney churchyard to have a look at the gravestones, which were known for their pithy epitaphs. He must have seen the most famous, the Carthage Stone; it stood near the church on the east side. It was brought from Tunis by Thomas Hughes in 1663:

Of Carthage wall I was a Stone,
Oh Mortals Read with pity!
Time consumes all, it spareth none,
Man, Mountain, Town nor City:
Therefore, Oh Mortals now bethink
You whereunto you must,
Since now such Stately Buildings
Lie Buried in the dust.

Pepys's trips to the East End were not all work related. Often, on fine, warm days, he and his wife, friends, family or colleagues took a hackney carriage and travelled the great road to Mile End to drink ale and perhaps eat supper at their favourite watering hole, the Rose and Crown. Sometimes he went after a visit to one of the West End playhouses; sometimes just to round off an exhausting day at work, which often began at four o'clock in the morning. Out through Aldgate, they went, past the crumbling church of St Botolph, past the tall half-timbered coaching inns, through Whitechapel with its lumbering haywains, past Leonard Gurle's 'Great Nursery' at the bottom of Brick Lane, famous for its flowering trees and shrubs, honeysuckle, jasmine and lilac, and especially its apricots. On the other side of the road was the medieval church of St Mary's, in a great state of decay, and next to it the great windmill. Perhaps they saw some Jewish pedlars on their way, selling ribbons and trinkets from a tray. Cromwell had invited the Jews back in 1656 and they had settled around here. Pepys had been to a Portuguese synagogue, and thought it was the silliest thing he had ever seen: 'Lord, to see the disorder, laughing, sporting and no attention, but confusion in all their service.'

And so to Mile End, with its Green, a place for strolling and taking the air. It was the City's Hampstead Heath of those days, with three bowling alleys, taverns and pleasure gardens.

Sometimes Pepys went a little further afield, to Bow. On a fine, clear, March day in 1667, full of 'gayete de Coeur', the cocky young clerk of the acts was feeling well pleased with himself, having spent the morning persuading the king to stump up a good deal of money for the navy. Leaving Whitehall by coach, with navy surveyor Sir William Batten, they dropped off their colleague Sir William Penn at Mark Lane, picked up some meat, then set off in high spirits for Bow. At the Queen's Head who should they encounter but both their wives, Penn and his wife and some other friends. They drank, feasted on oysters and had the meat they had brought with them cooked and served. They had so much fun that they did not get home until dark.

Outings to Bow were a favourite for Elizabeth Pepys in particular, and many a spring or summer afternoon her errant husband bundled his petulant wife into a coach, perhaps to calm her down after a quarrel. They might go first to Hackney and then to the 'resort' of Bow, with its ancient picturesque bridge over the Lea, its weatherboard cottages and welcoming taverns; the Queen's Head was their favourite. Sometimes they took a picnic, and on one occasion at least they were invited to dine at the house of Sir Edmund and Lady Pooley there. It was a good party, with Batelier the wine merchant and his mother – who was in a panic because she had lost a spaniel she had borrowed as stud for her bitch. They sang and drank, and at about ten o'clock Pepys's party left for home.

The calamities of 1667 had Pepys longing to escape to the countryside to live with 'plainness and pleasure'. For Londoners, and for the navy especially, that year was not much of an improvement on the last two. The Dutch fleet sailed up the Medway on 12 June 1667, inflicting the most humiliating defeat ever experienced by the navy, burning ships at Chatham and towing away the English flagship, the *Royal Charles*, while a trumpeter triumphantly tootled out 'Joan's placket is torn'. Panic gripped London; Pepys thought 'the whole kingdom is undone'. The king and the Duke of York, his brother, went down to Chatham in the early hours of 13 June and supervised the sinking of English ships to prevent any more being taken by the Dutch, and then went to Tower Hill to encourage the militia men who had been summoned for the defence of London from the surrounding areas. The king assured the soldiers that they 'should venture themselves no further than he would himself'. The government was on its knees: there was no money to pay the sailors, and Pepys met a gang of mariners' wives in Wapping crying up and down the streets: 'This comes of not paying our husbands.'

The Dutch did not invade and peace was made, but all was far from peaceful in the streets of London. Popular rioting, which was to become such a feature of Charles II's reign, started in earnest on Easter Monday 1668 when brothels in Poplar, patronised by the seafaring community, were attacked by an angry mob. It all started with a band of sailors, recently demobbed from fighting the Dutch, who had been cheated by the whores in the house kept by Damaris Page, that 'great bawd of the seamen'. Soon rioting spread to other parts, Moorfields, Shoreditch, East Smithfield and Holborn. About 40,000 were said to be on the streets, shouting 'Down with the redcoats' and marching behind a green banner as the Leveller radicals had done before them. What had started with some angry Stepney sailors, became a general protest against, among other things, the lewd-ness of the court. These were licentious times, with the king and his court leading the dance and Pepys not far behind. It was a boom time for brothels and bawds: the madam of a fashionable establishment said that during law terms, the London season, she would 'here [*sic*] of nothing less than half a crown', and at other times 'a shilling would go down with her'. If the king did not give them liberty of conscience, moreover, they would see to it that May Day, the next apprentices' holiday and a favourite occasion for demonstrations.

Nonconformists were 'mighty high' with the expiry of the Conventicles Act. Pepys commented: 'Everybody is encouraged nowadays to speak and even print … as bad things against them [the bishops] as ever in the year 1640, which is a strange change.' Archbishop Seldon, alarmed by the growth of open dissent, made a special enquiry into the situation in 1669. The returns, which may have exaggerated the threat, show fourteen 'fixed' conventicles in Stepney parish, two Presbyterian (one the Brick Lane house, another at a warehouse near Ratcliff Cross), two Quaker (Ratcliff and Spitalfields), four Independent (one in Bethnal Green and one in Rose Lane, Spitalfields), three Anabaptist, one Anabaptist and Independent by turns (the original Baptist chapel in Old Gravel Lane). Some 3-4,000 people attended these chapels, and there were more who met in private houses, like those of Limehouse butcher Launder and Mr Cherry in Poplar. William Greenhill was preaching openly in 1669 on Sundays, at home in Worcester House where he lived with his sister, Audrey, just a stone's throw from Stepney church. On Thursdays he preached at the conventicle in Wapping's Meeting House Alley, now 'as big as in Cromwell's time'.

Following the enquiry a much harsher Conventicles Act was put through parliament in 1670. Robinson's soldiers attacked the Quaker's Ratcliff Meeting House in School House Lane, seizing the furniture and smashing the place up. In Spitalfields William Penn (later founder of Pennsylvania and son of Pepys's neighbour and colleague) was arrested, and the Wheeler Street chapel attacked. In the spring of 1672 the king made a further attempt to 'quiet the minds of [his] good subjects' and encourage 'strangers to come and live among us' by issuing a Declaration of Indulgence. It was short lived, being withdrawn the following year, but in operation long enough for Stepney Meeting to apply for a licence and regularise its position for the time being, for Richard Kentish, pastor at a house in Redmayd Lane, Wapping to apply for a licence for a house by the Hermitage, and for Edward Veal to register his meeting in Globe Alley.

Greenhill had died in October 1671, five months before the issue of the Indulgence. Sadly he never saw the building of the fine meeting house, which was erected with the help of the Dutch government in a corner of the orchard of Worcester House. The foundation stone was laid on 10 May 1674. The chapel was deliberately made in the form of a dwelling-house so that it could revert to such if necessary. Its roof was supported by four huge round wooden pillars, sent by the Dutch States General. In October 1675 the Meeting had enough money to buy the whole of the vast Worcester House property from Maurice Thomson for £800. Thomson, who had once stood so high in the parish, was under suspicion from the government for spying for the Dutch. Matthew Mead was pastor now and started a series of May Day lectures on a triangle of land facing Stepney Green, the old maypole site, to keep the apprentices off the streets, no doubt. One wonders if he got any of the young locals away from Francis White's 'night club', which he set up in 1675 in the fields near Stepney Church. This bold Shadwell vintner sold beer without a licence, and had music and 'other disports' to lure young people into his 'greate shedd or booth'. When they tried to close it down he declared that he didn't care a 'bog' or a 'fart' for any Justice of the Peace.

When Dr Clarke and his curate attended the parochial visitation the year following the abortive Declaration of Indulgence, they had something to say about Dissenting activities in Stepney's Trinity House. Pastor Mead preached there regularly and one Mistress Payne ran a school there, making her pupils attend on holy days, forbidding them to observe the holidays prescribed by the Church. William Ludinager (this name means teacher, so presumably they did not know his proper name) had a school at Bishop's Hall in Bethnal Green and took his scholars to conventicles. Mr Ellwood, the schoolmaster at Green Bank in Wapping, was formally excommunicated for teaching without a licence. One Willis kept a conventicle and preached near Ratcliff Cross in an outhouse of the brewery kept by Mr Raiment. Examinations of the clergy and vestry members in Bow and Shadwell (a separate parish since 1669) revealed no conventicles there.

The census of nonconformity, made three years later under the auspices of Henry Compton, Bishop of London, made nil return for Stepney, Mile End, Limehouse and Spitalfields, but Ratcliff Hamlet was said to have fifteen Dissenters and Wapping was one of the worst areas in the whole country, with fifty detected.

For Stepney's churchwardens the greatest problem was, as ever, poverty in the parish. Just before Christmas 1662 they applied to the Mercers' Company for relief for 'their numerous and necessitous poor'. In November 1671 the vestry discussed the question of the provision of a parish workhouse and parish almshouse, following the passing of an Act of Parliament in this regard. Lady Wentworth was to be approached for some land. Burial fees, a good source of income, were put up from 2*s* to 3*s*, and in May 1678 the parish clerk was set to search for any wills that might contain unpaid donations for the poor. In April 1680 the desperate vestry even went to the lengths of putting collection boxes in all taverns, victualling houses, alehouses, coffeehouses, brandyhouses and public places. By September 1683 some land adjoining the churchyard had been acquired, and a general plea was issued to all 'charitably disposed persons' to build houses for the poor on it. Some half of all East Enders were classified as 'poor' in the Hearth Tax returns, and it is not surprising that they could not afford to pay the swingeing Poll Tax levied in 1668, reckoned to be the hardest tax ever imposed. In Wapping and Shadwell they shut their doors when the collectors came.

The poor of Stepney were concentrated in the parish's southern and northern extremities. In the riverside hamlets poor folk might supplement their meagre incomes by kidnapping children and youths and selling them to the masters of merchant vessels bound for Virginia and Barbados. This lively white slave trade seems to have peaked in the mid- and late 1670s. In the north, meanwhile, the weavers of Spitalfields and Bethnal Green were in trouble. In the summer of 1675 there was serious rioting among the weaving community, as there would be intermittently for many years to come. Silk weaving was a long-established industry on the City's eastern side, and the hamlets had swollen, attracting weavers from the Continent and the countryside. In the 1670s the textile trade was severely depressed, dominated by a class of permanent journeymen who never made enough money to set up their own businesses, and were threatened by the now common use of engine looms. On a hot Sunday night in August rioting and loom smashing started in Moorfields, quickly spreading to Spitalfields, Stepney, Whitechapel and Bow, and the other weaving areas, Cloth Fair, Blackfriars, Westminster and Southwark. Such was the popular sympathy for the poor weavers that the commanders of the trained bands refused to harm them and the Royal Guards, under the king's bastard son the Duke of Monmouth, had to be brought in.

Like the rest of London and the country at large, the frenzied hysteria of the Popish Plot obsessed East Enders in 1678. There was still an ever-present terror of Jesuits 'under the bed', of Roman Catholic plotting, while nightmares of Smithfield faggots were kept alive by *Foxe's Book of Martyrs* and stirred up by the politicians for their own ends. With a barren queen and the prospect of the king's Catholic brother, James Duke of York, taking the throne, the threat seemed to becoming a reality. It was said that the Earl of Shaftesbury, the leader of the anti-papist faction, looked to the eastern suburbs for support. When Titus Oates and his fellows came up with a story of a plot to overthrow the government, involving the queen among others, everyone jumped on the bandwagon and the world went mad. Any covert activities were suspect; even Stepney Meeting came under attack and Pastor Mead's goods were seized. While lawyers and politicians were hunting down innocent men, Thomas and Jack Jackson climbed onto the roof of Stepney church and stole some of the lead. They were brought before the scathing Judge Jeffreys, Recorder of London at the Old Bailey sessions. He took the opportunity to raise a laugh from the court and only fined them £20 each: 'You are brethren in iniquity, Simeon and Levi. Your zeal for religion is so great as to carry you to the top of the church.'

The failure of the politicians now known as Whigs to exclude the Catholic James from the succession to the throne saw a High Church Tory reaction, and in the 1680s the government took reprisals against the Dissenters; this time there would be great trouble enforcing the law. Richard Hitchcock, sub-constable of Limehouse, told the magistrates in 1681 'Hang me, I will not inform'; and John Holby, constable of Stepney, declared that 'the law for suppressing of conventicles is against the law of Christ'.

Meanwhile the Quaker Meeting House in School Lane, Ratcliff was subject to attacks from hooligans. In December 1681 they appointed two bouncers to keep 'bouys and Rude people' from 'annoying our meeting house Doores'.

Stepney Meeting was under fire in 1682 as part of the repercussions of the real or pretended Rye House Plot to murder the king and his brother. Sir William Smith went with a strong guard to the chapel, pulled down the pulpit and broke it into pieces, and Mead was brought before the privy council. For the parish at large this was a year of great disaster. A kettle of pitch was knocked over in a barge-builder's shop, and fire broke out. Thomas Scattergood, the Quaker, saw 'a very great smoke' in the sky as he was returning from Gravesend, and feared that the conflagration would consume his meeting house in School Lane. Half of Ratcliff was burnt down, with between 4–500 dwellings lost and the Coopers' free school razed to the ground. Tents were supplied by the government, Nell Gwyn sent a cash donation and hundreds of the homeless camped out in the church.

The winters of these years were bitter cold, and in 1683–84 the Great Frost, which saw the Thames frozen hard for months, brought distress to the parish. There was larking on the ice upstream at Westminster, oxen roasted and all the fun of the fair, but downriver (and in Southwark) thousands of watermen were out of a job and their families were starving. Meanwhile the Ratcliff Quakers divided up their patch into four areas for the purposes of 'visiting poor friends', and snoopers were sent to visit 'the widow Smith of Bow concerning the disorders of her daughter and former manservant'. The widow reports that the couple were secretly married.

The sick king spent an 'unconscionable long time a dying', but finally left the country to the mercies of James, his misguided papist brother, on 6 February 1685. That summer Dissenters and a whole ragbag of malcontents rallied in support of Charles II's son, 'darling of his father, and the ladies', the Duke of Monmouth. Monmouth, who was married to the great heiress of Buccleuch, had been living in open adultery for some years with Lady Henrietta Wentworth, daughter and heiress of Stepney's lord of the manor. When she was not in Brussels with the duke (where he had gone into exile after the Rye House Plots) she lived with her mother in the Wentworths' Stepney house, a substantial property just to the north-east of the church, where Durham Row now is.

Monmouth's rebellion in the West Country was horribly crushed, the so-called Bloody Assizes being presided over by Judge Jeffreys. In the reprisals that followed Matthew Mead fled from Stepney to Holland once again. John Hathaway of Stepney was overheard saying 'I would fight for the Duke of Monmouth, and if that Monmouth had the better and the King was to bee killed, rather then the King should not bee killed, I would doe it.' He was fined and condemned to a public whipping, to be:

> Stript from the middle upwards, and be publicly whipt upon his back at the hinder part of a cart, until his body should be bloody, from a certain place called The Maypole in East Smithfield to a certain other place called Ratcliffe Crosse, and that he should be committed to Newgate Gaol, there to remain until he should have paid the said fine and undergone the said punishment.

Monmouth went to the scaffold on Tower Hill, proclaiming to the last that Henrietta was his 'wife before God'. She died of a broken heart at Stepney on 23 April 1686, less than a year after her lover's execution.

Within two years a momentous invitation was sent to William of Orange and his wife Mary, daughter of James II. The Dutchman and his queen took the throne from the hated Catholic James with no bloodshed. The Dissenters of the East End, and the French Calvinist refugees who had been recently flooding into the hamlet of Spitalfields, were left in peace. A day of solemn fasting and prayer at Stepney Meeting marked the Glorious Revolution.

Matthew Mead, who was a personal friend of Prince William's, came back to Worcester House, and when he died in 1691 was buried in an ornate tomb in St Dunstan's churchyard. King James's chancellor, the hanging Judge Jeffreys, was captured at a Wapping riverside pub. The Town of Ramsgate in Wapping High Street makes a claim for this honour: according to an account in *Notes and Queries* in 1886, taken apparently from Roger North, it was at a 'little peddling alehouse' called the Red Cow in Anchor and Hope Alley near King Edward's Stairs. Some said that he was spotted by a local scrivener who had suffered from his sarcasm in court. It would be nice to think that the Jackson brothers were still around, and remembered with relish the day he had fined them £20 for stealing lead off the church roof and had a laugh at their expense.

Part III

THE
EIGHTEENTH
CENTURY

Chapter 7

THE EAST END SURVEYED

These were the days of Spitalfields silk (Mozart is said to have had a waistcoat made of it), of powdered wigs and buckle shoes, of rattling stagecoaches, gin and roistering and cries of, 'Stop thief!' Jack the Lad Sheppard, the celebrated ruffian and burglar (MacHeath of *The Beggars' Opera* and Dickens's model for the Artful Dodger) roamed the streets; Captain Kydd was hanged at Execution Dock. In Whitechapel Dick Turpin had a shoot out, David Garrick took London by storm and Hannah Snell, the 'woman soldier', strutted on the stage of the New Wells. Captain Cook and 'Bligh of the *Bounty*' were the celebrities down by the riverside and the sailors of Wapping (peg legs and parrots) were much occupied with the long years of wars with France. In the Annus Mirabilis of 1759, a year of British triumphs, the East End's sailors shared in the glory of trouncing the enemy, notably at the resounding victory of Quiberon Bay. David Garrick wrote a song in their honour, which was sung at the Christmas pantomime in Drury Lane:

> Heart of Oak are our ships,
> Heart of Oak are our men.

With the Glorious Revolution of 1689 the toils and tribulations of Reformation and Revolution finally came to an end. Warring Royalists and Parliamentarians, Arminians ranged against Independents, Presbyterians, Anabaptists and the rest, were replaced in the public arena by the more civilised antagonists, High Church Tory and Low Church Whig or Latitudinarian. With the new regime and the new century Stepney parish retired from the political and religious limelight that had illuminated it for nearly 200 years to fight its own private battles. The sound of Jacobite drums was far away in the north, although there were local rumblings. Although dissent still flourished, the East End played no outstanding part in the struggle for the removal of nonconformist disabilities that occupied the eighteenth century or in the radical politics with which it was associated. Spirits 'inimical to government' were said to flourish in Spitalfields, Ratcliff Highway and other rougher parts of Tower Hamlets, and Spitalfields and Wapping had their share of the riots that beset eighteenth-century London.

We will stand back from the great affairs of state, the wars with France, the loss of the American colonies, the machinations of courtiers and politicians over at Westminster, and survey the east side of London as it had become during the 'late troubles'. Henceforth our story is of manufacture and of the seafaring communities that serviced the glittering new post-Fire capital and Britain's burgeoning trading empire during the golden years of naval victories and merchant enterprise.

At no time was London more magnificent, her folk more prosperous or her labouring classes more uppity. As Francois Misson said in 1719, 'A thousand worthless fellows call themselves gentlemen and esquire.' Wages and living standards were the highest in the world in this time of commercial and industrial boom. New money turned traders and manufacturers into gentlemen. Even humble lamplighters had silk stockings and East End prostitutes might charge a guinea a go. The sign of Whittington's cat hung in Whitechapel High Street as encouragement to the working populace, perhaps, that they too might become lord mayor. James Boswell observed: 'Foreigners are not a little amazed when they hear of brewers, distillers, and men in similar departments of trade, held forth as persons of considerable consequence. In this great commercial country it is natural that a situation which produces much wealth should be considered as very respectable; and, no doubt, honest industry is entitled to esteem.'

Hitherto we have looked through a glass darkly, but now there are maps of the whole East End. In 1702 Stepney was surveyed in detail for the first time, by Joel Gascoyne, and we can actually see the streets, fields and buildings laid out before us. In 1702 the vicar and churchwardens were ordered by the vestry to find a 'skillfull Geographer or Plattmaker to make a Draught of this parish'. Each warden was allowed a copy for a guinea after he had served his two years. The maps were paid for by Captain Mudd, founder of the Trinity Almshouses. There are many other maps of London that incorporate this area, notably Richard Newcourt's of 1658, Strype's Stow of 1720, John Roque's, published in 1747, Richard Horwood's of 1792–99. There are detailed accounts of London and its suburbs, 'tourist' guides and records in abundance: tax lists and insurance company records, tales from the Old Bailey – all of which tell us a good deal about East Enders. There are prints of some of the public buildings and even some caricatures of lowlife. Best of all, among the debris of modern living are some solid physical relics of the eighteenth-century East End.

Some relics

Apart from old St Dunstan of Stepney, Stratford Bow church and the Tower itself, there is virtually nothing surviving from the earlier periods except brickwork in cellars, hidden below ground. For the eighteenth century there are visible traces. In Spitalfields there are complete terraces of houses and, if you search around else-where, some houses, shopfronts, pubs and public buildings that allow a glimpse of life 300 years ago.

No searching is necessary to find the three towering Hawksmoor churches: Christ Church Spitalfields (1714–29), St Anne's Limehouse (1712–24) and St George's in the East (1714–26), with their Georgian parsonage houses, nor, indeed, to find the Royal London Hospital (1751): 'The Georgian contribution still recognisable as the centre of the present agglomeration of buildings', as Pevsner said, or the German Lutheran Church in Alie Street (1762). The two St Botolphs of Aldgate and Bishopsgate date from this period, as does St Matthew Bethnal Green (largely rebuilt 1861 and 1961). St Matthias Church in Poplar, the former East India Company chapel, is a rare Interregnum church, not that you would think so to view it from the outside; as Pevsner says, it is 'clothed in Victorian hidiosity'.

Dwarfed by massive new office blocks, the Hoop and Grapes, a seventeenth-century timber-framed building at No. 47 Aldgate High Street, still looks the part of an eighteenth-century hostelry. In 1794 the Hoop and Grapes was the wine shop of one Henry Newton. A little east further along the Whitechapel Road, at Nos 32–34, are the mid-eighteenth-century buildings of the celebrated bell foundry.

Whitechapel's affluent quarter in the eighteenth century was Goodman's Fields, an estate of fine houses newly laid out, lying south of the Whitechapel Road, immediately east of Aldgate: Leman Street, Mansell Street, Alie Street and Prescot Street. Having descended into one of the dreariest parts subsequently, it is now revived. A sprinkling of restored houses remain among the sparkling new office blocks and hotels, to remind us of a time when it looked like a street in Bloomsbury.

At the west end of Cable Street, there are a row of early eighteenth-century houses and further east in Cannon Street Road, seven from the later part of the century. Nos 77A and 79 New Road are from the period.

Along the Mile End Road, not far from the Blind Beggar, you will find, set back from the road on the north side, the pretty Trinity Almshouses, dating from 1695. Further east are some eighteenth-century houses, restored and easily recognis-able. Next to the retail park, once Charrington's Anchor brewery, is Malplaquet House, built in 1742. Ireland Row (Nos 107–13) is a terrace of eight-roomed houses built in about 1717, and nearby is a terrace of mid-eighteenth-century houses at Nos 131–39.

Opposite the Royal London Hospital are two houses of the period, Nos 265 and 267. On the south side of the road Nos 82 and 84 are eighteenth-century and in Assembly Row Nos 90–98 date from 1763–66. No. 88, where Captain Cook lived, is no longer there. East of the hospital is an almost complete street of houses from the 1790s in Parfett Street.

Around the truncated remains of old Mile End Green, in a leafy oasis, are the Georgian houses of Stepney Green. Nos 61 and 63 are the remnants of a terrace of seven houses built in about 1762. Nos 21 and 23 date from *c.* 1740 and Nos 11–18 are late eighteenth- or early nineteenth-century. No. 37 is the star of Stepney Green, a Queen Anne house and one of the finest in London.

Spitalfields is, of course, the prize, being less impaired by the rebuilder than most of the East End, and even where the buildings are new it is 'unmistakably ancient in flavour', especially the narrow way of Artillery Lane with a shopfront (No. 58) that is the finest example of its period in London. The new 'Old Spitalfields Market', selling nick-nacks for tourists and classy clothes, bears little resemblance to the old place where children were sent to find work. Restored and made more elegant than perhaps it ever was, Spitalfields is a stage-set of a place, with old houses lovingly restored in Fournier Street, Wilkes Street, Folgate Street and Princelet Street. Having fallen into slum and become the disgusting and diseased underbelly of proud Victorian London, these streets of old weavertown have become most desirable, never mind the clash and clatter of Banglatown and Brick Lane nearby.

Up Brick Lane is the Brick House, the former Truman's brewery, with its very grand Director's House, enlarged for Sir Benjamin Truman in 1745 and remodelled in the 1770s. Along the Lane a few eighteenth-century houses are left: a tenement block built for a tallow chandler in 1763–65 is at Nos 194–98 and weavers' 'long lights' are visible in Nos 125–27. On the corner of Fournier Street is a mosque that was a Huguenot chapel, dating from 1743.

In Bethnal Green little survives of the houses of the working weavers from this era, only a couple of houses in Club Row and Nos 113 and 115 Bethnal Green Road (1735). In Sclater Street, at Nos 70–74, are some weavers' houses dating from 1719, but they have been largely rebuilt. In the heart of the old village, by the Green itself, which survived the coming of the weavers as a residential part, there is the fine Netteswell House, next to the Museum of Childhood. It dates from 1705 but was remodelled in 1862; part of the cellars have been dated 1553. Nearby are three eighteenth-century houses at Nos 17, 19 and 21 Old Ford Road, built and part-lived in by Anthony Natt in 1753–55; he was a builder who retired here from the silk area. No. 2 Paradise Row is eighteenth century, as is No. 17 Victoria Park Square, while No. 18 dates from *c.* 1690.

Over in Bow, where these days a massive flyover wheels over a scrubby industrial mess beneath, only the church in the middle of the road and one solitary quaint old house, just by MacDonald's, are left. No. 223 Bow Road dates from the seventeenth century, and may well be the oldest house in this part of the East End.

South of Bow Road is Bromley, perhaps the most difficult part of our area to imagine as a village. It has no heart and is a nothing sort of a place: its parish church has gone, and there is only a patch of churchyard to remind us of St Mary's and its predecessor, 'Madame Eglantine's' nunnery. If you turn off Bow Road, going south from Gladstone's statue, and walk down Bromley High Street, ahead of you is an impressive eighteenth-century house (1720), a pub called the Rose and Crown until quite recently. It is rather ramshackle but dominates the little parade of shops that overlook what was once the village green, with stocks and a whipping post. If you swing round to the right and go into Rainhill Way, among the blocks of flats you will find part of the Drapers' Company almshouses, a nice little row that is clean and restored, now private houses, founded by a sailmaker called John Edmundson/Edmanson and dating from 1706. You will look in vain for the Old Palace that stood in St Leonard Street (remembered in Old Palace School), but you can see one of its rooms in the Victoria and Albert Museum. This was a house of twenty-four bedrooms, built in 1606, so splendid that it acquired royal connections. James I, they say, built it as a hunting lodge here, for which some of the old materials of the demolished nunnery appear to have been used. In the first thirty years of its existence it was used as the manor house, until Sir John Jacob completed the new manor house in the priory grounds.

About half a mile south from Bromley High Street, in Gillender Street, you will find Bromley Hall, stranded in an unlikely position by the roaring Blackwall Tunnel Approach Road. This is a restored Tudor house, once the manor house for Lower Bromley and used as a factory during the Civil War. It was remodelled in the late seventeenth century, and in 1799 it was bought by calico printer Joseph Foster. A little to its north is the Three Mills Conservation Area, which, being in Newham, is no part of our story. But its beautifully restored nineteenth-century mill buildings clustered around the channels of the Lea are a reminder of the old milling days in these parts. The mills were bought in 1727 by three Huguenot distillers, Peter Lefevre, John Bisson and John Debonnaire.

Going south, down towards the river is the current site for the St Katharine's Foundation in Butcher Row, with its Master's House, dating from 1784, rebuilt after the Ratcliff fire. By the Thames, in sailortown, there are a few good old buildings, but they mainly date from the early part of the nineteenth century: dock buildings and the fine Meridien House in Poplar High Street, built for the chaplain to the East India Company almshouses.

In Limehouse, however, backing onto the river is a fine terrace of early Georgian houses in Narrow Street (Nos 78–94), with the Grapes pub at the end. Limehouse Rectory is an eighteenth-century house at No. 5 Newell Street, with other houses of the period at Nos 11–23. Shadwell has what claims to be the oldest pub in London, the Prospect of Whitby, in Wapping Wall. It is probably on the site of a medieval brewery. The building dates from 1777, when it was given its present name, and it has a nineteenth-century frontage.

Wapping, having been gentrified, is quite an atmospheric place these days, with patches of well-tended grass and trees, cobbled ways and restored warehouses set among the high dock walls. Just near the Pierhead, off Wapping High Street, with its grand early nineteenth-century houses overlooking the river, is the quaint Town of Ramsgate pub (1758), with its slimy stairs going down to the river.

Nearby is the tower of the new church (built in 1790, the old one having been demolished), and the original parish charity school building, with its figures of a bluecoat boy and girl. The school was founded in 1690 but the extant building dates from 1756. If you continue east along the High Street and turn left up Wapping Lane past a parade of shops, tucked away in Raine Street, is another school, Raine's Hospital it used to be called. This is a little jewel, a delightful 1719 building backed by a rose garden and ornamented with swags, pediments and the injunction 'Come in and learn your duty to God and man'. The figures of bluecoat boy and girl stare out with black, unseeing eighteenth-century eyes at the angular slabs of modernity around.

An overview

In 1700, it has been said, you could see all London from the top of St Paul's, spread out beneath you, a panorama of buildings interspersed with pasture and farms. By 1800 it was all town as far as the eye could see. London was the biggest city in Europe. London moved west; according to Sir William Petty because of the prevailing wind, to escape the 'fumes, steams and stinks of the whole easterly pyle'. Richard Horwood's map of 1792–99 shows the mass of buildings north and south of Oxford Street, while to the City's east there was still much open ground. Defoe, writing in the 1720s, regarded the increase of buildings in St Giles and St Martin in the Fields as 'some kind of prodigy'; it stretched as far west as Tyburn (Oxford Street). Squares and estates of fine houses were laid out; Pall Mall and St James's in the 1670s and '80s, Seven Dials and Holborn were developed. There followed the golden age of Georgian architecture in the 1760s, when the Adelphi, Piccadilly, Berkeley Square, Cavendish Square, Fitzroy Square and Portland Place came into being. By 1775 Oxford Street and London's brilliant streetlighting were the wonders of the world. Archenholtz, a foreign visitor writing in 1780, observed a migration from east to west in the previous twenty years, commenting that the East End 'especially along the shores of the Thames, consists of old houses; the streets are narrow ... The contrast between this and the West End is astonishing.'

The quality moved west while the City remained the centre of commerce, but the East End grew too; London's eastern limit was accounted at Blackwall. It was Spitalfields, Bethnal Green (weavertown), Whitechapel and Wapping Stepney (sailortown) which grew the most. Defoe, writing at the beginning of the century, tells us of the 'numberless range of buildings called Spittlefields'; between Bishopsgate and Bethnal Green, he says, 'above three hundred and twenty acres of ground ... are all now closely built, and well inhabited with an infinite number of people' Streets between the Whitechapel Road and Rosemary Lane and east as far as Old Gravel Lane had been built since 1670; squares were laid out: Haydon Square, Wellclose and Princes, in Bishopsgate, Devonshire Square and Crosby Square.

The Foreigner's Guide to London, published in 1752, has little to say about the East End, except that it was full of people. East of the Tower, St Katharine's to Blackwall was 'very large and populous suburbs', with lots of sailors and no 'remarkable buildings', except the two churches (Limehouse and St George's in the East). Whitechapel and Spitalfields were 'quarters very large and populous'. The author notes only Wellclose Square as being 'very pleasant', with its Danish church having the prettiest pulpit in London; this was removed from the Chapel Royal in Whitehall by Queen Anne at the behest of her Danish husband. In Spitalfields, he says, there were said to be 100,000 weavers; Mile End was 'another great quarter' and Blackwall was where they built the East India Company ships.

Strangers

As they had done for many years countryfolk were pouring into London and the suburbs. Many of those who came to the East End were from East Anglia, but they came from all over the British Isles. In 1680 a third of Londoners lived in the eastern suburbs and hamlets. Between 1630 and 1680 the population of Stepney parish had nearly doubled, with the Great Fire bringing in a number from the City. In the eighteenth century immigrants were coming into London at a rate of something like 8,000 a year.

The foreign immigrants for which the East End is renowned were staking their claims. The rector of Limehouse, writing in the 1930s, described his churchyard as a 'sleeping world in miniature', with its Lascars, Negroes, Danes and Venetians. There were religious refugees and seamen and traders from anywhere in the world that London had trading links. As we have seen, 'Dochemen' had been around for centuries. One of the most celebrated was the leading clockmaker of his day, Ahasuerus Fromanteel, born in Norwich of Flemish stock going back and forth from Amsterdam. He set up shop in East Smithfield in 1629 and returned there in his old age. John Strype (d. 1648), the antiquarian's father, was a Dutch throwster who lived just off Petticoat Lane. Not all were Protestants: a branch of the Culveners, a Catholic family of tapestry workers from Brabant, settled around Brick Lane in the 1660s–'70s.

Numbers of French and Walloons had arrived in the sixteenth century, and had, firmly established themselves in Spitalfields by the mid-seventeenth century. But the greatest and the best-known arrivals were the Protestants who fled from France following Louis XIV's 1685 revocation of his grandfather's toleration edict. Fifty thousand Huguenot refugees are said to have come to London, numbers of them silk weavers from Tours and Lyons. Many joined the already established weaving community and created a true industrial suburb, stretching from Bishopsgate to Bethnal Green.

The arrival of German sugarbakers saw the former Wapping Stepney start its transformation into 'St George's in the Dirt'. Demand for high-quality sugar meant a huge increase in its import and production, and experienced bakers and refiners were recruited from Germany (mainly from Hanover) to work in Whitechapel and St George's in the East. According to Millicent Rose, sugar-baking was the lowest paid work of all; even the Irish refused to do it and the manufacturers were forced to recruit from Germany. Such was the concentration of immigrant workers that the area became known as Little Germany. The bakers had their own church in Alie Street (a German Lutheran church), founded in 1762 by Dietrich Beckmann, a rich local refiner; it is still there. In 1782 Major Rohde, a German sugarman of 86 Leman Street, was appointed as Whitechapel's 'upper warden'.

Little bands of 'Blackamoors', led by their masters, might be seen along the riverside, roped together and being led to auction; every spring slavers arrived at Wapping Dock and unloaded their grisly human cargo. It was quite the fashion to have a black servant. Little Susannah Mingoe, aged fourteen, was baptised from a house in Prescot Street in 1696.

By the end of the century there were said to be some 15,000 negroes in London, mostly in the riverside parishes. This is a contemporary estimate; there were probably not as many as this. 'No clergyman in England', ran an obituary for the rector of St George's in the East (1764–1802), 'ever baptized so many black-men and Mulattoes.' A lane was named after them, Blackamoor Alley in Green Bank, and there was a Blackamoor's Head in Wentworth Street and another in East Smithfield. One lad, known as Black John, worked at the Peacock in the Minories in the 1780s, and got taken to court for theft by the landlord, who suspected him of sleeping with his wife.

The problem of poor blacks roaming the streets was acute, especially after the loss of the American colonies when numbers of black soldiers and sailors arrived. In 1786 a Committee for the Relief of the Black Poor was set up, patronised by such luminaries as the Duchess of Devonshire. Out relief was offered to these desperate individuals from the White Raven in Mile End (a tavern where the Whitechapel Mission now is, at No. 212 Mile End Road) and at another venue in Lisson Grove. A scheme for shipping them off to Sierra Leone was proposed by Henry Smeathman, a botanist, and taken over by a man from Mile End New Town, Joseph Irwin. It was a disastrous affair, and Irwin was accused of corruption and ill-treatment. Of the 350 blacks and fifty-nine white women who were dispatched, only sixty survived.

'Lascars', Asian sailors who arrived on East India Company ships, were much in evidence. These 'poor sons of misery' were quartered in barracks on Ratcliff highway known as King David's Fort. In 1813 there were said to be 500 Chinamen in the fort.

The Jews were to start their takeover bid for Whitechapel, although so far their numbers were relatively small. When Cromwell allowed the Jews back into the country it was predominantly Portuguese and Spanish Jews of the Sephardim, from Iberia, Amsterdam and Morocco, wealthy and respected middle-class merchants and manufacturers who came. They were followed by the poorer Ashkenazi Jews from Holland, Germany, Russia and Turkey, who tended to join the already established trade in secondhand and stolen goods, notably in Houndsditch and Rosemary Lane's Rag Fair. Many Jews were involved in the tobacco trade; Abraham Cordoza/Cardoza, for instance, had a snuff mill in Whitechapel's Goulston Street, which was run by his widow after his death. The City was resistant to Jewish settlement, and in order to operate a retail business within its jurisdiction it was necessary to take up freedom of the City. Practising Jews were unable to take the Christian oath that was required, so taking to the suburbs was the only option. They settled on the eastern side of the City and in Whitechapel and Stepney, in Wapping Stepney, Bethnal Green and Mile End. The Dutch synagogue was in Duke's Place, Aldgate. The Portuguese synagogue was in nearby Bevis Marks; the wealthier members of the congregation favoured the newly built houses in Whitechapel's Goodman's Fields and Wellclose Square, along with the naval officers. Jewish cemeteries in Mile End were Sephardic: the Velho (Old) behind No. 253 Mile End Road (1657) and the Nuevo Beth Caim (the New) opened 1725; and Ashkenazi: Alderney Road, opened 1696, and the Brady Street cemetery, opened by the New Synagogue in 1761.

Scandinavian merchants and seamen came with the timber needed for the rebuilding of London after the Great Fire. Some stayed, establishing churches in Wapping Stepney, the Danish church in Wellclose Square (1696–1869) and the Swedish church in Princes' Square. Strong trading links with Portugal brought numbers into the East End from the sixteenth century; those who stayed might attach themselves to the Catholic Virginia Street chapel in Wapping.

None of these 'aliens' were popular. Jewbaiting was quite a sport, and Colquhoun claimed that they were responsible for a disproportionate amount of crime. But it was the Irish who seem to have generated most abhorrence. London magistrate Saunders Welch commented in 1753 that the 'uncontrouled importation of Irish vagabonds' was one of the main causes of 'supply of rogues to London'. Poverty-stricken, uneducated and used to living in tiny hovels with their pigs, the fighting Paddies were prepared to work for less than English labourers – not only that, they were papists. In the summer of 1736 Irish pubs were attacked when native labourers were laid off the building of the new church at Spitalfields and Irishmen were taken on at two-thirds rates. A brewer's cooper watched the rioters from the end of Red Lion Street (Leman Street), a terrifying mob of 4,000, with sticks and flaring torches, coming down Bell Yard (where the Whitechapel Art Gallery now is), bound for the Gentleman and Porter in Church Lane. The Irish came to any part where there was building work to be had, and notably to work as coal heavers and ballast men along the riverside, joining the Germans in the sugar factories, the French at weaving, and carrying sedan chairs and selling milk, while many took to the sea. Before the building of the Virginia Street chapel in Wapping in the 1760s they worshipped in a house in 'Branch Place', probably Rosemary Branch Alley (the bottom of Mansell Street) and in a converted pub in Rosemary Lane called The Windmill. The 'Returns of Papists' for 1767 show great numbers of Irish in St George's in the East, with a few in Spitalfields and Bethnal Green. By 1816 there were about 14,000 in 'the Shadwell parishes', where coalheaving was a major occupation.

London and its suburbs continued to increase, intermittently, during the eighteenth century. Arthur Young thought it was because of the improved coach service and the introduction of turnpikes (toll roads). In 1777 you could jump into a coach in the morning in the shires, and for perhaps 10s get to London the same day; in the old days a stagecoach 'was four or five days creeping a hundred miles'. The larger outparishes were more attractive to poor immigrants than the City and West End. This was partly because of lower rents and partly because of the settlement laws. In a vast parish like Stepney beadles and overseers were unlikely to be able to keep a close check on people coming in, in case they were going to be a charge on the parish. Magistrate Sir John Fielding said there were an 'amazing number of women' coming to seek work in service.

The working end of town

All around London overpopulated parishes were divided up; there were seventeen new parishes in all. Seven were created in Westminster, and Stepney, as we shall see, was shorn of over half of its domain: the industrial hamlets of Spitalfields and Bethnal Green, the small town of Bow with Old Ford and the busy riverside hamlets of Wapping Stepney and Limehouse, losing 6,000 of its 9,000 households. In 1700 Stepney had 86,000 inhabitants; by 1801, even without half its old territory it had 113,000 (including Wapping and Shadwell). The total population for the area in 1801 was 163, 208, greater than the City (128,129) and larger than any town in Britain outside London, except Dublin (170,000), while Marylebone and Westminster had 225,000 inhabitants.

In the east the old mansions of nobility and courtiers were divided up or given over to other purposes: Kirby's Castle in Bethnal Green became a madhouse, in Poplar a large Elizabethan house was converted into almshouses by the East India Company, and the manor house was leased to a cowkeeper. The Mercers' Great Place in Stepney village became the Spring Garden, while Worcester House and Bromley's 'old palace' were both divided up and used partly as schools.

The days when wealthy London citizens had country mansions in the area had become only a memory, and the 'aristocratic' establishments of the East End were the homes of the nouveau riches, the brewers, distillers, sugarmen, ropemakers, glassmakers, silkmen, East and West India merchants, naval contractors, shipowners, insurance-men and stockbrokers. When Dr Cawley came to Stepney as rector in 1759 he was disappointed to find no 'ancient families' in his parish and the 1,750 houses occupied by families 'in trade or immediate descendants of tradesmen'. For the author of the *London Guide* of 1782, written for an audience mainly interested in theatres and places of superior entertainment, the only notable public buildings in the East End were almshouses and schools, namely Bancrofts, the Trinity Almshouses and the Whitechapel home for penitent prostitutes (which had by then moved to Southwark).

Overwhelmingly, except in the weaving areas of Spitalfields and Bethnal Green and the outlying rural hamlets, this was a nautical place where men of all sorts and conditions took to the sea, employed by the rapidly expanding trading companies and, in time of war, by the navy. Wapping was England's 'nursery of navigation', and Stepney church was to become known as the 'Church of the High Seas'. The dock operation, which grew beyond belief during the century (imports rose from £2,894,737 in 1705 to £13,065,290 in 1797 and exports from £4,622,370 to £17,721,441), was still based at the chaotic and overcrowded Legal Quays in the City and the Sufferance Wharves, most of which were on the south bank. The great vessels were moored midstream and the cargoes were taken to and from the Legal quays by hoy or lighter. Many of these were manned by East Enders. Ships were berthed downstream as the Upper Pool was too congested, and colliers from Newcastle discharged their cargoes in Wapping and Shadwell. In all 40 million tons of coal was imported into London between 1670 and 1750, most of it from Newcastle. Without coal London would grind to a halt and its citizens would freeze in the terrible icy winters of the time, and the unloading and sale of coal was one of the most vital of local concerns. In the desperate winter of 1775–76, 40,000 more chaldrons were sent from Newcastle to London than had been sent in the previous year. Coalheavers needed nothing but brute strength, and could earn very good money.

In the 1690s most warehouses were still in the immediate vicinity of the Legal Quays; only five warehouses had been located in Wapping and Shadwell by 1693/4 and four in Ratcliff. As the eighteenth century progressed it was a different picture, with dock warehousing moving out east, where there was more room and land was cheaper. In about 1780 the East India Company built an enormous warehouse in Ratcliff's Broad Street (now the Highway). Horwood's map shows a vast tobacco warehouse west of Cartwright Street, off Rosemary Lane, and the East India Company had a tea warehouse in Barker's Gardens between Whitechapel and the Minories. Of 185 wharves listed in Boyle's View of London (1799) forty-four are in the East End. Of these there are eighteen 'landing wharves' and fifteen coal wharves, mainly in Wapping, Shadwell and Ratcliff. Wharves designated for other particular commodities were the East India Company's saltpetre wharf and a wood wharf in Ratcliff, a flour wharf in Wapping, and a ballast wharf and a dung wharf in Shadwell.

At the end of the seventeenth century the East End was not yet quite the 'working end of town', although it would soon become so. Manufacture of all sorts was well distributed around London in the 1690s, with the greatest number of firms still in the City. But there is a noticeable shift to the east from mid-century, with modern factory-like operations establishing themselves, with labourers rather than journeymen working for good wages under one roof. Notable among these were the distillers and sugar refiners, brewers, dyers, colourmakers, coopers, glass manufacturers, vinegarmakers and tobacconists. By 1820, 20 per cent of London's manufacturing firms were in the East End.

There were, as there had been for generations, foundries (notably the Whitechapel bellfoundry) and, of course, the making of cloth and silk-weaving for which Spitalfields is renowned, and the trades associated with ships and shipping: ropemaking, sailmaking, anchorsmithing, blockmaking, mastmaking. Apart from the building of East Indiamen at Blackwall, most shipbuilding was done on the south bank or downstream, but there were still a number of shipyards and shipwrights in Limehouse, Ratcliff and Wapping.

In those days when Madam Geneva ruled the roost, Dr Johnson said he had heard Lord Hervey remark that 'distilling was the most profitable of any [trade] now excercised in the kingdom except that of being broker to a prime minister'. Some of the East End's richest men were the malt distillers, 'prodigious dealers' who produced the raw spirit, who came into their own after the import of French brandy was stopped at the end of the seventeenth century. Among the most successful were John Woodham of Shadwell Dock and, outstandingly so, the Lefevres of Bow and Bromley.

There were breweries all over London. The biggest of all in the 1690s was the Red Lion in St Katharine Street, in East Smithfield. In 1703 it was owned by Alderman Sir John Parsons, who lived in Wellclose Square; in 1736 its vats held 54,000 gallons. When they spoke of 'Alderman's ale' in the alehouses in Rag Fair, it was Parsons' porter they meant. Oliver Goldsmith called it 'Parsons' black champagne'. The famous Black Eagle brewery in Brick Lane, Spitalfields was founded in 1669 by Thomas Bucknall, passing to Joseph Truman in 1694. Sampson Hanbury became a partner in 1780, and his son-in-law, Thomas Fowell Buxton, in 1811. By 1873 Truman, Hanbury and Buxton were the biggest brewers in the world. Charrington's Anchor Brewery in Mile End dates from about 1757, when it was owned by Messrs Westfield and Moss, who had started their operation in Bethnal Green. In 1766 John Charrington bought Westfield's share, thus starting the long association of the family with the East End. By 1807/8 it was the second largest brewery in London, and only ceased production in 1975. Also in Mile End Old Town was the White Swan of the Trinker and Green families, and innumerable smaller operations.

Cable Street acquired its name from the best-known riverside industry of ropemaking, and contemporary maps show numerous 'walks', where hemp was twisted into rope. In May 1676 three Stepney women were accused of stealing 'hemp enough to make halters for all the rogues in Christendom'. Though hard and dirty work, a 'good hand' might earn as much as 5s a day; workers in most other trades earned between 10s and 15s a week. For masters it was 'very profitable'. The leading ropemen in 1693–94 were Joseph Todd, with two walks in Wapping (Virginia Street and Wiltshire Lane), and David Bushall in Hermitage Street. In the second half of the century the Shakespear works in Ratcliff dominated the industry. Here were rope-walks 400yds in length, and cables were made 'from six to 23 inches in girth'. Lysons wrote of St George's in the East (Wapping Stepney) in the 1790s: 'The inhabitants are employed, for the most part, in ropemaking, and the manufacture of other articles for the rigging of ships. There is no other considerable manufacture in the place.'

Bowles Crown glass factory, London's leading glasshouse, opened in 1691 in Ratcliff, and folded in about 1794. Crown glass was an improved version of window glass, hitherto imported from Normandy. The demand was high for quality sheet glass for sash windows, which were replacing the old-fashioned casements with their diamond-shaped panes. There were four or five glasshouses in Cutthroat Alley (Sun Tavern Fields, now Brodlove Lane) in the seventeenth century, one, Nelson and Co., being started by a retired sea captain. On the south side of Goodman's Yard, in Lamb Alley, Michael Rackett opened a glass and bottle factory in 1678, which exported to the Continent. Another factory in Salt Petre

Bank, just west of Wellclose Square, belonged in 1689 to Philip Dallow, along with another nearby in White's Yard off Rosemary Lane. In 1738 Dallow sold the 'Great Glasshoues in Rosemary Lane' to a dyer from Norton Folgate for £2,000.

Eight of London's fourteen powderhouses were in this area, one of them in Bishopsgate's Gun Alley.

With the fashion for tea- and coffee-drinking, the sugar-refining industry, which had flourished in Stepney for 200 years, expanded beyond all recognition. It was a lucrative business in which 'Estates are frequently got'. Land Tax records for 1782 show eleven sugar houses in Whitechapel, including a large one owned by Jeremiah Glover in Angel Alley, east of Brick Lane, and Woolwrath Holtzmeyer next to the bellfoundry at Tile Gate (insured for £3,900 in 1777).

The sugar workers, mainly Germans, became known in the alehouses of Whitechapel for their pale faces and desperate drinking. It was gruelling work in the boiling house; according to Millicent Rose:' In this hot nauseating place the workers laboured nearly naked, their bare chests becoming encrusted with the melted sugar as they filled the moulds at the taps and carried them across the factory where the sugar was left to set.'

The East End was not yet known as a slum to contemporaries. Archenholtz may have been shocked at the contrast between sailortown and the spacious glories of the fashionable West End, but nothing like the later extreme east/west divide existed. London's most crowded and disreputable places were St Giles and the area round Charing Cross Road, where *The Beggars' Opera* was set in 1728. The final stages of Hogarth's *Harlot's Progress* were set in Drury Lane, where in 1751 a quarter of its 2,000 houses were gin shops; there were eighty-two lodging houses with prostitutes and receivers. Infant mortality in 1750–55 was almost twice as high in St Giles and Southwark as it was in Shadwell, for instance. In 1768–78 the percentage of children dying aged less than six in Whitechapel was only 15.3, as opposed to 43.9 in St Clement Danes. The physician to the London Public Dispensary identified five areas as 'notorious for their wretchedness' in 1801, namely St Giles (an Irish ghetto), parts of Rotherhithe and Upper Westminster, the area north-east of the City stretching from Gray's Inn Road to Bunhill Fields; and, the only black spot in the East End, East Smithfield.

Horwood's map shows a collection of country towns, set among swathes of hay- and cornfields, pasture, orchards and market gardens, dotted with barns and cowsheds, with warehouses and 'manufacturies', crisscrossed with ropewalks, a dense weavertown to the north with clusters of workshops on its riverside. They spoke of the 'rich pasturages in that extensive parish' (Stepney), and Gascoyne's map of Mile End was ornamented with cows and cowherds. Sheep were regularly driven along the highway. In 1772 the rector of Stepney collected his great tithe from 2,535¾ acres, and although there was 'no land' in Spitalfields, and precious little in Wapping, his old parish church was flanked by fields, stretching west to

Whitechapel and east to Bow. Where now the wide Commercial Road growls through an ugly sprawl of densely packed buildings, lay flat acres of rich farming land. Hay was the predominant crop, remembered now only in Hayfield Passage. Whitechapel's haymarket was still operational in the last century. In 1777 of the *c.* 1,000 titheable acres in Mile End Old Town and Bethnal Green only an eighth were under plough. Hay was the fuel of those days, the all-important commodity for fuelling horse transport. Without a ready supply of hay the capital would have ground to a halt. In the terrible winter of 1775/6, when deep snowdrifts prevented the haywagons from getting through, prices at Smithfield rocketed to over £3 a load.

In Bow, Bethnal Green and Mile End the farms were between 30 and 100 acres, mainly mixed. There were large dairy herds in the farms of north Mile End and a 'great cow yard' adjoining Stepney churchyard, while beef cattle were fattened in the lush pastures of the Isle of Dogs. One of the Mercers' tenant farmers lost £1,100 in 1715 by 'death of cattle' and in 1746 another lost 120 beasts through a 'distemper among horned cattle'. Some humble folk kept a single cow or a sow in their backyard; poor widow Lea of Stepney Green had a sow and William Green had four. In one of the dingy alleys off Petticoat Lane there was a 'hog sty', and pigs were to be found rooting around in the yards of weavers' houses in Spitalfields. In 1817 the bellman of the Ratcliff watch was ordered to give notice that all stray pigs should be impounded and returned to their owners only on payment of 5s and expenses. After a heavy night's drinking and being seduced into a 'desolate apartment', one John Rogers awoke in the early morning to see 'people milking their cows' in Cable Street.

As for centuries, the East End was to a large extent feeding the capital. The Isle of Dogs provided the best pasture in Europe, or so it was said; Poplar had 886 titheable acres, of which 795 were pasture. Beasts fed on this rich grass might sell for an astronomical £34 each. In 1720 an ox weighing 236 stone was sold at Leadenhall Market. Import of corn into the capital doubled between 1680 and 1720, and the windmills that gave Millwall its name appeared at this time; twelve were built between 1679 and 1740. There were market gardens in Limehouse and Bethnal Green, and a windmill next to Whitechapel church until about 1732.

Numbers of the manufacturers had farms as well as workshops: two Mile End brewers, Green and Wright, had farms of 32 and 24 acres respectively; in Bethnal Green in the 1770s Scott the brickmaker had 35 acres and Crump the dyer had 10 acres of pasture. Two calico printers of Old Ford, Jones and Napper, had farms locally.

Crime, medicine, the roads

James Paterson, writing in 1714, opined that each of Stepney's hamlets 'might make a sufficient City or parish of itself'. Before its division (1729–45) these were Bethnal Green, Bow with Old Ford, Limehouse, Mile End Old Town, Mile End New Town, Poplar with Blackwall, Ratcliff, Spitalfields and Wapping Stepney. The other parishes in the area were Whitechapel, Wapping (Whitechapel), Shadwell, St Katharine's and Bromley, the City's out-parishes of St Botolph's Aldgate and Bishopsgate, and the Tower liberties.

Parishes, hamlets and liberties ran their own affairs by and large, appointed their own officials, churchwardens, overseers of the poor, constables, headboroughs, to keep the peace, scavengers who 'paid the Raker, for cleansing the Streets, and carrying away the Dust'. Each place had its own almshouses, workhouse, schools, shops, taverns, alehouses, and local attorneys, apothecaries, barber-surgeons, wig- and hairdressers, midwives and nurse-keepers. Shadwell had its own waterworks, Mile End its assembly rooms, Goodman's Fields its theatres; there were markets in Spitalfields (fruit, vegetables and meat), Whitechapel (hay) East Smithfield (the Rag Fair, old clothes), Shadwell (meat) and Ratcliff and Bow. Stepney had a fair at Michaelmas and Bow a Green Goose Fair in the summer, remembered in Fairfield Road.

But this was no ordered nursery rhyme place, according to an Irish seaman and ropeworker who had taken to crime. 'Stepney, Whitechapel and Shadwell … are infested with too many vagabonds.' Records of cases tried at the Old Bailey often provide no indication of criminals' birthplaces, but where they do it is noticeable how many were East Enders, with as many, if not more, girls and women than boys and men. Oiled with cheap gin and hungry for a slice of the wealth they saw around them, many lads took to pickpocketing, housebreaking and highway robbery. The girls were not far behind. Some East End criminals haunted the 'court end of town' where pickings were richer, like Thomas Talbot from Wapping who, with his doxy Nosegay Nan, was so active that it was said 'Scarce a coach or a well dressed Gentleman could pass by at an unseasonable hour, without being plundered'. Others chose their home ground. The notorious Jack Sheppard said that the 'chief scenes of [his] Rambles and Pleasures' were Spitalfields and the Drury Lane area. Thomas Beck, a young Stepney seaman's son, went raiding about Wapping 'learing into Peoples' shops to see what … [he] could take away'. They stole cash and snuffboxes, silver thimbles, watches and buttons, periwigs and handkerchiefs, brandy, cheese, currants and sugar, tobacco, horses, cows, geese, chickens, and anything that might make a few shillings. They burgled shops and warehouses, broke into houses and picked pockets in markets, alehouses and on the streets. Clothes were valuable and easily disposed of at the secondhand clothes market at Rag Fair in Rosemary Lane. Many a tale was told of highway robbery, notably at the Mile End Turnpike (junction of Cambridge Heath Row and the Mile End Road) and along the road to Bow: pistols brandished in the moonlight; lanterns swinging in the dark; 'stand and deliver!' The cry was, 'Come boys, let us go and stop a rattler'.

Open spaces near the City were always dangerous places, like Whitechapel Fields, which stretched towards Stepney on the south side of the main road, east of the church, and Blackguard's Gambling Ground, between Petticoat Lane and Wentworth Street. Stepney's 7-acre churchyard was another bad spot. The whole-sale theft of merchandise from ships berthed along the riverside was a scandal and the occasion not only of the creation of a special river police force (set up in 1798) but the building of the secure enclosed wet docks that transformed the area in the next century.

Each place had its own system of police, with a watchhouse manned by a rota of men who, for a few pounds a year and supervised by the constables, were required to patrol the streets from dusk till dawn, on the look-out for crime and prostitu-tion, carrying a lantern and a stick, and calling out the time on the hour: 'Twelve o'clock and all's well'. In 1702 three men took it in turns to walk the streets around the notorious Rag Fair area; the Rosemary Lane watchhouse, with its 'cage', was near the heart of the notorious market. In 1694 the watch for the Liberty of East Smithfield used a pub as its headquarters, and it was complained that they were often drunk. A special watchhouse was stationed at the top of Bearbinder Lane in Bow (Coborn Road), where highwaymen and footpads lurked. The 'watch' has been derided for its inefficiency; a few old men with sticks was, perhaps, not much defence against the rising tide of crime, and victims and members of the public increasingly took matters into their own hands. The magistracy (much vilified for corruption) relied on gangs of informers and professional thieftakers: bailiffs, ex-cons, prison turnkeys, publicans who knew what was going on in their patch. It was the best known of all their takers, Jonathan Wild, who was respon-sible for the capture of Jack Sheppard. The system was regularised when Henry Fielding, JP and novelist, in 1748 drew together a paid force of informers, the Bow Street Runners. In 1770 the Bow Street Patrol consisted of sixty-eight men divided between Queen's Square, Westminster, Great Marlborough Street, Hatton Garden, Shoreditch, Whitechapel, Shadwell, Southwark and the City.

The crime rate was noticeably high in Whitechapel (Red Lion Street, the northern end of what is now Leman Street, seems to have been a particularly bad spot) and, to a slightly lesser extent, in Spitalfields and Wapping. Dick Turpin himself was around in Whitechapel in the 1730s, while members of his gang, the Gregories, were from Wapping's Old Gravel Lane. Accordingly it was well policed, with three beadles, twenty-two watchmen and sixteen headboroughs (petty constables) in 1760. Spitalfields had nine headboroughs and seventeen watchmen, while Limehouse had only four headboroughs and one watchman.

The tiny riverside parish of St John Wapping (Wapping Whitechapel) had ten watchmen, an indication of how rough things were down in sailortown. In Strype's day the Portsoken had sixty watchmen, which may account for the low level of crime there. Maitland notes five headboroughs for Mile End Old Town.

Offenders might be taken to the Middlesex Sessions house at Clerkenwell or the Old Bailey, to the Bridewell for 'correction', or to local lockups for debtors in Whitechapel, St Katharine's and Wellclose Square. Pillories (for sodomites and spreaders of sedition) stood near the Sun Tavern in Shadwell, in St John Street, Spitalfields and by the Victualling House on Tower Hill. William Tankling had three sessions in the pillory (and three years in Newgate) for raping a Shadwell toddler. He seduced the three year old away from her mother's doorstep by the offer of cake, and 'hurt her very much with his cock', giving her a dose of the pox so that she had 'a buboe on each groin'.

These years were notorious for the brutal penalties imposed for even minor crimes, and East End criminals and petty thieves, like all others in London, went to the 'fatal tree' to meet their maker – unless they were lucky enough to be transported to Botany Bay. Little William Stone of Wapping, only twelve years old, was hanged for stealing linen in 1698; Joyce Hodgkis of Limehouse, for murdering her brute of a husband in a passion of rage, was tied to a stake and burnt in 1714. Sometimes it was deemed necessary to bring home the horrors of a crime to the locals. Pirates were strung up at Wapping's Execution Dock, as they had been for years, their bodies left for three tides to wash over them as an example to all river and seaboard thieves. Petty criminal William Hitchin was condemned to be whipped and dragged at the 'cart's tail' through the streets of Whitechapel until 'his body be bloody'. When Robert Congden was executed for a particularly vicious murder of three people, a gibbet was set up in Ratcliff's Brook Street in front of the door of Captain Gitings' house, and, to make sure the rest of the East End was thoroughly aware of the penalties for such a crime, his body was then taken to the gallows between Mile End and Bow and hung up in chains. A 'great concourse of people' gathered at the gallows in Wapping on a January day in 1725, to watch 'Captain' Charles Towers swing. In 1768 and 1769 gibbets were set up in Sun Tavern Fields and in Bethnal Green for the execution of rioting coalheavers and weavers.

As far as medical attention was concerned, there were local apothecaries, physicians, midwives, nurse-keepers and barber-surgeons, for those who could afford their services. They were especially numerous in this area, servicing the seafaring community. In 1637 twenty midwives were licensed for Stepney parish (there were certainly many more), when even the busiest City parishes had five at most. There were also seven surgeons and a doctor named John Slaughter. Christian Harrell, the society physician who attended on Nell Gwyn's deathbed, went to Lady Wentworth's house near Stepney church to look after Lady Henrietta, the

Duke of Monmouth's mistress, when she was dying. When Hannah Fromanteel of Catherine Wheel Alley, the rich silk mill owner's widow, had a series of strokes in 1697–1700 she was attended by physician Sir Richard Blackmore and apothecaries John Sinner, father and son, one local and one from Stratford. At No. 27 Prescot Street in the 1720s there practised a specialist in melancholy, hysteria and hypochondria who offered to cure all 'dismal apprehension of the mind'. There was a ready market for quacks who sold potions and pills for all manner of ailments, hawking them round the markets and advertising in the press. A physician living in St Katharine's offered cures for 'all Melancholy, Hysterical and Hypecondriack Distempers … Fainting and Sinkings of the Spirit, grant Hurries … also Pains and Giddiness of the Head; Risings to the Throats, Sick Fits, Tremblings, Oppressions of the Heart, or any other Distempers caused by Vapours'.

Some of these medical men accrued considerable fortunes. Dr William Connop, surgeon and apothecary, had a thriving business in Mile End Old Town (1742–65), making enough money for his son's widow to finance a very luxurious life style for her second husband, Thomas Thirlwall, curate of Stepney.

As the century progressed there was increasing concern about those who could not afford medical fees. The East End got its own hospital in May 1741 when the London moved into Prescott Street from its original building in Moorfields, and thence to Mile End Old Town, to its present site by Whitechapel Mount, opening its doors to patients in September 1757. Its patrons were the nobility, it was maintained financially by the gentry and the fast-growing middle classes. In 1782 the Eastern Dispensary opened in Whitechapel's Leman Street, providing free medical advice, medicine and home visits. For the Jewish community there was an infirmary from 1747, also in Leman Street, moving to Mile End in 1792. In Boyle's list of 1799 are the Misericordia (for venereal disease), the Dispensary for Pregnant Women, the Eastern Dispensary, all in Great Ayliffe Street, and the Middlesex Dispensary in Prescot Street. For the insane there was Bethlehem, moved from Bishopsgate to Moorfields, and private madhouses, the best known of which was the Bethnal Green madhouse, which opened in 1726. In Whitechapel there was one in Angell Alley, and the gruesome sign of the 'madman's head' swung in Colchester Street; this asylum may actually have been located in Crack Braine Alley.

Streets were paved, albeit mainly with cobbles, which made a coachride an uncomfortable affair. In the 1690s paving was ordered for Bluegate Fields and Cannon Street near Ratcliff Highway, Old Gravel Lane, Whitehorse Street in Ratcliff, in Whitechapel the highway from the church to the Mount (the London Hospital), Ayliffe Street from Mansell Street to Goodman's Gate, Leman Street, Church Lane, the road from Bow Bridge to Bromley. From the 1720s roads in general, and the great Essex road in particular, were improved considerably by the introduction of tolls; the Mile End Turnpike is still remembered in the name

Mile End Gate. If you were abroad after dark you no longer had to rely on a link boy to light the way; except in the poorest alleys lanterns were hung from house porches or on posts.

London opened up to its suburbs: livery companies extended their areas of jurisdiction and the old city gates were demolished (in September 1760) to make access easier. The relief from the gate at Aldgate was bought by an antiquarian called Ebenezer Mussell, who incorporated it into the north side of his mansion in Bethnal Green, which he named Aldgate House.

Rich and poor

John Strype, who grew up in Spitalfields, said in the early years of the century that the 'province of Stepney' would have been one of the greatest towns in England were it not for London. There was 'Populousness, Traffick, Commerce, Havens, Shipping, Manufacture, Plenty and Wealth the crown of all'. In 1693/4 Wapping Stepney had 114 substantial merchants; Whitechapel and Mile End Old Town would have had a high proportion of the middling sort for most of the century. There were enough brick houses around, mahogany long-case clocks and tea tables, summerhouses and servants, sets of fine china plates and marble fireplaces, and even some stabling for the family coach. There were no dukes in the East End, admittedly; the *Foreigner's Guide* (1752) lists no 'taxi ranks' for sedan chairs, and the rental value of houses was, on average, a third of that in the West End and City. Nevertheless there were some very rich men. Ratcliff Highway and East Smithfield might have had some of the meanest houses in the capital, and St Katharine's was probably the most overcrowded, but some elegant squares were laid out in Wapping Stepney, and impressive houses were built on Stepney Green, some of which still stand. Cary's *Survey of the High Roads from London* (1790), a sort of tourists' guide to posh houses, shows seven 'gentlemen's' seats' set back from the highway east of the Mile End Turnpike. By 1801 this was Mile End Grove. In later years it became the scruffiest part imaginable. Estates of good solid middle-class housing were laid out in Spitalfields, and claimed the remaining farmland in Whitechapel.

The people of the Tower Hamlets shared in the general expansion of industry, trade and commerce; the first half of the century was a time of working-class prosperity. According to Dorothy George the industrial explosion of the eighteenth century 'absorbed much of that residuum of beggars and vagrants' which had worried the sixteenth- and seventeenth-century churchwardens and overseers. Coalheavers and ropemen might earn a packet; local wheelwrights in 1745 were in a 'combination to raise the prices of their wages'. Work was plentiful. London labourers might have silver buckles on their shoes (or at least Pinchbeck ones, as sold in Petticoat Lane), and were known everywhere for their cocky insolence. Wives of tailors and shoemakers did themselves up with gold and silver embroidery, but there was much poverty around. Wars brought booms and peace depressions, trade fluctuated, and for those dependent on it life was fraught with uncertainty.

Half the total number of East Enders listed in the Hearth Tax returns for the 1660s and '70s had been classified as poor (most of those in Stepney parish were in Ratcliff, Wapping, Shadwell and Spitalfields); justices reported in 1684 that 'The people of [Tower Hamlets] for the most part consist of weavers and other manufacturers of seamen and such as relate to shipping and are very factious and poor.' In 1690 the local constables told the magistrates that the majority of the inhabitants of the Tower Hamlets were 'generally very poor'. In Wapping, Ratcliff and St Katharine's sailors' families suffered from losses in the 'new hundred years' war' that occupied much of the century. In January 1694 it was reported at Hicks Hall that there had been a great increase of poor in Ratcliff because of the loss and disabling of men in battle. Pierce Walsh of Wapping, a second lieutenant on HMS *Salisbury*, got £2 a year in 1704 from the Fund for Maimed Soldiers and Sailors, little enough for someone who had had his jaw broken by a musket shot and had lost part of his tongue. In 1691 a chapelwarden of Wapping Whitechapel was accused of appropriating the money of the orphaned children of a mariner who had died at sea. As the century progressed weavers, especially in Mile End New Town and Bethnal Green, suffered, subject to the fluctuations to which the industry was prone. John Wesley visited Bethnal Green in 1777 and reported: 'Many … I found in such poverty as few can conceive without seeing it.'

London had a widespread reputation for generosity to the poor at this time. The povertystricken had been relieved by the Church since time immemorial, with the system regularised under Elizabethan legislation, which allowed for the imposition of a rate on householders. Each parish (or hamlet) looked after its own, sending off those who had not established their 'settlement' locally to be kept by another parish. Settlement was established by having been baptised, employed or apprenticed in the parish, or renting a substantial property, holding parish office or, in the case of women, marrying a man who was 'settled' there. Paupers (elderly, out of work, single mothers) were given a small cash dole to keep the wolf from the door: old Matthew Allen, aged seventy-two, of Spitalfields got 12d a week in 1690, Bridget Harman of Limehouse got 2s a week in 1692. At St Botolph's Aldgate in April 1776 sixty-three paupers were listed as receiving out-relief (mostly a shilling each), plus 'casuals'. Stepney parish, because of the great numbers of sailors living there, became a favourite place for parishes from all over the country to offload paupers who were, or claimed to have been, born at sea. If a constable found a vagrant 'old salt' wandering the streets of Liverpool or Bristol, he might get sent to Stepney.

Destitute children and babies were farmed out to local women, like Mother Bartholomew whom we met in Stepney's church house in the days of the first Elizabeth, and Nurse Bryant at Aldgate in the eighteenth century. In some places there were parish shelters, for example in Stepney in the 1590s, and in Whitechapel there were parish almshouses from about 1678. From the 1720s there were parish and hamlet workhouses that took in orphans and paupers. By mid-century the East End was peppered with poor institutions of one sort and another. As well as the workhouses set up by local parishes and hamlets for their own poor, there were a number of private 'pauper farms', where contractors housed and fed the City's 'dross'. Some City parishes had their workhouses out east: the house for All Hallows by the Tower, for instance, was in Redman's Row in Mile End (1739–49), until the neighbours complained about the dumping of 'night soil' in the street.

Almshouses: cosy little homes with pensions

Almshouses funded by the endowments of private individuals (usually local men made good) and corporations were quite a feature of the East End; there was a cluster of them around the Mile End Turnpike and strung out along the road to Bow. In 1766 there were eleven almshouses in Stepney parish; in 1773 twenty in the whole Tower Hamlets area. Some served the locals, while City livery companies evidently found it a suitable spot for their pensioners. As Sir Christopher Wren remarked, Mile End was 'much more wholesome than the neighbouring places'. More land was available at lower prices than in the cramped City; it was a pleasant, countrified atmosphere for the pensioners, not far away from their friends in town. Going east from the Mile End turnpike Strype says there were 'several well built almshouse belonging to certain Companies of London. One whereof much exceedeth the rest.' This was Captain Mudd's Trinity Almshouses, between Dog Row (Cambridge Heath Road) and Red Cow Lane (Cleveland Way), providing shelter for old masters and mates, sailors and their widows, from 1695; there were twenty-eight places with a pension of 16s a month. They are still there, but today are private houses.

Just inside the turnpike on the north side of the road were the Pennell (Drapers' Company) almshouses founded in 1698, with four rooms for freemen's widows and four for Stepney seamen's widows. They received pensions of 1s 8d a week together with coal and clothes. In Dog Row were Captain Fisher's Almshouses of 1711, run by Trinity House and housing six commanders' widows. They got £6 a year in Strype's day, and Captain Fisher's widow sent them a crown each at Christmas. To the west of the Trinity houses were the Skinners' Almshouses of 1698, with effigies of two old cripples over the entrance. These were endowed by Lewis Newberry for twelve poor skinners' widows; their pensions were £5 4s.

To the east of the Trinity houses were the Vintners' Almshouses for twelve poor widows, built here after the Great Fire. In Lysons' day each vintner's widow received an allowance of 5s 3d. In 1802 that good old vintner Benjamin Kenton, supplier of porter, beer and wine to London and America, who has a fine tomb in Stepney church, left money for the almshouse to be rebuilt. Kenton was a typical East End lad made good; his mother was said to have sold cabbages on a stall in Whitechapel Field Gate (now Fieldgate Street).

East of Red Cow Lane were Judge John Fuller's Almshouses, which had housed twelve single Stepney men of fifty years on this site since 1652. Further along, to the east of Globe Lane (Road) were Margaret Astill's Charity for the Poor of Cripplegate (1685) and 'the Jews' Hospital'. In 1792 the Jewish Portuguese community, who had a cemetery at the north-east corner of the hamlet, moved their hospital here from Leman Street, adding almshouses for twelve to it later. Adjoining the Jewish almshouses were Bancroft's Almshouses and School (where Queen Mary College now is). The Bancroft Almshouses (for twenty-four old drapers) and School-house (for a hundred boys) were built in 1735 with the ill-gotten fortune bequeathed by Francis Bancroft, grandson of Archbishop Bancroft, so much hated that at his death the bells at St Botolph's Bishopsgate rang out for joy. It was one of the East End's showplaces; the *Ambulator* (1774) waxes lyrical about its elegance – its chapel with portico and Ionic columns, its turrets, its fine iron railings. The almsmen got £8 a year plus coal.

Further east on the north side of the road at the entrance to Bow were the eight rooms for Shadwell seamen and widows, set up by Captain James Cook and his wife; they were usually full of widows. Opposite was Mrs Bowry's establishment for mariners and their widows, eight houses built in 1744 with each of Stepney's hamlets nominating an inmate. They were mainly widows. Fuller's, Bowry's and Cook's were all in the hamlet of Mile End Old Town. In Bromley parish were the Drapers' Company houses, an amalgamation of the eight endowed by Sir John Jolles, and twelve by sailmaker John Edmundson in 1706. Sir John Jolles, a lord mayor born in Bow, acquired great wealth and, being childless, was very generous to the locality. His almshouses, erected not long before his death in 1621, were for eight draper householders or their widows, with preference given to inhabitants of Bow and Bromley. One wing of the Draper's Company buildings still stands.

Near Stepney church, on the south side, were the almshouses endowed by Lady Jane Mico, widow of a Mercers' warden. They were sturdily built with ten widows safely inside, each with a pension of £8 13s 4d a year (£12 in the 1790s). There were grilles over the cellar windows and tenterhooks on the walls on the east side to keep vandals out. Each widow had a room 10ft 11in square, a cellar beneath and a little backyard or garden plot for herbs and flowers. They were very desirable little properties and one of the first occupants, the widow Bletchington, a former servant of Lady Mico's, was evidently concurrently holding another place at the Vintners' almshouses in Mile End. She was told firmly that if she did not give that up she would be ejected. According to Strype one grocer's widow in Dame Mico's houses had brought her husband a portion of £1,500. Also in Ratcliff hamlet, in Schoolhouse Row, were the Coopers' Company almshouses (and school) set up by the Gibsons long ago for the benefit of old barrelmakers and their widows. It housed fourteen widows, and each had a small garden and a pension of £5 a year, with coal. Toby Wood's Ratcliff almshouses, set up in 1613 also for coopers, gave £6 to each of its six inmates. Shadwell had George Baron's establishment in Elbow Lane from 1682, for fifteen women with £5 4s a year.

A large old house in Poplar High Street had been converted for the use of the East India Company's pensioners. It was bought in 1627 and originally housed twenty disabled seamen. In 1798–99 new almshouses were built for retired commanders and officers or their widows, the old building to remain for boatswains, gunners, carpenters and caulkers or their widows, 'but none inferior'. The chaplain's house from 1801 still stands. In Bow Lane, off Poplar High Street, were six tiny cottages grouped around a paved courtyard. These were endowed by Mrs Esther Hawes in 1686, and in 1940, says Millicent Rose, they still housed six old Poplar ladies, 'each with a window box full of geraniums'. Sir Henry Johnson, who bought the East India Company's shipyard, left money for six houses for 'poor aged ships' carpenters' in Blackwall's Globe Yard. These old fellows (who had to be over sixty and without a wife) were to do very well with an allowance of 2s 6d a week (in 1688). In the event, Johnson's son and heir did not follow his instructions, although he permitted seven existing cottages to be occupied rent free 'in the nature of almshouses'. It was not until 1755 that purpose-built almshouses were put up. Noorthouck mentions Captain Fell's house in Blackwall, which accommodated four families.

In Bishopsgate's Lamb Alley (just beyond Liverpool Street station) were two sets of almshouses. One was set up by Edward Alleyn, the local theatrical impresario, in 1614. Here were five men and five women with a small pension of £2 a year in 1773. The other, 'Mr Underwood's', accommodated sixteen widows, with 2s 6d per month in 1773. Just to the south was the City workhouse, of which more anon. Further north, in the Liberty of Norton Folgate, there were two sets of almshouses in Blossom Terrace, one specifically for weavers. Nicholas Garret, by a will of 1726, gave £1,600 for the building and maintenance of almshouses for six 'decayed members' of the Weavers' Company. Also in Spitalfields, off Wentworth Street, in Hope Court, were a set of almshouses for old women, set up by a mariner called Michael Yoakley and, from about 1669 six almshouses near the market in Crispin Street. There were the French almshouse in Black Eagle Street for forty-five men and women, with pensions of 2s 3d a week and coal and clothes. The main Huguenot refuge, La Providence, the French Hospital, was in Finsbury.

In Puma Court there survive the 1860s almshouses built to replace those built in 1728. Thomas Parmiter's almshouse (with a school) stood at the eastern end of St John Street in Bethnal Green. It opened in 1722 and in 1773 had six widows with a pension of £2 10s a year. In the same street were the Dyers' Company houses for six Company widows in receipt of 30s a year. On the south side of the Essex (Mile End) Road in Whitechapel were the almshouses founded by William Meggs in 1658, housing twelve local widows, each with a pension of £5 4s in 1773. Strype, writing in about 1720, noted a set of parish almshouses opposite, with sixteen rooms and sixteen poor widows, each with a pension paid by the parish. Down in Rosemary Lane were the Merchant Taylors' almshouses, founded in 1593, with twenty-six widows with £6 a year in 1773.

These nice little homes with an index linked pension and a garden were only for the favoured few and, as we have seen, these were overwhelmingly widows. Only some 300 places were available in the whole area, and not all were necessarily for locals. The parish workhouses, which appeared from 1723 onwards, were a very different matter. They were a much larger-scale operation; by 1777 there were about 600 people in the Whitechapel workhouse alone, and the inmates were of all sorts, with great numbers of children.

Workhouses and pauper farms

Following years of agitation about the 'problem of the poor', there was an Act of Parliament in 1723 to allow for the establishment of parish workhouses. East London was first off the mark, with institutions set up in Wapping in 1723, in Limehouse and Whitechapel in 1724, followed by St Katharine's the following year. As mentioned by Strype, Whitechapel had parish almshouses before the Act; these are referred to in the burial registers from 1678. Since 1699 there had been an experimental workhouse for all London in Bishopsgate, as previously mentioned. In half of it beggar children and orphans found in the streets were fed and given some rudimentary education to fit them for gainful employment; they wore russet cloth and each was pinned with a badge that sported a poor boy and a sheep. In the other half vagrants brought in by the two beadles were put to hard labour. In 1702 there were 427 children in the house, and 430 vagrants had passed through. Initially London parishes were required to contribute to its upkeep, but there was a good deal of resistance and, although it continued to function after 1751, it no longer took in parish children, only those 'found begging in the streets, pilfering on the keys, or lying about in glass-houses, and uninhabited places'.

Stepney's hamlet of Wapping may have been the first place to have a parish workhouse under the new Act. It was in Virginia Street, off the Highway, just south of Wellclose Square, and was set up in 1723. In 1777 the establishment (now the parish workhouse of St George's in the East) had 500 inmates. Wapping Whitechapel's workhouse was in Upper Well Alley. The first Whitechapel workhouse was in Ayliffe Street in 1724; it later moved to the High Street at Town's End; by 1776–77 it had 600 inmates. The Spitalfields house was in Bell Lane from 1728; there children were set to silk-twisting. There were 340 inmates in 1777. The Aldgate workhouse was off Gravel Lane from 1734; there were 300 inmates in 1736; another, for the Middlesex part of the parish, was established in Nightingale Lane in 1736. The Poplar workhouse was on the north side of the High Street from 1735. The Stepney (Ratcliff) workhouse (opened in 1725) was in White Horse Lane; there were 150 inmates in 1777. Houses opened in Limehouse and St Katharine's in 1725, and in Shadwell in 1726. A workhouse opened for Mile End Old Town in 1741, opposite Bancroft's, and for Mile End New Town in Spicer Street (now Buxton Street) in 1783. Bishopsgate workhouse took in 120 when it opened in Rose Alley in 1730; the children were put to spinning.

The Act allowed for the contracting out of the poor, and the City parishes initially opted for this solution to the problem of the poor, or supplied outrelief. Parishes came to an arrangement with private individuals who undertook the running of workhouses or pauper farms, as they were known. Of sixteen adult pauper farms identified in London in 1800, six or seven were located in Tower Hamlets; the only one in the western suburbs was the pauper flax mill at Hounslow. The East End farms were Paul Cadmer's small house for eighteen paupers from three parishes in the Minories, the Pond-side house in Bethnal Green, Overton's and Sykes and Newall's in Mile End, Barclay's, later Bya's in Grove Hall, Bow and Edward Deacon's two houses in Mile End and Old Ford. Samuel Tull (who also had a pauper farm in Edmonton) ran a net manufactory on the south side of Mile End Road in the 1750s, near the turnpike, where paupers were housed and put to netmaking. After Tull's death in 1764 it was left to his daughter and then his grandson, Samuel Overton, a small boy. It was, however, taken over by Mary Sykes in 1768 and following a Chancery dispute was known as Sykes and Overton's from 1769 to 1811. Mary Sykes was paid £450 a year for keeping the poor of St Faith's parish. The Sykes/Overton/Newall/Deacon operation was a large one, servicing forty City parishes as well as Poplar, Blackwall, Barking and the Minories. This was a fairly lucrative business. Sykes and Overton's had, in 1815, 350 inmates in Mile End and 170 at Old Ford.

Life in these early workhouses and pauper farms was not necessarily as horrendous as the later Victorian institutions evidently were, although there were some nasty tales told of exploitation and suffering. Paul Patrick Kearney, who waged a seven-year battle to get support from the overseers of St Dionysis Backchurch, claimed that the East End Rose Lane pauper farm run by Richard Bitch was a 'filthy dungeon'. No doubt some were terrible places, but in the main they seem to have been humane institutions, where paupers were well fed, with meat three times a week. Overton's at Mile End seems to have been a not uncongenial place in the 1790s. At the Ratcliff workhouse there were buns and porter on Good Friday and roast pork for dinner on Easter Sunday, when everyone was given a 'tip' of 6*d* with 3*d* for each child. Children were taught to read and write and were put to apprenticeships when the time came. Adults were put to work, spinning, sewing, picking oakum or making nets.

Conditions varied from place to place; the steward at the Limehouse workhouse in 1725 was a former seafaring man, and apparently ran the show on shipboard lines. By and large it was a more relaxed and casual atmosphere than one might imagine (though probably not at Limehouse!); the men in the Stepney house were said to 'lie abed as long as they like and retire when they chose and work as they please'. The account of the trial of old Mabell Hughes for causing the death of an orphan in her charge in 1755 provides a surprising picture of the kindly folk in the Aldgate workhouse.

There is little to suggest that the parish house was regarded with terror or as the last resort of the desperate. It was perhaps more of a community centre than a grim prison, where the parish fire engine and stretcher were kept, and meetings were held. In some places the local poor might use the workhouse as a drop-in centre, going there only for meals or even to get their washing done; a supply of lying-in clothing and linen was made available for pregnant girls. Inmates could come and go, with permission; Sunday afternoons were the usual time for visits to be made to friends and relatives. In the Ratcliff 'Town House' in London Street (there appear to have been two institutions in Ratcliff) in 1725 there were thirty women who either did spinning or silkwinding (in the house or at a factory) or went out as 'chars' or to sell fish, or anything that might 'make a penny'. Children at the Limehouse workhouse were sent out to be educated at local schools, and the sick from Deacon's were sent weekly by carriage to Guys or St Thomas's.

Schools

This was the heyday of the charity school, when the informed members of society believed that educating poor children would solve the problems of vagrancy and crime. 'It is with the ill nurtured cattal who do not go to school that our prisons are daily filled' wrote a London clergyman. Not only that, catechising children properly provided a bastion against Catholicism – the activities of the Popish James II were still fresh in the mind. Low Church divine White Kennett, who was parson at Aldgate (1700–8) and later a bishop, was one of the prime movers. He wrote that 'Every Charity School is, as it were, a Fortress and a Frontier garrison against Popery.' It is not by chance that some of the earliest parish charity schools were in the East End, notably at Aldgate, Wapping and Norton Folgate, where the populace at large were poor. On a Sunday you might see children nicely shod and neatly attired in their blue (Wapping), green (Ratcliff and Bethnal Green) or red (Mile End) uniforms, aprons, caps and bonnets parading along to church, their master and mistress in attendance. These were the bluecoat children, of the parish charity schools, the 'glory of the age' as Joseph Addison called them.

Many East End boys, and fewer girls, had some schooling in the eighteenth century, maybe just for a couple of years – even if it was in the workhouse. In fact, the vast majority of offenders brought to trial had been to school, or so they said. Even Jack Sheppard went to school; according to the account of his life supposedly written by himself, it was Mr Garrett's School in St Helen's, Bishopsgate; Defoe says that it was a workhouse. The same goes for the 'poor silly boy' Thomas Woolcot (led astray by rough types in a Wapping brandyshop and executed in 1731), John Osborn, a waterman's apprentice who took to crime, and Thomas Beck, whom we met raiding in Wapping (both were hanged in 1732). Admittedly sneak thief Beck went to 'Play and Game' when he should have been in class. Edward Jones, former apprentice to a gardener of Tom Turd's Hole off Ratcliff Highway, who was hanged in 1739 for murdering his wife, had attended Mr John Turner's school in Chamber Street, Goodman's Fields. Richard/Thomas Studder, a Whitechapel weaver's son, executed in 1742 for breaking and entering, had been sent by his father to school at Mr Russel's at the Hand and Pen in Baker Row (Vallance Road) His partner in crime Henry Hinton had been for two years at St George in the East parish school, but admitted to often playing truant.

There were a vast number of different types of school, many more than appear in any of the published lists. Visitation returns of 1778 show twelve schools serving the 3,000 people living in Limehouse alone. There were private schools, parish charity schools, workhouse schools, privately and company endowed schools, French schools, Jewish schools and schools for Protestant Dissenters. Noorthouck lists the following twenty-four East End 'free and charity schools within the Bills of Mortality' in 1773: Bancrofts' (Mile End) with a hundred boys, Davenant (Whitechapel) with sixty boys and forty girls, Bethnal Green hamlet with thirty girls, Bevis Marks (Portuguese Jews) with twelve boys, Christ Church Spitalfields with thirty girls and thirty boys, Corbet's French school in Spitalfields with fifty girls and fifty boys, East Smithfield Liberty with forty boys and thirty girls, East Smithfield School, founded by Sir Samuel Starling in 1673 with sixteen Aldgate boys, Grey Eagle Street French school with fifty boys and fifty girls, Keat's Street Independent (Congregational) school in Spitalfields with thirty boys, St John Street, Spitalfields, thirty boys (possibly Parmiter's?), London Workhouse School (vagrant children), Mile End Old Town with twenty-two boys and ten girls, Norton Folgate with sixty boys, Poplar Hamlet with thirty boys and twenty girls, Ratcliff Hamlet with thirty-five boys and twenty-five girls, Ratcliff School with sixty children, Ratcliff Highway Presbyterian with thirty boys, St Botolph Aldgate with fifty boys and forty girls, St Katharine by the Tower with thirty-five boys and fifteen girls, St George's in the East with fifty boys and fifty girls, Raines' with forty-eight girls, St John Wapping with thirty-eight boys and twenty-three girls, St Paul Shadwell with fifty boys and fifty girls, Shakespeare Walk Presbyterian with thirty boys. There were also two free schools in Bow, Gloster Ridley's school in Poplar and a very small parish charity school in Limehouse in 1779.

As elsewhere in London and the major cities, there were numerous small, private short-term establishments, many of them dame schools, some little more than child-minding affairs, run at home by 'poor women, or others, who necessities compel them to undertake it as a mere shelter from beggary'. Of Limehouse's twelve schools eleven were 'women's' schools. At the top end of the market were genteel ladies' boarding schools; one such was housed in Stepney's Worcester House from 1741 to 1762. To send your daughter to one of these, said John Wesley, was to send them 'headlong to hell'. There were a whole range of other institutions, like Mr Huet's at Bromley, where boys were trained up to be writers for the East India Company and John Canton's scientific academy in Spital Square (1718–82). The East India Company had opened a school in Poplar in 1647, attached to its almshouses, where the orphans of employees were given an education with a navigational bias.

The wealthy and the middling sort had private tutors for their offspring; the *Annual Register* noted in astonishment in 1759 that even the 'meanest of tradesmen keep a governess for their daughter': an exaggeration, no doubt. Stephen Martin Leake of Mile End Old Town (1702–73), Garter King of Arms, had his children taught French and Latin by a curate for two hours three times a week at 2½gns a month, and a Mr Curtis did their 'schooling'. His son, Thomas, was taught navigation for 3gns, and his daughter Nancy had dancing lessons. A handful of East End boys went to major City grammar schools, as did the son of John Shakespear, the 'millionaire' ropemaker. Twenty public school boys have been identified in Mile End Old Town from the second half of the century; they went to the City schools of Charterhouse, Merchant Taylors and St Paul's, one to Harrow and one to Eton. A French visitor described such boys as 'the most intractable and obstinate creatures that ever came out of the hands of nature'. A very few proceeded to Oxford or Cambridge, like Moses Colley, who went to Oxford with an exhibition from the Ironmongers' Company in 1762. His father, an Oxford man himself, was a curate at Stepney church. Twenty-one East End boys have been identified at the Inns of Court, an alternative to university, during the period 1732–1802, most from Mile End Old Town.

Before it became overwhelmed with poor weavers, Bethnal Green seems to have been a favoured spot for private schools, the most notable, although very short lived, being the 'courtly academy' for sons of gentlemen opened by courtier, painter and friend of Rubens Sir Balthazar Gerbier in 1649; Lysons describes him as 'an enterprising projector'. In addition to the more common branches of education he offered 'astronomy, navigation, architecture, perspective, drawing, limning, engraving, sortification, fireworks, military discipline, the art of well speaking and civil conversation, history, constitutions, and maxims of state, and particular dispositions of nations, riding the great horse, scenes, exercises, and magnificent shows'. In the 1690s a Mr. Haines had a grammar school in Bethnal Green and in 1694 Mrs Palfryman a boarding school, while the lexicographer Robert Ainsworth ran a 'considerable boarding school', providing an intensive Latin course, in about 1698.

For those who could not afford even the few pence charged by the dames, or for older children, there were a variety of free schools, endowed for the most part by local men made good. These schools offered clothing, moral and religious training, reading and some writing lessons and 'casting of accounts' to children between the ages of seven or eight and thirteen or fourteen; girls were taught to read and sew, and sometimes to write. When they left they were apprenticed (the school might pay when times were good) or went into service. Religion and moral teaching were paramount: boys at Bancroft's in Mile End had to 'refrain from Vice, and more particularly from Stealing, Lying, Swearing, Cursing, Profanation of the Lord's Day, and other enormous crimes'.

Of the endowed free schools there were eight in the area, nine if we include the old-established Ratcliff Free School run by the Coopers, the oldest grammar school in Middlesex. In Strype's day it educated thirty boys free and took some private pupils, offering Latin and Greek and arithmetic to both, and putting on entertainments of Classical verse-speaking for the locals on its founder's day. Its School Lane building was razed to the ground in the Ratcliff fire of 1794, but rebuilt. The heyday of the grammar schools was over, however, and the area had gone down. By 1818 Coopers' scholars were the sons of the working poor, provided with a minimal education; Latin was not added to the curriculum again until 1848.

Apart from the Gibson school, the oldest foundation, and that which claimed to be the oldest Protestant charity school in England, was that founded in 1665 by the famous Presbyterian minister of St Botolph's (ejected at the Restoration), Zachary Crofton. This was situated on Little Tower Hill in East Smithfield and Crofton's son was schoolmaster there when a new building was provided in about 1674 by brewer and lord mayor Sir Samuel Starling. It was for sixteen Aldgate boys, and was later amalgamated with the Aldgate parish school.

Raine's in Wapping (noted in our modern perambulation; fifty boys and fifty girls) was founded in 1716, and reorganised and endowed three years later by another local brewer, Henry Raine, who firmly believed in bringing up boys and girls for a useful trade rather than giving them money to 'loll and indulge themselves'. Go and look at this delightful little Georgian gem; especially the statue of the little girl.

This school ('two large commodious buildings' in 1738) was popularly known as the 'Hundred Pound School' on account of the mightily generous dowry it offered to a few girls. There was a valuable twice-yearly draw for 100 freshly minted gold sovereigns in a long silk purse; six girls were chosen for the draw and one got the prize together with £5 for a wedding breakfast, to be held in the Great Room of the school, following a ceremony in the parish church. The old brewer himself recounted his delight at watching the draw: 'I have seen, six poor innocent maids come trembling to draw the prize and the fortunate maid that got it burst out into tears in excess of joy.' Candidates had to be old girls of the school, of good character, aged twenty-two and engaged to 'an honest, industrious mechanic' from Wapping Stepney (St George's), Wapping Whitechapel or Shadwell. In later years they sang:

> Many a nymph and many a swain
> Did bless with joy the name of Raine.

The prize was much sought after, as £100 was a huge amount for an ordinary Wapping lass, and was perhaps worth the gruelling regime to which the girls were subjected. They started school at eight years old, and after two years were selected for transfer to the nearby boarding school, where they stayed for four years, behind locked gates, only seeing their parents for four days: at Christmas, Easter, Whitsun and Bartholomewtide. No girl was allowed out for any purpose, and in 1803 the trustees ordered that any girl who spoke to anyone (including relatives) would forfeit her next holiday and be expelled if she repeated the offence. Some managed to escape, it seems, and there were 'frequent elopements'.

Davenant's School lay on a detached part of the burial ground of St Mary's Whitechapel, about a quarter of a mile east of the church, on the north side of the main road. It was founded in 1680 by courtier, poet and rector, 'that ingenious young man' Ralph Davenant, for forty boys. At the same time Henry and Sarah Gullifer undertook to provide for the education of thirty poor girls: the girls were taught reading, knitting and 'plain sowing'. A free school in Bethnal Green was endowed by silk merchant Thomas Parmiter by his will of 1682; in 1722 a schoolroom was built (also almshouses) in St John Street where thirty boys were under instruction by 1765. Bancroft's School in Mile End (a hundred boys) was attached to the fine almshouses that had been founded by that old rogue Francis Bancroft in 1727. It was built and administered by the Drapers' Company. Alderman Sir John Cass founded a school for fifty boys and forty girls in the churchyard at St Botolph's Aldgate, in 1709; his statue stands in Duke's Place.

Bow had two free schools, one founded in about 1701 by the formidable heiress and breweress Prisca Coborn; this was for fifty children, boys and girls. From 1711 premises were shared with the boys from Jolles grammar school, who had hitherto had their lessons in a room over the market-place, which adjoined the church on its eastern side. The Jolles School was run by the Drapers' Company and had been founded in 1611 by Draper Lord Mayor Sir John Jolles, who stipulated that thirty-five boys should be educated 'in the feare of God and good manners', learning 'their Grammer, or lattin tongue, and the write and cypher'. By 1711, however, like the Coopers' School in Ratcliff, it had gone downmarket and was only teaching the rudiments.

A 'general nursery or college of infants' was set up by Sir Thomas Rowe in Clerkenwell in 1685. Here small numbers of pauper children from Middlesex urban parishes and Westminster were housed and taught reading, writing, religion and some trades. It also took seamen's children for a small fee. In Bishopsgate there was the great school attached to the London Workhouse with over 400 children; they wore russet and a badge with a boy and a sheep on it. After prayers and breakfast the children were set to work from 7 a.m. to 6 p.m., with an hour for 'dinner and play' and an hour to learn reading and writing: little enough, but sufficient, presumably, to fit them for their apprenticeships.

In the early years of the century individual parishes took up the task of educating poor children. John Strype revealed that there was:

Yet another sort of charity in this city, maintained by the Society for Promoting Christian Knowledge, very singular and extraordinary ... And that is the erecting of schools in many parishes of London and Westminster (especially the great parishes in the suburbs) called Charity Schools for the free education of poor boys and girls and also for their maintenance in apparel and afterwards disposing of them abroad in honest callings.

This 'singular and extraordinary' occurrence was the beginning of a systematic attempt to extend elementary education among the poor, although it started primarily as a method of dealing with vagrancy and of keeping the tide of popery, Dissent and irreligion at bay. White Kennett's instructions for the charity boys at Aldgate, *The Christian Scholar* (1705), which went into many editions and was widely used, is revealing. Only the 'most honest and hopeful boys' were to learn to write and cast accounts; for the rest religious instruction and reading sufficed. They were first and foremost catechised, taught to 'speak properly', to 'eschew idleness and evil company', to behave themselves decorously in church (no 'running or thrusting to be gone' at the end of the service), show respect to the clergy, refrain from telling tales, from hitting any boy younger than themselves, and from mocking their parents!

In fact, the SPCK (founded by clergyman Thomas Bray, who followed Kennett at Aldgate from 1708 to 1730) was coordinating a movement that had already begun. Dr Turner's charity school at Norton Folgate claimed to be the first parish charity school in the country (established in 1692 for seventy boys), though in fact Wapping's charity school in Cock Lane near the church predated it by two years. Kennett made the claim for Aldgate: 'It is no small Honour to this Parish ... that here was first laid the Foundation of these Charity Schools.' The response to the efforts of the SPCK was immediate and positive; within months of the founding of the society in 1699 charity schools were organised in Poplar, Whitechapel, Shadwell, Shoreditch, Holborn and other places. All the East End parishes, hamlets and liberties would now have their own schools, maintained by local subscribers and governed by elected trustees. Poor parents who could not afford even the 1d a week charged elsewhere might send their boys and girls to these schools from the age of seven or eight, to be cleaned up, clothed and taught to chant the catechism, read, write and cast accounts, ready for their apprenticeships at fourteen. At the Ratcliff hamlet school in Whitehorse Lane, in addition to the three Rs the children were taught singing by the church organist and the boys were taught to make and braid fishing nets. Parish schools were closely associated with the workhouses: in Mile End Old Town the school for twenty-one boys and ten girls was actually in the workhouse. Admission to parish schools was not free to all and sundry; in 1774 the Ratcliff School, for instance, insisted on recommendations from four subscribers for any child 'settled' in the hamlet, for those who were not six references were asked for. They were not in the main used by the really poor. For one thing there were simply not enough places to go round. In an overcrowded parish like St Botolph Aldgate, for instance, the relatively few places were scarcely enough for a population of 12-20,000 people.

Funds were raised in a variety of ways, by special sermons, from bequests and from local subscribers. At Ratcliff anyone who gave 2s 6d might become a trustee of the hamlet school. The Bethnal Green school in Church Row was supported largely by Huguenot gifts and bequests. Children from schools all over London were trooped off to a fundraising annual festival at a city church, attended by numbers of the great and the good: William Blake described them at St Paul's:

> 'Twas on a Holy Thursday,
> Their innocent faces clean,
> The children walking two and two, in red and blue and green,
> Grey-headed beadles walk'd before, with words as white as snow,
> Till into the high dome of Paul's they like Thames' water flow.

In red and blue and green they marched; the provision of sturdy serviceable clothing was all important, and the parish colours were worn with pride. One extreme form of punishment, much worse than beating, was to have your uniform removed so you had to turn up in the old rags that were perhaps all your parents could provide. 'Go to the habitations of such children before taken into a charity school,' wrote one observer, 'and … find them without shoes and stockings, perhaps half-naked, or in tattered rags.' At Ratcliff, as elsewhere, it was ordered that 'school clothing should be worn every day so that it may be seen what the children's behaviour is abroad'. The boys at this school were originally attired in a grey coat and waistcoat of Yorkshire broadcloth, lined leather breeches and black cap; the girls were dressed in grey Padua serge and sported straw hats with ribbons. From 1763 the uniform was changed to green, and to this day it is known as the Greencoat School.

There is no doubt that the charity school movement was a resounding success, and the 'Day the children walked to Christ Church' (or whichever venue was chosen for the annual service) was a great occasion. By 1816 the Poplar and Blackwall boys' school, founded in 1711, had educated 1,341, apprenticed 709, sent 66 to sea, and put 516 to service or out to friends. Many of the schools founded at this time went on to become National (Church of England) schools in the next century. It was the declared aim of the SPCK to rectify the 'visible decay of religion in this kingdom'. The parish schools were associated closely with the established Church, and it was feared by some that the clergy (many of them High Churchmen) who participated in the instruction of the parish children would inculcate the minds of their charges with High Church, even Jacobite, notions. A journalist wrote in 1723 that the parish children were 'taught to babble out High Church and Ormonde' (the Jacobite cry) as soon as they can speak'. For the Protestant Dissenters, who had always put a great emphasis on education, the parish school movement was a particular cause for concern.

Nonconformists, now allowed freedom of worship, lay relatively low after the Glorious Revolution. 'Occasional Conformity' allowed them to keep their official positions by taking communion according to the Anglican rite from time to time. It is said the main streams of Independence and Presbyterianism went into decline for some fifty years, but in the East End Dissent still rode high. A Parliamentary committee estimated that 100,000 people, a quarter of the population of London's suburbs, were Dissenters. Reasons offered against a Pound Rate in 1729 ascribed the low number of christenings performed in Spitalfields and Wapping Stepney to the high numbers of nonconformists.

Matthew Henry, a prominent Hackney minister, recommended that Dissenters should open their own charity schools, and one such was set up in Shakespeare Walk, Ratcliff Highway, in 1712, and another in Wood Street (Wilkes Street) Spitalfields in 1717. By *c.* 1760 there was a school attached to the Independent chapel in Nightingale Lane. Undoubtedly there were many small private or dame schools run by Godfearing women; an Act of 1714 exempted elementary schools from the penalties imposed on nonconformists by the Clarendon Code. Samuel Brewer, the go-ahead minister at Stepney Meeting from 1746 to 1796, set up his own charity school (for forty boys) in 1785.

More influential and significant were the Dissenting Academies, for which suburban Middlesex was well known, the foremost being at Newington Green (1675–1706) where Daniel Defoe was trained, and at Hoxton (1699–1729). Originally set up by ejected ministers, these institutions were like universities for boys of Dissenting families who were barred from Oxford and Cambridge, offering what was probably a higher level of education as well as training for the ministry; they were the precursors of theological colleges. The course at the Bethnal Green Academy covered logic, rhetoric, metaphysics, ethics, natural philosophy, the classics, Hebrew, and Jewish antiquities, besides theology. So highly thought of were these academies that knights and baronets, with no religious affiliation, might send their sons for a Dissenter's education to avoid the 'debaucheries of the Universities'.

Brewer taught in an academy in Mile End Old Town, where there was another, set up in 1783, which moved to Hoxton in 1791. There was an academy in Wellclose Square (1744–85) and one run by Edward Veale (1675–1708) in Wapping. The Bethnal Green Academy at Bishop's Hall started during the Interregnum under William Walker, and carried on until *c.* 1708.

Perambulation

So this was the eighteenth-century East End: still rumbling with Dissent, children at school (many of them), paupers (some of them) supplied with buns at Easter, some wealth, some poverty, some slums, some farmland, dark, overhung alleys and lanes still lined with hedgerows. There were old wooden houses and new brick ones, hovels, tenements and mansions. As all over London, rich and poor lived cheek by jowl: 'The different departments of life are jumbled together', opined Smollett's character Welshman Matthew Bramble on his first visit. Large prosperous manufactories kept company with scruffy little workshops, weavers' garrets, ropewalks, and tentergrounds, where newly woven pieces of wet woollen cloth were stretched to dry flat.

Along the riverbank were quays and wharves and warehouses, while great ships, stuffed with rich prizes, sugar, rum, tobacco and coffee, lay temptingly near the riverbank. Alehouse and taverns without number offered a 'clear Newcastle fire' and 'a pot of the best gin hot', served, in the better establishments, in a silver tankard.

Walking along the footpaths and ropewalks that crisscrossed the landscape you would have heard country sounds, the murmur of lowing cattle, the clink of milk churns, the whirring of windmills, along with the rapping of hammers and the clatter of looms, the rumble of hay- and brickcarts and the distant thunder of stagecoaches, rattling along the great Essex Road. The locals were rough seafaring men and gold braided officers, cowmen and market gardeners, French weavers, German sugar bakers, Jewish merchants and pedlars, Irish coalheavers, smiths, ropemen, slopsellers, shopkeepers of all sorts, footpads, pirates and highwaymen, doxies and good-time girls. Babies might be 'dropped', children and teenagers hanged; life was short and work was hard. And was all set against the backdrop of the forest of masts on the river (Defoe counted 2,000 ships). Poorer than the west, as populous as the City, it was a mix of a place, most accounted part of London but still a collection of independent suburbs, villages and hamlets, each with their individual characters.

Mile End Old Town, with its fine assembly rooms, its fat merchants and gentlemen sea captains, was as different from Mile End New Town, crammed with the poorest weavers, as it was from the rackety riverside. We will take a perambulation of this 'province', starting off at Aldgate. If you could afford it you could take a hackney carriage (1s 6d an hour according to the 1782 *London Guide*); there were stands at Aldgate, in the Minories, at Bishopsgate, in Goodman's Fields, Houndsditch, Spital Square, Spitalfields Church, at Whitechapel church and bars, in Wellclose Square, Prince's Square, Tower Hill, at the victualling office, in Burr Street, at Hermitage Bridge and Pelican Stairs in Wapping, at the Mile End turnpike, in George Street, Ratcliff Highway, at Ratcliff Cross and Poplar church.

Aldgate

Until 1761 the main route east out of the City was through the old gate, rebuilt since Chaucer's time but still medieval in appearance. All that remains today is the pump (a nineteenth-century reconstruction) and St Botolph's church, restored after bombing during the Second World War and after a fire in 1965. The gate, as we have seen, was taken down, and its façade used to ornament a house in Bethnal Green. It was an impressive crenellated structure, with office accommodation at the top and a pedestrian gate at the side. It had been rebuilt in 1609. On the top were a golden ball and a weathervane. Two stone sentinels with stone balls in their hands guarded the upper battlements 'as denying the entrance of any bold enemies'. On the City side, below the sentinels, was a golden figure of Fortune and, facing towards the East End, stood James I with a lion and unicorn. It was in a fairly poor state. When it was repaired in 1734 the figures were removed.

Coming out through the gate you would face one of the widest and busiest highways in London, the Essex Road, bound for Stratford, Colchester and Harwich. This part is known either as Aldgate High Street (just an eighth of a mile in length) or, confusingly, as Whitechapel. It was thronged with carts, carriages and wagons, cattledrovers and market folk. On the left, between Houndsditch and Petticoat Lane, was St Botolph's church, and to its east a row of towering half-timbered inns and taverns. From here stagecoaches, mailcoaches and wagons travelled to Stratford and all points east. On the other side of the highway were numbers of butchers' shops selling beef, veal, mutton and lamb, 'lying conveniently for driving and carrying cattle from Romford Market'.

St Botolph's parish was a long, narrow strip running down the east side of the City. It extended from Gravel Lane off Houndsditch in the north down to the river, meeting Whitechapel on the east at Somerset Street (now the top of Mansell Street) and Nightingale Lane, skirting round the tiny parish of Holy Trinity Minories and that of St Katharine by the Tower. It encompassed the City's oldest suburb, the Portsoken (the city part), and in Middlesex the old manor of East Smithfield, where once the Abbot of Tower Hill held sway. In 1760 there were 1,240 houses in the Portsoken and 1,435 in East Smithfield. Perhaps because the Portsoken (northern) part of the parish was part of the City and, as such, more closely guarded than the rest of the area, the crime rate was unusually low.

Aldgate, without the walls, was 'one of the most populous places within the bills of mortality'. Its population grew from about 11,000 in 1650 to about 20,000 in 1700; by 1748 the churchyard was full and another had to be acquired in Whitechapel. The streets and alleys were densely packed with houses, shops, warehouses and hostelries of one sort and another; there were coffeehouses and bawdyhouses and even a homosexual brothel, Muff's. With the highway and the river as its *raisons d'être* the streets were full of ostlers and porters, carriers, hackneymen, carmen and a good number of sailors. Aldgate was known for its butchers' shops and gunsmiths, its brewers, distillers, tailors and clothworkers, for the manufacture of glass, saltpetre and the burning of tallow.

In a wide, leafy churchyard stood the dilapidated sixteenth-century church. Here, on a snowbound January day in the year of the Great Frost (1684), when the Thames froze over for months, Daniel Defoe married Mary Tuffley, the daughter of a local cooper, rich enough to provide an enormous dowry but not enough to keep Defoe out of debtors' prison. The old church, a rather ramshackle place where chickens were allowed to peck around and washing hung up to dry, had to be pulled down in 1740 and a new one, 'massy and spacious', was designed by George Dance the Elder and completed at the end of 1743. Its magnificent organ (built by Renatus Harris in about 1705) is still there today, said to be the oldest in the country.

Unusually the church stands on a north-south orientation It was a wealthy church with a vigorous vestry, owning a good deal of local property and unusually well supported by the manufacturers and merchants, drapers, ironmongers, gunsmiths, vintners, brewers and butchers among its parishioners. Numerous benefactors, to the church and the poor of the parish, included Isaac Berkley of

Calcutta, an Aldgate man who evidently made a mint in India and left the church
3,000 rupees (£375). When in 1751 the vestry bought the impropriation of the
church, it was for the large sum of £13,000; henceforth the church was to be
under the patronage of the wealthy burghers of Aldgate. On a Sunday you might
see them, bewigged and in their finery, with skirted coats, gold buttons and silver
buckles, being ushered to their pews. The Parsons family were the local bigwigs
in the first half of the century: Alderman Humphrey (an active Tory and Lord
Mayor 1730 and 1740), who inherited the Red Lion Brewery from his father, Sir
John (Lord Mayor 1703–4), chaired vestry meetings and had the church's north
gallery fitted out at his own expense and made into a exclusive pew for his family.
A story was told that he met Louis XV at a hunting party who, being informed
that he was a '*chevalier de malte*', commissioned him to supply the French court
with his famous porter.

You might also see beggars crowding round the entrance to the church. Poverty
was a problem in the parish, as it had been in the sixteenth century, although
there were a number of rich men, most of them self-made in trade and manufacture. Houses on average were meaner than any in the rest of the conurbation,
especially in East Smithfield, which was known by the medical fraternity for its
'wretchedness'. In 1798, 61 per cent of its households were too poor to pay tax.
The 'Manor', as they called it, as it had been in the Abbot of Tower Hill's day, was
the roughest, poorest and most overcrowded part of London.

The two parts of the parish were run separately, and there was even a special
place in the churchyard for burying 'Manor women'. There were three charity schools and two workhouses. Alderman Sir Samuel Starling, who owned a
number of local breweries including one at the Hermitage, had erected a building
on Little Tower Hill to house the seventeenth-century East Smithfield school,
as we have seen. Alderman Sir John Cass endowed the school for ninety children that occupied part of the churchyard (1709). A workhouse for the Portsoken
was established by 1734 off Gravel Lane, where silk was wound and oakum was
picked, and another for the Manor in Nightingale Lane (1736), where there was
also a Dissenters' charity school.

Overseers of the poor were active, and pastoral care among the clergy at
St Botolph's was remarkable at a time when the Church of England, by and large,
lay slumbering. Two go-ahead incumbents, the celebrated White Kennett and his
successor, Thomas Bray, ruled wisely over their flock and parish for thirty years,
Kennet from 1700 to 1708, Bray from 1708 to 1730. Bray was founder of the
SPCK, an ardent missionary in Maryland and a close friend of Thomas Coram
of the Foundling Hospital. Both clergymen were known for their learning and
dedication to the care of their parishioners. Diarist Thoresby, visiting Dr Bray at
his house in Aldgate, was very surprised at 'the prodigious pains so aged a person
takes'. So concerned was the good doctor about the reluctance of his poor parish-

ioners to attend church that he left money for 'suits of mean but new apparel ...
mantuas and petticoats' for poor women to wear, so they were not afraid to come
to church. Prisons were visited and a tradition of social work started that is still
alive in St Botolph's today.

East of St Botolph's there was a row of inns. The Three Nuns and the Blue Boar
were the two main coaching inns; the Blue Boar was the staging post for the
Billericay, Brentwood and Malden coaches. Roque's map shows the White Bear,
The Crown and the Black Horse alongside them. All had long yards, like lorry
parks, for coaches and wagons, and stabling for horses. Since the Middle Ages the
sign of the Three Nuns had swung from a building on this site, named thus, no
doubt, because of its proximity to the nunnery in the Minories. Once it had been
a bellfoundry; its first mention as an inn is in Defoe's account of the Great Plague
of 1665, and it was still a pub in the 1960s. In Strype's day this was the staging
post for the Romford coaches, taking turns with the Saracen's Head on the City
side of the gate, and for the Chipping Ongar Carrier; a 1721 list adds Bishops
Stortford, Barking, Epping, Low Layton and Walthamstow.

Accusations of theft brought against a hackney 'higgler' in 1762 allow us an
inkling of what went on. When the carriers' wagons lumbered into the yard,
bringing wares from the Essex countryside, each bundle or basket had a bill of
lading in it that had to be checked off by the inn's book-keeper. In this case it was
Joseph Brooks, dealing with baskets of butter (from ten different dairies) and a
number of calves. The ostler fed the horses and put them in the stables.

Henry Fielding describes an early morning departure from a coaching inn. The
company rose early to be ready for a 7 a.m. departure, the coachman stowing half
a dozen of them 'with perfect ease into the place of four', guessing that the 'well
fed alderman' and the fat lady will take up less room; 'passengers', he says, 'are
properly considered as so much luggage'.

The Three Nuns and the Blue Boar were akin to commercial travellers' hotels-
cum-transport cafés; perhaps more upmarket were the Crown and the Pye taverns
in the High Street, where the church vestry met from time to time, and The
Bell in Church Row. They also met in The Peacock, the Bunch of Grapes and
Cary's Coffee House in the Minories, at the Queens Head on Tower Hill and the
Horseshoe Tavern by the victualling office and the Kings Arms on the corner of
Burr Street. In 1762–63 they met in the Crown and Magpie in the High Street,
kept by millionaire vintner Kenton. Cruikshank's picture of the interior of the
Coach and Horses in Nightingale Lane allows a look into the rough and tumble
of the alehouses in the Manor.

Leading off the highway to the north was Houndsditch, with its secondhand
clothes shops, brokers, joiners, brasiers, upholsterers and Jewish dealers. The
Dukes' Place and Bevis Marks synagogues were nearby and in the 1790s two
Polish synagogues were set up in Gun Yard and Cutler Street. Off it was Gravel

Lane, 'a large place with pretty good buildings', where the workhouse stood (from *c.* 1734), and a maze of mean courts and alleys.

The broad and spacious Great Minories was south of the church, with some good brick houses, newly built, with porches and porticoes, intermingled with old timber-framed buildings, like the Fountain; the Great Fire had not come this far east. Entick, writing in 1775, noted that elegant 'first rate houses' stood all along the west side, instead of the 'wooden hovels' that had been there before. Though the alleys and courts leading off were mostly 'nasty and beggarly', the Minories itself was a fine street; one thief reckoned that it was the 'best place to rob in, there being the most to be got'. There were coffeehouses, shops and taverns, like the Peacock where 'Black John' the potman slept with the landlady. Guns had been made in the Minories since Tudor times, and many of the signs swinging overhead advertised the presence of this most flourishing industry: in the late 1690s Richard Lowder worked at the sign of the Star, John Turvey at the Trophies, and there was a gunsmith's shop called the Fowler. Just south of the Fountain was a passage that led to Holy Trinity Church (now St Clare Street) in the Little Minories, rebuilt in 1706 and a relic of the old nunnery. Its tiny parish covered only 4 acres and the population was only a few hundred people. Any day of the week it was possible to catch a sailor and his girl, or even a City gentleman and his intended, who had come for a quick, quiet, cheap wedding without the public fuss of having banns called. 'Very few', reported a French visitor in 1697, 'are willing to have their affairs declar'd to all the world in a publick place, when for a guinea they may do it snug.' From about 1644 Holy Trinity Minories was the favoured church; the parish having been created at the Dissolution and owned by the Crown, was exempt from the bishop's visitation rights. Before the system was regularised by Hardwicke's Marriage Act in 1754 couples of all sorts and conditions resorted for a variety of reasons to marriage venues away from home. Londoners had a predilection for 'private marriage' and the notorious 'marriage shops' around the Fleet prison did a roaring trade, especially among poor seamen and weavers from the East End. The 'marrying churches' were on the east side: Holy Trinity itself (the most popular), St James's Duke's Place, St Botolph's, St Katharine's and St Dunstan Stepney.

A passage off the Minories to the east of the church (now Haydon Street) led to Haydon Square, laid out in the new fashionable style in 1682 and named after Sir William Heydon, Master of the Ordnance in the seventeenth century. Its 'very handsome houses', stables and coachyards, trees and garden were railed off; 'Very ornamental in the summer' was Strype's comment. In 1740 there was quite a cluster of 'eminent' merchants and traders in the Square: the Scandinavian firm of Alstrom and Clasom, Jonathan Collet, director of the Royal Exchange, David Crichton, merchant and insurer, Fisher, Johnson and Co., cornfactors, John Spicker, merchant and insurer.

Continuing south, past the Peacock (a pub of this name is still there), along another alley there was the glasshouse. It was in one of these glasshouses between Rosemary Lane and Ratcliff Highway that Defoe's Colonel Jack, a homeless orphan, snuggled down for warmth near the hot ashes, and where the 'Good old Master' of the factory reproved a gentleman customer for swearing like 'My black wretches that work there in the furnace'. A little way past the Glasshouse Yard you would have crossed Rosemary Lane, once Hog Lane (now Royal Mint Street and Cable Street), long notorious for its 'shiftless men and cutpurses' and for its secondhand clothes market, Rag Fair. Here were the Merchant Taylors' almshouses and, in an alley off it running south, known as Church Row, was the new churchyard for St Botolph's. And so on down towards the river, across Little Tower Hill, past the Naval Victualling House where beasts were slaughtered and the King's Brewhouse, where beer was brewed for the seamen (once the Abbey of Tower Hill and later the Royal Mint). Passing the rough precinct of St Katharine's and turning left along East Smithfield and then right, down Nightingale Lane, where the workhouse was from 1736, you would have arrived at Hermitage Dock and the Red Lion brewery.

This was the Manor: a different world, with its 'little low houses', sailors' cottages, alehouses without number, workshops and warehouses. There were coal wharves and landing stages for passengers. The maypole, which the Puritans had pulled down, stood on its old site (opposite the entrance to St Katharine's Marina) and there was the pillory, for entertainment of a grimmer sort. East Smithfield had the houses with the lowest rent of anywhere in London in the 1690s. Midcentury, Black Boy Alley in Salt Petre Bank was an 'ancient sink of pickpockets and thieves'.

Whitechapel

Returning to Aldgate High Street, about 200yds east from St Botolph's, past the coaching inns and butchers' shops, by the turning into Petticoat Lane (near Aldgate East underground station today), was Whitechapel Bars, which marked the end of the City's jurisdiction. In Strype's day there were posts with chains across the road. This and Temple Bar were the two busiest points of entry into the City.

Here we enter Whitechapel parish and the county of Middlesex. This is the East London's most famous place, albeit for its associations with an Edwardian murderer and the bubbling life in the Jewish 'ghetto'. Its history before the Ripper has been much ignored. Unlike its more romantic neighbour, Spitalfields, where fine rows of old houses remind the tourist of the olden days, there are only isolated examples of eighteenth-century housing among the office blocks, crumbling Victorian remains, scruffy little shops and bright Bengali cafés. It has been built over, bombed, redeveloped, many of its streets and landmarks renamed. Even the parish church at its heart is no longer there. Let us take a closer look, and try to recreate the town of Whitechapel known to Daniel Defoe and Dick Turpin, who lived here in the 1730s. And town it was. Described by many a modern commentator as a 'village on the east of London', by the end of the century Whitechapel had in its 170 acres twice as many inhabitants as the whole town of Ipswich. As the great 'province' of Stepney was split into six, (1729–45), Whitechapel parish took pride of place. It had more shops, more coffeehouses and taverns, more chapels, more variety of trades, more rich men and more poor men than any other of the East End's Middlesex places. It had theatres and hospitals, prisons and courthouses, markets and manufactories, brothels, schools, almshouses and workhouses. It was the most cosmopolitan part of all London, with Germans, Spaniards, Portuguese, Flemings, Dutch, French, Turks, Poles, 'Lascars', and home-grown merchants with foreign connections who thought nothing, or so it seems, of a trip across 'the pond'. It was four times bigger in extent than Aldgate, with more open ground; a gate just beyond the church (now Altab Ali Park) on the south side of the Whitechapel Road, known as the Fieldgate, led onto the path to Stepney across Whitechapel Fields, where footpads lurked. It was here, early one morning in 1715 that one of the parish headboroughs, cutting 'tuffs for his larks', spotted a couple of burglars burying their ill-gotten gains. Many local lads and lasses were strung up at Tyburn for turning to crime. Whitechapel's crime rate was much higher than that of Aldgate, perhaps because of the proximity of expanses of unlit common ground, perhaps because the policing was less intensive than in the adjoining city parish; there were twenty-two watchmen as opposed to Aldgate's sixty in 1760.

Towards Mile End, on the north of the highway (opposite the Royal London Hospital) was Whitechapel Green. From here fields stretched down towards the river and across to Stepney.

Whitechapel's ribbon development started in the early Middle Ages and buildings spread north and south. Since the 1580s the Wentworth lords of the manor released land for building along both sides of the Whitechapel Road. Although there was overcrowding in parts, overall there was less density of habitation than in Aldgate. In 1760 there were said to be 2,792 houses, roughly the same number as in the much smaller parish of St Botolph's. St Mary's church has served the locals since the thirteenth century and long ago became independent of the mother parish of Stepney. The west-east extent of the parish was originally from the Bars to just beyond the church Sometime in the seventeenth century it was extended along the Essex Road to Mile End, taking a long strip out of Stepney. The parish boundary with Mile End is the stone bridge that crosses the Black Ditch running from Spitalfields to join the Thames at Poplar, just before the turnpike.

The main streets in Whitechapel are the Essex (Whitechapel) Road, probably the widest highway in London, and two long lanes: Petticoat Lane, going north to Spitalfields, which it shares with Aldgate and Stepney; and Rosemary Lane (Royal Mint Street and Cable Street), running east-west down near the river. So often does the parish clerk have to make entries for these that he abbreviates them to PCL and RML. Between 1720 and 1747 the turnpike road to Wapping, New Road, was built at Town's End. Since the 1680s Goodman's Fields, the south-west part of the parish, until recently farmland, had been developed as a middle-class residential district. There was a concentration of habitation on the City side of the parish. East towards Mile End it was less built up, but this changes as the century progresses.

The seafaring riverside strip, Wapping Whitechapel, had its own chapel of ease, St John's, built in 1617; by now it had broken away completely from the mother parish. Building had gone on apace in Whitechapel parish (423 houses in 1656–77), with alleys and courts proliferating towards Spitalfields. Houses had to be hastily erected for the weavers who were flooding in, and a 'new town' was created for them, just east of Brick Lane. This was christened Mile End New Town; we shall look at it more closely in due course.

Like Aldgate, there was a mix of rich and poor in Whitechapel, of workshops and middle-class living, of a few fine squares and numerous squalid alleys, dominated by the 'rattlers' and wagons that 'choked up the loaded street' and turned its main artery into a pot of gold. How many local fortunes were made in the tall gabled inns that fought for business along Whitechapel High Street? Millionaire vintner Benjamin Kenton started off as a potman in the Angel and Crown in Goulston Street, just near the Bars. The victuallers of Whitechapel were by far the largest group of rich self-made men.

Whitechapel's gentry, of whom there were a surprisingly large number, were by and large sea captains and scions of successful merchant and manufacturing families. They were to be found, along with wealthy Jewish families, predominantly in Goodman's Fields and Wellclose Square. The best address seems to have been Prescot Street, the first London street to have its houses assigned numbers; Queen Anne's celebrated admiral, Sir Cloudesley Shovell (d.1707), lived there for a time. The fifth land tax division (Goodman's Fields) paid twice as much as the first division (the Brick Lane area). The wealthy and middling sort were not confined to these estates; they were jumbled together with the poor, as we have noticed. Expensive properties were to be found along parts of the Whitechapel Road, and it was still customary for manufacturers to live on site, as is witnessed by the magnificent Director's House, built by Truman the brewer in Brick Lane in the 1740s. Henry Raine, the rich brewer who endowed the school in Wapping and lived at his Star Brewery there, was of the opinion that men of business should not buy a country house until middle age; he was forty before he 'lay abroad from [his] business'.

The majority of residents were working families, living in multi-occupation tenements or small houses. Nearly everybody rented: publicans, tradesmen and artisans let out rooms, with the lowest of the low inhabiting cellars or lodging houses. Immigrants clung to fellow countrymen, Welsh with Welsh, Irish with Irish, huddled together in houses that were crammed to the gunwales, perhaps as much to keep warm in those freezing eighteenth-century winters as for economic reasons. Off the main streets there was a maze of courts and alleys, with weavers and throwsters and workers at other textile trades, metalworkers and mariners, many more of the latter in the first half of the century. Rich people were enough of a rarity for the parish clerk to note by his entry for the christening of Captain Jasper Hicks's baby 'quality'. In 1692 the churchwardens told the Sessions that paviors consulted about paving the high road from Ayliffe Street to the Mount reported that the houses fronting the street were very small and not above £3 per annum, some of them 'belonging to fatherless children and widows'.

A bewildering variety of trades is noted by the parish clerk in his registers at the opening of the century. There were metalworkers: gunmakers and smiths, a brasier, pewterer, bellman, anchorman, locksmith, gunlockmaker, ironmonger, blowing-hornmaker, clockmaker, cutler. He made mention of the 'lead house' in Buckle Street, 'the Guns' in Red Lion Street, the 'Cross Guns' in Lambeth Street, the 'Pewterers Plater' on the Green and a gun forge in Rupert Street. In the High Street there was a clockmaker. The textile industry and allied trades were represented by a good number of weavers and throwsters, a matmaker, pack-thread-spinner, fringemaker, pinmaker, needlemaker, twinespinner, hatter, several clothworkers, stockingmakers and tailors, a shearer, pattenmaker, mantua-maker, dyer, a worsted seller. Fowler the hatter had a shop in White Lyon Street. There was a worsted shop in Hooper Square, and various signboards announced the presence of the industry: the Shears and the Clothworkers' Arms in Chamber Street, two Childs Coats, one in Petticoat Lane and one in Goodman's Yard (1698), the Glovers in Graces Alley, the Throwsters' Arms in Church Lane (1698), the Mantua in Goodman's Yard, the Hat and Feathers in Petticoat Lane.

Tobacco was an important local trade. Several pipemakers were noted and there was a tobacconist shop in Brick Lane. For the building trade there were a plumber, plasterer, the Bricklayers' Arms in Church Lane, a sawyer, carpenters, turner and joiner. There are glasiers and a glass-seller, paviors and stonecutters (for the new road paving), a combmaker, a hemp-dresser, a skinner and a pellman, an upholsterer, a brushmaker, and several brewers, distillers and coopers. Bakers were numerous; there were a pastrycook, a gingerbread-baker, a grocer, several butch-ers, milkmen, cheesemongers, a mealman, two sugar 'finers', several victuallers and a cook. On Christmas Eve 1699 the sexton buried 'a man that cried cakes and pies'. There were oilmen, several tallow-chandlers and horners. Representing road transport there were a carter, a carman, a horse-keeper, horse-courser, a horse-seller, a farrier, a wheelwright. For the seafaring side there were many sea captains, mainly in Goodman's Fields, two customs officers, one in Hooper Square and one in Rosemary Lane, an excise manager, Josuah Pix, clerk to the navy office in Prescot Street, tide-waiters, watermen, and ordinary seamen. There were shoemakers, one apothecary, barbers in abundance, a prisonkeeper, a watchman, a schoolmaster, gardeners, porters and labourers, a nightsoil-man, a drummer, a few soldiers. By the Nags Head (opposite the church) there was a seed shop, and Thomas Adderton the undertaker worked from the sign of the Three Coffins. Three gentlemen featured, two in Mansell Street and one in Prescot Street.

The pursuits that made men's fortunes were indicated by the numbers who had wills proved in the senior probate court. Between 1700 and 1800 there were 2,442 from Whitechapel: at the top of the list came 320 mariners. We know that there were a number of sailors in Whitechapel and many wealthy naval officers, but this number of testators is greatly magnified by the fact that sailors were required to leave wills, even the lowest of the low, to make sure their back pay was properly disposed of if they died at sea. The next group was the victuallers (innkeepers) of whom there were 121. Then came the weavers of silk, linen, ribbon, tape, haircloth and sailcloth; of these there were forty-two, and twenty-two throwsters and dyers. There were thirty-four bakers, twenty-nine butchers, twenty coopers, nineteen sugar refiners and boilers (many German), twelve brewers, twelve tailors (of whom three are also victuallers), ten distillers, ten gunmakers, eight coachmen and coachmasters, eight barbers, eight glassmen (cutters, dealers and grinders), eight apothecaries, six smiths, five tobacconists and one tobacco-pipemaker, five corn-chandlers, four farriers (the blacksmith was a very important man hereabouts, with many hundreds of horses pulling coaches and wagons along the great road every week – and needing to be shod), four horners, three vinegarmakers, two pawnbrokers, two ropemakers and one starchmaker. As to the merchants and brokers their numbers were not large, but they were often men of considerable wealth.

Along the Whitechapel Road, from the Bars (Aldgate East) by way of Petticoat Lane, to the London Hospital

At the Bars, 'stage coaches to the neighbouring villages ply at all hours of the day'. It was here that Defoe's Moll Flanders waited in all her finery to 'assist' ladies descending from their coaches with valuable parcels. The Bars were where Petticoat Lane branches off to the north and Somerset Street/Mansell Street to the south. Until 1972, when the eponymous clothing shop was burnt down, the junction was Gardiner's Corner, the 'gateway to the East End'. These days it is the junction of Commercial Road, Commercial Street and the Whitechapel Road.

Before travelling along the coach road towards the church and then to Town's End, we will take a turn up Petticoat Lane, to become Whitechapel's best-known street. Once Hog Lane, down which pigs were driven to market in Whitechapel, it had acquired its new name by James I's reign, when Ben Jonson's Vice Iniquity included it in his tour of the more insalubrious parts of the suburbs. Large houses had been divided up and new small ones built. Down a paved alley east of the lane, in Spitalfields hamlet, had been a 'large fair house' with 'good garden before it' built and occupied by Hans Jacobson, James I's court jeweller, and subsequently by John Strype, a Dutch Huguenot silk throwster, the antiquary's father (d. 1648). By 1723 it had been divided into six dwellings. The Petticoat Lane Tabernacle (there by 1711) was a 'very low and dark' little place, crammed between houses. The textile industry was much in evidence; the tenter grounds had been there at least since 1576 when an Italian merchant called Benedict Spinola had, according to Stow, twenty tenter grounds constructed on the 8 acres of land 'on the back side of Whitechapel'; 'many clothiers dwelt here'. The arrival of foreign weavers was the occasion of 'contiguous rows' of housing appearing on both side of the lane. Some wealthy Huguenots had houses here in the 1690s: Raphael Duboyce with stock valued at £200, James Duboyce with stock of £200, Francis Poussett with stock of £300. For much of the eighteenth century the lane was known mainly for its horners, who prepared horn for lanterns, inkhorns and other commodities. They had a 'common warehouse' in Wentworth Street. Lantern 'leaves' evidently provided good pickings for thieves: Jonathan Adams had 150 lantern leaves stolen and Mary Spratley lost thirty-six. When a Mr Edward died in 1744 at his country house in Romford, the press reported that he had an estate of £60,000 accrued from his horner's business in Petticoat Lane.

Although there was not much sign in the first half of the century of the clothes market it would later become, there were weavers around and tailors and hatters advertised their wares at the sign of the Child's Coat and the Hat and Feathers. John Smyth (d. 1722) had a wool warehouse. There were bowling alleys, 'garden houses', coffeehouses, builders' yards, alehouses and brandyshops, where sheeps' heads and hog's faces are sold and washed down with a dram. You might encounter girls selling 'sieves' of oysters, pedlars, and a whole gallery of rogues. Petticoat Lane had not gone up in the world since Jonson's day; it was a haunt of low-life, especially pawnbrokers and receivers of stolen goods 'Notorious pilferer' Thomazine Tally passed some silver items to a 'broker' there in 1687, a 'fence' kept a house near the Marlborough's Head (1731) and Philip Lacy, a well-known thief and receiver, kept a brandyshop at the end of the Lane in 1735. Malt stolen from a warehouse at Queenhithe was stashed away in a Petticoat Lane hideaway.

There were enough Irishmen around to make it worthwhile for Archibald Paydon, landlord of the Black Lion, to serve a special dish of salt fish and potatoes for them on St Patrick's Day. A couple of Paddy ruffians, 'stout well-made men', were executed in 1749, Lawrence Lee, a coal heaver turned highway robber, and his partner Peter Murphy. One of their victims, who went to seek them out, found his stolen wig in a box, pistols, powderhorns and 'implements for making bullets' in the Petticoat Lane house, and a young girl who claimed to be Lee's niece, sporting two suspiciously valuable rings. Most of the loot, of gold, silver and diamonds, had been offered to a Jewish receiver, Nathan Ashur, who, fearing he might be 'brought into some scrape', betrayed them to the local constable.

Cheap, fiery spirits, locally distilled, were on offer here, as at thousands of outlets in the capital, sold by chandlers, weavers, barbers and the like. A lodger at the Goat alehouse, John Marsland, forty-four and 'drunk and idle', a seaman in the 'Guinea trade' turned street trader, sold a home-distilled brew in the Lane as French brandy 'to such as could not discern the difference'. He infected his wife with the pox and she was sent to Bedlam; he then raped his thirteen-year-old daughter and gave her a dose. She was rescued by a kindly uncle who saw to it that the brute paid the penalty; he went to the gallows.

As the century progresses Jews would congregate here and set up their old clothes shops. A list of members of the Sephardim attached to the Bevis Marks synagogue in 1803 included the following residents of the Lane: Abraham Azulay from Morocco via Hamburg, arriving in 1784 to 'seek a livelihood', Italian tailor Angelo Bendetti from Rome, arriving in 1802, Samuel Sukami/Souhami, cap maker, who came from Smyrna via Amsterdam in 1783/4, and Zipporah, wife of Nissim Zerach, arriving from Berlin in 1763. Rachel Serrano, watch-stringmaker, came with her parents from Marseille via Leghorn in 1780. Old clothes dealer Isaac Ramos and his wife Rosa (from Amsterdam and Bordeaux) arrived in 1792 and 1791 respectively. In 1768 labourer David Monteiro came from Amsterdam, while David Ottolenghi accompanied a 'young gentleman' from Leghorn in 1774 and moved from Woolpack Alley to the Lane. Abraham Levy, dealer in old clothes from Modena, was there by 1784, and his wife Esther had come with her parents from Amsterdam the previous year. Judah Delmonte, Dutch clothes and slipper dealer came to London in 1786 and set up his business in Boars' Head Yard. Gartermaker Samuel Paz Cardozo had come with his father from Braganza in 1732. Josiah de Calver, a Jerusalem silkworker, came as a gentleman's servant in 1788. Henoch Cohen from Nice via Leghorn arrived in 1771. Phinas Bornanel, a Dutch tailor who had 'lost his business in his own country', took up residence in 1796 in Cooks' Buildings. Mordecai Mendes, a labourer from Amsterdam, arrived in 1776 and married a widow who had travelled to London with her former husband, also from Amsterdam. Zipporah Mendoza, wife of a Dutch leather dealer, lived in Mulberry Court in 1792.

Returning to the main road and proceeding east, we would have passed 'considerable inns': the Castle, which was there in Strypes's day, is remembered today in Old Castle Street. Coaches for Barking, Ongar and Chelmsford and wagons for Chelmsford left from the Pied Bull in 1721. In 1771 the principal inns were the Blue Boar, the George Inn, the Nags Head, opposite the church, the Red

Lion (top of Leman Street), the Talbot Inn, the White Hart and the White Horse. In 1795 the Bull was the inn for postcoaches.

Between today's Goulston Street and the Whitechapel Art Gallery are busy streets and alleys going up towards Spitalfields: Moses and Aaron Alley, Newcastle Street, Catherine Wheel Alley, George Yard, and Angel Alley, where there was a madhouse. Houses, some of them quite substantial, are interspersed with workshops and breweries, sugar factories and silkworks. Goulston Square is a pretty leafy enclave. One of the households in Catherine Wheel Yard (off the Alley) has left an account of itself from the opening years of the century. It is a sad little tale, with no major repercussions for the outside world, but it draws together some of the strands of Whitechapel life at the time.

Had the shutters been open at the parlour windows and the candles lit, you might have witnessed a bizarre sight. A couple of maids, dressed in funny clothes, are jigging dolls about as if in a dance, having pillow fights and making the little dog bark at a parrot in its cage. They are trying to lift their widowed mistress 'out of her melancholy fits'. This was the Fromanteel house, with a little parlour, a great parlour, an ale cellar and stables and silkworks at the back. The sobbing widow, in her early forties, was Hannah, whose recently deceased, and much loved and much older husband Mordecai, High Constable of the Tower Division, of Flemish stock, was a throwster of great wealth, said to be worth as much as £30,000 (c. £4 million in today's' money). Silk throwing was, as we have noted, a major local industry. It was easy, repetitive work, and the Fromanteels would have given employment to many women and children.

Mordecai was the nephew and close friend of the most famous clockmaker of his day, Ahasuerus Fromanteel, who had been, until his death in 1693, living in Maidenhead Court in the south of the parish, in the Dutch quarter near St Catherine's. Some of his pieces were in the house: a 'new clock and corrall set in gold' and a 'regulator'. Hannah was the daughter of a local tallowchandler. The couple were Dissenters, and worshipped at the Presbyterian Hand Alley chapel in Bishopsgate (although they and their one child, a baby son, were buried in the parish church). Frequent visitors to the house were the Hand Alley divines, the famous historian of the 'sufferings' of ejected ministers Edmund Calamy, and the extraordinarily influential Welshman Dr Daniel Williams, adviser to William III and founder of the theological library that bears his name.

When the rich throwster died, in March 1697/8, Hannah was devastated. Everyone agreed that they had been a loving couple and that she had helped him in his business. Their one child, a little boy named after his father, had died in infancy. Hannah's wealth, her diamonds and pearls, were of little comfort to her in her loneliness, and she went into a decline, spending all her time crying and apparently having a series of strokes. Medical attention was of little avail: Sir Richard Blackmore, the physician, and local apothecaries John Sinner, father and son, came to the house in Catherine Wheel Yard. One of her maids said she had become 'like an Ideott or a Naturall'.

The trustees of Mordecai's estate, John Drake, another silk throwster, living in Wentworth Street, and Andrew Prime, ironmonger (another Fleming and a relative), kept the poor woman under virtual house arrest. Relatives were denied access to her house and a sinister 'keeper' called Fuller was employed, a woman who came daily by coach from the City to guard the widow and her money. The maids were bribed and, under Fuller's instructions, put on the shows of dancing dolls and pillowfights to keep the distracted widow quiet, or perhaps to drive her completely mad. Now Hannah's family, or some of them, were in 'low circumstances', and whether or not she was in her right mind she managed to summon her lawyer and three old friends. She executed a will and several codicils that benefited her poor relations, even leaving £5 to her nurse's granddaughter. Hannah lasted only a couple of years after her husband, dying in 1700. The executors Drake and Prime tried to overthrow the will on grounds of her incapacity, but were unsuccessful: the poor relations all got their little pots of gold.

Parallel to the highway was Wentworth Street, developed in the 1650s. The boundary with Spitalfields lies along the middle of the road. There were some very large properties on the Whitechapel side, fewer on the north side. Alderman George Heathcote, a lord mayor and said to be the richest commoner in England at his death, paid £20 land tax for two sugarhouses and a dwelling-house here in 1742.

About a quarter of a mile from the Bars Brick Lane led north up to Truman's brewery and Spitalfields.

The south side of the Whitechapel road was used for a haymarket three times a week; in the 1690s it was in Peacock Court, in 1782 in Swan Court. There were more butchers' shops and slaughterhouses. Whitechapel had long been known for its butchers: 'Beware the butchers' hooks of Whitechapel' warned a character in Beaumont and Fletcher's *Knight of the Burning Pestle* (1607).

A little beyond Brick Lane, on the south side of the highway, was the parish church, standing on the site of the ancient chapel that gave the village its name. The medieval building having fallen into decay, St Mary's was pulled down and replaced in 1669–73 with a larger church to serve the swelling community, a 'coarse irregular building' according to Noorthouck, with different shaped windows ornamented with 'thick festoons'.

The Great Windmill whirred on its eastern side, and to the south-east was an extensive grove of mulberry bushes (now Mulberry Street). In 1790 a fine large chapel was built here by Selina, Countess of Huntingdon for the followers of her Calvinistic Methodist sect. Charles Wesley played the organ at the opening service. These worshippers were known for their lusty singing and attracted a good number of locals. Sion chapel must have been a thorn in the flesh for the parish clergy, who were so very close at hand.

After the death of the reverend courtier Ralph Davenant, who founded the school, the rector of Whitechapel was the prominent Whig (Low Church) clergyman William Payne (1681–97). He was probably best known locally for his part in an abortive government initiative to try and stop the marriage trade at the church in the Minories. His successor Richard Welton (1697–1715), a Huguenot hater, was of a very different stamp: a Jacobite High Churchman who openly preached that the Stuart name was 'the glory of the country'. He caused a great uproar by having Bishop White Kennet (the Whig incumbent at Aldgate, mentioned above) depicted as Judas in an altarpiece that was put up in the church in 1713. After he was thrown out of his benefice for refusing to take the oath of allegiance to the Crown (in 1715), he started an illegal 'nonjuring' chapel in Goodman's Fields, and finally took off for America in 1724.

Obadiah Shuttleworth, the celebrated violinist and composer, born in Spitalfields, was organist at Whitechapel church in the early years of the century, moving on to St Michael Cornhill in 1724.

In those days when advowsons were sold to the highest bidder at Mr Christie's Great House in Pall Mall, Whitechapel church, along with Stepney and Wapping was purchased in 1708 by Brasenose College, Oxford. For the rest of the century the church was supplied with a series of Oxford dons, the first of whom, Robert Shippen, was principal of the college, 'a quiet and devoted Jacobite' and a leader of the Tory opposition to chief minister Walpole. He was rector from 1719 to 1745, but probably was little concerned with the church or parish. This may have been just as well: according to the college historian, he was a 'mere Hocus Pocus and very unfit for the cure of souls'. The curates here were kept busy with burials. The death rate was high, as it was all over eighteenth-century London, and the clergy at St Mary's were burying eighty or ninety people a month mid-century; in the 1690s there were three burial grounds, the Lower, the Green and the Gravel. In the cramped insanitary conditions they died of tuberculosis, cholera and typhus, smallpox, 'excess of drinking' and accidents. Children were found dead in the streets, or 'overlaid' by their mothers; toddlers with smallpox were picked up at the roadside. In 1743 little Jane Prescot, evidently found in Prescot Street, was put to a parish nurse in Black Lion Yard and perished from convulsions, aged just one week.

Just beyond the church on the north side, after the Nags Head (there is a Nags Head on the site today), the Green Dragon and the Black Lion (remembered today in Black Lion House), was Great Garden Street (Greatorex Street) leading up to Mile End New Town and Gurle's Ground, where the famous nursery stood. This was the first large nursery in London, started in 1643, when it was a 43-acre site. Gurle (who became the king's gardener and supplied fruit trees for

Woburn Abbey) died in 1685, but a son or a grandson was in possession of part of the garden site in 1719. In 1779–80 Great Garden Street was cleared to make it a 'convenient way' into Mile End New Town.

East along the south side of the highway after the church, past the windmill just before the gate leading to the path across the fields to Stepney, there was the famous bellfoundry. In 1738 the Artichoke inn premises were taken over by a local bellfounder. The Whitechapel Bell Foundry still functions today on the very same site and is, according to the *Guinness Book of Records*, the oldest manufacturing company in Britain. From 1619 and for most of the seventeenth century the Bartlett family ran the foundry in premises north of the highway. After the lull in trade brought about by the Puritans during the Interregnum, business looked up, especially with the building of Wren churches after the Great Fire. The inscription on their bell at Christ Church Southwark (1700) reads: 'Lambert Made me Weak, Not Fit to Ring, But Bartlett Amongst the Rest Hath made me sing.' A Wiltshire man, Richard Phelps, who had a large property in Horse Shoe Alley off Petticoat Lane, took over the foundry in 1701 and ran it very successfully for thirty-seven years, making, among many others, the great hour-bell at St Paul's. When Phelps died he left the foundry lease to Thomas Lester, his foreman, along with all the stock and equipment, and 'my little engine for extinguishing fires'. Lester, who lived nearby the works in Catherine Wheel Alley, moved to the Artichoke Inn site. Together with Thomas Pack, his partner from 1752, Lester was responsible for the making of Philadelphia's Liberty Bell, originally commissioned by the Assembly of the Province of Pennsylvania in November 1751 to celebrate the anniversary of Penn's charter. Admittedly it was cracked and had to be recast, but it is good to think of the bell made by a Whitechapel founder proclaiming America's freedom to the world, summoning the citizens of Philadelphia to hear the first public reading of the Declaration of Independence. It was inscribed with the words 'Proclaim Liberty throughout all the land unto all the inhabitants thereof' and was later adopted as a symbol by slavery abolitionists, who dubbed it the Liberty Bell. Lester's nephew, William Chapman, went into partnership with Pack after Lester's death in 1769, and in 1781, after Pack's death, Chapman took William Mears into partnership. The Mears family maintained connections with the foundry for 125 years, making such famous bells as Big Ben itself.

Leaving the foundry, on the north side of the highway (from Greatorex Street to Vallance Road) there were houses and more inns, the Cross Keys and the King's Arms, with sugar refineries and ropewalks behind by the end of the century. We are now entering Towns End, where Whitechapel adjoins the hamlet of Mile End. Set among gardens were the old parish almshouses (with sixteen widows), which were replaced by the workhouse on the same site between 1765 and 1768. Behind was the overflow parish burial ground and next to it Rector Davenant's schools in Davenant Street.

Whitechapel Green (behind the underground station) is past the workhouse, the schools and Baker's Row (Vallance Road). In the 1690s Whitechapel's village green had a ducking pond at its eastern end, the manor's dog pound, a blacksmith, a 'music house' and was all set about with shops and drinking establishments: the Children in the Wood, the Pewter's Plater, the Pottage Pott, the Eagle and Child, the Golden Horn, the White Horse, the Grave Maurice. With the coming of the turnpike at Dog Row in the 1720s (Cambridge Heath Road) and the building of the London Hospital, Towns End lost its country feel. By the 1790s the southern part of the Green had been built on; soon the pond would be filled in and stables built on the site.

On the south side of the Green (marked today by Court Street) stood a Court of Record with a debtors' prison attached. A petition of some mariners in Charles II's reign reads: 'For want of good observation, by bad steerage they are fallen into the great eddy of Whitechapel prison.' This was the franchise prison of the Manor of Stepney: 'Lord Wentworth's jayle' was well known and greatly feared. Before the 1725 reforming legislation, men and women were arrested for debts of a few pence, 'usually for vexation and revenge'. Families were destroyed thereby and innumerable poor creatures were put on the parish. By 1800 the prison was empty and the debtors' court had moved to Brick Lane.

Opposite the parish almshouses, on the south side of the main road, were the rather more select Meggs's almshouses, where twelve local widows were housed in what appears to have been a splendid building After the relocation of the workhouse and presumably the rehousing of the parish widows, Meggs's seems to have been adopted by the parish. In November 1793 the vestry raised money to buy flannel waistcoats for 'the brave British soldiers' fighting the French in Flanders, 'against the severity of the ensuing winter'. The balance of the sum collected (£9 13*s*) was given to the Meggs's widows.

With its pauper institutions, its debtors' prison and courthouse, its charity school, its cemetery, its hospital (from 1757), its house for stray dogs, farriers and all the bustle of the Mile End turnpike nearby, this was perhaps not the most desirable part of town, made less so by the opening of a pauper farm in the 1750s. A short distance south-east of Meggs, in a continuation of Fieldgate Street (now Stepney Way), Samuel Tull, high constable of Edmonton, had his 'net manufactory' from 1755 to 1765. In the 1790s it was run by Edward Overton, his wife and sons, and had some 400 inmates, eight to a room, taken from all over the City, its eastern suburbs and even rural Essex. In 1792 the Whitechapel vestry decided to redraw the parish boundary so as to offload Overton's on to Mile End. Overton's does not appear to have been a sinister Victorian hellhole. From the evidence supplied in the prosecution of inmate Ann Fell it seems that Edward Overton and his wife supervised the house personally, and there was some competition to get a place there. Fell was accused of stealing 3gns from an old widow called

Rachel Keen, who seems to have lived a pleasant enough life, comforted with gin and small beer, and in receipt of a £10 a year pension from Goldsmith's Hall. When she went to collect it she went by coach, and took her lunch at the Bunch of Grapes, just by the hospital.

The London Hospital for the 'Charitable Relieving Sick and Wounded Manufacturers and Seamen in Merchant Service, Their Wives and Children', built on its present site between 1752 and 1759, along with the Mount which adjoined it (the remains of the Civil War fort) and the Mile End turnpike (made in 1722–26), are the best-known landmarks in this part of town. 'The London' was one of six London hospitals or infirmaries set up in the eighteenth century, and brought a greatly improved form of medical attention to the East End poor. Private medical practitioners of one sort and another, as we have seen, offered their services to those who could afford to pay. For the poor, places might be found at the two old hospitals of St Bartholomew's or St Thomas's in Southwark, where a precious few might be taken in 'upon the charity of the house', unless they were incurable or had the pox. In 1740 the East End acquired its own hospital; it was 200 years since the Spital beyond Bishopsgate had been closed down and 150 years since Lazarcottes at Mile End disappeared. 'The London' started life in Moorfields, a small affair set up by a group of enthusiasts, professional and business friends. It moved within months to one of the large houses in Prescot Street, rented at 24gns a year in 1740. The site is now marked by Magdalen Passage. Although the rules were that patients had to be recommended by a governor, on payment of a penny (often returned) anyone might petition to be treated. John Harrison, from St Thomas's, one of the initiators of the project, was appointed surgeon, along with a Huguenot as physician, Dr Andrée from Rheims. Another of the prime movers, Josiah Cole, was the hospital's apothecary. Nurses were recruited locally and paid £14 a year, £9 for night 'watches' (half as much as artisans). In 1742 there were 30 inhouse patients and 150 outpatients on the books, and a special house or 'lock' for syphilitic patients had been opened in a house farther down the street. Demand grew apace, and while four adjoining houses were added in Prescot Street (by 1757; one of them for Jewish patients) a larger purpose-built edifice was rising at Town's End (1751–59). It opened its doors in 1757, although building went on for another two years. Designed by Boulton Mainwaring, a leading local JP who was surveyor to the magistracy, according to Sir John Summerson it 'forecasts the arrangement of the typical Victorian hospital', with its 'ward wing and tiers of privies in the angles'. Meanwhile the old infirmary premises in Prescot Street were taken over by a home for prostitutes (1758), of which more anon.

A picturesque painting of the projected hospital shows an impressive Classical style, looking for all the world like a grand country house in an idyllic setting among trees and fields; the Mount adjoining is a pretty hillock covered with ornamental trees. It was here that the medieval manor house of Asshews had stood; more recently it was the Red Lion Farm, property of a wealthy local land-owner named Arthur Bailey. Farmland spread south towards the river and there were some houses and groves of trees to the east around Mile End Green, but it was not quite the peaceful rural place that one might imagine from maps and the painting. As well as the noisy rough and tumble of the coach road and a large distillery on the opposite side of the highway, there was Minish's 'hartshorn' factory nearby. Here ammonia was produced by the distillation of bone. The works stood 'amidst a vast assemblage of stinks; on a dunghill, adjacent to a vitriol manufactory, a bone house and a laystall [a mound of human manure] ... contiguous to a ditch full of common soil'. Minish was sued by the hospital trustees for creating a public nuisance. The action came to nothing, however, with one witness assuring the court that the smell in the wards was worse than anything that came in from outside, and another declaring that the 'smell of ham boiling in his own Kitchen was more disagreeable than the smell at the Defendant's works'.

In 1782 there were 120 inpatients (Barts had 428) in eight wards. Treatment was free and there was no deposit demanded for burial expenses as at St Thomas's, where 17s 6d was taken for this purpose. Though returnable, this was a large sum for a poor family whose weekly outgoings might amount to £1. Patients usually had to have a letter of recommendation from a governor, but there was the equivalent of an A&E department that took patients regularly with no questions asked. The hospital's stated aim was the relief of 'manufacturers and seamen', and beds were filled by the victims of industrial accidents and wounded sailors. Riverside brawls also brought in a good many.

When Commodore Anson's *Centurion* docked in the summer of 1744, having famously circumnavigated the world in an expedition against the Spanish, with all but one of its marines dead, there was a spate of fights that took surgeon Harrison and his brother (who also worked in the hospital) to the Old Bailey to give evidence. There was a major fracas in the Aldgate watchhouse in late August involving survivors from the ship, local publicans and a 'great possy of people' brandishing cutlasses, all drunk. Watchman James Sparkes was badly wounded and taken by the beadle into the hospital, where he died after a couple of weeks. A fortnight later the mob outside the Hamburgh Arms on Tower Hill 'rose so high' that onlookers thought the tavern might be demolished. This time a British soldier got into a fight with a Dutch member of Anson's crew; the soldier was stabbed and died from his wounds in the hospital four days later.

The hospital had noble, even royal, patrons: in 1765 the king's brother, the Duke of York, was president, followed by the Duke of Gloucester. Financial support came from bodies of annual subscribers from the gentry and middle classes. Henry Woodsall from St Martin in the Fields did the printing in the 1760s. This was a considerable expense, costing between £50 and £100 a month. As with any organisation that depended on charitable giving, there was a good deal of PR to be paid for; thousands of copies of special begging sermons by notables were distributed and the forms for letters of recommendation were printed. The Drapers' Company made an annual subscription in return for the hospital taking their boys, and there were generous subs from the East India Company, from private individuals in Madras and Bombay and from the Hudson Bay Company. Among the governors (1791–92) we find appearing as 'sponsors' for patients Major Rohde, the Leman Street sugar baker, John Charrington, the Mile End brewer, Lord Mayor Paul le Mesurier of Aldgate, Isaac Lefevre, Limehouse malt distiller, David Samuda, the immensely wealthy Sephardic Jewish Jamaica merchant of No. 19 Leman Street, Henry Engell, the sugarbaker of Wellclose Square, who recommended an old bricklayer of St George's. John Roebuck, who kept a grocery shop by the maypole in East Smithfield, recommended a teenage boy with 'diseased glans'. Elijah Goff, the coalman of Old Gravel Lane, recommended a young sailor; Rector Mayo of St George's recommended Mary Shaboe, aged thirteen, a labourer's daughter with a bad foot; she stayed in for over three months. Arthur Shakespear, the 'millionaire' rope manufacturer, recommended John Taylor, thirty-six, a ropemaker, with a 'wounded face', an industrial injury incurred at the Shakespear works no doubt.

The opening of the hospital was good for local trade. Thomas Lawton of Wapping supplied the earthenware chamber pots (ten dozen in August 1766), glassware (phials, retorts and so on) came from John Collett in the Minories, plastering work was done by George Wellings of Somerset Street. Peter Cooke, a Whitechapel tinman, provided kettles and saucepans, Gilbert Ford, an Aldgate brazier, warming pans. Keeping the patients warm was a considerable expense: during the course of the century the Thames froze over during eight winters. Fitzer and Woodham, Shadwell coal merchants, were delivering fourteen sacks a day in the winter of 1766; there were also deliveries of small coal and charcoal from another supplier. Firewood came from Richard Wetherell, an Aldgate man. Mrs Catherine Lewis of Spitalfields provided herbs and leeches, including twenty-four-dozen bunches of St John's wort in August 1768. Meat came from Thomas Gurnell of Assembly Row in Mile End: patients had 8oz of meat for their dinner – except the Jews, who had to survive on bread, presumably from choice. Spirits were supplied by John and William Baggs, distillers of Shadwell Dock, and beer by Robert Wastfield/Westfield of Mile End's Anchor Brewery (later Charrington's). This was the patients' staple drink: they were given 3 pints each in summer and a quart in winter. Mr Robert Phipps, upholder of Aldgate, supplied blankets, pillows and mattresses, and saw to the 'beating of flocks' (3s 6d a day). Flock mattresses were shaken three times a month. He also supplied the curtains. From his fellow Aldgate vestryman, John Watts, the hospital bought bedpans, spoons, pots and badges. John Adams, Aldgate turner, maintained wooden items, like the 'washing masher', and supplied brooms, brushes, crutches, pails, mops and cinder sieves. Thomas Wrigglesworth, instrument-maker of the Minories, was responsible for forceps, tonsil scissors, amputation knives, fracture cradles, needles, saws and hooks, and a very great quantity of lint. The windows (588 panes) were cleaned, at 3*d* a pane, by a firm of glaziers run by a Huguenot widow living in Ratcliff Highway, Mrs Magdalen Gilman *née* Hanat. She married wealthy glazier Robert Gilman of Montagu Street, Spitalfields in 1751, and when he died she carried on the business. She remarried in 1771 and died in 1778 'suddenly in her chair'. John Pott of Mansell Street supplied a quantity of vinegar.

By the end of the century the pleasant spot of Mile End Green, which lay to the east of the hospital with a few houses, large gardens, groves of trees and bowling greens, was built over. A grid of new streets of 'affordable housing' was laid out in the 1790s; those in Parfett Street still stand today.

Goodman's Fields, Rag Fair (Cable Street) and Wellclose Square

Leaving Town's End and going back west towards the City, after a left-hand turn, less than a quarter of a mile past the church, going south, was Red Lion Street, now the top end of Leman Street. This was the entrance to Goodman's Fields, Whitechapel's showpiece of upmarket residential living, at least for a time.

Before we take a closer look, it is worth bearing in mind that eighteenth-century Goodman's Fields had the reputation of being an unsavoury place of brothels, bagnios and 'many cheap places of low entertainment'. Unwittingly and incidentally this was mainly David Garrick's fault. His extraordinary overnight success at his London debut (as Richard III) in the Goodman's Fields Theatre here in 1741 took Whitechapel into the limelight for about twenty years mid-century. It engendered vast public interest, now as then, and with it adverse remarks about the area, made by contemporary authority figures and outraged locals, have been endlessly repeated. This bad press has been made worse by confusion between 'Garrick's' theatre and the 'drinking theatre', the New Wells, set up by William Hallam. The latter achieved some notoriety thanks to the corruption and antics of its landlord, JP Sir Samuel Gower. Theatres were, as in Shakespeare's day, widely thought of as nests of sedition and immorality; a series of satires directed at chief minister, Sir Robert Walpole (1720–42), made the government jittery. Noorthouck wrote:

> The grand jury of Middlesex in the month of May 1744 made a laudable presentment of several public places of luxury, idleness and ill fame, which tended to corrupt the morals of the people. These were, two gaming houses near Covent Garden, kept by the ladies Mordington and Castle; Sadler's-wells near the New river head; the New-wells in Goodman's-fields, the New-wells near the London spa in Clerkenwell; and a place called Hallam's theatre in May fair.

Playhouse-phobia, the short-lived stay of the Magdalen Hospital for Penitent Prostitutes in Prescot Street (1758–72) and the presence of the workhouse in Alie Street (1724–65) have rather distorted the view of this generally rather well-behaved sort of place, described in 1761 as having 'handsome streets inhabited by merchants and affluent people'.

Goodman's Fields was developed, as was much of new London, by landed gentry, in this case the Lemans of Northaw in Hertfordshire; its streets were named after branches of the family: Leman, Prescot, Mansell and Alie. It was bounded by Alie/Ayloffe/Ayliffe Street on the north and Rosemary Lane on the south, arranged in a grid around a square of tenterground; it measured about three-quarters of a mile north to south and an eighth of a mile west to east. Thoroughfares were built over the fields in the 1680s and '90s, lined with three, four- or even five-storey houses, with long gardens, stables and coachhouses at the back. Some were quite as fine as any West End mansion, big enough to accommodate the hospitals and manufactories that took over many as the years passed, although much demolition and rebuilding went on. A four-storey house at No. 55 Prescot Street, auctioned in 1778, was described as having two rooms on each floor, a large garden, shed, stables and a yard with a back entrance, with a ground rent of £101 a year, par for the course for a good London townhouse of the period. In most houses the kitchen was in the basement, with two parlours on the ground floor, a dining room and bedrooms above, and servants quarters at the top. A few steps led up to the front door, where a lamp hung from an iron bracket. Leases of these fashionable properties were taken by sea captains and men of business, especially big-time silk throwsters and, mainly in the second half of the century, by wealthy Jewish immigrants and German sugarbakers.

'As one wanders around these thoroughfares,' wrote Cecil Roth in 1940, 'now dingy and neglected, the eye is caught by noble Georgian frontages, beautiful lights over the entrances, exquisite pieces of moulding, handsome bow windows [*sic*] and (through an occasional open doorway) dignified oak staircases, which make it possible to revive in the imagination those more spacious and more simple days when this was the heart of London Jewry.' Today it is no longer 'dingy and neglected'; it is being seriously smartened up, with modern hotels, glassy office blocks and inviting cafés and pubs. Some dozen of the old houses still survive from those 'more spacious days', though nothing from the initial period of development; there is even still a bit of a green square in the middle. The developers have even revived the old name of Goodman's Fields. Roland Goodman, who kept his dairy herds here in Tudor times, would be gratified.

Once these fields had belonged to the nuns in the Minories. Old Goodman bought them at the Dissolution and his son, or grandson maybe, sold 'Goodman's Fields Manor, properly called Barnes Manor', to a merchant and lord mayor, Sir John Leman of Beccles in Suffolk. Leman had made a huge fortune selling dairy products to Londoners, hence his interest in the Goodman pastures, perhaps. His grandson, Sir William Leman (d.1667), a treasurer of war under Cromwell, was created a baronet by Charles II, and the family's Whitechapel estate was developed under the auspices of his son, the second baronet (d.1701). This Sir William inherited on his father's death in 1667, and the building of Prescot Street (named after his mother's family) was underway by 1678; building plots were still available in 1694 on the west side of Leman Street at 1s or 1s 8d a foot, and thirteen houses were in the course of construction in Red Lion Street. There were fifty-five houses in Leman Street, thirty five in Precot Street and seventy-two in Mansell Street. The second baronet had incurred serious debts, and the sale of building leases on his London manor would have been a welcome addition to his income. He instructed his executors to 'lease and mortgage' the Barnes manor land if necessity arose. His heir and grandson, another William, also referred to the heavy debt charged on the manor of Goodmans Fields. The second baronet married Mary Mansell, daughter of Sir Lewis Mansell of Margam; hence Mansell Street. The Lemans were connected by marriage to the Alies – hence Alie Street.

By the time Strype wrote his account of the area in the 1720s, 'Goodman's Fields are no longer fields and gardens, but buildings, consisting of many fair streets, as Maunsell Street, Pescod or Prescot Street, Leman Street etc. and Tenters for Clothworkers, and a large passage for carts and horses out of Whitechapel into Wellclose; besides many other lanes.' The residents were rich throwsters, merchants, bankers company directors and the like, among them Joseph and John Phillimore, throwsters of Leman Street, cousins of Robert Phillimore who laid out the estate in Kensington.

Sephardic Jews were the first of the 'sons of Abraham' to come to Goodman's Fields; it was a short walk to their synagogue at Bevis Marks, where the congregation was established in 1657 and a synagogue opened in 1701, and it was outside City restrictions. In the 1720s there were only about a thousand of them in the country. Numbers increased from mid-century; there were nice properties to be had, and, one presumes, a welcome from friends and relatives who had made earlier settlement. A good many of the 'Marranos', as they were known at home (crypto-Christians), were cultivated and rich. They came from Spain and Portugal and their colonies, from Italy, Holland, Turkey and North Africa, to benefit from Britain's relatively liberal ethos and to get a slice of London's boomtown trade. Life here seems to have suited them. Lysons notes their longevity; between 1743 and 1792 twenty-one people aged ninety-plus were buried in their Mile End cemetery, and Samuel Calormo made his century. Isaac Penha, a Portuguese apothecary, on Bevis Marks's books in 1803, said he had come 'flying from the Inquisition, my mother having been burned alive for Judaism'. Many came to 'seek a livelihood' or expand their trade. Laudadio Frachette arrived in 1751, a language teacher from Mantua, to 'establish a house of trade being at that time possessed of a very good property'; Angelo Delmar, a feather merchant, came from Leghorn via France to Prescott Street and then Mansell Street in 1780, 'in search of some property'; Isaac Calvo, a Portuguese student, came from Smyrna via Jerusalem in 1782 'with a view to being admitted to a university'; Solomon Treves of Italy and Gibraltar, clerk on a British ship, came, he said, 'for no particular reason, principally to introduce myself to some of my relatives and to seek livelihood'. The De Los Rios family from Amsterdam arrived in Leman Street in 1796/7: the widow Jochebet Machovra and spinsters Esther, Rachel and Rebecca joined their family there. There were enough Sephardic Jews by 1747 to warrant the opening of the Beth Holim, hospital for Spanish and Portuguese Jews, in Leman Street. It got off to a very bad start, with accusations made of corruption and ill-management, and was the subject of a vicious cartoon 'The Jerusalem Infirmary'. One of the characters depicted is Dr Vaz da Silva (one of the founders), saying 'Gonorrhoea and the French disease for all gentlemen!'. From 1790 it opened its doors to Ashkenazi patients as well, and in 1792 moved to Mile End, to a site on the main road near the cemetery; Lysons says it had forty beds. By 1820 it was an old people's home, its former function having been taken over by The London.

One of the richest Marrano families to come to London was the Da Costa Villa Reals from Lisbon. Newspaper reports of their arrival in England in 1726 credited them with goods worth £300,000. Widower Abraham Da Costa Villa Real, an old man when he arrived, took a house in Prescot Street. He had visited London in his youth, in the days of Charles II; either he or his brother was one of the first of their ilk to be admitted to the Stock Exchange in 1673. He went back to Lisbon, however, only to return many years later in 1726, when his son Jose/Joseph, who had made a new fortune as providetore general to the royal Portuguese army, was accused of Judaism by the Inquisition. Jose brought with him fifteen other members of the family, as well as his seventy-three-year-old father. The household in Prescot Street in the 1730s comprised Abraham, now over eighty, his wife's granddaughter Judith alias Leonora (the family all made open profession of Judaism on arrival and took Jewish names), a Mulatta slave girl he had brought from Portugal and a 'single young woman' called Luiza, 'who lives in my house and in my company'. At his death he left Luiza a paltry £50 and a few household items in recompense for her 'services to me'. He left his step-granddaughter a marriage portion, and two gold chairs wrapped up in paper and labelled 'Judith'.

The wealthy old man brought his girls from Portugal with him; John Sivall of Prescot Street brought his 'curious talking parrot' from North Africa. When he went bankrupt and the house was put up for sale the unfortunate bird was left behind with the furniture. Jacob da Costa Villa Real, old Abraham's son, another Goodman's Fields resident, brought with him a Portuguese bedstead, Portuguese candlesticks (silver), 'Portugal sheets' and twelve dining chairs with Spanish leather seats. The luxurious furnishings of his house were itemised in a probate inventory: a very fine crimson silk damask counterpane trimmed with gold lace, crimson harrateen curtains at all the windows, in the dining room twelve walnut chairs with black Spanish leather seats, blue and white china teacups, punchbowls, decanters, turkey carpets, a long-case clock. In the parlour were three card tables.

Not all the Sephardim were so fortunate. When Deborah Mendes Alvares, matron of the 'hospital for delivering poor married women of the Jewish persuasion', died in 1790, her estate was hotly disputed by poor relatives. Raphael Mendes Alvares claimed he was her nephew, son of Moses, an apothecary, whose mother had been burned alive by the inquisition, and one Sarah Melina/Milano. The opposition argued that he was illegitimate and, therefore not eligible to inherit. A couple of very old Jewesses from the congregation at Bevis Marks, among others, testified (with relish) that Raphael's parents had never married: 'Go along, you whore with your bastard!' her neighbours would call after his mother, who was, they said, of a pauper family that had been long maintained by the synagogue's charity. A woman who had been a patient in the Beth Holim when Moses, Raphael's father, was in his death throes there, remembered the dying man calling for his mistress so that he could make an honest woman of her at the last. The matron of the hospital and Moses' father shut the doors in her face until he was dead. She was then let in and sobbed over his body, loudly cursing the old man and the matron.

The Ashkenazi Jews, who came in far greater numbers, arrived slightly later than the Sephardim; there were only perhaps 120 arriving a year in the first half of the century and 150 in the second. A trickle of immigration had started in the late seventeenth century, and after the establishment of the Great Synagogue in Duke's Place in 1722 London gradually became a place of refuge for Jews from various parts of Europe. The early arrivals were mainly from Hamburg, where the large Jewish community was subject to bouts of persecution; in 1744 a number came from Bohemia, expelled from Prague by the Empress Maria Theresa. There followed Dutchmen (the Netherlands was in economic decline) and Poles, after the partition in 1772 brought most Polish Jews (the largest Jewish community in Europe) under the repressive regime of Catherine II, Empress of Russia. By the 1790s there were six synagogues in the east side of the City and the East End. As well as the Great Synagogue there were two in the City: the Hambro in Fenchurch Street (1707) and the New in Leadenhall Street (1761). There were three minor congregations, two specifically Polish, in Gun Yard (1792) and Cutler Street (1790), both off Houndsditch, and one in Rosemary Lane (1747/8) The Great Synagogue tried, without success, to restrict the flow by refusing to offer relief to those who came without good cause. Numbers increased after the 'Jew Bill' of 1753, which freed foreign-born Jews from commercial discrimination.

By the end of the century there were something in the region of 20,000 Jews in London; of these the overwhelming majority were Ashkenazi and very poor. We shall meet the poor Jews when we get down to Rag Fair. The rich 'German Jews', of whom there were some, like their Sephardic brothers chose to live in Goodman's Fields or Wellclose Square.

Leading lights at the synagogue in Duke Street were the banking Goldsmid family. Aaron Goldsmid (d.1782), son of a Hamburg merchant, came to Leman Street from Amsterdam in 1765; his house at No. 25, shared with his eldest son, George, with whom he was in partnership, was large, insured for £2,000 in 1781. His second son, Asher, a diamond merchant and bullion broker to the Bank of England, lived in style at No. 44 Mansell Street. One January evening in 1790, just after dusk, Asher went downstairs with a poker when he heard a noise and found his servant, Michael Levy, in a state of shock. He had caught a gang of (Jewish) burglars, or so he said, in the act of stealing two crystal chandeliers. The presiding magistrate evidently had doubts about the story, and the three men were let off. Asher's younger brothers, Benjamin and Abraham, set up as brokers in 1777 and became the largest loan contractors of their day. Among other enterprises they raised cash from the Netherlands to bail out the spendthrift Prince of Wales. They left Goodman's Fields for the City and had splendid country houses as well. Both were known for their philanthropy, to both Jewish and Christian concerns, and both tragically committed suicide. Their sister, fat, luxury-loving Polly Goldsmid, married Baron Lyon de Symons, another diamond broker, of Viennese stock. The couple set up home at No. 3 Prescot Street. Poor Polly was the victim of a Gillray caricature showing a very stout, plain, highly rouged woman, with a feathered headdress and enormous breasts spilling out. It is labelled 'A Lyoness'.

Asher Goldsmid was ticked off by the chief rabbi, Hirshel Levin, for wearing leather boots instead of cloth slippers at the synagogue at Yom Kippur. The rabbi complained, 'We want to be like them. We dress as them, talk as they talk, and want to make everybody forget we are Jews.' As Israel Zangwill commented, it was a lax generation. Attendance at synagogues lapsed and kosher rules were ignored. Traditional Jewish ways were abandoned by many, especially the magnates, who got themselves into 'society' if they could. The granddaughter of old Abraham Da Costa Villa Real of Prescot Street married a viscount; the Goldsmid brothers hobnobbed with William Pitt. Beards were shaved off, turbans discarded and long flowing robes were replaced with buttoned coats and breeches. In his portrait in the National Gallery Abraham Goldsmid looks for all the world like an English country squire. They bought themselves country houses along the riverside at Richmond, where they lived during the summer months. Asher Goldsmid, like many others, retired to Brighton. At the end of the century the rich started leaving Whitechapel, going west to Piccadilly and Park Lane, to Bloomsbury and Islington. Asher's son became the first professed Jew to receive a hereditary peerage.

The 'fair streets' of Goodman's Fields were not just rows of smart houses. Taverns, ale and coffeehouse keepers did a good trade and shops with bow windows displayed their wares, offering the necessities of life and luxury items for the new consumer society. Captain Thomas Bowney (1650–1713), ship owner and traveller, had a china-shop in Mansell Street where he sold Delftware and Japan bowls. There were grocers, chandlers, shoemakers, barbers, fishmongers, butchers (the Haunch of Venison in Leman Street, 1699) and cheesemongers; John Pearson, cheesemonger of Prescot Street, had a firkin of butter stolen from outside his shop. There was a pawnbroker at the sign of the Three Blue Balls in Mansell Street in the 1730s, and another by the theatre. Alie Street had a school, at the sign of the Hand and Pen, and for over forty years the workhouse. The theatre arrived there in 1729. Six houses in Prescot Street were taken over by the Infirmary, which was followed by the Magdalen in 1758. In one of the large Leman Street houses was the Jews' Hospital (1747–92). By the 1790s there was the Misericordia (for venereal diseases), the Dispensary for Pregnant Women in Alie Street, the Eastern Dispensary and the Middlesex Dispensary in Prescot Street.

No tour of London, it was said, was complete without a visit to the 'sweet singers of Israel at Goodman's Fields'. These sweet singers were the Seventh Day General Baptists or 'Saturday Baptists', who had a chapel in Mill Yard from 1692. An academy was attached, where for a few years in the 1760s the celebrated Tom Paine (reformist radical, supporter of Revolutionary France and Republican America) taught, much hated by the boys for his harshness. It is strange to think of a man who regarded the tenets of Christianity as 'fabulous inventions' teaching at a Baptist school. Its regular attenders numbered about a hundred mid-century. As in years gone by, home-grown Protestant Dissent flourished in Whitechapel, and there was a cluster of chapels in Goodman's Fields. Baptists of one sort or another dominated. In Prescot Street was the oldest established Baptist congregation, which had moved from Wapping (where it had been for forty-three years) in 1730. Alie Street had two Calvinist Baptist chapels, established in 1753 and 1756, and in Somerset Street (Mansell Street) was the Presbyterian chapel (from 1756), which had previously been in Gravel Lane off Houndsditch.

Taverns and alehouses proliferated, especially after the theatre opened. Many householders hung a bunch of grapes sign outside their door, and 'extortionate prices' were charged for punch, ale and spirits. John Buckmaster kept the George alehouse in Mansell Street from 1744 to 1757. There was the Three Tuns in Alie Street (1745), the Fleece and the Theatre Tavern, where the landlord sold theatre tickets. A tap house attached to the livery stables in Mill Yard was frequented by 'persons of fashion', who kept their horses there and enjoyed the bowling green, until it was taken over by the manager of the New Wells theatre and brought downmarket. In 1782 Charles Cox was the landlord of the Black Horse and French Horn in Alie Street, and George Gowreing kept the Brown Bear in

Leman Street (still there at No. 139). Like the City and the West End Whitechapel had its coffeehouses, among them the Black Boy in Leman Street, Hink's in Red Lion Street (1690s) and Pidgeon's in Alie Street (1734). Not all of them were what they seemed. Brothels or bagnios often called themselves coffeehouses; one such was the Turk's Head bagnio in Alie Street, kept by Elizabeth/Eleanor Roberts (d.1748). Procuring and prostitution went on, of course, and if the enemies of the theatre are to be believed the trade got a boost with the arrival of the players in Goodman's Fields. Widow Hutchinson kept a house of ill-repute called the Star and Garter in Alie Street, and girls were said to be sent regularly to the Bridewell from the tenements around Mill Yard, owned by corrupt magistrate Sir Samuel Gower. It may be of significance that the house for penitent prostitutes, The Magdalen, was sited (albeit briefly) in Prescot Street. In January 1754 the Whitechapel constables' expenses for the prosecution of bawdy houses was £350.

It was a bustling place. Early in the morning, before it was light, the night-soil-men carted away the sewage in covered wagons. The watchman called out reassuringly every hour, on the hour, and as dawn broke Jewish dealers set out from their cellars around Rosemary Lane, off to the West End to collect old clothes. Work for apprentices, for throwsters, weavers and sugarmen started at six, or with the light. Furnaces were stoked in the glasshouses, and looms started to clack. Turncocks from the London Bridge Water Company turned the water on and off at the pipes. Maids lit fires and opened shutters, letting the sunshine flood in through the tall windows on to walnut furniture and multicoloured turkey carpets. Amid the snorting and stamping of horses, the rumble of carriage wheels, the rattle of rolling barrels, shopkeepers opened their doors, boys played marbles in the streets, servants scurried about their business, naval captains, bank directors, diamond merchants, sugar refiners and textile magnates strode or rode about theirs. One morning Asher Goldsmid, off to the Royal Exchange with a very fine yellow diamond tucked in his coat pocket, was robbed. Women folk might be seen, managing their billowing skirts into hackney carriages, bound for the fashionable shops of the West End.

As night fell the lamplighters were abroad as carriages and cabs took the quality about their cardplaying, their dancing, their drinking, their debating. 'Even the lowest class have their clubs,' wrote a visitor; there was one called the Hercules in Rosemary Lane. Burglars were always afoot, and the cry of 'Stop thief' rang out almost as often as the watchman called out the time. In the early years of the century the watch had a special round here. Lights twinkled from a hundred hostelries, inviting the locals to come in for a 'pint of hot'. At six o'clock sharp, October to May, the doors of the playhouse opened and an excited crowd gathered to see the spectacular performances that delighted their eyes and stimulated their sexual appetites.

Theatres, music houses and an entertainment of another sort

We have seen something of how Goodman's Fields was affected by the 'Company of Comedians' in Alie Street and their fellows. Now it is time to go to the play, and to see what was really going on.

Playgoing and 'music houses' were all the rage. There had been a theatre in Lincoln's Inn and Drury Lane since the Restoration (both had royal patents) and the Haymarket opened in 1720. The East End joined the craze early on. Stephen Scudamore, a gentleman, and actor George Paul were summonsed for running a 'booth for dancing on the ropes and other unlawful excercises' in Wellclose in 1670. Five years later, as we have seen (p199), Francis White, a bold Shadwell vintner, had music and 'other disports' to lure young people into his 'greate shedd or booth' in the fields near Stepney church. Whitechapel parish register entries refer to a 'music house' at Towns End (in 1690, 1699 and 1700) and one in Cable Street (in 1700). Down near Rosemary Lane, in a yard by the Ship Tavern between Chamber Street and Prescot Street, was a 'booth or theatre' that was said to have opened in 1703. Nothing more is known about these establishments. In 1729 Thomas O'Dell, an actor from Dublin, opened a theatre, without patent or licence, in a converted throwster's shop in Ayliff Street (Alie Street). A public outcry ensued; there was a protest meeting in a tavern in the Minories and a scorching sermon was preached at St Botolph's: 'Whores are dog cheap here in London. For a man may slip into the playhouse passage, and pick up half a dozen for half a crown.' It was said that Whitechapel, a place of industry and commerce, vital to the country's economy, would be corrupted, and crime and prostitution encouraged, if Mr O'Dell's project went ahead. It did – and was successful, taking about £100 a week. There were regular performances of popular plays and musicals and a team of mainly Irish actors; the production of a 'new opera' named *The Merry Throwster* must have gone down well with the locals. In the summer of 1731 O'Dell sold his rights to one of the company, 'eminent comedian' Henry Giffard.

Things went well under the new management, and a purpose-built playhouse was commissioned, designed by Shepherd, architect of the new house in Covent Garden. It was on the east side of Alie Street, near the junction with Mansell Street. Doors opened for the 1732–33 season. Hitherto the customers had been largely of the 'middling sort' and local artisans; Israel Zangwill in his novel set in Goodman's Fields conjures up the scene:

The audiences – mainly Germans and Poles – came to the little unfashionable playhouse as one happy family. Distinctions of rank were trivial, and gallery held converse with, and pit collogued with box. Supper parties were held on the benches ... a portly jewess sat stiffly, arrayed in the very pink of fashion in a spangled robe of India muslin, with a diamond necklace and crescent, her head crowned by 'terraces of curls and flowers'.

In 1735 nobles and 'parliament men' started to attend, and the programme was changed at the last minute 'if persons of quality have a special request'. Tickets were sold at venues near the West End theatres, in nearby coffeehouses and taverns and in Pinchbeck's toyshop in Fleet Street. There were Restoration comedies and the newly fashionable 'sentimental comedies', musical shows with special effects; playbills enticed the locals with promises of 'new Scenes, Machines, Flyings and other Decorations'. Shakespeare's plays (their own versions) were interspersed with dancing of 'grotesque characters'. John Ravenscroft, 'the wait of Tower Hamlets' and a fiddler much in demand at balls, played here in the band and delighted all with his hornpipes. There was 'farce, Harlequinery, buffoonery, dumb – or deserving to be dumb – entertainment', after pieces and antics. A rendition of 'The Jolly Waterman' by Mr Bardin must have appealed:

Come all ye Jolly Watermen that on the Thames do ply
Haul up your boats and wet your throats for rowing makes us dry …

Perhaps this suggests that the average waterman (or taxi driver) might be able to afford a ticket – at 1s 6d in the gallery, 2s 6d in the pit.

Rents shot up and pubs and brothels opened up all around, or so it was said. Following an anti-government performance, *A Vision of the Golden Rump*, and the 1737 Licensing Act that it triggered, it was closed, but reopened, calling itself the 'late theatre' and getting round the law against charging for the performance of straight plays by sandwiching them between musical entertainments, for which there was a charge, and offering the plays *gratis*.

On 19 October 1741 Alie Street was the triumphant scene of David Garrick's debut on the London stage as Richard III, and all the town went 'horn mad' after him. The Duke of Argyll declared he was superior to Betterton; there were 'a dozen dukes of a night at Goodman's Fields'. But Whitechapel's moment of theatrical glory was brief. The furore attracted the attention of the authorities, and in 1742 the theatre was again closed down, this time for good, with a final production of the good old favourite *The Beggars' Opera*. It was demolished in 1746.

Towards Stepney Fields, near the bottom of Leman Street and off to the east, was Mill Yard, a narrow alley running up from Cable Street through gardens, with a sailcloth factory, a Baptist chapel, stables with a taproom and bowling green, and a row of tenements. Here, very convenient for Rag Fair, the New Wells, another theatre, was constructed by actor William Hallam, later to be known as the 'Father of the American Stage', together with his brother Lewis. The landlord was Sir Samuel Gower, a rich local developer and a leading Middlesex magistrate, who had made his fortune making sailcloth and lived next door to the taphouse. Gower's Walk, off Commercial Road, marks the site of his property today. As well as the Whitechapel factory and houses around, he had sailcloth works in Old Ford called the Buckhouse. Work started on the premises in about 1737, costing Hallam £1,500 (the equivalent of about £130,000 today), and the doors opened in 1742. Here 'pantomimes and enterludes' were performed, puppet shows put on and 'perspective views' as well as 'straight' comedies and tragedies. It must have been a great coup when in 1750 the Hallams secured the services of the celebrated self-publicist Hannah Snell, the toast of London, who had fooled both the army and the navy and fought disguised as a man. She strutted about dressed as a marine, singing 'All ye noble British spirits'.

In 1751 there was a great to-do and public outcry. Gower faced serious accusations from his fellow justices of laxity in the issue of licences and of conniving at the goings-on in the Turk's Head bagnio. Whitechapel vestry had ordered the Wells to be closed down as a 'disorderly house' in May 1749 and, presumably because of Gower's connivance, no action had been taken. The whole business was part of an ongoing feud between two gangs of thieftakers: the Mitchell gang, led by Ralph Mitchell of Deptford and supported by Gower, and the Carlows, a rival gang that was under the protection of another JP, Thomas Quarrill. At all events Gower apologised and the affair seems to have blown over, but that was the end of the New Wells. The Hallams took off for America, where they achieved fame running the American Company. The Mill Yard theatre was subsequently converted into a warehouse, and was burnt down in 1809.

The 'illegitimate theatre' struggled on in the East End as elsewhere. In October 1778 'vagabonds infest[ing] the Tower Division' advertised a forthcoming show at Whitechapel's Angel and Crown. Constables were ordered to arrest all actors. In June 1787 yet another theatre opened its doors in Whitechapel, with a production of *As You Like It* together with Garrick's farce *Miss in her Teens*. The Royalty was a plain brick building in Well Street, off Wellclose Square, with a splendid interior lit by ten cut-glass lustres suspended over the boxes, and the 'best elevated pit' in any theatre. It was the enterprise of 'Plausible Jack' Palmer, a Drury Lane actor who seems to have hoped that his theatre would be protected from the law by virtue of its being in the Tower Liberty. The usual objections were raised by 'respectable and opulent merchants and other Gentlemen residing in the vicinity of the Tower', but, subject only to minor kerfuffles, all was well. The Wellclose Square theatre continued to entertain the neighbourhood for about forty years, until it burnt down in 1826. Its customers were not just the 'mumpers of Knockfergus' (beggars of Cable Street) as one report put it, but some of the most refined and respectable of local families. Little Jane Mayo, a 'miss in her teens' and daughter of that most revered of clergy, the Revd Herbert Mayo, rector of St George's in the East, was a regular in the summer of 1788. She saw a musical drama called

The Deserter (twice), *Don Juan,* 'a musical pantomime', *Hero and Leander,* a 'comic burletta in two acts', and heard a rendering of Gray's 'Elegy' given by Plausible Jack himself.

Dukes (and duchesses) had come to Goodman's Fields to see David Garrick, and they started coming again some seventeen years later to an entertainment of another sort: sermons at the house of young whores, at No. 21 Prescot Street, which took over from the London Hospital in 1758 and is remembered today in Magdalen Passage. An outing to the Magdalen provided a titillating performance from the dandy-chaplain, Dr William Dodd ('If a man look on a woman to lust after her …'), flashing his diamond rings, and an exciting opportunity to view (penitent) young prostitutes *en masse*. Even members of the royal family went, and as much as £1,000 might be raised at one session. A year after it opened there were a hundred girls, a seventh of them under fifteen and several under fourteen. A third of the inmates 'had been betrayed before that age' (fourteen). Here is Walpole's account:

> This new convent is beyond Goodman's Fields, and I assure you would content any Catholic alive. The chapel is small and low, but neat, hung with Gothic paper and tablets of benefactions. At the west end were inclosed the sisterhood, above an hundred and thirty, all in greyish brown stuffs, broad handkerchiefs, and flat straw hats with a ribband pulled quite over their faces. As soon as we entered the chapel, the organ played, and the Magdalens sang a hymn in parts; you cannot imagine how well. The chapel was dressed with orange and myrtle, and there wanted nothing but a little incense, to drive away the devil – or to invite him. Prayers then began, psalms, and a sermon; the latter by a young clergyman, one Dodd; who contributed to the Popish idea one had imbibed by haranging entirely in the French style, and very eloquently and touchingly. He apostrophised the lost sheep, who sobbed and cried from their souls – so did my Lady Hertford and Fanny Pelham, till I believe the City dames took them both for Jane Shores.

One tourist guide was at pains to explain that it was not a house of correction but a 'secure retreat'; the inmates were 'not reproached' and were given the option of using assumed names. In 1772 it moved to Southwark and in 1869 to Streatham, becoming an approved school for girls. It finally closed down in 1966. Many thousands of 'lost women' were said to have been restored to their families and society thanks to the Magdalen. The unfortunate Dr Dodd came to a sticky end, however. His extravagant lifestyle took him into debt and he was tried for forging a bond, amid a great clamour from the press. In spite of Dr Johnson's endeavours on his behalf, he was hanged in June 1777.

Wellclose Square: seamen, sugarmen, magicians

Leaving the dukes and the (recovered) lost women, we will leave Goodman's Fields and go south-east, crossing Rosemary Lane and taking a closer look at Wellclose Square, where the Royalty theatre stood.

Squares, like those of the new West End, were something of a rarity in this part of town. In Bishopsgate there were Devonshire Square and Crosby Square, and off the Minories Heydon Square. Between Cable Street and Ratcliff Highway there were two. Wellclose, also called Marine Square, was the best known, with the Danish church (1696), designed by Caius Cibber, at its centre. Here was 'the prettiest pulpit in London', removed from the Chapel Royal in Whitehall by Queen Anne at the behest of her Danish husband. The square was about the same size as St James's Square and was created at the same time as the Goodman's Fields development, in the early 1680s. The other was Prince's Square, later Swedenborg Square, laid out in the 1720s and dominated by its Swedish church. Many Scandinavian timber merchants were settling in London at this time because of the demand for wood in the rebuilding of the capital following the Great Fire. Prince's Square was in Wapping Stepney (St George's in the East). There is nothing left of these elegant squares: the last of the eighteenth-century houses were pulled down in the 1960s. Prince's Square was still a 'picturesque old place' when George Sims wrote his *Off the Track in London* in 1911. When Millicent Rose wrote of the East End (1940s–51) Wellclose Square still survived, with houses from the 1690s on its south side, some from the mid-eighteenth century on its north, 'a tall warmly coloured group', and the Old Court House turned into a paintworks, with its fine staircase 'done up in shiny cocoa brown'.

The relatively recent demise of Wellclose, and the furore that accompanied the demolition of its old houses, has endowed it, perhaps, with a rather more upmarket reputation than it perhaps deserves. The records of the Four Shillings in the Pound tax show that most houses there in the 1690s were only of a moderate value, compared with the much finer properties in Prescott Street and Leman Street. The exception is the mansion that was occupied by the brewing alderman Sir John Parsons, who funded the development; this may have been why he got into debt. The *Foreigner's Guide* of 1752 describes the square as 'very pleasant', but Noorthouck, writing twenty years later, was rather less enthusiastic:

> The south east corner of Rosemary-lane leads to Wellclose square, situated between Knock Fergus and Ratcliffe-highway; and which is by some called Marine-square, from the number of sea officers who live there. It is a neat square of no great extent; its principal ornament is the Danish church, situated in the center, in the midst of a church-yard well planted with trees, and surrounded by a handsome wall adorned at equal distances with iron rails.

Before the 1680s Wellclose, as its name suggests, was a field with a well, crossed by a stream that had fed Crassh Mills, the great twin watermills at the end of Nightingale Lane. It was a rough spot for duels, illegal conventicles and places of entertainment. Once part of East Smithfield Manor, its eastern half belonged to Wapping Stepney and its western to Whitechapel and Aldgate. It was Crown property after the Dissolution and was formerly adopted in 1686 as part of the Tower Liberty, along with part of the Minories (used by the Ordnance) and the Old Artillery Ground; the Liberty's court of record (mainly for debtors) was moved there from Tower Hill. It stood on the south side, at the corner of Neptune Street until the last century, along with its gloomy prison – accessed through a pub, the King's Arms. The gaol was known as the Sly House; one of its cells can be seen today in the Museum of London.

The square was the creation of the West End speculator Nicholas Barbon, son of Praisegod Barebones of the Barebones Parliament, in partnership with brewer Sir John Parsons. They were also responsible for the new estate on the Old Artillery Ground and another development on Little Tower Hill. Barbon was an extraordinarily successful wheeler and dealer who lived in greater style than he could afford to impress his customers and investors, dressing 'as richly … as a lord of the bedchamber on a birthday', according to Roger North. Taking advantage of the post-Fire building boom he bought land and threw up houses for the growing middle classes, using some of his gains to fund the first Fire Insurance Company. In January 1682 £3,200 was paid for Wellclose. The site was cleared and two-storey houses with attics built around a central garden space, with roads radiating out from the corners. The best houses were on the east side, with long gardens stretching towards Prince's Square. The smart new houses, convenient for the quays of Wapping and in a leafy setting, well above the marshy riverside, were soon snatched up by naval officers and wealthy merchant seamen. Perhaps the most famous of its seafaring men was Thomas Bowrey, a Wapping man who explored and traded in the East Indies, writing accounts of his adventures with pirates and cannibals. He lived in the square from 1691 to his death in 1713, compiling the first English-Malay dictionary, which was published in 1701. There were shipbuilders (Hugh Raymond in 1720) and affluent men of business, Jew and Gentile, silkmen and timber-merchants, some from Norway, Denmark and Sweden, like George and Ernst Wolf, the German-Norwegian brothers. Joseph Kell (d. 1745) was living there in the first half of the century; he had a deal yard in Woodbridge and owned several ships, kept pistols in his bedroom and had five caged canaries birds to sing to him. As the years passed houses were rebuilt and embellished, but some stayed the same. It was not long, however, before the square was 'spoilt for quiet living' and the houses dwarfed by the arrival of towering, smoking sugarworks.

The first sugar firm noted in Wellclose Square was that run by John Macklean and Rudolph Ireson in 1724–29. Many others followed. Carsten Dirs from Hoya near Hanover appeared in 1746–48. He had his 'dwelling house' in the square, a refinery (run in partnership with Carsten Holthouse) and a pub called the Prince of Denmark in one of the streets that ran off the square, Shorter Street. To begin with the refineries were in the streets off the square, but by the 1770s they were in the square itself, the ubiquitous sugarmen having started moving in during the 1720s. The 'fumes and stinks' of the refineries must have lessened the attractions of Wellclose. There were also the goings-on at the courthouse and its prison, and all the bustle of marine life. Recruiting for the navy at the King's Arms in 1771, Lieutenant Bryne had his pocket picked. But the juxtaposition of good living and working slum was a commonplace all over London and the square continued, for some years at least, to be regarded as desirable. In 1787 widow Elizabeth Dancer inherited a fortune from an aunt, and decided her house in Prince's Square was 'not good enough for a person of her family and fortune'; she planned a move into Wellclose.

Free spirits and intellectuals seem to have been drawn to this quarter; writers and colourful eccentrics kept strange company with the hard-headed men of commerce. Most strange, and most long-term of residents, was Dr Falcon, the Jewish cabbalist. In 1742 this learned and devout Jew escaped from Westphalia, where he had been sentenced to be burned alive. For forty years (1742–82) Baal Shem, alias Chayim Samuel Jacob Falk, alias de Falk, alias Dr Falcon (1708–82) practised his magic arts in his house in Wellclose, ran a private synagogue and received a stream of eminent visitors. Stories about his miracles spread like wildfire: it was widely believed that an incantation from the 'sorcerer' might fill his cellar with coal in an instant. Had you looked through the window at twilight, before the shutters were closed, you might have seen him sitting on a throne, wearing a golden turban, performing his rituals in a room lit by silver candlesticks. Dr Falcon was a rich man, and locals spoke of the gold he had buried in Epping Forest. Sometimes at midnight, it was said, he could be seen driving his coach hell for leather down the Mile End Road, muttering incantations, dressed in a long robe, his white hair trailing out behind him – on his way to inspect his hoard. Aaron and George Goldsmid, whom we met in Leman Street, were probably his closest friends. A story circulated that when Falk was dying he gave Aaron a small sealed packet, warning him that if he opened it he and his family would be cursed for ever. Aaron could not resist, and broke the seal to find the contents were papers with cabbalistic symbols. He died that day. It was no part of the contemporary gossip, but perhaps it is worth remembering that two of Aaron's sons subsequently committed suicide.

Prophetic dreams, angels, visions and miraculous powers were also the stock in trade of the Swedish mystic Emmanuel Swedenborg (1688–1772), who took lodgings in the square (among other places) during his visits to London, his favourite city. Like his Jewish neighbour, the Baron, as he was known locally, attracted a number of visitors who had heard of his powers: one such described him as 'an old fool who pretends to keep angels and spirits in bottles'. For some he was a clairvoyant who might put them in touch with their dead loved ones; others revered him as a great Christian mystic, a philosopher of a new brand of Christianity. The authorities in Sweden branded him as a heretic and, as a regular attender at the Swedish church in Prince's Square, he ruffled the feathers of the more orthodox pastors there. He had been a brilliant scientist who may have had a schizophrenic breakdown. Soon after his death Swedenborgian societies sprang up, and some still exist today; Prince's Square was renamed Swedenborg Square in 1938. At all events he was a kindly, gentle man, who kept sweetmeats in his pockets for children and lived simply on bread and milk, with the occasional dish of eels or pigeon pie.

Another occasional local resident in the 1770s–80s was an English eccentric, the wealthy tenant of No. 32, Thomas Day (1748–89). He was a child of the square, born there in 1748, the son of a wealthy landowner who was also a customs collector: the house went with the job. After an Oxford education he lived in Lichfield and had country estates elsewhere, but evidently used the Wellclose house as his London base. Day was a tall, dark, stooping, dishevelled man, notoriously lacking in any social graces, prone to 'long dismal catalogues' on the evils of women and endless discussions of metaphysics. Though he was called to the bar he never practised, and devoted his time to writing and radical politics. He was an avid devotee of Rousseau's philosophy, an animal lover, an abolitionist and a friend of negroes. This prophet of the Enlightenment was a member of that most exclusive and prestigious association of philosophers, inventors, scientists and manufacturing men, the Birmingham Lunar Society. Anna Seward, the Lichfield poetess, one of Day's circle, reckoned they only had any regard for him because he was rich. Day is remembered for his *History of Sandford and Merton*, credited as the first book written specifically for children, but best known for his extraordinary 'pygmalion' experiment, supported, apparently, by the Birmingham 'Lunaticks'. Having made a couple of marriage proposals and having been rejected, still aged only twenty-one, he took two pretty foundling girls of eleven and twelve, one dark, one fair (one from Dr Coram's celebrated hospital) and trained them up to suit his requirements, like Sophie in Rousseau's *Emile*. They were to dress as modestly as 'mountain maidens', eschewing luxury but adept at cultural discourse. He would choose between Sabrina and Lucretia (as he named them) when they were ripe and ready. To harden her up and make her as 'fearless and intrepid as Spartan wives', he dropped hot wax on Sabrina's arm and fired a pistol at her petticoats. The initial stages of this regime were carried out in London, presumably in Wellclose Square, and then the three of them went to Avignon. It all went awry. Lucretia was packed off to be apprenticed to a milliner on Ludgate Hill, and Sabrina married Day's old schoolfriend Thomas Bicknell. Day married a rich man's daughter, who promised to apply herself to improving reading and never to go to Bath.

Protestant nonconformity flourished in the cosmopolitan, free-thinking society of Wellclose. Dr Daniel Morton ran a small Dissenters' academy in his house in the square between 1744 and 1762. Dr Henry Mayo, prominent radical writer and pastor of the Independent chapel in Nightingale Lane, lived here from 1762 until his death in 1793. He was editor of the *London Magazine* and, from 1785, tutor at the Homerton Academy. With dinner parties at home every Monday night and frequent visits to gatherings held by the glitterati and literati, his seems to have been a fulfilled and comfortable life. Bated at one such gathering by the mighty (and very rude) Dr Johnson, for his notions of religious toleration, he maintained a 'steady perseverance', while the playwright, Oliver Goldsmith, lost his rag in the cleric's defence. For his 'calm temper' and failure to take offence Johnson dubbed Mayo the 'literary anvil', and presumably kept on hammering away at him. If Dr Mayo was happy in his worthy public endeavours and enjoyed his social networking among the intelligentsia, things at home were not so good. By the time he was thirty-six, and had lived in the square for seven years, he had lost two wives in childbed and was left with three little girls: Jane, aged four, Elizabeth, aged two, and baby Rebecca. He did not marry again and was clearly protective of his daughters, as we shall see for good reason. Elizabeth married a man called Adam Plowman, and when the good doctor was approaching death in the spring of 1793 he wrote a will that insisted Plowman should not touch a penny of the money he left Elizabeth from her mother's marriage settlement. The widowed husband of Rebecca was warned off similarly, and Jane, still single, was forbidden to marry without the consent of his executors. Aged twenty-one, Rebecca had taken off with a sailor, a neighbour in the square, one James Craigie; he was a widower originally from Orkney, much older than herself. They were married well away from home and from Dr Mayo's disapproval, in Hornsey chapel. Rebecca only survived a year after the runaway marriage, like her mother dying after giving birth to a baby girl. Jane was left at home with her father, who died within three years, leaving money for his granddaughter; this was 'never to be subject or liable to the debts, creditors, losses, control engagements of Mr James Craigie'. The residue of his estate was left to Jane, and just in case she too might succumb to an unsuitable marriage, or perhaps just to marriage at all, he specified that the interest on his capital was to be paid to her half yearly 'without receipt or concurrence of any husband'. She would lose her inheritance if she married without the consent of her father's executors. Succumb she did, moreover to her widowed brother-in-law Craigie, and without benefit of matrimony. A child was born to the couple, a boy, and only after that did they marry, in August 1797, just a couple of months after the birth. The wedding was in Marylebone in secret, one presumes so as not to forfeit

Jane's inheritance. Craigie died the following year. What happened to Dr Mayo's favourite daughter thereafter, her niece Rebecca and her son remains a mystery. One can imagine the gossip that went on around the tea tables in Wellclose Square and in the pews at the Nightingale Lane chapel.

Dr Johnson would have approved of the firm line his friend took with his wayward daughters. He observed to Mrs Thrale:

> Madam ... were I a man of rank, I would not let a daughter starve who had made a mean marriage; but having voluntarily degraded herself from the station which she was originally intended to hold, I would support her only in that which she herself had chosen; and would not put her on a level with my other daughters ... when there is gross and shameful deviation from rank, it should be punished.

Rag Fair

Walking for just a few minutes north from the fragrant gardens and well-polished interiors of Wellclose Square, you would find yourself among all the noisome clatter, shouting and trafficking of Rosemary Lane's Rag Fair, one of London's most colourful and notorious spots. Everyone knew of the East End's famous secondhand clothes market, which had been flourishing at least since Charles I's executioner sold his sovereign's pomander there. You could buy yourself new breeches, or any imaginable item of wearing apparel, for a fraction of the price you would have to pay a regular tailor. Not just 'penny rags' were to be had: on his escape from Newgate Daniel Malden, one of Dick Turpin's associates, bought himself an outfit there costing 45*s* (about £200 in today's money): a scarlet coat and a waistcoat with gold buttons, a plain hat and wig. You could pick up a whore (reputedly the cheapest in London); they hung round in doorways, their faces 'like crumpled parchment', their odour of 'tarpaulin and stinking cod' on account of 'continual traffic with seamen's breeches'. You could also dispose of ill-gotten gains.

Rosemary Lane was an ancient way, extending from Tower Hill to Ratcliff, known as Hache Street and then Hog Lane. How and why the name was changed in the seventeenth century is a mystery. Perhaps the overpriced bunches of rosemary on offer during the 1603 plague were sold here. The stretch from Church Lane to Prince's Square (Back Lane to Christian Street) was called Cable Street, because of the ropes made there, and the next stretch east (as far as Cannon Street Road) was Knockfergus, thought to have been so-named by Irish settlers in Elizabeth's reign. The market extended along Rosemary Lane and Cable Street, and was thus in the three parishes of Aldgate, Whitechapel and Wapping Stepney. Rocque's map (1745–46) shows three 'Exchanges' or market-places, the Great Exchange near the bottom of Mansell Street, opposite the Victualling Office, the

Old Exchange, and the New Exchange, side by side, set back from the road just near the bottom of Leman Street, between Mill Yard, where the theatre was, and Church Lane (now Back Lane). The houses in the lane were a mixture of old and new. In Blue Anchor Yard, at the west end, there were in 1694 five tenements, 'a parcel of unfinished houses' and thirty small houses. Richard Edgoose had a house here. Perhaps he was descended from the medieval limeman. The local watchhouse, with its cage, was located at the bottom of Mill Yard, at the heart of the market. The shops along the lane, some of them as small as dog-kennels, had canopies hanging over the footway to protect the 'old clo' from the weather. Gowns and breeches, coats and cloaks were hung out of windows and laid on the ground; the 'New Change' was described in 1739 as 'a Place like a Square where people bring old cloaths and lay them down for sale'. Artists drew the scene, and it even featured in popular songs. One ballad tells of a countryman who comes up to town to see the Crown jewels and the lions in the Tower. On his way he finds himself in a 'laneful of second hand taylors'. There are stalls with 'cheap left of cloaths for Spitalfields beaus', 'fustian frocks for bakers', ruffled shirts, children's bedlinen, stockings 'not darned above quarter', beaver hats 'for curates and Quakers', periwigs of all sizes and colours. Not only are clothes sold, but also stale bread and cheap stinking meat (mutton from Leadenhall and beef from Honey Lane); quacks have trays of pills, worm powders and corn plasters. 'Fast food' is on offer: 'sweet plum pudding, smoking hot, a groat a pound', pancakes fried in dripping, sausages and black pudding. And all among the smelly throng weave pickpockets and prostitutes.

All sorts of stolen goods were received and sold by the 'brokers' here. When Micajah Perry's tobacco warehouse in the Minories was raided in 1724 the tobacco was sold here. Thomas Blew stole a basket of loaves from Leadenhall Market and sold it at Rag Fair. Edward Overton of the pauper farm had two mahogany tables stolen in 1782, and they turned up at a broker's in the market, Elizabeth Hicks of No. 36. The landlord of the Blue Boar was well known for receiving stolen clothes, and the Sun and Wheathead harboured thieves. One of the numerous brandyshops was kept by the mother of Jack Sheppard's partner in crime, Joseph 'Blueskin' Blake. Next door to the Hayfield, a good place to pick up a prostitute, lived one of the major receivers, Isaac Alvarez Dacosta.

The market functioned every day except Saturday, the Jewish Sabbath, for this was predominantly a Jewish operation; although there were plenty of native costers (and criminals) around, and many alehouses were kept, and dwellings occupied, by the Irish. 'Down with the wild Irish' was the cry when a mob riot broke out here in August 1736: an Irishman called Grogram was reported to have eaten a cat alive for a wager in the Black Lion in Salt Petre Bank, just off the market. By Mayhew's day Rag Fair was all Irish, but until then it was mainly Jews who plied their trade. Rowlandson's watercolour, painted in about 1801, shows some of the signboards: 'Moses Moncera, Old Hats and Wigs bought sold or exchanged', 'Widow Levy dealer in old Breeches' and 'Most money given for Bad Silver' by Moses Estardo.

Over the eighteenth century the Jewish population of London rose from about 750 to 15-20,000, the majority, as we have seen, being Ashkenazi. By 1747/8 there was an Ashkenazi synagogue in Rosemary Lane. Patrick Colquhoun asserted that the immigrants were completely uneducated and mostly very poor. Barred from the City and the parish workhouse, many of them tradeless and unable to take apprenticeships with Christian masters, they lived by their wits, hawking anything that might make a few pence. All over London you might encounter them, with trays of oranges and lemons, sealing wax, clocks, cheap prints, buttons, slippers, glass ware, plaster statuettes, trinkets, ornaments and all sorts of bits and bobs. But it was for the sale of old clothes that they were best known. Colquhoun reckoned there were 2,000 Jewish old clothes men in London in the 1790s. It was a thriving trade. Off in the early morning they went to collect cast-offs from the better parts of town. Bearded and bedraggled, for the most part, some still sporting the long caftans and wide-brimmed hats they had worn at home, they were a common and striking sight all over London. The cry of 'Old Clothes' rang out as often as 'Stop thief'. With their carts and bundles they trudged back to Rag Fair, to stitch and mend, and lay their wares out ready to sell in the market in the afternoon. Trading and hustling went on until it was dark.

Changes

By the end of the century Whitechapel was fast hurrying towards the industrial slum that it was to become. The duckpond on the Green was filled in, the great windmill by the church was no more and the air was thick with the smoke from sugar refineries and breweries, while the great Essex road growled and rumbled by, carrying ever greater volumes of traffic. In 1801 the population was 23,666, with an overall density of about 139 people to the acre. This was less than Aldgate, St Giles, Saffron Hill and busy City parishes, but as Horwood's map shows there was still a good deal of open ground in Whitechapel, especially in the east side of the parish, so the City side would have been very overcrowded. The huddle and crush of housing, warehouses and factories on the City's eastern flank, which comprised Aldgate and Whitechapel, was as populous as one of the biggest cities in the country, Norwich. Tower Hamlets' Court of Requests, opposite Whitechapel church, was the busiest by far of the five London courts for small debts in the 1820s, hearing, according to one estimate, as many as 30,000 cases a year.

Many of the fine houses designed for aspiring living were converted to industrial use or pulled down and replaced by new manufactories, like Thomas Slack's sugar house on the west side of Mansell Street. There were more and larger factory operations: throwsters' shops, breweries, sugar refineries, a white lead factory, vinegar-makers, makers of colours, tobacconists, soapboilers, snuffmakers and starchmakers. Thomas Pearson, silk throwster of Leman Street, was employing 800 people in 1755, of whom a good number worked in his silk mill, others at home. Samuel Hawkins insured his silkworks, also in Leman Street, for £3,000, and James Montgomery, in partnership with Henry Dyson and John Anthony, insured No. 26 for the same amount in 1781. Two 'spinning grounds' with warehouses are noted in 1782, one in Great Garden Street and another in Mill Yard. The throwsters eventually left the area, as we shall see, but the sugarmen remained. In 1782 there were eight sugarhouses in the Leman Street area alone (three in Leman Street itself, two in Rupert Street, two in Lambeth Street and one in Buckle Street). Brewing flourished, as it had done since medieval times. Tickle and Williams had an enormous brewery in Castle Street for which they paid over twice as much land tax as the governors of the London Hospital. Charles Page had one in Great Garden Street and the Bullocks had a big brewery between Angell Alley and Brick Lane. Opposite the London Hospital was Samuel Liptrap's distillery, insured for £5,200 in 1777.

The splendid boulevards, Leman Street, Precott Street, Mansell Street, and the pretty squares were soon to be changed beyond recognition. In Goulston Square in the 1770s Daniel Pincot had a works where he produced artificial stone, while Wellclose was becoming overborne by the sugar refineries. The heyday of the Goodman's Fields development was over by the early years of the new century, and the wealthier members of the Jewish community were leaving for the West End. 'We hear', reported the *Hebrew Intelligencer* in 1823, 'that a well known gentleman has expressed his determination of quitting the neighbourhood of Goodman's Fields, which, he declares, no longer sufficiently select for him.' Some stayed on: Rebecca Mendes da Costa died there in 1840.

Weavertown: Spitalfields and Bethnal Green – 'a numberless range of buildings'

Let us set out for Spitalfields, turning off the Whitechapel Road just opposite St Mary's church (Altab Ali Park) and heading north up a narrow, muddy track called Durty Lane (Osborne Street; it was widened in 1778). This was the way into Brick Lane, and leads up to Ben Truman's brewery (a working brewery until 1988) and a dense industrial complex, where every other man is a silk-weaver, a throwster, a dyer, a twister, a patternmaker, a silk merchant, a mackler or a piece-broker (these were middlemen who sold silkwork to shopkeepers). Weavertown covered the land between the Old North Road out of Bishopsgate, the Whitechapel Road and Dog Row in Bethnal Green (Cambridge Heath Road), taking in Stepney's hamlets of Spitalfields and Bethnal Green. It absorbed the liberties of Norton Folgate and the Old Artillery Ground, took in the new hamlet called Mile End New Town and stretched north into Shoreditch. All this part of town was talked of as Spitalfields. It comprised, largely, land that had belonged to the priory known as the Spital, much of which had passed into the hands of the Wheler family of Buckinghamshire in the 1590s, and the St John's (Earls of Bolingbroke) and Stepney manorial land, sold off (1630s–'60s) by the impecunious Earl of Cleveland to pay his debts. The main thoroughfares within weavertown were Petticoat Lane on the west and Vallance Road (Baker's Row) on the east, with Brick Lane running north south. The centre of Spitalfields town lay to the west of the lane, around the market (where the Old Spitalfields Market is today) and the new parish church, Christ Church (now in Commercial Street).

It was not an unrelieved succession of textile workshops and weavers' houses, although there were a very large number. Bricklayers, plasterers and carpenters had come to the area to cash in on the building boom, Truman's brewery had a considerable workforce, and by 1740 there was a large sugarhouse in Brick Lane. Parish registers for 1730–35 show the usual range of other local occupations: tobacco-cutters, clock- and watchmakers, snuff-box-makers, brewery workers, distillers, coopers, braziers and smiths, founders, pewterers, plumbers, sandmen, bricklayers, stonecutters, turners, reedmakers, chairmakers, carmen, chairmen, coachmen, shoemakers, victuallers, vintners, butchers and herbmen, apothecaries, cheesemongers, poulterers, grocers, tallow chandlers, charcoalmen, stationers, wigmakers, barbers, postmen and market porters, sailors, attorneys, dancing-masters, schoolmasters, excisemen. As well as the ubiquitous weavers, dyers, throwsters and 'draw boys', there were staymakers, framework knitters, hot-pressers, tailors, woolcombers, pattern-drawers and hatters.

From the time of Charles I the number of houses and inhabitants in the Spitalfields hamlet was growing so much that in 1635 Stepney vestry decided that this northern part of the parish should have its own warden. A Dutch Huguenot was, appropriately, selected, one James Dantier/Dentier. By 1642/3 it was the third most populous of Stepney hamlets, after Limehouse and Ratcliff, and in 1650 it was populous enough to warrant consideration as a parish. The population of Spitalfields and Bethnal Green combined was probably in the region of 2,000.

Woollen cloth had been made here since the sixteenth century. In 1669 'the inhabitants of the pleasant locality of Spitalfields petitioned the [Privy] Council to restrain certain persons from digging earth and burning bricks in those fields, which not only render them very noisome but prejudice the clothes which are usually dryed in two large grounds adjoyning, and the rich stuffs of divers colours which are made in the same place by altering and changing their colours'. With the new fashion for silks, satins, brocade and velvet, a ready market in the lords and ladies who now came to town for the London season (October to April) and the *nouveau riches*, the weavers of these luxury fabrics joined the local textile industry and soon came to predominate. It was claimed that in 1661 there were 40,000 men, women and children employed in London as silk throwsters. Many of the silkworkers lived and worked in the immediate vicinity of Aldgate, Whitechapel, Bishopsgate and Shoreditch, whence they gradually spread towards Spitalfields.

In 1711 there were said to be about 500 houses in Norton Folgate, the Artillery and Spitalfields hamlet. By the late 1720s the place was quite transformed, with rows of new houses and humbler tenements-cum-workshops. Where cattle had grazed at the time of the Restoration was now one of the busiest of London's markets. Stepney's ancient parish church had spawned three new chapels of ease to accommodate the weavers and their families by 1711, one in Norton Folgate, one in Petticoat Lane and one in Mile End New Town, not to mention the numerous chapels erected by French refugees, and the home-grown Protestant nonconformist chapels that bore witness to the East End's traditional inclination to Dissent. Defoe reckoned that the whole of weavertown had 200,000 inhabitants in the 1720s. The hamlets of Spitalfields and Bethnal Green became so swollen that they were made parishes of their own, with their own large churches. In 1738 Christ Church was said to be a 'great and populous parish'. In 1760 it had 2,224 houses, guarded by seventeen watchmen and nine headboroughs, and lit by 235 lamps in the winter. Sleepy Bethnal Green would be changed beyond all recognition.

Walking around you would have heard the clack of looms from garret windows. This was no factory operation, although there were some large workshops; most of the weaving was done at home. Passers-by, shopkeepers and children playing in the streets might have been speaking in a strange tongue; even some of the scavengers spoke no English. Shop and inn signs proclaimed the presence of the foreigners: Le Chien Noir in Cock Lane (Redchurch Street), La Navette (the Shuttle) in Brick Lane, La Cloche in Booth Street (now part of Princelet Street). Shoreditch was 'Chardiche', Petticoat Lane 'Pettitcostelaine', and Truman's brewery 'Le Grand Brasserie'.

Protestant refugees from Catholic France arrived in great numbers from 1685, making Spitalfields their own and quite transforming the indigenous silk industry. These 'gentle and profitable strangers', according to tax records, constituted perhaps a quarter of the population in these parts in the following decades. The poor, however, did not pay tax: they rented a room, and might not appear in the records, even as tenants. The percentages might have been much higher. In an area of a few hundred acres the French had twelve churches of their own, of which two at least had seating for over 1,000 people. As far as the silk industry was concerned, the Huguenots made such a firm imprint that one might imagine there were no natives at all working at the loom. This was, of course, far from the truth: 'How many country weavers come daily to town', commented a journalist in 1719, 'and turn their hands to different kinds of work that they are brought up to.' By the 1730s there was an increasing number of Irish weavers and throwsters. One such was John Milton's son-in-law, Abraham Clarke, a weaver who came over from Dublin in the 1680s.

Brick Lane

Brick Lane, weavertown's main north south artery, has been so-called since 1550 or before, since the Spital's farmlands were dug up for bricks and loaded carts trundled down to Whitechapel. Even before the Dissolution the clay on priory land was used to make bricks; the southern part of Lolesworth Field, known as 'le bryk place', was let to Hugh Brampston in 1509–10. The Brampstons/Bramstones were brick manufacturers. Clothwork has been done around here certainly since the days of Elizabeth. What had been little more than a track across the fields at the time of the Armada was beginning, by the 1590s, to acquire some habitation: weavers' cottages and lodging houses. Stepney's parish clerk noted burials from the 'brick kilns' and 'the tenters'. When 18 acres between Wentworth Street, Petticoat Lane and Artillery Lane were sold in 1639/40 there were sixty-nine houses here, including the White Cock, the Red Cock and a bowling alley.

By the 1640s on the south-west side of the lane there were nurseries with currant bushes, a 'spinning ground', nineteen tenters and 'little houses' for the tentermen to keep their tools in. Lines of houses had already appeared in Rose Lane (now Commercial Street) and Wentworth Street, the latter named after the lords of the manor. In the 1650s houses were built along Brick Lane, starting on the east side, and new streets were laid out on the west side: Thrawl Street, Flower and Dean Street (in 1881 'perhaps the foulest and most dangerous street in the metropolis') and Fashion Street, named after the Fossan brothers who developed it. These were mean houses for the workers: tall, narrow, jerry-built properties with low rents of between £2 and £5 a year. Flower and Dean Street was only 10ft across at its west end, and the properties in Thrawl Street were all made of timber. John Jenney, the draper, whom we met having trouble collecting plague rate before the Civil War, built some houses in Rose Lane and Wentworth Street in the 1660s. He insisted that the tenants of one such should not be anyone 'who shal be or become burthensome or chargeable to the parish or parishioners of

Stepney'. When Sir Christopher Wren tramped around Brick Lane on foot in 1671, it being impassable by coach, he found 'adjoyning Durty lands of mean habitation', but brick houses with 'sufficient Conveighance for the water' were built on either side. Like so much of the development in seventeenth-century Spitalfields, the houses had been hastily thrown up by local builders and did not last very long. John Flower and Gowen Dean were Whitechapel bricklayers.

Among today's spangled array of neon signs, curryhouses and leather-shops there is still some trace of the mid-eighteenth-century weavers' houses and workshops. On the corner of Sclater Street stands a large tenement block built by developer and tallow chandler Peter Mansell in 1763–65. It is four storeys high, with fifteen rooms in all; shops on the ground floor, living quarters on the first and the rest intercommunicating workshops. Nos 125–27 was a similarly arranged large property, built in 1778 on the site of an earlier house, and occupied in 1720 by a weaver from Poitou called Peter Fromaget. This has been restored and, although it has lost its top floor it looks the part, with weavers' windows and a contemporary plaque: 'Here is Scalter Street'.

'A Spacious High way ... for passage of Carriages and Horsemen' was promised to John Carter when he applied for permission to build on the north-east side of the lane in 1671. Roque's map of 1746 shows Brick Lane as a wide road, sweeping through a squalid slumland of tiny courts and workshops. In 1771 the lane was paved, and described as a 'great thoroughfare for carriages'. One of the finest vehicles to be seen going up and down must have been the one from the Truman coachhouse, along with the lumbering dray-horses pulling their loads of barrels, brimming with the black porter that made Ben Truman a millionaire and a household name. The brewery then, as now, dominated the middle section of the lane, between Wilkes Street, Brick Lane, Quaker Street and Black Eagle Street. A brewhouse had been here at least since 1669. In 1694 it was taken over by Joseph Truman and much extended by Benjamin, who joined the firm in 1722. By 1739 it had 296 publicans on its books, and in 1766 was producing 83,000 barrels of porter a year.

Sir Benjamin, knighted in 1760 for his generous contributions to the war effort, built himself a mansion on the brewery site, which doubled as a dwelling and company headquarters. He was in residence there by the 1760s, having moved from his house in Princelet Street. This magnificent Director's House is still there (as is the house in Princelet Street), and Gainsborough's portrait of the Lord of the Lane hangs there in splendour. Apropos of the refurbishment of the house, done in the 1770s, he wrote:

> I think it proper to declare that the Motive for my laying out a very Considerable Sum of Money in Alterations and Improvements above mentioned is to make my House more complete for the Reception of Mr. and Mrs.

Villebois [his granddaughter and her husband] and their said two sons and to induce them to spend some part of their time in Spitalfields especially in the winter season. I need not enlarge on the pleasure it must give Mr. Villebois for tho' no sharer in the Management of the said Trade He will soon form an Idea from the regular manner in which the same is conducted how beneficial a Trade is carrying on And how comfortable a prospect there is for his said two sons my great grandchildren.

These two little boys, John and Henry, were also painted by Gainsborough: two little black-eyed children, resembling, no doubt, their French father, Villebois, who was a dancing master.

Around the brewery: a New Town

The area west of the brewery and stretching up north toward Bethnal Green was known as the 'New Town' for rating purposes. Streets here were first laid out in the 1650s and '60s: Wheler Street, Quaker Street, Black Eagle Street, Grey Eagle Street, Monmouth Street, Phoenix Street and King Street. The landlord was Sir William Wheler of Westbury, a friend of Pepys's patron, the Earl of Sandwich, 'a Comely Old Gentleman with a round plump Face'. Sir George Wheler (apparently no relation), who inherited part of Spitalfields via his father from Sir William, tells a story of how, aged sixteen, he was taken by his father to see Lady Wheler soon after her husband's death. It was September 1666 and young George, up from the country, was fascinated to see 'London lye in its ruines, the fire had not yet done smoking'. Presumably the visit was to negotiate with the widow, who was put out that her husband had left his property out of the family. The boy took his precious cage of songbirds as a present to appease the old lady. It does not appear to have done so. Lady Wheler obstructed the inheritance, but died in 1670.

The new houses were ill-constructed. Within sixty years an 'old ruined messuage' in Quaker Street had to be rebuilt, and 'ruinous houses' in the same street were rebuilt in 1735–36. In the meantime George and his father lost about half of their Spitalfields estate to Sir Charles Wheler, heir to the baronetcy.

Young George grew up to be a celebrated travel writer and antiquarian. A great advocate of the Huguenots, he went to France in 1681 to collect evidence of their sufferings. According to the diarist John Evelyn, George was 'a very worthy, learned, ingenious person, a little formal and particular, but exceedingly devout'. He entered holy orders and took his local responsibilities very seriously, endowing and building his own chapel in 1693, where he encouraged some services to be taken in French.

Mile End New Town

Off to the right of the lane, to the east, was Gurle's Ground, where the famous nursery had been, and beyond that another 'New Town' built for the weaving explosion, on land sold by the Wentworths in the mid-seventeenth century. This was Mile End New Town, 2 miles in circumference, lying between Old Montague Street, Vallance Road, Buxton Street and Spital Street. Building started in the 1680s, with a few houses put up in what is now Greatorex Street and continuing spasmodically. By 1690 there were enough people living there for it to be established as a separate hamlet of Stepney parish, acquiring in due course its own workhouse, parish officers, poor law officials and vestry house, in Spicer Street (now Buxton Street). The worthies of Stepney vestry, run by the rich men of the much superior Mile End Old Town, found this poverty-stricken weaving neighbour an embarrassment, a nuisance and a drain on their resources. It was a straggly place of jerry-built houses, with patches of open ground; the 12 acres left of Gurle's great garden were not built over until the end of the century. In 1792 there were 620 houses in all, most of them three storeys high with narrow 15 ft frontages: none remain. There were, presumably, like the Bethnal Green multi-occupation workshop tenements, several families in each house. Coverleys' Fields, on the north-east side of the hamlet (towards Vallance Road), seems to have been a sort of 'industrial park', with Truman's warehouses (1776–79), a large dyehouse (1745–58) and just a few scattered houses. In 1810 the rector of Stepney reported that Mile End New Town was 'crowded with poor'. It was not generally regarded as Huguenot territory: there was no French chapel, and it became mainly occupied by the Irish and English who came flocking in to find work in the silk industry. It was never a place for the quality, or, indeed, the middling sort, unless the family had come down in the world. Deborah, Milton's daughter, married an Irish weaver and they settled in Spitalfields. Reduced to poverty after his death, she went to live with her daughter, Elizabeth Foster, who ran a chandler's shop in Pelham (Woodseer) Street. The press got hold of her (Joseph Addison discovered her illustrious connections) and she sold her story, receiving a stream of nosey visitors at the shop. According to Voltaire, who heard about it on a visit to London, 'in a quarter of an hour she was rich'.

The little town did not get its own church until 1841. There had been plans to detach it from Stepney and add it to the new parish of Bethnal Green in the 1740s, but they came to nothing, and for a short time, towards the end of the eighteenth century, the new town had its own chapel of ease to Stepney church, with a school attached. The chapel was just south of Church Street, between Old Montague Street and the Whitechapel Road. By 1795 the chapel and the school had been taken over by the Methodists, and remained a Nonconformist chapel for years to come.

Mile End New Town has been swept clean; it became the direst of slums. Nothing at all is left that dates from this era: these days there are just a few Victorian cottages (Woodseer Street, Underwood Road and Deal Street) stranded among a positive wilderness of modern flats.

The west side of the Lane, north of Fashion Street, is a very different place, as we shall see. Before we go there we will make a closer acquaintance with the French families who made such an impression on the area and its industry.

The French

The French had been seeking refuge from popish oppression in Norton Folgate and Bishopsgate for over a hundred years, but the massive influx came with the Revocation of the Edict of Nantes in 1685. By 1603 Petty France, near St Botolph's church, was so called, and the names listed for Spitalfields in the 1642 Protestation Returns are one third French or Dutch. Louis XIV's campaign of religious persecution started in 1661 and refugees started to come in fairly small numbers. In 1671 Pearl Street (now Calvin Street, off Brick Lane) had three brick houses with workshops specifically designed for a French broadloom weaver. No doubt there were more.

Large-scale immigration started with the 'dragonnades' of 1681, when the French king had troops quartered in Protestant homes, smashing the furniture, torturing women, sending men to the galleys and abducting children if the occupants refused to convert to Catholicism. Refugees from France, reported an English pamphleteer, 'come hither in troops almost every day, the greatest part of them with no other goods but their children'. One of thousands was John Jacob Marmoy, a ribbon weaver from Metz, who came with his wife and children, and found lodgings in Phoenix Street, off Brick Lane in the 'New Town' area near the brewery. When their ship docked near the Tower, the *Impartial Protestant Mercury* reported that it carried 322 of those 'distressed, poor Protestants'.

In the spring of 1685 they started coming in droves, shiploads arriving at Dover, Rye, Southampton, Dartmouth and Plymouth. It has been estimated that between 1670 and 1710 over 50,000 refugees reached English shores and another 10,000 made it to Ireland. By 1700 there were about 20,000 of them in London, perhaps half in Spitalfields. The old Walloon and French church in Threadneedle Street (dating from 1550) had 8,000 people on its books in 1688, with a busy annexe in Spitalfields in a chapel called l'Hopital. Some 5 per cent of Londoners were Huguenots. At the close of the century there were twenty-eight congregations in and around London.

Mostly the immigrants were town-dwellers, artisans with little or nothing to their name, although there were some from other walks of life. Of the 13,050 who arrived in London in 1687 and noted by the French Relief Committee, 140 were 'quality', 143 ministers, 144 lawyers, physicians, traders and burghers, the rest being artisans and workmen. Many of them were silk-weavers, while some took to the weaving when they got to London. They were also renowned as clockmakers, papermakers, doctors and lawyers, but were engaged in all manner of trades and callings.

Back home workshops were closed down, French industry all but destroyed and the towns depleted. Under cover of night and in disguise the desperate folk made their escape. The young Dalbiacs were smuggled out in hampers; Captain James Dalbiac of Spital Square was a master-weaver with a considerable workforce. A Courtauld ancestor, a young boy, was brought out of the Huguenot town of Saintonge by a family servant, hidden in a donkey's pannier covered up with vegetables. If caught the men were sent to the galleys and the women to prison for life. Workers followed their masters; congregations came with their pastors, many from Brittany, Normandy and Picardy and from the silk-weaving cities of Lyons and Tours. In Lyons 12,000 men had worked making velvet and satin; in Tours a huge force of 40,000 had produced silk and taffeta.

How were they received? The climate of Protestant Dissent in this part of London was congenial; the congregation at the chapel in Bethnal Green's St John Street offered the immigrants the use of their place of worship. The influx, moreover, came at an opportune moment. Charles II had been battling with the Exclusion Crisis, an attempt by the Whig faction to prevent his Catholic brother, James, from succeeding to the throne. Anti-popish feeling ran high; the annual pope-burning procession, between 1679 and 1681, was sent on a detour round the east side of London, to stir up sympathy to a cause close to the heart of East Enders. The Earl of Shaftesbury, who masterminded the operation, is said to have looked especially towards Spitalfields for popular support, to exploit not only popular anti-popery but also the radical politics and frenzied distress of the weavers at the decay of their trade.

In 1681 Charles II, as a tactical measure, offered letters of denization (similar to permanent residency status today) free of charge, and further privileges and immunities. He also authorised a public collection on their behalf. 'We love you as a God on earth, for such you are,' proclaimed one pastor. People were 'especially liberal' in their giving when the new Catholic king did, indeed, take the throne (February 1685): 'They began to think it [persecution] might be their own case,' said White Kennet. For whatever reason, probably because of the force of public opinion, James II continued his brother's policies towards the Huguenots; a Royal Bounty fund was set up, with some individuals receiving as much as £1,000; and letters patent authorised the setting up of French chapels. In 1688 James was dispatched, and replaced by the Protestant William III.

Food, clothing and shelter were on offer from the French families who were already settled in London, and the churches in Threadneedle Street and at the Savoy gave succour and practical help. The Marmoy family received 4*s* a week from the Threadneedle Street church in 1698. There were soup kitchens and friendly societies sprang up; the Charitable Society of Saintonge and Angoumois still exists today. In due course French almshouses were built in Black Eagle Street for forty-five men and women, with pensions of 2*s* 3*d* a week, coal and clothes. The main Huguenot refuge, La Providence, the French Hospital, was in Finsbury. In 1723 there were 123 inmates, and the numbers rose considerably thereafter. Here they admitted the insane, the sick and poor widows. Among them were Louis Lardant from Normandy, paralysed by his 'douleurs' and transferred from the Bethnal Green madhouse in 1767, Henry la Roche, an asthmatic weaver (from 1752), Priscille Laurent, an eighty-two-year-old widow from Hog Lane (Petticoat Lane) crippled with rheumatism (from 1772). The hospital was munificently patronised: the most unlikely gift was sixty-three bottles of champagne, sent in 1787 by the Princesse de Lamballe, Marie Antoinette's best friend.

For ordinary Londoners the arrival of the Huguenots must have been alarming: the sheer numbers of foreigners swarming into their lodging houses and workplaces, renting houses and rooms, setting up businesses and shops left, right and centre, planting their chapels everywhere. Never had there been an invasion on this scale. But in the climate of anti-popery sympathy was widespread for the poor wretches who had suffered so much at the hands of a Catholic power, though probably more among the 'haves' than the 'have nots'. The diarist Evelyn spoke for the former:

> The French persecution of the Protestants, raging with the utmost barbarity, exceeded even what the very heathens used. The French tyrant demolishing all their churches, banishing, imprisoning, and sending to the galleys all the ministers; plundering the common people, and exposing them to all sorts of barbarous usage by soldiers sent to ruin and prey on them; taking away their children; forcing people to the Mass, and then executing them as relapsers.

Lady Rachel Russell, herself of French stock, wrote in a letter: "Tis enough to sink the strongest heart to read the accounts sent over: how the children are torn from their mothers and sent into monasteries, their mothers to another, the husband to prison or the galleys.'

It was not all plain sailing when they arrived, and although the Huguenots probably came in for less stick than subsequent immigrant groups it has to be remembered that Londoners were known for their xenophobia; they hated the French (with whom they were locked in battle for most of the century). On stage and in cartoons they were mocked as effete, puny, lantern-jawed poseurs.

Some might be deserving of pity, but they still took jobs that might have gone to Englishmen, worked for less money, seduced local women and generally did all the things that immigrants are usually accused of. As we have seen, 'Charles Lepoxon' and 'Jaques Monsieur' feature in the list of Spitalfields inhabitants in the Protestation Returns of 1642, surely rude nicknames. In the summer of 1683 there were riots against the 'trade abuses' of the French weavers; a troop of horse was sent into Whitechapel and the militia were out in Bishopsgate's Devonshire Square. Richard Welton, High Church rector of Whitechapel from 1697 to 1715, attacked the newcomers with ferocity: 'This set of rabble are the very offal of the earth, who cannot be content to be safe here from the justice and beggary from which they fled, and to be fattened on what belongs to the poor of our own land and to grow rich at our expense, but must needs rob our religion too.' 'No Jews, no wooden shoes' (the latter referring to Frenchmen) was the cry when the government proposed to naturalise foreign Protestants in 1753. Frenchman P.J. Grosley met with a 'volley of abuse at every street corner' on his visit to London, which he ascribed in part to the fact that the Protestant refugees 'reduced to beggary ... had ... exhausted the charity of the English'. At all events, though, considering the size of the invasion there was surprising little trouble, and the riots that plagued the industrial suburb on and off throughout the century were not 'race riots' but about wages and perceived threats to the weavers' livelihood. Without any doubt the Huguenots did great things for the economy and revived a severely flagging industry. The huge sums of money that had been spent on the import of 'English taffeties' from France (said to be 200,000 livres a year before the Revocation) now went into the pockets of Spitalfields masters, not all of them French. In addition quantities of brocades, silks and velvets were manufactured for foreign export.

Some complaints were made that the French only took on their own countrymen as apprentices, but, in the main these quiet, law-abiding, hard-working pious folk (not rough, drunken papists like the Irish, or strangely attired, like some of the Jews) settled in happily. Pastors made sure that children did not make too much noise in the streets and publicans were asked to keep an eye open for any French customers who drank too much. Strype claimed that the strangers 'may serve as patterns of thrift, honesty and sobriety as well', but he would say that; his father was a Huguenot, albeit Dutch, not French.

Rapidly the newcomers became part of their host society, those who had come with money and status becoming magistrates, vestrymen, tax commissioners, commissioners of sewers, officers in the army and navy and serving in the militia. Dr Andrée from Rheims was one of the initiators of the London Hospital and Colonel Peter Lekeux, along with many compatriots, was a hospital governor. Even the 'London's' windows were cleaned by a French widow's firm. It was a community led by good citizens, solid and respectable members of society.

Of the 134 'principal manufacturers of Spitalfields' who formed an association to send volunteers against Bonny Prince Charlie in 1745 (to 'manifest ... inviolable attachment to his [the king's] person and government') 95 were Huguenots. This is hardly surprising; the last thing the Frenchmen wanted was the Pretender to take the throne and impose a popish regime like the one that had dealt so cruelly with their parents and grandparents. Nevertheless it was quite a sacrifice for men of business: 1,736 members of their workforce were offered up. Of the silkmasters in Fournier Street, Peter Campart offered seventy-four men, Peter Bourdon promised twenty-eight, and there was a contribution from Judith Signeratt and her son-in-law, Gedeon Bourdillon. James Dalbiac of Spital Square put himself down for eighty.

The immigrants bred spaniels and pigeons, cultivated their gardens, growing tulips and dahlias, and held flower shows. Weaving garrets were hung with cages of linnets, goldfinches, chaffinches and greenfinches, which sang to relieve the tedium of the working day. Sunday family outings were taken to the pleasure gardens at old Ford and Bow. In the twilight old men might be seen sitting on their doorsteps drawing on a pipe, while the delicious aroma of French cooking wafted out into the evening air. 'Before the arrival of the refugees', wrote the Victorian chronicler Samuel Smiles, 'the London butchers sold their bullocks' hides to the fellmongers always with the tails on. The tails were thrown away and wasted. Who could ever dream of eating oxen's tails? The refugees profited by the delusion. They obtained the tails, enriched their *pots-au-feu* with them, and revelled in the now well-known delicacy of ox-tail soup.' Native neighbours, sitting down to a dish of the 'roast beef of old England', thought little of their culinary skills. As David Garrick (of Huguenot stock himself!) wrote at the beginning of the Seven Years War:

Beef and Beer give heavier Blows
Than Soup and Roasted Frogs

The Frenchmen were sociable and some were intellectually inclined, with a special interest in mathematics and science. Best known of the numerous Spitalfields clubs and societies was the Mathematical Society. Members first got together in a tavern called the Monmouth Head, Monmouth Street, in 1717, assembling on Saturday evenings to employ themselves 'in some mathematical exercise'. Anyone who could not answer a question posed to him by a fellow member had to forfeit 2*d*. James Leman, the celebrated silk designer of Steward Street in the Artillery Ground (1688?–1745), collected mathematical and musical instruments. Weaver John Dollond, founding father of the opticians, studied maths and astronomy in his spare time, and set his son up in an optical workshop in Vine Court.

Initially the strongest French presence seems to have been around the market, in the 'new town' area, north-west of Brick Lane in the vicinity of Truman's brewery, spreading over to the east side of the Lane into George Street and north into Bethnal Green's Hare Street and Fleet Street. There were French families in the Artillery, with only a few in Brick Lane itself in the early days. The two earliest known Huguenot chapels in Spitalfields were L'Eglise de L'Hôpital, on the corner of Black Eagle and Grey Eagle Street, and the Bethnal Green church of St Jean (much favoured by immigrants from Picardy) not far away, in St John's Street. The 'French Charity' headquarters was in Corbet's Court.

Mid-century Brick Lane, the brewery area and the west side of Bethnal Green appear, from the Maison de Charité records, to have been where most of the poorest Huguenots were living. The wealthier members of the community, masters and merchants, were to be found in the Old Artillery Ground in the early days, later in the smart new houses built in 1720s and '30s in Spital Square, Elder Street and Folgate Street, and in the streets around the new parish church: Church Street (Fournier Street), Wood Street (Wilkes Street) and Princes Street (Princelet Street).

Chapels proliferated. L'Hôpital, the first 'official church', set up in 1687 as an annexe to the established church in Threadneedle Street, initially at least seems to have been the busiest. The congregation grew quickly, and by 1765 they had to have a new building. One congregation met in the market itself, calling itself Du Marché, and there were two in Crispin Street, the main street on the west side of the market. These were the Crispin Street chapel (1693–1716) and La Patente, operating with a royal licence, which was there from 1689 or 1698 until 1740, when it moved to Brown's Lane (Hanbury Street). A congregation started off in Petticoat Lane (c. 1691–1701) under a reformed priest called Labourie, who subsequently got himself into trouble and fled to America. In 1695 Labourie alienated his flock, most of them moving to a new chapel at Parliament Court in the Artillery in about 1695, where the Sandys Street synagogue now is: this dates from 1870. There were an astonishing twelve French chapels in weavertown, and one in Wapping. Some held over 1,000 people; others were probably very small; of some we know virtually nothing. As well as the three described above, there were six more in Spitalfields itself. In Bethnal Green there were two in addition to St Jean, one in Slaughter (Sclater) Street (1721–35) and one in Cooks (Cock) Lane.(1731).

In 1742 a large and austere edifice, L'Eglise Neuve, the largest and grandest of the Huguenot churches, was built on the corner of Church Lane (Fournier Street) and Brick Lane. It is the only French church building that survives to this day, the celebrated monument to the changing face of Spitalfields. In 1815 it housed an institution for converting Jewish children, from 1820 to 1869 it was a Methodist chapel, then it became a synagogue and now it is a mosque. This fine new church, with a school attached and its cellars let to Truman's 'Grand Brasserie' for storage, was built to replace L'Hôpital as a daughter church to Threadneedle Street, and perhaps in a spirit of competition with the overpowering Christ Church nearby. But the heyday of the French church in Spitalfields was over. As the foreigners' children began to speak English as their first language, played with, and went on to work with and intermarry their native neighbours, the French chapels started to lose membership. Many journeymen and tradesmen were caught up in the whirlwind of John Wesley's new Puritanism, while merchants, masters, lawyers and doctors, and those who did well for themselves, might take their families to the smarter parish church: in modern terms, it was good for networking. Dr Welton and his High Church cronies apart, relations between the Church of England and the French church had always been quite cordial, and the form of service used in the French 'conformist' chapels was a translation of the English liturgy. Even Calvinist congregations started to adopt this form, as it mean that their pastor would be funded by the Royal Bounty.

The son of the first pastor of L'Eglise Neuve, Ezekiel Douespe, a good friend of Herbert Mayo, rector of St George's in the East, became a Church of England vicar. One of the first lecturers appointed at Christ Church when it opened in 1729 was John Dubourdieu, and there was a Huguenot organist, Peter Prelleur. John Rondeau, master-weaver of Wilkes Street, was the sexton for nearly thirty years (1761–90). David L'Heureux was organist at Stepney church, also at Hackney and Bow, where he rented a large house. Monsieur L'Heureux was rather full of himself and had to be told to cut down the length of the 'voluntaries and interludes' to which he treated Stepney's congregation on Sundays.

Of the twenty-eight French churches in London in 1730 only eleven were left in 1782. As early as 1715 the congregation at Crispin Street had dwindled from 1,200 in the 1690s to 170. Jacob Bourdillon, pastor for fifty years, deplored the feeble remnants of a congregation left to him when he preached at his jubilee in 1781. Sir Samuel Romilly remembered as a child, in the 1760s, being made to go with his family back to the Artillery chapel, as a 'sort of homage to the faith of his ancestors'. It was a dreary experience: 'A large uncouth room, the avenues to which were crowded courts and dirty alleys, and which, when you entered it, presented to the view only irregular unpainted pews and dusty unplastered walls; a congregation consisting principally of some strange looking old women, scattered here and there, two or three in a pew; and a clergyman reading the service and preaching in a monotonous tone of voice, and in a language not familiar to me.' The old chapels were deserted, and finally abandoned to English Nonconformists. The Artillery hung on until 1786, when it was taken over by Baptists, then the Unitarians and finally the Ashkenazi in 1890. St Jean was adopted as a chapel of ease to Bethnal Green parish church.

By the 1780s the French identity was disappearing. Hardly any of the refugees went back home. As Spitalfields went down, the successful moved into more salubrious parts of town, some to distinguish themselves in other walks of life and marrying into the English aristocracy. Masters were already leaving by the 1740s, and as the silk industry declined some operatives went north to the flourishing cotton manufacturing towns in search of work, or followed the departure of the silk-throwing industry to rural Essex. Mostly they disappeared into the morass of East London, with the tradition of pigeon fancying and aviaries on the roofs of Bethnal Green houses as a reminder of the days when 'Jacques Monsieur' ruled the roost.

The Weaving

'The English government had long envied France her possession of the silk,' wrote Samuel Smiles. Henry VIII had brought silk workers over from Rouen, and, in 1609 Robert Therie or Thierry was admitted to the freedom of the City, 'being the first in England who hath made stuffes of silk, the which was made by the silkworm nourished here in England'. In the event silkworms never prospered here, and raw silk was imported mainly from Italy. In 1629 the Silk Throwsters were incorporated, and ten years later, the ancient city company of Weavers started admitting silk weavers. By 1685 the English industry, mainly the making of ribbons and handkerchiefs, was well established in Bishopsgate, Whitechapel, Spitalfields and Shoreditch, also in Southwark, Westminster and parts of the City, with some 100,000 people, it was claimed, dependent on the trade in London at large. With the new wave of immigrants a terrific boost was given to the industry, which expanded twenty-fold between 1664 and 1713. In the last quarter of the century between 12-15,000 looms were at work, operated by some 30,000 weavers. The fame of Spitalfields drew weavers from other parts of London and indeed all over the country, including Huguenots who had initially settled elsewhere.

The skilled Frenchmen were expert in creating the wonderful flowered silks seen in dresses and waistcoats in the portraits by Gainsborough and Reynolds, and on show today in the Victoria and Albert Museum. These figured silks are said to have come originally from the Spitalfields workshops of three Frenchmen: Lanson, Mariscot and Monceaux. The leading artist who supplied the designs was another refugee, Christopher Beaudoin. The secret of 'Lustring' manufacture was brought from Lyons. This fine, glossy, black silk had been for some time a favourite with the English market; now it was made at home. The Royal Lustrings Company was incorporated in 1692, and an act was passed prohibiting the import of foreign lustrings and alamodes. Velvets, brocades, satins, heavy silks known as paduasoys, watered silks, black and coloured mantuas, ducapes, watered tabbies, and stuffs of mixed silk and cotton came off the looms of

Spitalfields. Although there was some smuggling in of prohibited French materials, home industry now dressed most of the fine lords and ladies at court, the gentry, the *nouveau riches*, and even, if we are to believe reports of the time, the wives and the daughters of butchers and bakers and candlestick-makers. Bales of silk were loaded onto ships sailing to the American colonies, whose direct trade with continental Europe was forbidden. Mary Dandridge, who married George Washington, is said to have worn gowns of Spitalfields design and manufacture. The probate inventory of Isaac Delaneuve, dated 1701, shows he had an extensive trade in Maryland.

The refugees soon taught the people of Spitalfields to create these fabrics. Of the leading men in the silk industry listed in Kent's *Directory* for 1740 under half have French names. The raw silk (which cost about 44s a pound in 1701) was usually imported by a silk merchant, who sold it through a broker to a silkman, who supplied the master-weaver. Either he or the silkman had it thrown (made into thread) and dyed. According to the author of *A General Description of All Trades* (1747), all throwing had been done by 'foreigners' in Elizabeth I's day. It was easy work and poorly paid, with women and children as young as seven much employed either at a 'factory' or at home. A member of the Merzeau family, French throwsters who had moved from Whitechapel to Spitalfields by 1774, described the throwing process: 'A drum, round about which a strap passes, embraced in its course two or three dozen clumsy bobbins, and returns round a small roller at the end of the mill to which a blind old man, fit for no better work than this, groaningly turns the drum around.' Girls were hired as winders for 3s a week at Spitalfields Market. Sometimes they worked through the night. Throwing soon left London for the country, where waterpower was used. In 1661 it was said that the Company of Throwsters oversaw 40,000 men, women and children; an exaggeration, no doubt, but there was a huge workforce. By 1823 there were only about a hundred in all London.

The mercer, perhaps with a West End shop, put in his order and the master-weaver then instructed his foreman, who measured out the warp needed. The journeyman weaver collected it from the master's shop or house. Isaac Campart of the Old Artillery Ground dealt for twelve years with a mercer called James D'Argent of St Swithin's parish. The weaving was done at home or in the master's garret, well lit with wide windows, on looms hired or supplied by the master. Thomas Poor had seven looms and four or five journeymen, who 'sleep in his shop'. It was piecework, and the weaver was paid at a certain rate per ell. Although women were not supposed to weave they usually did, and it was a family affair: small children helped at the minor tasks of quilling and picking. The size of the operation varied: there were small masters and large masters, and numerous humble workshops with only a couple of looms, one for the weaver and one for his wife.

The house of Thomas Short (d.1725) in Mile End New Town was probably typical of many. In the kitchen were the range and spit, some pewterware, a couple of brass candlesticks, a table and an old chest of drawers. Adjoining it was the bedroom, with a sacking bottom bedstead with 'China' hangings, a small feather bed, a chest of drawers, a deal table and some chairs. In the workshop on the first floor were three silk looms, one double wheel and jack, a chest of drawers and another bedstead (perhaps for Thomas's son, aged nine when his father died). On the next floor was another loom, a double wheel, a jack, a turner and bobbins. Thomas was worth £8 17s in all, with £1 12s owed to him by a relative for 'shop goods'.

This 'mobbish part of London'

Rioting, so common in late seventeenth- and eighteenth-century London, was a regular feature of Spitalfields life; the quote above, describing weavertown, is from Horace Walpole. Bands of weavers often took to the streets in their thousands to express their grievances. Francis Belin, a French weaver, kept a store of eighty pistols in his house, and the militia was always on the alert.

When orders for silks stopped coming in, as they did if fashion suddenly changed (to a preference for muslin, for instance) or the court went into mourning, looms were 'put up' and journeymen's families, as one doctor put it, were left 'without fire, without raiment, without food'. The industry was known for its extreme fluctuations occasioned by a variety of circumstances: ships might be prevented from bringing in the precious raw silk, there might be military action or bad weather; manufactured silk smuggled in from France might ruin the market. Masters were known to go bankrupt; between 1710 and 1770 eighty-three Huguenot masters did. Like their descendants at the dock gates in later years, men looking for employment gathered inside the railings before the church on Monday and Tuesday mornings in the hope of being hired. One week there was roast beef; the next it was off to the soup kitchen. When things were bad the weavers, men and women, took matters into their own hands. As Grosley, a visitor to London, and many others observed, journeymen and mechanics had grown 'insolent' in their prosperity. When wages fell or work was wanting, 'They enter into associations, they refuse to work, they revolt.'

The community was in uproar in 1675 when engine looms came in. 'In the year 1697,' wrote Noorthouck, 'the silk weavers in London grew very tumultuous and outrageous, on account of the great importation of silks, calicoes, and other Indian manufactures, imported by the East India company, and worn by all sorts of people. They even attempted to seize the treasure at the East India house.' During the better-known calico riots of 1719 women who were wearing cotton had their dresses soused in ink and acid, and mercers' shops selling foreign stuffs had their windows smashed. In 1765 a great procession of weavers, with banners and flags flying, marched to parliament when the king was there to give his assent to the Regency Bill, protesting that they were reduced to starvation by the import of French silks. When silk sales slumped in the 1760s the workforce was reduced by half and piecework rates were cut. The distress was acute and weavertown was in panic; the 'cutters' were abroad. Bands of weavers, run by 'committees' of journeymen, broke into workshops and houses, cutting the silk from looms if the operatives had agreed to a cut in wages. Cutting was done both as a punishment for weavers who accepted a lower rate of pay and as a way of forcing master-weavers to pay into their 'union' funds. The usual rate was 6*d* per loom, although as much as 2*s* or 4*s* might be demanded. It was all highly organised, with the various branches of the trade represented by different committees: 'The Bold Defiance' for the half-silk, half-worsted weavers, the 'Dreadnought', for the broad silk workers, the 'Independent' and the 'Sloop'. After dark in the Northumberland Arms in the Artillery's Gun Street, the White Horse in Wheler Street, the White Hart in Vine Court, both in Spitalfields parish, and the Dolphin in Bethnal Green's Cock Lane, masked members of the committee waited in an upper room. In the crowded tap rooms below the weavers gathered, and one by one went up the stairs to pay the dues demanded. Each was given a written receipt; those for the 'Bold Defiance' bore the tag 'Success to trade'. If they fell behind with payments for two consecutive weeks, their looms were cut. Thus was Spitalfields held to ransom. In 1766 cutting was made a capital offence, but still it went on.

Houses of the principal manufacturers were attacked, even if there were no looms inside and threatening notes were pushed under their doors. In the early hours of one summer morning Peter Auber, master-weaver of Spital Square, received one from the 'Defiance Sloop' demanding that he should pay 6*d* per week for each of his workers: 'We give you now an Egg Shell of honey, but if you refuse to comply, we will give you a gallon of Thorns.' In the summer of 1769 Lewis Chauvet of Crispin Street (a large-scale manufacturer of silk handkerchiefs, director of the French Hospital and a governor of the 'London'), had had enough. He offered a £500 reward (enough to keep a family for life) for information leading to the arrest of committee members. Two men came forward: Thomas Poor of Shoreditch, an Irishman, and Daniel Clarke of the Artillery. The finger was pointed at John Doyle and John Valline/Valloine, among others. Poor claimed he had been 'reduc'd to penury' by the committees' activities, but he had another axe to grind. What prompted him to shop the cutters was a private quarrel; it was only when Doyle got Poor's wife Mary put into the Bridewell for assaulting him that he went scuttling off to the 'Blind Beak', magistrate Sir John Fielding, to claim his reward. Mary said it was she who went. The cutters took reprisals, attacking Poor's looms on 8 August, cutting the silk on thirty-six of Chauvet's looms and smashing up Daniel Clarke's house and workshop in Artillery Lane. This last raid was led by Thomas Haddon, a tall man disguised as a woman wearing a black bonnet and talking in a squeaky female voice. Some particularly fine garnet satin with 'leopard spots' was destroyed.

The authorities took action. On 30 September, between 9 and 10 p.m. at the Dolphin, the usual assembly of journeymen and cutters was raided by Sir John Fielding's men, with soldiers for support. One was shot and killed in the fracas. The weavers got out of an upstairs window and escaped over the rooftops, all except one Daniel Murphy, who was found shivering under the bedclothes in the landlord's bed, with a blunderbuss beside him and a note in his pocket from 'the Conquering and Bold Defiance': 'Gentlemen, Send you [*sic*] Donation this Night to the Dolphin ... at this time you must either conquer and flourish or starve and perish ... and will be for ever bond slaves ... support the just Cause in hand and assist those innocent men who is cruelly and falsely swore against.'

On 6 December John Doyle and John Valline were hanged outside the Salmon and Ball in Bethnal Green as a dire and terrible warning to the locals. Doyle, with the rope around his neck, protested his innocence to the last: 'Let my blood lie to that wicked man who has purchased it [his death] with gold, and them notorious wretches who swore it falsely away.' That day a mob of between 4-5,000 attacked Chauvet's house: 'Pull the house down! Hang him!' Daniel Clarke was subsequently stoned to death by the mob.

How much this was 'trades union' activity and how much gang warfare between rival journeymen is difficult to say. Rudé claimed it was the latter. Certainly there is no record of the funds accrued (said to be over £1,000) being used to support those in need; probably it was used to hire the room, buy the pistols, cutlasses and knives, and other necessary expenses. In due course the weavers won their battle. Following further agitation in 1771 the famous Spitalfields Acts of 1773, 1792 and 1811 (in force until 1824) brought in wage and price regulation that calmed things down. In the long run this legislation paralysed the industry, and sent the weavers off to other parts of the country that were not subject to the statutory rules.

By the end of the century Spitalfields silk-weaving was past its prime; it would struggle on still manned by the descendants of the refugees with more and more Irish and poor folk coming in from the English countryside. The last prosperous time for the industry was the boom that followed in the wake of the Napoleonic Wars (1816–26). Unable to cope with competition from France and from the new cotton manufacturers of the north it collapsed in the 1830s. In 1834 1,000 houses stood empty in Mile End New Town. The final death blow was dealt in 1860 when a treaty with France allowed the import of French silk. Many redundant silkworkers went to the docks; the women, most of them, becoming part of the notorious Whitechapel sweated industry, the 'rag trade'.

The poor

It is a nice story – that of the clever, thrifty, Huguenot housewives inventing oxtail soup – but who would eat cows' tails if they could afford something better? Overwhelmingly the people of weavertown were poor, especially in Mile End New Town and Bethnal Green; English, French and Irish alike – 'The manu-facture being a continual refuge for the indigent and distressed', as petitioners to the Lustring Company put it in 1695. Even when the industry was booming and regular work was to be had, wages were low for the ordinary weaver who made handkerchiefs, ribbons and plain broad silk, perhaps only 10s a week. It was the skilled man who produced the elaborate patterned materials who made the money (perhaps a guinea a day), and a master might 'live quite handsomely' said the author of *A General Description of All Trades* in 1747. A velvet weaver of French descent recalled in 1838: 'There was never a time in my recollection when some in the weaving trade could not earn very large sums and others next to nothing.'

The weaver was a byword for poverty. He was pale from long hours confined in his garret and prone to arthritis, his fingers sore and bent from the fiddly work. Families were small, with rarely more than two surviving children to a household; many died in infancy. Milton's daughter Deborah lost eight of her ten babies. Children might be put to work at the age of six or seven, filling their fathers' quills and picking the silk clean. Weavers were, or became, a 'diminutive race'; 'Hardly a man or woman above 5ft 4in among them', noted Charles Booth's researcher when watching the crowd at a Bethnal Green funeral in 1898, the result of generations of deprivation, no doubt. Even their heads were said to be smaller than everyone else's. Poet John Bancks, himself a Spitalfields weaver said he was:

> Branded with Weaver's odious Name
> Thro' all the World, a Mark of Shame

He dreamt of having a country seat, with a cosy wife to share it, but:

> rigid fate condemned me to the Loom;
> Of all she utters, sure the hardest doom.

His 'slim volume' was sold at John Knotts at the sign of the Queen's Head in Dorset Street, just south of the market (Duval Street in 1952, now gone), for 6*d*.

Contemporary references to the poverty of the area abound. In 1693 and 1696 the 'great distress' of Spitalfields weavers was publicised; in 1729 Spitalfields parish was 'burdened with a Numerous poor', with 'great decay of trade and fall of rents'. By the 1740s houses were being divided into lodgings and in 1754 the old workhouse was replaced by a larger one in Mile End New Town. In 1774 the poor of the Old Artillery Ground were said to be 'lately much increased', and the Christ Church vestry clerk in 1807 wrote of 'the very peculiar Circumstances' of Spitalfields and Mile End New Town, which were inhabited almost entirely by 'poor Persons'. In 1814 £11,000 was spent on poor relief.

Some grim tales are to be told of poverty and despair. John Bedford, the hatter, lived in Corbets' Court (where the brewery leisure centre now is: tourists sitting there sipping their beer might give him a thought). Business was slack and he was 'in poor circumstance'. His wife had been taken off to hospital, probably to the 'foul ward', leaving him with a tiny baby girl to cope with. The child cried all night and drove him distracted; he flung her on the bed, crying 'Be damn'd you bitch and cry till you burst!' He went from one neighbour to another trying to get someone to nurse his daughter for the small amount he could afford (1s 6d a week). At only six or eight weeks baby Jane died and her father, unable to apply for free burial locally, having undertaken not to let the child become a burden to the parish, smuggled the body off to Bethnal Green. With the help of friends there she was buried under an assumed name. As might be expected questions were asked about the child's death, and the father came under suspicion for starving and beating the little mite. Neighbours were divided in their opinions: Sarah Barnes, a soldier's wife and an old acquaintance, said he was a fond parent: 'If he had three farthings' he would buy a half quatern of sugar for the baby. He was acquitted.

For the most part people managed. Most weaving families had but one room to sleep, eat and perhaps work in, for which they paid about 1s a week. Dr Johnson was told that a man of the middling sort might live in a garret at 18d a week, so the lot of the poor was not quite as removed from his superiors as might be imagined. Rarely did anyone actually starve, and there was always the soup kitchen, some small sums available from the parish (for the French from various charities), the pawnbroker, almshouses for a few, the workhouse if need be, and, then as now, a chance to win on the lottery. A hopeful author submitted an oft-told lottery tale to the *Spectator* of 7 December 1711. The wife of an idle, drunken weaver had saved up to buy a lottery ticket. While she was out he went rootling around looking for cash and came upon the ticket hidden in a trunk. He sold it. In the meantime the wife found out that her number had come up with the amazing prize of £500. Excitedly she shouted up to her husband in the garret, calling him down to have a drink to celebrate their good fortune. When she learned the truth she fainted away, and 'is now run distracted'. The author thought it might make a good play.

The soup kitchen has a long history here. In the 1670s a Mr Emson kept a 'café' (a victualling house) with a takeaway service in Folgate Street (White Lyon Yard), where poor weavers and throwsters went at 9 a.m. for 'Messes of Broath'.

The Maison de Charité, set up in 1689 in Corbet's Court, provided food and sometimes shelter for Huguenot families with young children and for the old and destitute. It was known as 'La Soupe' or the 'Bread House'. In 1797 a soup kitchen for needy families was opened in Brick Lane, where soup was sold for a penny a quart and potatoes at 2*d* for 15lb. A plaque now marks the spot.

On Sunday evenings many a weaver's wife went off to the pawnshop. The brokers, of whom there were a great number, many weavers themselves, did a good trade, not least in stolen goods. When a Spitalfields girl was suspected of stealing two prayerbooks from St Paul's a couple of vergers went on the rounds of the local pawnbrokers, and found the missing items in one in Paternoster Row (Brushfield Street). Hannah Killgrew pawned 17yds of velvet that she had stolen, the property of James Dalbiac, master-weaver of Spital Square. In Fashion Street a pawn business-cum-chandler's was run by an elderly Welsh widow called Margaret Williams, rich enough to attract the attention of a man in his twenties. Daniel Thomas, also Welsh, a lowly porter in a city china shop, came to Fashion Street on his master's business and, with an eye to the main chance, courted her. The old woman and the young man were married at Christ Church in November 1757, keeping it from the widow's daughter and son-in-law for several months. For eight years they lived happily enough, and then the old lady died. Daniel being, as his maid reported, 'of a very covetous and avaricious temper ... always continually enquiring and seeking after any old woman that had a great deal of money', quickly set his sights on another rich widow. She turned him down, and he turned his attention to yet another, Mistress Horner, who ran the Dolphin in Whitechapel. Preparations were made for a wedding, but Daniel was taken ill and died. As he was illegitimate and a childless widower, his estate was liable to be confiscated to the Crown. A good deal of money and property was at stake, and an expensive and protracted lawsuit ensued at Doctors Commons, with all sorts of tricks pulled out of the bag by neighbours and others hoping to cash in. A Fleet marriage was invented, with a girl called Kitty Hill put forward as the pawnbroker's true wife and heiress, and a whole gang of witnesses was called, including another pawnbroker from Thrawl Street, Robert Eyre.

James and Ann Merceron, parents (probably) of the notorious Bethnal Green extortionist Joseph, made a mint at their pawnshop in Brick Lane and became property developers.

The Old Town, the market, the new church, Fournier Street and its neighbours

Leaving the brokers counting their money, and the poor weavers in their garrets, we will take a turn around the smart part of the town to the west of Brick Lane (around Christ Church and today's Old Spitalfields Market) and take a look at the heart of Spitalfields. Here there were the market, the 'town hall', a huge new parish church (1714–29) and elegant houses, built in the 1720s and '30s and occupied by master-weavers, silk merchants, lawyers, bankers and the clergy. Many of these houses still stand. Of all London, the long-gone world is best observed in these few, magical streets: 'Some of the Georgian doors might open at any moment, one feels, to allow a silk merchant in knee breeches to step forth.' There are no wide boulevards like those in Goodman's Fields, nor any properly laid-out squares like Wellclose. Streets are narrow but straight, unlike other parts of Spitalfields, where lanes and alleys still wander about in the old-fashioned way. The new houses were of dark red brick, three storeys high, good sized with about ten rooms, some plain, some ornamented, according to the taste and status of the occupants. The famed 'weavers' garrets, the top storeys with wide windows to let in maximum light, are in the main later additions.

The new estates lay to the north and to the east of the market-place, the former around Spital Square in Norton Folgate, the latter near the church. On the west of the market was the Old Artillery Ground, favoured by the masters of the silk trade before the new estates were built. The market area was the hub of the parish, with its 'town hall', almshouses and a cluster of French chapels. Since 1669 the meeting place for the hamlet (a parish from 1729) had stood in Crispin Street, the busy street that in those days ran along the west side of the market-place. A watchhouse occupied the ground floor of this public building and the upper room was used for meetings. It was in Crispin Street, at No. 39, where the silk manufacturer Lewis Chauvet (whom we met in the cutters' riots of 1769) had his dwelling-house and workshops.

On Thursday and Saturday the streets round here were lined with carts and thronged with traders in all sorts of provisions, which they sold from stalls or 'sheds' in the paved market-place, or from shops in the rather splendid market house, a cruciform structure with deep-pitched roofs, Doric columns and tall clocktower. At the south-east corner there was a slaughterhouse. Richard Skelton, who had a 'green shop' in Rag Fair, bought his vegetables at Spitalfields; Elizabeth Craydon bought potatoes in the market to 'sell about the streets'. All among the hubbub of herbwomen and butchers, mealmen and bakers, there were a number of children and young folk. This was weavertown's 'employment exchange', where girls and boys 'stand to be hir'd'. Thomas Beck, the young sailor's son who played truant from school and was hanged for highway robbery in 1732, was put into the market by his desperate mother after he had embarked on a life of crime in his early teens. He was hired, briefly, to draw worsted damask for 3s 2d a week, but ran away.

Looking along Paternoster Row (now Brushfield Street), on the south side of the market, you could see the towering white edifice of the new church. Early in the morning the steeple-keeper rang a bell to get everyone out of bed and to work:

A Quarter before six I ring my Bell,
As every honest labouring Hand can tell:
The Porters, Joiners, Bricklayers, Market Folks,
Are all in Arms, and crack their harmless Jokes:
The jolly Dyers, now, whose gaudy Trade,
Decks both the Duchess and the Chambermaid;
Wak'd by my Bell they straightway quit their Room,
And then prepare their colours for the Loom.
The Weavers, Draw-boys, Throwsters now arise,
Jump up in bed and rub their sleepy Eyes,
Slip on their cloaths and then to work they hie,
Nor think it time to lay their Labour by,
Till eight at Night, I give them their Dismission,
And then they homeward go by my permission.

Christ Church was consecrated in 1729 as parish church for Spitalfields, its enormous size, height and splendour bringing a new grandeur to the area. New streets were laid out on its northern side, lined with desirable properties. These were Church (now Fournier) Street, Wood (now Wilkes) Street, Princes (now Princelet) Street (the part west of Brick Lane) – some of the best-known streets in modern London, built all of a piece between 1718 and 1728. The developers were two wealthy lawyers, Charles Wood and Simon Michell, who had bought this part of the Wheler estate. Much of the work was done by local carpenter Samuel Worrall, who became a gentleman thereby, lived in one of his own houses and consorted with the prestigious Le Keux family and pastor Bourdillon.

From time immemorial Spitalfields had belonged to Stepney, becoming a separate hamlet in the early part of the seventeenth century. By the opening of the eighteenth century Stepney was an unwieldy parish, with only one church, and four or five chapels of ease servicing its 86,000 souls. St Dunstan's, Stepney, was a good walk from Spitalfields and Bethnal Green, and before they got their own churches some of the families of weavertown had made use of Shoreditch church, the small chapel of ease in Petticoat Lane, or the wooden proprietary chapel erected in 1692 by landlord Sir George Wheler on his estate in Norton Folgate, just off White Lyon (Folgate) Street. The building of the Wheler chapel proved to be a troublesome venture, much opposed by the Bishop of London, who only agreed to consecrate the chapel if one Luke Milbourne was put in as minister. Sir George, who was in holy orders himself as well as being lord of the manor, tried to run the show, deciding the form of services and even taking them himself. There was a major incident in 1695 and Milbourne took half the congregation off with him, holding services in a local shop. A petition went to parliament asking for a proper chapel of ease or a church for Spitalfields. By 1792 there was a school for twenty boys and twenty girls attached. After the building of Christ Church the chapel continued to function; with only a handful of baptisms a year, it seems to have been used by only a few families. No doubt the wishes of the inhabitants of Spitalfields hamlet was taken into consideration when it was decided that they should have their own parish church.

Stepney's hamlets had been virtually autonomous for some years; a proper division of the parish had been mooted in 1650 but came to nothing. In 1711 the decision was made to make three of the hamlets into parishes: Spitalfields, Limehouse and Wapping Stepney. Bethnal Green and Poplar were on the original list, but they would have to wait. By Act of Parliament £350,000 was voted by the newly elected High Church Tory government for the building of a number of 'Blenheim' churches in London, in celebration of the Duke of Marlborough's victories and in response to a plea from the people of Greenwich, whose church roof had fallen in. The money was to be raised by a tax on coal that was brought into London; this grand gesture on the part of the government would remedy the church's severe accommodation crisis as well as stemming the tide of Nonconformity, or so they thought. It was decided that fifty churches were needed, five being allocated to Stepney. The basis was one church for every 4,750 people. In the event only twelve were built in all, three in Stepney, one of which was Christ Church. Nicholas Hawksmoor, a pupil of Sir Christopher Wren, as surveyor to the 'Commissioners for Building Fifty New Churches in London and Westminster and their suburbs', was to design the three new East End parish churches. They were giants, towering above the humble rooftops of the East End. They proclaimed the victory of the British in Europe, and of the mighty Established Church over the creeping malaise of Dissent.

Building work started on Christ Church in 1714, on a site where there had been four tenters, a spinning ground and some old 'ruinous and ill-tenanted' tenements. After hitches and complications (including a pitched battle when cut-price Irish labourers were employed) the church was finally consecrated on 5 July 1729. It was Hawksmoor's most extravagant and most expensive church, costing about £40,000, including the parsonage house; the original estimate had been just over £9,000. The churchyard extended from Brick Lane to Red Lion Street. It had a 'best ground,' a 'middle ground' and a 'poor ground'; the latter had to be extended in 1791. One critic described Hawksmoor's church as 'one of the most absurd piles in Europe'. Herbert Pritchard, who had been serving as Stepney's 'Spitalfields Portionist', was made rector. There were two lecturers, one Huguenot, John Dubourdieu, and John Lewis, and the curate, Thomas Wright, came from St Dunstan's. The clerk of Stepney parish got £16 by way of compensation for fees lost.

The rectory was a grand house, built in 1726 at a cost of £1,456 8s 10d. It was the first house built in a new street, named Church Street (now Fournier Street), running along the north side of the church. It is still there (No. 2 Fournier Street) as are all of its fine neighbours. These days this is Spitalfields' most famous street, almost completely Georgian, with the best houses on the south side. They were built as residential properties but started to be used commercially by 1743. No. 14, Howard House (1726), is the prize. Sydney Maddocks, writing in the 1930s, waxed lyrical:

> The handsome staircase is carved in hardwood. Fluted columns with Ionic capitals are placed on every turn, and the balusters are each varied in a slight degree from one another, the different lengths, too, giving variety. There are a hundred stairs and each one is deeply carved at the end with a triangular design of hops, barley, and wild roses. The spacious hall is panelled and from it there is a vista of where once a garden smiled but where now all is forlorn. When the day is done and these business premises are left in solitude, the old hall and the stairs could very well become quaint Fancy's playground, where
>
> ... if you lie in hiding
> And hardly breathe at all
> You will see the grey-clad weaverfolk
> Like shadows on the wall,
> Dim shadows on the moonbeams
> Of people of old France
> Come trooping from the attics –
> Salute, chassé, advance.

The 'people of old France' who lived and worked in this house mid-century (1740s and '50s) were the French weaving firm of Signeratt/Seguret and Bourdillon. Weaver Gedeon Seguret lived in the Old Artillery Ground. He died in 1732, leaving his estate to his wife, Judith and his two daughters, Judith and Mary. He was quite a rich man with a house in Club Row, let out to a French widow. His widow evidently continued the business, as many Huguenot widows did, moving into Fournier Street and joining forces in due course with Mary's husband, Gideon Bourdillon, brother of pastor Jacob.

At Nos 4 and 6 was, in 1750 and 1766, Peter Campart and Company, weavers of 'striped and plain lutestring mantua and tabby'. This firm was a large enough operation to offer seventy-four of its workers to fight against Bonnie Prince Charlie in 1745. Campart's personal estate was estimated at £44,600 at his death in 1772

(£2 million today). At No. 10 was James Lardant in the 1750s, a weaver of 'silk, mantuas and tabby', and at No. 12 in 1750 was George Garret Esq., an English master-weaver and a trustee for the Spitalfields almshouses. On the other side of the road at Nos 23 and 25 were Reuben and John Foxwell, worsted stuff-weavers (in 1743 and 1773) and in the fine house at No. 27 (formerly No. 21) was master silk-weaver Peter Bourdon (d.1732), headborough of the hamlet in 1712, his wife Margaret and his son Peter, with whom he was in partnership. Bourdon made enough money to buy himself a country mansion in Dagenham, to buy a lease on a Princelet Street house for his daughter and son-in-law, a family vault in Christ Church and to leave his wife £3,500 (£400,000 today), property apart. Peter junior lived on in the house after his father's death for some twenty-five years. In 1759 the house was occupied by Obadiah Agace, a weaver of silk mixed with worsted.

Fournier Street is much celebrated for its weavers' houses, but there were also a number of clerical residents, the rector apart. Along with the textile 'millionaires' lived many of the pastors who tended their French flock and officiated at L'Eglise Neuve, which stood at the Brick Lane end of the street. Gedeon Patron, minister and secretary of the Threadneedle Street church, was the first occupant of No. 1 on the north side and later lived at No. 33 (in 1766). At No. 37 (references date from 1766 and 1783) lived the kindly Jacob Bourdillon, brother of the weaver at Howard House and minister of the French churches in Petticoat Lane and the Artillery. His well-appointed house was probably one of the 'temporal ... favours incomparable' for which he gave 'a thousand thanks to [his] creator'. At No. 12 (at least between 1759 and 1766) lived Benjamin Francois Houssemayne du Boulay, born in Paris, minister of the Threadneedle Street and probably of L'Eglise Neuve. His neighbours at Nos 20 and 33 were also ministers at the two churches, Louis de la Chaumette (in 1766) and Paul Covenant (in 1759).

The French pastors were much more of a presence in Fournier Street than the Anglican clergy. The rectory probably often lacked its master, with only the servants left to keep it in order for his return. John Prichard, who was rector from 1738 until his death in September 1782, aged eighty, evidently spent a good deal of time out of town, leaving parochial duties to his curates. His will gives his address as Windsor; it is a scrappy document, appointing Charles Mayo (his great-nephew and son of the rector of St George's) as executor, with no mention of his own daughter, Gertrude, who seems to have been something of a black sheep, going by a number of aliases and living in sin with a dodgy lawyer. Not only did the rector's daughter get into trouble; one of his curates, Richard Green, was accused of raping his landlady's servant. The account of the trial gives us a glimpse of the pleasant life led by the comfortably off living in these handsome streets around Christ Church.

Leaving Fournier Street we turn into Wood Street (Wilkes Street); it was here that the Revd Richard Green had lodgings. Wood Street was (and is) much like

Fournier Street, good three-storey houses occupied by the middling sort, including master-weavers: John Rondeau (1723) at No. 4, Abraham Deheul at No. 5 (1743–50), John Fremantle and Co. at No. 14 (1750–73). Mid-century there was an inn called the Three Tuns and a china shop, and in the 1780s or '90s the Spitalfields Dissenters' Charity School moved here. Adjoining the Three Tuns, in a 'double brick house lined with a wainstcoat', was the residence of Edward Rodenhurst, an exciseman. Here he lived with his wife, Mary, a baby girl and a servant girl called Elizabeth Jervis. During Mr Green's stints at Christ Church, 'the time the other clergyman had gone to Oxford', he lodged with the Rodenhursts. One April day in 1769 the jolly young parson ('naturally chatty and merry') offered his landlord and lady tickets to go to see Nicholas Rowe's tragedy *The Fair Penitent*, the most popular play of its time. He had a bad cold and this, presumably, was why he was not going himself. Edward Rodenhurst decided to forgo the outing, but escorted his wife to the theatre and collected her when it was over, having spent the evening with a neighbour. When the couple got home, late at night, Mary popped into the tavern to fetch them a pint of beer and they sat down to supper, prepared by the girl Jervis. The servant seemed distressed, and her mistress followed her down into the kitchen to see what was wrong. Mary had come home from one tragedy to another, or so it seemed. According to the girl, Richard Green had come home while master and mistress were out, flung her and the crying toddler onto the couple's bed and ravished her. She told the court: 'He pulled my petticoats up, and lay with me. There came wet from him, and blood from me.' Whether he did or not we shall never know. Perhaps Elizabeth Jervis was aiming at blackmail: there was talk of a threat to send a 'lawyer's letter'. The justices found Green innocent; his character witnesses were impeccable and his alibi fairly sound. All the offending evening he had been in the Three Tuns, enjoying a feast of lobster and salmon, radishes and cheese, washed down with bottles of wine. According to his two companions (one of whom was a local wheelwright), the parson was only out of their company for a very short time.

Off Wood Street was Princes (Princelet) Street, the third of the new streets on this estate. It is now lined with restored houses of the period, with only No. 19 (now a museum) looking as if it is nearly 300 years old. This was the house of Peter Abraham Ogier (d.1754), part of the great Poitevin weaving clan. Ben Truman lived at No. 4 (in 1724) before he moved into the Director's House in Brick Lane. Samuel Worrall, the builder, had his house and timber yard at No. 18, Henry Coates, the rich dyer, had a 'mansion' and dye works on the corner with Brick Lane. At No. 23 was Thomas Excelbee (1720), lieutenant-colonel in the Tower Hamlets Militia and Warden of the Weavers' Company (1729). John Sabatier and his family, wife Susannah, his two daughters and two sons, lived at No. 16 (1738–53) before moving into Church Street. A hundred looms supplied Sabatier with flowered silk and a great deal of money. He retired to Chichester in his sixties, leaving the business to his son, another John, and enjoying the income from his considerable property portfolio. He called himself 'gentleman' and sported a diamond ring, a gold seal ring set with a garnet and a set of cornelian sleeve buttons.

Probably the most famous Wilkes Street resident was a woman, the silk designer Anna Maria Garthwaite, a clergyman's daughter from Leicestershire. A blue plaque marks the house (No. 2) where she lived from 1728 for over thirty years, with her 'dear and loving' widowed sister Mary. Anna Maria became the pre-eminent designer of her generation, famous for her floral silk designs with a three dimensional effect produced by shading. Hundreds of her designs, of which there were over 1,000, have survived, and can be seen today in the Victoria and Albert Museum. Hers was an all-female household: her sister, her niece, her women friends, two maids. She left her gold snuff box to a neighbour, a woman.

Norton Folgate: Spital Square

Anna Maria may have taken her snuff from a gold box, but the respectful tread of footmen was in the main confined to Spital Square, over on the west side of the market, lying at the centre of the once lawless liberty of Norton Folgate. At Nos 34–35 Spital Square lived Huguenot Sir Isaac Tillard (d.1726), from Devon, lord of all he surveyed: a JP, a Land Tax commissioner and a colonel in the Tower Hamlets Militia. His grand house was purchased in 1716, along with a good deal of property around, from the third Earl of Bolingbroke, whose family had been the chief landowners in Norton Folgate since the days of Charles I. Tillard continued the development of the area started by the third earl in about 1697, building or rebuilding between Blossom Terrace in the north and Spital Square in the south. The Square, which was not really a square but streets laid out in a cruciform shape, stayed a secluded spot into the nineteenth century, protected from the busy streets around by bollards, like a modern gated estate. It had the best houses in Spitalfields, built at varying dates between *c.* 1700 and the late 1730s. They were not all of a piece, like the houses that lined its fellows, White Lyon (Folgate) Street, Fleur de Lis Street, Blossom Street and Elder Street, but were of different designs; all were spacious with long gardens. This was 'millionaire's row', where the number of families with coaches was a cause of comment (twelve in 1751). It was home to the wealthiest merchants and masters, the Dalbiacs, the Ogiers, Samuel Totton, silk-broker (1758–62), John Vansommer, gold and silver flowered silk-weaver (1750–75), John Lekeux, lawyer (1727–31) and many others. Benjamin Goldsmid, whom we met in Whitechapel, had a house here in 1803. Some of these families were very rich. A journalist commented, during the depression in the silk trade in 1765, that the price of silk might be reduced by 'master weavers putting down their coaches and their country seats and their livery servants' rather than starving the poor journeymen.

Houses in Elder Street, Blosson Street, Fleur de Lis Street and White Lyon (Folgate) Street were more modest than those in the square, although they had their wealthy occupants. The very fine house at No. 30 Elder Street was the home of a weaver called Isaac Dupree in 1724. He was one of the richest locals, well Anglicised, of a pre-1685 immigrant family and apprenticed to an English master. His marriage to an English girl, Sarah Cash, the daughter of a Shoreditch throwster, brought with it money and property. He built Nos 28 and 30 Elder Street, had an additional three houses on lease in Elder Street, two in Fleur de Lys Street, three further in Mile End New Town and two in Montague Street. He kept his chaise at his country seat in Stamford Hill.

White Lyon Street (now Folgate Street) was a seventeenth-century street, almost completely rebuilt in the 1720s. Originally White Lyon Yard, it was named after the large brewery that had been there at least since 1671, with its storehouses, granaries, hop-lofts, malthouse and stabling. Nearby was Robert Pickard's dyehouse (c. 1704). Norton Folgate's courthouse was in an old house in this street from 1744, shared by the boys of the charity school. In Blossom Street was a small girls' school, the workhouse and two sets of almshouses, one for the parish and one for weavers, 'very handsome'. Just south of White Lyon Street was the Liberty's place of worship, the Wheler chapel. There was no French chapel within the Liberty itself, although those around the market were not far away.

Only No. 37 is left of the very fine houses in Spital Square, most of which were demolished in the 1920s and '30s and the rest in the 1960s. No. 37 is now the headquarters of the Society for the Preservation of Ancient Buildings. It is said to have been the house of master-weaver Peter Ogier III, whose portrait hangs in La Providence in Rochester and whose skull was minutely examined by the Spitalfields Crypt Project. In 1765 Ogier had £3,000-worth of stock in his warehouse; he was director of La Providence, upper bailiff in the Weavers' Company and a governor of the London Hospital.

Elder Street has a good number of early eighteenth-century houses, and there are a few in Folgate Street, including No. 18, Dennis Severs' house, now a 'living museum', where by candlelight you can eerily experience 'the grey-clad weaver-folk, Like shadows on the wall'.

The Old Artillery Ground

Immediately south of Spital Square and Sir Isaac's new houses was the Old Artillery Ground, its 5 acres probably the most densely packed of anywhere in Spitalfields. Anciently part of the priory's land, called the 'tasel' field, where clothworkers of old had grown teasels to raise the nap on cloth, since the Dissolution it had been a place of guns and gunpowder, leased from the Crown by the Artillery Company and transferred to the ordnance office in 1658. A wall enclosed the ground, where there was a shooting range, master-gunner's house and storehouses. Pepys came here to watch a new gun called Punchinello being tried out.

At the time of the main Huguenot invasion the ground had just been sold off by the Crown to Nicholas Barbon and his associates It was a piecemeal, hotch-potch development, with seventeen different builders being granted leases. Low-grade buildings, tall narrow houses, were hastily thrown up along new straight streets: Duke Street/Fort Street, Stewart Street and Gun Street. At its southern tip was Old Artillery Lane and its eastern extension, the notorious Smock Alley, where Ben Jonson's devil had flown.

The Artillery Ground was an independent liberty, free of the City; it had its own vestry, and meetings of the leading inhabitants were held in the parish house in Fort Street (1766). The workhouse in Gun Street (1731), then Fort Street (1791), was at some time presided over by widow Judith Griffiths, 'mistress of the poor', who left her silver teaspoons, tea caddy, sugar tongs and milk pot to her two daughters.

No carriages could pass into the Ground from Bishopsgate or the market area; the only access for vehicles was from the south, which, combined with the high brick wall that enclosed it, must have encouraged a sense of separateness from the world around, perhaps a feeling of security for the immigrants. Be that as it may, before the building of the new estates around Spital Square and Church Street in the 1720s and '30s this was where the better-off members of the Huguenot community chose to live. Gedeon Seguret (d.1732) lived in the old Artillery Ground, but his widow, daughter and son-in-law moved to Fournier Street. Isaac Campart's house (d.1725) was in the Artillery and his son, Peter, moved into Fournier Street. Gentlemen of the Le Keux family lived here: John (d.1726) and Peter (d.1743), as did master-weaver Daniel Auber (d.1748) and watchmaker Robert Auber (d.1750). In 1769 Peter Auber was in Spital Square. In Steward Street lived the silk designer James Leman (?1688–1745), the son of a refugee, who achieved high office in the Weavers' Company. He moved into the City, taking with him his collection of coins and medals, mathematical and musical instruments and 'reptiles in glasses'.

One of the earliest French chapels was here (*c.* 1691), in Parliament Court, but it was by no means an immigrant ghetto; there was quite a sprinkling of English gentlemen living in the new Old Artillery and a number of wealthy families. By the end of the century it was a different picture, the 'crowded courts and dirty alleys' that Sir Samuel Romilly noted around the chapel characterising what was now a poor area, full of silk and woollen workers, with 1,428 people in its 185 houses in 1801.

Bethnal Green

Romance has had a field day in Spitalfields, with talk of Gallic refinement and picturesque pursuits, with its beautifully restored Georgian houses and its magnificent church. Not so its poor relation, Bethnal Green. So little survives here of the 'more spacious days', and what does has been so overborne by the slum it became in the next century that it is easy to be retrospective. Its growth was rapid and extraordinary (it grew eightfold between 1664 and 1743) and horrified contemporaries, especially those who were responsible for keeping order and looking after the poor. Stepney's most sleepy, out-of-the-way hamlet grew from a village with less than 1,000 people into a great seething suburb, notorious for its poverty, the home of poor weavers and labourers, many of them French. It became a parish of its own, detached from Stepney in 1743, with a large church, St Matthew's, and two (or three) French chapels. In 1743 the population was 15,000, in 1795 19,000.

In fact, most of Bethnal Green's 755 acres was pleasant enough in aspect for most of the eighteenth century, and there were a surprising number of gentry and wealthy Huguenots in residence. However harsh the toil was at the loom, however crowded and mucky the streets, you were never far from fields and gardens. Although there was marshy land and stagnant ponds to be negotiated, the fields and paths of Bethnal Green were still a place for strolling.

Bethnal Green hamlet had been part of Stepney Manor, sold off to various individuals by the impecunious Wentworths in the 1650s and '60s. The hamlet's growth, which dates from the 1670s, was almost entirely on its south-western tip, an outcrop of Spitalfields, housing in the main occupied by poor weavers. Silkweaving predominated for the whole of the century, but gradually other related industries began to establish themselves. Lysons noted an 'extensive cotton manufacture' in St John Street, where from 1783 Messrs Paty and Byrchall employed 'from 200 to 300 hands'. At the end of Pollard's-Row was 'a new manufacture lately established by Messrs. Hegner, Ehrliholtzer, and Co.' making 'water-proof flaxen-pipe hose for fire-engines, brewers, ships, etc'.

In 1664 there were 215 houses in the hamlet, in 1743 1,800, the vast majority of them in what Lysons called the 'town part'. Two hundred houses were built between 1719 and 1724, mostly on the Red Cow estate across the top of Brick Lane. Over to the east, around the Green, the old heart of the village (where the Museum of Childhood and the underground station now are), there was still leisured living, trees around the pond by the tumbledown Tudor chapel, market gardens, hayfields and large country houses. As Millicent Rose wrote, 'The two halves of Bethnal Green were distinct and even incompatible.' In between the two halves was farmland. The 'town part' of Bethnal Green, merging into Spitalfields, constituted territorially only a small part of the hamlet in the first part of the century, although it was much more heavily populated than the rest. This would be changed by the 1790s as the tentacles of weavertown stretched north and east, absorbing the farmland and gardens and taking hold of the old village. When 'cutters' Valloine and Doyle were hanged it was over in the heart of the village at the Salmon and Ball. By the 1830s tradesmen's houses lined all the main roads and on the eastern side of the Green, apart from that, all housing was occupied by weavers and labourers.

The 'town part'

We will start our tour at the watchhouse at the crossroads at the top of Brick Lane. Here Cock Lane, an ancient way, some 300 years old at least, had led out of Shoreditch and wandered up to the bishop's palace, which long ago had been Bethnal Green's *raison d'être*. It took its name from the Cock alehouse, which had been there in Henry VIII's day; as it went east it became known as Rogue Lane (1642) and Whores Lane' (1717). In 1722 there were seven alehouses in Cock Lane, and later in the century its Dolphin tavern was the headquarters of the weavers' notorious Bold Defiance. With the new development of housing round here, the road was straightened and extended, and its eastern part became Church Street, leading to the new parish church. It became the New Bethnal Green Road and is now the Old Bethnal Green Road.

Either side of the watchhouse in the early years of the century, fanning out north towards Shoreditch and to the east towards the village centre, were market gardens; in 1703 there were nine of them. Nurseries were a feature here from the early seventeenth century, when they began to spring up all around London's periphery. Before the weavers arrived they were the lifeblood of the hamlet. Radishes, spinach, onions, cauliflowers, sugarloaf cabbages, carrots, peas (a 'dainty' for the ladies) were cultivated for the growing demands of metropolitan tables, and flowers were grown for cutting by Huguenot wives.

By the end of the century the gardens had nearly all gone, eaten up by housing. Satchwell's garden, remembered in Satchwell Street, had shrunk from 6 acres to 2 acres by 1792. Kemp's garden, adjacent to Shoreditch church, carried on until 1817. From Nicol Street to Truman's Brewery, spreading eastwards almost as far as the church, was all weavertown. The great 4-acre garden north of the west end of Cock Lane, part of the freehold land long owned by the Nicol family, became the Old Nicol, by the late nineteenth century the country's worst slum, immortalised in Morrison's *Child of the Jago*. At Goodwell's and Border's Gardens, up near Shoreditch church on the Hackney Road, the potting sheds and summerhouses, the rows of cabbages and onion sets, became the direst of places in Victorian times, Nova Scotia Gardens. When the cottages here were 'erased' for the building of St Thomas's church in 1857 it was a 'huge mountain of refuse', almost certainly the famous dustheap that features in Dickens's *Our Mutual Friend*.

By the 1770s only 3 per cent of the inhabitants of the parish were of the 'middling sort'. From the days of Charles II, when the 'town part' started to be built up, the hamlet's industrial quarter was a poor place. Because of the 'great increase of inhabitants and great charge of the poor' Stepney vestry had appointed a churchwarden for the hamlet of Bethnal Green in 1685, a Mr William Malin, probably a Frenchman; previously it had been tacked onto Mile End. In 1696 it was reported that there were only 200 people in the hamlet who had enough money to contribute towards the paving of the highway. In 1743 it was said that 'Increase of Dissoluteness of Morals and a Disregard for religion' had led the 'better sort of people' to move 'from their habitations in the said Hamlet, to the great Impoverishment thereof'. Objections were made to the provision of a parish church on the grounds that the hamlet was too poor to sustain one: 'The inhabitants … consist chiefly of journeymen weavers and other inferior artificers … who can scarcely support themselves'; the rest of the community consisted of 'bakers, butchers, chandlers and such like trades'. Overseers of the Poor were busy offloading pauper families to other parishes, like widow Mary Sier and her three young children who were dispatched to Canterbury in the summer of 1737. When John Wesley visited in 1777 he was appalled by the terrible conditions, and a dispensary doctor writing in 1792 summed up the distress of the poor silkweavers of Bethnal Green: 'It is not in the power of language to describe their long and continued miseries.'

There were two or three French chapels here, one of which may even have been the first to be set up, possibly before 1685. This was the former Dissenters' chapel in St Jean Street, not far from Truman's, abutting on to Spitalfields proper. There was another in Slaughter (Sclater) Street nearby (1721–40) and there may have been another in Cock Lane in 1731.

About a hundred of the 520 people assessed in the 1693/4 tax have French names, with the highest proportion in Club Row (twelve of thirty-one names); a quarter of the names in Cock Lane and Carter's Rents are French, and there are sixteen of seventy-two in St John Street. There are only eight of fifty-eight in Brick Lane and none at all over to the east in the village or Dog Row (Cambridge Heath Road). Tax records, as we have seen, give only a very rough indication of the relative size of the Huguenot population, as they take no account of the impecunious families moving from lodging to lodging. Almost certainly Bethnal Green's 'town part', especially in the early days of immigration, was as French as the hamlet of Spitalfields, if not more so.

'Dirty and melancholy' streets were crammed with tall, narrow dwellings, with the characteristic 'long lights' (weavers' windows) and alive with the hum of looms. Most were built for multi-occupation, with workshops at the top: there were no big houses to be subdivided. Few masters were to be found in Bethnal Green; there were some in Sclater Street. It was a rare family, with an income of perhaps £20 a year, that could afford the £7–10 rent for a whole house. They were 'mostly Lett out by the Owners … in two or three distinct parts or tenements, by Reason of the Great Poverty of the inhabitants'. One room per family was the norm, for which the rent was about 1s a week. Lysons said there were usually three or four families per house. In 1763 a third of the housing was said to be in the hands of just a few landlords, building tradesmen like the pawnbroking Mercerons and the Wilmots of Wilmot's Folly.

With money in short supply and cramped, squalid living conditions, babies struggled to survive. Before St Matthew's was built, every day three, four, five or more corpses were brought over to Stepney church from Bethnal Green's industrial quarter; most of them were infants and small children. A typical day was 6 August 1734; seven bodies were buried, five of them from Bethnal Green, three of them the children of paupers, two of weavers, four of them with French names. From Nicol Street, Thomas Street, Club Row, Bacon Street, Church Street, Cock Lane, Slaughter (Sclater) Street, Austin Street and Carters' Rents they came, to see their precious bundles interred in Stepney's famous churchyard.

Contemporaries and some historians, notably Dorothy George, put it all down to 'Madame Geneva': 'Children are born weakly & Sickly and often look Shrivled & old, as they had Numbered many Years.' Gin and other hard liquor was sold off barrows and vegetable stalls; you could get a dram at any chandler's or tobacconist's shop; one in six of the houses in Holborn, Westminster and the Tower divisions sold it. All London was awash with gin (until the Gin Act of 1751), but when a committee appointed to look into the 'pernicious' habit reported in 1726, the finger was pointed especially at the Bethnal Green weavers. There were said to be at least forty weavers selling liquor in the hamlet; ten years later there were ninety. All week the weavers drank 'on tick', and at the end of the week there was no money to take home to their families. Judith Defour, a simple-minded girl who worked as a throwster, went to visit her toddler in Bethnal Green workhouse, a bastard child sired by a weaver who lived by Spitalfields market. Egged on by a bad lot called Suzy, she strangled her little daughter to get the price of a bottle of gin, left her body in a ditch and sold the outfit just bought for her by the overseers for 1s 4d. Her mother said she 'was never in her right mind'; the chaplain at Newgate observed 'I have not seen one so stupid.' She was sentenced to be hanged.

The children who survived might have some education, although there were only places for sixty children at the parish school set up in Church Row in 1763. Parmiter's in St John Street had been set up for thirty boys in 1722. Mostly they worked with their parents, and some were apprenticed out in due course if their family could afford the fee. Some tales may be told of the goings-on in the workshops of Bethnal Green. Richard Kindrick complained to the justices in 1702 that his son, apprenticed to a French weaver called David Paton, had been beaten 'as black as ones hatt' and set to attend to his master's racing pigeons on the roof instead of going to church.

Parish apprentices, put to local men from workhouses all over London, were notoriously badly treated. One such was poor little Tom Salter, an orphan sent from the Newington workhouse to an elderly master-weaver in Bethnal Green. Edmund Gilbert, who, though he cut a 'tolerable figure' locally, living well and spending an lavish 7s a week (*c.* £30 today) on prime cuts of meat, was a peevish, morose and bad-tempered individual, known to ill-treat his boys. When he went out they were locked in the house, and in the freezing winter weather Tom had to go into the yard and break the ice to wash his clothes. Beatings were a twice-daily occurrence, and the neighbour reported terrible shrieks and screams coming from the Gilbert household 'that made one's heart bleed to hear them'. Eventually the boy died from the blows, aged nearly fifteen. Terrible though this was, it is good to hear that the prosecution was vigorously promoted by the parish, with church-warden James Mussell putting in an appearance. These are isolated incidents. For every cruel master there must have been many decent men.

The trek to St Dunstan's was a long one, and the old chapel of St George in the village, used for services in Cromwell's day, was in ruins by 1716 and 'turned into houses' by 1720. About fifty years after the Huguenot invasion the hamlet got its own church, located in the new industrial quarter, and was made a parish. Such was the size of the population that Stepney's parish clerk lost half his income in baptism, marriage and burial fees. Striking off in a easterly direction from the Brick Lane watchhouse, past the remants of Satchwell's nursery, you would come upon St Matthew's, lying on the south side of the road, a squat brick build-ing with a small square tower. Designed by George Dance the Elder, and very different from Hawksmoor's Spitalfields wonder, it was consecrated on 15 July 1746. Hard-working curates ran the show at St Matthew's, with the gently reared Brasenose dons who were rectors little in evidence. Ralph Cawley, rector of Stepney, reported in 1763 that the rector of Bethnal Green was never there at all. His curate occupied the parsonage house, while he spent the summer with his family in the country, reading prayers to his brother's family; he was 'much in town' in the winter. William Loxham (1766–1809) hardly set foot in the parish, apparently frightened off by the 'aggressive system' that operated in the vestry. In due course the vestry was to become a high-powered racket, dominated in the first half of the next century by the crooked magistrate Joseph Merceron (parish treasurer from 1764) of the pawnbroking family. He was eventually imprisoned for misappropriation of funds, licensing of pubs used for debauchery and organis-ing bullock hunting in the churchyard.

The village

Shaking off the dust of the weaving quarter, and setting off along Church Street (the Old Bethnal Green Road) in the direction of the village, you would soon be in a very different environment. A little way past the church, on the north side, in Saffron Close (Coates Lane) was a large farm belonging to a former Brick Lane dyer called Thomas Coates (d.1740). The backdrop of a watercolour of the farm, painted in 1773, has a pleasant country air about it, but there are houses in view and a coaching inn called the George on the main road.

By the 1770s the approaches to the village along the new road had been laid out as a residential estate, Wilmot Street and Square, with the Lord Camden public house and a bowling alley. This was the project of David Wilmot, a local labourer/builder who amassed a considerable fortune through his property-dealing, became parish treasurer and a JP, and built himself a grand and extravagant house where Coates's farmhouse had been. The locals rudely nicknamed it Wilmot's Folly; as the magistrate responsible for arresting two weavers who were hanged in 1771, he was not a popular man.

The village and its environs were a pleasant place, with a number of gentry families in residence. Some were those who had done well for themselves in the hustle bustle of weavertown, like Thomas Coates. It was regarded as a remote spot: when a site near the Green was considered for the London Hospital, it was thought to be 'too far from Town for the physicians and surgeons to attend'. Near the village and clustered around Dog Row (Cambridge Heath Road), to the south, were nurseries. Market-gardening continued in this part of Bethnal Green well into the next century. There were farms and cottages scattered in the fields, with rows of small houses, some dating from the mid-seventeenth century, lining Dog Row, with more buildings near the Mile End Turnpike. A lane leading off Dog Row to the west led to Sir Robert Darling's house. Darling was a seriously wealthy man, prominent on the vestry and with property all over the country. Instructions in his will included directions that his nephew and heir John Bosworth should take his name, and on no account should marry anyone worth less than £10,000.

To the north-east, where the bishop's palace had been (now Victoria Park) was Bishops Hall, a 100-acre farm, part of an estate acquired by the Southeby family in the late seventeenth century. James Sotheby, who came into the estate in 1700, grew white jasmine, red honeysuckle, grapes and 'double-flowered pomegranate' against the farmhouse, and apricots, peaches, plums, cherries and nectarines on the garden walls. It was mainly an arable farm, with a dairy herd of about eighty beasts.

The village itself nestled around the Green. Bought by the well to-do residents from Lady Philadelphia Wentworth in 1671, the Green was let out as garden and meadow and the income went to the poor. It has survived (as a park), as have a handful of eighteenth-century houses, enough for the modern observer to get the feel of the place in its market-gardening days. Netteswell House, next to the Museum of Childhood, dating from 1705, is still there, although much changed; and nearby are the three beautiful (unspoilt) houses at Nos 19–21 Old Ford Road. Anthony Natt, a carpenter from the 'town part', built them in 1753–55, and lived in one of them. Kirby's Castle, where Pepys had strolled in the beautiful gardens in days gone by, still stood on the south-eastern edge of the Green (where the library is today). It was popularly thought to be the site of the Blind Beggar's house. By 1727 it was a private madhouse, and continued to be for nearly 200 years, the only place in Bethnal Green to be accounted worthy of note in the *New Complete Guide* of 1771. A report in the *Gentleman's Magazine* allows a glimpse of what went on behind closed doors in this grim place. In the spring of 1772, when the blossom on the fruit trees must have made the Green a pretty sight, a woman was decoyed to the madhouse by her husband, and shut away. She was put in 'a little apartment the stench of which was intolerable', chained and handcuffed. After a couple of days her husband had a change of heart and took her out. While confined she had befriended another woman in a similar plight whom she tried to rescue, and a *habeas corpus* was issued. The keepers still refused to release her, and the Justice concerned went himself to the house and insisted on interviewing the woman. He said he would not go again for £5,000 as 'the place was so intolerably nasty'.

Over on the other side of the Green (between Old Ford Road and Victoria Park Square), opposite the ruins of St George's chapel, was another mansion. In Tudor times it was known as The Great Corner House. Rebuilt during the Civil War and occupied in 1683 by a seafaring man and India merchant, Sir John Goldsborough, it was a three-gabled house with numerous rooms. There were a great and little parlour, a withdrawing room, hall, piazza, painted wainscots, tapestry, Indian chintz hangings and Dutch painted tiles. Goldsborough was very rich; when he set off for India, letting out the Corner House; he took with him £4,000 (worth about £300,000 today) in cash as 'Adventure in money'. Local bigwig, JP, leading vestryman and antiquarian Ebenezer Mussell leased the Corner House in the middle of the eighteenth century and made it into something quite extraordinary. He added an extra wing and built onto it the reliefs from the gate at Aldgate, which had just been demolished. It was renamed Aldgate House and became one of the local sights.

Lysons tells us that every inn in the village sported a sign depicting the Blind Beggar or Bess, his daughter. This comment suggests that Bethnal Green was something of a tourist spot, a place for a day out to enjoy the fresh air and have a look at Mussell's remarkable edifice, and to take some refreshment at one of the many hostelries. Of the eighty-two alehouses listed in Bethnal Green in 1722, only thirty-seven were in the 'town part'. There were the more upmarket taverns, like the Green Man, south of the Green where manorial courts were sometimes held (there by 1750), the well-known Salmon and Ball, at the junction with the Bethnal Green Road where the two weavers were hanged, Wilmots' Lord Camden and the Gibraltar, which gave Gibraltar Row its name.

Aldgate House was rented out to Israel Levin Salomons in 1765 and Abraham de Mattos Mocatta in 1769. By 1779 this part of Old Ford Road was known as Jews Walk and Bethnal Green had started its long association with the Jewish community. Celebrated Jewish boxer Daniel Mendoza lived at No. 3 Paradise Row from 1788; *The Times* reported in 1788 that the inhabitants of Bethnal Green were 'mostly French Jews'. This was patently not the case, but there were enough Jews to cause comment.

As to the French, a few Bethnal Green 'gentlemen' of French descent appear in the will archive, but they are mainly over in the 'town part', like John Jacob Marmoy gent (d.1781) of Virginia Row (near Arnold Circus) The Mercerons and the Renvoize families were landowners and active in local affairs; Peter Renvoize the elder (d.1790) lived over to the Spitalfields side in Church Street, and had properties in Thomas Street (between Cock Lane and Hare Street) and on the north side of Bethnal Green Road. No streets or alleys have French names. As to the more humble descendants of the refugees, many took English forms of their names (famously L'Heureux to Happy), and by the end of the century they were hard to identify.

Mile End Old Town and Stepney Village

At the south end of Bethnal Green's Dog Row, where it joined the Essex (Mile End) Road was the manor dog pound and the turnpike, the tollgate into London from the east. The junction of Cambridge Heath Road and the Mile End Road is still known as Mile End Gate. These days its famous landmark is the Blind Beggar pub, where one of the Kray twins shot a rival gang member in 1966. On the City side of the gate is Whitechapel and on the country side the hamlet of Mile End Old Town. In area it is much greater than any other of the East End villages, apart from Bethnal Green, being about four times as big as Whitechapel and nearly seven times larger than Spitalfields parish.

Eighteenth-century Old Town, for many years the country retreat of city grandees, was a self-important place, fairly select, with some half of its folk of the middling sort, rows of neat villas and a good amount of new money around. The hamlet had a leisured, comfortable feel about it, in marked contrast to the hustle and bustle of its westerly neighbour, Whitechapel. It was much favoured by successful seafarers, especially East India Company men, naval officers and widows;

some of them were Huguenot, some Jewish, like old Esther Jesuvan Alvares, who left a pair of silver shoe and knee buckles to her little grandson. By the end of the century it was becoming something of a manufacturing place: Lysons noted three large breweries, Charringtons, Jackson and Bicknell, 'Mr Minish's hartshorn manufacture', Cooke's workshops making patent sponges for ships, two major ropewalks and the West Ham waterworks.

The population, although it had grown by 1801, was still relatively sparse, with only about 10,000 people living in its 677 acres, while Whitechapel had 23,666 in 170 acres and Spitalfields parish about 15,000 in 73 acres. As we have seen, Christopher Wren said, the hamlet was 'more wholesome' than the surrounding parts', lying amid farmlands and gardens.

Today, at the busy junction at Mile End Gate, the White Hart pub stands like a sentinel, as an inn of this name has done for at least 250 years on the corner of Cambridge Heath Road. The vista east towards Bow affords a change of tempo, as the stalls and clutter by Whitechapel station peter out and the road widens out into a tree-lined avenue, almost like a Paris boulevard, sweeping eastward. Its route, these days, is taken between massive blocks of flats on the right and, on the left, the towering neo-Classical edifice of what was Wickham's, the East End's only department store.

Beyond the flats a few Georgian houses remain, smartened up, in what was once Assembly Row, where Captain Cook lived. On the opposite side of the road are the magnificent Trinity Almshouses, Mile End's showpiece then and now. Strype noted 'a beautiful structure, having a very fair Entrance at Two Gates and a chapel at the further end'. Further along, on the north, either side of the Anchor Retail Park, is a row of early Georgian houses (Ireland Row, *c.* 1717) and, hiding behind railings heavily draped with honeysuckle and ivy, Malplaquet House, built in 1742. In the eighteenth century the road was lined with houses such as these, with shops, their bow windows twinkling, and comfortable taverns. It was a country town of a place, set among farmland and hayfields, remembered today only in the name Hayfield Passage.

From the Turnpike (Mile End Gate) to the Plough Inn (Mile End underground station)

We will take a tour of the village, starting at the bustling turnpike like the fat man in a tricorn hat, lolloping along in his chariot in Rowlandson's picture. The print shows two imposing square tollgates, well lit with lanterns, and five barred gates spanning the highway.

Lighting was important; this, along with all the other London turnpikes, was a dangerous spot, where in spite of the guards, highwaymen had good pickings.

Captain Griffith, on his way home to Mile End late one Saturday night in October 1729, was robbed of some items here, including his wife's spectacles. The thieves got away in the general chaos as a flock of sheep was hustled through the gates.

Mid-century, from here as far as Thieving Lane (Globe Road by Stepney Green station) there were buildings lining most of the road and spilling out southwards. It was still largely a ribbon development along the arterial road, which gave easy access to the City. Lady Philadelphia Wentworth had sold this land to pay off the debts incurred by her father-in-law, and by the 1690s there were about 230 houses in the hamlet, some of them quite large; as Strype said, 'many good Houses, inhabited with divers sea Captains and Commanders'. By 1741 there were in the region of 400 houses, and more were built in the 1760s; Noorthouck noted in 1773: 'Here the spirit of building is carried on with such alacrity, that the great road from Mile End turnpike is almost inclosed on both sides with regular well built houses to the village of Bow.'

A little to the south of the turnpike was one of the many inns, the Four Swans. Rooms were let out and food supplied to the residents, as was common practice. A weaver/pawnbroker and his wife, Corbet and Mary Vezey, paid 7s a week in 1731, for which they got several rooms, kept clean by the management, a weekly change of bedlinen, and meals brought up to them. The menu was lavish, including roast goose and giblet pie, fillet of veal, mutton chops and plum pudding. One day, just before Christmas 1731, a large crowd gathered around the inn: old Mary Vezey had thrown herself out of one of the garret windows. A beadle who happened to be passing noted her wasted body and, when he went up to her room, a sinister thing: a stale loaf hanging by a piece of string. Mistress Vezey died soon after, and her husband, who had previously been arrested for ill-treating his wife, was accused of causing her death. Already she had given an account of her sufferings to local JP Captain Stephen Martin Leake, and with her dying breath she repeated it. She had been locked up in her garret room without fire, water to wash, a proper chamberpot or decent food for a year or more: witness the stale loaf. She stank, and was so weak she could only crawl. When she cried for a little warm beer her husband horsewhipped her. Meanwhile Corbet had another woman. All this, she said, was because she had a 'small estate in the country' worth £7 or £8 a year with which she refused to part. The landlady, who happened to be Corbet's sister-in-law, said this was all rubbish; the loaf was hung on a string to keep it away from the mice, and the old lady was well fed. Corbet admitted to keeping his wife under lock and key to stop her stealing from him, protesting that he had 'loved her as I loved my Life' before she took to pilfering. Expert medical witnesses said she had died from consumption or asthma, and the court found him innocent; he lived for another ten years.

Near the Four Swans was the best house in the neighbourhood, built in 1738 by the widow Fitzhugh on Littlefield, land bought from local surgeon and apothecary Richard Lee. The three-storey house with a fine Portland stone stair-case and seven marble chimneypieces was set back from the road in extensive grounds with curving forecourt walls, and coachhouses and stables made of brick. Mary Fitzhugh's life was as different from Mary Vezey's as could be imagined. Her loving husband William, an East India Company captain, died in 1731, leaving her a wealthy woman; she had £9,000-worth of East India stock and, according to her will, had property worth more than £12,000. The family became famous for their import of Chinese porcelain; the basic blue design was known as Fitzhugh.

Genteel widows, though most of them not quite as wealthy as Mary Fitzhugh, were evidently drawn to Mile End Old Town; there was quite a collection of them. Of 234 Old Town wills proved in the senior court between 1700 and 1800 there were a remarkable eighty made by women, mostly widows, some spinsters and a sprinkling of wives. In 1780 one in seven of all taxpayers was a woman. It is difficult to say whether this was because it was a safe, pleasant place to live, or whether it was because the prevalence of seafaring men meant women were likely to be left widowed, with some cash. At all events it must have created a Cranford sort of society in Mile End, where the tea-table reigned supreme. Huguenot widow Elenor Christale, of the Trinity Ground, left the curate Hugh Colley a guinea. Perhaps she put on her best cap when he came to tea.

Rattling along the main road we would pass on the left a row of almshouses. The very grand and highly ornamented entrance to the Trinity Almshouses, its massive gates held between two tall columns, with its topping of stone balls and model ships, its statues and stone crests, announce firmly to passers-by that they are in the land of the seafarer.

What with the widows and pensioners, Mile End must have had quite an elderly as well as a nautical air. There were altogether fourteen different insti-tutions housing pensioners and paupers. Around the turnpike were, as well as the Trinity, the Drapers' (later moved), Captains Fisher's, the Skinners' and the Vintners'. Further east are Fuller's, the workhouse for Cripplegate and the Jews' Hospital east of Globe Road, then Bancroft's, followed at the approaches to Bow by Cook's and Bowry's. Opposite Bancroft's was the parish workhouse, and south of Assembly Row the All Hallows' Barking workhouse in Redman's Row (from 1738). If you include Overton's pauper farm near the hospital, taken over as part of Mile End in 1792, there were something in the region of 680 pensioners and paupers. Widows predominated in the privately endowed and livery company almshouses; there were usually more widows in the Trinity than 'decayed masters and pilots'. They were comfortable little homes, and the inmates of a different calibre from those in the workhouses. Old Dinah Josselyne of the Vintners' was hardly on the breadline; she had a precious collection of silver for her tea-table, milk pot, strainer and spoons, and enough cash to make it worth her while making a will to benefit her children.

32 Wapping parish school. Photograph by Yvonne Hughes.

33 Figure of blue coat girl on the old Raines School building in Wapping. Photograph by Yvonne Hughes.

34 Sailmakers' almshouses, Bromley. Photograph by Yvonne Hughes.

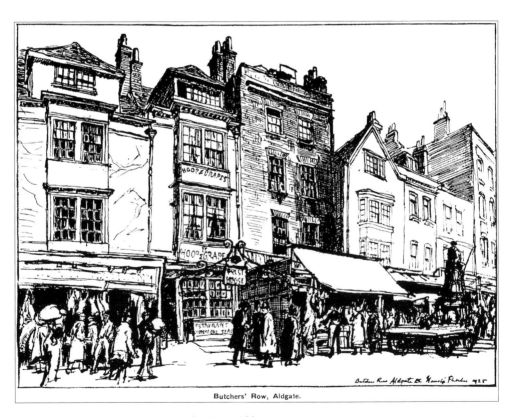

Butchers' Row, Aldgate.

35 Eighteenth-century houses in Butcher Row, Aldgate.

Right 36 St Botolph's church, Aldgate. Unusually the church stands on a north-south orientation.

S.ᵗ BOTOLPH ALDGATE.

This Church is dedicated to S.ᵗ Botolph the British Saint, a Man of so exemplary a character that four of the Churches of London have been dedicated to his Memory. It is believed to have been founded about the time of William the Conqueror, and in 1418 M.ʳ Rob.ᵗ Burford, a wealthy Parishioner, caused a New Steeple to be built, and various additions to be made. Becoming at last much decayed it was judged requisite to be taken down. The present structure was completed in 1744 and stands contrary to general usage, North and South. The Rector is the Rev.ᵈ Hen.ᵗ Hutton, M.A.

Below 37 Around the hospital and turnpike, Whitechapel, *c.* 1790 Richard Horwood.

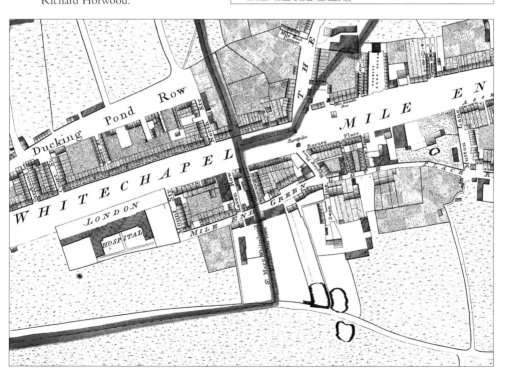

38 St Mary's church, Whitechapel, drawn by Thomas Shepherd.

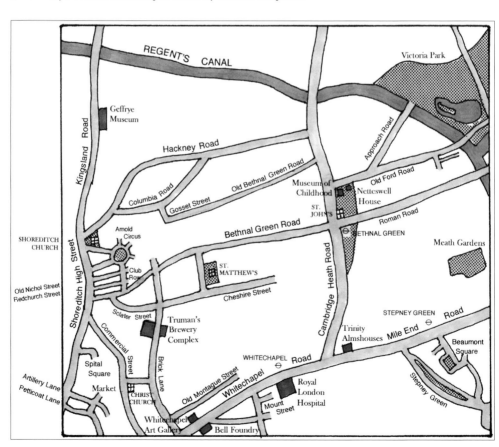

39 Spitalfields and Bethnal Green today. Map by Jane Seal.

Right 40 Spitalfields on Gascoyne's map, 1703.

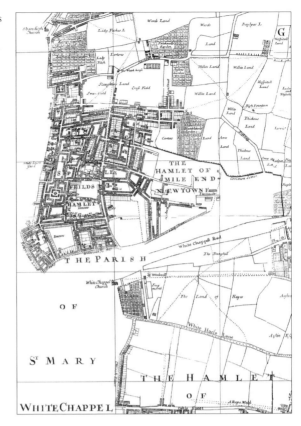

Below 41 Weavers' cottages in Puma Court. Photograph by Yvonne Hughes.

42 Christ Church, Spitalfields, in an engraving published in 1836.

The Mirror

OF
LITERATURE, AMUSEMENT, AND INSTRUCTION.

No. 766.]   SATURDAY, MARCH 5, 1836.   [PRICE 2d.

CHRIST CHURCH, SPITALFIELDS.

A LITTLE to the eastward of Bishopsgate-street lies Spitalfields, originally a hamlet of the parish of St. Dunstan, Stepney. In the reign of Queen Anne, when the Legislature had determined to erect fifty new churches in the metropolis, this populous district was found to require one of the number. The separation accordingly took place; and the first stone of the intended church was deposited by Edward Peck, Esq., one of the Commissioners, in 1715, as we are informed by the inscription upon that gentleman's monument within the church; though the Parish Clerks' Remarks state 1723; which has been followed by others. The site was purchased for 1,260*l.* and the chosen architect was Nicholas Hawksmoor, Esq., who was a pupil of Sir Christopher Wren. Mr. Hawksmoor's estimate was 13,570*l.*; but he expended 14,418*l.* 3*s.* 6*d.* The Church was

VOL. XXVII.   L   766

43 Anna Garthwaite's house. Photograph by Yvonne Hughes.

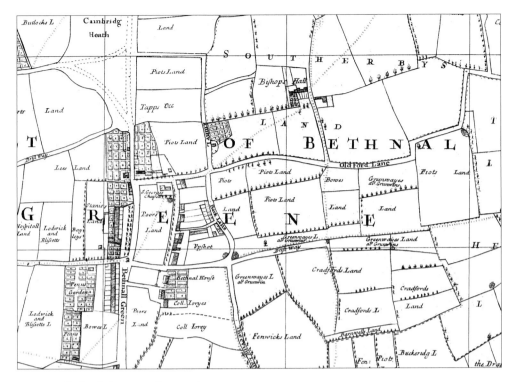

44 Bethnal Green on Gascoyne's map, 1703.

KIRBY CASTLE, BETHNAL GREEN. (THE BLIND BEGGAR'S HOUSE).

45 Kirby's Castle, Bethnal Green – by 1727 a private madhouse.

46 Aldgate House, Bethnal Green, 1808.

47 The White Hart on the site of the turnpike, Mile End Road. Photograph by Yvonne Hughes.

48 Looking along Mile End Road to the east: the entrance to Mile End Old Town today. Photograph by Yvonne Hughes.

49 Wickam's department store. Photograph by Yvonne Hughes.

Left 50 The Trinity House almshouses today. Photograph by Yvonne Hughes.

Below 51 Mile End Turnpike, by Thomas Rowlandson, 1798. *(City of London Corporation)*

VIEWS of LONDON. Nº 5

Entrance from MILE END *or* WHITE CHAPLE TURNPIKE

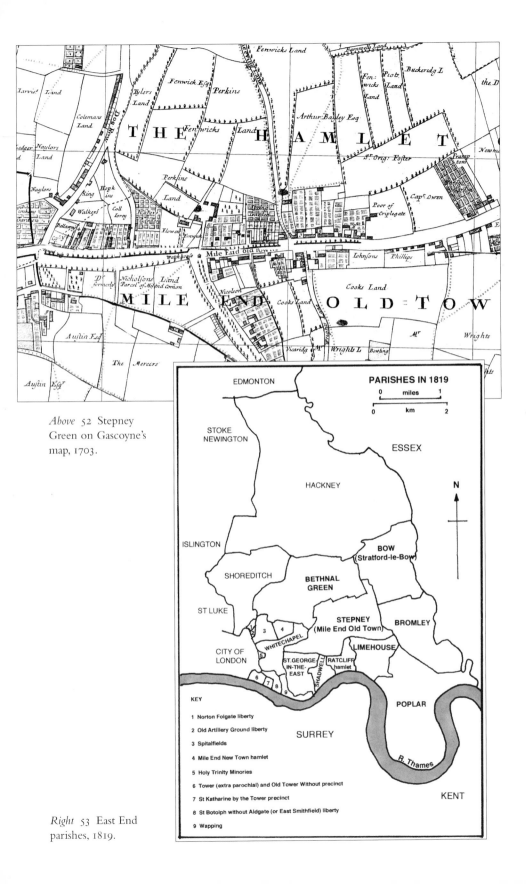

Above 52 Stepney Green on Gascoyne's map, 1703.

Right 53 East End parishes, 1819.

The following labels appear on the maps:

THE HAMLET

MILE END OLD=TOW

PARISHES IN 1819

EDMONTON

STOKE NEWINGTON

ESSEX

HACKNEY

N

ISLINGTON

BOW (Stratford-le-Bow)

SHOREDITCH

BETHNAL GREEN

ST LUKE

STEPNEY (Mile End Old Town)

BROMLEY

CITY OF LONDON

WHITECHAPEL

LIMEHOUSE

ST.GEORGE IN-THE-EAST

RATCLIFF hamlet

SHADWELL

POPLAR

SURREY

R. Thames

KENT

KEY

1 Norton Folgate liberty

2 Old Artillery Ground liberty

3 Spitalfields

4 Mile End New Town hamlet

5 Holy Trinity Minories

6 Tower (extra parochial) and Old Tower Without precinct

7 St Katharine by the Tower precinct

8 St Botolph without Aldgate (or East Smithfield) liberty

9 Wapping

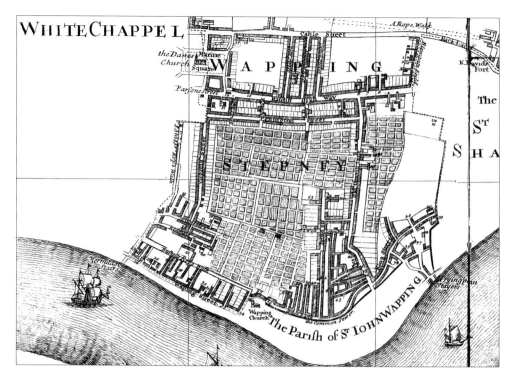

54 Wapping Stepney on Gascoyne's map, 1703.

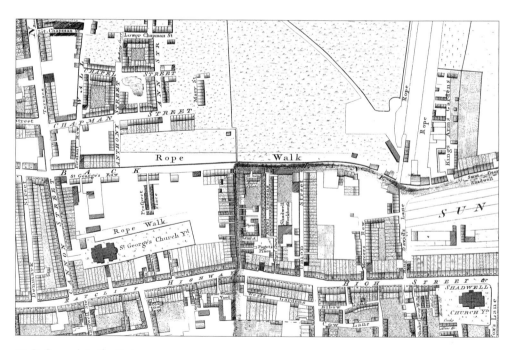

55 St George's in the East, c.1790.

56 The Prospect of Whitby, Wapping Wall – the solitary fragment of eighteenth-century Shadwell.

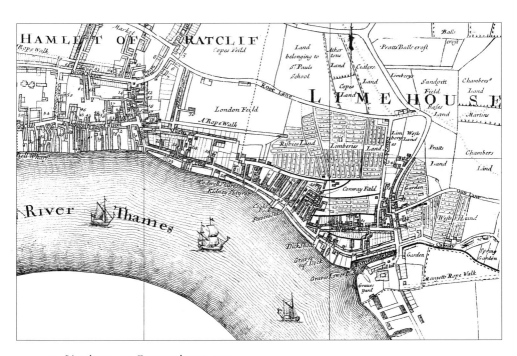

57 Limehouse on Gascoyne's map, 1703.

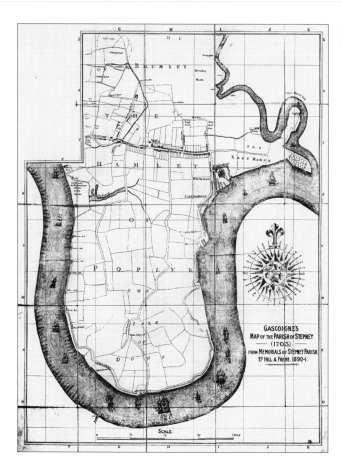

58 Poplar and the Isle of Dogs on Gascoyne's map, 1703.

59 The East India Company chapel, now St Matthias's, Poplar. Photograph by Yvonne Hughes.

2423.—The Idle Apprentice sent to Sea.

60 In the background of this engraving, entitled 'The Idle Apprentice sent to Sea' (after Hogarth), four of the twelve windmills at Millwall can be seen.

61 A view of Bow, 1783; the artist is not known. *(City of London Corporation)*

62 Early nineteenth-century houses in Sidney Square, Stepney. Photograph by Yvonne Hughes.

THE PEOPLE'S PALACE FOR EAST LONDON
THE FOUNDATION STONE OF WHICH IS TO BE LAID BY THE PRINCE AND PRINCESS OF WALES. JUNE 28

63 The People's Palace, Mile End: the foundation stone was laid in June 1886 by the Prince and Princess of Wales.

On the opposite side of the highway from the almshouse was Lady Leake's Grove, where hundreds of birds nested, and behind it seven exclusive houses occupied by the elite of Mile End, among them the Leake family themselves and silk merchant Francis Cokayne, lord mayor in 1750–51. Lady Leake was Christian, wife of the 'Brave and Fortunate' Admiral Sir John Leake (1656–1720), probably the most famous local, said to have been the best sailor of his day and five times Admiral of the Fleet, well known for the relief of Londonderry and taking Gibraltar. The couple had six children, of whom only one survived childhood. All Lady Leake was left with was her scapegrace son. Captain Richard Leake married badly, ran through his money, then lived on his father until his death aged forty-three. His grandfather, it was said, had predicted at the boy's birth that he would be very vicious, very fortunate, so far as prize-money was concerned, and very unhappy. He must have been a nasty old man. The admiral's heir was his brother-in-law Captain Stephen Martin, his former flag captain, who added Leake to his name on inheriting his estate. He was the justice who interviewed Mary Vezey. By the 1790s the Grove was covered in houses, but was called Lady Leake's Ground for another hundred or so years. Stephen Martin Leake, the captain's son, was Garter King of Arms.

After Red Cow Lane (Cleveland Way), a little way north of the road was the brewery, there by the 1720s. Taken over by Robert Westfield/Wastfield in 1757 and by John Charrington in 1766, it grew and grew, and by 1809 it was the second biggest in all London. Nearby was the house of Captain Richard Haddock, comptroller of the navy from 1739–49, son of Admiral Sir Richard Haddock.

Assembly Row, on the south side, between Mutton Row and Stepney Green, was built in the 1760s by Ebenezer Mussel, whom we met in Bethnal Green. It was here that Captain Cook took a house, moving upmarket from Wapping in 1765; his family were living in the Row when he landed at Botany Bay in April 1770. It was a modest enough house for such a great man, with eight small rooms and a 15ft frontage; you can see some of the furniture in the National Maritime Museum. As its name suggests, this was the site of Mile End's Great Assembly Rooms, which lay behind the Row, remembered today in Assembly Passage. The hall was used for public meetings and, no doubt, for balls. Probably its most exciting time was 10 March 1770, seven weeks before Captain Cook discovered Australia, when radical John Wilkes held a rowdy anti-government meeting here, promoting his Bill of Rights. Apparently he had good support among the locals.

Further along on the north side, just before Globe Lane (Road) and set back from the main road, was the Spring Garden, known as the Jews Spring Garden, perhaps because the sons of Abraham took their entertainment here, perhaps because of the proximity of the Sephardic cemetery and the Jews' hospital, which were on the other side of Globe Lane. In 1743 it was kept by Mr Dove Rayner, a good-humoured man of 'agreeable mirth' according to the *London Daily Post*.

Nearby, before reaching the burial ground, on the other side of Globe Lane, was the town's chief farrier's shop, kept by Caleb Simmonds from 1735 to 1748; between 1768 and 1784 it was a bakery.

Opposite the Spring Garden, at the junction with Whitehorse Lane, was Mile End's main coaching inn, the Whitehorse. This tavern and the Trinity Almshouses are the only local landmarks noted in the *New Complete Guide* of 1771. It had about seventeen bedrooms, hung with tapestries, mirrors and paintings, beds dressed with crimson, blue or green silk hangings, equipped with clocks, tea-tables, warming pans, thirty chamberpots, thirty-one pairs of sheets, candlesticks, fine china, glasses and cups for chocolate and coffee. In the bar the drinks on offer were mainly beer and 'mountain wine', costing about 7d a pint. (£2.50 today). There were loads of hay and eight horses in the stables. Joseph Bolton, the land-lord (d. 1741), had a tortoiseshell tobacco box, various wigs, a walking cane and a number of books.

About a dozen or so taverns and inns were interspersed with shops along the north side of the road; the main ones were the Globe, the Three Colts and the Swan. In all, the town had about forty hostelries mid-century, including the intriguingly named Why Not Beat the Dragon, which may have had some connection with a racehorse, whose owner William Connop made a fortune in his apothecary's shop (1742–65). Other shopkeepers were Mark Hammil, the linen draper (1741–71), Thomas Humphrey, the butcher, and Henry Hollely, the chairmaker.

From Globe Road on the left there was the Jews' old burial ground and Bancroft's school and almshouses (now Queen Mary and Westfield College), a palace of a place, its central block resembling the Royal Hospital at Chelsea. Opposite, on the south side of the road, was the parish workhouse. After Bancroft's there was the Jewish Neuvo Beth Caim, the West Ham waterworks, Cook's alms-houses, and then James Gordon's famous nurseries; we are now in the vicinity of Mile End underground station. After The Plough tavern there are open fields fan-ning out northwards with seven gentlemen's residences facing them on the south side of the main road, all set in their own grounds and superior enough to warrant a place in Cary's *Survey of the High Roads from London*, a guide to posh houses. In the next century the monstrous City workhouse was to be built here; it still stands.

The nursery, just north-west of The Plough, was quite a sight, with its rows of greenhouses. James Gordon took over and expanded an existing nursery in 1738. It rivalled the Chelsea Physic Garden and made Gordon rich and famous; he had a seed shop in Fenchurch Street and another nursery in Bow. Swedish botanist Daniel Solander, who sailed with Cook on his first voyage to the Pacific, was most impressed when he visited the Mile End establishment, but rather horrified at the cost of the plants. Gordon thought nothing of charging £15 for a magnolia, about six months' wages for a poor weaver.

Stepney Green: 'A small strip of Eden'

Leaving the hurly-burly of the road, with its wagons and chaises, its mailcoaches and flocks of sheep, we will return to Assembly Row to take a stroll south to Stepney church and village, branching off the highway just near Captain Cook's house.

The main access route to the village was anciently White Horse Lane, by the White Horse Inn. By the early eighteenth century there was another way, a little to the west. This was a wide stretch of avenue called Mile End Green, later Stepney Green, with the watchhouse at the top. The name is all that is left of the common that once extended from Whitechapel church as far as Stepney village. 'A small strip of Eden' was what Walter Besant called Stepney Green in 1882. It still is today, a quiet place of old trees and gardens, with a few Georgian houses and, best of all, the finest, prettiest house in all East London, No. 37, a survival from the reign of Queen Anne.

Between 1669 and 1684 the northern strip of the Green was enclosed and planted with rows of trees as a screen, and by the 1760s the east side of the road-way was strung with large properties, with two rows of smaller houses, 'The Thirteen Houses' on the west side and Mapp's Row on the east. Since medieval times the Green had been the resort of wealthy City men later it became known for its sea captains and colonial merchants. But Mapp's Row and its 'miserable cottages, one storey high – a very great nuisance', as a Victorian surveyor put it, took up a good third of the east side of the street.

With all this talk of moneyed Mile Enders, we should not forget that the majority of the inhabitants were ordinary families, the like of which might be found in Mapp's Row. If you look at the baptisms in Stepney church for 1750, for instance, you will find in its sixty-one entries (as parents) two gentlemen, five seamen, one soldier, one schoolmaster, one apothecary, two farmers, five carpenters, one bricklayer, two turners, one sawyer, one mason, one tilemaker, one painter, one gardener, two weavers, one blacksmith, one cooper, one brewer's servant, one distiller, one victualler, one vintner, one butcher, one wheelwright, one netmaker, one cordwainer, one coachmaker, one peruke-maker, one tailor, one upholsterer and seven labourers. By the 1780s nearly half of the hamlet's houses were small ones, with five rooms or fewer.

Be that as it may, it would be a shame to spoil the image of Stepney's best street, and behind the rows of Lombardy poplars, limes, elms and horse chestnuts, there were large houses where maids flitted about polishing the mahogany furniture. Before the Thirteen Houses or Mapp's Row came to Stepney Green, veteran seaman Sir John Berry (d.1690), Admiral of the Red, a colleague of Pepys, had a house where Nos 61 and 63 now are. It had a coachhouse and stables, marble flooring and eight marble fireplaces, a counting-house, a master bedroom ('great chamber') with lemon-coloured damask bedhangings, tapestries on the walls and twelve 'great damask chairs'. Berry had risen through the ranks, the son of a poor Devon clergyman; he was knighted for rescuing the Duke of York's ship at the Battle of Solebay, and after his retirement from active service in 1688 was comptroller of the victualling accounts. Although one of Mile End's most eminent men, it was his wife who, albeit posthumously, achieved most local notice. Dame Rebecca Berry remarried aged forty-six, ten months after her husband's death, rather speedy even for the eighteenth century, but only lived six years to enjoy her new life. Her second husband, Thomas Elton, an elderly gentleman and apothecary of Bow, had an extravagant monument set up when she died, perhaps in a spirit of competition with his dead rival, whose memorial bust was in the church, adorned with cupids. Dame Rebecca's memorial was a large oval plaque, set into the wall on the outside of the church, bearing the arms of the Elton family, with three fishes on it, and some complimentary words about the lady's temperament:

> ... her peaceful mind,
> ... still was gentle, still was kind.
> Her very looks, her garb, her mien,
> Disclos'd the humble soul within ...
> Ne'er vex'd with this, ne'er mov'd with that.

The plaque became quite an attraction. It was known as the Fish and Ring and, for reasons that are not apparent, the notion arose that Dame Rebecca was the heroine of a popular ballad called 'The Cruel Knight'. The story tells how a knight hears the cries of a woman in labour and has a premonition that he will marry the child. He makes repeated attempts to kill her. When she is grown he takes her to the seashore and flings a ring into the sea, forbidding her ever to see him again unless she can find the ring. She becomes a cook, finds it in a cod that she is preparing, and they marry.

East India Company Captain Thomas Heath MP lived in the Berrys' old house from about 1703. He was a Whig MP, a director of the Company who got very rich by marrying the daughter of Virginia merchant and local landowner Arthur Bayley. A terrace of seven houses was built on the site in the 1760s, of which Nos 61 and 63 survive.

Before she was widowed and built Fitzhugh House over by the Turnpike, Mary Fitzhugh lived on the east side of the Green, with her husband Captain William from 1713 to 1731. No. 37, built in 1694 for Dormer Sheppard, a merchant, was bought in 1714 by Lady Mary Gayer, widow of Sir John, Governor of Bombay. Her monogram is still on the gate. Laurence Sullivan, an East India Company director, lived in the house from 1757 to 1763, where he was paid a visit by the Robert Clive (Clive of India) in 1760. From 1764 to 1811 it was the home of Isaac Lefevre, distiller and banker. Down towards the village, on the same side, was the vicarage, with 3 acres of orchard, occupied from 1679 to 1718 by the Revd John Wright and his wife Dorothy. Thomas Dod, a barrister's son from Cheshire, took up residence in the vicarage as Spitalfields Portionist with his bride Mary after Wright's death. Whatever high hopes the Dods might have had of their new life, it was to end in tragedy. Mary Tod bore him four children, two of whom died. Ten days after the death of his toddler son Dod himself followed him to the grave, leaving Mary pregnant and with two young children. He was buried in the chancel near the Colet tomb, where you can read his memorial tablet and inspect his coat of arms. Rector Ralph Cawley had the vicarage (it was now a rectory) rebuilt in 1764. According to a rather jaundiced incumbent, writing in 1841, it was 'as gloomy as a dungeon', on marshy ground and enclosed by trees.

Worcester House, the great rambling mansion where in Cromwell's day Maurice Thomson had lived and ruled the village, stood at the south-west end of Stepney Green, with its Tudor gatehouse, known as King John's Palace. It was now divided into three: part a girls' boarding school (1741–64) and part private dwellings. Captain Samuel Jones, deputy governor of the Hudson's Bay Company and churchwarden (1750) lived there (1741–86) with his family and a flock of servants; the Joneses had three menservants in 1780s, the most in all Mile End. Approached through the orchard of Worcester House was the solid edifice of Stepney Meeting, looking like a rather grand private house. It was built in 1674 for Matthew Mead. Independence went into decline after 1715 for some forty years and Stepney Meeting, which had played such an important part in the religious revolution of the previous century, was almost abandoned. In 1743 there were only seven men and twenty-five women, perhaps because of the poor preaching of the minister, John Hubbard. With the arrival of the celebrated Dr Brewer in 1746 things started to improve, and by 1796 the congregation numbered about 250. Brewer knew how to appeal to his flock, enlivening his preaching with anecdotes and making sure he knew which ship had just docked so he could address the crew directly in his sermons.

Stepney village and Stepney buns

Stepney village, not so long ago a select spot with country mansions, was quite a place for 'trippers' in the eighteenth century, with its bowling alleys and pleasure gardens. The *Ambulator* of 1774 commented: 'The village … is but small, and consists of few houses besides those of public entertainment; vast crowds of people of both sexes resorting thither on Sunday, and at Easter and Whitsun holidays, to eat Stepney buns, and to regale themselves with ale, cider etc.'

South of Dr Brewer's chapel, opposite the church, was the large, half-timbered Mercers' Great Place, once the home of the Colet family and residence of Thomas Cromwell. It was occupied by the early years of the eighteenth century by two taverns, the Spring Garden and the Green Dragon, each with its own pleasure garden. The Spring Garden was well known, a downmarket and much smaller version of Vauxhall. Here, under the lamps twinkling in the elms and poplars, the tars took their girls to drink and disport themselves. What would the stern reformer John Colet have thought of such goings-on in his family home! According to *Low Life*, published in 1764, the pleasure garden was the 'evening resort of holiday makers'.

Also near the church was a tavern called the King's Head, where the Cockney Feast was held every year in aid of a charity for putting poor parish boys out as apprentices, mainly at sea. Proceedings kicked off with a sermon in the church, given one year by the historian John Strype, who was a licensed preacher and cousin of the famous East India Company seaman Robert Knox. After this there was a grand procession, with charity boys walking two by two, led by eight stewards and accompanied by a band, and followed by a throng of locals, parading through the streets of Limehouse and Ratcliff, and ending up at the tavern.

A fair was held every year at Michaelmas, which drew in customers from all around. From 1664 to 1694 it was held on land that was still part of the common, on the main road, where Assembly Row was to be built. After this was enclosed by Dr John Nicholson it was moved to a site south of the Spring Garden on the south side of what is now Stepney Way. By the early years of the next century Stepney Fair was a fully fledged funfair, with rides for children (arms and legs were often broken), sideshows and all manner of booths. In 1820 a Romford farmer had a booth for 'Wonderful Travelling Deceptions'. Gangs of youths got into fights and were taken off to the watchhouse to cool off. In 1823, 300 constables and police officers were put on guard.

A more leisurely, and permanent attraction was, surprisingly perhaps, the churchyard and its gravestones. The ancient parish church, which lay in the hamlet of Ratcliff, stood in an enormous 7-acre churchyard. 'Sometimes', wrote Strype, 'they bury more in a Week in this single Parish than are buried in that Space of Time in all the Parishes of London within the Walls'. St Dunstan was the mother church for most of the area and the hub of a great 'province', until it was shorn of its overgrown children: Spitalfields, Wapping Stepney, Limehouse and Bethnal Green, Bow, and Poplar (1729–1817). Looking up at the white stuccoed church, well shrouded with trees, its tower topped with a golden cupola, you would have seen the outlines of the fifteenth-century structure, but 'defaced' with 'strange brick porches with little grated windows'. It seemed to John Paterson in 1714 that the building was too small for its purpose, 'Very unproportionable for a spacious parish and innumerable inhabitants'. By 1792 it was 'hurrying fast to decay'. The churchyard was not, on the face of it, much of a pleasure park. It was a notorious place for 'drops', or foundlings, where poor girls dumped babies that they could not care for. Hogs rooted under the elms, poplars and sycamores, and horses were put out to graze among the crumbling tombstones, 'street soil' and dumped builders' rubbish. After dark it was the haunt of local prostitutes, and bodysnatchers were at work. In 1737 Thomas Jenkins, one of the gravediggers, was dismissed for selling bodies. Even after the clearance of the 1780s it was so dangerous that when the large sum of 10s 6d was offered to guard it no one was prepared to take the job on, and 14s had to be paid for a private 'neighbourhood watch', with blunderbusses at the ready. However insalubrious the churchyard may have seemed to the vestry, it was a popular tourist spot, which featured in most guidebooks. We met Samuel Pepys taking a walk there in the last chapter. The *Spectator* noted on 24 October 1712 that 'The people of that parish have a particular genius for an epitaph', and for many years to come a stroll round Stepney churchyard, with an inspection of the wise, witty and sometimes sarcastic verses on the mossy tombstones, was accounted a good day out for Londoners.

We will take a walk round, starting with William Wheatley (d. 1683):

Whoever treadeth on this Stone,
I pray now tread most neatly:
For underneath this Stone here lyes
Your honest Friend Will. Wheatley.

The inscription on the tomb of Mad Hatter Roger Crabb (used as a model by Lewis Carroll) is worth taking to heart:

Tread gently, reader, near the Dust
Committed to this Tomb Stones trust;
For while 'twas Flesh it held a Guest
With universall Love possest;
A Soul that stem'd Opinions try'd,
Did over sects in triumph ride …
Wouldst thou his religion know,
In brief, 'twas this: To all to do
Just as he would be done unto …

The Hatter was a vegetarian and eccentric who enjoyed much local notoriety for his strange habits; Strype said he was a 'Philadelphian or Sweet Singer'. He wrote an autobiography, *The English Hermit or The Wonder of the Age*. After seven years' service in Cromwell's army and a cracked skull, he was ill rewarded by two years in prison. Thereafter he set up a hatshop in Chesham, 'got God' and stopped eating meat or drinking alcohol, gave his property to the poor and lived on a rood of land at Ickenham, eating bran, grass and leaves, and drinking water. Some say he lived in a tree. The caption on the woodcut of him in his pamphlet, published in 1655, reads:

Roger Crab that feeds on herbs and roots is here;
But I believe Diogenes had better cheer.

He died at Bethnal Green in September 1680.

Over to the north of the church lies the Wilkes family. William, of the Goldsmith's Company, and Sarah, his wife; they had a daughter, named Alice. On 25 June 1698 Alice died, aged nine, and was buried with her dead mother. Two years later her father followed, aged thirty-seven, unable to bear the grief. The inscription on the little girl's tomb, once to the north of the west end of the church, read:

Farewell dear Flower, no sooner came thy early piety to bloom
But Death hath cropt thy tender Bud
And laid thee in this mournful Tomb;
With her who like thee lay so near the Heart
As made it even Death itself to part.
With Patience he the Torment did endure,
But endless Love desin'd another Cure;
Think on't with Joy, here but his Body lies.
For Wilkes is fled and triumphs in the skies.

One wonders what gossip had been spread around the parish about Sarah Hartland, just twenty-five years old, who was buried on 4 December 1696 on the north side of the churchyard?:

Whose Heart too tender for to bear
From nearest Friends such Calumnies,
Receiv'd a Wound, and so she fell
To Death, a mournful sacrifice;
But did ascend in Peace and Joy
To him who did her Prayers hear
And will as in the Noon-day light,
Her spotless Innocence declare.

To the north-east (now Durham Row), was the grand 'Manor House', known more often as Lady Wentworth's House, where the ill-fated Duke of Monmouth had visited his mistress, Lady Henrietta. Here the grieving heiress came home to die, with her mother, Lady Philadelphia, in 1686. Lady Wentworth was a feisty woman, who had often presided at manor courts in person and had done all she could to keep afloat, selling off property and mortgaging to pay off her father-in-law's debts. At Henrietta's death there was a great to-do over the estate, with Lady Lovelace, her elderly aunt, fighting tooth and nail for the manor and everything else her niece had to leave. Claims were made that Vicar Wright, in cahoots with Lady Philadelphia's 'business manager' and agent, Sir William Smith, (apparently a known wheeler dealer, who specialised in defrauding the aristocracy) had concocted a will benefitting Lady Philadelphia and got the dying woman to sign it when she was wracked with pain and insensible.

Lady Philadelphia sold the manor to Lord Montgomery in 1695 but was still living in the manor house at her death the following year with a flock of servants, including her butler, John Fells, son of a Stepney farmer. Her will, witnessed by curate Isaac Sharpe and made just a month before she died (4 May 1696), gave generous legacies to all her servants, to Dr Wright the vicar and for the local poor. She left £2,000 for a monument to be raised to her 'dear child' at Toddington, the family's country house. It was a sad and solemn procession that left Stepney in the early days of May 1696, taking the body of the last Stepney Wentworth to the family vault in the Bedfordshire countryside.

From that point the lordship of the manor passed through various hands. Still they were property owners and interfered in local affairs. In 1704 the lord of the manor told the Whitechapel constables to inspect weights and measures, and in 1745 he was involved in a dispute with the vestry over the election of officers. The manor's steward attended the Court of Record (debtors' court) in Whitechapel, and the manor took tolls from the Whitechapel haymarket.

Over on the east (Limehouse) side of the churchyard, enclosed behind a brick wall, stood the Tudor parsonage house. This was the very large house shown on the Mercers' map of 1615, a rambling and ramshackle edifice with cottages, out-houses and pigsties; no rector had lived there for some time. It was repaired in 1696 and used as a vestry house and accommodation for the curates.

St Dunstan's church and the parish divided

On entering this 'very old, low, dark building', you step down 2ft into the dim, musty nave, pewed with oak, its walls clad with oak wainscoting to a height of 8ft and with wooden galleries on three sides. Over the altar gold cherubs, and the figures of Moses and Aaron, can be discerned in the flickering light, if the chandeliers are lit, and behind them the black and gold tablets of the Commandments and the Law. All around are the sepulchral monuments of naval officers, and the whole is dominated by the organ, with its magnificent carved case and King David at his harp. The rood screen has survived, and there is a three-decker pulpit, with seats for rector, curate and clerk. The church is full of baize-lined private pews, square boxes like animal pens, to which their owners or renters had keys and where they sat in comfort with cushions and rugs. Sir John Berry's box, just south of the pulpit, had been the subject of a dispute in 1693 when several people, including Mrs Greaves, the curate's wife, had started using it. The children from the charity schools sat at the back of the church on forms. Women pew openers were paid 11*d*; one such was Mrs Jenkins, wife of the bodysnatching gravedigger.

For nearly forty years this was John Wright's church. He was vicar from 1679 and rector from 1710 to 1718. He had been there when the bells rang out with a special welcome for William III's arrival in 1689. Vicar Wright stayed firmly in post when between 3–400 'non-juring' clergy were forced out of their jobs for refusing to take the oath of allegiance to the new regime, although his sympathies were High Church. He and his curate, Isaac Sharpe, came under fire from the Dissenting press; Daniel Defoe and another pamphleteer called John Tutchin accused them, among other things, of charging for baptisms. All over the country those who stayed loyal to the banished regime, Jacobites and non-jurors, expressed their disapproval of the new monarchs by their actions in church: when it was time to pray for the royal family they rose from their knees, slammed shut their prayerbooks or turned the leaves over noisily. Little of this behaviour would have been noticed in Stepney church.

On 19 February 1708 Brasenose College purchased the patronage of Stepney from William Lord Montgomery, First Earl of Powis, who had bought it from the Wentworth family. Although it was quite usual for eighteenth-century Oxford and Cambridge colleges to buy advowsons for the support of their married fellows (who were not allowed to be resident in college) the Bishop of London was much against the scheme, and supposed it would meet with 'universal opposition'. The purchase was nevertheless confirmed by an Act of Parliament in April 1711. It included other advowsons, among them Whitechapel and St John Wapping. This was the beginning of Brasenose College's long rule in the East End, which lasted until 1864. The act united the vicarage and rectory of Stepney under the title of rectory. On the death or departure of the existing incumbent it was to be divided into two 'portions', and the college was to present two men as portionists, one for Spitalfields and one for Ratcliff. The scheme came into operation when vicar John Wright died in 1718, with the twin rectors, one in the vicarage and one in the parsonage, taking it in monthly turns to run the parish. With the creation of new parishes the experiment came to an end in 1743.

Meanwhile plans were afoot for the proper division of the parish (see above). Money voted by parliament was on offer for new churches for London and Stepney's vestry recommended that Limehouse, Spitalfields and Wapping Stepney needed their own churches. The East India Company's chapel in Poplar was reckoned to be large enough to serve as a parish church for that hamlet. Bethnal Green was not yet considered. The parish clerk and sexton were very worried about the great loss of fees, although both they and the rectors received some measure of compensation; Spitalfields and Wapping Stepney had to pay St Dunstan £100 a year and Limehouse £50 a year. Perhaps the curates welcomed the prospect of less work, as indeed they might; burials dropped from 2,755 in 1725–29 to 460 in 1780–84. As to the vestry, there is no indication that anyone was particularly opposed to the measure; there was, as far as we know, no rumpus created by the sea captains of Mile End. In all probability they were glad to free themselves of the troublesome poorer hamlets, which they were often called upon to subsidise. Spitalfields, the nursery of low life and home of rioting weavers, was no great loss. Ordinary folk seemed to want their new churches, and were continually petitioning to have them completed when work came to a halt for lack of cash.

The three vast Hawksmoor churches (Christ Church Spitalfields, St George's in the East, and St Anne Limehouse) that were built were all made parochial, and all belonged to Brasenose. By Act of Parliament of 24 March 1729 Bow was finally accorded independent status, and £3,500 was voted from public funds for its endowment. Bethnal Green had its own church built in the 1740s, while plans to make Poplar chapel a parish church came to nothing until 1817; in the meantime the chapel was rebuilt by the East India Company in 1776. While work started on the enormous modern edifices that would dwarf their old Gothic mother church and seize away half her flock (the tower of St George's in the East was a massive 160ft, as compared to St Dunstan's 92ft), the strange new system of twin rectors or portionists was introduced. At least the clergy in charge would now be resident in the parish, in theory. One of the twin rectors might saddle up and ride over the fields to baptise in the better houses of Bethnal Green or Spitalfields, and honour their parishioners with a Sunday sermon, but for the most part it was the curates who took services, buried the dead, baptised infants and conducted the numerous weddings that came St Dunstan's way. The church was to become well known, like Holy Trinity Minories (mentioned earlier) as a venue for couples wanting a quick, quiet wedding; they came in their hundreds. Weddings became a significant source of income: in the 1690s a wedding by licence cost 4s; later in the century the rector charged 10s for a marriage by licence and 5s for marriage by banns, with an extra charge if the couple were not resident in the parish.

The newly married Oxford fellows who one by one came to Stepney had a rough ride. They came from their cushioned bachelordom to marriage and children, from their ivory tower stronghold of Jacobitism, where conversation was exclusively college business, 'Tory politics, personal anecdotes and private scandal'. There was virtually no religious instruction and certainly nothing that might equip them for running a mercantile and industrial parish with an overriding tradition of Low Churchdom and Nonconformity (there were said to be nineteen Nonconformist chapels in Stepney in 1711) or to deal with the machinations of a powerful, hostile vestry. There were fights about fees charged for baptisms, marriages and funerals, about the choice of key parish officials and in general about who was in charge, the rector or the sea-captains and merchants of Mile End Green. Like the seventeenth-century Puritans, Nonconformists resented having to pay to shore up the crumbling old parish church. The situation was exacerbated by the attitude of the high-handed clergy at the helm, and the exclusivity and corruption of the select vestry (until it was disposed of).

The first sole rector after the portionist experiment ceased in 1743 was Robert Leybourne, Spitalfields Portionist, rector of the new church at Limehouse (appointed in 1729), nephew of the Principal of Brasenose, Robert Shippen, whom we met in Whitechapel. Leybourne was disastrous for Stepney, a tactless, autocratic man with little interest in the parish, spending much of his time in Oxford and preaching fashionable charity sermons in Bath. He was rarely in attendance at vestries in the 1730s and the parish was run by a few powerful locals, notably Ratcliff Warden, Henry Jones and Alderman Francis Cokayne, lampooned during his time as lord mayor for his injustice. If the inscription on the rector's wife's tomb in St Dunstan's (presumably devised by him) is to be taken seriously, his domestic persona was much like his public face: Mary Leybourne's 'sole ambition', it says, was to 'please her husband'. He fell out with both the Limehouse and Stepney vestries, the former for sending his curate to their meetings instead of going himself, the latter over fees and appointments, control over the size of the vestry, whose right it was to let out ground for tombstones, and virtually any other serious matter that arose.

It was the curates (four of them were licensed in 1739–40) who kept the show on the road. Hugh Colley was effectively vicar from 1747 for forty years. Why this popular, hard-working cleric, gently reared and Oxford educated, never got preferment seems strange. Perhaps it was his temper: he was indicted for assault at the Middlesex Sessions in 1746; although he was found not guilty, mud sticks. John Entick, a Classical scholar, historian and radical activist, was the most celebrated of Stepney's curates. He was arrested for writing an attack on the government and had an affair with the wife of one of the masters at Bancroft's, where he too was on the staff. Dr Cawley, a wealthy man from Wigan, was rector from 1759 for eleven years. During his time at Stepney he married Ann Cooper, a relative by marriage of Jane Austen. According to the author, who was briefly taught by Mrs Cawley as a seven year old, she was a 'cold, stiff woman'. Presumably with his forthcoming marriage in mind, in 1763 Cawley asked for permission to demolish the tumbledown rectory with its three or four cottages, 'hog stye and other mean buildings', and use the material to build a new house. Brasenose agreed, and it was completed in 1768, a two-storey house

with a garret, lying a little to the east of the old vicarage. The rector paid the
£690 it cost out of his own pocket.

Between 1774 and 1778 Stepney vestryhouse was a battleground. For over a
hundred years Stepney had been governed by a 'select vestry', a self-perpetuating
and probably corrupt body run by a few rich men. This changed: from May 1778
any householder might turn up at the meetings to have his say and cast his vote.
It started, or appears to have started, in June 1774, with an unseemly fracas at
a vestry meeting. The vestry leader, Captain Gilbert Slater of Mile End Green,
an East India Company man who had sailed to China and India, and whose
ships had raided in the Caribbean, assaulted John Nixon, nominated as Mile End
Old Town warden, and threw him out of the meeting. Nixon was a clerk in the
cashier's office of the Bank of England, earning £60 a year in 1755 and £200 in
1780, well down the socio-economic scale from Slater. A lawsuit at the King's
Bench ensued, initiated by Nixon, which the grandees regarded as an attempt to
overthrow their select vestry, which indeed it was. While the American colonies
were declaring themselves independent, Stepney's fight went on in the courts,
culminating in a coup on 5 May 1778. A great meeting of 'many inhabitants'
was called by the churchwardens of Mile End Old Town and Mile End New
Town, and voted in favour of having an open vestry. From that time, for many
years, the government of Stepney parish was an extraordinarily democratic affair,
with hundreds of ratepayers turning up to vote for the election of parish clerk,
sexton and organist, and to debate other matters of moment such as the imposition of church rates. In 1814, 2,241 votes were cast in the election of the lecturer.
There were, almost certainly, a number of Dissenters among the individuals who
attended these mass meetings and voted in the ballot; the rector reported in 1778
that Dissent 'is growing apace'; there were seven or eight chapels in his parish and
the Methodists were on the increase.

In March 1789 300 parishioners confronted new rector Braithwaite at a vestry
meeting to elect a new parish clerk. The rector refused to take the chair, which
was taken by the Ratcliff warden, and there followed an angry debate over whose
right it was to appoint parish clerk. Two weeks later, on 17 March, 645 inhabitants gathered to vote for the clerk. Braithwaite had taken refuge in Oxford,
where he seems to have stayed put, sending messages of protest. This little English
drama, which incurred no bloodshed and rocked no dynasties, was played out as
revolution was brewing in France. One cannot help but speculate how different
things might have been if there had been some vehicle for the people of Paris to
voice their grievances and impose their rights. It seems rather silly to compare
the storming of the Bastille with the election of a parish clerk in Stepney, but the
democratic vestries of London surely played their part in protecting the country
from revolution.

Down to the riverside: Whitehorse Street

Leaving the squabbling in the vestryhouse, we will set off south down Whitehorse Street (now Whitehorse Road) towards the river and Ratcliff Cross, the 'town centre' of the hamlet of Ratcliff. It was a walk of just under 1 mile from the church to the riverbank, from the leafy village with its bowling greens and pleasure gardens to the busy centre of riverside activity in Stepney's ancient port. Whitehorse Street was flanked by fields, with just a single row of houses on each side, belonging to the Mercers' Company. First we would have passed a great cowyard just south-east of the churchyard, then the Mercers' almshouses on the other side of the road, a neat row of smart little homes with the Company's coat of arms and a bust of Dame Mico, the foundress, over the entrance. A little further south from 1779 was the burial ground for Stepney Meeting, its almshouse and a small charity school (1785). Dean Colet House, the old High Master's house, belonging to St Paul's School, was now two houses, in the Classical style, with the weatherboarded gabled buildings of the workhouse next door, on the corner of Salmon Lane. On the other side of the road was the parish school – little girls in straw hats with ribbons, boys in leather breeches busy plaiting nets. As the road veered round to the right and became Brook Street, there was the watchhouse at the top of Butcher Row, the entrance to the commercial and industrial riverside complex with the Cross at its hub. Jonathan James rolled into the Ratcliff watchhouse at four in the morning one April, and 'declared that his present Majesty King George the Second and Sir Robert Walpole Knight were rogues and villains like unto the Watchmen belonging to the said watchhouse'.

It is time to take a walk along the riverbank and breathe in the air of sailortown.

Sailortown: the riverside from St Katharine's to Blackwall

According to the *Foreigners' Guide* (1752), in the five 'contiguous places' (St Katharine's, Wapping, Shadwell, Ratcliff and Limehouse) 'the little streets, lanes, alleys and courts swarm with people, and are so considerable, that they contain as many houses as several capital cities in Europe'. Wapping, once 'one great wash', had thirty-seven households per acre in the 1690s, and by 1801 the parish of St George's in the East, old Wapping Stepney, had over 20,000 people in its 244 acres.

The hamlets on the north bank of the Thames from the Tower to Limehouse comprise a roughly triangular patch of land, about 2 miles east-west and a little under a mile north-south. To the east of Limehouse, where the river loops round creating a peninsula, is the old Stepney Marsh, now the Isle of Dogs, an area of 836 acres, with the villages of Poplar and Blackwall across its neck. At the opening of the century, apart from the Liberty of St Katharine's, Wapping Whitechapel and Shadwell, all the area belonged to Stepney parish. By the end Limehouse had become independent, as had Wapping Stepney, now called St George's in the East. Although there were seven distinct places, Wapping being divided in two, they were to a degree much of a muchness.

Everything here was concerned with the expanding seaborne empire, with all things maritime: with the manufacture of ropes, sails, anchors, blocks (pulleys for ropes), masts and rigging, with charts, maps and nautical instruments, with victualling, watering and manning the ships. When Strype updated Stow's survey in the 1720s Wapping stood 'exceeding thick with buildings, and is very populous; having been much improved by human industry'. There was, as we shall see, a great deal of money around, and extremes of wealth and poverty lived side by side. It was the heyday of London's sailortown; monuments in the churches were those of notable mariners, and you would be sure to have met gold-braided sea captains in bicorne hats striding or riding about their business. Jack tars you would have met in abundance, sporting their trademark pigtails, baggy trousers and 'bum-freezer' jackets, leaning on the bars in alehouses or rambling about, their pockets jingling. Although the pre-eminence of Limehouse as a shipbuilding centre had gone, there were still many shipwrights. There were ships' bakers and marine store dealers, instrument-makers, laundresses who washed the seamen's clothes, and slopsellers who sold them, ratcatchers who went aboard to get rid of vermin, lodging houses, brothels and pawnshops. Between the Pool of London and Blackwall in the 1720s, Defoe noted, on both sides of the river, three wet docks for laying up ships, twenty-two dry docks for repairing them, and thirty-three shipyards for building merchantmen.

Any East Ender who could afford it invested in trading enterprises; it was rare for the will of any local man of reasonable substance not to mention a part share in a merchant ship. A glance at contemporary newspapers leaves us in no doubt that ships and shipping were of prime concern for the 'chattering classes' of those days. The all-important coming and going of vessels was noted, cargoes might even be listed and in wartime, prizes itemised. Ships to be auctioned at Lloyds' Coffee House were advertised in the press: the *Nancy* brigantine, lying at Union Stairs, Wapping, the good ship *Yeomans* and *Sawcolt*, 'suitable for the Virginia Trade', lying at Ratcliff, and countless others. The riches that came in with every tide were very great. An enormous expansion of trade and the recovery of British shipping after the doldrums of the previous century brought wealth and activity to the riverside on an unprecedented scale. Patrick Colquhoun estimated that at the end of the eighteenth century £75 million (about £2,412,750,000 today) of floating property lay in the Thames in a single year. Between 1705 and 1751 the number of vessels in overseas trade increased from 1,335 to 1,682; by 1794 there were 3,663. Cargo tonnage rose from 234,639 in 1751 to 620,845 in 1794. The coastal trade doubled between 1750 and 1796; in 1795 there were 11,964 coastal ships using the port, of which some two-thirds were colliers. The vessels themselves were larger than before: the number of London-based ships of over 200 tons rose from 205 in 1732 to 751 by 1792. The river was a thick forest of masts. As well as the large ocean-going vessels there were smaller coastal ships, the myriad lighters and hoys used for carrying the cargoes to shore and hundreds of little 'taxi boats'.

Colquhoun described the merchandise: the East Indiamen brought 'tea, china, drugs, nankeens, muslins, calicoes, long cloths, cotton yarn, pepper and spices, salt petre, indigo, raw and manufactured silks, sugars etc.'. From the West Indies came 'sugar, rum, coffee, cocoa, pimento, ginger', from Africa 'fruit, wax, gums, elephants' teeth, palm oil and wine', from North America 'tobacco, rice, indigo, cotton, corn, oil, skins, and naval stores', from Eastern Europe 'hemp, linens, tallow, ashes, iron, masts, deals'. Linen was imported from Ireland and liquor from the Channel Islands. The mainstay of the coastal trade was coal from Newcastle, with corn from Kent and Essex, fish from Yarmouth, butter and cheese from East Anglia. Exports, which exceeded imports considerably in value, were 'linens, woollens, haberdashery etc.' sent to the Indies, 'liquor, arms and gunpowder' to Africa. To the Continent went 'British manufactures and East and West India goods'. Ships discharged their cargoes upstream at the City's Legal Quays or the Sufferance Wharves, on the south bank, and at St Katharine's, where the total quay frontage was less than 1,500ft, a third of that of Bristol. The congestion was appalling, with vessels queuing up for a week or more. The larger ships were berthed in the Middle and Lower Pool, all along the riverside from St Katharine's to Limehouse. East Enders worked as stevedores (who loaded), lumpers (who unpacked), porters (carrying merchandise from hold to lighter) and as watchmen (guarding the wharves).

Smuggling and theft were rife; ships and lighters loaded with valuable cargoes were continually prey to the waterside gangsters and petty thieves, and anyone who had mind to help themselves, like the ratcatchers who went aboard and the children ('mudlarks') who prowled about on the shore at low tide. According to Colquhoun it was regarded as a legitimate pursuit, and men 'who would shudder at the idea of committing a burglary, or robbing on the highway', were happy to seize sugar by the hundred weight'. Sometimes they were caught; more often they were not. Thomas Handley landed a horde at Ratcliff in 1742: 346lb of teas, 4½lb of coffee and 51yds of handkerchiefs; and no duty paid. Rum, sugar and ivory were stolen when the *Peggy and Jenny* docked at Limehouse Hole at Carter's Dock, and the goods were taken to the Black Swan in Ratcliff. The *Wiltshire*, lying off the Cross after its voyage from the West Indies, lost 2cwt of sugar while lying at Ratcliff. The *Augustus Caesar* lying at Bell Wharf had 80lb of ginger stolen from her lighter. Lighters were often cut adrift and plundered when they got to shore. Anchors, ropes and all sorts of equipment was taken, as well as cargoes. There were night plunderers, known as 'light horsemen'; day plunderers, called 'heavy horsemen', and 'scuffle hunters', who hid stolen goods under their long aprons. West India merchantmen, with their riches of rum and sugar, suffered the heaviest losses, and at the end of the century it was estimated that four out of five of the Company's ships were 'game' and the officers or watchmen in cahoots with the thieves. Patrick Colquhoun was persuaded by them to set up a force of river police in 1798, but it was not until the construction of the fortress-like enclosed docks in the next century that the situation was effectively remedied.

Sailors

'When one goes into Rotherhithe and Wapping, which places are mainly inhabited by sailors, but that somewhat of the same language is spoken, a man would be apt to suspect himself in another country. Their manner of living, acting, dressing, and behaving are so very peculiar to ourselves.' This was the opinion of magistrate John Fielding. If every other man in Spitalfields was a weaver, every other man in St Katherine's, Wapping and Shadwell had at least some marine or river experience. They were a rough lot. Seafaring labour was here for the taking by the great merchant trading companies, the East India Company, Russia Company and Hudson's Bay Company. Until the 1880s there was no such thing as joining the navy, except for officers, and the Royal Navy recruited from the same pool. There were the men who plied for passenger hire, the lightermen who manned the barges for unloading the ships, fishermen and others who had been reared to work on the river. On offer, too, for manning the ships, were men who had no trade or were on the run: boys fleeing from ill-treatment by their masters, weavers who had been laid off in Spitalfields, orphans with no one to help them, and out-of-control teenagers. George Peters, a Ratcliff Highway carpenter's son, had been trouble since he was out of the cradle, swearing so as to 'pollute the very air', mixing with rough types and 'proficient in every kind of mischief'. His parents, 'fearing the fatal tree', put him to sea, thinking it might 'bring him to leave off his wicked habits'. He joined a man of war and then a collier, but returned to his life of crime; and his parents' fears were confirmed. Thomas Trevis, a Shadwell boy who, with his father dead or gone and his mother in the workhouse, had worked at rigging and then gone north on a coal boat, thought of volunteering 'when the press for seamen begun', but turned to burglary instead.

The charity known as the Cockney Feast and then the Marine Society, set up in 1756 for manning the navy for the Seven Years War in 1756, sponsored lads for sea service. In 1773 the Society sent off fourteen-year-old Isaac Scott (just 4ft 5in tall), a silkwinder's son from Spitalfields, a drawboy, and John Lank, a weaver's boy of Norton Folgate, also fourteen. In 1774 went Charles Holmes from Bethnal Green, Thomas Francis, a carpenter's son from Norton Folgate, who used to make toys, Thomas Tolley, another Spitalfields weaver's drawboy, and George Mackenzie, aged thirteen, from Whitechapel. George's only relative was a step father and he lived with a twine spinner. Among lads sponsored in 1775 were Thomas Tansey from Aldgate, who had worked with a tobacco spinner, and in 1780 Joseph Howard, who had been living with his mother in Rosemary Lane, working as an errand boy, Robert Hobbs, who had worked with his father, a Petticoat Lane shoemaker, and Thomas Townend of Bethnal Green, son of a brewer's servant, who had worked in a rope ground.

For the skilled and unskilled there was a chance of escape and the possibility of making a good living, or even a fortune, if they survived the harsh conditions at sea, and promotion from the ranks to officer in the navy was not uncommon; Admiral Berry, whom we met in Stepney church, had done so, and Captain Cook himself joined up as an able seaman. As Millicent Rose wrote, 'A great part of the riches that flowed up the river with every tide was paid for in East End courage and East End lives.' The need for serviceable men in time of war was urgent: during the Seven Years War the navy was employing some 85,000 men, as opposed to 10,000 in peacetime. There were something in the region of 80,000 men in the merchant service, ripe for poaching.

The Black Boy and Trumpet in St Katherine's was the East End's naval recruit-ment centre at this time. It was here, almost certainly, that in June 1755 James Cook, who had come south on a collier boat from Whitby, volunteered, having 'a mind to try my fortune that way'. At the opening of the American War of Independence the *Middlesex Journal and Evening Advertiser* (20–23 January 1776) reported the opening of 'several more houses of rendezvous … in Wapping and Shadwell' to man the ships that were being fitted all over the country. A gang of sailors, with an officer in charge, would set themselves up in the tavern and take on volunteers. The bounty offered was generous: in the 1750s a man might get £7 for volunteering as well as two months' advance wages, another £5. Once signed up the men were put on tenders and taken down river to the Nore or Portsmouth, or wherever they were needed.

As well as the reasonably well ordered recruitment operation in St Katherine's, raids were made, and unwilling, often drunken, men were seized for the navy from the alehouses and taverns or in the street. Only men who might be suit-able were pressed: those who were dressed in the distinctive seafaring garb were especially at risk. Everyone was scared of the press gang. Samuel Clements said that he carried a loaded pistol just in case, and Charles Cleaver was so frightened of being pressed that he dared not go into St Katharine's precinct. It was a vicious system, though accepted by most as a necessary evil, and hugely liable to abuse. It was easy enough to put the press gang onto someone you had a grudge against.

Thomas Milward had something against Wapping ropemaker William Clarenbolt and set the gang onto him, so he dared not go to work.

One ganger, Richard Eades, has left an account of himself. Son of a Southwark soldier, he apprenticed himself to a fisherman but failed to complete his apprenticeship, taking to sea as a servant with Captain Townsend of Plymouth on a man-of-war. He then went with Captain Rook of the *Sunderland* to impress men in the Channel – most pressing was done at sea. When this stint was over he hung around in Portsmouth, spent all his cash and returned to London, only to be pressed himself in a pub next to the Black Boy and Trumpet. He escaped, took to thieving with a gang of whores and was hanged, aged nineteen, for stealing a silver watch in Rag Fair.

It was not just the press gang that seafarers had to be afraid of. Demand for seamen for the merchant service was such, especially when the navy was luring volunteers in with generous bounties, that there was quite a trade in selling men. Crimps, or Wapping landlords as they were known, used various means to entice naval seamen from their ships, then sold them to the highest bidder. The unfortunate dupes were allowed to get behind with their rent and were then offered the choice of going to gaol for debt or being sold off. Alternatively the landlord or his heavies waited until they were drunk, then knocked them out and dragged them off to a buyer. One such crimp or kidnapper was Thomas Gater of the King of Prussia's Head in Shadwell. Although well known to the authorities, they were powerless to do anything about his activities.

However rough and ready their introduction to the sea, and however dangerous, gruelling and demoralising their life aboard ship, the sailors earned good money. Lads might earn as much as eight times more than their cousins who ploughed in Mile End or herded cattle in the Isle of Dogs, and at least double what was made by an ordinary Spitalfields weaver, who had rent to pay and food to buy. Food was plentiful, if basic and monotonous: ships' biscuits and pickled beef and pork, rather than oxtail soup. An able seamen in the navy got net pay of £11 7s 6d a year, with the added bonus of prize money, and small pensions might be paid out by the Greenwich Hospital. There were pensions for widows and for the wounded, and for officers there was half pay, a retainer paid for those no longer serving and a variety of other pensions. Pay in the merchant service was higher, but not always reliably delivered. Stephen Smith came home from a Jamaica run in the *Lovely Ann* with 10gns to spend on lodging at John Tevamlow's pub at Ratcliff Cross in the form of a promissory note from his employer. The West Indies trade paid very well, with as much as £40 offered for a voyage home to England. Thomas Robinson thought the £25 offered to him for a run to London from Jamaica on a sugar ship 'a great price'.

Not that much of the paypacket stayed in their pockets. Back home after months of confinement and abstinence sailors were ready to squander their cash on pleasure, and the landlords and girls of Wapping were eager to oblige. A 'black eye'd Susan' plying her wares at Rag Fair conned a sailor out of 2gns to 'please his inclination', according to a folksong. A surgeon who 'keeps a light at his door' in the Minories, and another on Tower Hill, advertised a 'speedy and safe cure for the pox'.

Servicing the navy and the trading companies' ships was big business for the locals in other ways. It was not all jack tars and larking in sailortown, whatever Dr Johnson might have thought. In January 1729 the *London Evening Post* reported that in nine weeks 1,000 oxen and 1,500 hogs had been slaughtered at the Victualling Office on Tower Hill. At the height of the Seven Years War (1760) the navy was consuming 96,700cwt of beef and 41,400cwt of biscuit. Casks of provisions were packed and distributed from the London victualling office and its branches at Plymouth and Portsmouth. The victualling office, once the Abbey of Tower Hill, was vast, complex and employed many people; there were a bakehouse, a slaughterhouse, hogpens and a hog hanging house, a cutting-house, a salthouse, where the meat was salted for preservation, a picklehouse, a coopers' workshop, stables, offices and a watchhouse. Outraged press reports in the bitter January of 1776 claimed that the 'mercenary harpies' at the victualling office were selling off 'perished salt provisions' cheaply to the poor of Wapping and Limehouse.

Local bakers made biscuits for the sea service on a mammoth scale: J.P. Malcolm noted the 'mansions of rich ship-bakers'. Joseph Curtis's Wapping house, with its adjoining bakehouse and counting house, was one such. Curtis was a very wealthy man, rich enough to advance money to the City authorities for the building of Blackfriars' Bridge, buy part shares in four vessels and leave £20,000 in specific legacies alone. All the accoutrements of the gentry were to be found at his fine house by Wapping Dock: chariot, stables and coachman, marble fireplaces, silver plate, paintings on the parlour walls, a diamond ring. He seems to have been a kindly and generous man with a multitude of friends, if the number of legacies in his will is anything to go by. Joseph Norwood, foreman at the bakery, was given an annuity and the old man's best hat, wig and clothes and all his shoes. Local brewers, coopers and distillers also did very well out of the sea service, as did butchers. Brothers Peter and Samuel Mellish, who provided meat for the navy during the Seven Years War and the American War of Independence, both died rich men. Samuel, of Upper Shadwell, had enough of a fortune to set up his eight bastard children, seven by his housekeeper. His daughters Charlotte and Esther had establishments of their own in Hampstead, one in Church Row; Fanny had her own house in Mile End; and his two sons called themselves 'esquire'. Peter's sons William (d.1798) and Peter jnr, who were born in Wapping High Street, inherited the business, and were responsible for supplying all the navy's fresh beef and live oxen, salt beef and pork for the whole area from Yarmouth to

Portsmouth, as well as London. Their slaughterhouse was in Shadwell, their cattle were pastured on the Isle of Dogs, and they had a country seat at Woodford and estates at Chingford.

Bad times: flood, fire, frost and riot

If weaving was a precarious trade, life was much more risky for the seafaring and waterside families. Young women were often widowed and children orphaned when ships went down or sailors were killed by pirates or in battle; there were sixty-three years of war between 1695 and 1815. At home families were at risk from flooding; the 'great breach' of 1660 brought the loss of thousands of pounds' worth of property in Limehouse, and Wappingers had a continual battle with the river, which was their lifeblood, being 'burthen'd with vast Charges in Keeping up their Damms or Fences towards the Water'. There was also a high fire risk among the flimsy timber workshops, with tar and pitch lying around and furnaces on the go. Locals petitioning for their own parish church were worried about the long trek to Whitechapel; their houses might catch fire while they were gone.

Wapping High Street was rebuilt after the fire of 1673, in which many houses owned by the Bridewell were lost and Sir William Warren's timberyard went up. Seventeen plots, wharves and houses between Wapping Dock and Frying Pan Stairs were destroyed. In 1682 a kettle of pitch was knocked over in a barge-builder's shop and fire broke out in Ratcliff. St Katharine's had a 'dreadful fire' in 1672 and Limehouse in 1716. In July 1794 there was a catastrophic fire in Ratcliff, when another bargebuilder's yard went up. This one belonged to Daniel Cloves in Cock Hill; he had insured it for £700 in 1786. The flames spread quickly, consuming 458 houses and 20 other buildings. Tents were pitched in nearby fields for the homeless and a subscription fund was set up. So immediate and generous was the response that the hamlet soon recovered.

Riverside folk were especially at the mercy of the weather. If the wind didn't blow the ships were becalmed, and if it blew too hard they might be lost. For sailortown the greatest drama of the opening years of the new century was probably the Great Storm of 26–27 November 1703. A hurricane blew in from the Atlantic, killing 8,000 people, the worst storm ever to have hit these islands. 'The ships in the river Thames were all blown from their moorings,' wrote Defoe. 'From Execution Dock to Limehouse Hole there were but four ships that rid it out; the rest were driven down into the bite from Bell Wharf to Limehouse, where they were huddled together and drove on shore, heads and sterns one upon another.' Some 700 ships, 'some very great ones', lay between Shadwell and Limehouse, their rigging torn and their masts smashed. The *Russel*, laden with bale goods for the Streights, was sunk at Limehouse and the *Sarah*, bound for Leghorn, sank at anchor at Blackwall. Only the ships in Howland's great enclosed dock on the south bank were spared.

In the bitter winters of the late seventeenth and eighteenth centuries (known as the Little Ice Age) the river often froze over for weeks, or even months. All the bustle was stilled in snowy sailortown, and a great hush lay across the icy waste: you could walk from ship to ship. There was no work for the watermen; some were found frozen to death in their wherries. When the snow began to melt after the Great Frost of 1683–84 a terrible thick fog enveloped the river: 'No vessel could stir out or come in,' wrote diarist John Evelyn. In the harsh winter of 1775–76 watermen and fishermen went begging from house to house, and coal prices shot up to 40s a chaldron.

Contrary winds and freezing conditions affected, among others, the coalheavers. If the coalboats could not get in, for whatever reason, there was no work. In spring sometimes 300 arrived at a time from Newcastle to heat the houses and stoke the furnaces of London. As the century progressed increasing numbers of poor Irish took to the work of coalheaving and as ballast men. They were a profligate and rowdy bunch, 'the very Dogs of mankind', spending all their wages on drink on Friday, getting into fights and then crawling home to the scruffy rooms they shared with pigs, or so it was said. There were said to be some 670 coalheavers in Wapping and Shadwell in 1768, of which some two-thirds were Irish. They earned good money ($£50$ a year), but the trade was subject to fluctuations, mainly because of the weather. Rather like the sailors, they were under the thumb of 'Wapping landlords'. In the first half of the century the trade was in the hands of local publicans, middlemen or 'undertakers' as they were known, who undertook to supply labour for the discharge of cargoes. One such was Samuel Batts (d. 1743), Captain Cook's father-in-law, who kept the Bell at Execution Dock. The men were constantly in debt to the undertakers and trouble was always rife. A brutish lot, the heavers terrorised the local watermen and operated a fierce closed shop. If the master of any collier boat had the temerity to use his own men to unload the coal into lighters, he was asking for trouble. The master of the *Freelove* made this mistake, and his crew were attacked by the outraged heavers.

An attempt to regularise the business was set up in 1758 under the supervision of the alderman of Billingsgate Ward who became responsible for registering the gangs, of fourteen to sixteen men. They had to apply to the alderman for work and were assigned to shipowners. Each was required to pay 2s towards a widows, orphans and pensions fund. The system was abused and serious trouble broke out in May 1768, when food was in short supply and heavers' wages were being withheld, or so they claimed. John Green, publican of the Roundabout Tavern in Old Gravel Lane, was the alderman's local agent, who assigned work and took the money for the pension scheme. In May a gang led by James Farmer, known as 'Terrible', launched an armed attack on the Roundabout. Green shot at them from a window and saw them off; as they went they set up 'an Irish howl', calling out 'The Bougre has got no Ball[s]' and vowing to take revenge. A few days later great numbers of heavers were parading around in Stepney Fields, in the streets of Wapping and Rotherhithe, brandishing sticks and cutlasses. They went for Green's pub again, terrorising the lodgers (an elderly seafaring man, a shoemaker and a sailor's wife); Green's mother-in-law, an old woman of seventy-four, was found hiding behind a chest in the garret. Wapping folk, fearing an uprising, started to 'remove their goods and chattels'. Press reports were alarming: 'The coal heavers are grown a terror to the whole neighbourhood of Stepney and Wapping.' Armed gangs paraded around the streets, shouting '£5 for a sailor's head, £20 for a master's'. Reprisals were swift and vicious, and the executions of rioters at Sun Tavern Fields were said to have been watched by 50,000 people. What with the coalheavers rioting and the Wilkite riots of the following year, London was in uproar. 'What times we are in!' exclaimed Mary Mayo, wife of the rector of St George in the East.

For six days in the early summer of 1780 a storm of crazy anti-popery, stirred up by the unhinged Lord George Gordon and following the government's Catholic Relief Act, saw mob attacks on prisons, Catholic homes, chapels and magistrates' houses, focusing mainly on the Holborn and Newgate area and then spreading to anywhere where Catholics were known to live. The mob were hell-bent on the chapel in Wapping's Virginia Street (where Tobacco Dock now is). Local Irishmen formed themselves into a body to defend it, and their priest went off to enlist help from the government. Soldiers were sent and entered the narrow alley to find the mob was already there, throwing furniture and bedding out of the windows of the priest's house. The chapel was utterly destroyed, and Father Michael Copps only managed to escape from the rioters by jumping over a wide ditch. Some thousand people lost their lives in these riots, the worst in eighteenth-century Britain. In September 1781 the Whitechapel vestry raised money to repair damage done by the 'late riots'.

The routes through sailortown

There were three main routes through the triangle of sailortown, as today, running east-west: Cable Street in the north (once Hache Street), Ratcliff Highway through the middle (the medieval *Vicum de Shadwell*), and Wapping High Street by the riverside. Of these the riverside route was a relative new comer, having been created in about 1570, after the draining of the marshy land in west Wapping. In between these roads were rows of new north-south streets and a maze of courts and alleys.

It was a 2 mile walk from the Tower to Limehouse. In modern times glassy blocks of luxury flats and expensive warehouse conversions have obscured the river frontage for most of the route, but in the eighteenth century you could walk almost all the way along the riverbank, passing by narrow passages where you might glimpse masts and sails, and listen to the clinking of iron chains and the measured working of oars. Every few hundred yards or so there were wharves, privately owned and closely guarded, and steep, slimey stairs leading down to the water; Wapping Old Stairs by the Town of Ramsgate at Wapping Pier Head is still there today. What skulduggery went on after dark down these gloomy stairs can be imagined. Early one morning in September 1764 a waterman's apprentice down by the riverside at St Katharine's spied the corpse of a new-born baby in a barge, its tiny head poking out from a bag.

Striking east of the Tower, along by St Katharine's, you would pass the Parsons' brewery at the Hermitage, going thence along Wapping (High) Street, and Wapping Wall to Pelican Stairs (the Prospect of Whitby). The riverside route continued along Lower Shadwell (the King Edward VII Memorial Park), took a turn inland along Broad Street (The Highway) and went back down to the riverbank along Narrow Street and Fore Street to Limehouse Kiln Dock. Sheds and workshops, warehouses, yards and dwellings, large and small, lined the way. Hannah Snell, whom we encountered on the stage at the New Wells, kept one of the thirty-six drinking houses that offered refreshment, lodging and goodness knows what else along Wapping High Street and Wapping Wall. At the end of her colourful career she went mad and died in Bedlam.

Wider, busier and older than Wapping's 'filthy straight passage', lying to its north, was the notorious Ratcliff Highway. Starting off life as an Iron Age trackway, it lumbered and rattled its way from east of the Tower to Ratcliff Cross, cutting through the middle of Wapping Stepney and Shadwell. Some of the meanest houses in London line the road, with worse in the side streets and alleys – Tom Turd's Hole among them. Some of the houses were old ramshackle timber structures; some had been rebuilt. There were dwellings, vermin-infested doss-houses, alehouses, brandyshops, chandlers' shops where you could get a dram along with your candles and groceries, slopshops where sailors could get cheap secondhand clothes (there was no uniform for ordinary sailors), pawnbrokers and bawdy houses. Here 'the sailors of the world reeled … from drinking-bar to dancing-room, and from dancing-room to back courts and alleys, where they were always robbed, frequently injured, and occasionally murdered'. Appropriately enough, the most successful and notorious whore and brothelkeeper of her day, Damaris Page (?1610–69), had turned to property speculation and built some houses along Ratcliff Highway.

Towards the west end, when the Highway became Upper Shadwell and Broad Street were better brick properties. On its north side were the residential squares,

Wellclose and Prince's, and the mammoth new church of St George's in the East dwarfing its lowly neighbours. Further east the road passed by Sun Tavern Fields, with its ropewalks, the Bowle's glass manufactory and Cooper's School. On the south side were the marshy streets and alleys of the newly drained parts of Wapping Stepney/St George's in the East and the church and new town of Shadwell.

The volume of traffic along the Highway was heavy, it being the main route east before the coming of the docks and the construction of the great Commercial Road (1802–6). Wagonloads of merchandise, especially coal, jostled with all manner of vehicles, with pedestrians, with cattle and sheep. Richard Cook was walking along with his coal cart, drawn by three horses, one day in spring, when a little boy ran under the wheels and was crushed to death. Hackney carriages spanked along, taking sea captains' wives and daughters to the fine houses in the better parts of Wapping, and ladies of lesser respectability to Ratcliff Cross or Shadwell Market. One evening in February 1732, when all day the rain was so heavy that 'Heaven and Earth had come together', you would have seen hackney coach No. 383, driven by a young lad called Showland Wright, taking two women from the City to Ratcliff Cross. You might meet fortune tellers along your way, like the 'cunning man' at the Golden Ball who told Katherine Gibson what had happened to her money, as well as sellers of nosegays and perhaps some poor wretch being whipped at the cart's tail from the watchhouse at Wellclose as far as Shadwell church. Prostitutes plied a lucrative trade. Ann Carter was hanging about on the Highway late one night in May 1730 when she picked up Erasmus Bowen on his way home from a club. She took him to the Three Tobacco Rolls and thence to her lodgings, where she took money from him. When taken to court she was acquitted by the judges, as she claimed the guinea she had removed was payment for services rendered. Not cheap. Moll James and Black Peg operated from a bawdy house at the Three Tobacco Rolls and Sugar Loaf. and Grace MacMullin, a 'Scotch woman of the town', a notorious housebreaker's moll, kept a low lodging house for sailors near the King's Arms.

The northernmost route, Cable Street, was Rosemary Lane and home to the notorious Rag Fair at its western end, and to many Irish, to whom it became Knockfergus, but like the Highway it became more respectable as it proceeded east past the great East India Company barracks, King David's Fort. Elizabeth Wells had a brothel in King David's Lane, handy for the barracks.

Sometime between 1720 and 1747 a wide New Road was built, leading up to Whitechapel's Town End. from Knockfergus, with an southern extension down into Ratcliff Highway. In 1754 it was made a turnpike road.

St Katherine's by the Tower

Remember the chap up from the country to see the Crown jewels and the lions at the Tower whom we met at Rag Fair? The conqueror's mighty fortress, although it still housed soldiers, was best known by this time as a tourist attraction. The animals, tigers, leopards, panthers and apes, and an elephant or two as well as lions, were 'kept remarkably clean and healthy in capacious dens'. Visitors were warned against meddling with them; one had been killed when a orang-utan had thrown a cannon ball at him. The Crown jewels were disappointing, viewed through a grate 'like that of a nunnery': an attendant showed the items one by one in the candlelight.

Even the ghastly entertainment periodically offered at the block on Tower Hill ceased mid-century. Here the dashing Duke of Monmouth calmly met his end, declaring at the last that Lady Henrietta, heiress to Stepney Manor, was the 'choice of his ripened years' and a 'lady of virtue and honour'. Those Jacobite rebel lords the Earls of Derwentwater and Kilmarnock were beheaded on Tower Hill. Soon after the 1715 rebellion Joseph Addison paid his 6d to go into the menagerie, in the company of a Tory friend with Jacobite sympathies:

> Our first visit was to the Lions. My friend, who had a great deal of talk with their keeper, enquired very much after their health, and whether none of them had fallen sick upon the taking of Perth, and the flight of the Pretender? And hearing they were never better in their lives, I found he was extremely startled, for he had learned from his cradle, that the Lions in the tower were the best judges of the title of our British Kings, and always sympathized with our soveraignes.

The very last public execution was that of Lord Lovat on 7 April 1747, watched by a crowd of only 400, very modest by eighteenth-century standards.

To the west and north of the Tower lived merchants and gentry in good new houses, but not so to the east, in the patch that for centuries belonged to the Hospital of St Katharine, exempt from both the ecclesiastical jurisdiction of the Bishop of London and the secular jurisdiction of the City.

The main thoroughfares were St Katherine's Lane and Butcher Row, running down from East Smithfields, with Pillory Lane on its eastern side, where were the rambling buildings of the Hospital and the ancient church that serviced the locals. Like Holy Trinity Minories it was a marriage venue and issued its own licences. A master ran the hospital with a chapter of three brothers, with an income of £40 a year each, and three sisters with £20 each. There were ten bedeswomen with £8 a year; profits from their estates were divided between them.

Along the waterfront were wharves and landing stages. With 75 houses per acre, St Katharine's was the most overcrowded and possibly the most insalubrious part of the East End, a place of 'foul building and foul living'. 'All them rummy streets the t'other side of the Tower' was how one old man described the precinct to Henry Mayhew. The devil still lurked in the precinct, as he had done 200 years earlier when Ben Jonson had him 'drinking with the Dutch'. In its 14 acres some 2,000 people lived (2,652 in 1801) and worked: seamen's cottages, workshops and warehouses were jammed and crammed together in Dark Entry, Cat's Hole and the other pestilential alleys and courts.

As the only part of the East End's waterfront where foreign cargoes might be legally landed, St Katherine's probably had the feel of the City's port area proper, with its wharves and warehouses. The so-called 'Sufferance Wharves' had existed since 1663 and customs duties were paid on site, without the masters having to go to the Legal Quays.

When it came to assessing for the county rate, little St Katharine's was worth more than extensive Mile End Old Town, with its grand residences. Tax records for 1693/4 show that the mass of small dwellings were interspersed with valuable industrial and commercial properties. Thomas Freeman had a property worth £70 a year and £600 in stock, Samule Twyn also had a £70 property and £300 in stock, Emmanuel Dudson had a property worth £80 a year and £150 in stock. The latter is described in his will as a waterman, with 'shipping, lighters, hoys, smacks and pinkes'.

The precinct had its own workhouse, watchhouse, two burial grounds, a charity school, a fire engine which was kept in Water Cock Alley and a parish nurse, one Goody Price in 1699. There were a gaol, a pillory and 'two courts, in one of which actions of debt for any sum are tried weekly on Thursdays, and in the other, which depends upon the civil law, are decided ecclesiastical matters'. It also had the royal barge house. It was here, as we have seen, that the navy had its local recruitment centre at the Black Boy and Trumpet, where there was the greatest concentration of seamen, river-workers and what we would now call dockers. There were also a number of hatters, shoemakers, tallowchandlers, wigmakers, glaziers, wheelwrights, coopers and distillers, and of course the ubiquitous victuallers. There were customs officials (tide waiters), who worked at the Sufferance Wharves, and slopsellers, like Christopher Holyland, known as Joseph Wilson, who left everything he had to his girlfriend, Charlotte Finch.

At this time St Katharine's had been for many years the first place where many foreign immigrants set foot on English soil, known for its Dutch and Flemish settlers. The Flemish church has gone by now, but the 'Doche' were still there. The famous clockmaker Ahaseurus Fromanteel (d. 1693) retired, as an old man, to a house in Maidenhead Court, off St Katharine's Lane, where presumably he felt at home. Florence Cornelius, a ship's master, lodged at the sign of the Dutch Beggar and John Schroder kept the City of Amsterdam and Spread Eagle by the waterside. In 1784 the inhabitants included 328 Dutch, 69 French (mainly hatters), 8 Danes, 5 Poles, 2 Spaniards, 1 Italian and 12 Scots.

Wealthy men did not live in St Katherine's, although it was not all grinding poverty. The precinct's poor relief officers were kept busy, to be sure, but mainly with the wives and children of sailors who never returned home. Some of the locals did well for themselves: if you looked through the windows of wharfinger and lighterman William Goodwin's house, which adjoined his wharf and backed on to the river, you would have seen a long mahogany table, sparkling with silver and all set with porcelain ware. Goodwin wore a valuable ring, had silver shoe buckles, and when he rode about he sported silver spurs on his heels.

In 1824 the precinct was obliterated for ever; 1,250 houses were pulled down, the Hospital moved to Regent's Park and two wet docks were constructed, enclosed within Thomas Telford's six-storey yellow brick warehouses. Today it is a marina, with expensive yachts and restaurants.

Wapping Whitechapel: 'Wapping in the Wose'

If you took the river route eastwards from St Katharine's you would find yourself in the parish of St John Wapping, Wapping Whitechapel, a small straggle of a place, full of 'narrow ill built streets'. Most of it was once known as Wapping in the Wose. It was separated from Wapping Stepney, its much larger neighbour, by the common sewer. Dr Johnson told Boswell to explore Wapping, where he might see 'such modes of life as few could imagine'. Presumably he was talking about the low life among the seafarers, rather than the dinner table he knew so well in Wellclose Square.

Wapping Whitechapel was divided into two distinctive parts. On the west (St Katharine's side) was a strip of land stretching south from the mother parish of Whitechapel, running east of Nightingale Lane (Thomas More Street). At the riverside the parish turns east along Wapping (High) Street, at which point it is only the width of the street. It broadens out when you get to the church (Wapping Pierhead and the Town of Ramsgate) into an area about 350ft from north to south and 900ft in length. It was bounded on the north by Green Bank and the common sewer, stopping on the east just before New Gravel Lane (Garnet Street).

At some unknown date, perhaps when the marsh was drained in the sixteenth century, the riverside part of Wapping was detached from Stepney and added to Whitechapel parish. By 1617 there were enough inhabitants for the hamlet to acquire its own little wooden chapel of ease. Pepys set off with some colleagues to attend the funeral of a naval captain there, but 'it being dirty, we would not go to church'. He went home and to the pub instead. Like him, before they got their own chapel the 'looser sort' of Wappingers went to the alehouse instead of trekking to Whitechapel church. In 1694 the chapel was accorded parish status.

Wapping Whitechapel was now its own place. In 1760 there were ten watchmen and seven headboroughs.

The first rector of the independent parish was, of course, a fellow of Brasenose, John Russell (1694-1723). From the tenor of his will he seems to have been a tetchy and overbearing individual, who had trouble with two of his four sons. Peter left home; when he made his will his father did not know whether he was alive or dead. John, his eldest son, thirty-one when his father died, was a Fellow of Merton College Oxford, and chaplain to White Kennet, Bishop of Peterborough His father strongly disapproved of the woman John wanted to marry: 'I think her name is Elizabeth [Clark] but she is commonly called in the said College Chloe … I give him nothing … if he marry the said Clark.' The old rector left his wife his lottery tickets and a life interest in his estate, making sure his two friends, Messrs Pitman and Woster, kept an eye on her. He could trust them: they 'do not serve my family for reward'. From 1748 to 1800 the rector was George III's celebrated 'mad doctor', Francis Willis. He had little to do with Wapping or, indeed, with the Church, being much occupied with the running of his lunatic asylum in Lincolnshire.

Wapping in the Wose was a swampy place. By 1756 the church was sinking and the graves in the churchyard were filling up with water; the sexton had to empty newly dug graves with buckets before he could bury the corpses. The church was rebuilt on firmer ground next to the school house in Cock Alley (Scandrett Street). Noorthouck thought the tower looked like an overgrown chimney. The school, maintained by a 'charitable society' of thirty local worthies, was rebuilt at the same time. In Milk Alley, near the church, was a French church, with a congregation of seafarers from Jersey and Guernsey and Huguenot refugees. Evidently the congregation were on good terms with the parish church. When minister M. de la Prade fell into arrears with the rent, the rector of St John's interceded to prevent the church from closing down. An offshoot of Stepney Meeting was set up in 1704, near Wapping Old Stairs. One of the congregation was 'a pious and experienced Christian' woman, the mother of John Newton, slave ship captain-turned-clergyman, author of the hymn 'Amazing Grace'.

The main thoroughfares were the riverside Wapping (High) Street and Old Gravel Lane (Wapping Lane), which ran north-south, joining the riverbank to Ratcliff Highway. The main highway was, of course, the river, as is clear from the number of wharves and stairs: Union Stairs and Bell Dock, Wapping Old Stairs, Gun Dock, Wapping News Stairs, Dung Wharf, Gun Wharf, Execution Dock Stairs, Wapping Dock Stairs, King Edward Stairs, Frying Pan Stairs.

Since Tudor times the hamlet had been busy with ships and shipping and had grown accordingly. Its eighteenth-century inhabitants were 'chiefly seamen and depending on Sea Trade'. Along with Shadwell, its neighbour, it had a remarkable concentration of mariners; in Gun Alley, just east of the church, lived William Peckover, gunner of Captain Bligh's *Bounty* (1789).

According to the rector of Whitechapel, the inhabitants of the hamlet in 1693 were 'accounted wealthy people'. This comes as rather a surprise: Wapping was known for the racketing of its sailors, its whores, coalheavers and dingy alleys – perhaps Execution Dock gave it a bad name. As a matter of fact, Wapping had more than its fair share of gentlemen and rich families. Best known and possibly the richest local in the 1660s–'90s, one of a number of timber merchants, was Sir William Warren, who imported timber from the Baltic and supplied the navy with masts. He had a great yard and several wharves, property in Wapping Stepney's King Street, worth £55 a year and occupied by seventeen tenants. Sir William Warren Square is marked on Blome's map of 1720, near King Edward Stairs (just north of the underground station). Zachariah Cockfield, ships' chandler and a prominent local Quaker, had a timber yard near Wapping Old Stairs. He was a sailor's son and came to Wapping from Whitby in 1737 to marry the daughter of wealthy Quaker Joseph Sheppard. Sheppard had a number of wharves and warehouses, a timber yard in Cinnamon Street and nautical shops in Wapping Wall. Cockfield took over his father-in-law's business and died a gentleman with extensive property in Yorkshire and West Ham, having retired to the Quaker heartland at Upton.

Blocks or pulleys for ropes aboard ship were needed in vast numbers, and blockmakers were much in demand. Samuel Lash (d.1700), 'the Kings Majesty's Blockmaker for making and fitting blocks and carriages for the use and Service of His Majesty's Navy and Ordinance', had his dwelling-house, workshops and stables in Old Gravel Lane, and a house (rented out) on the south side of Wellclose Square. Among his considerable collection of silver was a tankard made from 'wreck silver got from a Spanish ship by Sir William Phipps'. Lash mixed with the gentry, including the Gouldsboroughs of Bethnal Green's Great Corner House, and was very proud of it. Like so many of the *nouveau riche*, he was troubled with an 'extravagant, obstinate and troublesome' son.

When assessed for tax in 1761 the parish was liable for double what St Katharine's had to pay, and only slightly less than the much more extensive Wapping Stepney. Most of the dwellings, though not all, were smallish, but there were some valuable industrial premises. Fire insurance policy records for 1777–78 include Thomas Coxhead, timber merchant and dealer in provisions at the Hermitage, insuring his premises for £8,900, John Boddy, 'sail maker and dealer in ships' stores' at Execution Dock, insuring his for £6,500 (Boddy had a country house at Plaistow), Wilkinson, dealer in china and glass, insured for £4,000, Roger Evans, linen draper at King Edward Stairs, for £3,100, James Hunt and John Rixon, coopers, for £2,400, Parkers, the brandy merchants at the New Stairs, for £2,200, John Parker, sailmaker and marine dealer, for £2,000, Henry Fletcher, shipwright and timber merchant, for £1,800. This was at a time when substantial houses, such as those in Assembly Row and Goodman's Fields, were usually insured for about £500 and the greatest of the sugar refineries was insured for £10,000; most of the larger ones for sums between £2,000 and £3,000.

As well as employment in the marine trades, and the heaving and sale of coal, there was a deal of cobbling and wigmaking in the first half of the century, and, of course, brewing. Horwood's map (1792–99) shows Pichard's, a very large brewery, south of Brewhouse Lane.

Wharves were owned by tradesmen and used for their own purposes, or rented out. Peter Mackattie (d.1747) leased two wharves with houses and warehouses; John Wood (d.1764) owned a coal wharf. Henry Beal, of St Katharine's, had a coalyard and wharf in White's Yard, in the East Smithfield part of the parish. Beal was evidently an old-fashioned Dissenter: he called his son Increase and had a property in Goodman's Fields 'at the sign of the Bible'. Wharves in 1799 were Godsall's coal wharf at Wapping Dock, Henley's coal wharf, Laverick's flour wharf, Phoenix coal wharf, Townesend coal wharf and Wheatsheaf coal wharf.

Of twenty-eight people buried in St John's churchyard in January 1747, fifteen are 'poor' or pensioners; of thirty-two buried in January 1755 (only eight were adults and the rest were mainly toddlers), five were in the workhouse and seven more classified as 'poor'. Elizabeth Fellemy, aged twenty-five (poor and paid for by the parish), was put in the same coffin as her two year old – to save money no doubt. The vast majority of the dwellings were occupied by the labouring classes, most of them the families of seafarers, often left destitute.

Most of the 'mean' houses were not those in the riverside strip, some of which were quite large, but in the west side of the parish, part of the old Manor of East Smithfield. Here, on the east side of Nightingale Lane, where the London Dock would be built, were Longs Yard, Black Jack Alley, Ten Foot Way and Meeting House Yard, with its chapel where Dr Mayo of Wellclose Square officiated. Rents were very low at the beginning of the century, less so later on. Good brick houses were to be found, especially on the waterfront, for example the mansion of Joseph Curtis, the biscuitmaker (d.1771), and that of George Kitson, ships' chandler, by Wapping Old Stairs. Execution Dock was, far from being just an East End Tyburn, a great exchange where merchants had offices and shops. The hanging of pirates still went on there, however. Captain Kidd, the gibbet's most famous victim, met his end there at low tide on the morning of 23 May 1701, having enraged the East India Company by raids on their ships. The seizure of ships was a serious danger to the economy, and the death meted out to offenders was the most terrible. They were hanged on a shortened rope so that they died slowly, without the merciful 'drop' that quickly broke the neck.

Some of the parish survived the incursion of the docks in the next century, although this ripped the heart out of the area. Just a little of the eighteenth century is still there, around Wapping Pier Head, which was the village centre. A pair of bluecoat children stand above the entrance to the 1756 school building and the tower of the church (rebuilt in 1790) is still there. Nearby is the Town of Ramsgate (1758) and Wapping Old Stairs, descending into an unfamiliar, empty river.

Wapping Stepney/St George's in the East: the money-making place over the ditch

'Over the ditch', as they used to say (referring to the common sewer) was Wapping Stepney. The hamlet had not been much of a place hitherto; its riverside strip had been poached by Whitechapel, with only a 53ft river frontage, retained by Frying Pan Wharf. In the course of the century Wapping Stepney became the 'moneymaking' parish of St George's in the East, with weddings of the 'better sort' in its church reported in the press. Thereafter it became St George's in the Dirt, but that is another story. The hamlet covered an area of 244 acres, the larger part lying south of Ratcliff Highway, with fields stretching up to Whitehorse Lane (Commercial Road). The southern part was crossed by Pennington Street, parallel to the highway (in modern times the headquarters of Rupert Murdoch's newspaper empire), with two main north-south roads, Virginia Street on the west and Old Gravel Lane (Wapping Lane) on the east. Today a truncated version of Virginia Street has survived, turning down off the Highway by Tobacco Dock, while Pennington Street and Wapping Lane still take their old route. The area between them, much of which remained garden ground because it was too wet to build on, became the London Dock, and in the twentieth century was covered in tiny new houses and blocks of flats made to look like warehouses, all arranged around water channels: not so different from old Wapping.

Wapping Stepney grew enormously during the eighteenth century, becoming a parish of its own in 1729. Development started in the 1670s. New streets, like Broad Street, were laid out in the south-east part of the hamlet, near the river. North of the Highway, on higher and drier ground, Barbon's grand square at Wellclose arrived in the 1680s and its neighbour, Prince's Square, in the 1720s. Three fine churches were built. Most imposing was Hawksmoor's 'strong and magnificent pile' of St George's in the East, with its pepperpot turrets and its high tower 'in the manner of a fortification, with a staff on the top supported by stays like a mast, for an occasional flag'. It was badly bombed in the Blitz, but its shell remains. For the Scandinavian timber merchants and seamen ('very numerous in this parish') was the Danish church in Wellclose and the Swedish church in Prince's Square, both now gone. The Irish coalheavers worshipped in the Catholic chapel in Virginia Street, built in the 1760s.

From 1780 there was a spate of building; according to Lysons: 'The increase of population in this parish, since the year 1780, has been very considerable.' By the 1790s there were some 3,700 houses in the parish and by 1801 the inhabitants numbered 21,170, on a par with St Andrew Holborn or Bethnal Green. Even the swampy part south of Pennington Street was built on, although Horwood's map shows part still undeveloped. The drainage gardens, planted with trees to draw moisture from the soil, were 9ft below road level and had to be approached by stairs; the cellars of the houses were often full of water. William Daniell's engraving of Old Gravel Lane reminded Millicent Rose of a model of Old London Bridge, with its houses overlooking drainage ditches on either side. Even the best streets were said to be soaking wet.

'Tit for Tat or the Merry Wives of Wapping', a ballad sung in local taverns, no doubt, tells the tale of a naval officer and gentleman, offering 50gns for the favours of a sailor's wife. As elsewhere in the capital rich and poor lived on top of one another, but in Wapping it was especially remarked upon: 'Houses erected here', wrote a contemporary, 'are almost without exception mere hovels, when compared to the habitations within the City of London', but 'exceedingly useful, opulent and worthy members of society are scattered through the streets and lanes'. The 'useful and opulent' inhabitants were sea captains, merchants of the great trading companies and manufacturers. At the end of the seventeenth century Wapping Stepney had 114 substantial merchants, and the numbers grew. Manufacture, according to Lysons, was confined to ropemaking and the marine crafts. There were a number of shipwrights, mastmakers, blockmakers, mathematical instrument-makers and the rest, but there were also makers of pumps and fire engines, clay pipe-makers, glass manufacturers and, of course, the sugarbakers around Wellclose Square. Fortunes were made (and lost). These men had brick houses with mahogany furniture, long-case clocks, silverware and fine china. Some of them even had summer houses, and when time allowed might take up gentlemen's pursuits. Joseph Ames (d.1759), a ships' chandler and ironmonger, originally from Yarmouth, made a study of printing and became secretary to the Society of Antiquaries. Joseph Reed, from Durham, an 'eminent rope maker' and a Dissenter, produced the *Tradesman's Companion*; and a treatise on the monopoly of hemp. He also tried his hand at playwriting, with some success: 'His tragedy of Dido was received with great applause.' wrote Lysons, 'but acted only three nights, in consequence of a quarrel with Garrick, who had at first refused it, and was with difficulty persuaded to bring it on the stage.' 'These various publications', he adds, 'were all the produce of his leisure hours; for he never suffered his literary pursuits to interfere with his attention to a lucrative business.'

Coopers and the drink trade in all its manifestations did well; Henry Raine, a local brewer, richly endowed his famous 'Hundred Pound School'.

When St George's was opened in 1729 accommodation was assigned to the leading families, of which eleven were those of captains of merchant vessels. They and naval men congregated in Virginia Street, where there were ten sea captains in the 1690s. Another street favoured by the well-off seafarers was Broad Street (Reardon Street), parallel to Old Gravel Lane where, at the opening of century, James Yeames had a large shipyard. In later years Captain Bligh would take lodgings here; while he was away on his fateful expedition in the *Bounty* his twin daughters were taken by his remarkably beautiful wife to be baptised in the parish church. The most desirable residences were north of the Highway, in Wellclose and Prince's Squares and around the church. Servicing the residents were apothecaries, butchers, bakers, milkmen, slopsellers lamplighters, upholsterers, cheesemongers, grocers and victuallers in abundance. The first parish clerk was Sam Bright, barber and wigmaker. John Dilworth dealt in sugar, tea, figs, almonds and nutmeg (1764.) Howson Edwards, chemist and druggist of Old Gravel Lane, sold Daffy's elixir, Godfrey's cordial, Essence of Lemons, Hooper's Female Pills and 'All sorts of medicine for sea'.

As to the 'mere hovels', in Three Foot Alley, Five Foot Alley and the rest of the 'despicably parsimonious' streets, mostly they were home to ordinary mariners or their widows, Irish coalheavers, riverworkers and artisans. It is not without significance that one of the earliest workhouses was in Wapping Stepney, opening in Virginia Street in 1723. As one might expect in a place where rich and poor were so close, where rough Ratcliff Highway was minutes from two well-appointed residential squares, where tempting and valuable commodities were made and stored, and where life was precarious, there was a good deal of crime. If magistrate Welch was right in seeing Ireland as the main source of 'rogues', this was another reason why St George's was a troublesome place. Dick Turpin's Gregory Gang operated from the brandy shops in Old Gravel Lane in the 1730s. Thomas Kemp of Pennington (Penitent) Street, burgled in 1733, explained to the magistrates that he was a newcomer to the area and did not realise just how securely houses had to be bolted and barred. Euphemia Kendall of Prince's Square left a first-floor bedroom window open, and almost immediately a gang put a ladder up and took her silver. In Greenbank, centred around the Sun tavern between 1722 and 1724, was the New Mint or the Seven Cities of Refuge, a haunt of debtors and fugitives. Here local hero and ruffian, the audacious 'Captain Charles Towers' (whom we met at his execution) and 'General Webb' ran an 'alsatia' after they had been ejected from debtors' refuge in the liberty of the Southwark Mint. Exemption from the law was claimed on the basis that there had once been a mint in Wapping. A 'Book was kept … in which the Names of all the New Minters were enter'd, they paying half a Guinea at the time of subscribing, and obliging them selves to the utmost extent of their Power to rescue and set at Liberty any Person on the said List, whenever he was arrested or imprison'd'. Towers and his cronies roared around, often in bizarre disguises, attacking their hated enemies, the bailiffs, and dunking them in pits of human excrement. A mob of 200 were cheering them on when they assaulted bailiff William Jones and put him in the lavatory; when he emerged he had a turd in his mouth.

St George might hold his head up high (160ft) and proclaim the might of the Established Church, but in the lanes and alleys of old Wapping Stepney the workers were of another mind. Dissent, which had flourished in the East End since the early days, coming into the limelight in Cromwell's time, was still alive and strong, nowhere more vigorous than in this parish. Baptisms in the parish church were said to be appreciably fewer than might be expected, and Lysons noticed the extraordinary drop in the number of burials in the churchyard between 1730 and 1790, even though the population had risen steeply. Chapel was fighting Church, and winning, or so it seems. In Globe Lane and Wellclose Square were Dissenters' academies. Between Old Gravel Lane and Broad Street was the Baptist meeting house. In Broad Street was a Scotch Presbyterian chapel (*c.* 1669 to 1823) and there were two Independent chapels, one in Love Lane, at the junction of Green Bank and Old Gravel Lane, and another one that opened in New Road in 1780. Quakers are to be found, much involved in the drink trade and cooperage: from 1770 to 1779 there was a Meeting in Wapping in Blackamoor Alley.

Lysons says that in the 1790s the 'people called Methodists' met at three venues. John Wesley, whose father had briefly attended Edward Veale's presbyterian academy in Globe Lane, was setting Wapping (and the world) on fire. When he preached it was a thunderous drama. Rising slowly in a crescendo that often reduced his audience to sobbing hysteria, this strange and powerful mystic offered the sailors, artisans and traders direct, personal contact with the Godhead, calling them up to repent and be saved. His pyrotechnics culminated in the public shows of electric shock treatment for those 'possessed by the Devil'. He was a pioneer of this procedure, which was subsequently adopted by the medical profession, and seems to have achieved amazing results with the depressed and deranged. After a 'road to Damascus'-like conversion in 1738, Wesley launched into evangelical preaching, especially in parishes where the poor were numerous, preaching from pulpits, when allowed, and in the open air. Wapping, Ratcliff, Spitalfields, and Bethnal Green were fertile seedbeds for Wesley, who had notable success with lower tradesmen and artisans. With all its emotion and superstition, Methodism was no airy-fairy cult; it was a practical creed for the poor: 'Get all you can, save all you can; give all you can.' It offered ordinary men and women a place of importance in the organisation, if they were prepared to work for it. In the year of his conversion Wesley preached several times in St John's Wapping, and in October he was at St Georges and the following February delivered his first sermon at Spitalfields, which was to become one of his strongholds. In March 1764 he opened a new chapel in Wapping. By 1784, when he finally broke away from the hostile Established Church, there were an astonishing 356 chapels around the country. 'This pretending to extraordinary revelation and gifts of the Holy Ghost is a horrid thing-a really horrid thing,' said Bishop Butler.

What opinion Herbert Mayo, rector of St George's (1764–1802), had of his charismatic rival is not on record. With Wellclose and Prince's Square gone, and the smart properties of sea captains and lords of industry leaving no trace at all, his Georgian rectory by the church is probably the best place for the modern visitor to contemplate life for the opulent Wappingers. Very highly thought of was Rector Mayo, an enlightened man by all accounts, a friend of negroes (of which there were many in his parish) and of Huguenots, and an exemplary pastor. There was, however, another side to Hubert Mayo. He was greedy. The rector was the grandson of a baronet, who had married well. Although the Mayos lived in some style, with regular visits to Bath, flocks of servants and expensive tuition for their sons, it seems that Dr Mayo may not have been averse to fleecing some of the well-heeled among his flock. One such was Elizabeth Dancer, a 'bustling' and demanding widow who couldn't keep her servants. She was burgled at her house in Prince's Square in December 1784, and after that was too frightened to keep any cash in the house. She handed her financial affairs over to the rector, who took on the task of paying her bills, her rent, her tradesmen. When she died, by now a wealthy woman having inherited a fortune from a lunatic aunt (one Lady Snell), there was trouble. A will benefiting the rector's family was contested by Mrs Dancer's family, who argued that the rector and his wife had wormed their way into her affection only after she had come into her fortune. His 'love of accumulating' was spoken of. Various letters were produced in court to prove that the friendship between the household in Prince's Square and the rectory was long term and intimate, and that Mayo had put himself out to help the widow. When Mrs Dancer was house-hunting in the parish in 1769 Mayo had offered her a bed in the rectory at any time and found her a property on the south side of Prince's Square, which in the event turned out to be unsuitable because the drains were smelly. In 1787, when she decided to go upmarket into Wellclose, the rector arranged for her to buy the house of a merchant friend, Mr Collett. In the event he came back and no purchase was made, so Mrs Dancer moved into another house in the square, belonging to George Wolfe Esq. The rector lost his case.

Nine years later Mayo was again at Doctors' Commons, this time over £850 left to his family by a widowed West India merchant of Broad Street, Thomas Mapstone, governor of Christ's Hospital and the London, who grew China roses in his garden and left teaspoons and stayhooks to the old 'Nanny' who had served his family for thirty years. On this occasion the Mayos were successful.

Dr Mayo's 'love of accumulating' has, quite by chance, provided us with an insight into the lives of the children of the 'quality'. One of the exhibits produced in the litigation over Mrs Dancer's estate was the diaries of his daughter Jane, written by her when she was twelve to fourteen years old. The only East End children we have met on our perambulation so far have been the sons and daughters of the working poor, either marching along in their school uniform or going to a terrible death for some minor misdemeanour. Jane Mayo's life was very different from those of the children in the grubby courts and alleys, at work at the loom or the mast from an early age. Her account of it is a reminder of how pleasant and civilised life could be in eighteenth-century sailortown. The diary is no riveting Pepysian affair; it is as boring as children's diaries tend to be, and leaves much to the imagination. Even though she was only twelve, she seems to have been 'in society', and there was an endless round of afternoon visits to and from neighbouring merchant families in Wellclose and Prince's Square, supper parties and card playing. On one occasion, at Captain Barker's, she won £26. More exciting than tea-drinking were the balls, held in private houses and at Raine's Hospital, where her father was the treasurer, and the frequent outings to the theatre. She walked a lot, even as far as Hackney, to have tea with Dr Markham, took strolls locally, with her elder sister or a friend, around the City and in the Museum Gardens in Bloomsbury. A highlight was a visit to Buckingham Palace in June 1787, when she saw the queen and the six princesses. She notes the numbers of her mother's lottery tickets and makes shopping lists: blue ribbons, gloves, gauze, a paper of pins. Perhaps she (or her much-loved Mama) wore a massive cartwheel hat perched on a huge curly wig, like the one shown in the illustration in her diary. There were music lessons and dancing lessons, with no mention of anything else in the way of education, while her brothers Charles and Paggen went off to Oxford. Charles became a professor and Paggen a physician. Occasionally a dancing partner is mentioned, but Jane never married; neither did her sister Rebecca. They ended their long and comfortable lives living in a cottage on their brother Charles's estate in Cheshunt, Lime Cottage at Churchgate, with their maidservant and a niece.

In 1800 the work of constructing the London Dock was begun. In the parish the whole or part of twenty-four streets, thirty-three courts, yards, alleys and lanes were demolished. 'Most of these houses were of a mean and wretched description,' wrote local historian Maddocks, 'and the loss of them was a distinct gain to the neighbourhood.' In due course the better houses north of the Highway would be gone as well. Jane Mayo's childhood home, her father's church and the Raine's school building, where she went to dance, are all that remain of eighteenth-century St George's in the East. The houses where she took tea and played cards in Wellclose and Prince's Square hung on for a couple of hundred years, but now have vanished without trace.

Shadwell

To the east of Wapping was Shadwell; according to Lysons it was 'very small, being only 910 yards in length, and 760 in breadth', very slightly larger than Wapping Whitechapel. It stretched from New Crane Stairs to Bell Wharf (opposite the bottom of School Lane) and up across the Highway to Cable Street, taking in Sun Tavern Fields. The Highway was called Upper Shadwell along this stretch. The area south of the Highway was known as Lower Shadwell.

What had been riverside meadows belonging to St Paul's since the Middle Ages, with a line of wharves with some sailors' cottages, workshops and wayside taverns in the early sixteenth century, became in the seventeenth an industrial town, full of workers in the marine trades and sailors. The eastern part had been drained in the Middle Ages and the western part, with west Wapping, in Henry VIII's day. In the old days the Dean and Chapter's manor house had stood where the church now is, and there were two tide mills, fed by channels that emptied themselves 'into divers ditches' with makeshift bridges built over them. In 1649, when, as Judge Jeffreys said, there were no deans and chapters, their land was sold for £9,500 to a man called Winterburn. By 1650 there were about 700 houses, some 'good houses and orchards', and in 1656 a chapel of ease was built. St Paul's got their land back after the Restoration, and by 1664 the inhabitants of the hamlet numbered some 7,000.

In 1669 speculator Sir Thomas Neale, Master of the Mint (more famous for Seven Dials and Neale's Yard), leased from the Dean and Chapter all the eastern part of Lower Shadwell, which comprised two-thirds of the township (the Edward VII Memorial Gardens). He got parish status for the hamlet and built 289 houses, along with a market and a waterworks. With a great fanfare of publicity, Neale was sued (unsuccessfully) for 7½ acres of east Shadwell in 1684 by Lady Theodosia Ivy, a troublesome and litigious lady. She had been thrice married, and was the daughter and heiress of local brewer John Stepkin, a descendant of the Stepkin who had built Wapping Wall. The land, she claimed, was her rightful inheritance. It was a protracted proceeding, presided over at Kings' Bench by the great Judge Jeffreys, and attracted a good deal of public notice, probably because of Lady Ivy's celebrity. She was 'famed for her wit and beauty,' rich and spoilt, and had achieved notoriety some years before in an alimony dispute with her second husband. Thomas Ivy was, apparently, 'a trade fellow but welthie, which [he] had gotten in the East Indies'. He claimed she had squandered his fortune; she said that it was her fortune, and that his 'harsh and cruell usage' had sent her running barefoot, late at night, from their house in Charterhouse Square back to her father's at the Hermitage.

Lower Shadwell's main north-south routes, going down to the river from the Highway, are New Gravel Lane (Garnet Street), built to bring gravel down from

Sun Tavern Fields, Shakespeare's Walk and Fox's Lane. Wapping Wall runs along near the river and turns up into Fox's Lane, named after the Mr Fox who built houses here in the first half of the seventeenth century. These two roads used to be the marsh wall; witnesses in the Ivy case remembered Fox's Lane when it was called Wall Marsh (Walmarsh) Wall. It was sometimes still impassable at high tide. Shakespeare's (Shagsby's) Walk was named (by 1720) after the local ropemaking family. After the ropeworks moved to Sun Tavern Fields (by 1700, see below) it became a residential quarter, with trees planted down the middle. Landmarks were Shadwell Dock, in the centre of the waterfront, the market and the water-works over to the east; a pump driven by four horses raised water from the river, which was then piped to houses from the Tower to Stepney. There was a charity school, a Dissenters' school, almshouses and three chapels, Presbyterian, Calvinist and Wesleyan. Taverns and alehouses there were by the score, or more.

Though more respectable than Rag Fair, the market was a place for pickpockets and fun and games. Mary Crafts picked up William Chapman as he was having a pee in Wellclose Square. There followed some goings-on in Sun Tavern Fields, and finally they ended up at Shadwell market:

> He wanted to have me again upon the Stalls,' she told the magistrates; 'he did pull up my Petticoats quite over my Head, but 2 Men coming up, God bless you, says I to them, for coming, and then he charged me with taking his Watch. Esther Morris, a Dealer in old Cloaths, and John Warner, a Hackney Coach man, said they had never heard any Harm of the Prisoner and she was acquitted.

St Paul's church stood on the Highway, as it does today, though rebuilt. The first minister, in the Protector's time, was the celebrated Puritan divine Matthew Mead It is modest and unassuming, appropriate for a church that started out as an Independent chapel, and for a working town without any pretensions. In no way did it compete with the splendour of St George's. According to Noorthouck it was a mean brick edifice, ornamented only with stone balls, with a plain low turret only 60ft tall.

Sun Tavern Fields, north of the highway, was the only open ground in the parish by the end of the century. Before the arrival of the Sun Tavern it was known as Ratcliff Fields, where ballast was dug. By about 1700 the Shakespear ropeworks was here and a mineral spring was discovered in 1745, which briefly gave the name of Shadwell Spa to the area – but it never took off as a fashionable health resort.

'The money-making parish of St. George', wrote Sydney Maddocks, 'looked askance at the neighbour who offered so little and wanted so much in the way of charity.' Maybe it did. Shadwell was developed largely all of a piece, and many of the original houses were small ones, built for sailors and artisans. Here seamen, watermen and lightermen, coalheavers and shopkeepers, and ropemakers, coopers, carpenters and smiths, lived in small lathe and plaster or weatherboard houses, two storeys and a garret high, with one room on each floor. There were even smaller dwellings, mainly occupied by widows. By the mid-eighteenth century many would have been rebuilt, but they are still little houses (£2–7 rack rent), smaller on average than those you might find in Wapping, and with some sign of multi-occupation. In Milk Yard Captain Lawrence had thirteen small houses, three of which were subdivided, and Messrs Duffin and Wilson had ten, of which four were subdivided. In Fox's Lane Edward Graves had a medium-sized house (£10 rack rent), 'let in tenements'.

Shadwell had a bad reputation, like Wapping, was said to be 'infested with vagabonds' and was troubled with an increasing number of Irish come to heave coal. However, like its neighbouring parishes it had its fair share of rich families, and men calling themselves 'gentlemen', making money from industry or commerce, leasing or buying small houses for letting out and living close by their works and their 'rents'. David Trinder (d.1774), a cooper, owned ten little houses in Collins Court. Captain Malbon had fifteen tiny houses off Fox's Lane, called Malbon's Rents. Those who left wills that went to the senior probate court between 1700 and 1800 numbered nearly 3,000, of which 1,866 were mariners, 92 victuallers (publicans), 64 shipwrights and 64 gentlemen, 33 coopers, 31 merchants, of which 12 were coalmerchants, 30 surgeons, 10 apothecaries, 7 ropemakers, 6 distillers, 4 sailmakers, 4 anchorsmiths, 2 mastmakers. Apothecaries, surgeons and shipwrights (some of them) would have been working on board ship, at least part of the time. There are a few plumbers, woodworkers of one sort and another, tailors and tallow chandlers. Thirteen 'leading inhabitants' were listed in the 1774 directory. John Woodham, distiller of Shadwell Dock, had premises insured for £6,000 and a coachhouse and stables behind the waterworks, and was one of the wealthiest men in Shadwell. In Wapping Wall were Richard Dowding, cooper and beer merchant, Benjamin Everington, who sold sacks, and Joseph Grieve, ships' chandler. David Trinder, the cooper, had a mammoth operation, with eleven warehouses in Lower Shadwell, as well as the company's headquarters (with an annual rent of £40), warehouses elsewhere in Shadwell and property in Ratcliff. Best known of the Shadwell industrialists was the old-established firm of ropemakers, run by the Shakespears, with their works first at Shagsby's Walk and then in Sun Tavern Fields. For over 150 years the Shakespears made ropes in these parts. They did very well for themselves, as we shall see when we look at their mansion in Ratcliff.

Substantial brick houses for the better off were mainly along the waterside and along the highway at Upper Shadwell. Here lived the industrialists, sea captains and professional families. Sea captains seem to have congregated in Love (formerly Cutthroat) Lane by Sun Tavern Fields, and Upper Shadwell, where some of the best houses were. One of the grandest Upper Shadwell houses in the 1750s–'70s was occupied by lawyer Micajah Malbon, who had a country estate in Barking. It was to a notary's in Upper Shadwell that widow Amy Davis, among many other seafaring folk, went to draw up her will before she set off as a nurse on the hospital ship *Antelope* in 1703. She never returned home.

Women ran small businesses. Sarah Boulton had a fancy shop selling hats, china and glass in Upper Shadwell, Judith Ansell sold lace, Margaret Wharton had a hat shop, also in Upper Shadwell, and Mary Stevenson sold shoes in New Gravel Lane.

A neighbour of the Malbons in Upper Shadwell, though living in a much smaller property, was John Blackburn, former landlord of the Bell alehouse at Execution Dock. His stepdaughter, Elizabeth Batts, married Captain Cook, and the couple took over the house at No. 126 Upper Shadwell, living there from their marriage in December 1762 until 1765/6, when they moved to Assembly Row in Mile End. A blue plaque on the Highway marks the site today.

In 1748 Cook, a Yorkshire lad, came down to London on a collier boat from Whitby, owned by John Walker, a Quaker, and may have made the acquaintance of Elizabeth at the Bell, where her father, and presumably her stepfather, were coal undertakers. A story was related by the artist John Constable that Cook had 'stood sponsor for a little girl in Barking church', declaring 'if the infant lives I will marry her'. Elizabeth was only fourteen years younger than her husband, so the tale seems unlikely to be true. The couple were, however, married in Barking church, where there were probably family connections. By the time Cook married he had served in the navy, joining as an able seaman in June 1755. At his discharge in 1762 he got £300, which presumably enabled him to marry. Within eight years he was landing at Botany Bay and claiming New South Wales for Britain. Little did the East Enders imagine, when the news finally filtered back home, that many thousands of their children, grandchildren and great-grandchildren would end up living in this vast new continent on the other side of the world, and that the names of Shadwell, Mile End, Wapping, Poplar and Limehouse would be as familiar to those exiled descendants, and their descendants in years to come, as they were to them.

The year after Captain Cook first came to London, Shadwell's most celebrated woman was married in Virginia to a man called Peter Jefferson. This was Jane Randolph, born in 1721 and the daughter of a mariner of Shakespear Walk named Isham. She was probably taken to America by her parents. Her son Thomas became the third president of the United States, growing up in a Virginia farmhouse named Shadwell.

From mid-century the population was in decline. In 1760 there were 1,696 houses; in the 1790s only 1,300. The population in 1801 was 8,828, having dropped from 13,002 in 1710.

Appropriately, perhaps, the solitary remnant left today of eighteenth-century Shadwell is a pub, the Prospect of Whitby in Wapping Wall, but even that has a Victorian face. Shadwell Basin, now an ornamental lake, covers the western half of the little town and the Edward VII's Memorial Gardens lie over the market-place where William Chapman had Mary Crafts up against the stalls, or tried to.

Ratcliff: a vanished place, a royal mistress and some Shakespears

East of Shadwell is Ratcliff, 2½ miles in circumference, extending from Cutthroat (Brodlove) Lane to about an eighth of a mile east of the Link tunnel into what is now Limehouse, and up as far as St Dunstan's church. These days, as an entity, it has all but disappeared. The oldest of the riverside hamlets, by the seventeenth century a thriving commercial and industrial centre, has become anonymous. Even the famous road that used to bear its name is just called the Highway now. Eaten up by Limehouse and Wapping, with Commercial Road struck through its middle, it is only remembered in byways: Ratcliff Cross Street, running between Commercial Road and Cable Street, Ratcliff Lane, leading east off Butcher Row, and Ratcliff Cross Stairs in Limehouse. Nothing concrete of old Ratcliff remains, except, of course, the East End's most venerable piece of heritage, the church of St Dunstan, and a solitary eighteenth-century ship owner's house, in Butcher Row.

The hamlet covered an area about the same as Whitechapel. In 1870 it was 112 acres, but had lost some land to Limehouse by then. It was two separate areas of settlement, that around the church in Stepney village, to its south, and the port/riverside part. They were linked, as they had been since the Middle Ages, by Whitehorse Street (now Road) and divided by Cable Street (called Brook Street) and the Highway (called Cock Hill and Broad Street).

Stepney village was still countryfied, somewhere for Londoners to go for a day out, but the riverside part of Ratcliff, like its sailortown neighbours, was a dense complex of dwellings, workshops and warehouses; a truly enormous one was built by the East India Company at Cock Hill (the Highway) in 1780. Thirty-six warehouses were lost in the 1794 fire. The dock has been in use for at least 400 years, probably many more. Ratcliff is an old place, used to river commerce and accustomed to industry. Domesday peasants probably lived around Butcher Row (the main street leading down to the Cross), the kings' ships were built here in the fourteenth century and at the time of the Wars of the Roses there was a major brewery. From Tudor times the sons of its seafarers have toiled at their lessons in the Cooper's School, sugar has been baked and anchors, masts and sails made and fitted. For Elizabethan sailors Ratcliff Cross was the London rallying point, and in the early years of the seventeenth century a number of city shipwrights of the Shipwrights' Company moved out to Ratcliff because of 'fear of fire' and the noise caused by their work. The newly formed Rotherhithe Corporation claimed jurisdiction over them but lost their case, and the Company's headquarters, Shipwrights' Hall, was moved to Butcher Row. Trinity House also took a house in Butcher Row.

By that time a third of the population of vast Stepney parish was living in the hamlet; it had grown greatly between about 1590 and 1630. In 1641, because it 'is of late so largely increased', Stepney vestry allowed it a churchwarden of its own; St Dunstan's has a Ratcliff warden to this day. From 1664 there was a weekly fair at the Cross.

At the opening of the eighteenth century this was the most built up of the riverside hamlets, with a large population of over 20,000 (more than Whitechapel) with a great 'multiplying of buildings'. By the 1770s the only open ground was 34½ acres of hayfield and an acre ploughed, up towards the church. Stout houses for sea captains lined the Highway, and moored along the riverbank were East and West Indiamen, heavy with treasure.

It had three schools by the end of the century, the old Coopers' School in Schoolhouse Lane, the hamlet's charity school and a school for poor Dissenters, which opened in 1783, taking in forty pupils. There was also a Presbyterian cemetery, a flourishing Quaker meeting house, an Independent chapel, a workhouse from 1741 and a parish or town house. For misbehaviour there was a pillory; John Painet and Samuel Green were put in it for 'sodomitical practices'. Town meetings might be held at the Ship Tavern, at the corner of Broad Street and Ratcliff Cross, and there were hostelries by the score. You could have oysters with your beer and a game of billiards at the King's Head and Billiard Table at the Cross. At the Queen's Head in Whitehorse Street guests slept three in a bed, and John Baskerville had the silver buttons stolen from his coat, which he had left slung over a chair.

The people drinking in the alehouses and busy in the workshops were shipwrights (there was a Noah's Ark Alley), coopers, brewers, distillers, glaziers, sugar- and biscuit-bakers, timber merchants, ropemakers and workers in all the variety of marine trades. Sailors abounded and there were chandlers, pawnbrokers, slopsellers, apothecaries, quacks and fortune-tellers. Rachel Smith pawned a gold ring and a wig she had stolen to a 'Cunning Woman' to tell her some news of her sweetheart.

Working hard in the distilleries, cooperages and breweries were Quakers, who had established themselves in a meeting house in School Lane in the previous century, with a sister chapel in Wapping (1770–79). They were taking a firm hold in the area, like Methodism recruiting largely from the artisan classes. They looked after their own poor and had a system of 'house visits', dressed in plain grey clothes, eschewing the gaudy and any form of show; they refused to swear on the Bible, take their hats off in deference to authority or join the militia. For the rector of Stepney and other clergy they were a thorn in the flesh on account of their refusal to pay tithes. One such defaulter was Benjamin Batts of Ratcliff Square, who may have been a relative of Elizabeth Batts who married Captain Cook. Their ostentatious piety, odd clothes and old-fashioned way of speaking ('thee' and 'thou') made them objects of ridicule, fair game for a spot of scandal.

Most famous by far of the local Quaker community was Hannah Lightfoot, daughter of a Wapping cobbler called Mathew who married Mary Wheeler, a packer's daughter from Goodman's Fields, in 1728. Hannah was born in 1730 in Wapping, and was only two when her father died and was buried in St John's: 'a Quaker of Wappin'. She was brought up by relatives in St James's, and after marrying a Baptist called Isaac Axford at Keith's Mayfair chapel was expelled by the Quakers and seems to have disappeared. For reasons that are not clear a story began to be circulated that she became the mistress of the Prince of Wales, later George III. On 10 December 1759 Lady Sophia Egerton wrote to her uncle, Count William Bentinck: 'It has often been buzz'd that H.R.H., in spite of his reserve, was not wholly insensible to the passion of Love: and I am assured that he kept a beautiful young Quaker for some years, that she is Dead, and that One Child was the produce of that intrigue.' The story continued in circulation for years, and was even being cited as a precedent for morganatic marriages when Edward VIII's liaison with Mrs Simpson was under discussion in 1936!

When the hamlet was assessed for tithes in the 1770s the rector noted a number of poor people, but, as with all the riverside places, poor and rich were 'jumbled together' and there were men (and women) who made money. Seventeen men were listed as 'leading inhabitants' in 1774. Thirteen of these ('manufacturers' and 'dealers') lived in the southern part of the hamlet, three in fashionable Stepney Causeway, a new road that ran up to the church from Brook (Cable) Street, and one up in Stepney village. This last was Gilbert Slater, the East India merchant and industrialist whom we met presiding over the vestry meetings. The list includes two ropemakers, John Huddy and John Shakespear, Richard Vaux, distiller, and Andrew Seymour, oilman (both of Butcher Row), John Matthew, ships' chandler and tinplate-worker and Spencer Burgess (both at the Cross), John Lungley, wine merchant at Cock Hill. Cooperage has been a local trade for 200 years or more, witness the Coopers' School and almshouses. Both were burnt down and rebuilt in 1694 and 1794, staying put until the 1890s. It comes as no surprise, therefore, to find one of the most valuable properties in Ratcliff in 1764 was that belonging to David Trinder, the cooper whom we met in Shadwell.

Ratcliff was famous for its glass; some samples of Bowles Crown glass were still around in the last century, maybe some still are. Approached through an archway, proudly bearing the family coat of arms, was the Bowles glass factory, dwelling-house, stables and orchard, on 6 acres of land that lay between Sun Tavern Fields and Schoolhouse Lane. The site is even today marked by Glasshouse Fields off the Highway. For about a hundred years Crown glass was made here; it was London's foremost glasshouse.

Since the days of James I glass had been made in Ratcliff. Operating under a royal patent, a Frenchman called Abraham Bigoe had a factory in 1621, probably just producing drinking vessels. John Bowles's story is no fairytale of a poor man made good; unlike so many of our East End manufacturers and merchants, he came of an wealthy gentry family from Kent. His first factory was in Southwark; and he moved to Ratcliff in about 1691, perhaps in need of a larger site for his expanding business. His original premises were near the watchhouse at the top of Butcher Row, moving later to Glass House Fields, perhaps taking over the Nelson factory that was on this site. It was a large operation, with three glasshouses 'newly erected' in 1738; there were a kiln, a 'flashing house', a warehouse, two millhouses, an ashhouse, mixing-rooms, a counting-house, a woodyard, two coalyards and stables. Crown glass was widely used for the newly fashionable sash windows, for the twinkling shop windows of the West End, for carriages and mirrors. It was not cheap. In 1746 1s 4d a foot was paid for new windows in the Great Dining Room at Hicks Hall for 'the best Ratcliff Crown glass'.

In Stepney Causeway, at the end of an avenue of trees, was one of the best houses in Ratcliff, the residence of the Shakespear rope 'millionaires'(from about 1701 until about 1820). The locals called Arthur Shakespear (d.1818) the 'Squire'. They were proud of their illustrious name and claimed descent from the bard's grandfather. A bust of William Shakespeare was displayed on a shelf in the fine panelled dining room and they adopted the poet's coat of arms, 'there being but one known'. The founding father of the rope dynasty was a John Shakespear (b.1619), possibly of gentry stock. He had a ropemaking business in the area by 1656; it supplied the navy. His premises were just west of Shadwell chapel in what came to be known as Shakespear's or Shagsby's Walk, the street where little Jane Randolph was born. John died in 1689 and by 1700 the works, now under the care of his son Jonathan, had moved north of the Highway to a site in Sun Tavern Fields, and the family took a house in what would become Stepney Causeway. Alderman John, Jonathan's son, inherited the ropeworks from his brother in 1749. They comprised four long sheds, a wheelhouse, a hemp-house, a tar-house, a rigging-house and stables totalling 2,160ft. Business flourished, and at his death he left £31,000. The business went to his son, Arthur (the 'Squire'), who married a rich heiress of a noted Whig family from Yorkshire, and paid £2,000 to make himself MP for Richmond (1798–1808). He acquired a house in fashionable Albemarle Street, although still keeping the splendid one in the Causeway, where the staircase was 'so wide you could drive a coach and four down it, and a hall so large you could turn the horses round'.

In the small hours of a moonlit Saturday in June 1781, Arthur Shakespear's coachman was driving his master home to Ratcliff from an evening spent in the Ranelagh pleasure gardens when they were robbed. The Squire gave the court a concise and vivid account:

> The chariot was stopped just opposite St. George's church. There was a violent noise, and I saw, through the blinds, a kind of flash upon the chariot's stopping; I drew my watch out of my fob, and concealed it in the best way I could under my arm. Immediately the door of the near side of the carriage was opened, and two fellows with cutlasses and pistols demanded my money ... I gave my money to the comrade of the person I take to be the prisoner ... they uttered horrid imprecations the whole time; they then demanded my watch ... the other door of the carriage was opened, and there were two fellows at it, both armed with pistols and cutlasses, or hangers, threatening to pull me out, and to cut me to pieces ... I was a little alarmed: I desired them not to use me ill, I had given them every thing I had. One of the men on the near side of the carriage insisted I should not be hurt: he said to the two fellows on the left-hand side, D—n your blood! you would not hurt the gentleman after you have got every thing he had? Upon which they shut the door, and we drove on.

Limehouse

Like Ratcliff, its next door neighbour, Limehouse is an old place, one of the oldest identifiable industrial sites in east London, as its name suggests. Here lime for building has been produced for at least 400 years. Its dock, a considerable inlet, has been in use since time immemorial and shipbuilding has been a local trade since the fourteenth century. From Tudor times it has been a place of seafarers, and Stepney vestry was for years controlled by the rich and powerful Limehouse ship-building fraternity and East India Company magnates. In the eighteenth century it still had a very salty air; even the workhouse was run like a ship.

The population had grown greatly in its heyday (from *c.* 1590 to 1630) and in 1642 the hamlet was about as populous as Ratcliff. By the opening of the eighteenth century it was far less crowded than Ratcliff, with fewer houses, and the population declined in the following years. In 1710 there were about 7,000 people; by 1778 there were only 3,429. There was a good deal of open ground, with pasture stretching up towards Mile End and over to Poplar. Ropewalks and ship- and timberyards dotted the landscape.

Most of Limehouse was clustered around the streets close to the river: Three Colts Lane, which ran north-south down to Lime Kiln Dock, Church Lane, parallel to it, and Fore Street (once Forby Street, now Narrow Street), hugging the shore. Limehouse Causeway struck off east towards Poplar and up north of the main village. Rose Lane followed the route now taken by Commercial Road and East India Dock Road. Church Lane (part of which survives as Newell Street) happened to go up to the church, but was called that before the parish church was ever built, or even thought of, so presumably it was the first part of the trek up to Stepney church. In 1767 work started on Limehouse Cut, a canal that would link the Thames with the Lea near Bow, leaving the Thames halfway along Narrow Street.

Houses and workshops came and went, and were rebuilt after the 'great fires' that regularly ravaged the parish, the worst being in 1716. Others were reported in 1765, 1775, 1805, 1809 and 1811. Houses, flourmills, granaries, blockmakers' shops, timberyards and oil and colourmen's warehouses went up. Damage in one instance was estimated at £60,000.

At the opening of the century market gardens flanked the riverside village, the two largest, adjoining one another, being Limberie's Land (7 acres) and Risbie's Land. John Limbrey was victualler to the navy in Cromwell's time; we met him serving on Maurice Thomson's reforming vestry. Limehouse Rectory stands on part of Limbrey's garden ground. Captain Henry Risby's market garden was about the same size, and he also had a ropewalk. Risby was an Elder of Trinity House, an East India Company man and also engaged in the Virginia trade; evidently a man of wealth and standing. A sketch of his fine house, with a dome on the top, is drawn on Gascoyne's map. The only other mansions accorded this honour by Gascoyne are those around Bethnal Green.

The pattern of settlement did not change a great deal during the course of the century, although the garden acreage was reduced and ropeyards proliferated. When the new church of St Anne's was built on high ground away from the shore, up near the main highway, it stood among fields. By the 1790s it had drawn some habitation north from the riverside and there were houses along the northern section of Three Colts Lane, and some new terraces, accompanying the rectory west of the church, in what is now Newell Street. Some of these stand to this day. The better off favoured the new houses up towards the church.

North of Rose Lane there were dairy farms; Roque's map shows a very large cowhouse just near the church. The fields of north Limehouse were 'a beautiful pastoral country adorned with villages ... parks and meadows containing countless herds of cattle'. A ship's cook, with a wife and five children in County Durham, one Christopher Saunders, had sex with a cow belonging to Mr Knight at the sign of the Blue Anchor. Abraham Denning, the cowman, spied him from the hayloft of the barn, climbing onto a bucket and taking down his breeches.

Down by the river shipbuilding, which had been the glory of Limehouse in the days of the Petts, was still one of the main industries, less so as the century progressed. No vessels of any great tonnage were made here, with only barges and small craft being built from scratch, but ships of all sorts were repaired and reclassed; Lysons noted three dockyards used principally for repairs.

It was not a wealthy place, affected perhaps by the decline in the prosperity of the Blackwall shipyard in the 1720s. According to Maitland (1729) only one Limehouse family was of sufficient standing to have its own carriage. It was rigging, blockmaking, oarmaking, sailmaking and all the subsidiary marine crafts that were the chief moneymakers for the locals. 'Then indeed,' Dickens's Captain Cuttle, a Limehouse rigger, remarked, looking back to the good old days, 'fortunes were to be made, and were made.' Captain Cuttle, of *Dombey and Son*, was of course a fictional character, but he was based on Dickens's godfather, Christopher Huffam (or one of his fellow riggers), whose house at No. 12 Church (Newell) Street the novelist used to visit as a boy. Dickens remembered from his childhood 'anchor and chain cable forges where sledge hammers were dinging upon iron all day long ... rows of houses with little vane-surmounted masts uprearing themselves from among the scarlet beans. Then ditches, then pollarded willows and more ditches ... all other trades swallowed up in mast oar and block making.' This was about twenty years after the end of the eighteenth century, but assuredly the description holds good for our period.

Huffam's father Solomon (1736–1804) was a rigger who started off in a fairly modest way. By the time he died he had indeed made a fortune and owned half of Narrow Street. He had a 'long warehouse' in Risby's Walk, which was let out to a firm of chandlers. In Narrow Street he had a wharf, six freehold houses next to Green Dragon Alley, four tenements on the north side, which included a blacksmith's shop and a pub called the Three Foxes, a workshop let out to a bargebuilder and another leasehold property. He had two leasehold houses in Church Street, one of which he occupied himself; presumably the house known to Dickens.

Lysons said that the 'principal manufactures' in the 1790s were 'Mrs. Turner's of sailclothes, and Mr. Hall's of pot-ashes. The late Charles Dingley, Esq. erected a saw-mill of his own invention, which still exists, but has not been employed for many years.' Narrow Street was the hub. Here at Dukes' Shore (Dunbar Wharf) was the watchhouse with its cage; there were only one watchman and four headboroughs in 1760. The workhouse was towards Ratcliff in Green Dragon Alley. Among the shops, yards, wharves and warehouses were taverns and alehouses; the Grapes survives among them from this era, said to be the Six Jolly Fellowship Porters immortalised in *Our Mutual Friend*. For a few years (1745–48) there was a porcelain factory at Duke's Shore, where blue and white china known as Limehouse ware was made.

A small parish charity school was founded in Church Lane in 1779 for fifteen girls. In 1786 ten boys were admitted, one of the first being little William Bone, aged nine, who was only allowed two years' education before he was set off to sea. For forty-four years from its opening the schoolmistress was Mrs Haggis, engaged at a paltry salary of £1 a year, with accommodation and fuel supplied. Before this school was founded Limehouse had shared Poplar's charity school, set up in 1737 by Gloster Ridley, lecturer at St Anne's and chaplain at the East India Company's chapel. The unusually small number of Limehouse children provided for by the parish facilities is possibly explained by the well-attested prevalence of nonconformity. When St Anne's was consecrated the rector publicly thanked the Dissenters for their support, and by the mid-nineteenth century they constituted a good half of the parish. So when the rector of Stepney, making his returns to the diocese in 1778, reported eleven 'women's schools' and one 'man's school' in Limehouse, he may have been referring to private Dissenting establishments, probably mainly dame schools. Surprisingly there was no chapel in Limehouse, although there was an Independent chapel in Ratcliff's Queen Street nearby.

In view of the relatively small number of inhabitants, it also seems surprising that the hamlet was chosen as a site for one of the new Blenheim churches. The original plan was for Poplar and Blackwall to be included, but the East India Company objected to Hawksmoor's St Anne's, which rose like a great white ship (a white elephant?). It has been said that 'a sailor might be deceived by a distant view in supposing it a very large ship coming towards him under an easy sail with a flag flying at her maintop'. Work started on the church in 1712. It was completed in 1724, but stood empty and unused for five years, while attempts were made to raise money to pay the clergy and for running costs. Wren had insisted that there should be ample room for the poor to stand, as there were many who could not afford to rent pews. There had to be pews as well because, he added, 'There is no stemming the tide of profit.' The final cost of the building was £32,232 8s 7d, with an additional £550 for a parsonage house. Meanwhile the inhabitants petitioned to say that the building was too big for the area, asking quite reasonably that Ratcliff and Poplar should be included in the new parish. They were not and eventually, in September 1729, the church was opened in response to popular demand. They had a good party at the consecration, with 'sweet meats and hot wine'. Robert Leyborne, the new rector, whom we met fighting with Stepney vestry, preached, complimenting the king and government and dear dead Queen Anne: 'Notwithstanding her long and expensive war did not hinder her promoting the worship and service of God.' He thanked the Dissenters especially for 'being so ready to sign the petition' to have the church consecrated. And so into the vestry for refreshments: the bishop nibbled a little and the clergy and laity 'scrambled' for the rest.

Like other of the Brasenose churches, Limehouse does not seem to have had much attention from its rectors. In 1766, it was reported, the rector of Limehouse was forced by his 'nerves' to live in the country, to sleep in dry air and take a daily draught of chalybeate water. The curate, Mr Hogarth, attended to his duties.

What with the fires, the construction of the Limehouse Cut, the driving through of Commercial Road and East India Dock Road (1802–10), the Regent's Canal, the Blackwall Railway (1839) and all the crashing through of roads, tunnels and flyovers that accompanied the arrival of the docks and modern Docklands, it is astonishing that there is anything left of the old days. But the church is still there and some houses in Newell Street. Take a walk along Narrow Street, view its eighteenth-century houses and visit the Grapes. Dickens said it had a bar to 'soften the human breast'. Perhaps it still does.

Poplar, Blackwall and the Isle of Dogs

Limehouse Causeway led into Poplar, just one line of houses strung across the neck of the peninsula with the great shipyard at the east end in the village of Blackwall, and the marshy waste of the Isle of Dogs looping down to the south. In medieval times Stepney Marsh, as it was known, had been a lively part of Stepney parish, but those days are long gone.

Since the Great Flood of 1448 washed in, creating Poplar Gut (later the West India Docks), the Isle of Dogs (836 acres) had been virtually uninhabited. Apart from isolated farmhouses down in the marsh and the manor house north of the main street, the only habitation in Stepney's hamlet of Poplar and Blackwall was along the High Street, with a small cluster of buildings around the shipyard and dock. Two lanes ran down the peninsula, Angell Lane/Gun Lane and to its east Arrow/Harrow Lane, which led, via the ruins of the medieval chapel with its farmhouse, to the horse ferry to Greenwich at its tip. By the end of the century, although the dock had been developed and expanded, the hamlet was still sparsely populated, having 4,493 inhabitants and about 600 houses in 1,158 acres.

Before we take a stroll along the High Street, we will go up North Street, the lane leading up towards Bow Road, and take a look at the manor house; the site is now Wade's Place, off the East India Dock Road. The grand old Elizabethan house, with two wings, was built by a Mercer and sheriff called John Maynard, who 'kept a grett howse and in the time of Cryastymas ... had a lord of mysrulle'. From about 1590 it was occupied by the Dethicks, of German descent, Lords of Poplar Manor. Sir Gilbert Dethick was Garter King of Arms (1500–84) and, the heralds having no establishment of their own, he hosted their meetings at Poplar. It was Sir Gilbert's son, 'Master Garter' Sir William Dethick (1547/8–1612), who granted the coat of arms to John Shakespeare (the bard's father, not the rope-maker). This Garter was a notoriously bad-tempered man, much given to violent tantrums, disrupting several important funerals; he even attacked his own brother. No kindly paternal lord of the manor, he must have scared the living daylights out of his Poplar tenants.

At the opening of the eighteenth century Henry Dethick (1623–1707), Sir William's grandson, lived in the manor house. The last member of the family to serve at the College of Arms, he was Richmond herald, register of the Commissary Court of Westminster and deputy lieutenant of Tower Hamlets. He had four brothers, Gilbert, William, George and Thomas, the last also living in Poplar and part-owner of the manor house. Evidently there was bad blood between Henry and Thomas; perhaps one, or both, took after their grandfather. Thomas suspected that Henry was going to hang on to some of the prize possessions which he, Thomas, had from his mother, including two pictures of birds inlaid with 'Florence stones' that were displayed over the fireplace in the main parlour. Henry accused Thomas of stirring up trouble about the brothers' inheritance of property held of Stepney manor, where the custom was 'gavelkind' (partible inheritance): 'They talk of Gavelkind … but I know of no such thing.' At all events, Thomas died in 1703 and Henry in 1707, possessed of a 'small estate', or so he said, and that appears to have been the end of the Dethicks' long residence in Poplar. In 1717 the house was sold to·a wealthy Quaker, a Whitechapel butcher, one Jeremiah Shirbutt (remembered in Shirbut Street), who leased it to a cowkeeper for £120 a year. In 1823 the old house, 'in a dilapidated and dangerous condition', was demolished. 'The property', says Sydney Maddocks, 'then belonged to Mrs. Wade (d. 1821) the widow of Jeremiah Wade, a most hospitable lady and one who was generous to the poor. She built and resided in the present commodious house, which in her time was surrounded by an extensive garden.'

The Dethicks had owned most of the High Street, a narrow road, 30ft wide, which extended for two-thirds of a mile. It was lined with about 250 houses, mainly small ones, shops and inns. Here, on the north side opposite Arrow/ Harrow Lane, was the town house where the 'ancients' of the hamlet met to decide matters of local importance. In 1770 a proper 'Town Hall' was built on the south side of the road, just east of Gun/Angell Lane. The High Street being the main route from the passenger port at Blackwall, it had always been known for its wayside taverns; in 1800 there were eighteen of them. The better properties were on the north side of the road, where drainage was better than it was on the south. Most of the men living here were artisans, working in the shipyards or at distilleries and cooperages. Of the 500 tenements in the hamlet in 1766, 300 were 'too mean' to be charged Poor Rate and 'all live by their trade', said the rector of Stepney.

The Dethicks may have been lords of the manor, but the lords of all they surveyed in Poplar had been, since they planted their dock at Blackwall in 1614, the magnates of the East India Company. Even after their yard was sold off in 1652 their presence was strong. Time was told by the shipyard bell at Blackwall, locals worked at the construction of their ships and manned them, went to their chapel on Sundays, drank coffee at the India Coffee House in the High Street, and sent their children to the Company's School. About halfway along the High Street (between Hale Street and Woodstock Terrace) were the Company's almshouses, a large Elizabethan house converted in 1627 into accommodation for pensioners. Meridien House, built for the chaplain in 1801, marks the spot where disabled old Company sailors and lonely old Company widows were sheltered at the end of their lives. A crook named Hugh Greete was, strangely, the founding father of the almshouses, for which he left money in his will. Greete was a jeweller, commissioned to buy diamonds in India on the Company's behalf, but was caught out taking the best stones for himself; he died in prison in 1619. Nevertheless the terms of his will were carried out and, the Blackwall yard just having been acquired, Poplar was chosen as the site.

Behind the almshouses, was the Company's chapel, later the church of St Matthias, which still stands.

Locals had been wanting a local place of worship since 1633 when they petitioned the Company, asking for a chapel to be built near the almshouses. Gilbert Dethick, lord of the manor at that time, left £100 for this purpose when he died in 1639, and more sums of money were contributed by local worthies. Its completion in 1657 was thanks to the money and efforts of Maurice Thomson, the tobacco magnate and governor of the Company, whom we met running Stepney parish in Cromwell's day. A school was opened at the same time. Sir John Gayer, Governor of Bombay, whose widow bought No. 37 Stepney Green, was a major benefactor of the chapel. Although a proprietary chapel, it served as a parish church for Poplar and its rights were jealously guarded by the Company. Attempts to attach the hamlet to Limehouse and put it under the jurisdiction of the new parish, and Brasenose College, were firmly quashed. Dr Landon, minister of the chapel, acting on the Company's behalf, petitioned the Fifty Churches Commission in 1718, asking for Poplar to be a parish of its own. The chapel was surveyed, but reckoned to be in too poor a state to be used as a parish church. In July 1724 notice was given to the inhabitants to give reasons why they should not become part of Limehouse. The clerk of the East India Company wrote a strong letter, however, and that was the end of that. Poplar remained as it was until 1817 when it was made a parish; in the meantime the East India Company restored the chapel. Lysons said it was a 'large and stately' brick building with nave, chancel, two aisles and a small wooden turret at the west end. Pevsner described it as a 'handsome simple chapel', unfortunately now enclosed by an exterior of 'uncommon ugliness' with a Teulon bell turret of 'unprecedented Victorian shape'.

At the end of the High Street was Blackwall, the dock and the shipyard, the hamlet's *raison d'être*. Blackwall's natural harbour had made it a shipbuilding and repairing place since the Middle Ages. Jacobean seafaring expeditions had set off from here and it had long been a passenger port, where travellers could embark and disembark, avoiding the long river route into the City. The arrival of the East

India Company's shipyard gave a terrific boost to the area, which continued after the yard passed into private hands.

Among the coats of arms displayed in the Company's chapel's windows were those of Sir Henry Johnson, who had paid, among others things, for the painting of the building. Johnson was by far the richest and most important local man in Charles II's reign. He had bought the East India Company's Yard in 1652 when the Company was at a low ebb and made a great success of it, continuing to build East Indiamen and also ships of the line: twelve ships were built between 1670 and 1677. Grateful for his services, the king came and stayed in Johnson's magnificent Blackwall house when he conferred a knighthood on him in 1679. Sir Henry lived in flamboyant style, his walls ornamented with murals of great ships, including the famous *Sovereign of the Seas*, built by his cousin Pett. His heir, another Sir Henry, was very grand, with property all over the place and a town house in Bloomsbury Square. Ironically he became lord of the manor of Toddington, the Stepney Wentworths' old family seat, when he married, as his second wife, Martha, Baroness Wentworth.

While the second Sir Henry was busy at his social climbing, and off in Africa (he died in 1718 on a posting as Governor of Cape Coast Castle for the Royal African Company), things fell apart in Poplar. It was reported in 1723 that Sir Henry senior had 'imployed great numbers of people in the trade or business of building ships which was a great support and advantage to the said Hamlet, but since his death the Hamlet, and particularly that part called Blackwall, is gone very much to decay'. There was much poverty and distress, and many local people left to find work elsewhere. Blackwall shipyard was not long in the doldrums; it was taken over by the Perry family in 1746, and in 1784 was said to be the biggest private yard in the world. In 1799 John Perry built the spacious new Brunswick Dock at Blackwall, capable of receiving twenty-eight East Indiamen and fifty to sixty smaller ships. Here the cavalry destined for the Continent to fight in the Revolutionary Wars would embark.

Nearly as important as the shipyard, both for the Company and the navy, was the pastureland of the Isle of Dogs, which supplied much of the vast quantities of beef needed to feed their sailors. In the 1690s the largest farm was of 81 acres, belonging, appropriately enough, to a man called Bull. The fields were said to be the best pasture in Europe, and cattle fed on the rich grass might sell for an astronomical £34 each. In 1720 an ox weighing 236 stone was sold at Leadenhall Market. It was here that the Mellish brothers, major naval suppliers in the second half of the century, had their herds. It was not all beef: corn was ground here on a considerable scale in the windmills on the western side of the Isle of Dogs, which gave Millwall its name. Not all were flour mills: among those nine named on a 1750 plan there are Lead Mill and Oil Houses.

Before we leave Poplar and Blackwall, hard at work servicing Britannia, we will take a look at some of the local pubs. Rather remarkably, Blackwall acquired quite a reputation for *haute cuisine*; perhaps it wasn't *that* haute, but certainly some of the taverns were deemed a fashionable place for the quality to go for a feast of whitebait. This was quite a feature of the London season from mid-century, which apparently started at Breach House in Dagenham, where the commissioners for rebuilding the wall had eaten 'whitebait suppers'. Blackwall's Plough and Artichoke (and pubs in Greenwich) became best known for the delicacy, along with Folly House, a little south of the village. This last was in a pleasant spot, with ornamental and kitchen gardens and a terrace overlooking the river with a landing stage. In 1800 an enterprising local coal-merchant bought and extended it, and added a row of shelters or 'bowers' for the patrons to enjoy the river view from the terrace.

A far cry from the fashionable riverside Folly was the White Horse. This was the large and busy tavern in Poplar High Street at the junction with North Street. It was there at least from 1690 and continued to serve the people of Poplar with liquor until demolished in 2003. Here, in the 1750s and '60s, the landlord and landlady were not all they seemed. The story *The Female Husband*, as told by a contemporary journalist in 1766, begins like this:

> About 34 years ago a young fellow courted one Mary East, and for him she conceived the greatest liking, but he going upon the highway, was tried for a robbery and cast [sentenced to death], but was afterwards transported; this so affected our heroine, that she resolved ever to remain single. In the same neighbourhood lived another young woman, who had likewise met with many crosses in love, and had determined on the like resolution; being intimate, they communicated their minds to each other, and determined to live together ever after; after consulting on the best method of proceeding, they agreed that one should put on man's apparel, and that they would live as man and wife in some part where they were not known.

The girls, aged sixteen and seventeen respectively, managed a series of pubs, one at Limehouse Hole, for some years, with Mary East playing the man's part and calling herself James How. They saved hard and bought the White Horse in Poplar and other houses. All went well, and for nearly thirty-four years her disguise went undetected. Having established herself as a citizen of repute and of good name, she held various parish offices, serving as headborough and overseer of the poor; a James How appears as 'servant' to Mr Darking, warden at Stepney church in 1759. Although her effeminacy was remarked upon, nobody seemed to think it strange that they never entertained or employed any servants: Mary 'used to draw beer, serve, fetch in and carry out pots always herself'. At last all was revealed, of course. Stories vary slightly. Some say her true sex was revealed by her dying partner, who wanted to make sure their nest-egg (£4,000 or £5,000) was properly disposed of.

At all events an old acquaintance, who had been blackmailing her for some time, sent a gang of thugs parading as law officers, who threatened her with prosecution. It seems that in her panic she blurted out the truth to the friend who came to her assistance. All ended well; the thugs were put in the pillory and Mary, rather ill at ease in her new female attire, told the press. 'After her house is lett or sold, and her affairs settled, she intends retiring into another part to enjoy with quiet and pleasure that fortune she acquired by fair and honest means, and with an unblemished character.' Perhaps she did – but imagine the tittle-tattle over the teacups.

Hardly anything survives of old Poplar; the High Street is now a backwater, quite overborne by new Docklands and marginalised by the two mighty highways, one on either side. The East India chapel is still there, in its Victorian guise, but Mary East's pub is not forgotten: a statue of a fine white horse marks the spot.

The outliers: Bow, Bromley and Old Ford

Finally we will leave the hammering and racketing of the overcrowded riverside and, as Pepys did, take in the fresh air of the pretty little town of Stratford Bow and its adjoining villages of Old Ford and Bromley, lying just 1½ miles north of Poplar High Street. Bow is a picture postcard place, with its quaint old bridge spanning the main channel of the Lea, which winds in various branches through reeds and banks of irises: 'gliding down from the north' it 'falleth into the Thames about Limehouse', says Stow. It is a little town apart, which had been fighting for its independence from Stepney for 200 years. Industrial activity along Lea side increasingly spoilt its peace.

Bow Bridge is the end of Middlesex and the beginning of Essex. The town's prime position, where the great Essex (Mile End/Bow) Road crosses over the important river highway of the Lea, made it a busy place in the old days. Barges nosed their way down from Ware and Enfield, bringing grain to be ground in the mills at Bow and Stratford. Bow had been famed for its bakeries, but by about 1600 the breadcarts no longer trundled their way into the City. The east London flour mills became concentrated in the Isle of Dogs, and Bow, once the most populous of Stepney's hamlets, was a relatively quiet place, with only a few inhabitants. The famous mills, on both the Middlesex and Essex sides of the river, were increasingly given over to distilling and to dyeworks, heralding the transformation of the area into the industrial park that it became in the next century. Bow became famous for its bright red dye and its blue and white china, though the latter was actually made on the other side of the Lea at Stratford.

With the creation of the Limehouse Cut (1767–70), the canal that provided a route from the Lea at Bromley to Limehouse, the town was bypassed by the water route that had been its *raison d'être*. At the end of the century there were only 330 houses and the inhabitants numbered about 2,000, less than a tenth of Wapping or Bethnal Green. About half of the parish's 565 acres was still arable farmland, and there were 13 acres of nurseries.

Leading north from the main highway was the road to Old Ford (the line of the Blackwall Tunnel Approach Road), following the banks of the Lea, going thence to Hackney across the marshes, and turning west to Bethnal Green. Bearbinder Lane (the line of Tredegar Road) ran roughly parallel to the main road about a quarter of a mile to the north, turning down to join it at the watchhouse at the beginning of Mile End (the end of Coborn Road). Less than a quarter of a mile further north was a footpath that one day would become Roman Road. South of the highway was Bromley High Street, with St Leonard's church at its eastern end, and with Bromley Lane and Four Mill Street leading down to Poplar.

Old Ford was a tiny place, a cluster of houses near the riverbank around what is now the east end of Old Ford Road and Wick Lane, north of Bow town. The poet and dramatist Thomas Dekker, who was well acquainted with London's suburbs, had some hundred years earlier chosen the hamlet as the scene for a lord mayor's house, where deer were chased through the thicket and brushwood, and the daughter of the house sat and thought of her lover amid pinks, roses and violets. Probably it had not changed much since then, although the presence of a massive dyehouse must have altered the character of the place somewhat.

Bromley adjoins Bow, but it was an independent village. There, in 1692, Thomas Collett took a house 'for his wife's taking the air in the summer time'. When the century opened it was an old-fashioned country place, with its two great manor houses, wonderful gardens, stocks and a whipping post. The lord of the manor, Sir William Benson (d. 1712), was in residence at the very grand Bromley House, which dwarfed the tiny church beside it, the remains of 'Madame Eglantine's' lady chapel. The *Ambulator* of 1774 describes Bromley as a 'pleasant village near Bow,' but the arrival of the Limehouse Cut, which took navigation direct from the Thames just north of Bromley Hall, brought change. In 1799 Bromley Hall was bought by a rich calico printer.

Starting a perambulation of the town of Bow from Mile End, the first landmark was the watchhouse, just beyond Gordon's nurseries, a well-known danger spot where highwaymen and footpads lurked. As you approached the town, on your left was the field where the 'Greengoose fair' was held in June, remembered in today's Fairfield Road, by the theatre. A green goose, as well as being a delicacy, was a whore or cuckold, as the poet John Taylor wrote:

At Bow, the Thursday after Pentecost,
There is a fair of green geese ready rost,
Where, as a goose is ever dog cheap there
The sauce is over somewhat sharp and deare.

The fair was a major attraction, bringing in folk from the City and outlying parts, and was by no means confined to the field; all Bow was *en fête*. Players, puppeteers and stallholders set themselves up in 'booths and sheds' all along the road, obstructing the traffic. Naturally a good deal of beer and brandy was consumed at unlicensed premises. It was said to cause 'terror, damage and annoyance' to the good folk of Bow, but must have been much welcomed by publicans and shopkeepers. Repeated attempts were made to suppress it, but it carried on until the primmer and better regulated times of the nineteenth century.

As the town came into view you would have seen, as now, the medieval church in the middle of the road, but partially screened by some old houses. On the far side of it, adjoining the graveyard, was a small market-place and the gabled market house, where the children of Sir John Jolles' school had their lessons in an upper room. Here too was the town cage or lock-up. On the south side of the church the road was lined with inns and shops, while on the north side of the church were residences, including the rector's, and a fine old house now used as the workhouse. It was, according to an account written in 1816, 'plentifully ornamented with stucco and carving, but neither possesses any armorial allusions'. I hope the paupers appreciated their superior surroundings.

The church was not very busy, with, for example, only eighty baptisms, marriage and burials recorded in 1725. Like St Dunstan's it was a marrying church, where a couple might come for a quiet wedding, away from prying eyes, but it did not issue its own licences. The hamlet was granted autonomy on 16 March 1729 and Dr Robert Warren of Hampstead became its first rector, but £20 a year was still paid to the old mother church, and the rector of Stepney still took tithes from them; they included an alum basketmaker of St Benet Paul's Wharf who paid for his acre of osier beds.

Dissent, though perhaps not at prevalent as in Ratcliff, Wapping and Limehouse, has a presence; there was by 1816 a Baptist chapel with a school and a Methodist meeting house. The parish clerk noted in his registers quite a few Quakers, whose bodies were taken off to West Ham for burial. John Funston, the Quaker farmer from Mile End, had a coal wharf by the Lea and Edward Wilkinson, Quaker apothecary and surgeon, arrived in the 1750s. Wealthy Jews were also beginning to sample the delights of rural Bow and in about 1792 the stockbroking Ricardos made their home there. Twenty-year-old David Ricardo, the economist, fell in love with Priscilla Ann Wilkinson, a liaison unwelcome to the proud Dutch/Portuguese Sephardic family. The couple eloped, and it was said that David's mother never spoke to him again.

Beyond the church was the bridge, still the ancient structure but much repaired. Although Bow was still 'bearing the aspect of a country town', in the early years of the nineteenth century along the Lea side, north and south of the town centre were gathering distilleries, dyehouses, calico printing-houses and breweries.

The best-known (and best-loved) brewer in the days of the later Stuarts was a woman, Prisca Coborn; in 1698 she had 922 barrels of strong beer and 238 barrels of small beer in her cellars. She became a local legend, a very grand and generous old lady, and the four days when her £10 annuities for the poor were distributed in Bow (especially for those 'who have great charges of children to maintain') were known as Coborn Days. These were Good Friday, Maundy Thursday, St Bartholomew's Day (her birthday, 24 August) and 30 January. Prisca, as might be expected in Bow, came from a baking line on her mother's side. Her maternal grandfather, Thomas Skorier, owned land locally and in Essex which she would inherit, becoming a wealthy woman. Her father, John Forster, was minister at Bow chapel from about 1611, and continued to preach there after he gave up the living in 1620. At the ripe old age of fifty-three, in 1675, Prisca married brewer Thomas Coborn (Colborne), recently widowed. He died very soon after the wedding, leaving her a baby, Alice, to bring up, which she did, according to the monument in the church, with 'unexampled care and a liberal education'. Alice died tragically, aged sixteen, on the day she was to be married; the story was that she was buried in her wedding dress. Madame Coborn, as she was known, ran the brewery herself; her will includes bequests to eleven of her 'servants' there, to her 'house clerk' and 'broad clerk' and to all her women customers (victuallers). She was clearly rather a feminist. Her devotion to her mother is clear – she asked to be buried in the church with her mother, although her husband's corpse was there, and her love for her stepdaughter was manifest. Her funeral, if her directions were followed to the letter, must have been an extraordinary affair, with her coffin attended by thirty poor women of Bow and thirty poor women of Bromley, not to mention thirty members of the clergy. Her manor of Colville Hall in Essex, with 250 acres of land, was left to Stepney parish for the benefit of seamen's widows; a bell was struck in her honour in 1806 and still hangs in the belfry, inscribed with her name. Colville Hall in White Roding still stands. She left money for the relief of clergy widows and their children. But her most lasting monument is her school, the descendant of which, the Coborn School for Girls, in the dark Edwardian slum days gave Bow girls a genteel and inspiring introduction to life. Prica died in November 1701, in her eightieth year. The clerk noted in the parish register that 'She Lyes upon her mother 4 foot Deep. The deceased did Desire that she might never be Disturbed.' The residue of her estate was left for the foundation of a free school for fifty children, boys and girls; if her executor thought fit these children might join the Jolles School. Unusually for the time the girls were to be taught to write as well as to read. The local clergy and churchwardens, who were to take over the running of the school after the death of her executor, were reluctant to let it pass into the hands of the Drapers' Company, and initially there was a separate building for the Coborn children on the north side of the High Street. This situation did not last long, and in 1711 they joined the Jolles children.

As well as men (and women) in the drink business, there was the usual mixture of trades that might be expected in a place of this sort: millers, tanners, bargemen, blacksmiths, a few clothworkers and quite a number of coachmen, coachmakers and wheelwrights. The manufacture of sailcloth and sails was a big local business. The almshouses taken over by the Drapers' Company were founded by a sailmaker, and Sir Samuel Gower, the JP we met in Whitechapel, had sailcloth works in Old Ford, called Buckhouse; his turnover, he claimed, for this and his Whitechapel factory, was £10,000 a year

It was, however, for its dyehouses and calico printers that Bow became renowned. Cheap cotton printed with bright, bold designs became popular after the East India Company began to import calico, much to the distress of the silk industry. A newly invented bright red dye was all the rage. This was developed by a Dutch chemist called Drebbel, and his son-in-law, Dr Johannes Sibertus Kuffler of Leyden (1595–1677), set up a dyehouse in Bow; the product became known as Bow dye.

The Selmans of Old Ford were one of the richest manufacturing families; their scarlet dyehouse is marked by Gascoyne in Wick Lane, the only considerable building in the hamlet, remembered today in Dye House Lane. During the last two decades of the seventeenth-century Daniel Selman set himself up in Old Ford, possibly starting in a relatively modest way, and went into partnership with one John Warner. At his death in 1727 he was a rich man, Daniel Selman Esquire. He was buried in the prime spot in the church and had a good estate, which included a house in St James's rented out to a Chancery master. 'All the benefits of [his] Trade' were left to Lister/Leicester (1708–79) his nineteen-year-old favourite son, child of his old age and second marriage. Lister's birth had meant so much to the dyer and his wife that its exact time (four minutes after eight at night) was recorded in the parish register. The young man expanded the business, acquiring a good deal more property, including some of Sir Samuel Gower's, and, like Gower, became a very active JP. He made a good age and left everything to his daughter Helena, the wife of John Lefevre, a distiller of Huguenot descent. Thus were the two richest Bow manufacturing families united; in 1789 Helena was granted a coat of arms in her own right, and her grandson became a viscount.

The Lefevres are remembered in Lefevre Walk near Wick Lane; there used to be a Lefevre Road as well, but that has gone. This family did very well indeed for themselves. Isaac Lefevre (d.1746) was a Spitalfields dyer who expanded into Bromley and Stratford. His brother Peter was part-owner of the Clock Mill in 1727. His daughter Magdalen married William Currie (d.1781), a wealthy Poplar distiller; their son became an MP, married Lord Byron's daughter and commissioned Sir Charles Barry to rebuild his manor house in Surrey, Horsley Towers. Isaac's sons were distillers. Peter Lefevre (d.1787) of Bromley was part owner of the Clock Mill. Isaac junior had his Limehouse Hole distillery insured for £10,000 in 1778, and lived in the Queen Anne mansion at No. 37 Stepney Green (1764–1811). Probably the eldest son, John, was the richest, helped no doubt by his marriage with the Selman dyehouse heiress. His distillery in Bromley's Four Mills Street was one of the most valuable of London business properties, insured for £12,000. There was a spirit warehouse, a stillhouse, a dwelling-house, a rectifying-house, granaries and three windmills. Together with his brother Isaac he went into partnership with their brother-in-law William Currie, and opened a bank in Cornhill. Much of Bromley was owned by John Lefevre; he also had property in Old Ford, Bow, Wapping, Hackney, Edmonton, Essex, Buckinghamshire and a country estate in Hampshire, Heckfield Place, with 200 acres. His daughter Helena (d. 1834) married Charles Shaw, who took her name, and their son was Sir Charles Shaw-Lefevre 1st Viscount Eversley of Heckfield (1794–1888), the longest-serving speaker of the House of Commons.

These days Currie's Bank belongs to the Royal Bank of Scotland, Heckfield Place (rebuilt) is now a 'world class luxury hotel', Barry's Horsley Towers offers 'unforgettable weddings', while Madam Coborn's school flourishes out in the leafy suburbs of Upminster.

As to Bow, Bromley and Old Ford, they were scarred by factories, gasworks and railways, sliced up by arterial roads and covered in mean little houses, although there were some good ones, as we shall see. All that is left of the old Green Goose days in Bow is the church in the middle of the road and one seventeenth-century house stranded in the High Street. In Bromley there are only the sail makers' almshouses.

Our tour is over. We have seen something of the contrasts and varieties of the towns and villages that will become one agglomeration in the next fifty years. We have met Irish coalheavers, French weavers, German sugarbakers, Jewish pedlars and bankers, Lascars and Negroes, multi-millionaire industrialists and merchants living cheek by jowl with jolly jack tars, anchorsmiths, rope-twisters, sailmakers and carpenters, lightermen and watermen, tobaccomen, brewers, publicans, milk-maids, cowherds and market gardeners, bedesmen and genteel widows, pirates, highwaymen, footpads, prostitutes, apothecaries, physicians, midwives. Within a very short time all the places will be joined up and, as their separate identity is lost, their people will become simply Old East Enders.

FROM DOCKS TO DOCKLANDS

You may think this is an upside-down book. Most histories of the East End, or anywhere else, get fuller and longer as modern times approach, and there is more to be said, or at least more available evidence. Not so this history. It has been my intention to remind the reader that there was life on the east side of London before Jack the Ripper, before the dock companies and the Jews made it their own, before the terrible dark days of the 'submerged', of music halls, street markets, and all the fun of the slums. I hope I have shown how different, separate and important the little towns and villages were before they all merged and became the East End that everybody knows about. For those wishing to bring the story up to date, there are manifold reminiscences and serious studies. There are Victorian and Edwardian relics on the ground in abundance: dock buildings, restored warehouses, row upon row of houses, workhouses, model dwellings, public libraries, public baths, town halls and churches.

Like Sir Hubert Llewellyn Smith, who in the 1930s embarked on the East End's story, 'I hate to see how this vast area is popularly regarded as a mere aggregate of dull and common place poverty, interesting only as an object of philanthropic effort or social research, or as a show-place to gratify a morbid curiosity to learn how the poor lived.' Most of his life's work was doing just that, and the notion of 'the fields beneath' clearly fascinated him. My account really stops, as his did, with the coming of the docks, and the transformation of our 7 square miles that followed.

But something, albeit scanty, has to be said about what happened next, and the 'problem of the poor' has at least to be acknowledged.

Cockney Corinthian

When Francis Place did a tour of inspection from the Tower to Limehouse and back along Ratcliff Highway to Rosemary Lane in the early years of the nineteenth century, he noticed the children were lice-free, cleaner and wearing shoes, which they had not done in his youth. 'I carefully observed the children and can safely say they are equal and in many respects superior to the children of tradesmen in much more wealthy districts.' Dorothy George concludes her masterly work on eighteenth-century London optimistically. Things got better for the poor, but, then, as everybody knows they got much, much worse. But before that, were some good times for East Enders.

In the opening years of the new century came the docks. Houses were demolished and the seaborne commerce of the capital shifted from the Legal Quays down river to the East End, changing it from sailortown to the Docks. London was to become the greatest port in the world, and the enclosed docks its wonder. The first was the West India Dock, two stretches of water covering 164 acres, secure and enclosed with high walls and tall warehouses, at the north-west corner of the Isle of Dogs. It was opened by William Pitt himself on 21 August 1802, and the West India Company was granted a twenty-one-year monopoly for the import of sugar, rum and coffee. The London Dock opened in Wapping in 1805, taking 11 acres of land and 120 houses, 24 streets, 33 court yards, alleys and rows, two cooperages and a glasshouse from St George's in the East. Originally all wine, brandy and spirits (except those from East and West Indies) had to unload here. In 1806 the East India Dock opened at Blackwall. With the opening of these deep water docks the medieval porterage brotherhood lost their old monopoly for unloading and a new type of labourer appeared. Originally there were only about 900 of them; by the 1850s there were 10,000. Labourers arrived from all over the British Isles; it was noted in the 1810 visitation returns that a whole colony of Irish labourers had arrived in Poplar. In October 1825 work began on the demolition of St Katharine's: 11,300 householders were thrown out, and Telford's elegant and efficient dock took the place of the rackety old precinct. This was one of the largest projects of its kind yet undertaken in London.

The arrival of the docks did not immediately reduce the place to a slum; initially it was rather the reverse. The riverside and its hinterland were a busy humming boomtown, where the merry songs of the well-paid dockmen rang out in the well-ordered new workplaces. With money coming in, shops were filled with luxury goods and a new middle class came to live and work in the East End: excise men and customs officers, well-paid stevedores, dock foremen and insurance men. Squares of 'Cockney Corinthian' were laid out in imitation of the West End in Stepney: Trafalgar, Beaumont and Arbour, offering elegant homes to professional and merchant families. Houses were 'neatly and solidly furnished from top to toe, with every modern convenience and improvement: with bath rooms, conservatories, ice cellars; with patent grates, patent door handles, dish lifts, asbestos stoves, gas cooking ranges'. Seafarers and merchants who had grown rich in the East and West Indies were still around, as Sydney Maddocks wrote: 'In many a home hereabouts the picture of a fine, tall vessel in full sail, the coral in the case, the curious shells, the vases from India and the Far East told their story.' The square laid out on Lord Tredegar's estate in Bow in 1835 was the prize, with its beautiful 'South Kensington' houses where, says Millicent Rose, occupants might keep a pet pony for their children and played croquet in the long back gardens.

The new Commercial Road (1802–6) and East India Dock (1806–12) Road were lined with substantial properties. Villas popped up all along Bow Road and in the new streets of Poplar, where the population grew from 4,493 in 1801 to 43,523 in 1851, and a fine white Portland stone church (All Saints'), was built, at great expense, by public subscription in 1821–23; it had an Ionic porch and a Classical interior.

The *Mirror* reported the opening of the Eastern Institution in Commercial Road in March 1839. With its fluted Doric columns, gas-lit crystal chandeliers, benches with 'handsome stuffed cushions and mahogany backs' and elegantly laid out gardens, it spoke of the new flamboyant wealth. In Beaumont Square the millionaire philanthropist John Thomas Barber, calling himself Beaumont, built his Institution, a forerunner of the People's Palace. There, in surroundings of classical splendour, locals came for the 'meeting together for mental and moral improvement and amusement in their intervals of business freed from the baneful excitement of intoxicating liquor and for the cultivation of the general principles of natural theology'.

Efforts were made to create an attractive residential district in Stepney. In 1842 the rector anticipated the neighbourhood becoming 'more respectable'. St George's in the East reached the zenith of its respectability in the 1820s, declining sharply thereafter following the opening of the London Dock and the proliferation of sugarhouses, which brought in more poor Germans to live in increasingly overcrowded conditions. In 1829 the curate William Quekett, arriving to take on his new job in what he had mistakenly thought was St George's Hanover Square, was horrified at the slum he had come to.

In the north of the area weavers enjoyed the boom in their trade (the last) that followed the Napoleonic Wars. Bethnal Green was covered in small houses built for weavers. But the good times were brief: a great depression hit the silk industry, and in 1834 over 1,000 houses stood empty in Mile End New Town.

While Old Ford was still a 'small village pleasantly situated on the banks of the river Lea', little Bromley grew out of all recognition. It spawned a 'new town', a truly horrible place, with a bridge named Stink House Bridge down on the banks of the Limehouse Cut, whose banks were crowded with factories making vitriol, pitch varnish, grease naphtha, manure and animal charcoal. James Dunstan, in his account of 1862, remembered a 50-acre field, where potatoes, cabbages and onions had grown, now covered in houses.

The docks transformed the area, and the coming of the railways in the 1830s changed life for the man in the East End street unimaginably. Not only was there massive clearance of land to make way for the monsters, together with noise, smoke and soot as they roared past your backyard, blackening the washing and ruining your vegetable patch, but they took the better-off out to the suburbs. As Canon Barnett, the saintly vicar of St Jude's Whitechapel, put it: 'It is this practice of living in a pleasant place which impoverishes the poor. It authorises, as it were, a lower standard of life for the neighbourhoods in which the poor are left ... it leaves large quantities of the town without the light which comes from knowledge, and large masses of the people without the friendship of those better taught than themselves.' Daniel Vawdry, rector of Stepney for five miserable years (1842–47) and moaner *par excellence*, had his own complaint. He found the railways 'a most intolerable nuisance', finding himself 'cut off between the extremes of my estate'.

In 1839 the Registrar General reported that the East End had the highest mortality rate in London and that there was 'massive overcrowding, insanitary conditions and polluted air'. Still there was some open ground around Bow and Bromley, and sheep grazing on Stepney Green. Dickens in *Our Mutual Friend* noted the stumps of some windmills in Ratcliff.

Bethnal Green in the 1840s was in the last stages of its transition; Whisker's gardens off Old Ford Road, with its sixteen or twenty 'summer houses' had 'choicest dahlias' and tulips carefully cultivated. If you took a walk round Stepney Green in the spring twilight of these years, among the limes, elms and Lombardy poplars, the horse chestnuts hanging heavy with blossom, you might sniff the scent of the well-tended flower gardens, although there was more than hint of soot in the air. Before the shutters were closed and the gasmantles lit, you could see through the windows of the gracious old houses, maids scuttling about in their starched caps, tending to the needs of the good, respectable folk safely ensconced within: the families of customs officers, wholesale ironmongers, rope manufacturers, surgeons, ships' insurance brokers, ships' masters. At No. 22 was the superintendent of the Commercial Gas Company, at No. 21 the ship-owning West India merchant Charles Sugrue with his Jamaican-born wife and daughters, who taught at St Dunstan's Sunday School. There were two Dissenting ministers: at No. 11 the Wesleyan minister for the Spitalfields Division and at No. 4 John Kennedy, pastor of Stepney Meeting.

A pall of fumes and despair was falling over the East End when the Great Exhibition opened in 1851, celebrating the triumph of man over nature and of Britain over everywhere else. Model ships from Blackwall were exhibited, artificial limbs, eyes and noses from J. Fuller of Whitechapel, a huge hemispherical bell from Mears at the bellfoundry, twine and nets from S. Tull at Mile End, improved watercocks from Fraser, Noakes and Vincent of Brick Lane, improved rudder fastenings from Young, Dowson and Co. of Poplar, a speedometer for steam engines by W. Yates of Bromley, marine soap from Old Gravel Lane, daguerreotypes from Mile End, beers from Truman and Hanbury, cigars and printed leather from Spitalfields. J. Sculey from Wapping decided to remind visitors of past glories and displayed Captain Cook's quadrant and compass, 'as used by the celebrated mariner'. In June 65,000 people were attending on 'shilling days'; the queen danced a polonaise at a ball to encourage trade. Miss Angela Burdett Coutts (fabulously wealthy heiress and one of the greatest benefactors the East End would ever know), was at the ball, sporting a magnificent broad baldrick of emeralds and diamonds. She is remembered in Burdett Road, which was named in her honour, and in Cockney rhyming slang: the term for 'boots'.

The launch of Brunel's *Great Eastern* in 1858, the largest ship of its day, was the pinnacle of Poplar's boomtime. Thousands of trippers came to view her. Most of the immense wealth generated by the new docks flowed into the City; Poplar's heyday came with the expansion of its shipbuilding industry. In 1837 one of the first iron ships was built, and by 1848 there were thirty-eight shipbuilding firms, as well as ironfounders, blacksmiths, sailmakers and ropemakers. Workers came in from Scotland, Ireland, Wales and Italy. The area between Cubitt Town and Millwall Dock would soon become covered by heavy industry.

The abyss

The repercussions following the crash of the bankers Overend and Gurney in 1866 brought a dramatic and sudden end to the Poplar shipbuilding trade, which relocated to the Clyde near the source of iron. Skilled ships' fitters turned carpenters or joiners and joined the Shoreditch furniture trade or went to Scotland. Many, especially the older men, went to the workhouses. From this time, says Millicent Rose, 'an air of desolation begins to spread through Ratcliff, Shadwell and Wapping'.

The year 1866 saw the end of the boom in the building trade and of railway construction. The winter of 1866–67 was bitingly cold, and the river froze over. That winter 10,000 of the 40,000 population of St George's in the East (mainly dockers) were out of work. The sugarbaking industry that had dominated in St George's also collapsed, because of the introduction of sugar bounties; the workforce dropped from 1,437 to 616 in the twenty years after 1861. Meanwhile the final death blow came to Spitalfields and Bethnal Green in 1860, when a treaty with France allowed the import of French silk. Unemployed silk workers took to dockwork or joined the burgeoning rag trade, which provided cheap ready-made clothes. It had started with the making of outfits for sailors. Whitechapel in particular became notorious for its sweated industries, with small tailoring work-shops and seamstresses working from home. Needlewomen in the 1860s made about as much a week as dockers had made in a day when the docks first opened. By 1888 there were 1,015 tailoring workshops in Whitechapel.

Meanwhile the population explosion went on apace; the affluent years saw couples marrying younger, having more children and living longer. Medicine was improved; smallpox inoculation all but banished one of the major killers. People poured into the East End in search of work; Bethnal Green grew from 22,310 in 1801 to 126,061 in 1881, tiny Bromley from 1,684 to 64,359, Poplar from 4,493 to 55,077. The growth of these places is astonishing.

Waves of starving Irish folk had arrived following the Great Famine of 1845 and 'Irish nests' appeared in Ratliff, Limehouse, Spitalfields, Whitechapel, Shadwell and Wapping and St George's. Paddy's Goose on Ratcliff Highway was, accord-ing to Charles Dickens junior, 'The uproarious rendezvous of half the tramps and thieves of London'. Then came the poor Jews. From 1881, when the czar was assassinated, there came into the East End a great influx, families fleeing from pogroms in Poland, Lithuania, Germany and the Austro-Hungarian empire. There were said to be 30,000 of them, mainly in Whitechapel and Spitalfields, spreading out to St George's, Stepney and Bow. Whitechapel ghetto was a place of solid, sodden poverty, with 3,000 souls per acre, as opposed to 800 in the gentile parts. Most of the newcomers joined the rag trade.

As the port expanded even more, immigrants arrived from wherever in the world that Britain traded. By the 1880s the Chinese were established in Limehouse, famous for its opium dens, laundries and restaurants and their patch, around Pennyfields, was known as Chinatown. From the late nineteenth century Somali seamen were to be found in the Cable Street area, and a street in Shadwell was named Tiger Bay because of the Goans there.

With the collapse of the major industries there was a tremendous and lasting labour surplus, and in the long economic depression that lasted from 1873 to 1896 the East End descended into the 'great joyless city of two million people' that Walter Besant described. There were no hotels, no cabs, no grass (except in Victoria Park), no gentlemen, except the clergy and do-gooders, who ventured, warily, east of Aldgate pump in their fine clothes and, for the most part, went away again. In 1891 Charles Booth classified half the populations of Whitechapel, St George's and Bethnal Green as poor.

Work, when you could get it, was irregular and low paid, notoriously at the docks, where conditions and pay became scandalous, resulting in the great strike of 1889. For a variety of reasons London became 'over docked', and the opening of new docks downstream, the Victoria and the Albert in East and West Ham and the Tilbury docks, meant less work was on offer in Wapping and Poplar. Men queued up at the dock gates in the hope of getting a day's work.

In the early autumn every year thousands of East Enders, men, women and children, crammed into midnight trains from London Bridge and rattled down to the hopfields of Kent: in the mid-1870s about 35,000 of them. They stayed for the hop harvest, living in bleak shacks with earth floors, surrounded by festering heaps of rubbish, earning a little cash to supplement what income they had from London work. All the family joined in; it was gruelling work and the pay was poor. 'They treat us like beasts', one hopper told the rector of Stepney; 'Hopping is hell' said another. Still, it was the nearest thing anybody got to a holiday, and there were fun and games in the local pubs, and 'hoppers' marriages': all you had to do was jump over a rope and you were spliced.

Thrown out of the trades they were reared to, men took to chimneysweeping, woodchopping, cobbling, cabbing, hawking, setting up stalls and taking work as messengers, sandwichmen and theatrical extras, and all the range of casual work that is to be found on the fringes of a wealthy consumer society. Lighterman Gaffer Hexham in *Our Mutual Friend* rowed about the river at Limehouse under cover of dark, searching for bodies he could sell. Children might fix the bristles in scrubbing brushes – 1*d* for filling a hundred holes. Flowergirls took a turn as prostitutes, and seamstresses augmented their meagre earnings by selling themselves, for appreciably less than their eighteenth-century counterparts. The match girls, 'smart as paint', risked the terrible disease of phossijaw for the relatively high wages offered by Bryant and May at their match factory in Bow. A statue of W.E. Gladstone, paid for by factory owner Theodor Bryant, stands in the middle of the road by Bow church. The locals said it had been erected 'with the blood of the match girls'.

Developers took advantage of the demand for housing and covered the East End in terraces of tiny cheap two-storey houses, which were then subdivided to squeeze in as many tenants as possible. Most families had just one room. Those who could not even afford to rent a room resorted to the terrible low lodging houses where you paid 2*d* a night. If they couldn't afford that, they might be allowed to huddle on the stairs. The government's attempts at slum clearance in the 1870s and the construction of model dwellings made the situation worse, if anything. The poor couldn't afford 5*s* a week for a Peabody flat, and many were left empty or taken over by the better-off Jews, who were more accustomed to flat-dwelling than their indigenous neighbours. Evicted families, needing to stay near their work, crowded into nearby areas. Whitechapel became more over-crowded than ever as a result of the clearances in St George's. Those who could afford railway fares moved out to the suburbs, to Pooterland and beyond, following the 1883 Cheap Trains Act and the coming of omnibuses and trams. Only the very poor were left behind.

By 1885 the first home factory was set up on the west side of beautiful Tredegar Square. The gracious Queen Anne house at No. 37 Stepney Green became a Home for Aged Jews and the Signeratt/Bourdillon house in Fournier Street a home for working boys. In Stepney Causeway, once lined with some of the best houses in Stepney, Dr Barnado opened his shelter for homeless children. The *Great Eastern* was broken up in 1888 at Liverpool, where in her last days she was used as a funfair.

There were no adequate means for dealing with the poverty problem. Under the new Poor Law (1834) great workhouses were built, where conditions were deliberately harsh to discourage malingerers. If an able-bodied man went into the workhouse his family had to enter with him. From 1867 separate infirmaries were built, and later there were experiments with farm colonies for families and 'cottage settlements', and 'scattered homes' for children in the countryside. Thousands were still on out-relief. Alexander Heriot Mackonockie, ritualist vicar of St Peter's London Dock, reported in 1883 that all his parishioners were on poor relief and they were all Irish. Poplar workhouse had nearly 2,192 inmates in 1888, as well as 'casuals' who went in for 'a night's kip on the spike'.

The Bitter Cry of Outcast London, a pamphlet produced in 1883 by two Congregational ministers, made an enormous impact. They took for their study Shadwell, Ratcliff and Bermondsey, where they found 'pestilential human rookeries' inhabited by 'stunted, misshapen, and often loathsome objects', 'courts reeking with poisonous and malodorous gases arising from accumulation of sewage and refuse', the bodies of dead children left to rot, roofs overlaid with the putrefying corpses of cats, dogs and rats. Incest was rife, and nobody got married or went to church (39 of 4,235 in St George's in the East) or chapel. *The Bitter Cry* sold like hot cakes and the Great Victorian Conscience was given another stir.

The well-to-do went 'East Ending' in droves. Universities opened 'settlements', like that at Toynbee Hall in Whitechapel and Oxford House in Bethnal Green, where young men might spend a short time experiencing how the other half lived. While the Charity Organisation Society tried to pull together the myriad different charitable endeavours, in churches and chapels (of which there were now a huge number) saintly men and women, clergy and laity alike, worked indefatigably to alleviate the suffering. It was not always welcome. Arthur Morrison, Poplar novelist, relayed a conversation that has the ring of truth about it. Kiddo Cook, an inhabitant of the terrible slum described in *A Child of the Jago*, meets the local vicar, based on the Revd Arthur Osborne Jay. Kiddo, 'smirking and ducking' with mock affability', emerges from a pub and offers the parson a quart pot:

'An' 'ow jer find yerself, sir? … Hof'ly shockin' these 'ere lower classes, ain't they? Er-yus; disgustin', weally. Er – might I – er-prepose – er – a little refreshment? Ellow me.'

The parson, grimly impassive, heard him through, took the pot, and instantly jerking it upwards, shot the beer, a single splash, into Kiddo's face. 'There are things I must teach you, I see, my man' he said, without moving a muscle, except to return the pot.

There were boys' clubs and men's clubs, penny banks, brass bands, boxing clubs, sewing clubs, outings to the seaside, jumble sales, sales of work, temperance societies, maternity societies and parish nurses. There was mission upon mission: the George Yard Mission in Whitechapel, the King Edward Mission in Spitalfields, the Nichol Street Mission, the Out and Out Mission in Bow, the London Cottage Mission in Salmon Lane, where soup was ladled out every Wednesday, after grace had been sung to the tune of 'The Old Hundredth'. Frederick Nicholas Charrington, scion of the great brewing house, took up the cause of temperance, and set up the magnificent Great Assembly Hall at No. 31 Mile End Road in 1872. On Sunday evenings the first 700 people queuing outside the Hall were given a hot meal in return for taking the pledge. Thousands flocked to get free food and hear the evangelists preaching, among them Harry Orbell, layreader and union leader, later a member of the Labour Party's executive. The rector of Stepney said it was the 'work of the Devil': Charles Booth had noticed that although the churches and charities of the East End were fighting the same fight there was no co-ordination, and in fact a good deal of conflict between them.

How things got better (slightly) from 1900

'We may take it roughly that the great city is divided into three parts: there is the West End, where the richer people live, and where there are good shops; and the City, which was the first part of London, from which all the rest has sprung; and beyond the City on the other side is the East End, where poor people crowd together.' Thus wrote Geraldine Mitton in *The Glory of London*, published in 1905. The East End was universally regarded as a place quite apart from the rest of London, but observers were able to find its good points. 'Life goes quite as merrily … There is a Continental bustle … People know each other here. Friends on buses whistle to friends on the pavements … no where else in London, in England, is fruit so eaten.' With Edwardian times we enter the East End of the popular imagination, the good old days of eel and pie shops, rhyming slang and street markets: Petticoat Lane, Roman Road, Chrisp Street, where 'rollicking Cockney girls' in their ostrich feathers and sham fur coats swagger, and costers shout out, selling baked potatoes, crockery and cheap clothes. There were music halls, the Wonderland in the Whitechapel Road, the Paragon in Mile End, Foresters' Music Hall in Cambridge Heath Road, the Marlow in

Bow, the Queens and the Hippodrome in Poplar. On Sunday East Enders might take the train to Hampstead Heath ('Appy Hampstead' they called it) or go to the pub. 'The church bell wakes them,' wrote Booth of Mile End, 'they get up and adjourn to the public house from one to three, dine soon after three, sleep and either go again to the public house in the evening or to the park.' The *Daily News* survey of 1903 showed that only about 5 per cent of all East Enders went to church or chapel. Inspector Pearce, taking Charles Booth's researcher round Bethnal Green just after Christmas 1897, commented that the inhabitants 'form a great family party'. He noticed especially, in the brightly polished windows of the little houses, even in the poorest streets, there were Christmas trees, decorated with sugar plums and candles.

The 1900s were not such bad years for the East Enders as the 1870s and '80s had been. Although there was still widespread poverty, food was much cheaper; the London loaf cost less than it had done since 1762. The deprivation discovered by Booth, and drawn in his famous poverty map, was less acute than that investigated by Henry Mayhew in the 1850s. One of the blackest spots in the whole of the conurbation was, ironically, where 300 years before poor pregnant girls and old soldiers had huddled together in the parsonage barn, Stepney's first poorhouse. This was Eastfield Street and the streets parallel to it, lying in the Limehouse parish of St John the Evangelist.

Although there was still a long way to go the old East Enders, in these high bugle-sounding days of Empire, were beginning to climb out of the abyss. Most children were enrolled at elementary schools, although there was a good deal of truancy. In June 1886 the foundation stone of that great cultural institute and leisure centre in Mile End, the People's Palace, was laid. 'Nothing we know too well', said the Prince of Wales in his speech, 'can really turn the East-end into a garden, can take away the dismal monotony of its streets, or can destroy the squalid type of life which the vast majority of its inhabitants are doomed to live ... but it is also true that a little brightness, a little enjoyment, and such chances of learning as are to be given by the People's Palace count for far more in the case of these people than they would in the case of people more richly furnished with good things.'

The first moves were being made towards the revolution that would eventually deal with the poverty question. In this revolution Sir William Beveridge, architect of the welfare state and Clement Attlee, leader of the great reforming post-war government, were to play a vital part; both had been volunteers at Whitechapel's Toynbee Hall. Trades unions were organising themselves into fighting forces and the intelligentsia were investigating socialism. In February 1900 the two movements together forged the Labour Party. By 1906 there were twenty-nine Labour men in Parliament, among them Will Crooks for Poplar, the son of a ship's stoker and a seamstress, who had spent some time in the workhouse. In 1908/10 the first state old age pensions were introduced; the welfare state was launched.

In 1899 the County of London (LCC) was formed and the area allocated three boroughs: Stepney (incorporating Whitechapel), Bethnal Green and Poplar. The ancient parishes, hamlets and liberties were no more of any account. By the 1920s east London had extended itself into Essex, with West and East Ham, Ilford, Forest Gate, Walthamstow and Romford. In 1921 the American firm of Ford opened a factory in Dagenham, but most of the new industrial development was in west London. These were the days of flat-chested girls who peeped from under cloche hats and showed legs in silk stockings. The West End danced to American jazz, flocked to American 'flicks' and drank American cocktails, while lines of mock-Tudor semis introduced a new, clean, electric-powered monotony in the outer suburbs. Those who could afford it were abandoning the dark, old Victorian inner city, making for the new places where Hoovers buzzed and there was only the wireless for company. For those left behind in the East End, the dockers and rag trade workers and their families, it was a hard time, with much anger, unemployment and distress, but people did not starve.

Things were not as bad as they had been forty or fifty years before, although the East End was still a pretty grim place and unemployment was rife, as it was countrywide in the inter-war years. The 1911 National Insurance Act had introduced a limited health and unemployment insurance scheme, and there was some out-relief to be had in the form of small grants from the Poor Law Guardians; food, coal and clothing tickets might be distributed to the needy. The burden of poor relief, in the main, lay with individual boroughs, and in 1921 one in five of the breadwinners in the borough of Poplar were out of work. George Lansbury, later leader of the Labour Party, led a council revolt; they refused to levy the rates until the wealthy boroughs took a share of the burden, and organised a protest march that was joined by thousands. Their banner read 'Poplar Borough Council, Marching to the High Court and Possibly to Prison, To Secure The Equalisation of Rates For Poor Boroughs'. There was enormous popular support and a bill was rushed through Parliament, which more or less equalised tax burdens between rich and poor boroughs. In May 1926 came the General Strike, with workers all over the country coming out in sympathy with the miners who had refused to accept a cut in wages.

Sir Hubert Llewellyn Smith's poverty survey of 1930 showed that the worst areas of London were Stepney, Poplar, Bethnal Green, Bermondsey and North Kensington. Unemployment in Stepney and Poplar was between 15 per cent and 20 per cent. When the government proposed a 10 per cent cut in national insurance benefits to deal with the economic crisis of 1931, Father Groser, the Christian Socialist incumbent at Christ Church, Watney Street, started a campaign. He wrote: 'There were to be cuts in social services and for the unemployed. We ... started a campaign by leaflets and open air meetings in which we tried to point out that the causes of the present crisis lie at the root of the devilish and inhuman capitalist system under which we live.' But the cuts were duly made by Ramsay MacDonald, Labour prime minister, who thereby earned the enduring hatred of East Enders. In 1934 Labour won the LCC elections and its new leader, Herbert Morrison, proclaimed: 'Let Labour build a new London'. Morrison initiated the creation of the Green Belt, but it was Hitler who was primarily responsible for a new London, certainly a new East End, and Morrison gave his name to the shelters where Londoners retreated during the Blitz.

'Black Saturday', 7 September 1940, when the 'poor old docks copped it', was the most concentrated assault on Britain since the Spanish Armada. The planes covered 800 square miles of sky, and the glow of the burning warehouses could be seen a hundred or more miles away. The raids went on night after night until the following May; the East End was bombed by an average of 200 planes nightly, for 57 nights in succession, with 788 high explosive bombs falling on Stepney alone. By 11 November 1940 four out of ten houses in Stepney had been damaged. It was a world of wailing sirens at dusk, hustling down to the public shelters, into the crypts of churches and Stepney Green, Mile End and Bank underground stations, waving goodbye to children sent off to the country for safety, fire-watching, and making the best of it all. Whole streets disappeared, and evacuation reduced the population of the borough of Stepney from about 200,000 to 80,000. On 13 June 1944 the first German flying bomb hit London, and blew up on the LNER at Bow Viaduct. Night and day the 'huge dragons' came with light in their tails. The last bomb that fell on London was on Hughes Mansions in Whitechapel's Vallance Road, on 27 March 1945. On 8 May 1945 Germany collapsed; what church bells were left rang out, and the women of Stepney threw up their skirts to reveal hastily put together red, white and blue knickers, and did 'Knees up, Mother Brown'.

The East End was left empty, torn and bleeding. The mass exodus continued in the post-war era. It was a derelict place in decline. Jennifer Worth, author of *Call the Midwife*, who remembered it well, wrote: 'Pre-war Stepney ... was the home of thousands of respectable, hard working, but often poor East End families. Much of the area was filled with crowded tenements, narrow unlit alleyways and lanes and old multi-occupant houses.' In the 1950s these still often had a single tap and lavatory for up to twelve families; large families occupied single rooms. The Second World War changed matters for the worse. In a massive case of urban blight, the area was scheduled for demolition, but this did not take place until twenty years later. As houses were privately owned, they could not be sold on the open market – so, perhaps inevitably, landlords became more and more distreputable as time passed – letting virtually derelict rooms for very low rent, and allowing brothels to flourish in former shop premises. Overcrowding worsened – thanks to wartime bombing, and the loss of housing stock – and in the 1950s this was exacerbated by the arrival of thousands of Commonwealth immigrants, desperately searching for somewhere to live.

By the time the new borough of Tower Hamlets was formed in 1965, the Jewish tailors were leaving, or had left. In 1905 G. Sims, in his *Trips about Town*, opined that the well-clad and shod Jewish children he saw on the streets would 'Make a bold fight with fortune'. And so they did, most of them making for the sunnier climes of north London. The sweatshops were gone, the sailors' boarding houses closed, the warehouses empty; and soon the docks would lie bereft of ships. The docks and the rag trade, which had supported East End families for so many years, were on their way out. Huge cargo ships, demanded by the advent of containerisation, could not get up the river. In 1967 the East India Dock and St Katharine's closed, followed by the London Dock the next year. The West India Docks closed in 1980 and the Royals in 1981. The rag trade was ruined when its producers were undercut by the import of cheap stuff from India, Hong Kong and Taiwan. By the 1970s the Jewish community had left. Mills and factories were closing; one of the East End's oldest trades, the refining of sugar, which had gone on since the days of the Ratcliff Sugar House 400 years earlier, was no more when Tate and Lyle closed their Plaistow plant. By 1981 the workforce in Tower Hamlets had fallen from 210,000 pre-war to 87,000.

Meanwhile the East End received its latest batch of poor exiles, from the Indian sub-continent. It was in the 1950s, following Partition, and in the 1970s, after the creation of the state of Bangladesh, that mass immigration began. By the time the twenty-first century dawned about a third of the inhabitants of Tower Hamlets were South Asian, mainly Bangladeshi, a far higher proportion than ever the Jews constituted. You could say it has become East India Company territory again, as it was hundreds of years ago. Brick Lane has become 'Banglatown' and mosques have replaced synagogues. On the site of the house once owned by Sir Walter Raleigh's brother-in-law is the massive East London Mosque, in the Whitechapel Road. A 90ft tall silver minaret, topped with a bright crescent moon, towers over the old Huguenot heartland, marking the site of the Brick Lane Jamme Masjid, once L'Eglise Neuve. The Church of England secondary school on the site of the Mercers' Great Place (now an amalgam of Sir John Cass's seventeenth-century City foundation and the old Mile End charity school, the Red Coat school) has an 80 per cent Muslim intake.

The regeneration of the East End promised by the Docklands Development Corporation in 1981 came to pass, in part, with the creation of the new town called Canary Wharf on Stepney Marsh. Tall glittering glass towers rose on the grim old Isle of Dogs around lakes made from the dock basins. New roads and tunnels rendered the place unrecognisable, and along the riverside at Wapping warehouses were converted into luxury flats, with new blocks built to look like them and dinky houses, as small as those that had covered Shadwell 300 years before.

Meanwhile the Georgian houses of weavertown and those in Limehouse's Narrow Street were lovingly restored, and Old Ford began a new life. It has scrubbed up nicely; the Victorian and Edwardian villas are painted and primped, smiling over the glorious expanse of Victoria Park. The park has been there since 1845 but has never looked so good as it does now, done up for the Olympic Games. Tredegar Square is smart again, as are the nineteenth-century houses along Bow Road, and there are hanging baskets on lampposts in Roman Road market. You can find the Lea, if you really try, at Old Ford Lock perhaps; it is a pretty, quaint spot, with a lock-keeper's cottage. Whitechapel's Goodman's Fields have been rechristened, and those left of the old houses restored. The once gracious boulevards shine with modern hotels, restaurants and office blocks.

Tower Hamlets has fifty Conservation Areas (Islington has forty, Newham nine and Hackney twenty-nine) and about 2,000 listed buildings. There is a museum in Docklands, a living museum in Spitalfields, a ragged school museum and a museum of immigration. St George's in the East has a website that tells you absolutely all you need to know about old Wapping Stepney. The Spitalfields Trust preserves what buildings are left, when it can. There are historical and genealogical societies, and organised walks.

What with all the changes that came with Docklands, and the kerfuffle and smartening up in anticipation of the 2012 Olympic Games, you might imagine that the whole place has gone up in the world. In spite of the billions of pounds poured into the projects that have gone a long way to transforming its appearance, and although there are pockets of high life, Tower Hamlets remains a poor place, which offers, as it has done for hundreds of years, a home to poor refugees. It is still the East End, thank God.

SOURCES

Abbreviations used in source list

Ancestry	London records @ *www.ancestry.co.uk*
BL	British Library
BNC	Brasenose College Archives
Boyle	View of London, *1799*
CMH	Centre for Metropolitan History
Cox, Stepney	History of Stepney Church, *2008 (unpublished MS at THLHL)*
George	Dorothy George, London Life in the Eighteenth Century, *1951,1973 ed.*
G'hall	Guildhall. *Most of the manuscripts formerly in the Guildhall Library are now at* LMA
Guillery	Peter Guillery, The Small House in Eighteenth Century London, *2004*
Four Shillings	Four Shillings in the Pound Aid, CMH, *1992*
Frere	ed. G.W.Hill & W.H. Frere, Memorial of Stepney Parish vestry minutes *1579–1662, 1890-1*
Harben	Harben's Dictionary of London, *1918*
London Lives	*www.londonlives.org: database of records of eighteenth-century London*
LAMAS	London and Middlesex Archaeological Society
Land Tax	Records of land tax LMA (Ancestry)
L&P	Letters and Papers of Henry VIII
LMA	London Metropolitan Archives
LH	Royal London Hospital Archives
Ll. Smith	Sir Hubert Llewellyn-Smith, The History of East London, *1939*
LPL	Lambeth Palace Library
LSE	London School of Economics
Lysons	Daniel Lysons, Environs of London, *1795/6*
McD	Kevin McDonnell, Medieval London Suburbs, *Phillimore, 1978*
Maitland	William Maitland, The History of London, *1756*
Molas	Museum of London Archaeological Service

Noorthouck	*J. Noorthouck,* A New History of London, *1773*
OB	*Old Baileyonline*
par.reg.	*Parish registers, LMA (Ancestry)*
PCA	*Pre-Construct Archaeology*
PCC	*Prerogative Court of Canterbury wills, TNA*
Rose	*Millicent Rose,* The East End of London, *1951*
Sess.	*Calendar of Middlesex Sessions & sessions records @ londonlives*
stgite	*St George's-in-the-East website*
Stow	*John Stow,* Survey of London *(first published 1598), ed. Wheatley, revised 1956*
Strype	*A Survey of the Cities of London and Westminster by John Stow revised by J. Strype, 1720*
Survey	*Survey of London*
TNA	*The National Archives*
THHOL	*Tower Hamlets History online*
THLHL	*Tower Hamlets Local History Library*
Thornbury	*W Thornbury,* London Old and New, *1878*
VCH	*Victoria County History,* Middlesex *vols 1,2, 11 &* London *vol.1*
VM	*vestry minutes*

Chapter 1

VCH, McD, Ll. Smith, Francis Sheppard, *London A History,* 1999, Stow

B. Cherry, C. O'Brien and Nikolaus Pevsner, *The Buildings of England: London 5: East,* 2005

Harvey Sheldon and Laura Schaaf, 'A Survey of the Roman Sites of Greater London', *Collectanea Londiniensis,* LAMAS, 1970

Cathy Ross and John Clark, *London: The Illustrated History,* Museum of London, 2008

David Bird, 'The Origins of Roman London', *London Archaeologist,* vols 7–10, 1994

PCA site summaries 1998 & 2005

Robert Cowie and Lyn Blackmore, *Early and Middle Saxon Rural Settlement in the London Region,* MoLAS, 2008

A.G. Vince, *Saxon London,* 1990

ed. Derek Keene, Arthur Burns, Andrew Saint, *St Paul's The Cathedral Church of London,* 2004

John Blair, *The Church in Anglo-Saxon England,* Oxford, 2005

John Clark, 'King Alfred's London and London's King Alfred', *London Archaeologist,* vol.9 (1999)

W.R. Lethaby, *London before the Conquest,* 1902

H.A. Harben, *Dictionary of London,* 1918

Stow

Cox, *Stepney*

Chapter 2

VCH Mx I & II; *VCH* London I

J. Cox, *Domesday Exhibition Catalogue,* PRO, 1986

Michael Wood, *Domesday: A Search for the Roots of England,* BBC, 1986 ed. Derek Keene, Arthur Burns, Andrew Saint, *St Paul's The Cathedral Church of London*, 2004

I. Grainger, D. Hawkins, L. Cowie and R. Mikulski, *The Black Death Cemetery, East Smithfield, London*, MoLAS Monograph 43, 2008

ed. M. Chibnall, *The Ecclesiastical History of Orderic Vitalis*, vol. II, Oxford, 1969.

Stow

ed. D. Whitelocke, *The Anglo Saxon Chronicle*, 1961

Francis Sheppard, *London a History*, 1999

Gover, Mawer and Stenton, *The Place Names of Middlesex*, English Place Name Society, XVIII, 1987

Harben

TNA Ancient Deeds: A 1817, C 799, A 2543-5, A 1978, A 7319

C.N.L. Brooke, 'The Composition of the Chapter of St Pauls' 1086–1163', *Cambridge Historical Journal*, vol. X, 1951

Oxford DNB

A. Morey and C.N.L. Brooke, *Gilbert Foliot and his Letters*, Cambridge, 1965 & *Letters & Charters of Gilbert Foliot*, ed. ibid, 1967

English Episcopal Acta 15 & 126

George F. Tull, *North of the Tower, The Story of St Botolph-without-Aldgate*

Chapter 3

Caroline Barron, *London in the Later Middle Ages*, Oxford, 2004; Gwyn A. Williams, *Medieval London*; Cox, *Stepney*; McD. Ll. Smith. Stow, *VCH* Mx & *VCH* London 1

ed. R. Sharpe, *Calendar of Letter Books of the City of London*, 1899–1912

ed. R. Sharpe, *Calendar of Wills … in the Court of Hustings, 1258-1688*, 1899-1890

London Commissary Court wills: Guildhall MS 9171, LMA, Ancient Deeds: TNA

G.F. Vale, *Old Bethnal Green*, Bethnal Green, 1934

A.J. Robinson, *The Green: a history of the heart of Bethnal Green*, 2nd ed., 1986

E.G. Donoghue, *The Story of the Bethlehem Hospital*, London, 1914

M.B. Honeybourne, 'The Leper Hospitals of the London Area'. *LAMAS*, vol. 21 pt 1, 1967

eds W.H. Hale and H.T. Ellacombe, *Accounts of the Executors of Richard Bishop of London*

E. Ekwall, *Two Early London Subsidy Rolls*, Lund, 1951

H.G. Richardson and G. Sayles, 'The Early Records of the English Parliaments', *Bulletin of the Institute of Historical Research*, 5, 1928

T.F. Tout, *Edward I*, 1893

Sylvia Thrupp, The Merchant Class of Medieval London, 1903

A.R. Myers, *London in the Age of Chaucer*, London, 1972

TNA/E 36/279 & Guildhall MS 25, 422 (Black Prince)

Stepney Court Rolls: TNA/SC12/11/31, SC 6/1139/1; LMA Guildhall MSS 10, 312 & 25, 422

R.E. Glasscok, *The Lay Subsidy of 1334*, 1975

Carolyn Fenwick, *The Poll Taxes of 1377, 1379 & 1381*, 1998–2005

TNA/C3/168/63: Akeshull

P. Morant, *History and Antiquities of the County of Essex*, 1816

Calendar of Miscellaneuous Inquisitions, 1307–1349 (whale)

Thomas Walsingham, *Historica Anglicana*, ed. H.T. Riley, 1864

eds M.M. Crow and C.C. Olson, *Chaucer's Life Records*, 1966

*The Black Death Cemetery, MoLAS Monograph
43*, 2008

TNA/SC2/191/60

TNA/E 134/19 Eliz.4 (Poplar Manor)

Ruth Bird, *The Turbulent London of Richard
II*, 1948

A.K. Hardy, *The Church in London*, 1977
(British History Online)

TNA/ E 40/2640, E 210/6778, 820, 9089,
E 326/2313, 2322, 2326, 7083 (East
Smithfield houses)

ed. Silvester Davies, *St Albans' Chronicle 1395*,
Camden Society, 1861

Chapter 4

C. Barron, *London in the later Middle Ages*;
ed. C. Barron and Nigel Saul, *England
and the Low Counties in the late Middle
Ages*, 1995; Jane Cox, *London's East
End*, London, 1994; McD; Alison Weir,
Lancaster and York; *VCH* London 1,
Religious Houses

Wills: Brampston, Hugh & John, Gibbons,
Crosby, Staunton, Rich. Dryver, Rich
Etgoos, Shrouesbury, Waryn, Honyngton:
PCC/TNA. Gymer, Stepkyn, Sheffeld,
Camberleyn, Fen, Wm Dryver, Joan
Dryver, Alice Etgoos, Colte, Graunger,
Syward, Batte, Bryce, Buntyng, Browne:
London Commissary Court, G'hall MS
9171, LMA. Wm Dryver jnr., Colston:
Hustings. Gregory's and Greyfriars
Chronicles @ *British History online*

Commissary Court Correction Book
1489–91, Guildhall MS 9064/4 LMA
(Mistress Say)

Alien Subsidy Rolls: TNA/E 179/141/69,
72, 94, E 179/235/69

'a pynt': Guildhall MS 25,287 LMA

East Smithfield Court Rolls: TNA/
SC2/191/55,6

Peter James & St Katharine's: Guildhall MS
9065, LMA

Sylvia Thrupp, 'Aliens in and around
Fifteenth Century London', *Studies in
London History presented to P E Jones*, ed.
A.E.J. Hollaender and William Kellaway,
1969

C. Jamison, *The History of the Royal Hospital
of St Katharine by the Tower*, Oxford, 1952

Great Flood jurors: TNA/C145/314/55;
tenants: TNA/SC6/1140/24

Letters and Papers of Henry VIII, IV.

Walford, *Village London*, 1883

H.F. Westlake, *Parish Guilds of Medieval
England*, 1919

S. Brigden, *New Worlds, Lost Worlds*, London,
2000

S.E. Lehmberg, *The Reformation Parliament*,
Cambridge, 1970

J.B. Trapp, *Erasmus, Colet and More*, London,
1991

Jean Imray, 'The Mercers' Company and
East London', *East London Papers* vol.6
no.2, 1963

Mercers Company Archives: Colet MS
1/226

'Purgatorie': TNA/SP1/116/106

King's house in Bethnal Green: *Letters and
Papers Henry VIII* pt II, 1474

Bow meeting: G'hall MS 9531/12 f. 58, LMA

Chapter 5

'calf's call': TNA/SP1/116/106

population: ed. E.L. Beier and Roger Finlay,
*The Making of the Metropolis, London
1500–1700*, Harlow, 1986; Ll. Smith,
Chantry Certificate: TNA/E 301/34

J.P. Boulton, 'The Limits of formal Religion', *London Journal* 10 no. 1, 1984, ed. J. Cordy Jeaffreson, *Middlesex County Records*, Old Series vol. 1, 1886 (alehouses)

Brian Tuke: *Letters & Papers of Henry VIII*, III, 1528

J.J. Scarisbrick, *Henry VIII*, 1968

shipwright's will: Davye LMA/DLC 355.

Armada Map BL Ad. 44839

L&P II pt.II

will: Gymer G'hall MS 9171/10/137

M.B. Honeybourne, 'The Leper Hospitals of the London Area' *LAMAS*, 1967

M.F.J. McDonnell, *A History of St Paul's School*, 1909

J.H. Lupton, *Life of Dean Colet*, London, 1887

C. More, *Life of Sir Thomas More*, 1726

Cox, *Stepney*

J. Imray, 'The Mercers' Company and East London', *East London Papers* vol. 6, no. 2, 1963

Colet's Charge: Colet MS, John Cheke's Register of Lands, Mercers' Company Archives

Poyntell: TNA/C1/1050/35

Colin Churchett, *Coopers' Company and Coborn School Anniversary History*, 1986

Coopers' Company Accounts, G'hall MS 5606/1

J. Weever, *Ancient Funeral Monuments*, 1631

L&P passim

VCH Mx 1 & London 1

R.C. Palmer, *Selling the Church*, 2001

E. Duffy, *The Voices of Morebath*, 2001; *The Stripping of the Altars*, 1992

S. Brigden, *New Worlds, Lost Worlds*, London, 2000

S.E. Lehmberg, *The Reformation Parliament*, Cambridge, 1970

R.B. Merriman, *Life and Letters of Thomas Cromwell*, Oxford, 1902

S. Brigden, *London Churches at the Reformation*, 1989

ed. S.T. Bindoff, *History of Parliament*, 1982

Diarmuid MacCulloch, *Tudor Church Militant*, London, 1999

lease Great Place: Mercers' Company Court of Assistants 26/7/1534

G. Moorhouse, *The Pilgrimage of Grace*, 2002

Stepkyn: Madge Darby, *Judge Jeffreys and the Ivy Case*. History of Wapping Trust, 1989

Wapping brewery: TNA/E178/1469 34 Eliz.

Wriothesley's Chronicle, Camden Soc, 1877

Richard Cromwells' will and inventory: BL/Ad 34,393 f.7

Darnley: J. Weever, *Ancient Funeral Monuments, 1631*

wills: LMA/DC/L 335-6

ed. J. Nicols, 'Underhill's Diary', *Narratives of the Reformation, Camden Soc. Ist ser. 77*

G. Burnet, *A History of my own Times*, 1906 1724

MacCulloch, *Tudor Church*

Wriothesley's Chronicle

Chantries: TNA/E 301/34, E315/68 f. 409, LMA/DC/L/335f.116

H.B. Walters, *London Churches at the Reformation*, 1939

Dryver will: PCC 1578

Ridley: ed. Ives, Gina Alexander in *Wealth and Power in Tudor England*, 1978

Wentworth: *Troubles connected with the Prayer Book of 1549, Camden Soc. 37*

Greyfriars Chronicle

ed. J.G. Nichols, *Diary of Henry Machyn*, 1848

D.M. Loades, *Politics and the Nation 1450–1660*, 1974

Strype, *Ecclesiastical Memorials*, vol. III pt 1

D.M. Loades, *Mary Tudor, a Life*, 1989

J. Foxe, *Actes and Monuments*

Aldgate: G'hall MS 9235/1, LMA

C. Burrage, *Early English Dissenters*,
Cambridge, 1912

wills: G'hall MS 9171/14/21,2 & 13/146v,
LMA

Sparrow, *Articles of Visitation*, 1677

John Thomas: will: LMA: DC/L 288/1f.351;
children: Stepney par. regs. (*Ancestry*)

Nicolson, *Power and Glory*

Stephen Gosson, *Pleasant Quipps for Upstart
Newfangled Gentlewomen*, 1596

Anderson, *The Shield of our Safety*, LPL

J.S. Burn, *History of Foreign Refugees*, 1846

Lay Subsidy 1598: TNA/E179/142/239

ed. Scouloudi, *Return of Aliens in the
Metropolis*, Huguenot Society LVII, 1953

B. Jonson, *The Devil is an Ass* (first
performed 1616)

Frere

par. regs Stepney: LMA

Middleton, *Seven Deadly Sins of London*

Chettle, *Kind Harts Dreame*, 1592

ditchers: G'hall MS 9065A/2

William Bullein, *A Dialogue against the
Pestilence*, 1573

T.R. Forbes, *Chronicle from Aldgate*, London,
1911 and 1971

Warde: Coopers' Company Acts of Court,
G'hall MS 9172/190

Borgine: G'hall MS 9172/190

Miller: Sess.

eds E. Greenlaw, C.G. Osgood, F.M.
Padelford, Ray Heffner, *Edmund Spenser:
The Works A Variorum including the Life of
Edmund Spenser*, AC Judson, 1945

berbs: TNA/SP1/67/107

Poplar Town Book THLHL

Frere

par. reg. Aldgate & clerk's memoranda book:
LMA

East Smithfield court roll TNA/SC2/191/59

Map: TNA/MPB 4/A&B.

Jonson, *The Alchemist*

Stow

Frere

Janet S. Loengard, 'An Elizabethan Lawsuit:
John Brayne, his Carpenter, and the
Building of the Red Lion Theatre',
Shakespeare Quarterly, Vol. 34, no. 3,
Autumn 1983

H. Berry, 'The First Public Playhouses',
Shakespeare Quarterly, vol. 40, 1989

C. Phillpotts, *Red Lion Theatre Whitechapel.
Documentary Research Report*, MoLAS for
Crossrail, 2004, at www.crossrail.
co.uk

Cox, *London's East End*

Wilson & Kydd: Step. bur. reg; DNB;
will LMA/Archdeaconry of London
1594/3/11v

ed. W.G. Perrin, *Autobiography of Phineas Pett*,
Navy Records Society, 1918

wills: LMA/G'hall MSS 9171, 2;
DC/L/335-6; TNA/PCC

Chapman, Johnson and Marston, *Eastward
Hoe*, printed 1605

Willoughby and Frobisher: *Principal
Navigations*, Hakluyt Society, extra series,
1903–5

ed. K.R. Andrews, *English Privateering Voyages
to the West Indies 1588–1595*, Hakluyt
Society, series II, vol. III, 1959

D.B. Quinn, *England and the Discovery of
America 1421–1620*, 1974

Throckmorton: Hales MS vol. II,
Canterbury Cathedral Library

Poyntell: TNA/C1/1050/35

Poplar map: TNA/MPB 3

The earliest reference to the 'Ile of Dogges':
par. reg. Step. 23/4/1587

Survey of London, vols 43 and 44: *Poplar,
Blackwall and Isle of Dogs*, 1994

J.G. Birch, *Limehouse through Five Centuries*, 1930

Madge Darby, *Judge Jeffreys and the Ivy Case*, History of Wapping Trust and *Waeppa's People*

VCH 11

Survey

Frere

Stow

Cox, *London's East End*

Hales MS (*above*)

A.L. Rowse, *Raleigh and the Throckmortons*, 1962

Raleigh Trevelyan, *Sir Walter Raleigh*, 2002

Anna Beers, *Bess*, London, 2004

W.M. Wallace, *Sir Walter Raleigh*, 1959

W. Kemp, *The Nine Daies Wonder*, 1600

J. Cox, *East End Ancestry*

par. regs Bow

Chapter 6

Watts, *Dissenters*

C.V. Wedgwood, *Thomas Wentworth a Re-evaluation*, 1961

C.V. Wedgwood, *The King's Peace*, 1955

T. Dekker, *The Wonderful Year*, 1603

Bennet Johnson's will: G'hall MS 9172, LMA

Frere

DNB

par.reg. Step

banquet: Minutes of East India Company 9/4 & 23/5, 1614, BL

ed. G.G. Harris, *Trinity House Transactions 1609–1635*, London Record Society, 1983

C.R.B. Barrett, *The Trinity House of Deptford Strond*, 1893

ed. W.G. Perrin, *Autobiography of Phineas Pett*, Navy Records Society, 1918

Puritans' speech: BL/Thomason E 168/7

Charles Banks, *The English Ancestry and Homes of the Pilgrim Fathers*, New York, 1929

Dekker, *The Seven Deadly Sins of London*, 1606

'Many lewd': BL/Lansdowne MS 16 f.90

Frere

par. reg.

sess

Benjamin Wooley, *The Herbalist*, 2004

Wellington, 'A Record of the Mercies of God.', G'hall MS 204

Wills: LMA/ Commissary Court 1625

Strype's Stow

Hooth: LMA/ G'hall MS 9064/18

London Commissary Court Act Book 1619–1631 & Consistory Court Act Book 1633–5, LMA

Salmon will: TNA/PCC, 1641

Jeremiah Burroughs, *Moses his choice*, 1659, LPL

K. Lindley, *Popular Politics and Religion in Civil War London*, 1997

Paul S. Seaver, *The Puritan Lectureships*, California, 1970

BL/Thomason E 168/7, E80/12. E173/23, E181/1 (sects, churchwardens, Utye, Pym)

Protestation Returns: Parliamentary Archives

Christopher Hibbert, *Cavaliers and Roundheads*, 1993

Mariners' protest: BL/Thomason/E 168/7, 181/31, E 132/15

William Stampe, *A Treatise on Spiritual Infatuation*, The Hague, 1653

J. Walker, *Sufferings of the Clergy*, London, 1714

'Oh Stepny': Thomas Edwards, *Gangrena*, 1646

S. Schama, *A History of Britain*, 2002

Mrs Warden's Observation..: BL/Thomason E 115/20

Acts and Ordinances of the Interregnum

W. Foster, The East India Company, 1933

Barker and Jackson, *The History of London in Maps*, 1990

William Lithgow, *The Present Surveigh At London*, cited in W.G. Ross, *Military Engineering during the Great Civil War, 1642–9*, London, 1984

ed. K. Lindley and David Scott, *The Journal of Thomas Juxon*, Camden Fifth Series vol. 13, CUP, 1999

L.G. Ward, *Stepney Meeting House, a History*, 1978

Murray Tolmie, *The Triumph of the Saints*, CUP, 1977

Christopher Hill, *God's Englishman*, 1970

S.R. Gardiner, *History of the Great Civil War vol. iv*, London, 1894

N.A.M. Rodger, *The Command of the Sea*, 2004

Keith Thomas, *Religion and the Decline of Magic*, 1971

Tim Harris, *London Crowds in the Reign of Charles II*, London, 1987

W Loftie Rutton, *Three Branches of the Family of Wentworth*, 1891

Sess

trans. and eds Maurice Exwood and H.L. Lehmann, *The Journal of William Schellinks' Travels in England*, Camden Society fifth series, vol. I, 1993

W. Beck and T.F. Ball, *The London Friends' Meetings*, 1869

John Selwood, *An Invitation of Love to all people: but especially to the inhabitants of the parish of Stepney*, 1678

ed. A G Matthews, *Calamy revised*, 1934

Antonia Fraser, *Charles II*, 1979

B. Capp, *Cromwell's Navy*, 1989

Daniel Defoe, *A Journal of the Plague Year*, 1722

Cox, *East End*

Churchwardens: G'hall MS 9583/2f.138, LMA

Visitation: G'hall MS 9537/16

Slander suit: Court of Arches depostions, LPL/Eee 1/202-3

William Foster, *The East India House*, 1924

Pepys' Diary *passim*

Claire Tomalin, *Samuel Pepys; the unequalled self*, 2002

L.G. Ward, *Stepney Meeting House*, 1978

Visitation: 1673: G'hall MS 9537/20, LMA

ed. Ann Whitman, *The Compton Census of 1676*, 1986

Mercers' Company Court of Assistants

Poll Tax; TNA/E 179/143/350

G.W. Keeton, *Lord Chancellor Jeffreys and the Stuart Cause*, 1965

Minutes of Quakers Ratcliff Meeting, 1684, Library of the Religious Society of Friends

Chapter 7

Major sources, used throughout the section.

Maps

Newcourt, 1658, Ogilby and Morgan, 1676, Wm Morgan 1682, Gascoyne 1703 (BL), Roque 1747, Richard Blome 1720 & 1755 (Wapping), *Actual Survey of London and Westminster*, 1725, Horwood 1792-9, Cary's New and Accurate Plan of London and Westminster 1792, Fairburn, 1802, Cross's New Plan, 1853, WH Smith, 1875.(BL Crace and Mernick Map Gallery).★

Records and reference works

Old Bailey proceedings @ oldbaileyonline;
PCC wills, TNA; par. regs. for Aldgate,
Bethnal Green, Bow, Shadwell, Stepney,
Limehouse, Spitalfields, St George in the
East, Wapping, Whitechapel, LMA @
Ancestry

Four Shillings in the Pound Aid, CMH★; Land
Tax records, LMA @ *Ancestry*★

London Lives: Aldgate parish records, fire
insurance, sess. etc★

Sess

Directories @ *Ancestry*★

DNB

Books

Boyle; Cox, *Stepney;* Dilworth (parish
officers)★; George★; Guillery★; Lysons★;
Maitland; Noorthouck★; Rose★; Strype;
Thornbury; *VCH* Mx 2, 1911, vol 11,
Stepney, Bethnal Green, 1969★; *Survey
of London*, Bromley by Bow, vol. 1, 1900,
Spitalfields and Mile End New Town, vol
27, 1957, Poplar, Blackwall and the Isle of
Dogs, vols 43–4, 1994★

★ These sources are only specified in the list
below if a section is especially dependent
on them.

Jane Moody, *Illegitimate Theatre in London*
at www.assets.cambridge.org citing
pamphlet in support of the Royalty
Theatre in Wellclose Square

For listed buildings see www.british-
listedbuildings.co.uk/england/
greater+london/stepney and www.list.
english-heritage.org.uk>Tower Hamlets

Pevsner, *The Buildings of England*

Peter Guillery, *The Small House in Eighteenth
Century London*, 2004

Guillery

Tom Ridge, *Central Stepney History Walk*,
1998 @ moderngov.towerhamlets.gov.uk

ed. Millicent Rose, *The East End of London*,
1951, 1973

Survey, Bow, 1900

ed. Godman, *The Old Palace of Bromley by Bow,*
Survey of London, monograph 3, 1901

David Barnett, *London, Hub of the Industrial
Revolution*, 1998

Dorothy George, *London Life in the
Eighteenth Century*, 1925

Daniel Defoe, *A Tour through the whole Island
of Britain*

Elizabeth McKellar *The Birth of Modern
London*, 1999

R.B. Shoemaker, *The London Mob*, 2004

J.G. Birch, *Limehouse through five Centuries*,
1930

Hans Kreft, 'Rediscovering the Fromanteel
Story' @ www.kunstpedia.com.

Dirt: J. Hollingshead, *Ragged London in 1861*

Obituary: stgite

TNA/pathways/black history

OB Peazy

Daniel Lysons, *Environs of London*

Todd M Endelman, *The London Jews of
Georgian England*, 1979

C. Roth, *The Great Synagogue*, 1950

G Rudé, *Hanoverian London*, 1971

Craig Spence, *London in the 1690s*, 2000

VCH Mx 2

Cawley: LPL/Terrick 14

Strype's *Survey of London*, 1720

coal: *Middlesex Journal and Evening Advertiser*
16–18 Jan. 1776

manufacture distribution: Spence

Boswell, *Life of Johnson*

D Morris, *Mile End Old Town 1740–1790*,
2002

'hemp enough': OB May 1676

A General Description of All Trades, 1747

Nelson: *Four Shillings in the Pound Aid*,
CMH, 1992

Francis Buckley, *Old London Glasshouses*,
London, 1915

Sale of glasshouse: LMA/M93 f. 471

Stephen Inwood, *A History of London*, 2000

Tithe records: LMA/P93/
DUN/200,202,207, 1772-5

Rogers: OB

Windmills: *The Isle of Dogs, a brief history*,
Island History Trust, 2000

J. Paterson, *Pietas Londiniensis*, 1714

ed. William Maitland, *The History of London*,
1756

'vagabonds': OB Carey 1750

OB *passim*

*John Sheppard's Narrative of his Life and
Actions*, Newgate, 1724

Sess: 1693,4, 1702, 1705,

John L McMullen, 'The New Improved
Monied Police', *British Journal of
Criminology* vol. 36, no. 1, 1996

D. Barlow, *Dick Turpin and the Gregory Gang*,
1973

H.W. Dilworth, *The History of London in its
Ancient and Modern State*, 1760

Midwives: LMA/G'hall MS 9537/15

Cox, *Stepney*

LMA/VM Stepney 1726

W. Thornbury, *London Old and New*, 1878

Mussell: PCC 1764

D. Morris and K. Cozens, *Wapping
1600–1800*, 2009

OB *passim*

Sess. 1690,1

Tim Hitchcock, *Down and Out in Eighteenth
Century London*, 2004

Londonlives

Morris, *Mile End*

J. Noorthouck, *A New History of London*, 1773

Peter Marcam, *An East End Album*

Kenton: DOM, *Circuit of London*

Tessa Murdoch and Randolph Vigne, *The
French Hospital in London*, 2009

Tull: TNA/C12/393/22

Elaine Murphy, 'The Metropolitan Pauper
Farms 1722–1834', *London Journal* vol. 27
no. 1, 2002

Hitchcock

S. Maddocks, *'White Horse Street'*, 1935,
THHOL

George

Kennet: Oxf. DNB

*John Sheppard's Narrative of his Life and
Actions*, Newgate, 1724

Visitation: LPL/Lowth 4

Morris, *Mile End*

Liza Picard, *Dr Johnson's London*, 2000

G.A. Sambrook, *English Life in the Eighteenth
Century*, 1940

Colin Churchett, *Coopers' Company and
Coborn School Anniversary History*

Llw. Smith

Kennett, *The Christian Scholar*, 1705

PCC: Starling, Raine, Jolles

J.V. Pixell, *A Short History of the Hamlet of
Ratcliff School*, 1910

Dissenters: *The Commission for Building Fifty
New Churches*, 1986, intro

OB: John Smith 1763

L.G. Ward, *Stepney Meeting House, a History*,
1978

I. Parker, *Dissenting Academies*, 1969

Bramble: *Humphrey Clinker*, 1771

Aldgate

Whitechapel High St/Aldgate: OB Fordham
1809

Muffs: OB Milton 1728

PCC: Tuffley 1686

Defoe's uncle Henry Foe had a big house in
the High Street; Hearth Tax, 1666

A.B. Beaven, *Aldermen of the City of London*, 1908

PCC:Starling 1674, Bray 1730

A List of Flying Coaches, Stage Coaches, Waggons and Carriers, 1721 at www. London.ancestor.com

The *Three Nuns* was rebuilt in 1876: www. deadpubs.co.uk

Cruikshank, *AllMax in the East End*

Jewishgen.org

Tony Benton, *Irregular Marriage in London*, 1993

J. Cox, *Tracing your East End Ancestors*, 2011

Sir John Summerson, *Georgian London*

Elizabeth McKellar, *The Birth of Modern London*, 1999

The victualling operation moved to Deptford in 1740s; in 1780s the office moved to Somerset House

Tuffs: OB Thomas Gowen

Raine; TNA/PCC, 1738

Petitcoat Lane Tabernacle: Paterson, *Pietas*

warehouse:*A General Description of All Trades*, London, 1747

Edward: *The Penny London Morning Advertiser*, 6 August 1744

OB: Adams & Spratley, 1768, Williams & Nixon, 1736. oysters: Bullingbroke 1737, Paydon 1732, Lee, Marsland 1739

'Aliens at Bevis Marks 1803', *Migration and Settlement, Proceedings of the Anglo American Jewish Historical Conference*, 1970

Fromanteel: TNA/ PROB 18/26/43 & 27/19,51,53 (Drake v Prime*)*: wills: PCC, 1698. 1701, Commissary Court 1665

Sir John Hawkins, *A General History of the Science and Practice of Music*, 1776

Brasenose College Annals B.: Monograph XIII, 'Robert Shippen'

Gurle: *Roderick Floud, 'The hidden Face of British Gardening', DNB, VCH*

Phelps: PCC 1738

Workhouse & parish boundary: LMA/P83/ MRY/1/90

Pond: LMA/M 93/273

The Grave Maurice survived until recently at No. 269; it was patronised by the Kray brothers

gaol: S Maddocks, 'Whitechapel', 1933, THHOL

Overton: PCC 1797

The London: www.bartsandthelondon.nhs. uk/about-us/our-history

A.E. Clark Kennedy, *London Pride*, 1979

LH: patients' lists & tradesmens' accounts

William Dunlap, *History of the American Theatre*

London and its Environs Described, published by R. and J. Dodsley, 1761

Roth, *Great Synagogue*

Leman wills: PCC 1632, 1701, 1742

The Genealogy of the Family of Phillimore, 1922

Alfred Rubens, *Anglo Jewish Portraits*, 1935

A.M. Hyamson, *The Sephardim of England*, 1951

Abraham da Costa: PCC, 1737

M.J. Lauda, 'Kitty Villareal and the da Costas', *Transactions of the Jewish Historical Society of England* 13, 1932–5

Jacob da Costa: TNA/PROB 3/33/5

Mendes Alvarez: TNA/PROB 24/100-1, PROB 18/99

Endelman

synagogues: jewishgen.org

OB 1790

The Universal Jewish Encyclopaedia

I. Zangwill, *King of the Schnorrers*

'sweet singers': sgite

Paine, *The Age of Reason*

Three Tuns & Fleece: BL/Burney Collection: Notes on the History of Goodman's Fields Theatre

Gower: Sess. 1750–1 *londonlives*

Constables' expenses: LMA/P93/MRY/1/90

Hercules: bur. reg. 1698

Asher: OB 1792

Beazley, *Historical Account of London Theatres*

Burney Collecion BL

The Jolly Waterman sung by Mr Bardin at the Goodman's Fields Theatre, 1733-4

F.T. Wood, 'Goodman's Fields Theatre', *The Modern Language Review*, 1930 vol. 25

Gower & Hallam: londonlives, PCC, 1757 (Gower)

A New Song sung by Hannah Snell at the new Wells. [1750], Madden Ballads vol II

Ruth Paley, 'Thief takers in London in the Age of the McDaniel Gang *c.* 1745–1754 in D. Hay and F. Snyder, *Policing and Prosecution in Britain 1750–1850*, 1989

S. Maddocks, 'Wellclose', 1934, THHOL

Jane Mayo's diary: TNA/PROB 18/99

London Guide, 1782

Mogg's New Picture of London, 1844

Gerald Howson, *The Macaroni Parson*, 1973

Parsons' debt: TNA/PROB 5/5635

Barbon's enterprise: TNA/C8/357/139 & T/27/6 p.368

Kell: TNA/PROB 3 /44/33

stgite

Hoya: PCC 1777

Byrne: TNA/ADM 106/1194/209

Dancer: TNA/PROB 18/99/10

Falcon: *The Universal Jewish Encyclopaedia*; Morris, *Wapping*; PCC 1782

Cyriel Sigstedt, *The Swedenborg Epic: the Life and Works of Emmanuel Swedenborg* at www.swedenborgdigitallibrary.org

David Cody and Richard Goerwitz *Emmanuel Swedenborg* at www.victorianweb.org/religion/swdbor.html

Jenny Uglow, 'Educating Sabrina', *Guardian*, 5 October 2002

Mayo: family: *Ancestry*.co.uk, *TheGenealogist, FamilySearch*; will PCC

Boswell, *Life of Johnson*

OB

Latroon, *The English Rogue*, 1665

The Georgian Underworld, @ www.rictornorton.co.uk

Humours of Rag Fair [1750], BL

Lucy Moore, *Con Men and Cutpurses*, 2000

Irish: stgite; *The Penny London Morning Advertiser* 6/8/1744

www.locatinglondon.org.static/Population.htm

Slack: lease @ clara.net.com

Pearson: OB Barker

Pincot: milelewis.net/Australia-buildings

Da Costa; PCC 1841

Survey

ed. Charles Marmoy, *The Case Book of La Maison de Charité de Spittlefields 1739–41*, Huguenot Society of London vol LV, 1981

S. Smiles, *Huguenots in England and Ireland*, 1876

A Further Examination of the Weavers' Presence, 1719

D. Masson, *Life of John Milton*

Jerry White, *London in the Nineteenth Century: A Human Awful Wonder of God*, 2007

Fromaget: PCC 1735

Truman: DNB; PCC 1780. The Director's House was built in 1745 and later modified

ed. E.G. Wheler, Sir George Wheler, *Autobiography*, 1911

Rector: LPL/Randolph 12/45

Masson, *Milton*

'The Dragonnades': www.museeprotestant.org

Marmoy: www.rogerwilliams.net/family_history/huguneot/ancestry.htm

Catherine Swindlehurst, 'An unruly and presumptuous rabble', in E. Barrett, R. Vigne, C. Littleton, *Huguenot Integration in late 17th and 18th Century London, From Strangers to Citizens*, 2000

Robin Gwynn, 'Marital problems and the position of women in the French church of London in the later seventeeth century', Gwynn, *Huguenot Society Proc.* XXVI no. 2, 1995

Smiles, Huguenots

Tim Harris, *London Crowds in the Reign of Charles II*, 1987

R.L. Poole, *A History of the Huguenots of the Dispersion at the recall of the Edict of Nantes*, 1879

ed. C.F.A. Marmoy, *La Providence: The French Protestant Hospital*, Huguenot Society, 1977

Tessa Murdoch and Randolph Vigne, *The French Hospital in London*, 2009

Nathalie Rothstein, 'Huguenot Master Weavers 1700–1750', *From Strangers to Citizens*

Garrick: "William Hogarth' @ www. Artoftheprint.com

wills: Leman: PCC 1745; Dollond: PCC 1750.

pattern of settlement: TNA/RG 4/ 4615, 4645; *Four Shillings*

Robin Gwynn, 'England's First Refugees', *History Today*, vol. 35, issue 5, March 2012

George B. Beeman, 'Notes on the History of the French Churches in London,' *Huguenot Society Procs* VIII, 1909

Marmoy, *Case Book*

Douespe wills: PCC 1770, 1782, 1795

L'Heureux: LMA/Stepney VM, 1766,1774

Romilly: Smiles

A.K. Sabin, *The Silkweavers of Spitalfields and Bethnal Green*, BG Museum, 1931

Linda Baumgarten, *What Clothes Reveal*

Theya Molleson and Margaret Cox, *The Spitalfields Project vol. 2, The Anthropology, The Middling Sort*, CBA Research Report no. 86, 1993

LMA/ G'hall 9174, 1701

night work: OB Defour, 1734

Campart: TNA/PROB 24/61

Short: LMA/G'hall MS 9174/43, 1725

Rudé, *Hanoverian London*

Belin: LMA/G'hall 9174, 1715

Cutters' riot: TNA/TS/11//818/2696; OB: Norris, Horsford

Chauvet: Murdoch, *French Hospital*

Lady de Wint, 'The Spitalfields Silk Cutters' @ www.eastlondonforum.com

LSE/Booth B 350

The Weaver's Miscellany, 1730

Bedford: OB 1762

A True and Perfect Relation of that Execrable and Horrid Fact committed in White-Lion Yard ... Published to prevent false reports, 1674

Prayer Book: OB Manton, 1769

Williams: TNA/PROB 24/84, 1771

E.V. Lucas, *A Wanderer in London*, 1904

Beck: OB

poem: Rose

Worrall: will of sister, Elizabeth: PCC 1783

G.L. Barnes, *Stepney Churches*, 1967

Wills: Seguret PCC 1732, 1748; Jacob Bourdillon PCC 1786; Campart PCC 1772; Bourdon PCC 1732

Prichard: OB Richard Green 1769; will PCC 1782

Gertrude Prichard: OB Richard Mason, 1757

Richard Green OB 1769

Garthwaite: PCC 1763

F.A. Young, Guide to the local *Administrative Units of England*, vol. 1,1979

Dupree: PCC 1746. Isaac's grandfather was
  Stepney weaver John Dupree (d. 1674
  PCC); family: *Ancestry.co.uk*
Skull: Molleson
Ogier: Murdoch
The Old Artillery Ground
Griffiths: PCC 1782
Of 244 testators in the PCC 1686–1800, 61
  have French names
VCH
Guillery
'Increase of dissoluteness': BNC/ Stepney 55
'The inhabitants…', House of Commons
  Journal 3/3/1733/4
gin: OB Justices' working douments 14, 15
  Jan.1736
OB Defour 1734, Gilbert 1745
Cawley: LPL/Osbaldeson 7, 1763
Merceron: LMA/MR/B/R 1, 3
The village
Coates: TNA/PCC 1740; watercolour in
  Llw. Smith
1/9 of PCC Bethnal Green testators
  1686-1800 are 'gentlemen'
Darling: TNA/PCC 1770
Gents. Mag April 1772
Goldsborough: TNA/PCC 1696
Great Corner House: Gascoyne (BL)
Revoize: TNA/PCC 1790
Morris, *Mile End*
Alvarez: PCC 1780
Vezey: QB 1731
Fitzhugh: PCC 1731, 1746; Christale: PCC
  1763; Josselyne: PCC 1773
pictures at www.spitalfieldslife.com
Sir John Leake, *History of Parliament*; PCC
  1720; Morris
Warwick Wroth, *The London Pleasure
  Gardens in the Eighteenth Century*, 1896
Bolton: TNA/PROB 3/40/43
Besant, *All Sorts and Conditions of Men*

Tom Ridge, *Central Stepney History Walk*, 1998
Surveyor: BNC/Stepney 181
Cox, *Stepney*
Berry: PCC 1690
N.A.M. Rodger, *The Command of the Ocean*,
  2004
Tod: par. regs.; PCC 1727
Gloomy rectory: BNC/Stepney 181,
  Vawdrey to Brasenose
Baptist College: lithograph *c.* 1845 in Peter
  Marcan, *An East End Album*, 1987
Spring Garden: S. O'Donnell, *London 1753*,
  exhibition catalogue, 2003; BM Crace
  XXXIII/80
Cockney Feast: Strype. appendix chap 12.
  The feast was discontinued in 1784, its
  function being taken over by the Marine
  Society
Cox, *Stepney*
Wentworths: THHOL: engraving of house.
  Law suits: TNA/PROB/24/ 125, PROB
  20/237. PROB 32/66/59. PROB
  18/11,12,21,29. Lady Philadelphia's will:
  TNA/PCC 1696
Lord of Manor: LMA/P93/MRY/1/90
Cox, *Stepney*
Dissenting press: *The Observator* 13/6/1706;
  *An Appeal to the Church of England by [-]
  curate of Stepney* (BL)
Cokayne: '*The Wise men of Gotham*', a
  cartoon lampooning him for his injustice
  and Jacobitism, connectedhistories.org
John Stoughton, *The Ecclesiastical History of
  England: The Church of the Revolution*, 1874
Tony Benton, *Irregular Marriage in London
  before 1754*, 1993
M.W. Patterson, *A History of the Church of
  England*, London, 1909
James: OB 1733
Ships' advertisements: *Daily Journal*, 30 June,
  7 July 1736

P. Colquhoun, *A Treatise on the Commerce and Policing of the River Thames*, 1800

Hermione Hobhouse, *Survey of London vols 43 and 44 Poplar, Blackwall and the Isle of Dogs*, 1994

T.S. Willan, *The English Coasting Trade*, 1938

Arthur Bryant, *Liquid History*, 1960.

Theft from ships: OB

R.J. Mitchell and M.D.R. Leys, *A History of London Life*, 1958

Fielding: Guillery

N.A.M. Rodger *The Wooden World*, 1986

Peters, Trevis: OB

Marine Society @ *londonlives*

Julia Hunt, *From Whitby to Wapping*, 1991

Clements, Cleaver, Clarenbolt, Eade, Smith, Robinson: OB

Humours of Rag Fair

ad.: *London Evening Post*, Nov. 1728.

Plan of the Victualling Office at Tower Hill, 1776, BL/Crace.

'harpies': *Middlesex Journal and Evening Advertiser*, 16–18 Jan

Curtis: PCC 1771; Morris, *Wapping*

Janet MacDonald, *The British Navy's Victualling Board 1793–1817*, 1998

Mellish: TNA/PCC 1777, 1784, 1795, 1798; Land Tax quota @ *Ancestry*

Madge Darby, *Waeppa's People*, 1988

Fire of 1673: TNA/MPE/494

S. Maddocks, 'Ratcliff', *THHOL*

Defoe, *The Storm*, 1704

Birch, *Limehouse*

Bryant, *Liquid History*

coal heavers' riots: TNA/TS/11/818/2696

Liza Picard, *Dr Johnson's London*

Mayo: TNA/PROB/18/99/10

J. Paul de Castro, The *Gordon Riots*, Oxford, 1926

Gacoyne, Rocque, Cary's *New and Accurate Plan of London and Westminster*, 1792

baby: sess. @ *londonlives*

Snell: Darby, *Waeppa's*

George Sims, *Off the Track in London*, 1911

Page: TNA/PCC 1669 (as Damaris Dry)

Cooke, Wright, Gibson. Goodwin, Woolfe, Carter: OB

Moll James: OB Osborn 1732

Henry Mayhew, *London Labour and the London Poor*, 1849–61

Darby, *Waeppa's*

Picard

William Thornton, *New, Complete and Universal History*, 1784

William Fellows, *A Plan shewing the Situation of the Foreign Sufferance Wharfs*, 1796, BL/Crace

Dudson: TNA/PCC 1714

Cornelius: *londonlives*

Goodwin: TNA/PCC 1714

streets: Noorthouck

Darby, *Ivy*, *Waeppa's*, *Captain Bligh in Wapping*, 1990

Pepys, *Diary* 13/4/1661

Russell: PCC 1723, Foster's *Alumni*

Newton: *Oxf. DNB*

PCC 1700–1800: 53 gents' wills plus numerous sea captains

Cockfield: Julia Hunt, *From Whitby*

Lash: TNA/PCC 1700

Beal[e]: TNA/PCC 1736, 1776

hanging: Fiona Rule, *London's Docklands*, 2009

Maddocks, 'St George's in the East', 1933 *THHOL*

ditch: *Four Shillings*

Darby, *Bligh*

Morris, *Wapping*

sgite

Yeames: TNA/PCC 1706

Kemp: OB Banks; Kendall: OB Simmonds 1734

New Mint: OB Richard Edwards 1725, sess. 13/1/1725, OB Orchard and Towers 1725

W.Beck and T.F. Ball, *The London Friends Meeting*, 1869

J Stoughton, *Ecclesiastical History* of England, 1874

ed. Edward C Raynor, *John Wesley's Journal*

J.H. Plumb, *England in the Eighteenth Century*, 1950

Mayo: DNB, TNA/PROB/18/98/40, &99/10; PROB/31/787/487 &818/72

PROB /20/684; PCC 1799 (Mapstone), PCC 1848 (Jane Mayo); 1841 census

M.J. Power, 'Shadwell, the Development of of a London suburban community in the Seventeenth Century,' *London Journal* vol. 4, no. 1, 1978

Darby, *Ivy*

S. Maddocks 1935 THHOL

OB 1736

Hunt, *From Whitby*

Shipwrights: Llw Smith. According to Maitland the hall had disappeared by the 18th century and the members met at 'different places'

Population: East London History Group Population Study, 1968, George, appendix.

open ground: LMA/P93/DUN/207.

OB 1727 (sodomy), Doller 1750 (oysters), 1736 (Baskerville), 1714 (Smith)

shipwrights: PCC 1690–1800, 12 Ratcliff shipwrights' wills 1690–1735; thereafter only 2

Lightfoot:Oxf. DNB, par reg. 4/2/1732/3, BL Egerton MS 1719 f.81

Bowles: Maddocks, 'Ratcliff', THHOL, 1725 map, Stepney Manor Court Book 1735–8 f. 473, LMA

Shakespear: OB Gough 1781, C.C. Stopes, *Shakespeare's Family,* 1901, Jonathan Shakespear's account of his life @

Ancestry, PCC 1775; staircase: Mrs Riddell, *The Race for Wealth*, 1866

Population: George appendix; Dilworth; LPL/Lowth 4

Birch, *Limehouse*

Limbrey: Frere

Saunders: OB 1776

ship building: PCC 1700–1729: 13 shipwrights; 1730–1820: only 8

Huffam: TNA/PCC 1804, The Huffam Family Tree @ hougham-huffam.org

Barnes, *Stepney Churches*

rector's nerves: LPL/Terrick 14 ff.502-3 *Survey*

Dethick: PCC 1703, 1707

Maddocks, 'Poplar in the past', 1933, THHOL

Taverns: Fairburn, *An Accurate Plan of the Docks for the West India Trade*, 1800, BLCrace

Rector: LPL/Terrick 14

Barnes, *Stepney Churches*

Johnson:*Survey*, Rose, peerage.com, *VCH Bedfordshire* (the latter confuses father and son)

Plan of the River Thames from the Tower to Blackwall taken by the Corporation of Trinity House, 1750, BL Crace

deadpubs.co.uk

'Mary East, the Female Husband', *Homosexuality in Eighteenth-Century England: A Sourcebook*, 6 December 2003, www.rictornorton.co.uk

Survey

Lysons

Dekker, *The Shoemakers Holiday,* 1599

Maddocks, 'Old Ford', THHOL

poem: John Taylor, 1633

fair: sess. 1709, 1719, 1763, 1768, 1776

workhouse: J. Norris Brewer, *London and Middlesex* vol. IV, THHOL tithe: LMA (above)

Ricardo: Endelman, *The Jews of Georgian England*

Coborn: cellars: OB Warren 1698, *VCH mx* 2, M.E. Fransella, *Prisca Coborn and her School* (?1970s), PCC 1702

Selman: Bow par. reg. PCC: 1727, 1779 Marr. to Lefevre: Bromley par. reg. 23/5/1765

Lefevre: TNA/PCC 1746, 1758, 1780, 1787, 1789 Horsley Towers: exploringsurreypast.com

Sir Charles Shaw-Lefevre: *Ancestry*

Postscript

S. Inwood, *A History of London*, 1998

W.J. Fishman, *East End 1888*, 1988

G. Stedman Jones, *Outcast London*, 1971

Gavin Weightman and Steve Humphries, *The Making of Modern London,* 2007

J. Cox, *History of Stepney Parish* (unpublished MS, THLHL)

Ed Glinert, *East End Chronicle*, 2005

Visitation: LPL/Randolph 12/45

G.A. Sala, *Twice round the Clock*, 1859

Liza Picard, *Victorian London,* 2005

curate: R.H. Hadden, *An East End Chronicle*, 1880

Mile End New Town: VM Stepney 5/8/1830, 21/3/1834

James Dunstan, *The History of the Parish of St Leonard Bromley*, 1862

Bethnal Green: Rose, 1851 census

Great Exhibition Catalogue

Illustrated London News, June 1851

Henry Mayhew, *London Labour and the London Poor*, 1849–61

Hoppers' file, St Dunstan's Church archives

Arthur Morrison, *A Child of the Jago*, 1896

E.V. Lucas, *A Wanderer in London*, 1904

St John Beverley Groser, *Politics and Parson*, SCM, 1949

Jennifer Worth, *Call the Midwife*, London, 2002

INDEX

Individuals who appear in lists, or make a single appearance, perhaps as an example of something are omitted, as are authors of quotes or givers of opinions and non-East Enders (by and large).